Praise for *Life Beyond the Classroom*

Fifth Edition

"The most up-to-date, comprehensive, and authoritative source on transition to adult life. It provides practical guidelines without watering down the complexities of the transition process."
—**Linda Bambara, Ed.D.,** Professor of Special Education, Lehigh University

"The new edition is excellent, as I expected, with a top-notch group of contributors who offer high-quality chapters on an important set of topics. The new and improved instructional supports are an added bonus."
—**Hank Bersani Jr., Ph.D.,** Professor of Special Education, Western Oregon University

"An excellent *real-world* look at transition services . . . an asset to new and current staff entering the field of transition services education."
—**Richard L. Rosenberg, Ph.D.,** Lead Vocational Coordinator,
District Teacher of the Year 2009–2010,
Professor, California State University, Los Angeles

"A rich, comprehensive, and up-to date presentation of recommended practices in the field of transition. . . . Though its scope is encyclopedic, it remains accessible, hopeful, and motivating."
—**Paula F. Goldberg,** Executive Director, PACER Center

"An essential book for professionals and parents based on evidence-based practices and research that will assist adolescents and young adults in reaching their maximum potential."
—**Jennifer Sellers, Ph.D.,** Consultation, Training, and Transition Specialist &
Distance Learning Coordinator; Chairperson for the Alabama Interagency Autism
Coordinating Council, Transitional Services Work Group; parent of a son with ASD

"A text for those of us committed to making a positive difference in the lives of students with disabilities. All key challenges and opportunities are addressed in a comprehensive, up-to-date manner."
—**Lyman Dukes, Ph.D.,** Associate Dean, College of Education, Associate
Professor, Special Education, University of South Florida St. Petersburg

"A unique and beneficial book . . . a most welcome edition for those of us concerned about individuals with disabilities at the secondary level and beyond."
—**Edward A. Polloway, Ed.D.,** Rosel H. Schewel Distinguished Professor of
Education and Human Development, Dean of Graduate Studies, and
Vice President for Community Advancement, Lynchburg College

"A comprehensive textbook that will allow educators to focus on outcomes and results in the classroom and community settings. It is a must-have textbook for transition courses!"
—**Cynthia Allen Nixon, Ed.D.,** Associate Professor, Francis Marion University

Life Beyond the Classroom

Life Beyond the Classroom

TRANSITION STRATEGIES FOR YOUNG PEOPLE WITH DISABILITIES

Fifth Edition

by

Paul Wehman, Ph.D.
Virginia Commonwealth University
Richmond

with invited contributors

PAUL·H·
BROOKES
PUBLISHING CO®

Baltimore • London • Sydney

Paul H. Brookes Publishing Co.
Post Office Box 10624
Baltimore, Maryland 21285-0624
USA

www.brookespublishing.com

Typeset by Spearhead Global, Inc., Bear, Delaware.
Manufactured in the United States of America by
Sheridan Books, Chelsea, Michigan.

The individuals described in this book are real people or composites based on the authors' experiences. Some names and identifying details have been changed to protect confidentiality. Real names are used by permission.

Library of Congress Cataloging-in-Publication Data

Wehman, Paul.
    Life beyond the classroom: transition strategies for young people with disabilities / by Paul Wehman with invited contributors. — 5th ed.
      p.   cm.
    Includes bibliographical references and index.
    ISBN-13: 978-1-59857-232-2 (alk. paper)
    ISBN-10: 1-59857-232-6 (alk. paper)
    1. People with disabilities—Vocational guidance—United States.   2. Youth with disabilities—Employment—United States.   3. Youth with disabilities—United States—Psychology.   4. School-to-work transition—United States.   I. Title.
    HV1568.5.W43 2013
    331.3'4087—dc23

                                                            2012011718

British Library Cataloguing in Publication data are available from the British Library.

2017   2016   2015   2014   20113

10   9   8   7   6   5   4   3   2   1

Contents

I INTRODUCTION

Paul Wehman
Meet the Faces of Transition in America
Defining Transition
2010 Survey of Americans with Disabilities: Much Work
   Remains to Help Persons with Disabilities Gain Employment
National Longitudinal Transition Study-2: What Happens to
   Youth When They Leave School?
Gallup Poll Employer Results: The News Is Not All Bad
Is Business the Answer to Improving Transition Outcomes?
Making the Journey to Adulthood: The Importance of Setting Goals
Evidence-Based Transition Research: The Foundation for
   Recommended Practices
Related Disability Legislation
Challenges that Affect Youth with Disabilities
Transition Themes for Success: Why Do Some Students
   Succeed and Others Do Not?
Conclusion
Study Questions
Online Resources

Michael L. Wehmeyer and Karrie A. Shogren
What Is Self-Determination?
Self-Determination, Disability, and Empowerment
Assessments, Methods, and Strategies to Promote Self-Determination
Conclusion
Study Questions
Online Resources

Pamela Targett and Paul Wehman
Parent and Student Involvement as Key Components of Successful Transition
Barriers to and Strategies for Involvement
Supporting Improved Outcomes
Conclusion
Study Questions
Online Resources

About the Online Companion Materials

Attention Instructors! Online companion materials are available to help you teach a course using *Life Beyond the Classroom, Fifth Edition.*

Please visit www.brookespublishing.com/wehman to access

- Videos for every chapter that bring key concepts to life for your students
- Customizable PowerPoint presentations for every chapter, totaling more than 300 slides
- Activities for every chapter that help students practice key skills, such as writing transition plans and conducting assessments
- Quick "at-a-glance" introductions to each chapter, showing objectives, takeaway points, and study questions, to help you plan your syllabus and lessons
- A convenient test bank with multiple-choice and short answer/essay questions

About the Author

Paul Wehman, Ph.D., Professor and Director of the Rehabilitation Research and Training Center, Virginia Commonwealth University, 1314 West Main Street, Richmond, Virginia 23284

Dr. Wehman is Professor of Physical Medicine with joint appointments in the Departments of Rehabilitation Counseling and also Special Education and Disability Policy at Virginia Commonwealth University. He serves as Chairman of the Division of Rehabilitation Research in the Department of Physical Medicine and Rehabilitation. Dr. Wehman has his Ph.D. in behavioral disabilities from the University of Wisconsin–Madison.

As one of the original founders of supported employment, he has worked closely with business and industry since 1980 and has published more than 200 articles and authored or edited more than 40 books primarily in transition, severe disabilities, autism, traumatic brain injury, and employment for persons with disabilities. He has been the Principal Investigator on over 40 million dollars of grants during his career.

As the father of two young adults with disabilities, he brings a strong parental as well as business perspective to his work. He is highly active in speaking to professionals, parents, advocates, and businesses on transition and employment for people with autism, traumatic brain injury, spinal cord injury, and other developmental disabilities. On a daily basis he works with individuals with disabilities, communicates regularly with professionals in the world of business related to disability and diversity, and is active in teaching and mentoring medical students, residents, and doctoral students in rehabilitation medicine, special education, rehabilitation, and psychology. A major focus of Dr. Wehman's work is on expanding the partnerships with businesses of all sizes so that more persons with disabilities can gain entrance into the workplace and retain employment successfully.

He is a recipient of the Kennedy Foundation Award in Mental Retardation in 1990 and President's Committee on Employment for Persons with Disabilities in 1992. Dr. Wehman was recognized as one of the 50 most influential special educators of the millennium by the *Remedial and Special Education* journal in December 2000. He is also Editor-in-Chief of the *Journal of Vocational Rehabilitation*.

About the Contributors

Edwin O. Achola, M.Ed., Adjunct Faculty, Department of Special Education and Disability Policy, Virginia Commonwealth University (VCU), 1015 West Main Street, Richmond, Virginia 23284

Mr. Achola is adjunct faculty in the Department of Special Education and Disability Policy at VCU. He currently teaches the secondary education and transition planning class designed for practitioners in the M.Ed program and those seeking special education endorsement. He is also teaching an undergraduate special education introductory class. Mr. Achola has worked as a general and a special educator with both high and middle school students in Kenya and the United States.

Amy J. Armstrong, Ph.D., CRC, Associate Professor and Chair, Department of Rehabilitation Counseling, VCU, 730 East Broad Street, Richmond, Virginia 23298

Dr. Armstrong is Chair and Associate Professor in the Department of Rehabilitation Counseling at VCU. She has been involved in advocacy, education, and employment issues related to individuals with disabilities for more than 25 years. Her interests include the employment of individuals with significant disabilities, community reintegration, resilience, leadership, and personal/professional transformation. She received an M.A. in rehabilitation counseling from Michigan State University and a Ph.D. in education from VCU.

Kira Austin, M.Ed., Program Specialist, Virginia Department of Education Training and Technical Assistance Center at VCU (VCU T/TAC), 10 East Franklin Street, Suite 200, Post Office Box 843081, Richmond, Virginia 23284

Ms. Austin is a faculty member with the VCU T/TAC. As a program specialist she provides training and technical assistance to 27 counties serving more than 200,000 students. In this capacity, her expertise includes autism spectrum disorders (ASDs) and positive behavior interventions and supports. Her research interests also include paraprofessional training, personnel preparation, and transition planning for individuals with ASDs. Ms. Austin serves as a member on the Virginia State Directed Project for ASD. She is also a Ph.D. candidate in the Special Education and Disability Policy Program at VCU.

Emily C. Bouck, Ph.D., Associate Professor, Special Education Program, Department of Educational Studies, College of Education, Purdue University, Beering Hall of Liberal Arts and Education, 100 North University Street, West Lafayette, Indiana 47907

Dr. Bouck is Associate Professor of Educational Studies in the Special Education Program at Purdue University. Dr. Bouck's scholarship is dedicated to improving the in-school and postschool outcomes of secondary students with high incidence disabilities—particularly students with mild intellectual disability—through advances in two strands of scholarship: functional curricula and standard academic curricula.

Kimberly S. Boyd, M.T., Special Education Coordinator, Clover Hill High School, 13301 Kelly Green Lane, Midlothian, Virginia 23112

Ms. Boyd received her master's in teaching degree in special education from VCU and is currently a third-year doctoral student in the Department of Special Education and Disability Policy, also at VCU. Her professional areas of interest include working with students with intellectual disability and the improvement of transition services for all students with disabilities. Ms. Boyd currently works as a special education coordinator for a public high school.

Lori W. Briel, M.Ed., Coordinator of Postsecondary Initiatives, VCU, Rehabilitation Research and Training Center (VCU-RRTC) on Workplace Supports and Job Retention, 1314 West Main Street, Post Office Box 842011, Richmond, Virginia 23284

Ms. Briel is the VCU-RRTC Coordinator of Post Secondary Initiatives at VCU in Richmond, Virginia. She has extensive experience coordinating demonstration projects related to career development for college students with significant disabilities, preparing youth with disabilities for college, and collaborating with university and community services to enhance the success of students with disabilities in college. Ms. Briel has contributed to professional development products including web sites, web casts, and fact sheets. She has coauthored several journal articles and book chapters in these areas.

Valerie Brooke, M.Ed., Director of Training and Employment Services, VCU-RRTC, 1314 West Main Street, Richmond, Virginia 23284

Ms. Brooke has been a faculty member at VCU and working in the field of employment for people with significant disabilities for more than 30 years. Ms. Brooke is Director of Training and Employment Services at VCU-RRTC and serves as Principal Investigator on several grants promoting employment for individuals with disabilities. Ms. Brooke has served on the Editorial Board for the *Journal of Vocational Rehabilitation* since 2000 and is interested in all issues that have an impact on the employment and inclusion of people with disabilities.

Erik W. Carter, Ph.D., Associate Professor, Vanderbilt University, Department of Special Education, Box 228, Peabody College, Nashville, Tennessee 37203

Dr. Carter is Associate Professor in the Department of Special Education at Vanderbilt University. His research and teaching focuses on evidence-based strategies for supporting access to the general curriculum and promoting valued roles in school, work, and community settings for children and adults with intellectual and developmental disabilities. Before receiving his doctorate, he worked as a high school teacher and transition specialist with youth with significant disabilities. He has published widely in the areas of educational and transition services for children and youth with significant disabilities. He has coauthored four books, including *Peer Support Strategies for Improving All Students' Social Lives and Learning* (Paul H. Brookes Publishing Co.) and *Peer Buddy Programs for Successful Secondary School Inclusion* (Paul H. Brookes Publishing Co.).

Charles Dillard, M.D., Pediatric Physiatrist, Children's Hospital of Richmond at VCU School of Medicine, 2924 Brook Road, Richmond, Virginia 23220

Dr. Dillard is Assistant Professor in the Department of Physical Medicine and Rehabilitation, Children's Hospital of Richmond at VCU (Children's Hospital of Richmond). He completed his residency in physical medicine and rehabilitation in 2008 at VCU Medical Center, and during his residency he served as Chief Resident and received the Physical Medicine and Rehabilitation Clinical Excellence Award.

Tony Gentry, Ph.D., OTR/L, Assistant Professor, VCU, Department of Occupational Therapy, 730 East Broad Street, Richmond, Virginia 23298

Dr. Gentry is Assistant Professor of Occupational Therapy at VCU, where he directs the Assistive Technology for Cognition Laboratory. Over the past decade, he has conducted a series of studies investigating the utility of handheld computers, smart phones, computer games, and biometric devices as assistive technologies for people with brain injury, autism, polytrauma, and other conditions.

Elizabeth Evans Getzel, M.A., Director of Postsecondary Education Initiatives, VCU-RRTC, 1314 West Main Street, Richmond, Virginia 23284

Ms. Getzel is Director of Postsecondary Education Initiatives at VCU-RRTC, a grant-funded center focusing on education and employment needs of individuals with disabilities. She currently directs projects on supported education in postsecondary education for college students with disabilities, collaborative career planning for college students with autism, supported education for veterans with traumatic brain injury and spinal cord injury in college, Project SEARCH®, and college opportunities for individuals with intellectual disabilities and other developmental disabilities. She has authored or coauthored journal articles and book chapters on transition, career development, postsecondary education, and employment and is the coeditor of the book, *Going to College: Expanding Opportunities for People with Disabilities* (Paul H. Brookes Publishing Co.).

Howard Green, M.S., Deputy Director for Corporate Programs, Bridges to Business, National Organization on Disability, 5 East 86th Street, New York, NY 10028

Mr. Green is the Director for the Bridges to Business Program for the National Organization on Disability. For the past 2 years he has worked with many businesses to assist them with their disability employment initiatives. He has worked with projects that have included companies such Lowe's, Sam's, J.B. Hunt, Tyson, Toys "R" Us, JC Penney, Sodexho, and Aetna. For the past 20 years, Mr. Green served as a faculty member at VCU, where he also served as Director of Employment Services. In addition, he has provided technical assistance and consultation to businesses, community rehabilitation agencies, and vocational rehabilitation staff. Mr. Green is known as a national trainer on building relationships between business and rehabilitation programs. He has provided a number of training activities across the country on business development for the employment of people with disabilities. Before his work with VCU, he worked as Marketing Director for the Virginia Department of Rehabilitative Services. He has been involved with a number of projects and programs that have assisted both the supply side and the demand side of employment for people with disabilities. Mr. Green has been active with the U.S. Chamber of Commerce, VCU Business Roundtable, U.S. Business Leadership Network, and SHRM. In addition, he currently serves on the Board for the Virginia Business Leadership Network and is a board member for National APSE.

Cary Griffin, M.A., Senior Partner, Griffin-Hammis Associates, LLC, 5582 Klements Lane, Florence, Montana 59833

Mr. Griffin is Senior Partner at Griffin-Hammis Associates. He provides training and consultation on customized wage and self-employment to community rehabilitation programs, school personnel, state and federal programs, university programs, businesses, families, and individuals with disabilities.

John J. Gugerty, M.S., Researcher, Wisconsin Center for Education Research, University of Wisconsin–Madison, 366 Educational Sciences Building, 1025 West Johnson Street, Madison, Wisconsin 53706

Since 1975, Mr. Gugerty's professional life has focused on improving career aspirations, preparation, employment opportunities, and outcomes for youths and adults with disabilities and other risk factors that challenge their learning, performance, and success. Toward that end, he has collaborated with Univeristy of Wisconsin–Madison colleagues, professionals in other institutions of higher education, state agencies, local agencies, community-based organizations (including parent advocacy groups), and secondary schools from around the country on 18 multiyear, federally funded projects and numerous state-funded efforts. His current work focuses on evaluation of math-science and advanced placement programs in Wisconsin districts that have high enrollments of students from low-income backgrounds, students with disabilities, or other factors that impinge on their performance and success.

Carolyn Hughes, Ph.D., Professor, Vanderbilt University, Department of Special Education, Box 228, Peabody College, Nashville, Tennessee 37203

Dr. Hughes is Professor of Special Education at Vanderbilt University. Dr. Hughes's research program extends over 25 years in the areas of transition to adult life, self-determination, support strategies for students with intellectual disabilities and autism, and social interaction among general education high school students and their peers with disabilities. Dr. Hughes has published numerous books, chapters, and articles addressing social interaction and self-directed learning skills among high school students with disabilities and mentoring programs for high-poverty youth.

Sunyoung Kim, M.Ed., Doctoral Student, Special Education, University of Wisconsin–Madison, 1000 Bascom Mall, Room 461, Madison, Wisconsin 53706

Ms. Kim is a doctoral student in the Department of Rehabilitation Psychology and Special Education at the University of Wisconsin–Madison. Her research interests are in transition and evidence-based interventions for young children with autism spectrum disorders. Ms. Kim received her M.Ed. degree in early childhood special education from the University of Texas at Austin, in 2009. Before her graduate work, she was a preschool teacher in South Korea.

Jennifer Todd McDonough, M.S., CRC, Associate Director of Training, VCU-RRTC on Workplace Supports and Job Retention, 1314 West Main Street, Post Office Box 842011, Richmond, Virginia 23284

Ms. McDonough has been a faculty member at VCU and working in the field of employment for people with disabilities for more than 15 years. She is Associate Director of Training at VCU-RRTC and Project Coordinator for the Vocational Rehabilitation Service Models for Individuals with Autism Spectrum Disorders Disability and Rehabilitation Research Project. Ms. McDonough is a national expert on Social Security disability benefits and work incentives as well as the Virginia Project SEARCH Statewide Coordinator.

Margaret J. McLaughlin, Ph.D., Associate Dean for Research and Graduate Education, College of Education, and Professor, Department of Special Education, University of Maryland, College Park, Maryland 20742

Dr. McLaughlin has been involved in special education all of her professional career. She earned her Ph.D. at the University of Virginia and has held positions at what was formerly the U.S. Office of Education and at the University of Washington. She has been studying the impact of educational reform on special education since the late 1980s and has written extensively on topics of students with disabilities and standards, assessment accommodations, finance reform, and on the disproportionate representation of minority students.

Cynthia Pearl, Ph.D., Project Director, University of Central Florida, College of Education, Department of Child, Family, and Community Sciences, Post Office Box 162202, 4000 Central Florida Boulevard, Orlando, Florida 32816

Dr. Pearl is Coprincipal Investigator and Project Director for two personnel preparation grants through the U.S. Department of Education, Office of Special Education Programs. She has directed Project ASD, Preparing Teachers to Work with Students with Autism Spectrum Disorders, at the University of Central Florida since the fall of 2003 and Project SPD, Special Educator Preparation in Severe/Profound Disabilities, since the fall of 2007.

W. Grant Revell, Jr., M.S., M.Ed., Research Associate, VCU-RRTC on Workplace Supports and Job Retention, 1314 West Main Street, Post Office Box 842011, Richmond, Virginia 23284

Mr. Revell works as Research Associate at VCU and has extensive experience in the areas of policy analysis, state systems development, and funding related to state-level and national implementation of employment supports for individuals with significant disabilities. He has served as Project Director and Project Associate for a variety of national technical assistance and research projects. Before coming to the VCU-RRTC, he worked as a state program supervisor and as a vocational rehabilitation counselor at the Virginia Department of Rehabilitation Services.

Carol M. Schall, Ph.D., Director, Virginia Autism Resource Center, VCU-RRTC, 1314 West Main Street, Richmond, Virginia 23284

Dr. Schall is Director of Technical Assistance of the Autism Center for Excellence at VCU. She is Principal Investigator of a randomized clinical trial of Project SEARCH for students with autism spectrum disorders. Her research interests include the monitoring of psychotropic medication for individuals with autism spectrum disorders, transition from school to work and adulthood, and training for parents and professionals on serving individuals with developmental disabilities. She is also on the board of the Association for Positive Behavior Support. Dr. Schall is coauthor of *Autism and the Transition to Adulthood: Success Beyond the Classroom* (Paul H. Brookes Publishing Co.).

LaRon A. Scott, Ed.D., Assistant Professor, Department of Special Education and Disability Policy, VCU, 1015 West Main Street, Richmond, Virginia 23284

Dr. Scott is Assistant Professor in the Special Education and Disability Policy Department at VCU. His current work and research includes improving special education teacher preparation, transition planning for students with disabilities, student-directed individualized education programming, and professional development for special educators. He has coauthored a book on transition instruction titled *Universal Design for Transition* (Paul H. Brookes Publishing Co.) and has served as contributing author in books and chapters related to self-directed individualized education programs and transition planning. He was the recipient of the Division on Career Development and Transition, Transition Teacher of the Year award in 2008.

Karrie A. Shogren, Ph.D., Assistant Professor, Department of Special Education, University of Illinois at Urbana-Champaign, 270D Education Building, 1310 South 6th Street, MC 708, Champaign, Illinois 61820

Dr. Shogren is Assistant Professor of Special Education at the University of Illinois at Urbana-Champaign. Dr. Shogren's research focuses on self-determination, transition, and systems of supports for people with disabilities. She has published more than 50 articles and book chapters on disability and education issues.

Kim Spence-Cochran, Ph.D., Coordinator of Educational and Training Programs, Center for Autism and Related Disabilities, University of Central Florida, Post Office Box 162202, 4000 Central Florida Boulevard, Orlando, Florida 32816

Dr. Spence-Cochran has been the Coordinator of Educational & Training Programs for the Center for Autism & Related Disabilities (CARD) at the University of Central Florida (UCF) since 1999. In addition to her job at CARD, Dr. Spence-Cochran is a member of the Project Autism Spectrum Disorders Grant Advisory Committee at UCF and is adjunct instructor for both the College of Education and the Department of Communication Sciences and Disorders at UCF. She serves on the Editorial Board of the *Journal of Vocational Rehabilitation* and the Editorial Review Board of *Assistive Technology Outcomes and Benefits,* and serves nationally as a consultant and expert witness for individuals with developmental disabilities.

Kevin Sutherland, Ph.D., Professor, Department of Special Education and Disability Policy, VCU, 1015 West Main Street, Post Office Box 842020, Richmond, Virginia 23284

Dr. Sutherland is Professor of Special Education and Disability Policy at VCU. Before receiving his Ph.D. from Vanderbilt University in 2000, he was a teacher of students with learning and behavior problems in both public school and residential treatment settings. Dr. Sutherland's research focuses upon intervention development and evaluation for school settings. He is currently coeditor of *Behavioral Disorder.*

Pamela Sherron Targett, M.Ed., Director of Special Projects, VCU-RRTC on Workplace Supports and Job Retention, 1314 West Main Street, Richmond, Virginia 23284

Ms. Targett has worked in the disability employment field since 1986. From that time until 2009, she oversaw the daily operations of a supported employment program to serve individuals with the most severe disabilities and served in various roles on a number of federally funded demonstration projects. Her special interests include issues in transition to work for youth with the most severe disabilities, developing employer partnerships, and job restructuring as well as supported employment for individuals with traumatic brain injury. Today, she is Director of Special Projects. In this capacity she provides support on a variety of projects and is heavily involved in the design and implementation of online education courses.

Colleen A. Thoma, Ph.D., Professor, Department of Special Education and Disability Policy, VCU, 1015 West Main Street, Post Office Box 842020, Richmond, Virginia 23284

Dr. Thoma earned her doctoral degree from Indiana University, where she began her research on self-determination in transition planning. She is currently Professor in the Department of Special Education and Disability Policy in the School of Education at VCU, where she teaches courses in both the Ph.D. and M.Ed. programs. Her research interests include preparation of teachers to support self-determined transition planning, student-directed individualized education program development, universal design for transition, postsecondary education transition programs for students with intellectual disability, and the impact of student self-determination on transition and academic outcomes. She was elected as a member of the board of directors for the Council for Exceptional Children (CEC), and before that, served on the executive board of CEC's Division on Career Development and Transition for 6 years, including 1 year as President. She has authored and coauthored multiple journal articles, book chapters, and conference proceedings related to transition, instructional strategies, and self-determination, including three books: *Transition Assessment: Wise Practices for Quality Lives* (coauthored with Caren L. Sax; Paul H. Brookes Publishing Co.), *Universal Design for Transition* (coauthored with Christina Bartholomew and LaRon Scott; Paul H. Brookes Publishing Co.), and *Getting the Most Out of IEPs: An educator's Guide to the Student-Directed Approach* (coedited with Paul Wehman; Paul H. Brookes Publishing Co.).

Audrey A. Trainor, Ph.D., Associate Professor, Special Education, University of Wisconsin–Madison, 1000 Bascom Mall, Room 438, Madison, Wisconsin 53706

Dr. Trainor is Associate Professor of Special Education at the University of Wisconsin–Madison, where she teaches graduate courses in qualitative data analysis and multicultural issues in special education. She also teaches undergraduate courses in special education teaching methods. Focusing on learning and emotional/behavioral disabilities, Dr. Trainor's research examines the perceptions and experiences of adolescents during the transition from high school to adulthood. Dr. Trainor received her Ph.D. in special education from the University of Texas, Austin, in 2003. Before her graduate work, she was a special educator in North Carolina. Dr. Trainor is the 2012–2013 President for the Division on Career Development and Transition of the Council for Exceptional Children.

Zachary Walker, M.A., M.B.A., Doctoral Student, University of Central Florida, 4000 Central Florida Boulevard, Orlando, Florida 32816

Mr. Walker is completing his doctorate in special education at the University of Central Florida. He is an educator and consultant partnering with schools in the United States, Europe, Central America, and the Caribbean. His work with teachers focuses on transition, teaching and learning, and technology.

Michael L. Wehmeyer, Ph.D., Professor, Department of Special Education; Director, Kansas University Center on Developmental Disabilities; Senior Scientist, Beach Center on Disability, University of Kansas, 1200 Sunnyside Avenue, Room 3136, Lawrence, Kansas 66045

Dr. Wehmeyer is Professor of Special Education; Director, Kansas University Center on Developmental Disabilities; and Senior Scientist, Beach Center on Disability—all at the University of Kansas. He is Past President of the CEC's Division on Career Development and Transition and the American Association on Intellectual and Developmental Disabilities (AAIDD). He is Fellow of the AAIDD and the American Psychological Association. Dr. Wehmeyer's research is in the areas of self-determination, access to the general education curriculum for students with severe disabilities, technology use by people with cognitive disabilities, and the conceptualization of supports in the definition of intellectual disability.

Michael D. West, Ph.D., Research Associate, VCU-RRTC, 1314 West Main Street, Richmond, Virginia 23284-2011

Dr. West is Research Associate with the VCU-RRTC. His research projects have included national surveys of supported employment policies and practices, a study of students with disabilities in higher education in Virginia, states' use of Medicaid Home and Community Based Waivers to fund employment services, and return to work (including self-employment) for severely disabled veterans. Dr. West also is involved in research and demonstration efforts related to Social Security disability reform at the VCU-RRTC.

Katherine Mullaney Wittig, M.Ed., Project Coordinator, Post-High Program, VCU-RRTC on Workplace Supports and Job Retention, 1314 West Main Street, Post Office Box 842011, Richmond, Virginia 23284

Ms. Wittig is an instructor with the VCU-RRTC and has more than 25 years of experience with the secondary transition process for youth with disabilities. As Project Director for Post-High Programs, Ms. Wittig works at the VCU-RRTC with students, families, school divisions, colleges and universities, adult agencies, and employers to enhance successful outcomes for students with disabilities. She recently coauthored *Transition IEPs* with Paul Wehman (2009), and has authored or coauthored several book chapters and newsletter or journal articles regarding the transition process.

Preface

We live in the most challenging times. The 21st century has not been kind to many people and families in America. The recent invasion on American soil with the 9/11 tragedy, the recession that followed, Hurricane Katrina in New Orleans, the financial crash of 2008 in the United States, and the resulting destruction of housing markets and high unemployment rates have left millions of Americans shaken and worried. We cannot write a book on transition from school age into adulthood for thousands of young people with disabilities without understanding the context in which they live. All young people with or without disabilities are faced with new financial, family, employment, and educational challenges as they grow up. There is less money available for programs to help them, and this will continue to be the case for the foreseeable future.

So, is it all dark and grim? Is there no hope? Are there no ways out of what seems like hopeless gridlock among our national leaders? The answer to these and other similar questions is that, of course, there is every reason for hope and optimism for the future. This energy and pessimism that seems to have permeated our society in the past 5 years will be eradicated by strength. Historically in this country there have always been difficult times and, in the end, leaders emerge. To overcome these extraordinary challenges, we have to look directly at our strengths and then build off of those.

Let us take a second and review what some of these strengths are as a lead in to this 20th anniversary of *Life Beyond the Classroom,* its fifth edition. First, the baby boomer generation, those between 50 and 70 years old, are the parents of the emerging youth with disabilities, and these baby boomers have grown up with the most education, the most knowledge, and the greatest networks in the history of the United States. These parents will not let their children fail. They will infuse all of their passions, energies, and networks into giving their children whole lives.

One only needs to look at the power of Autism Speaks and its national grass roots efforts, or to examine the drive behind establishing access for youth with intellectual and developmental disabilities into colleges, or the burgeoning number of Business Leadership Networks around the country to know that failure is not an option for these parents and business leaders.

Second, let us examine the power of technology, especially mobile and wireless technology. The role of information technology is exploding as this is written. The technology needs to be harnessed to become an equalizer for young persons with disabilities who need to read better, who need to communicate better, and who want to socialize more with peers without disabilities. There are seemingly no limits to how information technology can level the playing field with those who have no disabilities. And there is more to come. Look at what basic research and biomedical technology are doing to help palliate diabetes, rheumatoid arthritis, and congenital heart problems, or the important research on Down syndrome that has focused on the importance of early intervention on intellectual functioning. As these research findings emerge, they are going to change the entire future for thousands of young people with illnesses and disabilities.

Third, let us understand the tremendous influence of business. We talk extensively in this book about business being the social engine of America. The fact is that millions of American employers and workers also have children and family members and friends with disabilities; they increasingly "get it" and want to become involved in opening their doors and knowledge to young people with disabilities. As we move forward in this next decade, business can and will play a crucial role in filling the gap picking of publicly funded programs through public–private partnerships.

Fourth, and finally, we know more about transition—what works and what does not work—than we have before in history. As the reader will see as she or he goes through this edition of *Life*, evidence-based research has simply exploded with increasingly good quality articles available in print or on the Internet. If parents and teachers want good, credible information, it is easily at their fingertips. If they want to know whether internships work, there are the examples of Project SEARCH® and the Marriott Bridges program. If they want to know about how technology improves life for people with autism, this information is one click away. For parents who want to know about access to college or community-based instruction, again, there are many articles and chapters that will tell them how to help advocate for their children to get into these programs.

In short, the education and employment of young adults with disabilities in the United States remains, more than ever, a leading national priority. The education of individuals with disabilities is critical to the foundation of adult adjustment and success in work and the community. Without an education that focuses on the development of personal competence, life skills, and employment opportunities, young adults with disabilities are greatly challenged in the complex modern society in which we live. In the fifth edition of *Life Beyond the Classroom*, the contributors and I emphasize the importance of work, transition planning, business, living skills, assistive technology, high-stakes testing, postsecondary education, multiculturalism, social skills training, parents and families, and secondary curriculum. The field of transition has expanded dramatically, and these topical areas, in their own way, will influence employment, postsecondary education, and community integration. The need for accurate, clear, and up-to-date information on how to make successful transition a reality is stronger than ever, and this new edition of *Life* provides this learning platform.

In *Life Beyond the Classroom*, unlike other books related to the transition field, we focus on people with disabilities and their respective strengths. We specifically dedicate chapters to the recommended methods of transition planning and intervention for youth with intellectual, physical, emotional, and learning disabilities, and autism. These chapters were developed to meet the unique needs of a wide variety of students.

We ask the reader to think about the faces of transition who are on the cover of this book and discussed in Chapter 1. They represent the thousands of young people waiting to fulfill their full potential into adulthood. We rely on evidence-based research for our program decision making, but our motivating passion and drive come from the desire to elevate lives. We have expanded our offerings to include social skills training and parent and student voices, as well as multicultural influences on transition planning.

Having high aspirations for success can influence the actual outcomes of people with disabilities—a major theme of this book. We live in a rapidly changing society, both politically and technologically, and it can become easy to feel inept or overwhelmed. However, positive self-esteem and confidence can directly affect one's level of success. There are substantial doubts on the part of many in society about the quality and credibility of education for young people with disabilities. We believe that the only way to change these views is for young people with disabilities to demonstrate their competence on college campuses, in shopping malls, in recreational centers, and in the workplace. Societal attitudes only change when everyone can see the successful behaviors of individuals with disabilities—many of whom have never been given the opportunity to perform well.

Whatever the political climate, there will always be young adults in need of education and work opportunities. In addition to the emphasis on evidence-based academic research and high-stakes testing, inclusive employment will continue to be the targeted outcome. Transition from school to adulthood has remained a major priority of state legislatures, as well as the U.S. government, primarily because intelligent and informed people know that the country's future rests on the education and employment of its young people, thousands of whom have specialized needs or disabilities. As society becomes more complex and as technology and jobs become more specially designed, upgraded equipment and facilities and more sophisticated approaches to training will be required. Greater work experiences in the community, more intensive apprenticeships, greater use of business mentors, and employment during school all constitute a more successful approach to transition planning, according to observations made since 1980.

The issues that face high school–age youth with disabilities and their families as they prepare and plan for completion of special education are the same in this edition of *Life Beyond the Classroom* as in previous editions. These issues have, however, become more complex, complicated, and challenging as our society demands greater levels of knowledge and competence in young people. Educators at the high school level must therefore be informed about postschool services, especially postsecondary college outlets, because they will be the major source of information to concerned parents and their teenage students about what awaits them after they finish school.

We believe that this fifth edition of *Life Beyond the Classroom* will successfully touch the lives of thousands of university students and professionals who wish to accumulate more information and knowledge in the important areas of education and employment for young people with disabilities. The challenge is greater than ever. There is a critical need for professionals to take a more significant leadership role in the community on behalf of people with disabilities. Advocacy and involvement are essential to making transition work in a community. This book is based on the notion that any community can have a successful transition program, but individuals with disabilities and their families and advocates must be actively involved and committed to envisioning successful employment and community outcomes for students after high school.

Acknowledgments

With this publication, *Life Beyond the Classroom* now enters into its fifth edition, a 20-year anniversary. This book has reflected the steady growth of knowledge, changes, improvements, and future aspirations for all who are interested and concerned about young people with disabilities. This book has been, from the beginning, a team effort made up of the best collaborators and contributors for whom an author could ask. I would like to specifically thank each person for the time they took and for the thoughtfulness they put into each chapter.

Michael Wehmeyer and Karrie Shogren gave us the self-determination chapter. Mike is known to most of us in the special education field as the father of the self-determination movement. His grace and humility are only outpaced by the proliferation and quality of his work. Karrie is the prototype emerging nationally known scholar in self-determination. She is intensely dedicated to making things better for people with disabilities. I am so lucky to have her participation.

Pam Targett provided leadership on the voices of families and persons with disabilities. I thank her for her work and will acknowledge her further in this section.

I thank Kira Austin, an up-and-coming Ph.D. student, and Kathe Wittig. Kathe has been a friend my entire career and remains as passionate about transition today as the first day I met her.

I am indebted to Audrey Trainor, another of the "young guns" who is now defining the future of transition. Her efforts at multicultural transition planning are a superb addition to the fifth edition of *Life*. What a wonderful career she has ahead of her.

My long-standing colleagues Vicki Brooke, Grant Revell, Jennifer McDonough, and Howard Green have once again come forward to help me with one of the most important chapters (coordinating community resources) in this book. They have always been there for me, and I am fortunate to count them among my very best colleagues and friends.

I also thank Kim Spence-Cochran and her colleagues. Kim is an outstanding clinician and educator who knows what is going on at the grass roots of service delivery. I cannot believe we were lucky enough to have her contribute again for this chapter.

We have one of the top-five educators and researchers in the country, especially in special education leadership, Margaret McLaughlin. I am grateful and amazed that she has the time to do all of the things she does. She gets her work in before anyone else, it is top quality, and I am so glad she again agreed to write the chapter on high-stakes testing.

Emily Bouck from Purdue responded immediately to my call for the recommended guidelines for secondary curriculum. Emily is one of the top young national leaders in transition who will be providing guidance to the field. I am so pleased she could write this chapter.

A long-time colleague and friend, Colleen Thoma, and her colleagues were willing to offer the all-important assessment and teaching chapter. Colleen has been a national leader in transition for many years and is known by many for her service and scholarship.

Erik Carter and Carolyn Hughes agreed to do the social skills chapter despite having an enormous amount of grants, books, and articles already on his plate. I felt this book would not be complete without this contribution. Erik and Carolyn have been extraordinarily prolific and are among the premier transition researchers nationally.

Long-term friends Amy Armstrong (who has always been there for me for more than 20 years) and Tony Gentry, a brilliant occupational therapist, who is also a friend, wrote a terrific chapter on technology. I am blessed to have both of them as colleagues.

Elizabeth Getzel contributed, once again, to two chapters—one on learning disabilities along with John Gugerty and another on postsecondary education along with Lori Biel. I thank all of them for their exceptional work, and I am especially grateful to Liz for her values, leadership, and tenacity for making postsecondary education a reality for so many young people with disabilities. We have worked together for close to 30 years and there is not a better colleague.

Kevin Sutherland and his colleagues joined me in greatly improving the chapter on emotional and behavioral disorders. His work on bullying and antisocial behavior in middle schools has been nationally recognized, and I am so glad he could help.

One of my very favorite people—Carol Schall, an extraordinary expert on autism and also positive behavior supports—agreed to update the chapter on autism and transition. Carol and I work together closely every day on autism education and service delivery. There is not a finer and more knowledgeable person than her, and anyone who has worked with her knows the level of autism experience she brings to the table. What a terrific colleague she has been to work with every day.

I thank Mike West, Pam Targett (again), and Chad Dillard for their labors on the last chapter related to orthopedic, health impairments, and brain injury. Chad is a young physician dedicated to the rehabilitation of young people with illnesses and disabilities; I am so glad he accepted the invitation to write on this most important topic.

In addition to these contributors, I thank Roberta Martin, my administrative assistant and person who keeps my professional life straight, for her efforts in organizing the continual mass of paper and flow of communication related to permissions, bios, and, in general, arranging work flow. She has been a delight to work with every day.

I also thank Jeanne Roberts, who typed all 1,200 manuscript pages, organized the hundreds of references that poured in, and made it all seem very easy. She is just an incredible word processor, and problem solved every issue that came up. She is incredibly skilled.

I also want to thank my family—my wife, Lele, and my children—for putting up with me during this project, especially during the spring and summer of 2011 when I spent many a Sunday morning in the office trying to get everything done and organized.

I need to reserve a very special thank you to Pam Targett who served as my assistant editor and proofreader and contributor to the labor that went into this book. Pam is fast and thorough and knows the field extremely well and was willing to take extra time out of her work schedule to help me get this project completed.

I want to thank the thousands of parents and professionals who have used the *Life* books in the past and who have given me feedback on how to make it better. I also say thank you for your courage, passion, and dedication to making lives of young people with disabilities better, especially in these challenging times. In our field, we draw from the leadership and excitement of our best professionals and most dedicated and outspoken parents and families.

I want to thank the Paul H. Brookes Publishing Co. for the opportunity to make this the best possible book it can be in the transition and secondary special education area. I am grateful for the production and marketing efforts that were necessary and want to say thank you to Steve Plocher for his rapid response time to all corrections made.

Finally, I want to say thank you and acknowledge publicly the work and dedication of Rebecca Lazo, who is Senior Acquisitions Editor for Paul H. Brookes Publishing Co. Rebecca has worked on *Life* with me for the past 10 years and her investment in it and enthusiasm about it has motivated me to do the best I can on this project. Many of our colleagues in transition have come to know her and are also aware of her infectious enthusiasm for helping children and youth with disabilities. Her passion for making Brookes' books the very best comes out in the day-to-day working with her and her team. She is not only good at recruiting projects but also at administratively following through to maintain a top-flight product. I thank her for her generous commitment to seeing this fifth edition through, especially with the greater efforts toward reaching larger audiences.

To my children, Brody, Cara, Ragan, Peyton, and Blake,
who, in the past 10 years, have taught me more about the transitions that occur
from school to adulthood than any college professor could ever hope to learn

I

Introduction

Transition

New Horizons and Challenges

PAUL WEHMAN

After completing this chapter, the reader will be able to

- Describe the role of business in promoting employment for young persons with disabilities
- Describe evidence-based transition research and recent findings
- Describe the requirements that are placed on educational systems by the Individuals with Disabilities Education Improvement Act of 2004 (PL 108-446) regarding transition
- Discuss the importance of goal setting in transition planning
- Describe the major transition themes involved with helping young people with disabilities grow up and achieve their life goals
- Discuss the challenges faced by youth in school-to-adulthood transition

Transition from school to adulthood for young people with disabilities remains one of the most exciting and fulfilling aspects of special education and rehabilitation. As children become teenagers and move into early adulthood, there are many transitions that they face. For young people with disabilities, this is no different except that there are invariably additional complex challenges that must be overcome. It is the successful mounting of these challenges that generates much passion and happiness in the minds of students, family members, and professionals.

Consider, for example, the young man with severe dyslexia, a reading disability, who is able to utilize special Kurzweil technology and graduate from high school, walk the stage for graduation, and go to college. Or, consider the 21-year-old student with significant autism who works in an internship in a hospital sterilizing surgical tools for the ambulatory surgery unit, whose experience culminates in a job offer. Think about the 15-year-old student who experienced a **traumatic brain injury**, was in the hospital for 3 months, and now goes on to finish high school and enters community college in a nursing program. When young people with disabilities succeed—the look of joy and tears on the faces of mothers and fathers, the gratification of that teacher or counselor who spent hundreds of hours with that person—well, these are career makers. This is why people want to go into special education and rehabilitation. This is why often the best of the best back away from other careers and say: *This is what I want.*

Most parents and families want successful, fulfilling futures for the young people in their family. But, with many young people with disabilities, the bar has often been set too low, and it is the job of professionals to raise the bar and then follow through with success. To those readers of this book who are new to the field, recognize the greatness you will experience when you are able to change lives as described here. For those of you who have been doing this for years, do more and do it better and draw on all of the many new advances in the transition field. For those parents of young children, aim high and aspire for the best for your child. Advancements to transition for youth with disabilities are occurring rapidly; what we see now as work and community outcomes will not be the same in 10 years—they will continue to significantly improve.

The purpose of this book is to help give you the information—the power—to effect change. Knowledge is power. Once the knowledge is there, then the motivation and leadership can follow.

Meet the Faces of Transition in America

To best appreciate the power of successful transition into adulthood and the challenges that must be met and overcome, it is essential to look directly at people who have been successful despite incredible barriers. On the cover of this book are the pictures of four young people with different disabilities who are transitioning into successful adulthood. They each have different personalities, families, and issues.

Teresa   Teresa is a 24-year-old with Down syndrome and is very social, with a large, extended friends-and-family network; she went to a regular high school and made a lot of friends. Her mother and father had high expectations that she could work and helped her get a weekend job at a bagel shop. Teresa has some academic skills and basic computer knowledge, which made her a good fit for her position in which she was hired as an administrative assistant in a local university near her home. After several months of job coaching to acquire a work routine and appropriate operation of office equipment, the most challenging area for Teresa has been acquiring acceptable work behaviors. With the assistance of a several co-workers providing **natural supports**, she is able to receive regular reinforcement for on-task behavior, checks for accuracy, and redirection on conversations that are for a lunchtime get-together. Teresa is approaching her second-year employment anniversary date and is advancing her computer skills on the job. She has friends on Facebook, communicates regularly with those with and without disabilities, and is viewed as a positive force in the work environment.

So what has Teresa taught us? First, she has been a product of an inclusive high school environment, which has helped her integrate into a normal work site. Second, she had a weekend part-time job, so she has work experience. Third, she took advantage of the family–friend network of placement as her employer and father had been professional acquaintances. Fourth, she benefited greatly from the use of a job coach. Fifth, she demonstrated outgoing, friendly social skills. Finally, she had a highly supportive family. There are other parts of her success story but the take away is this: *Her Down syndrome label was minimized to nothing.* She entered a workplace with support that allowed her to leverage her skills into acceptance and success.

Kalyn   Kalyn, 21, came into **Project SEARCH®** (see Chapter 7 and Chapter 13), a business-based transition program, saying she wanted to work full time at St. Mary's Hospital. She came with supportive parents and from a regular high school. At 21 years old, this young adult with severe **autism spectrum disorder** has achieved her goal. Kalyn is employed as a surgical care technician and she works in the main operating room. Her duties include stocking supplies throughout the department, including the blanket warmers, sutures, and physicians' scrubs. In addition, she prepares patient rooms as patients exit to be ready for new patients. Kalyn is a bundle of energy, which can cause challenges in the workplace. Focusing her energy and controlling her speed is her biggest challenge. She is an emotionally charged young woman and cries easily. Kalyn's **employment specialist** has created a strict schedule and checklist outlining duties and times so that she can stay focused while at work. Kalyn enjoys meeting her goals, so the checklist and schedule have been critical in keeping her on task. Over the course of her three 10-week Project SEARCH rotations, Kalyn worked on her social skills in a business setting. She learned how to maneuver her way through crowded hospital halls without stepping in front of visitors and guests and walking at a professional pace. Through her internships and employment, Kalyn has created a life for herself where she is truly a part of her community and is looking forward to more independence as a result of her employment.

When one reviews why Kalyn was offered a job, several points come to mind. First, she showed personal attributes of enthusiasm and tremendous determination to learn this rather complex job. Second, the 9-month internship was a critical opportunity for her to showcase these attributes and demonstrate her vocational capacity. Third, the use of co-workers—in this case, surgical nurses, supports, and some employment specialist's help—was a critical bridge to unleash her underlying potential. In the end, Kalyn was no longer considered as one with autism—instead, she is now a surgical technician.

Bess   Bess is a 23-year-old woman referred to a large business office through a local school transition program. Bess has multiple pterygium syndrome, which causes webbing of joints and muscle contractures. She uses a motorized wheelchair for mobility. Bess began working at the office in April 2006 on an internship basis, which was subsequently developed into a permanent part-time position. Bess performs office work, including data entry, making copies, sorting mail, duplicating CDs/DVDs, and packaging products. Throughout the years, Bess has taken on more responsibilities and duties. Her data entry skills are excellent. She is fast and accurate.

Bess also has become more independent and social. Initially, she was quiet and dependent on her personal assistant. Her personal assistant provided aid for communication, instruction, reassurance, and bathroom breaks. Now, Bess travels by herself throughout the building and uses the elevator. She takes the initiative to ask for additional work and helps other co-workers. Her personal assistant does not stay on site anymore but is quickly available if Bess contacts her by cell phone for a bathroom break. This has given Bess autonomy, freedom, and self-confidence.

When Bess first started working, new duties may have caused her to doubt her abilities and to ask for assistance before trying something difficult on her own. Now she is willing to try new tasks independently. If she needs assistance, she will ask her supervisor or co-workers for clarification. Bess has so many assets that she brings to the workplace. She is positive and has a strong work ethic. Bess is a dependable employee and presents herself professionally to co-workers and university guests.

Bess is an extraordinary young lady who, for close to 20 years, was considered by her school district to have severe intellectual disabilities. So she was treated this way and subsequently her potential was suppressed. Real work for real pay prefaced by a 1-year on-the-job internship was the only way to show her skills, which were hidden by complex physical challenges. She receives **personal assistance services**, she receives **assistive technology** supports, her job tasks have been redesigned, and has specialized transportation—yet, in the end, she not only is doing well in her job, but she is also gaining more competence as she continues to work. Her job is becoming an important therapy for her to feel better about herself. Bess is transitioning from school to adulthood. Bess is now an administrative assistant, and, at least at this worksite, the hard-to-pronounce name of her syndrome means nothing.

Pharoah (PJ)   At 18 years old, Pharoah (PJ) was in a private school with other students with disabilities and challenging behaviors. Fast forward to 1 year later, PJ, who has **autism**, has completed three rotations at a local hospital through Project SEARCH and was offered a position working in the mail room. He is sorting mail, using the meter machine, and delivering packages throughout the seven-story facility, as well as binding documents for distribution. Through the use of positive behavior supports he has learned to accept criticism without outbursts. In addition, staff use a system of checking in and out with him to assess his mood and concerns each day. This helps PJ stay in touch with his feelings. But Project SEARCH has taught PJ more than just work skills; PJ's grandmother states that through the supports of Project SEARCH she has seen his social skills blossom, and now he has friends. This is something she never thought she would see for her grandson. With the right supports and tools, this young man has created an independent life for himself.

What have we learned through the success to date of PJ? We know that positive behavior supports were crucial (see Chapter 19) because he had a history of behavior problems and a long time period in a special school. These behavioral challenges could have caused a rapid end to his internship or job termination, so experienced behavioral help was critical. Second, the internship has these 12-week rotations; without these opportunities to show his capacity, he would not have been hired. Finally, PJ's grandmother helped maintain his participation in community activities as he was growing up. This investment in the community served him well as he adjusted to a fast-paced hospital environment reflected by many different staff and patients.

This book is about how to reach people like Teresa, Bess, Kalyn, and Pharoah (PJ); their parents; and the community and school personnel who serve and support them. There are millions of young people with disabilities in the United States, and a significant number of them are in middle and secondary schools. Table 1.1 shows the distribution of these children in 2009–2010 across disabilities. Throughout the country, these young people with disabilities are leaving the public schools and looking for postsecondary opportunities in 2- and 4-year colleges and the workforce, searching for their rightful places in the community. Table 1.2 shows by state the number of students with disabilities ages 14–21 years who exited school during the 2008–2009 school year. What teachers, rehabilitation counselors, transition specialists, and parents must ask is this: Are we prepared to help those young people seamlessly move from school into the workplace and community? Have we begun the planning early enough to make a difference?

Table 1.1. Number of students ages 6–21 years served under IDEA during 2000–2001 and fall 2009 of the 2009–2010 school year

Disability category	Number served		Percent change in number
	2000–2001	2009–2010	
Specific learning disabilities	2,887,217	2,486,419	−13.9
Speech or language impairments	1,093,808	1,107,428	1.2
Intellectual disabilities	612,978	461,337	−24.7
Emotional disturbance	473,663	405,475	−14.4
Multiple disabilities	122,559	124,529	1.6
Hearing impairments	70,767	70,650	−0.2
Orthopedic impairments	73,057	57,972	−20.6
Other health impairments	291,850	678,970	132.6
Visual impairments	25,975	25,848	−0.5
Autism	78,749	333,234	323.2
Deafblindness	1,320	1,365	3.4
Traumatic brain injury	14,844	24,402	64.4
Developmental delay[a]	28,935	104,528	261.3
All disabilities	5,775,722	5,882,157	1.8

From http://www.ideadata.org/arc_toc11.asp#partbCC retrieved on July 12, 2011.
Key: IDEA, Individuals with Disabilities Education Act.

[a]States' use of developmental delay category is optional for children ages 3–9 years and is not applicable to children older than 9 years of age.

Table 1.2. Number of students ages 14–21 years with disabilities served under IDEA, Part B, who exited special education, by exit reason and state: 2008–2009[a]

State	Exiting total	Graduated with diploma	Received a certificate	Reached maximum age[b]	Transferred to regular education	Moved, known to be continuing[c]	Died	Dropped out[d]
Alabama	7,734	1,678	2,308	367	547	2,177	21	636
Alaska	1,565	512	138	10	193	398	5	309
Arizona	11,558	4,910	–	26	972	4,304	25	1,321
Arkansas	8,775	3,364	79	11	487	4,147	18	669
California	63,087	14,630	7,214	802	7,124	26,343	141	6,833
Colorado	10,017	3,050	204	93	919	4,027	50	1,674
Connecticut	6,378	3,556	95	148	1,037	651	12	879
Delaware	2,069	569	56	x	161	944	x	322
District of Columbia	1,469	617	98	x	42	31	x	673
Florida	48,470	11,588	5,968	–	2,850	22,364	112	5,588
Georgia	19,088	4,579	3,532	–	1,544	6,241	38	3,154
Hawaii	2,122	1,199	24	216	443	190	9	41
Idaho	2,921	684	497	61	447	903	8	321
Illinois	35,272	14,263	140	341	2,942	14,032	68	3,486
Indiana	18,189	5,898	1,325	82	1,292	6,822	70	2,700
Iowa	7,383	3,479	161	40	1,347	844	19	1,493
Kansas	7,349	3,113	–	80	981	2,170	17	988
Kentucky	8,138	3,365	382	25	884	2,585	24	873
Louisiana	7,556	1,461	1,514	37	1,356	825	27	2,336
Maine	2,973	1,557	31	18	464	401	5	497
Maryland	11,211	4,112	727	86	1,175	3,440	34	1,637
Massachusetts	13,074	7,775	429	385	8	2,065	31	2,381
Michigan	27,836	10,359	309	–	2,423	9,763	70	4,912
Minnesota	8,458	5,757	–	6	475	1,511	14	695
Mississippi	4,391	807	2,028	22	173	898	18	445
Missouri	14,459	7,100	9	91	1,591	3,345	24	2,299

State	Exiting total	Graduated with diploma	Received a certificate	Reached maximum age[b]	Transferred to regular education	Moved, known to be continuing[c]	Died	Dropped out[d]
Montana	1,898	852	15	0	210	531	5	285
Nebraska	2,625	1,591	20	62	573	61	12	306
Nevada	4,071	703	841	52	415	1,173	17	870
New Hampshire	3,475	1,825	149	21	649	295	6	530
New Jersey	26,092	14,234	–	348	1,206	6,990	44	3,270
New Mexico	3,328	1,486	510	x	377	626	x	321
New York	53,884	15,937	6,277	286	2,888	20,604	104	7,788
North Carolina	18,691	6,484	1,022	30	2,241	5,307	48	3,559
North Dakota	1,465	576	x	24	182	440	x	231
Ohio	28,103	7,674	5,493	1,220	663	11,152	62	1,839
Oklahoma	11,971	5,134	–	11	678	4,637	31	1,480
Oregon	9,018	2,224	1,054	260	1,139	3,115	15	1,211
Pennsylvania	33,871	18,731	128	149	2,035	10,380	60	2,388
Puerto Rico	3,844	1,712	202	0	513	448	19	950
Rhode Island	3,439	1,205	38	60	474	1,277	7	378
South Carolina	9,021	2,308	62	306	610	2,696	37	3,002
South Dakota	1,443	577	–	18	280	425	5	138
Tennessee	16,326	5,758	1,803	36	1,050	6,555	51	1,073
Texas	51,036	16,251	10,700	36	9,022	7,819	142	7,066
Utah	5,671	2,476	267	67	429	1,630	13	789
Vermont	–	–	–	–	–	–	–	–
Virginia	21,188	6,007	4,836	10	4,838	3,645	49	1,803
Washington	11,950	4,511	240	–	–	5,383	20	1,796
West Virginia	4,515	2,122	260	5	312	985	9	822
Wisconsin	11,850	6,075	200	120	3,271	507	21	1,656
Wyoming	1,498	408	47	x	233	520	x	265
Bureau of Indian Education schools	801	147	x	x	46	342	0	220
50 states, District of Columbia, and Puerto Rico (including Bureau of Indian Education schools)	692,616	246,990	61,486	6,107	66,211	218,964	1,660	91,198
American Samoa	119	50	x	x	41	20	x	x
Guam	307	183	–	x	82	15	x	21
Northern Marianas	44	20	–	0	10	x	0	x
Virgin Islands	196	56	x	0	20	x	0	90
U.S. and outlying areas	693,282	247,299	61,508	6,112	66,364	219,020	1,661	91,318

Source: U.S. Department of Education, Office of Special Education Programs, Data Analysis System, OMB #1820-0521: "Children with disabilities exiting special education," 2008–2009. Data updated as of July 15, 2010.

Key: –, data not available; x, data suppressed to limit disclosure; IDEA, Individuals with Disabilities Education Act.

Note: Please see the Part B Exiting Data Notes on http://www.IDEAdata.org for information the state submitted to clarify its data submissions.

[a]Data are from a 12-month reporting period.

[b]Children may exit special education services because of maximum age depending on state law or practice or order of any court.

[c]Moved, known to be continuing, is the total number of students who moved out of the catchment area or otherwise transferred to another district and are known to be continuing in an educational program.

[d]Dropped out is defined as the total number of students who were enrolled at some point in the reporting year, were not enrolled at the end of the reporting year, and did not exit through any of the other bases described. For the purpose of calculating dropout rates, the Office of Special Education Programs counts students moved, not known to continue, as dropouts.

Defining Transition

So, what is transition? What does this term mean? Transition has been defined in the **Individuals with Disabilities Education Improvement Act (IDEA) of 2004** as follows:

> Transition services means a coordinated set of activities for a student with a disability that:
>
> A. is designed to be within a results-oriented process, that is focused on improving the academic and functional achievement of the student with a disability to facilitate the student's movement from school to post-school activities, including
>
> - post-secondary education,
> - vocational education,
> - integrated employment (including supported employment),
> - continuing and adult education,
> - adult services,
> - independent living, or community participation;
>
> B. is based upon the individual student's needs, taking into account the student's strengths, preferences and interests; and
>
> C. includes instruction, related services, community experiences, the development of employment and other postschool adult living objectives, and, if appropriate, acquisition of daily living skills and functional vocational evaluation. (34 C.F.R. 300.43[a]; 20 U.S.C. 1401[34])

The **individualized education programs (IEPs)** for students ages 16 years and older must specify **transition planning**. Some states have moved this to age 14 (Virginia, Delaware, Rhode Island). According to IDEA, the IEP must include a statement of

- Appropriate measurable postsecondary goals based upon age-appropriate transition assessments related to training, education, employment, and, where appropriate, independent living skills
- The transition services (including courses of study) needed to assist the (student) in reaching those goals (34 C.F.R. 300.320[b] and [c]; 20 U.S.C. 1414 [d][1][A][i][VIII])

The law also requires local education agencies to provide students with disabilities exiting high school with a Summary of Performance documents for transition students with disabilities, resulting in inconsistency across the field (Richter & Mazzotti, 2011).

There is now accountability in transition planning. Section 616 (b) of IDEA 2004 requires states to develop and submit a **state performance plan (SPP)** to the Office of Special Education Programs (OSEP). There are 20 indicators that are seen as key in this SPP. The SPP format consists, in part, of targets for each indicator, as well as activities intended to improve results for students with disabilities. There are four indicators from the SPP directly related to transition:

1. **Indicator 1** reads:

   Percent of youth with IEPs graduating from high school with a regular diploma compared to percent of all youth in the State graduating with a regular diploma.

2. **Indicator 2** reads:

   Percent of youth with IEPs dropping out of high school compared to the percent of all youth in the State dropping out of high school.

3. **Indicator 13** reads:

   Percent of youth with IEPs aged 16 and above with an IEP that includes appropriate measurable postsecondary goals that are annually updated and based upon an age-appropriate transition assessment, transition services, including courses of study, that will reasonably enable the student to meet those postsecondary goals, and annual IEP goals related to the student's transition services needs. There also must be evidence that the student was invited to the IEP Team meeting where transition services are to be discussed and evidence that, if appropriate, a representative of any participating agency was invited to the IEP Team meeting with the prior consent of the parent or student who has reached the age of majority. (20 U.S.C. 1416[a][3][B])

4. **Indicator 14** reads:

    Percent of youth who are no longer in secondary school, had Individualized Education Programs (IEPs) in effect at the time they left school, and were:

    A. Enrolled in higher education within one year of leaving high school.
    B. Enrolled in higher education or competitively employed within one year of leaving high school.
    C. Enrolled in higher education or in some other postsecondary education or training program; or competitively employed or in some other employment within one year of leaving high school. (20 U.S.C. 1416[a][3][B])

These indicators are important. They provide a method to track what is happening with youth with disabilities, influencing school divisions in all states to improve the way transition planning is developed within IEPs.

There is a growing emphasis on academic performance and educational outcomes for students with disabilities. This focus is demonstrated, in part, by the federal requirement to collect postschool outcome data from these former students (i.e., Indicator 14). Rabren and Johnson (2010) introduced two states' (Alabama's and Washington's) approaches to collecting postschool outcome data and offered recommendations and suggestions for implementing such data systems. The background and history of how these states developed systems to collect, analyze, and report postschool outcomes and how their data collection instruments were developed are described. Similarities, differences, and limitations of these systems are presented and recommendations for future research are provided.

In addition, Alverson, Naranjo, Yamamoto, and Unruh (2010) examined ways to collect outcome data on postschool employment, postsecondary school, and/or training enrollment of young adults with disabilities. To examine how these data have been collected, they conducted a literature synthesis of follow-up and follow-along studies to answer four critical questions:

1. What data collection methods were used?
2. What were the sample characteristics?
3. What variables were examined?
4. What postschool outcomes were identified?

They reported the answers to these questions, discussed the limitations of these syntheses, and made recommendations for state researchers collecting postschool outcomes data as well as education professionals.

At a minimum, the IEP should address each of these areas, including instruction, community experiences, and development of employment and other postschool adult living objectives. In many cases, each of these areas, and possibly some others, will be included in students' IEPs; however, **transition services** may be provided by the education agency or, as outlined in Section 300.348 of the regulations, by agencies outside the school. Steere and Cavaiuolo (2002) provided functional examples of how outcomes, goals, and objectives can be tied together (Figure 1.1). Furthermore, there is an increasing interest in providing **self-determination**, self-advocacy, and financial management objectives. Whatever the case, these objectives must be written into the IEP and the responsible agency noted. IDEA and its reauthorizations require that transition services be provided to all students by the time they are the appropriate age. We must now ask ourselves this: How we are doing? What concerns are being addressed?

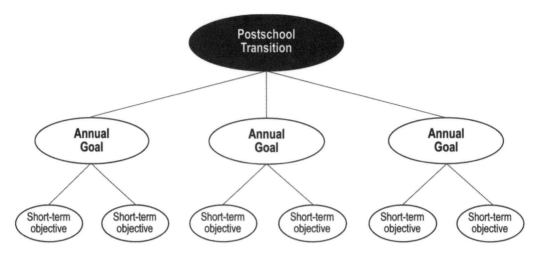

Figure 1.1. Relationship of postschool outcomes to annual goals and short-term objectives. (From Steere, D.E., & Cavaiuolo, D. [2002]. Connecting outcomes, goals, and objectives in transition planning. *Teaching Exceptional Children, 34*[6], 54–59; reprinted by permission.)

2010 Survey of Americans with Disabilities: Much Work Remains to Help Persons with Disabilities Gain Employment

Kessler Foundation and National Organization on Disability (2010) commissioned Harris Interactive to conduct a series of surveys exploring the quality of life and employment opportunities for people living with disabilities. The 2010 Survey of Americans with Disabilities marked the sixth effort over the past 24 years to measure the gaps between people with and without disabilities on different indicators and to track them over time. These indicators include employment, income, education, health care, access to transportation, socializing, going to restaurants, attendance at religious services, political participation, and life satisfaction.

Although there has been modest improvement in a few areas, the general implication of the indicators is that now, 20 years after the passage of the **Americans with Disabilities Act** (ADA; PL 101-336), there has yet to be significant progress in most areas.

Among the Findings

For example, employment success represents the largest gap between the two groups—those with disabilities and those without. *Of all working-age people with disabilities, not just young people, only 21% say that they are employed, compared with 59% of people without disabilities—a gap of 38 percentage points.* People with disabilities are still much more likely to be living in poverty. People with disabilities are less likely than those without disabilities to socialize with friends, relatives, or neighbors, once again suggesting that there are significant barriers to participation in leisure activities for this population. The second-largest gap between people with and without disabilities is regarding Internet access. Eighty-five percent of adults without disabilities access the Internet, whereas only 54% of adults with disabilities report the same—a gap of 31 percentage points.

Social networks can help individuals then locate job leads or be introduced to businesses, and Internet can be used to research businesses where a person may want to apply for work. The fact that these outcome data continue to be so poor is most discouraging (Wehman, 2011a; Rusch & Wolfe, 2008). We explore reasons for this through this chapter and the balance of the book. Work is a critical outcome that can bridge the quality of life one can experience. Transition from school to adulthood is an important means for this to happen (Wehman, 2011b; Test, 2008).

National Longitudinal Transition Study-2: What Happens to Youth When They Leave School?

The National Longitudinal Transition Study-2 (NLTS-2) was commissioned to begin in 2001 by the U.S. Department of Education, OSEP (2001–2011), and the Institute of Education Sciences (U.S. Department of Labor, 1997). It is a follow-up of the original NLTS, which was designed and conducted from 1985 through 1993. NLTS-2 includes 11,270 youth nationwide who were ages 13–16 years at the start of the study (2000). Information was collected over 10 years from parents, youth, and schools and provided a national picture of the experiences and achievements of young people as they transition into early adulthood. The data from the NLTS-2 Wave 5 2009 Parent and Young Adult Survey offers an update on what happens when youth leave school.

Employment

The survey reports on employment data and indicates that, among young adults with disabilities who had been out of high school 1–4 years, 59% had a current paid job outside the home, leaving 41% unemployed. Close to half (47%) reported that they had help with finding a current or most recent job. One fourth of those polled reported working in food preparation and serving-related occupations (13%) or sales and related occupations (12%).

The mean number of hours worked per week was 36 at their current or most recent job. The mean hourly wage reported at current or most recent job was $10.40. Thirty-eight percent reported earnings of $8.50 or less, with 16% reporting earnings between $7.25 and $8.50 per hour; and 22% earning less than $7.25 per hour.

Almost half or 48% were employed for less than 12 months in current or most recent job. Half of those individuals were employed for less than 6 months, with the remaining employed for 6–12 months. The reasons reported for leaving previous or most recent job were quit (54.0%), fired (11%), laid off (14%), and temporary job that ended (21%).

Carter, Austin, and Trainor (2011b) used the NLTS-2 data to examine the early work experiences of youth with severe disabilities (i.e., **intellectual disabilities**, autism, multiple disabilities). They explored the extent to which various student-, family-, school-, and community-level factors were associated with paid work experiences during high school. Findings highlighted the elusiveness of early work experiences for many youth with severe disabilities and called attention to malleable factors that may play roles in shaping employment success during high school.

Differences in some aspects of youth's early post–high school employment experiences were noted among youth in different disability categories, related to whether or not the youth were currently working or had worked since high school. It is worth noting that some youth had an agency stay in touch with them postemployment.

Postsecondary Education

We know that postsecondary education can positively affect employment outcomes (Flannery, Yovanoff, Benz, & Kato, 2011). Hence, it will be helpful to see what the NLTS-2 data say as well.

Related to postsecondary education, the survey reports that, since leaving high school, 43% of youth with disabilities have enrolled in 2-year or community colleges and 9% were attending at the time of the interview. While attending, 18% reported receiving services or **accommodations** from the college. The top-three accommodations or services received were testing accommodations (80%), human aides (60%), and material/technology adaptations (40%). Among those young adults who no longer attended 2-year college, 31% graduated or completed the program whereas 69% indicated leaving for another reason.

Young adults or parents also reported on 4-year college or university experiences. Eighteen percent of youth with disabilities reported taking a class at a 4-year postsecondary school with 5% doing so when interviewed. Ten percent of those who were attending or had attended indicated receiving services or accommodations. Types of help included tutor/help with subject (63%), writing center (27%), and study center or other help (30%). Forty-three percent reported that they graduated or completed the program, and 57% reported that they left for another reason.

Gallup Poll Employer Results: The News Is Not All Bad

In another national study (Siperstein, Romano, Mohler, & Parker, 2006), The Gallup Poll conducted a major survey of what people in the United States feel about people with disabilities in the workforce. Employers' negative attitudes and fears have long been perceived to be a barrier to the employment of individuals with disabilities. In accordance, attitude literature on the employment of people with disabilities has focused almost exclusively on employers (Luecking, 2008). However, the successful employment of people with disabilities is also heavily contingent on the views of the consumer, because of their influence over business practices. Consumer attitudes toward companies that hire individuals with disabilities were assessed through a Gallup Poll of 803 persons. The findings indicated that most respondents (75%) had direct experience with people with disabilities in a work environment and that these experiences were very positive. Table 1.3 and Table 1.4 also show how Americans who responded to this survey felt about giving their business to companies who hired persons with disabilities. These results were very favorable.

These findings present dramatic new evidence of how American society values individuals with disabilities, not only as co-workers but also as providing a reason to do business with a company that employs persons with disabilities. This is meaningful because,

Table 1.3. Participants' favorability ratings of companies that demonstrate social responsibility

	Much more favorable	More favorable	Same	Less favorable	Much less favorable
Offers health insurance to all its workers	46%	48%	3%	1%	<1%
Helps protect the environment	36%	56%	6%	2%	0%
Hires people with disabilities	32%	60%	5%	1%	1%
Donates money to disaster relief	31%	56%	7%	4%	1%
Stops doing business with countries known to treat their people badly	31%	44%	5%	14%	6%
Supports a cause you care about	29%	60%	9%	2%	<1%

From *Journal of Vocational Rehabilitation*, 24, Siperstein, G.N., Romano, N., Mohler, A., & Parker, R., A national survey of consumer attitudes towards companies that hire people with disabilities, pp. 3-9, Copyright 2006, with permission from IOS Press.

Table 1.4. Participants' perception of the benefits of employing people with disabilities

	Strongly agree	Agree	Neutral	Disagree	Strongly disagree
Helps people with disabilities lead more productive lives	47%	49%	1%	3%	<1%
Helps other employees have better understanding of persons with disabilities	40%	50%	3%	5%	1%
Shows their customers that they care about all workers	40%	53%	3%	4%	1%
Are companies you would prefer to give your business to	33%	54%	6%	4%	1%
Often takes advantage of people with disabilities	5%	14%	4%	51%	22%
Creates problems within their workforce	2%	12%	3%	60%	20%

From *Journal of Vocational Rehabilitation*, 24, Siperstein, G.N., Romano, N., Mohler, A., & Parker, R., A national survey of consumer attitudes towards companies that hire people with disabilities, pp. 3-9, Copyright 2006, with permission from IOS Press.

despite the mediocre employment rates to date for people with disabilities, the Gallup Poll would suggest that business and society are ready for workers with disabilities.

Tracey   Tracey is a 16-year-old student who has a difficult time controlling his impulses and his erratic behavior. His condition has deteriorated over the years. A few years ago, his elementary school teacher reported that he would get overly disturbed by things that happened. According to his father, things seemed to escalate about the time he was divorcing Tracey's mom. Tracey's father noticed that Tracey seemed to be withdrawn. He also started to get into fights at school. His father said he had to send him to live with his grandparents for a while because going back and forth to school to attend meetings about disciplinary problems was jeopardizing his job.

Tracey has a negative attitude, and if you ask him about his future goals in life, he gives you a blank stare and shrugs his shoulders. When he gets home from school, he lies on the couch and plays video games. Once bored, he watches wrestling matches on television. He does not have any responsibilities. His grandmother does almost everything for him—basically to keep the peace. Once she asked Tracey to take out the trash and he threw the garbage across the room out of anger. Afterward, he ran into his bedroom, slammed the door and locked it—he did not come out until late the next day. Another day of school was missed.

Should it be surprising that Tracey gets poor progress reports from school and there are ongoing reports that he is totally withdrawn and closed up? Should it be surprising that Tracey is sluggish around the house and indifferent to the authority of adults? Should it be surprising that Tracey does not want to continue in school and has no interest in higher education or a job?

Thousands of young people who have disabilities face these problems. The issue is not that these students lack potential; it is they do not have goals. In addition, there may be little or no attention to a plan for transitioning from the classroom to adulthood. There simply is no plan for the future. However, life beyond the classroom requires a blueprint—a plan for life. Having a plan in place is essential for all youth, disabled or not. A blueprint helps ensure that each student progresses toward building a successful and happy life at home, at work, and in the community. Students build their lives a day at a time, and all involved must put their best into the building even when they cannot see the end. There is hard work ahead. Personal views, decisions that are made, and activities that take place build the "house" that the student will live in tomorrow—parents, teachers, and others must help guide them so that the student builds it wisely. If not, the student could end up living an unfulfilled life without meaning—or, even worse, in ruins.

Is Business the Answer to Improving Transition Outcomes?

Business is the social engine in America. Everyone needs to work. Everyone needs a paycheck and benefits. We are so often defined by whether we have a job, what it is, how long we have worked there, and what it is we do. Americans strongly focus upon this aspect of their lives.

Young people with disabilities need to be a part of the work community. This job can be private-sector employment, public-sector employment, **self-employment**, or other opportunities, but the only way for the country to significantly turn around these protracted dismal employment outcomes is by partnering with business, getting business at the table with schools and community programs to understand the vocational capacity of young people with disabilities. Dyda (2008) has discussed how jobs change lives and the relationship between social capital and shared value exchanges that emphasizes use of face-to-face contact in conjunction with everyday life interests.

McMahon (2011) eloquently portrayed how potential employment of his son, Dan, an engaging young man, would help American business and economy in the following letter to the *Washington Post*:

My son, Dan, is 17 and has epilepsy. Here are five ways that hiring Dan can help reduce the budget deficit.

1. You can both cut and protect Medicare and Social Security. Right now, 13.6 million Americans like Dan draw $172 billion from Social Security and $150 billion from Medicare or Medicaid. If they were added to the officially unemployed, we would call this the Greatest Depression, not the Great Recession. If you hire Dan, he will not find himself on these programs.
2. Do you favor new revenue? Dan will be contributing the moment you employ him.
3. Do you favor stimulus? Dan will spend every penny of his new wages, almost immediately. Dan puts gas in his car and buys clothes and video games; he saves nothing. The wages you pay Dan will go directly into the economy.
4. Love private-sector health care? Put Dan on your insurance, and he won't end up on medical assistance.
5. Value innovation? Innovation creates wealth. Innovation is automatic if you operate in an extreme environment. Check out NASA, NASCAR, or the military. Like every worker with a disability, Dan brings his own "extreme environment" to your business. He may require you to rethink how you do things. That's a good thing. Thousands of inventions—think Jacuzzi and cruise control—have resulted from accommodating people with disabilities.

Dan's so attractive, a competitor may beat you to him. But worry not. There are 54 million Americans with disabilities, and when they all have jobs, our national debt will be under control.

                                                                                        Brian T. McMahon, Richmond

Why Should Business Want to Hire Young People with Disabilities?

There are numerous reasons why business should be interested in hiring young people with disabilities. First, and perhaps most obvious, when placed into a proper job with the supports and plans like we saw with Teresa, Bess, Kalyn, and Pharoah (PJ), young people with disabilities become not good workers, but outstanding workers. *Outstanding* is defined as working every day, producing a high level of reliability, and being highly productive. Productivity in basic business language means how much work is produced with the lowest amount of labor expense.

Second, the public (i.e., potential customers) prefer companies that hire workers with disabilities. In looking at Siperstein et al. (2006); Burge, Ouellete-Kuntz, and Lysaght (2007); and after review of Tables 1.3 and 1.4, it is pretty clear the public and co-workers prefer companies with strong hiring practices of individuals with disabilities.

There is a third reason businesses are open to hiring young people with disabilities. People who work in companies and their suppliers and their customers often have children, youth, and adults with disabilities in their families. The sensitivity that many employers and supervisors feel toward including young people with disabilities is very high, but schools and rehabilitation programs have not figured out the best ways to maximize the possible long-term relations that can exist here. Businesses will increase their likelihood of hiring when they have more exposure to workers with disabilities. Luecking (2008) astutely pointed out,

A very encouraging aspect of the Hernandez, Keys, and Balcazar (2000) review, and several more recent studies (e.g., Luecking & Fabian, 2000; Unger, 2002), is finding that employer views about disability tend to positively change with exposure. Simply stated, employers with prior contact with people with disabilities tend to hold more favorable attitudes toward workers with disabilities than those who have not. With respect to people with typically stigmatized disabilities, such as intellectual and psychiatric disabilities, employers have consistently been more positive about these workers when appropriate supports are provided

(Fabian, 2004; Morgan & Alexander, 2005). In fact, in many cases where employers are given specific consultation from rehabilitation professionals, they are willing to go well beyond the Americans with Disabilities Act requirements for reasonable accommodations by providing an array of supports to workers with significant disability (Unger, 2002, p. 5).

Finally, most businesses are good stewards in the community. They sponsor Little League basketball teams, church functions, health functions, and often engage in significant philanthropy. The prospect of hiring young people with disabilities and helping to give them a start in the world of work is highly consistent with this social responsibility philosophy that so many companies, in both private and public sectors, believe in and practice.

In sum, parents and professionals alike must begin to think about development of business connections first. They must ask: Where are the jobs? What jobs are going to be available? Whom do I know who could help my child get a job? And, to be truly successful, teachers and counselors in our field must start understanding how business thinks—specifically, how am I going to sell my products and services and make a profit? What will make my business look good in the community? How can I save money on my monthly expenses? Is there a new set of products I should be introducing? And the one we want to hear the most: What workers will be the most productive and reliable?

Too often in education we think only about what we want: one job for one person. But to get there we need to understand the business community, establish trust, and ask for their advice.

This type of relationship can ultimately lead to business understanding that those professionals in the disability community might add value to their businesses and potentially help their company be more productive. This is the answer to dramatically cutting into the high unemployment rates over the next 5–8 years. Exclusively providing training without business linkages will not work.

What Can Schools and Community Programs Do to Encourage More Business Participation in the Transition Process?

There are several ways to engage business in the transition process, but being passive is not one (Carter, Swedeen, & Trainor, 2009). We must look at the different roles of community providers, schools, and the private business sector and at building partnerships.

Promoting Public–Private Partnerships

One of the leading organizations promoting **public–private partnerships** is the U.S. Business Leadership Networks (BLN), which consists of employers, corporate representatives, state and federal agencies, and **community rehabilitation providers**. Currently, there are 43 BLN chapters in 32 states, including the District of Columbia, with a growing interest within the business community for developing new chapters. The primary focus of a BLN is to promote the recommended practices in hiring, retaining, and marketing of people with disabilities. BLNs view people with disabilities as the largest source of untapped talent and they are confident that they can help businesses effectively access this talent pool through introduction and education.

There are existing public–private partnerships dedicated to promoting the employment of people with disabilities in different stages of development all across the country. Rehabilitation professionals are strengthening their relationships with businesses, which in turn are increasing the number of competitive job opportunities for individuals with disabilities (Goodman, Hazelkorn, Bucholz, Duffy, & Kitta, 2011). The national network for the public vocational rehabilitation programs recognizes the importance of business as a customer and has recently created a national **Vocational Rehabilitation (VR)–**business network to expand their partnerships through the support of the Council of State Administrators of Vocational Rehabilitation (West-Evans, 2006). Key to this public–private partnership is developing a coordinated approach to serving business customers through a national VR team that specializes in employer development, business consulting, and corporate relations.

On the surface, the challenge for developing new or expanding existing public–private partnerships looks easy, but it is important to realize that these relationships are not created overnight or through a single contact. A strong and successful association is created by developing open and honest communication where both parties feel at ease to ask sensitive questions (Wehman, Brooke, Green, Hewett, & Tipton, 2008). Furthermore, recognizing a common need or purpose and together developing strategies that will transform ideas into an organized approach and ultimately success for both parties is a great basis for growing a partnership. Over time, these positive fundamental alliances are turning into strong, trusting relationships and partnerships that hold great promise for increasing the employment rate and advancement of people with disabilities (Carter, Swedeen, & Trainor, 2009).

Critical Force of Vocational Rehabilitation and Community Rehabilitation Programs

Rehabilitation professionals are the key developer in public–private partnerships. They must acknowledge the employer as a customer and demonstrate how their resources and clients can meet the needs of the business. Accessing employers and obtaining their investment in partnerships is not always an easy task. Rehabilitation professionals must research the companies they are approaching so they can market to that company's needs, ultimately affecting the return on investment for all associated partners. Through active development, many companies are collaborating with the public sector and establishing initiatives to hire people with disabilities. These partnerships are developing because of the increased knowledge and awareness between the two sectors and the understanding of mutual benefits.

Business and Industry: Where Are the Jobs?

The American economy, as worldwide with any economy, experiences periods of expansion and retraction. Severe retractions, i.e., recessions, typically result in employee layoffs, unfilled positions, business closures, and higher rates of unemployment. After initial waves of down-sizing and cost-cutting, businesses find ways to get more output from their workers, their machines, and their technologies, fueling economic recovery. Redesigning products to make them cheaper to produce and re-engineering processes to reduce unnecessary costs at all levels have become a permanent focus of corporate America. Persons with disabilities could meet businesses' needs, especially younger individuals coming out of effective transition programs in school (Griffin, Hammis, Geary, & Sullivan, 2008; Phillips et al., 2009; Rogers, Lavin, Tran, Gantenbein, & Sharpe, 2008).

It would appear that many of the positive attributes of an improving economy should provide significant employment possibilities for people with disabilities. People with disabilities should have greatly expanded work opportunities and their unemployment rate should be rapidly declining.

So, will there be jobs for people with disabilities over the next decade? The answer is yes. Despite the recession, there will be jobs as baby boomers (i.e., people born between 1946 and 1964) move into retirement. Consider what Eisenberg said:

> Though the average retirement age is creeping up—and the growing share of Americans, by choice or necessity, are planning to work at least part time well past 65—demographers say there still will not be enough qualified members of the next generation to pick up the slack. So with 76 million baby boomers heading toward retirement over the next 3 decades and only 46 million Gen Xers waiting in the wings, corporate America is facing a potentially mammoth talent crunch. Certainly, labor-saving technology and immigration may help fill the breach. (2002, pp. 41–42)

Table 1.5.   Fastest growing occupations for individuals with a high school diploma or general equivalency diploma

1.	Home health aides	Home health aides provide basic care for people with disabilities, chronic illnesses, and cognitive impairments or who have age-related problems. Employment of home health aides is projected to grow by 50% through 2018. Home health aides earned a median annual salary of $20,460 and a median hourly wage of $9.84 in 2008.
2.	Home care aides	Home care aides, sometimes called personal care aides or companions, help elderly or disabled clients with activities of daily living, including personal hygiene, meal preparation, laundry, and housekeeping. We can expect to see a 46% increase in the employment of home care aides through 2018. Home care aides earned a median annual salary of $19,180 and median hourly wages of $9.22 in 2008.
3.	Physical therapist aides	Physical therapist aides, sometimes called physical therapy aides, help make therapy sessions productive. Employment of physical therapist aides is expected to increase by 36% through 2018. Physical therapist aides earned a median annual salary of $23,760 and median hourly wages of $11.42.
4.	Dental assistant	Dental assistants perform duties that may include patient care, laboratory work, and office work. There is expected to be a 36% growth in employment of dental assistants through 2018. Dental assistants earned a median hourly wage of $15.57 and a median annual salary of $32,380 in 2008.
5.	Medical assistants	Medical assistants perform administrative duties in physicians' offices. They may also perform some clinical duties as allowed by individual state laws. Employment in this field is expected to grow by 34% through 2018. Medical assistants earned median hourly wages of $13.60 and a median annual salary of $28,300 in 2008.
6.	Self-enrichment teachers	Self-enrichment teachers instruct students in a variety of subjects that generally are not part of a required curriculum. Students who take self-enrichment classes are interested in learning about these subjects for self-improvement or for fun. Employment in this field is expected to grow by 32% through 2018. Self-enrichment teachers earned median hourly wages of $17.17 and a median annual salary of $35,720 in 2008.
7.	Compliance officers	A compliance officer's job is to make sure an entity is conforming with, or eligible for, contractual obligations, government regulations, laws, or licenses and permits. There is expected to be a 31% increase in the employment of compliance officers through 2018. Compliance officers earned median hourly wages of $23.50 and a median annual salary of $48,890 in 2008.
8.	Occupational therapist aides	Occupational therapist aides prepare materials and equipment used during patients' occupational therapy sessions. They also perform clerical duties. Employment in this field is expected to grow by 31% through 2018. Occupational therapist aides' median annual earnings were $26,960 and their median hourly wages were $12.96 in 2008.
9.	Pharmacy technician	Pharmacy technicians assist pharmacists with the preparation of prescription medications for customers. They perform tasks that range from receiving written prescriptions to counting pills and labeling bottles. We can expect to see a 31% growth in employment in this field through 2018. Pharmacy technicians earned median hourly wages of $13.32 and a median annual salary of $27,710 in 2008.
10.	Medical secretaries	Medical secretaries perform clerical duties in medical offices, utilizing their knowledge of medical terminology, insurance rules, and medical billing procedures. Employment in this field is expected to grow by 27% through 2018. Medical secretaries earned median hourly wages of $14.27 and a median annual salary of $29,680 in 2008.

From Rosenberg-McKay, D. (2011). Top 10 fastest growing jobs with a high school diploma or GED. *Career Planning*. Retrieved from http://careerplanning.about.com on June 13, 2011; adapted by permission.

Tables 1.5 and 1.6 provide an excellent overview of which jobs are expected to be leading possibilities in this decade.

Making the Journey to Adulthood: The Importance of Setting Goals

The role of business in transition is essential, yet knowing where you are going is equally important. As noted earlier, this book is about goal setting, planning, implementing, and following through transition activities. The ability to help a child understand the importance of identifying and meeting goals in his or her life can make all the difference in the world to the transition from living at home to becoming established in the community with a job and friends (Williams-Diehm, Palmer, Lee, & Schroer, 2010).

Table 1.6.   Top 15 jobs with the largest projected increases in near future

Projected number of new jobs

1.	Food-preparation and food-serving workers, including fast food: Think Starbucks—as fast-food chains grow, so will their jobs.	673,000
2.	Customer-service representatives: Some jobs have moved abroad, but growth of Internet commerce will boost demand.	631,000
3.	Registered nurses: The biggest occupation in a burgeoning health field stimulated by an aging population.	561,000
4.	Retail salespeople: With 4 million workers, currently the largest occupation, growing with the total population.	510,000
5.	Computer-support specialists: Requires only a couple of years of college, and the pay is decent; growth is sure to stay strong.	490,000
6.	Cashiers (except gaming): In lockstep with retail and restaurant expansion; still, it is mostly a minimum-wage job.	474,000
7.	Office clerks, general: The job is being redefined combining more and more diverse tasks into one.	430,000
8.	Security guards: Involves minimal training and low pay (about $17,000), but terrorism fears have boosted hiring.	391,000
9.	Computer software engineers, applications: As long as computer upgrades are constant, so will be the jobs.	380,000
10.	Waiters and waitresses: High turnover and the expectation that people will continue to eat out more means lots of job openings.	364,000
11.	General and operations managers: As new companies start up and old ones branch out, the need for managers will expand.	363,000
12.	Truck drivers, heavy and tractor trailer: As the economy grows, so does the amount of freight carried by truck.	346,000
13.	Nursing aides, orderlies, and attendants: Booming mostly in response to the increasing emphasis on rehabilitation and long-term care of the elderly.	323,000
14.	Janitors and cleaners: Needed to meet the growing demand in new office complexes, schools, and hospitals.	317,000
15.	Postsecondary teachers: Includes teaching and research for colleges, universities, and trade and technical schools.	315,000

Source: Thottam (2003).

Paul J. Gerber, professor of special education and disability policy at Virginia Commonwealth University, notes, for example, that parents can play a pivotal role in the development of this skill: "They can help not only with goal setting but with analyzing, monitoring, and providing motivation along the way" (Stuart, 2010, p. 1).

Here are some general guidelines to keep in mind:

Be a goal setter, too—Model the type of goal setting you want to see in your child. As you set goals, tell your child about them as well as the specific steps you are taking to reach them. If you are starting a new exercise regimen, casually mention your weekly and long-term goals. When you hit your targets, make a big deal of it. But do not forget to mention the bumps in the road and what you are doing to surmount them.

Make goal setting a habit—Planning a long trip? Bring your child into the process, by asking questions such as "What are the top three things you want to see on this trip? What are two things you can do when you get tired in the car (or your sister really starts to bug you)? What is one thing you can try to address your fear of flying?" Then ask for ways you can help your child meet these goals.

Inspire self-confidence—Coach, cheerlead, and celebrate successes. When your child succeeds in reaching a goal, ask him or her what made the difference. This helps your child internalize what he or she needs to do to carry over the skill to the next experience.

Help overcome obstacles—Gerber emphasizes that failing to meet goals may be disappointing but can provide invaluable lessons for your child. Rather than ignoring the failure or berating your child for lack of follow-through, help him or her to systematically pinpoint the specific obstacles that got in the way. "If your child fails, help him or her to come back and reboot and do it a different way that will work better next time" (Stuart, 2010, p. 1).

What are the ways to help young people with disabilities transition into the community? Most parents know from experience that the best way to help their children obtain a higher level of achievement is to set goals in a stair-step fashion. The IEP is an educational program mandated by law (most recently, IDEA 2004) that states the goals, objectives, and timeline of activities necessary for educational program implementation. An IEP is developed for each student with disabilities; it is highly specific only to the student for whom it is designed (Capizzi, 2008). The IEP should also provide a plan for making the transition to adult life, which some have referred to as a **transition IEP** (Wehman & Wittig, 2009). Over the years, educators have learned that no amount of paper programs, interagency agreements, or even new teaching techniques will help a teenager grow into a successful adult without transition planning and follow-through. Ongoing reinforcement by educators, parents, and others in the community for doing positive activities is very important for students making the transition from youth to adulthood. Once again, these goals need to be performed in a successful way over an extended period of time. Functional life skills are an important consideration, and this is discussed in depth in several chapters that follow (Wehman & Kregel, 2011).

Many teachers wonder what they can do to help a child at home or in the community. What influence do they really have? The answer is, their influence is enormous. Students who have a purpose in their lives, who know how to set goals, and who have been reinforced for those goals are much more likely to succeed in the world of work and living in the community (Williams-Diehm et al., 2010). Teachers, guidance counselors, coaches, and other staff in the high school environment can have as much or more effect on their students than parents do during this critical developmental period. Many young people rebel against parental authority and are not interested in advice from their parents; high school staff may be able to help in a less emotional way to carve out goals in the areas of community service, academic performance supports, or other activities that will help develop and create a sense of self-esteem. Can you think of someone you know who has been rebellious, oppositional, or unwilling to respect authority? What impact does that person have on his or her class or family? Highly effective educators in middle schools and high schools look beyond the classroom to identify ways to elevate their students' abilities.

Evidence-Based Transition Research: The Foundation for Recommended Practices

This book is based on research that provides true empirical support for excellent practice. Since early 2000, there has been a somewhat more concentrated effort to study factors associated with successful transition outcomes, led notably by authors such as Test and his colleagues (2011).

Kohler (1993), in her original taxonomy of transition, indicated that, since 1985, there has been an increased focus on improving transition education and services for youth with disabilities. Three specific initiatives characterize this development:

1. Federal special education and disability legislation
2. Federal, state, and local investment in transition services development
3. Effective transition practices research

Outcomes of these initiatives include 1) an expanded perspective concerning transition education and services and 2) identification of practices that apply this perspective to individual student needs. Kohler and Field (2003) described effective transition practices in five areas:

1. Student-focused planning
2. Student development
3. Interagency collaboration
4. Family involvement
5. Program structures

Developing specific interventions and service arrays for individual students within each of the transition practice areas is essential for postschool success.

We cannot be successful with helping young persons with disabilities succeed in the workplace, in the community, or at home without knowing what practices are effective and which are not. There needs to be credible evidence that can be measured, replicated, and evaluated on the major elements that comprise the transition from school to adulthood process.

It is fortunate that there have been positive developments on this front over the past decade (Eaves, Rabren, & Hall, 2011). Kohler (1993); Kohler and Field (2003); Test, Fowler, White, Richter, and Walker (2009); and Landmark, Ju, and Zhang (2010) have provided leadership in organizing the explosion of research that has been published in transition (Alwell & Cobb, 2009a; Alwell & Cobb, 2009b; Cobb & Alwell, 2009; Cobb, Rabren, & Eaves, 2011). They have been able to begin the process of evaluating those practices that have limited, moderate, or strong evidence of working, an invaluable contribution to teachers, parents, and administrators struggling to determine recommended practices that work.

To bring this discussion from the abstract to the concrete, consider the teacher who has a student like PJ in her classroom. Remember, PJ has significant autism. The teacher is being told to expend large amounts of each school week on developmental reading and writing and in classroom activities. Yet, as Landmark, Ju, and Zhang (2010) reported, paid and unpaid work experiences are absolutely among the highest, most credible evidence for successful transition. Now this teacher has a rationale to change her practice and infuse much more real work for real pay opportunities into the school year (Wehman, Inge, Revell, & Brooke, 2007). Recall at the start of the chapter the importance of work for Teresa, Bess, Kalyn, and PJ. Internships, employment participation, and competitive employment provide a seamless transition for them into adulthood.

Evidence-based transition research also helps the school principal decide how much to promote general education **inclusion** (Halle & Dymond, 2009). We now know, for example, that participation in general education classrooms and earning a diploma lead to greater likelihood for successful outcomes such as employment for many students with disabilities (Williams-Diehm & Benz, 2008; Rabren, Dunn, & Chambers, 2002).

To many, research seems abstract, distant, and far removed from their classroom or school world; yet, without this foundation of knowledge, we are just guessing at student challenges like the following:

- Where should students be taught?
- How much time should be spent in the classroom or outside?
- What should the curriculum be, functional or literacy-based, or both?
- What kind of planning is required for a successful transition process?
- How much should the parents be involved and what is their role?
- What instructional procedures are most effective?

Landmark, Ju, and Zhang (2010) noted that the field of transition has evolved rapidly under the impetus of federal and state initiatives, federal legislation, an array of research and demonstration activities, and practitioner-initiated practices. Transition services were ensured by IDEA in its subsequent reauthorizations in 1997 and 2004. The most current reauthorization (i.e., IDEA 2004) requires that transition services be in effect by the time the child with a disability is 16 years old. It is also aligned with the **No Child Left Behind**

Act of 2001 (PL 107-110) in that states hold school districts accountable for how well students with disabilities perform on standards-based assessments and postschool outcomes. Recent federal mandates set more specific goals for transition services and require transition service to be an integral part of a student's IEP. These legal updates have influenced policy making and research focus in the field of transition.

What Evidence-Based Transition Practices Are Effective?

Perhaps the two papers that summarize the existing transition research best to date are Test, Fowler, Richter, et al. (2009) and Landmark, Ju, and Zhang (2010). They have done the extensive work associated with identifying which studies fit criteria that allow inclusion into the Kohler and Field (2003) taxonomy for transition research; inclusion criteria are necessary in order to decide which studies have the merit to be included and the taxonomy is important in order to synthesize the volume of different pieces of work.

Although it is beyond the scope of this chapter to discuss all of the studies and their implications, it is highly instructive to see which areas of transition research are rising to the level of evidence-based work that have implications for practice. In Table 1.7, we summarize from most substantiated to least substantiated those practices that are undergirded by good-quality research.

Paid or unpaid work experiences are far and away the most important research associated with good transition outcomes (Carter, Swedeen, & Trainor, 2009; Lindstrom, Doren, & Miesch, 2011; Williams-Diehem & Benz, 2008; McDonall & Cruden, 2009; Benz, 2002). This reflects 16 research studies and supports the comments made by Wehman in 2002 in public page testimony to President George W. Bush's Summit on Education Reform, Rusch and Braddock (2004), and, more recently, Certo, Luecking, Murphy, Brown, Courey, and Belanger's (2008) call for "seamless transition." Employment preparation also plays a successful role in transition planning, as does general education inclusion, parent involvement, social skills training, and self-determination training.

Test, Fowler, Richter, et al. (2009) also reviewed the research in transition and did an exhaustive report of all of the studies, identifying the type of designs used and the level of evidence (limited, moderate, strong). They found strong evidence for life skills training, but many of the other transition practices were moderate (22 total) and others minimal. The reader who wishes more comprehensive detail on the different levels of research study quality is urged to consult this paper.

What Does This Research Mean to the Teacher?

This synthesis of research should be used by the teacher and administrators in determining what to teach and where and how much emphasis to place on different topical areas.

Table 1.7. Evidence-based transition research

Practice by taxonomy category	Number of evidence-based practices
Student-focused planning	3
Student development	26
Family involvement	1
Program structure	3
Interagency collaboration	0

Source: National Secondary Transition Technical Assistance Center (2010).

Note: Currently, NSTTAC (2010) has identified 33 evidence-based practices in secondary transition. These 33 practices have been categorized by using Kohler's Taxonomy for Transition Programming (1993).

With that said, the teacher must be very careful to understand that the number of studies and the quality at this point are quite limited. Few of these studies would rise to a multicenter Phase 3 trial demanded by most drug companies on a drug that can be put onto the market. Furthermore, just because the community/agency planning only showed two studies supporting it in the Landmark, Ju, and Zhang (2010) paper, this does not mean it has no value; it means only that a limited number of credible studies have been undertaken on this particular aspect of transition.

Here is how Test, Fowler, Richter, et al. see the implications of this work for the teacher, and this is important:

> The current list provides practitioners with a starting point for implementing evidence-based practices. Are they guaranteed to work? No, but practitioners can be confident that practices with strong and moderate levels of evidence will produce similar effects with their students. Practitioners will still need to use their professional judgment to select practices for their students. To help them with this process, further information about each practice can be found at http://www.nsttac.org under "Evidence based Practices." At this website, each practice is described in terms of the supporting evidence, with whom it was implemented (i.e., disability labels, gender, ethnicity if provided), what the practice is, how and where it has been implemented, how the practice relates to State Performance Plan Part B Indicator 13 and national standards, where the best place to find out how to do the practice is, and references used to establish the current evidence base. (2009, p. 45)

The amount of prospectively designed large-scale transition from school to work studies is minimal. This is a significant problem that needs to be corrected in the decade ahead. This is partially because of the complexities of designing and maintaining the controls necessary longitudinally to measure employment changes for young people still in school. The identification of appropriate community living and adjustment variables has also been problematic (Wehman & Kregel, 2011).

However, Wittenburg and Maag (2002) did examine data sources in a large national study that evaluated economic outcomes of youth with disabilities. They drew on multiple databases from Social Security, VR, and special education. Many of the studies that were relied on in shaping the conclusions of the authors provide information for transition planning and practices discussed not only in this chapter but also throughout the book.

As a Teacher, How Do I Interpret This Research?

To many teachers, administrators, and professors, as well as parents, using evidence-based research as the primary guideline for transition practices may be confusing. Why is this? Because there are literally hundreds of articles published every day, some empirical, some not, some demonstrations, some creative ideas, some that are analyses of existing databases, and, in fact, they may suggest alternative approaches. The findings on some of the database reviews may not reflect the same areas of emphasis.

Hence, it is important to know how to interpret this increasing volume of transition or transition-related research. First, be aware that the studies reflecting the previously mentioned evidence-based practices have been carefully reviewed by skilled researchers and have been determined to have value in the classroom and community. Second, this does not mean that new innovative ideas, tips, and ideas have no value but, instead, that one should proceed with more caution as these ideas have not met the criteria of credible evidence by scientific standards. Third, database reviews provide a snapshot in time, are not controlled studies, and will often reflect old history; furthermore, findings can often be generated by simply having a very large number of people in the database to analyze. Finally, some of the research, such as the Gallup Poll or Harris Poll studies, are useful benchmarks for what people think at a certain point in time and may not necessarily be totally reflective of thoughts of everyone in the world.

Related Disability Legislation

To promote and regulate transition practices in schools, Congress has enacted a number of related laws that influence the transition from school to adulthood for young people with disabilities. Table 1.8 provides a brief description of key provisions on major legislation impacting special education and the rights of individuals with disabilities. This is followed by a closer examination of select laws. Together, they form an important foundation for understanding the transition process.

The Rehabilitation Act

The Rehabilitation Act of 1973 (PL 93-112) changed the name of legislation previously known as the Vocational Rehabilitation Act of 1918 (PL 65-178). This legislation mandated a priority to serve individuals with severe disabilities. It prohibited discrimination on the basis of disability in programs conducted by federal agencies, in programs receiving federal financial assistance, in federal employment, and in the employment practices of federal contractors. The standards for determining employment discrimination under the Rehabilitation Act are the same as those used in Title I of the Americans with Disabilities

Table 1.8.   Key provisions on major legislation impacting special education and the rights of individuals with disabilities

Year	Legislation	Brief description and key provisions
1954	Brown v. Board of Education (PL 107-41)	Ended the segregation of children solely based upon race in public schools.
1965	The Elementary and Secondary Education Act (PL 89-10)	First law in federal government to offer direct aid to states for educational purposes; provided money to assist states in educating students whose families fell below the poverty line. Money was also available to improve education of students in state schools for the deaf, blind, and mentally retarded (now called intellectual disability).
1966	Amendment to Elementary and Secondary Education Act (PL 89-750)	Created the Bureau of Education for the Handicapped in the Department of Health, Education, and Welfare, known today known as the Office of Special Education Programs.
1970	Education of the Handicapped Act (PL 91-230)	Expanded the federal grant programs under the Elementary and Secondary Education Act to offer grants to institutions to develop programs to train teachers to teach students with disabilities; regional resource centers established to offer technical assistance.
1973	Section 504 of the Rehabilitation Act (PL 93-112)	Civil rights legislation for people with disabilities stated it is illegal to deny participation in activities, benefits, or programs, or to in any way discriminate against a person with a disability solely because of that disability. Individuals with disabilities must have equal access to programs and services. Auxiliary aids must be provided to individuals with impaired speaking, manual, or sensory skills.
1974	Education of the Handicapped Act Amendments (PL 93-380)	Amendments to Education of the Handicapped Act of 1970. Required states receiving federal funding to adopt a goal of full educational opportunity for students with disabilities.
1975	Education for All Handicapped Children Act (PL 94-142)	Amendment to the Education of the Handicapped Act of 1970. Required students who receive special education and related services to receive a free appropriate public education. Schools must have on file an individualized education program for each student with a disability (education that was individually designed to address his or her unique need). Parents have the right to inspect school records on their child, and when changes are made in a student's educational placement or program, parents must be informed. Parents have the right to challenge what is in records or to challenge changes in placement. Students with disabilities have the right to be educated in the least restrictive educational environment. Students with disabilities must be assessed in ways that are considered fair and nondiscriminatory and have other specific protections. (Note: Since passage, there have been numerous changes to the law.)

Table 1.8.   *(continued)*

Year	Legislation	Brief description and key provisions
1981	Medicaid Home and Community-Based Services waiver program (PL 97-35)	Identified supported employment services as an appropriate means for assisting individuals with significant disabilities, eligible for Medicaid Waivers services.
		Under Section 1915(c) of the Social Security Act, Medicaid law authorizes the Secretary of the U.S. Department of Health and Human Services to waive certain Medicaid statutory requirements. These waivers enable states to cover a broad array of home- and community-based services (HCBS) for targeted populations as an alternative to institutionalization. Waiver services may be optional state plan services either that are not covered by a particular state or that enhance the state's coverage. Waivers may also include services not covered through the state plan such as respite care, environmental modifications, or family training.
		The four basic types of 1915(c) HCBS waivers available for states based on the target population's level of alternative long-term institutional care are: intermediate care facility–intellectual disability (ID) level of care for intellectually disabled and/or developmentally disabled individuals; chronic or rehabilitative hospital level of care for individuals who are medically fragile, chronically ill, or severely disabled; psychiatric hospital level of care for individuals who are severely or chronically mentally ill; and nursing facility level of care for individuals who are elderly, physically disabled, and/or cognitively impaired. To be a waiver participant, an individual must be medically qualified, certified for the waiver's institutional level of care, choose to enroll in the waiver as an alternative to institutionalization, cost Medicaid no more in the community under the waiver than he or she would have cost Medicaid in an institution, and financially eligible based on their income and assets.
1984	Developmental Disabilities Act (PL 98-527)	Acknowledged the employability of people with disabilities and made reference to a new model for employment called supported employment.
1986	The Infants and Toddlers with Disabilities Act Amendment to the Education for All Handicapped Children Act of 1975 (PL 94-142)	Extended all rights of the Education for All Handicapped Children Act (1975) to cover 3- to 5-year-olds with disabilities. Requires each school district to conduct a multidisciplinary assessment and develop an individualized family service plan for each preschool child with a disability.
1986	The Handicapped Children's Protection Act of 1986 (PL 99-372)	Granted courts authority to award attorney fees to parents and guardians if they prevailed in law suits. Nullified *Smith v Robinson*, which prohibited award.
1986	The Rehabilitation Act Amendments (PL 99-506)	For the first time, supported employment is defined in legislation and grant funding is available for national demonstration.
1987	Developmental Disabilities Assistance and Bill of Rights Act Amendments (PL 100-146)	Example of a value-laden public policy that put national goals into legislation promoting employment for people with disabilities.
1990	Individuals with Disabilities Education Act (IDEA; PL 101-476)	Amended the Education for All Handicapped Children Act (1975). Changed name of law to reflect "people first" language. Added two new disability categories (traumatic brain injury and autism). Provided comprehensive definition of transition services including a plan for transition in every individualized education program by age 16. Made provisions to make assistive technology more widely available. Nullified law protecting states from these types of lawsuits.
1990	Americans with Disabilities Act (PL 101-336)	Civil rights law designed to prevent discrimination based on disabilities. Requires that covered entities shall not discriminate against people on the basis of a disability. It includes five parts, called Titles, which address employment, public entities, accommodations, communication, and other more general areas. Employers who receive federal funding must provide "equal access." Qualified people include individuals with physical or mental impairments that substantially limit one or more major life activities such as self-care, walking, seeing, hearing, speaking, breathing, learning, and working.

Year	Legislation	Brief description and key provisions
1997	Individuals with Disabilities Education Act Amendments (PL 105-17)	Amended IDEA 1990. Included a number of changes to individualized education program requirements to improve outcomes. Specified participants on individualized education program teams and documentation to include annual measurable goals and explanation of methods by which students' progress toward goals would be measured; required teams to report progress toward goals to parents. Required revision of individualized education programs for students who failed to make progress. Added disciplinary provisions by expanding authority of school officials to protect safety of all children. Required states to report on the performance and progress of all students.
1998	The Reauthorization of the Rehabilitation Act (PL 105-220) through the Workforce Investment Act	Retained the core definition of supported employment that appeared in the 1986 amendments.
1998	Workforce Investment Act (PL 105-220)	Established a framework for the nation's workforce development system. The law replaced multiple existing training programs with state formula grants and created a nationwide network of locally administered One-Stop Career Centers, which would provide access to training and employment services for a range of workers, including low-income adults, low-income youth, and dislocated workers. Mandated coordination among a range of federal job training programs, including the Employment Service, adult education and literacy programs, welfare-to-work, vocational education, and vocational rehabilitation.
		Title I of the Workforce Investment Act authorized services for youth, adults, and laid-off workers. Eligible youth must be 14–21 years of age, low income, and meet at least one of six specific barriers to employment. A year-round youth program emphasizes attainment of basic skills competencies, enhances opportunities for academic and occupational training, and provides exposure to the job market and employment. Activities may include instruction leading to completion of secondary school, tutoring, internships, job shadowing, work experience, adult mentoring, and comprehensive guidance and counseling. The program emphasized services for out-of-school youth.
		Authorization of appropriations under the Workforce Investment Act expired in FY2003 but is annually extended through appropriations acts. Reauthorization legislation has been considered.
1999	The Ticket to Work and Work Incentive Improvement Act (PL 106-170	Created a Ticket to Work Program administered by the Social Security Administration to modernize employment-related services offered to Americans with disabilities. Through the Ticket Program, individuals with disabilities can get job-related training and placement assistance from an approved provider of their choice. This provision enables individuals to go to providers whose resources best meet their needs, including going directly to employers. The second measure expands health care coverage so that individuals with disabilities will become employed without fear of losing their health insurance.
2001	No Child Left Behind Act (PL 107-110)	Reauthorized the Elementary and Secondary Education Act. Specified that its provisions are for all students, including those with disabilities. Required annual assessments in reading and math in Grades 3–8 and 1 year of high school. Provided for literacy interventions through Reading First and Early Reading First. Gave entitlement to supplementary education services. Allowed increased parental flexibility in accessing other schools if theirs has poor performance.

(continued)

Table 1.8.   *(continued)*

Year	Legislation	Brief description and key provisions
2004	The Individuals with Disabilities Education Improvement Act (IDEA 2004; PL 108-446)	Reauthorized and amended IDEA. Sought to increase the quality of special education programs by increasing accountability for results. Individualized education program must include a statement of the special education and related services and supplementary aids and services, based on peer-reviewed research to the extent practicable. When the team develops a student's education program, the services provided should be based on reliable evidence that has been published in a peer-reviewed journal or approved by an independent panel of experts. Changed special education eligibility requirements including that parents, state, or local educational agency could request initial evaluation and determination to be made in 60 days. Individualized education program teams are required to examine programming that a student received in general education to ensure poor programming was not the cause of the child's problem. State education agency could no longer use a discrepancy formula to determine if student had learning disability; instead, states must let local educational agency use a process that determines if a child responds to a research-based intervention as part of the evaluation—known as response to intervention (RTI); RTI is designed to identify students' academic problems early on and then matches evidence-based instruction to their educational needs. Included the addition of early intervening services to the section of IDEA about way a local educational agency may spend IDEA funds.
2005	Indicator 13 and Indicator 14	The Individuals with Disabilities Education Act (IDEA) was reauthorized on December 3, 2004, and its provisions became effective on July 1, 2005. In conjunction with the reauthorization, the U.S. Department of Education through the Office of Special Education Programs required states to develop 6-year State Performance Plans in December 2005 around 20 indicators, on which data will be submitted annually (beginning February 2007) in Annual Performance Reports.
		Indicator 13 relates to transition services for students: "Percent of youth with IEPs aged 16 and above with an IEP that includes appropriate measurable postsecondary goals that are annually updated and based upon an age-appropriate transition assessment, transition services, including courses of study, that will reasonably enable the student to meet those postsecondary goals, and annual IEP goals related to the student's transition services needs. There also must be evidence that the student was invited to the IEP team meeting where transition services are to be discussed and evidence that, if appropriate, a representative of any participating agency was invited to the IEP Team meeting with the prior consent of the parent or student who has reached the age of majority." (20 U.S.C. 1416[a][3][B])
		Indicator 14 concerns itself with the outcomes that youth with disabilities achieve once they exit high school: percent of youth who had IEPs, are no longer in secondary school, and who have been competitively employed, enrolled in some type of postsecondary school, or both, within 1 year of leaving high school. (20 U.S.C. 1416[a][3][B])
2008	Americans with Disabilities Act Amendments (PL 110-325)	Amended ADA (1990). Provided new language for determining eligibility by expanding coverage. Changes in language were specific to major life activities regarded as having such an impairment and definition of disability.
2011	Americans with Disabilities Act Amendments	Amended ADA. Service animals extended to include miniature horses. Institutions may not deny service animals. Expands the list of auxiliary aids and services to include advances in assistive technology, primarily for the deaf, hard of hearing, blind, and low vision. Changes the documentation needed to determine eligibility for accommodation. Institutions should not make unreasonably burdensome requests for additional documentation when an individual has already submitted appropriate documentation. Wheelchairs and other mobility devices generally should be allowed in any areas that are open to pedestrians unless it can be shown that the vehicle cannot be operated in accordance with legitimate safety requirements. Institutions may consider factors such as the size, speed, and weight of the vehicle, the amount of pedestrians in the facility, the design of the facility, and the risk of serious harm in determining whether a particular mobility device will be allowed in a facility.

Act (PL 101-336). Section 503 of the act required reasonable accommodations on the job for people with disabilities who were otherwise qualified for a position.

Some other changes were made over the years. **The Rehabilitation Act Amendments of 1978** (PL 95-602) responded to consumer concerns for added involvement by the establishment of independent living centers. A focus on peer counseling and guidance emerged. **The Rehabilitation Act Amendments of 1986** (PL 99-506) enhanced support for rehabilitation engineering, with clear definitions for rehabilitation engineering services. In addition, support for special projects and demonstrations in **supported employment** were established. **The Rehabilitation Act Amendments of 1992** (PL 102-569) clearly outlined the intent of Congress to ensure consumer choice in career opportunities, with competitive employment the desired outcome.

Section 504

A major provision of the Rehabilitation Act is **Section 504**, which created and extended civil rights to people with disabilities. Section 504 provided opportunities for children and adults with disabilities in education, employment, and various other settings. For example, the Section 504 regulations require schools that receive federal funds to provide a **free appropriate public education** to each qualified person, regardless of the nature and severity of his or her disability. It also allows for reasonable accommodations such as special study area and assistance as necessary for each student. It also called for the establishment of the individualized written rehabilitation program today known as **individualized plans for employment**, which was a major step to ensure the enhanced involvement of a person with a disability in developing a rehabilitation plan of action.

Each federal agency has its own set of Section 504 regulations that apply to its own programs. Agencies that provide federal financial assistance also have Section 504 regulations covering entities that receive federal aid. Requirements common to these regulations include reasonable accommodation for employees with disabilities, program accessibility, effective communication with people who have hearing or vision disabilities, and accessible new construction and alterations. Each agency is responsible for enforcing its own regulations.

In high schools and universities, **Section 504 plans** are also designed to help students with disabilities gain accommodations for education. **Modifications** received under 504 plans, such as foreign language waivers, untimed tests, or word banks, do raise concerns about expectations for students. McGuire (2010) noted that Subpart E of the Section 504 regulations stipulates that "academic requirements that the recipient (institution) can demonstrate are essential to the program of instruction being pursued by such student or to any directly related licensing requirement will not be regarded as discriminatory" (§ 104.44[a]). This underscores a potential disconnect between secondary and postsecondary curricular choices. If a student intends to pursue a college major in international business, an exemption from foreign language at the postsecondary level is unlikely. Assuming that the student is determined "otherwise qualified" for admission, he or she may be surprised to learn that a foreign language waiver will not be granted at his or her college because foreign language proficiency is viewed as essential to an international business major. There may be options he or she would be well advised to explore *before* making a decision about his or her college of choice (e.g., availability of a study abroad program with options for demonstrating language proficiency).

The Rehabilitation Act Amendments of 1998

The Rehabilitation Act Amendments of 1998 (PL 105-220) governs the VR programs. It provides federal dollars, matched by state dollars to all states to give individuals with disabilities assistance with employment. The act required cooperation among educational agencies responsible for the transition from school to employment or postsecondary education. This means that the VR program works cooperatively with local education authorities to serve transition-aged youth and is a primary support resource for adults with disabilities who need employment services. The act mandated ongoing support, including assessment of employment needs, **job development** and placement service, social skills instruction, and intense services at home or at work to live independently or maintain employment. Education professionals, parents, and individuals with disabilities alike need to be aware of how the legislation provides protections and ensures certain services.

The two federal acts that most affect public education are IDEA 2004 and Section 504. Section 504 (not IDEA) relates to students with disabilities in postsecondary education settings. In addition, the definition and eligibility requirements are more restrictive in IDEA than in Section 504. This may result in some people being eligible for protections under Section 504 rather than IDEA. Section 504 may be enforced through private lawsuits.

Americans with Disabilities Act

The ADA was signed into law in 1990, and many have hailed the act as a civil rights law for all people with disabilities. The intent of the ADA is to end discrimination toward people with disabilities throughout society. This act was followed 1 year later by a comprehensive set of regulations that provide for accessibility, nondiscrimination, and greater access to workplaces, community facilities, public transportation, and telecommunications. Before its passage, people with disabilities had no legal recourse against those who discriminated against them. The Vocational Rehabilitation Act addressed discrimination in federally funded programs. The ADA extended into the private sector except churches and private clubs. The ADA intended to break down a wide array of artificial barriers that were unnecessarily and unfairly limiting the participation of individuals with disabilities in society including employment (Rozalski, Katsiyannis, Ryan, Collins, & Stewart, 2010).

More specific, under the ADA, employers are prohibited from discriminating against "otherwise qualified" individuals with disabilities during recruitment, hiring, evaluation, promotion, or any other facet of employment. Employers are further required to provide reasonable accommodations to enable individuals with disabilities to successfully perform their jobs, when accommodation can be provided without an employer sustaining an undue hardship. Reasonable accommodations may include such things as restructuring jobs or work schedules, modifying equipment, providing assistive devices, providing an interpreter or reading aids, or improving the overall accessibility of the worksite. It also requires employers to list essential functions to perform a job. Employers found to be in violation of the law face the same legal penalties as those found guilty of discrimination on the basis of gender or race. Educators, parents, and individuals with disabilities should take time to understand the relationships among the ADA, IDEA, and Section 504, which are very important to understand as they each provide certain guidelines and restrictions for services.

Amendments to the ADA signed into law on September 25, 2008, clarified and reiterated who is covered by the law's civil rights protections. The ADA Amendments Act of 2008 revises the definition of *disability* to more broadly encompass impairments that substantially limit a major life activity. The amended language also states that mitigating measures, including assistive devices, auxiliary aids, accommodations, medical therapies, and supplies (other than eyeglasses and contact lenses) have no bearing in determining whether a disability qualifies under the law. Changes also clarified coverage of impairments that are episodic or in remission that substantially limit a major life activity when active, such as epilepsy or posttraumatic stress disorder. The amendments took effect January 1, 2009.

Workforce Investment Act

The Workforce Investment Act of 1998 (PL 105-220) provided for a major reform of the nation's job training system. The act called for

- Streamlining services through a one-stop service delivery system
- Empowering job seekers through information and access to training resources
- Providing universal access to core services
- Ensuring a strong role for local workforce investment boards and the private sector
- Improving youth programs

Under the Workforce Investment Act, four principles guide the implementation of **One-Stop Career Centers**: universality, customer choice, integration of services, and accountability for results (Targett, Young, Revell, Williams, & Wehman, 2007).

1. Universality: Everyone can use the services, regardless of whether they have a disability.

2. Customer choice: Individuals choose what services they want to use.

3. Vocational training and employment programs are consolidated in order to ease access to services. However, funding for the various services and training is not integrated and will vary.

4. The Workforce Investment Act dictates the operators' standards of performance that must be adhered to in order for the center to continue to receive funding. Chapter 4 provides more information on how One-Stop Career Centers operate.

No Child Left Behind Act of 2001

The No Child Left Behind Act of 2001 (NCLB; PL 107-110), which reauthorized the Elementary and Secondary Education Act of 1965 (PL 89-10), was designed to improve academic performance of all students by reforming schools, increasing accountability, and challenging low student expectations.

It requires all students including students with disabilities to learn the general curriculum, to participate in state and local assessments, and to make gains in achievement toward the goal of making adequate yearly academic progress. When students (including groups of those with disabilities) fail to make annual progress, the school faces accountability.

The accountability system must be the same for all public schools and agencies in the state, and timelines must be in place to ensure that all students will meet or exceed the state-determined proficiency level (this is expressed as the percentage of students the state projects will be at or above grade level) no later than the 2013–2014 school year. The goal is for the schools to make genuine progress in closing the persistent achievement gaps between students who are disadvantaged or disabled and their peers.

The law requires that the state's assessment system is valid and accessible to students with disabilities under IDEA and Section 504. Assessment accommodations must be determined by the student's **IEP team**, must be based on individual student needs, and should be in place when students take classroom tests and assessments.

Accommodation has been defined as "changes in testing material or procedures that ensure that an assessment measures the student's knowledge and skills rather than the student's disability" (U.S. Department of Education, 2002). This is different and broader than the notion of adapting instruction or the accommodations contained in IDEA. No matter how broad the definition, however, out-of-grade-level testing is not an acceptable means for meeting either the assessment or the accountability requirements of NCLB.

Another major provision is for schools to employ highly qualified teachers and use **evidence-based practices** or research-validated practices. Both terms used interchangeably denote educational practices that have been documented through empirical research.

Thus, IDEA is aligned with NCLB as both require qualified teachers to use practices based on scientific research to strengthen basic and specially designed instruction. Under NCLB, highly qualified means the teacher has a bachelor's degree, is state certified, and demonstrates competence in the content areas he or she teaches.

NCLB and IDEA have focused attention on evidence-based practices for students at risk of failing or placement in special education. NCLB defines scientifically based research as "research that involves the application of rigorous, systematic, and objective procedures to obtain reliable and valid knowledge relevant to education activities and programs" (NCLB, 20 U.S.C. 7801 [37]). IDEA encourages the use of **response to intervention** as a process for identifying students who need more intensive instruction or intervention.

Ticket to Work and Work Incentives Improvement Act

As authorized by the **Ticket to Work and Work Incentives Improvement Act of 1999** (PL 106-170), the secretary of the Department of Human Health and Services established funding for the Ticket to Work program. The Ticket to Work program operates under the **Social Security Administration.** The goal is to help Social Security disability beneficiaries obtain employment and work toward greater independence and self-sufficiency including youth in transition (Fraker & Rangarajan, 2009). Under it, the Social Security Administration issues a ticket to an eligible beneficiary who, in turn, can assign the ticket to an employment network or state VR agency. If the ticket is accepted, the agency works with the beneficiary to create an individualized employment plan and, as indicated, provides specialized services such as career counseling and job placement.

There are other provisions under the act including work incentives and work incentive planning and assistance services (Miller, O'Mara, & Getzel, 2009). Work incentives are special considerations that make it possible for a beneficiary to explore work options while still receiving health care and cash benefits. Cash benefits continue for a defined time period and are eliminated only when the beneficiary reaches a level of earnings through his or her job, known as **substantial gainful activity**. If a beneficiary receives **Medicare**, he or she may be able to keep the coverage for at least $8\frac{1}{2}$ years after returning to work. For **Medicaid**, some states continue coverage whereas others allow beneficiaries who have returned to work to purchase coverage at affordable rates. Work incentive planning and assistance is also provided to beneficiaries under the program (Hemmeter, Jauff, & Wittenburg, 2009).

Challenges that Affect Youth with Disabilities

Despite the many positive advances that have occurred in transition over the past 2 decades, numerous challenges are still present. Special education services for young people with disabilities have all too often been considered in a vacuum. One only has to look at children as they leave elementary school and move into the world of middle and high school to begin to understand the multiple pressures that are affecting the way they behave.

Violence in the Public Schools and the Community

One of the most critical social issues facing all Americans is safety in the community. Violence is in many homes, in many communities, and, regrettably, in many schools (Rose, Monda-Amaya, & Espelage, 2011). At the time that we wrote the first edition of *Life Beyond the Classroom*, this type of violence would have never been thought likely or possible except in the most unusual or high-risk environments within urban areas. Violent events are increasingly common and are bound to have an adverse effect on the psychological outlook of children.

Thousands of young people with behavior disorders are already at risk for greater likelihood of inappropriate social behavior or even violent behavior and, when placed in schools and communities that allow this type of behavior to occur, are more inclined to further engage in such activity. IDEA 2004 is supposed to supply school personnel with guidelines for how to manage these students; yet, as Smith (2000) noted, this has been an ongoing and major challenge not yet successfully met. Understanding the importance of this negative societal development simply cannot be avoided, and violence must be combated with the use of greater communication, safety procedures, anger management classes, counseling, and psychological help.

Emphasis on High-Stakes Testing

With the passage of NCLB, state governors and education leaders have put a rising emphasis on testing competence in core academic areas, such as science, civics, foreign language, mathematics, and language arts (see Chapter 7). As well-intentioned as this powerful state- and federal-mandated emphasis on school reform and testing is, it has often placed undue hardship on thousands of students with disabilities who need reasonable accommodations to take tests and, more important, who need a different area of focus than the core academic areas (Nolet & McLaughlin, 2005; Ysseldyke et al., 2004). For example, students with intellectual disabilities requiring significant support may not need to know algebra and will not perform very well on algebra and geometry competency tests. They would benefit more from functional math skills to be successful in the community and in the workplace. However, if they do not pass these tests, they will not have the ability to receive a high school diploma in many states (Bouck, 2009a). Educational reform as it is constituted by NCLB has been a major barrier for thousands of teachers who are trying to empower students to be more independent in the community (Browder & Spooner, 2003), despite the hopeful tone of Wehmeyer, Field, Doren, Jones, and Mason (2004), who believed that school reform efforts would provide an opportunity to infuse instruction in self-determination into programs for all students.

Continual Poverty and Chronic Unemployment

Despite the significant efforts of thousands of rehabilitation professionals, well-meaning advocates, and legislators, over the past decades, 65%–70% of people with disabilities remain unemployed as noted by the Harris Poll outcomes discussed earlier in this chapter. (Kessler Foundation and National Organization on Disability, 2010)

A majority of people with disabilities are poor (Hughes & Avoke, 2010; Palmer, 2011), including asset poor (Palmer, 2011). The welfare and disability policies in this country do not allow individuals who rely on public benefits to accumulate assets or save. Although there are efforts underway to reverse this situation, major changes will be required in federal laws and policy (Davies, Rupp, & Wittenburg, 2009).

This problem has occurred despite the fact that the unemployment rate has hovered around 5%–6% nationally, and more jobs were created during the 1990s than in any other decade in American history. Some have suggested this problem is attributable to job discrimination (McMorris, 2000), but the issue is too complex for only one reason to be identified. Much of this book is devoted to discussing ways to resolve this problem, but whether it is discrimination, perceived incompetence, policy issues, transportation issues, or all of the above, the fact remains that this is a major societal barrier—there is no protracted history of individuals with disabilities gaining access to the workforce in a meaningful way, and, subsequently, any progress is going to require a significant change in attitude and policy. Many of the chapters in this book discuss this issue, particularly Chapters 8 and 9.

Peer Pressure and Social Acceptance

A final area to consider is one that all children have coped with—peer pressure. As children become older, there is increasing emphasis from their peers on how they look, how they talk, whom they spend time with, what skills they possess, how much money their families have, and, in general, what type of person they are perceived to be. As children move into middle school, this need for peer affiliation really begins to show itself, and, by the time high school and college arrive, the self-esteem that is derived from this type of peer relationship either is significantly developing or has not developed. Young people with disabilities have consistently had poor self-esteem, and one reason for that is poor peer relationships. The social isolation that often accompanies being labeled with a disability leads to poor social skills, a lack of understanding of typical social situations, and a general inability to fit in. One way to approach and manage peer pressure for people with disabilities is social integration into inclusive settings and explicit instruction in social skills (see Chapter 11).

Results of a high school exit survey by Repetto, McGorray, Wang et al., (2011) suggested that students with disabilities feel better about knowing what they want to do after high school and how to achieve their goals but have few interactions with friends in social activities. Conversely, students without disabilities feel better prepared academically and participate more with friends in social activities. Identifying these trends can also assist districts in improving school programs and student outcomes.

Transition Themes for Success: Why Do Some Students Succeed and Others Do Not?

Increasingly, we hear of success stories like Bess and Teresa and PJ and Kalyn and people will inquire: *How did they transition into a job? What help did they get? Why can't my student or child also have this kind of success?* The truth is we are getting closer and closer to being able to provide answers to these questions. The truth is that we have evidence-based research and multiple clinical demonstrations and reports of recommended practices that repeatedly are showing the way.

We must leave behind the thoughts that schools are exclusively preparatory in nature. School-based programs should offer experiences to help develop competencies that students will need in the future at work, college, and the community. The days must be behind us where school is viewed as an endpoint with no eye to the future. The concept of "seamless transition" must become a reality, truly operationalized in school systems throughout the United States—large ones in Philadelphia; small rural ones in Wise County, in the far southwest of Virginia; medium-sized ones like Cedar Rapids, Iowa; to suburban ones like Park Ridge, Illinois, near Chicago. All students in all school districts must have a plan that will move them into successful work and adult life.

It is clear that many skills contribute to success, but we repeatedly come back to several themes that are backed by the research practices reported earlier in this chapter. These include work and employment preparation, self-determination, social skills to deal with multiple situations, inclusion in school and the community, parent involvement, and going to college when possible.

Doing well is not necessarily earning the most money in the highest-status job or being the most famous or popular. Success is a very personal issue and relates to how happy one feels about oneself and the impact of one's life on others. To this end, we stress six major themes in this book. These are work, self-determination and self-advocacy, social competence, inclusion, parent involvement, and postsecondary education.

1. Vocational Competence and Employment Perspective

Vocational capacity, employment, and the opportunity to advance in a career is a major underpinning of success in American society (Burkhauser & Daly, 2011; Wehman, Inge, Revell, & Brooke, 2007). Individuals are defined by earning ability, the type of work that they do, the regularity with which they are employed, the type of environment in which they work, and long-term work potential. The United States is a capitalist society. It is a country that expects people to be productive in work. The use of the Internet, automation, greater efficiency in the workplace, and technology all empower workers. Individuals with disabilities must become competent. They must take courses, improve themselves continually, and be highly persistent to secure employment. Schools have emphasized academic skills too much and employment not enough. This must change so that individuals with disabilities can take their rightful place in American society (Butterworth, Smith, Hall, Migliore, & Winsor, 2010; Callahan, 2010). Students who work before graduation are known to have a much higher likelihood of employment after they age out of school at age 21 (Carter, Austin, & Trainor, in press).

Carter, Austin, and Trainor (2011) examined the early work experiences of a nationally representative sample of youth with severe disabilities (i.e., intellectual disabilities, autism, multiple disabilities). They used data from the National Longitudinal Transition Study-2 to explore the extent to which various student-, family-, school- and community-level factors were associated with paid work experiences during high school. They found that early work experiences for many youth with severe disabilities were elusive and called attention to malleable factors that may play a role in shaping employment success during high school.

2. Self-Determination and Self-Advocacy

Self-determination is the capacity to choose and to act on the basis of those choices (e.g., Wehmeyer, Lance, & Bashinski, 2002); see next chapter. The emphasis on self-determination for people with disabilities can be traced to the independent living and self-advocacy movements that emerged in the 1970s. Most people develop self-determination in childhood and adolescence as they receive greater responsibilities and freedom from their parents and teachers (Mithaug, Mithaug, Agran, Martin, & Wehmeyer, 2003). Individuals cannot self-advocate if they have not developed self-determination skills. Self-advocacy will, ultimately, be the way for young people to navigate the challenges they face.

Self-determination requires that the young person be provided with the knowledge, competency, and opportunities necessary to exercise freedom and choice in ways that are valuable to him or her. Little doubt remains that those people who are self-directed and have the initiative to be successful, have ambition, and practice a reasonable degree of work ethic, inevitability do better in life than those who do not (Cobb, Lehmann, Newman-Gonchar, & Alwell, 2009). There is, of course, room for debate regarding how much the schools are able to instill these important skills (Lee, Palmer, & Wehmeyer, 2009). "Whose Future Is It Anyway?," a self-advocacy program developed by Wehmeyer and Kelchner (1995), which is described in Chapter 2, and *The Transition Handbook*, developed by Hughes and Carter (2000; 2nd edition, 2012), are good tools for helping teachers get started in teaching this process. Likewise, papers by Wood, Karvonen, Test, Browder, and Algozzine (2004) and Test, Browder, Karvonen, Wood, and Algozzine (2002) do an excellent job of guiding teachers and students through the self-determination process when developing IEPs. Self-determination is related to personal attributes as well (Carter, Owens, Trainor, Sun, & Swedeen, 2009). This is true whether a person has an intellectual disability requiring extensive support and works in the back of a kitchen or whether the individual is recovering from a spinal cord injury and is considering a career in computer engineering.

3. Social Competence

Many believe that getting along with people, interpersonal skills, and social competence in a variety of environments are the most important features of success in life. Unfortunately, many young people with disabilities are ultimately unable to achieve this level of competence. Using effective social skills and knowing how to behave in a variety of challenging social situations can make the difference in successful outcomes in the workplace as well as at home and in the community. Young people who get into fights will not make friends. Young people who are verbally abusive will not end up with effective social relationships. Many of the precipitating factors that lead to violence or similar types of behavior in the classroom are predicated on poor social skills. Part of the resolution of this issue within the schools is a tighter administrative structure, but much of the problem is that some students simply do not know the socially appropriate way to behave. Role playing, counseling, and targeted instruction on certain social skills can go a long way toward overcoming this problem. This is an important theme that we repeatedly come back to throughout the book.

4. School and Community Inclusion

Perhaps one of the most useful applications of the original school "mainstreaming" concept has been collaborative teaching (Snell & Janney, 2005). In this approach, a special education teacher or paraprofessional works collaboratively in the general education classroom with the regular education teacher. This collaboration can take place in a tutoring mode, a team teaching mode, or any of a different set of collaborations that may benefit the students with disabilities or special needs who are in the classroom. There are many different models of collaborative teaching. For example, Walsh and Jones (2004) do a very nice job of identifying and developing four different models that can work with youth:

1. Collaborative scheduling A: Special educator splits class time between two different classes.
2. Collaborative scheduling B: Special educator splits time between two different classes on different days of the week; the schedule is modified on the basis of the needs of team members.
3. Collaborative scheduling C: Special educator's schedule is set weekly on the basis of activities planned for each class; the special educator serves as a resource for the team and does not have a rigid schedule.
4. Collaborative scheduling with a teacher's assistant: Teacher's assistant represents the special educator in co-taught classes as directed.

Keefe, Moore, and Duff discuss the challenges involved with collaborative teaching, despite its many options.

> The nature of high schools presents greater obstacles for co-teachers because of the emphasis on content area knowledge, the need for independent study skills, the faster pacing of instruction, high-stakes testing, high school competency exams, less positive attitudes of teachers, and the inconsistent success of strategies that were effective at the elementary level. (2004, p. 36)

Despite these points, the fact is that collaborative teaching opens up the doors for students to have many more opportunities to interact with nondisabled students and general education teachers (Jackson, Ryndak, & Wehmeyer, 2009; Ryndak, Moore, & Orlando, 2009). This means higher expectations of students with disabilities, higher aspirations by parents, greater access to activities for the general population, and, in general, much richer opportunities for enhanced self-esteem and adjustment (Murawski & Dieker, 2004).

The inclusion of students with disabilities into general education classrooms is a substantiated recommended practice (Landmark, Ju, & Zhang, 2010). Young people with disabilities cannot feel part of a high school if they do not have access to the general curriculum, access to all students in the school, access to extracurricular activities, and access to the same rules. Working in real jobs, shopping, volunteering in the community, and so on, cannot be performed competently without the foundation of being in a regular school. So how is this best done?

5. Parent Involvement

Parental involvement is one of the most significant factors in the transition outcomes for students from youth into adulthood (Grigal & Neubert, 2004; Lindstrom et al., 2011). Involvement means informed knowledge about what school and employment options are available and then the willingness to deal with the frequent oppositional or recalcitrant behaviors of high school youth. Why is it that students such as Bess, Teresa, PJ, and Kalyn are doing well? Clearly, their parents played a major role, not only in facilitating decisions and advocacy but also in staying the course over long periods of time and not giving up (see Chapter 3).

In a word, good parents are *awesome*. They *do* make a difference with their values and their contacts in the community and workplace, and the family and extended family all play a role. The transition to adulthood is both an exciting and a challenging time for young adults and their families. Although this period is critical for all individuals, for people with significant cognitive disabilities, development of appropriate supports during the transition process is crucial. Indeed, individuals with significant cognitive disabilities may be described by the supports they need in relation to the demands of specific environments. For example, these individuals may have support needs in areas of intellectual functioning, adaptive skills, motor development, sensory functioning, health care, or communication (Turnball, Turnball, Shank, Smith, & Leal, 2001), which necessitate identifying strategies and supports that will assist these individuals in being successful and achieving desired outcomes.

In sum, the majority of parents want to help and be involved and aspire for their children to succeed. This is a resource that must be brought to the table early in the process, not just because it is the right thing to do, but because it is the smart thing to do.

6. Postsecondary Education

A final theme that continually emerges throughout this book is the need for ongoing education and lifelong learning (Getzel & Wehman, 2005; Grigal & Hart, 2010a; Lindstrom et al., 2011). Many individuals with disabilities have difficulty in the workplace throughout their lives. They also have difficulty with social skills and personal self-esteem. One way to overcome that is education. Earning an associate's degree or a bachelor's degree from a 4-year college will be an outstanding asset to add to one's résumé, but being able to take courses and assimilate new information can also make a significant difference (Fisher & Eskow, 2004). Adding new skills to one's knowledge base, identifying new interests, hobbies, and avocations; and making new friends are all mediated in a very effective way through postsecondary education and lifelong learning experiences. Significant opportunities for individuals with disabilities to try different areas of learning are increasingly available, even to those with significant intellectual disabilities (Schmidt, 2005; Lindstrom, Flannery, Benz, Olszewski, & Slovic, 2009).

Madaus noted:

> The transition from high school to college can be a confusing and overwhelming time for students with learning disabilities (LD), their families, and the secondary-level professionals who assist them. In addition to the challenges that all students face when transitioning to college, additional obstacles confront students with LD. Chief among them is the move from the familiar model of special education services at the high school level to very different services at the college level. Not only does the scope of these services change considerably from high school to college, but there can also be a great deal of institutional variation in the way that these services are provided. Additionally, at the college level, significant changes occur in the legal rights of students, and there is a sharp reversal of parental and student responsibility. (2005, p. 32)

Conclusion

A new generation of teachers who fully comprehend the importance of transition in the special education curriculum and the adult services system is needed to empower young people with disabilities. This book proposes several basic tenets for professionals:

1. The student and family are usually right. Listen to the student. Listen to the family. What are they saying? What hints are they giving about what they need? These ideas are the critical features of a student-oriented transition program.

2. It is essential to look closely at what businesses and industry require of their workforce. The new generation of teachers will examine daily curricula and evaluate whether the skills, objectives, and activities they are currently emphasizing have direct relationships to what local employers need to maintain a dependable workforce. These teachers will also determine whether their curricula are being influenced by what businesses say is required and needed or by objectives generated by bureaucrats.

3. All young people with disabilities should have the opportunity to be included in the workplace and schools. Special schools, segregated work activity centers, and programs that are designed only for people with disabilities must become institutions of the past. People with disabilities consistently perform better in typical work environments and natural community environments. Perpetual segregation hinders transition. Integration must be an outcome, not a process, that educators, parents, and professionals work toward together.

This chapter has discussed a legislative and philosophical framework for promoting school to adulthood transition. Strategies for enhancing transition services for young people with disabilities are developed in subsequent chapters.

Study Questions

1. What are the four societal challenges that affect the transition process? Describe ways to help students with disabilities overcome each of the challenges that are identified.

2. What are some examples of how the IDEA objectives can positively affect the transition planning and employment outcomes of youth with disabilities?

3. How do three disability-related laws, aside from IDEA, affect employment of people with disabilities?

4. What are examples of three opportunities that help to empower youth with disabilities?

5. Search the Internet to learn what current research findings say about transition outcomes for youth with disabilities.

Online Resources

National Secondary Transition Technical Assistance Center: http://www.nsttac.org/

Data Accountability Center, Individuals with Disabilities Education Act Data:
https://www.ideadata.org/default.asp

U.S. Department of Education Transition Guide: http://www2.ed.gov/about/offices/list/ocr/transitionguide.html

The National Longitudinal Transition Study: http://www.nlts2.org/

The National Center on Educational Outcomes: http://www.cehd.umn.edu/NCEO/

Self-Determination

Getting Students Involved in Leadership

2

MICHAEL L. WEHMEYER AND KARRIE A. SHOGREN

After completing this chapter, the reader will be able to

- Explain what characterizes people who are self-determined

- Describe the role of educators in promoting self-determination

- Discuss some of the methods, materials, and instructional strategies that promote self-determination in the transition years

- Explain how efforts to promote self-determination contribute to student involvement with and progress in the general education curriculum

- Identify and utilize existing methods, materials, and strategies that promote student involvement in transition planning and decision making

- Explain why it is important to promote student involvement in transition planning and leadership development

- Describe how self-determination can be infused into 18–21 programs

Promoting and enhancing the self-determination of youth with disabilities has become recommended practice in transition services. The National Secondary Transition Technical Assistance Center identified self-determination as 1 of 16 evidence-based predictors of postschool employment, education, and independent living success (Test, Fowler, Richter, White, Mazzotti, Walker, & Kortering, 2009). This chapter defines *self-determination* and examines its importance to successful transition-related results. It then describes methods, materials, and strategies to promote self-determination and to support active student involvement in educational planning and decision making.

What Is Self-Determination?

The historical roots of self-determination for people with disabilities can be found in the normalization, independent living, disability rights, and self-advocacy movements and in legislative protections ensuring equal opportunities for people with disabilities (Ward, 1996). Promoting self-determination emerged as an instructional focus area in special education as a result of efforts to improve transition-related outcomes for youth with disabilities in the 1990s. As a result, there are numerous frameworks that can serve as a basis for instructional design, as well as specially designed instructional methods, materials, and strategies to promote self-determination (Wehmeyer, Abery, Mithaug, & Stancliffe, 2003; Wehmeyer et al., 2007; Wehmeyer & Field, 2007).

Although these frameworks propose different definitions of the self-determination construct, there is a general consensus in the field as to what characterizes *people* who are self-determined.

> [Self-determined people] know how to choose—they know what they want and how to get it. From an awareness of personal needs, self-determined individuals choose goals, then doggedly pursue them. This involves asserting an individual's presence, making his or her needs known, evaluating progress toward meeting goals, adjusting performance, and creating unique approaches to solve problems. (Martin & Marshall, 1995, p. 147)

Our own work to promote self-determination, and the framework that guides our presentation of relevant interventions in this chapter, has been based on a functional model of self-determination in which self-determination is conceptualized as a dispositional characteristic (enduring tendencies used to characterize and describe differences between people; Wehmeyer, 2005; Wehmeyer et al., 2007) based on the *function* a behavior serves for an individual (Wehmeyer, 2005; Wehmeyer et al., 2007). *Self-determined behavior* refers to "volitional actions that enable one to act as the primary causal agent in one's life and to maintain or improve one's quality of life" (Wehmeyer, 2005, p. 117). Within this model, self-determined behavior refers to actions that are identified by four *essential characteristics:*

1. The person acted *autonomously.*
2. The behavior(s) are *self-regulated.*
3. The person initiated and responded to the event(s) in a *psychologically empowered* manner.
4. The person acted in a *self-realizing* manner.

These four essential characteristics describe the *function* of the behavior that makes it self-determined or not. That is, it is the function that the behavior serves for the individual that defines it as self-determined, not any specific class of behaviors themselves.

The concept of causal agency is central to our perspective. Broadly defined, *causal agency* implies that it is the individual who makes or causes things to happen in his or her life. One frequent misinterpretation of self-determination is that it simply means "doing it yourself." When self-determination is interpreted this way, however, there is an obvious problem for people with more severe disabilities, many of whom may have limits to the

Table 2.1. Component elements of self-determined behavior

Choice-making skills
Decision-making skills
Problem-solving skills
Goal-setting and -attainment skills
Independence, risk-taking, and safety skills
Self-observation, evaluation, and reinforcement skills
Self-instruction skills
Self-advocacy and leadership skills
Internal locus of control
Positive attributions of efficacy and outcome expectancy
Self-awareness
Self-knowledge

number and types of activities they can perform independently. However, the *capacity to perform* specific behaviors is secondary in importance to whether one is the causal agent (i.e., caused in some way to happen) over outcomes such behaviors are implemented to achieve. Thus, people who have severe physical disabilities can employ a personal assistant to perform routine activities and, if such functions are performed under the control of that person (i.e., the person with a disability), it is really a moot point whether the person physically performed the activity. Likewise, a person with a severe intellectual disability may not be able to "independently" (i.e., alone and with no support) make a complex decision, or solve a difficult problem. However, to the extent that supports are provided to enable that person to retain control over the decision-making process and to participate to the greatest extent in the decision-making or problem-solving process, he or she can become more self-determined.

Self-determination emerges across the life span as children and adolescents learn skills and develop attitudes that enable them to be causal agents in their lives. The *essential characteristics* that define self-determined behavior emerge through the development and acquisition of multiple, interrelated *component elements* (Table 2.1). Although not an exhaustive list, these component elements are particularly important to the emergence of self-determined behavior.

Self-Determination, Disability, and Empowerment

The role of educators in promoting self-determination is to teach students the knowledge and skills they need to become causal agents in their lives. However, it is important that educators not forget that the self-determination focus in disability services, including special education, emerged from deeply held convictions pertaining to the rights of people with disabilities to have a meaningful voice in their own lives. Within the context of the disability rights and advocacy movement, the self-determination construct has been imbued with an empowerment and "rights" orientation. *Empowerment* is a term usually associated with social and civil rights movements (Wehmeyer, 2004). *The American Heritage Dictionary of the English Language* (2004) states that the noun *empowerment* originally evolved to mean "to enable" or "to permit," and only recently has shifted to mean more control or power.

Although it is a contemporary buzzword, the word *empower* is not new, having arisen in the mid-17th century with the legalistic meaning "to invest with authority, authorize." Shortly thereafter it began to be used with an infinitive in a more general way meaning "to enable or permit." Its modern use originated in the civil rights movement, which sought political *empowerment* for its followers. Since people of all political persuasions have a need for a word that makes their constituents feel that they are or are about to become more in control of their destinies, *empower* has been adopted by conservatives as well as social reformers. (2000, pp. 586–587)

It is worth noting the meaning shift or drift that has occurred with use of the term since its 17th-century origination and the current linkages between empowerment and issues of control over one's life. It remains less than convincing, at least when the term is applied to the disability movement, that how many people use the term remains, in fact, closer to the original sense of the term: to authorize or invest with authority. The problem with that meaning with regard to people with disabilities is, of course, that in the end when one (and in our field, typically a professional) has the power to invest someone else with authority, one also has the power, presumably, to withhold granting that authority. Power and control remain, fundamentally, with the granter in that circumstance. In a similar way, the more current meaning identified by dictionary scholars (to enable or to permit) seems to offer two synonyms that, in the end, are not equally effective in solving the "granting authority" problem. That is, the act of "permitting" implies authority on the part of one person to allow another to do something, or not. The meaning of *empowerment* or, more accurately, *empower*, as meaning "to enable," is closer to the sense of the term as used when associated with social movements, particularly the disability rights movement, which typically uses the term in reference to actions that "enhance the possibilities for people to control their lives" (Rappaport, 1981, p. 15). *Enable* refers to providing opportunities and resources for something to happen.

Consideration of what it means to empower someone with a disability is more than just a semantic exercise. Well-intentioned professionals across many disciplines mistake empowerment as something that one grants or gives to someone else, to the end that the effort falls short of the standard of enhancing the possibilities for people to control their lives.

There is, as such, a bit of a catch-22 to issues pertaining to empowerment and professionals in transition and rehabilitation, in that many such professionals genuinely want to do whatever they can to empower people with disabilities, but similarly do not want to err in assuming that any ultimate authority to grant power or control lies within them. The way out of this conundrum is through efforts to *enable* people with disabilities to exert greater control in their lives—to become causal agents in their lives—and, as a function of such actions, to become empowered to do so to a greater extent. For professionals in transition education, the route to enablement is by providing opportunities and supports that promote and enhance the self-determination of students with disabilities.

Is Self-Determination Important to Transition Outcomes for Students with Disabilities?

Promoting the self-determination of students with disabilities has become a recommended practice in secondary education and transition services for several reasons. First, self-determination status has been linked to the attainment of more positive academic (Konrad, Fowler, Walker, Test, & Wood, 2007; Fowler, Konrad, Walker, Test, & Wood, 2007; Lee, Wehmeyer, Soukup, & Palmer, 2010) and transition outcomes, including more positive employment and independent living outcomes (Martorell, Gutierrez-Recacha, Pereda, & Ayuso-Mateos, 2008; Sowers & Powers, 1995; Wehmeyer & Palmer, 2003; Wehmeyer & Schwartz, 1997), and more positive quality of life and life satisfaction (Lachapelle et al., 2005; Nota, Ferrari, Soresi, & Wehmeyer, 2007; Shogren, Lopez, Wehmeyer, Little, & Pressgrove, 2006; Wehmeyer & Schwartz, 1998).

Second, research across special education disability categories has established the need for intervention to promote self-determination, documenting that students with intellectual disability (Wehmeyer et al., 2007), learning disabilities (Field, Sarver, & Shaw, 2003; Pierson, Carter, Lane, & Glaeser, 2008), emotional and behavioral disorders (Carter, Lane, Pierson, & Glaeser, 2006; Pierson et al., 2008), and autism (Wehmeyer, Shogren,

Zager, Smith, & Simpson, 2010) are less self-determined than their nondisabled peers. Teachers believe that teaching students to become more self-determined is important (Carter, Lane, Pierson, & Stang, 2008; Thoma, Pannozzo, Fritton, & Bartholomew, 2008; Wehmeyer, Agran, & Hughes, 2000) and there are numerous curricular and instructional models identified to enable them to provide this instructional focus (Test, Karvonen, Wood, Browder, & Algozzine, 2000; Wehmeyer & Field, 2007). In a meta-analysis of single-subject and group-subject design studies, Algozzine, Browder, Karvonen, Test, and Wood (2001) found evidence for the efficacy of instruction to promote component elements of self-determined behavior, including self-advocacy, goal setting and attainment, self-awareness, problem-solving skills, and decision-making skills. Cobb, Lehmann, Newman-Gonchar, and Alwell (2009) conducted a narrative metasynthesis—a narrative synthesis of multiple meta-analytic studies—covering seven existing meta-analyses examining self-determination and concluded that there is sufficient evidence to support the promotion of self-determination as effective. Also, research documents the positive impact of efforts to promote student involvement in educational and transition planning (Martin, Van Dycke, Christensen, Greene, Gardner, & Lovett, 2006; Mason, Field, & Sawilowsky, 2004; Test et al., 2004) on more positive transition and self-determination–related outcomes.

Third, and importantly, causal evidence of the impact of interventions to promote self-determination on student self-determination status is increasingly available. Wehmeyer, Palmer, Shogren, Williams-Diehm, and Soukup (in press) conducted a randomized trial control group study of the effect of interventions to promote self-determination on the self-determination status of high school students receiving special education services under the categorical areas of intellectual disability and learning disabilities. Students in the treatment group (*n* = 235) received instruction using a variety of instructional methods to promote self-determination and student involvement in educational planning meetings over 3 years, while students in the control group (n = 132) received no such intervention. The self-determination of each student was measured with two instruments, *The Arc's Self-Determination Scale* (SDS; Wehmeyer & Kelchner, 1995) and the *AIR Self-Determination Scale* (AIR; Wolman, Campeau, Dubois, Mithaug, & Stolarski, 1994; both described subsequently) across three measurement intervals. Wehmeyer and colleagues found that students with intellectual disability and learning disabilities who participated in interventions to promote self-determination over a 3-year period showed significantly more positive patterns of growth in their self-determination scores than did students not exposed to interventions to promote self-determination during the same time period.

In summary, there is an expanding base of evidence suggesting that higher self-determination and increased capacity in the component elements of self-determined behavior results in better transition-related outcomes for youth and young adults with disabilities. The obvious next issue is how to achieve this important outcome.

Assessments, Methods, and Strategies to Promote Self-Determination

Efforts to enhance the self-determination of youth with disabilities should involve multiple, parallel activities focused on teaching skills related to the component elements of self-determined behavior and promoting active involvement in educational planning and decision making. We have already highlighted research establishing that students can acquire skills and knowledge pertaining to self-determination if provided instruction and that such instruction can positively impact transition-related outcomes for youth and young adults with disabilities. In the context of school reform efforts, such efforts take on even greater urgency.

Importance of Self-Determination to Access to the General Education Curriculum

The 1997 amendments to the Individuals with Disabilities Education Act (IDEA 1997) and their associated regulations included statutory and regulatory language intended to ensure that students with disabilities had access to the general curriculum. Section 300.347(a)(3) in IDEA 1997 required that the individualized education program (IEP) of students with disabilities include

> [a] statement of the special education and related services and supplementary aids and services to be provided to the child, or on behalf of the child, and a statement of the program modifications or supports for school personnel that will be provided for the child
>
> (i) to advance appropriately toward attaining the annual goals;
>
> (ii) to be involved and progress in the general curriculum;
>
> (iii) to be educated and participate with disabled and non-disabled children.

In fact, as reflected in the language in part (ii), what IDEA required was that students with disabilities be involved with and show progress in the general curriculum. The term "access to the general curriculum" refers to this requirement for student involvement and progress. The general curriculum was defined in the regulations as referring to "the same curriculum as for nondisabled children" (*Federal Register*, 1999, p. 12,592). The intent of these access provisions was threefold, as described by U.S. Department of Education officials:

1. That all students, including students with disabilities, would have access to a challenging curriculum

2. That all students, including students with disabilities, would be held to high expectations

3. To align special education practice with accountability mechanisms emerging through school reform efforts

The 2004 reauthorization of IDEA (IDEA 2004) contained all of the original IDEA 1997 mandates and added several new requirements, including that schools ensure that the IEP team includes someone knowledgeable about the general education curriculum and that the team meet at least annually to address any lack of expected progress in the general education curriculum. IDEA 2004 also changed the term to general *education* curriculum. Finally, the regulations to IDEA 2004 prohibited a student with a disability from being removed from the general education setting based solely upon needed modifications to the general education curriculum.

Spooner, Dymond, Smith, and Kennedy (2006) reviewed the approaches to promoting the access of students with disabilities, identifying a focus on self-determination as one of only a few such approaches. Wehmeyer, Field, Doren, Jones, and Mason (2004) identified two ways in which promoting self-determination will, in fact, promote access to the general education curriculum. First, state and local standards frequently include goals and objectives that pertain to component elements of self-determined behavior. By identifying where in the general curriculum all students are expected to learn skills and knowledge related to the component elements of self-determined behavior, teachers can promote self-determination and promote progress in the general education curriculum. Second, model processes that identify how to promote access to the general education curriculum emphasize the importance of curriculum modifications, adaptations, and augmentations that enable students to interact with curricular content. Teaching students the skills that enable them to be more self-determined, such as goal setting and attainment, problem solving, self-regulation and self-management, self-directed learning, coping and organizational, and leadership and teamwork skills will also enable them to more effectively interact with the general education curriculum. These are discussed subsequently.

There is now a clear evidence base that teaching students to self-regulate learning or teaching students self-directed learning strategies such as self-monitoring or self-instruction has beneficial outcomes for students with severe disabilities in educational goal attainment, including goals linked to transition-related outcomes and to the general education curriculum (Agran, Cavin, Wehmeyer, & Palmer, 2006; Agran, Wehmeyer, Cavin, & Palmer, 2008, 2010). Recently, Wehmeyer and colleagues have provided evidence that teaching students to self-regulate learning using the *Self-Determined Learning Model of Instruction* (SDLMI; Wehmeyer et al., 2000) results in the attainment of goals linked to the general education curriculum (Lee et al., 2010). Shogren, Palmer, Wehmeyer, Williams-Diehm, and Little (in press) conducted a group-randomized trial control group study examining the impact of intervention using the SDLMI on student academic and transition goal attainment and on access to the general education curriculum for students with intellectual disability and learning disabilities, showing the efficacy of the model for both goal attainment and access to the general education curriculum.

Assessment in Self-Determination

As is the case with instruction in any content area, assessment and instruction go hand in hand in efforts to promote self-determination. Determining instructional and curricular needs in the area of self-determination will involve a combination of standardized and informal procedures incorporating input from multiple sources, including the student, his or her family, professionals, and others. Informal procedures will be similar to those described by Clark (1996) with regard to transition assessment. Clark identified informal assessment from which transition-related decisions can be made as including

   a. Situational or observational learning styles assessments
   b. Curriculum-based assessment
   c. Observational reports from teachers, employers, and family members
   d. Situational assessments in home, community, and work settings
   e. Environmental assessments
   f. Personal future–planning activities
   g. Structured interviews with students
   h. Structured interviews with parents, guardians, advocates, or peers
   i. Adaptive, behavioral, or functional skill inventories
   j. Social histories
   k. Employability, independent living, and personal social skills rating scales
   l. Technology or vocational education skills assessments.

These types of assessment procedures enable planners to form a complete picture of student needs, interests, and abilities by gathering input from multiple sources, and are important for determining the same things as they pertain to the need for instruction to promote self-determination.

Norm-Referenced Measures of Self-Determination

The Arc's Self-Determination Scale   The SDS (Wehmeyer & Kelchner, 1995; available online at http://www.ou.edu/content/education/centers-and-partnerships/zarrow/self-determination-assessment-tools.html) is a 72-item self-report measure based on the functional theory of self-determination. A total of 148 points are available on the scale, with higher scores indicating higher levels of self-determination. An overall self-determination score, as well as subscale scores for each of the four essential characteristics of self-determined behavior—autonomy, self-regulation, psychological empowerment, and self-realization—can be calculated. The SDS was developed and normed with 500 adolescents with intellectual disability and learning disabilities and was demonstrated to have adequate reliability and validity (Wehmeyer, 1996). Subsequent research (Shogren et al., 2008) has verified the proposed theoretical structure of the SDS (i.e., four related, but distinct, subscales that contribute to a higher-order self-determination construct).

The SDS has been used to conduct research into the relationship between self-determination and positive adult outcomes (Wehmeyer & Schwartz, 1997) and quality of life variables (Wehmeyer & Schwartz, 1998) and the relationship between self-determination and environmental factors (Wehmeyer & Bolding, 1999, 2001) and to validate instructional strategies to promote self-determination (S. Lee et al., 2010; Y. Lee et al., 2011; Shogren et al., 2010; Wehmeyer, Palmer, Agran, Mithaug, & Martin, 2000; Wehmeyer, Shogren, et al., in press) and materials to promote student-directed transition planning (Wehmeyer & Lawrence, 1995; Wehmeyer, Palmer, Lee, Williams-Diehm, & Shogren, 2011).

One potential use of the SDS is to generate discussion about items the student finds interesting or problematic or wants to discuss more broadly. A second use of the SDS involves scoring it and comparing total, domain, and subdomain scores with scale norms and, more importantly, examining individual strengths and weaknesses across the domains. Less than optimal performances in any area of the SDS should be followed by learning opportunities and experiences that enable the student to make progress in that particular area, and any use of the SDS with individual students should focus on potential educational goals and objectives. This discussion, in turn, can consider possible educational programs and activities to address and meet these goals and objectives.

The AIR Self-Determination Scale   The AIR Self-Determination Scale (AIR; Wolman et al., 1994; available online at http://www.ou.edu/content/education/centers-and-partnerships/zarrow/self-determination-assessment-tools.html) assesses student capacity and opportunity for self-determination. The AIR has a Student (AIR-S), Educator, and Parent version. The AIR-S has 24 questions and also yields capacity and opportunity subscale scores. The capacity subscale consists of questions related to things students do related to self-determination and how students feel about performing these self-determined behaviors. The opportunity subscale consists of questions regarding students' perceptions of their opportunities to perform self-determined behaviors at home and at school.

The AIR was developed and normed with 450 students with and without disabilities in California and New York (Wolman et al., 1994). The AIR was demonstrated to have adequate reliability and validity in the measurement of capacity and opportunity for self-determination (see Wolman et al., 1994, for details). Recent research (Shogren et al., 2008) has confirmed the theoretical structure of the AIR Self-Determination Scale (i.e., two related subscales—capacity and opportunity—that contribute to a higher-order self-determination construct). This research also confirmed that, although the SDS and the AIR-S are related ($r = .50$), they are measuring distinct aspects of the self-determination construct.

Self-Determination Assessment Battery[1]   The Self-Determination Assessment Battery was developed by Field, Hoffman, and Sawilowsky (2004). It contains five instruments that measure cognitive, affective, and behavioral factors related to self-determination. In addition, these factors are assessed from the perspectives of the student, the teacher, and the parent. This battery of instruments was developed to assess knowledge, behavior, and affective components of self-determination from these varied perspectives and within the context of an intervention theory to promote self-determination forwarded by Field and Hoffman (1994). The five instruments in the battery are as follows (Field et al., 2004):

---

[1]Information on ordering the Self-Determination Assessment Battery can be obtained from the Wayne State University Center for Self-Determination and Transition Business Office at (313) 577–1638 or sdtalk@wayne.edu.

1. *Self-Determination Knowledge Scale (SDKS) Pretest:* The SDKS-pre- and SDKS-posttest are each 37-item structured response instruments for use with students with mild–moderate intellectual disability and learning disabilities, designed to assess their cognitive knowledge of self-determination skills as taught in the Field and Hoffman (1994) *Steps to Self-Determination* curriculum.

2. *Self-Determination Parent Perception Scale (PPS)* and

3. *Teacher Perception Scale (TPS):* The PPS and TPS are 30-item questionnaires administered to parents and teachers, respectively. The items in these questionnaires were also derived from the Field and Hoffman (1994) model of self-determination intervention. The teacher or parent rates the student on a variety of behaviors, abilities, and skills associated with self-determination.

4. *Self-Determination Observation Checklist (SDOC):* The SDOC is a 38-item behavioral observation checklist designed to be administered by classroom teachers or other appropriate personnel in the school environment. The student is observed for approximately 5 minutes during a class period. Behaviors that correlate to self-determination are checked.

5. *Self-Determination Student Scale (SDSS):* The SDSS is a 92-item self-report instrument that measures both affective and cognitive aspects of the student's self-determination. The items contain a brief stimulus, to which the student marks "That's me" or "That's not me." The SDSS yields a variety of subscale scores; the general subscales relate to a student's sense of global self-determination, whereas the specific subscales relate primarily to application in their education, home, and related environmental settings. The positive subscales indicate self-determination in areas of perceived strength, and the negative subscales indicate areas of perceived weakness in self-determination.

The Self-Determination Assessment Battery instruments have many possible uses in education. First, they can be used to assist in educational planning by identifying areas of similarity and discrepancy among the three perspectives of the student, teacher, and parent. This provides an opportunity for discussion among the student, teacher, and parent to determine the reasons for this discrepancy. For example, it may be that a student is exhibiting skills in the home that he or she is not displaying at school or it may be that the teacher and the parent were using different criteria to evaluate the student's performance. Because students are not only evaluated from different perspectives but also being assessed in three different areas (cognition/knowledge, behavior, and affect), examining the differences in the three different areas can also help to determine appropriate interventions.

All of these instruments clearly have varied uses for educational planning, both as discussion tools in educational planning meetings that can help to promote greater self-awareness and as tools that can help to identify appropriate educational interventions. In addition, the instruments can be used for program evaluation or research purposes. By using the instruments as pre- and posttests before and after an instructional intervention, data can be obtained that can help to assess the effectiveness of the intervention.

Infusing Instruction to Promote Self-Determination in the General Education Curriculum

Infusing instruction on component elements of self-determined behavior (Table 2.1) into instruction across content areas provides the first focus for promoting self-determination. This section briefly identifies some key strategies to achieve this instructional outcome.

Goal Setting

Goal-setting and attainment skills are critical to students with disabilities becoming more self-determined. Goals specify what a person wishes to achieve and act as regulators of human behavior. If a person sets a goal, then it increases the probability that he or she will perform behaviors related to that goal (Latham & Locke, 1991). The process of promoting goal-setting and attainment skills involves teaching students to

1.   Identify and define a goal clearly and concretely
2.   Develop a series of objectives or tasks to achieve the goal
3.   Specify the actions necessary to achieve the desired outcome

Goal-setting activities can be easily incorporated into a variety of transition-related activities and across multiple instructional areas, as well as in the educational planning process, including through student-directed planning activities such as those discussed subsequently.

Research has suggested some general strategies to follow to make goals both meaningful and attainable for students with disabilities. First, goals should be challenging for the student. They should not be so challenging that the student cannot attain them, as this will lead to frustration and withdrawal from participation, but they must provide enough motivation for the student to work to attain them. If goals are too easy, then there is neither motivation to engage in the work necessary to attain them nor a feeling of accomplishment after achieving them. Although it is preferable for students to participate in setting their own goals at whatever level is appropriate given the nature of their disability, if this is not possible and goals need to be set by teachers, then the student's preferences and interests should be incorporated into the goal to increase the student's motivation to pursue the goal. Goals that have personal meaning are more likely to be attained (Doll & Sands, 1998).

Choice Making

Choice making (e.g., the expression of a preference between two or more options) has been linked to multiple outcomes of benefit to transition. There is an emerging database showing that incorporating choice-making opportunities into interventions to reduce problem behaviors of children and youth with disabilities results in improved behavioral outcomes (Shogren, Faggella-Luby, Bae, & Wehmeyer, 2004). Cooper and Browder (1998) found that teaching young adults to make choices improved outcomes of **community-based instruction**. Watanabe and Sturmey (2003) found that promoting choice-making opportunities in vocational tasks for young adults with disabilities increased engagement in the activity.

In addition, by making choices, students, particularly younger children, learn that they can exert control over their environment. For students to fully understand the process of choice making, including the various effects of making certain choices, choices need to be real and meaningful. A variety of adaptive equipment, ranging from picture communication systems to computer technology, can be used to support students with more severe disabilities to indicate their preferences. Such strategies may be particularly helpful for students with autism, given their preference for information in a concrete, visual form. Choice opportunities can and should be infused through the school day. Students can be provided opportunities to choose within or between instructional activities. They can also choose with whom they engage in a task, where they engage in an activity, and whether they complete an activity (Wehmeyer et al., 2007).

Problem Solving

A problem is an activity or task for which a solution is not known or readily apparent. The process of solving a problem involves (D'Zurilla & Goldfried, 1971, pp. 107–126):

1.   Identifying and defining the problem
2.   Listing possible solutions

3. Identifying the impact of each solution

4. Making a judgment about a preferred solution

5. Evaluating the efficacy of the judgment

Developing effective social problem-solving skills is central to the process of becoming self-determined. These skills are central to a student's capacity to interact with other people and to cope with problems that arise in social contexts.

Limitations in social problem-solving skills have been linked to difficulties in employment, community, and independent living situations for people with **developmental disabilities** (Gumpel, Tappe, & Araki, 2000). Storey (2002) reviewed the empirical literature pertaining to improving social interactions for workers with disabilities and determined that problem-solving skills contributed to more positive workplace social interactions. O'Reilly, Lancioni, and O'Kane (2000) found that incorporating instruction in problem solving into social skills instruction improved employment outcomes for supported workers with traumatic brain injuries.

A number of strategies to promote problem solving have been evaluated for students with disabilities. Bauminger (2002, 2007a, 2007b) developed a curriculum to teach students with autism social and interpersonal problem-solving skills. Students were taught about social concepts, such as starting a conversation, and then were presented a vignette of a student having difficulty implementing the skill. Students went through an eight-stage problem-solving process with their teacher in which they

1. Defined the problem

2. Discussed the emotions associated with the problem

3. Defined the alternative social actions

4. Considered the consequences of each alternative

5. Made a decision about the best alternative

6. Role-played the solution with their teacher

7. Received homework to practice the social skill covered in the lesson at home with peers

8. Received feedback from the teacher on the homework

After 7 months, students generated more appropriate solutions to problems faced in social situations and initiated more social interactions with their peers.

Bernard-Opitz, Sriram, and Nakhoda-Sapuan (2001) developed a computer program to teach students with developmental disabilities social problem-solving skills. The program first presented pictures or videos of people experiencing social conflicts. The program guided students through an animated problem-solving process in which they were asked to generate alternative solutions. After identifying an alternate solution, a video clip of the actors resolving the problem was presented. As students had repeated experience with the program, they generated more alternative solutions. Bernard-Ripoli (2007) used video self-modeling as a strategy, combined with social stories, to assist a child with Asperger syndrome understand emotions pertaining to social interactions and social problem solving. In addition, problem-solving instruction is a component of many self-regulation strategies, discussed subsequently.

Decision Making

A decision-making process involves coming to a judgment about which solution is best at a given time. Making effective decisions typically involves (Beyth-Marom, Fischhoff, Quadrel, & Furby, 1991, pp. 19–59)

1. Identifying alternative courses of action

2. Identifying the possible consequences of each action

3. Assessing the probability of each consequence occurring

4. Choosing the best alternative

5. Implementing the decision

Although the ability to engage in this process develops with age, research has shown that young children can engage in a systematic decision-making process, often by reducing and simplifying the steps in the decision-making process, although they are not as effective as older students (Crone, Vendel, & van der Molen, 2003). Thus, working to promote systematic decision-making skills is best addressed at the secondary level, whereas at the elementary level, a focus on choice making and problem solving can support the development of effective decision-making skills later in life.

Studies have shown repeatedly that adolescents with disabilities can effectively participate in the decision-making process (Wehmeyer et al., 2007), want to be involved in decisions related to their life (Ruef & Turnbull, 2002), and benefit from instruction to do so. Teaching young women with intellectual disabilities to make more effective decisions improved their capacity to identify potentially abusive social interactions (Khemka, 2000). Datillo and Hoge (1999) found that teaching decision making to adolescents with intellectual disability in the context of a leisure education program improved their acquisition of socially valid leisure knowledge and skills.

To support students with disabilities to acquire decision-making skills, a number of strategies can be implemented throughout the student's educational career. Early on, students should be provided a wide array of choice opportunities and receive instruction regarding how to make effective choices, as discussed previously. As students age, they should be provided overt instruction in the decision-making process. When teaching decision-making skills, opportunities to make decisions should be embedded in the curriculum. By supporting students to make decisions in "real-world" situations, they will better develop their ability to conceptualize and generalize the decision-making process. The Virginia Department of Education's Self-Determination Project (http://www.imdetermined.org) provides free lesson plans and templates for student involvement in the IEP.

Self-Regulation and Student-Directed Learning

Each of the aforementioned areas is important to enable students to self-regulate their behavior and their lives. Self-regulation is the process of setting goals, developing action plans to achieve those goals, implementing and following the action plans, evaluating the outcomes of the action plan, and changing action plans if the goal was not achieved (Mithaug, Mithaug, Agran, Martin, & Wehmeyer, 2003). The skills associated with self-regulation enable students to examine their environments, evaluate their repertoire of possible responses, and implement and evaluate a response (Whitman, 1990).

Student-directed learning strategies involve teaching students strategies that enable them to modify and regulate their own behavior (Agran, King-Sears, Wehmeyer, & Copeland, 2003). The emphasis in such strategies is shifted from teacher-mediated and -directed instruction to student-directed instruction. Research in education and rehabilitation has shown that student-directed learning strategies are as successful—and often more successful—as teacher-directed learning strategies, and these strategies are effective means to increase independence and productivity. A variety of strategies has been used to teach students with disabilities how to manage their own behavior or direct learning. Among the most commonly used strategies are picture cues and antecedent cue regulation strategies, self-instruction, self-monitoring, self-evaluation, and self-reinforcement. These are briefly introduced next (see Agran et al., 2003, for a comprehensive treatment of student-directed learning strategies).

Picture cues and antecedent cue regulation strategies involve the use of visual or audio cues that students use to guide their behavior. Visual cues typically involve photographs, illustrations, or line drawings of steps in a task that support students to complete an activity that consists of a sequence of tasks. Audio cues include prerecorded, taped directions or instructions that the students can listen to as they perform a task. Emerging technologies, such as handheld computers, provide new and potentially powerful vehicles to deliver visual or auditory cues to learners. Picture cues and antecedent cue regulation strategies have been used to teach individuals with intellectual disability complex work task sequences and to promote on-task behavior and independent work performance (Agran et al., 2003; Mithaug et al., 2003).

Self-instruction involves teaching students to provide their own verbal cues before the execution of target behaviors. Students and adults with intellectual disability have been taught to use self-instruction to solve a variety of work problems, to complete multistep sequences, and to generalize responding across changing work environments (Wehmeyer et al., 2007). Graham and Harris (1989) found that a self-instructional strategy improved the essay composition skills of students with learning disabilities.

Self-monitoring involves teaching students to observe whether they have performed a targeted behavior and whether the response met whatever existing criteria were present. Teaching students self-monitoring strategies has been shown to improve critical learning skills and classroom involvement skills of students with severe disabilities (Agran et al., 2005; Hughes et al., 2002). Woods and Martin (2004) found that teaching supported employees to self-manage and self-regulate work tasks improved employers' perceptions of the employee and improved work performance.

Self-evaluation and *self-reinforcement* involve teaching the students to compare their performance (as tracked through self-monitoring) with a desired goal or outcome and to administer consequences to themselves (e.g., verbally telling themselves they did a good job). Self-reinforcement allows students to provide themselves with reinforcers that are accessible and immediate. Given access to self-administered reinforcement, behavior change may be greatly facilitated and both procedures have been shown to improve generalization of learning (Agran et al., 2003).

Self-Advocacy

Students with disabilities need to learn the skills to advocate on their own behalf. To be an effective self-advocate, students have to learn both how to advocate and what to advocate. There are ample opportunities for students to practice and learn self-advocacy skills within the context of the educational planning process. Too often, students' perspectives have been lost because they have not had the opportunities or the skills to express their perspective within the IEP, transition, or general educational planning meetings. A first step to enabling students to express their wants and needs during these meetings is educating students about their rights and responsibilities in these areas. They can be educated about their educational rights and responsibilities under IDEA; about their civil rights under the Americans with Disabilities Act (ADA) of 1990 (PL 101-336); or, more generally, about the rights available to citizens. Instructional strategies have been developed for teaching such knowledge to students with disabilities (Wehmeyer et al., 2007).

When one is teaching students how to advocate for themselves, the focus should be on teaching students how to be assertive, how to effectively communicate their perspective (either verbally or in written or pictorial form), how to negotiate, how to compromise, and how to deal with systems and bureaucracies. Students need to be provided real-world opportunities to practice these skills. This can be done by embedding opportunities for self-advocacy within the school day, by allowing students to set up a class schedule, work out their supports with a resource room teacher or other support provider, or participate in IEP and **transition meetings**.

Perceptions of Efficacy and Control

People who have positive perceptions of their efficacy believe they can perform the behavior required to achieve a desired outcome (Bandura & Cervone, 2000). Furthermore, individuals also have efficacy expectations, which are beliefs about the probability of the performance of a given behavior leading to the desired outcome. These two constructs are both necessary for the performance of the skills discussed previously. For example, if a student does not believe that he or she can perform a particular behavior, then he or she will not engage in it (i.e., if a student with a disability does not believe he or she has the requisite skills for communicating with his or her peers, then he or she will not make attempts to communicate). However, even if a student does believe he or she can perform a given behavior, but holds low expectations for the attainment of the desired result from the behavior because previous attempts to engage in the behavior have been ignored or disregarded, then he or she is still likely not to perform the behavior.

Research has shown that students with disabilities tend to have less adaptive perceptions of efficacy and outcome expectations than do students without disabilities (Wehmeyer et al., 2003). The same has been found concerning the perceptions of students with disabilities about their ability to exert control over their environment. People who believe they have the ability to exert control over their lives and outcomes tend to be described as having an internal locus of control, whereas people who perceive that others are largely controlling their lives and outcomes are described as having an external locus of control (Rotter, 1966). Students must be provided with opportunities to develop adaptive perceptions of their efficacy in performing given behaviors and their ability to exert control over their lives. By enabling students to engage in problem solving, goal setting, choice making, and decision making, they can learn that they have control over their outcomes and develop confidence in their ability to perform these behaviors and achieve their desired outcomes. Both teacher and classroom characteristics can influence students' perceptions of efficacy and control. Overly controlling environments can diminish students' perceptions of their ability to exert control and engage in actions that enable them to develop adaptive efficacy expectations. It is important for teachers to work to empower students to be active participants in their classrooms.

Self-Awareness and Self-Knowledge

For students to become more self-realizing, they must possess a reasonably accurate understanding of their strengths, abilities, unique learning and support needs, and limitations. Furthermore, they must know how to utilize this understanding to maximize success and progress. However, like perceptions of efficacy and control, self-awareness and-knowledge are not things that can simply be taught through direct instruction. Instead, students acquire this knowledge by interacting with their environment. Unfortunately, students with disabilities often learn to identify what they *cannot* do instead of what they can do. This skews students' perceptions of themselves and influences how they interact with people and systems they encounter.

Thus, it is important to promote *realistic* self-awareness and -knowledge in students with disabilities. For example, Faherty (2000) developed an approach to guide children and youth with autism spectrum disorders through the process of developing an understanding of their strengths, their abilities, and the impact of autism on their lives. The process has a number of activities that encourage students to think about their strengths and abilities and contains activities to support students to develop and reflect on how they learn, their sensory experiences, their artistic and technological abilities, their social and communication skills, their thoughts, and why they sometimes feel upset. It also helps students reflect on the people in their lives, including their school experiences.

Self-Determined Learning Model of Instruction

Like all educators, special education teachers use a variety of *teaching models,* which are defined as "a plan or pattern that can be used to shape curriculums (long-term courses of study), to design instructional materials, and to guide instruction in the classroom and other settings" (Joyce & Weil, 1980, p. 1). Such models are derived from theories about human behavior, learning, or cognition, and effective teachers employ multiple models of teaching, taking into account the unique characteristics of the learner and types of learning. A teacher may use the role-playing model to teach social behaviors, social simulation and social inquiry models to examine social problems and solutions, assertiveness training to teach self-advocacy skills, or a training model to teach vocational skills. Likewise, special educators employ more traditional, cognitively based models of teaching, such as the concept attainment model to teach thinking skills, the memory model for increasing the retention of facts, or inductive thinking and inquiry training models to teach reasoning and academic skills. The teaching model most frequently adopted by special educators is the contingency management model, drawing from operant psychology.

The common theme across these teaching models is that they are teacher-directed. Although they provide direction for strategy and curriculum development activities that can teach components of self-determination, none adequately provides teachers a model to truly enable young people to become causal agents in their lives. The *Self-Determined Learning Model of Instruction (SDLMI;* Mithaug, Wehmeyer, Agran, Martin, & Palmer, 1998; Wehmeyer et al., 2000) was developed to address this problem and is based on the component elements of self-determination, the process of self-regulated problem solving, and research on student-directed learning. It is appropriate for use with students with and without disabilities across a wide range of content areas and enables teachers to engage students in the totality of their educational program by increasing opportunities to self-direct learning and, in the process, to enhance student self-determination.

Implementation of the model consists of a three-phase instructional process depicted in Figures 2.1, 2.2, and 2.3. Each instructional phase presents a problem to be solved by the student. The student solves each problem by posing and answering a series of four student questions per phase that students learn, modify to make their own, and apply to reach self-selected goals. Each question is linked to a set of teacher objectives. Each instructional phase includes a list of educational supports that teachers can use to enable students to self-direct learning. In each instructional phase, the student is the primary agent for choices, decisions, and actions, even when eventual actions are teacher-directed.

The student questions are constructed to direct the student through a problem-solving sequence in each instructional phase. Teachers implementing the model teach students to solve a sequence of problems to construct a means–ends chain—a causal sequence—that moves them from where they are (an actual state of not having their needs and interests satisfied) to where they want to be (a goal state of having those needs and interests satisfied). To answer the questions in this sequence, students must regulate their own problem solving by setting goals to meet needs, constructing plans to meet goals, and adjusting actions to complete plans. The questions differ from phase to phase but represent identical steps in the problem-solving sequence. That is, students answering the questions must

1.   Identify the problem
2.   Identify potential solutions to the problem
3.   Identify barriers to solving the problem
4.   Identify consequences of each solution

These steps are the fundamental steps in any problem-solving process.

Because the model itself is designed for teachers to implement, the language of the student questions is not written to be understood by every student, nor does the model assume that students have life experiences that enable them to fully answer each question. Some students will learn and use all 12 questions as they are written. Other students will need to have the questions rephrased to be more understandable. Still other students,

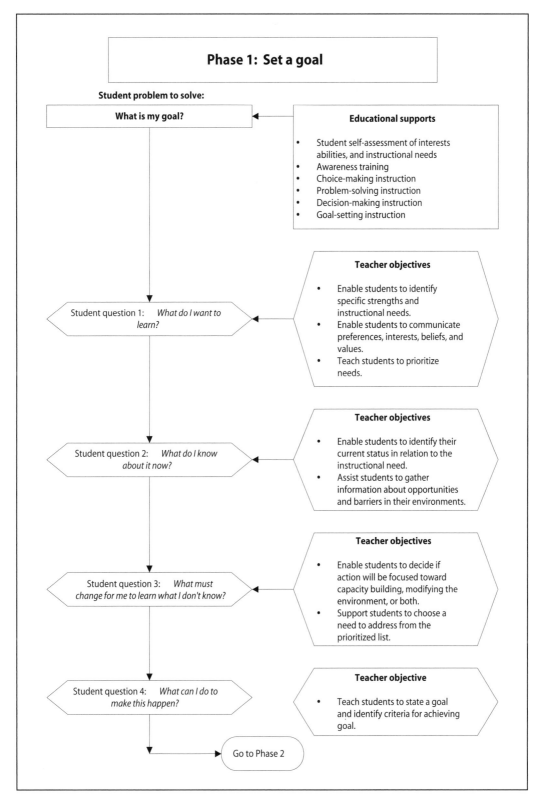

Figure 2.1. Phase 1 of the Self-Determined Learning Model of Instruction.

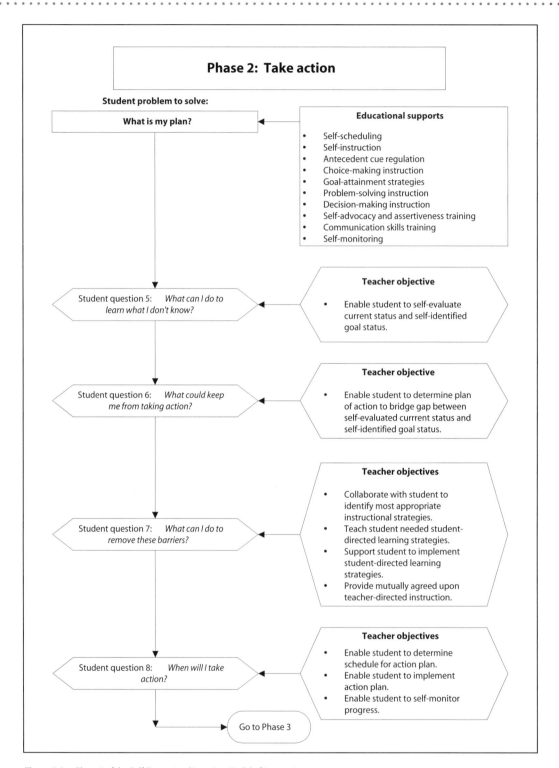

Figure 2.2.   Phase 2 of the Self-Determined Learning Model of Instruction.

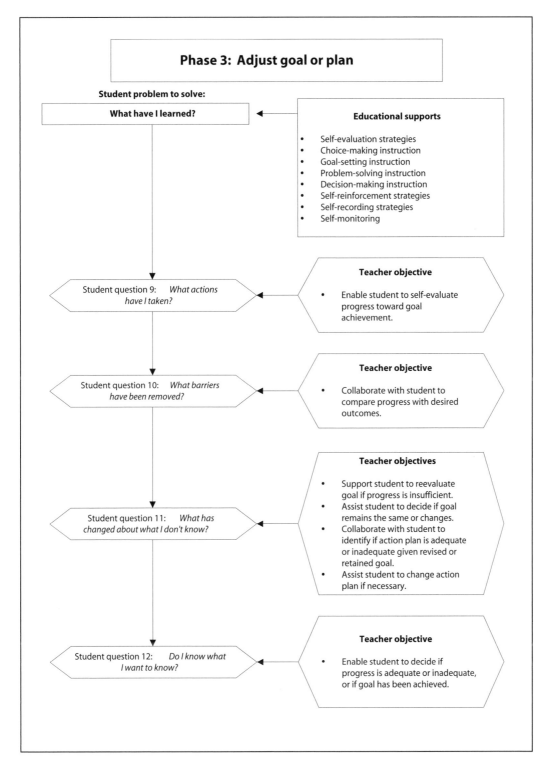

Phase 3: Adjust goal or plan

Student problem to solve:

What have I learned?

Educational supports

- Self-evaluation strategies
- Choice-making instruction
- Goal-setting instruction
- Problem-solving instruction
- Decision-making instruction
- Self-reinforcement strategies
- Self-recording strategies
- Self-monitoring

Student question 9: *What actions have I taken?*

Teacher objective

- Enable student to self-evaluate progress toward goal achievement.

Student question 10: *What barriers have been removed?*

Teacher objective

- Collaborate with student to compare progress with desired outcomes.

Student question 11: *What has changed about what I don't know?*

Teacher objectives

- Support student to reevaluate goal if progress is insufficient.
- Assist student to decide if goal remains the same or changes.
- Collaborate with student to identify if action plan is adequate or inadequate given revised or retained goal.
- Assist student to change action plan if necessary.

Student question 12: *Do I know what I want to know?*

Teacher objective

- Enable student to decide if progress is adequate or inadequate, or if goal has been achieved.

Figure 2.3. Phase 3 of the Self-Determined Learning Model of Instruction.

because of the intensity of their instructional needs, may have the teacher paraphrase the questions.

The first time a teacher uses the model with a student, he or she will read the question with or to the student, discuss what the question means, and then, if necessary, change the wording to enable that student to better understand the intent of the question. Such wording changes must, however, be made so that the problem-solving intent of the question remains intact. For example, changing student question 1 from *What do I want to learn?* to *What is my goal?* changes the nature of the question. The teacher objectives associated with each student question provide direction for possible wording changes. It is perhaps less important that actual changes in the words occur than that students take ownership over the process and adopt the question as their own instead of having questions imposed on them. Going through this process once, as the student progresses through the model, should result in a set of questions that a student accepts as his or her own.

The teacher objectives within the model are just that—the objectives a teacher will be trying to accomplish by implementing the model. The teacher objectives provide, in essence, a road map to assist the teacher to enable the student to solve the problem stated in the student question. For example, regarding student question 1, *What do I want to learn?*, teacher objectives linked to this question comprise the activities in which students should be engaged to answer this question. In this case, it involves enabling students to identify their specific strengths and instructional needs; to identify and communicate preferences, interests, beliefs, and values; and to prioritize their instructional needs. As teachers use the model, it is likely that they can generate more objectives that are relevant to the question, and they are encouraged to do so.

The model's emphasis on using instructional strategies and educational supports that are student-directed provides another means of teaching students to teach themselves. As important as this is, however, not every instructional strategy implemented will be student-directed. The purpose of any model of teaching is to promote student learning and growth. There are circumstances in which the most effective instructional method or strategy to achieve a particular educational outcome will be a teacher-directed strategy. Students who are considering what plan of action to implement to achieve a self-selected goal can recognize that teachers have expertise in instructional strategies and take full advantage of that expertise.

We have conducted research with students with disabilities to determine the efficacy of the model. Wehmeyer, Palmer, Agran, Mithaug, and Martin (2000) conducted a field test of the *SDLMI* with 21 teachers responsible for the instruction of adolescents receiving special education services in two states who identified a total of 40 students with mental retardation, learning disabilities, or emotional or behavioral disorders. The field test indicated that the model was effective in enabling students to attain educationally valued goals. In addition, there were significant differences in pre- and postintervention scores on self-determination, with postintervention scores more positive than preintervention scores.

Agran, Blanchard, and Wehmeyer (2000) conducted a study using a single-subject design to examine the efficacy of the *SDLMI* for adolescents with severe disabilities. Students collaborated with their teachers to implement the first phase of the model and, as a result, identified one goal as a target behavior. Before implementing the second phase of the model, teachers and researchers collected baseline data on student performance of these goals. At staggered intervals subsequent to baseline data collection, teachers implemented the model with students, and data collection continued through the end of instructional activities and into a maintenance phase. As before, the model enabled teachers to teach students educationally valued goals. In total, 17 of the participants achieved their personal goals at or above the teacher-rated expected outcome levels. Only two students were rated as indicating no progress on the goal.

Two recent studies have established causal evidence for the efficacy of the *SDLMI* to promote self-determination, access to the general education curriculum, and transition-related goals. Wehmeyer , Palmer, Shogren, Williams-Diehm, & Soukup (2010) conducted a randomized trial control group study of the efficacy of the *SDLMI* to promote self-determination. Data on self-determination using multiple measures were collected with 312 high school students with intellectual disabilities in both a control and a treatment group, and determined that students in the treatment group had significantly higher levels of self-determination as a function of receiving instruction with the model. As discussed previously, Shogren et al. (2010) similarly documented the efficacy of the *SDLMI* on student academic and transition goal attainment and access to the general education curriculum.

Student Involvement in Transition Planning and Leadership Development

Another important component of enhancing self-determination is promoting active involvement in transition planning. Test et al. (2004) conducted an extensive review of the literature pertaining to student involvement and determined that students across disability categories can be successfully involved in transition planning, and a number of programs, including those mentioned subsequently, are effective in increasing student involvement. Martin, Marshall, and Sale (2004) conducted a 3-year study of middle school, junior high school, and senior high school IEP meetings and found that the presence of students at IEP meetings had considerable benefits, including increasing parental involvement and improving the probability that a student's strengths, needs, and interests would be discussed. Research (Mason et al., 2004; Wehmeyer et al., 2000) has found that teachers value student involvement, though they fall short of actually implementing practices to promote this outcome.

Involvement in education planning, decision making, and instruction can take many forms, from students generating their own IEP goals and objectives, to tracking their progress on self-selected goals or objectives, to running their own IEP meeting. It is important to emphasize that it is not what the student does in the meeting that is critical, but, instead, the degree to which the student is an equal partner in and, to the greatest extent possible, in control of his or her planning. Students with intellectual disabilities can be involved in their educational program every bit as much as students with other disabilities. Student involvement may look very different in these cases, and students with more severe disabilities may not be able to make independent decisions or solve problems, but that is not the criteria by which we should judge student involvement. It is, instead, the degree to which the student is actively engaged in his or her planning and education program.

There are multiple advantages to student involvement. Test and colleagues (2004) reviewed studies examining efforts to promote student involvement and concluded that there was clear evidence that such efforts enhanced student involvement in educational planning. Student involvement in the educational process is a good way to teach and allow students to practice skills important to self-determination (e.g., goal setting, decision making, negotiation), self-advocacy, leadership, and teamwork.

There are several programs designed to promote student involvement, and space restrictions allow only a brief description of several resources.

Virginia Department of Education's Self Determination Project

I'm Determined, the Virginia Department of Education's (2011) Self Determination Project, provides a comprehensive web site of lesson plans, resources, and templates for educators, parents, and youth. Created by teachers and students from across the Commonwealth, this free and user-friendly web site (http://www.imdetermined.org) comprises pages geared for educators, parents, and youth at the elementary and secondary age levels.

Examples of resources on this site include videos depicting youth describing their involvement in IEPs, student-scripted dialogues about the importance of self-determination in the goal-setting process, and a very compelling youth credo-of-support film, among others; a template for a Good Day Plan, in which a student must honestly describe how often a good day occurs, an action plan to achieve that type of day, and the supports needed to attain it; guidance for teaching about goal setting and attainment; teaching tools, brochures, and lesson plans to promote student involvement in the IEP; and a special set of lessons called Life Lines, which assist students with making choices, making decisions, and solving problems.

ChoiceMaker Self-Determination Transition Curriculum and Program

The *ChoiceMaker Self-Determination Transition Curriculum* (Martin & Marshall, 1995) consists of three sections: 1) choosing goals, 2) expressing goals, and 3) taking action. Each section contains from two to four teaching goals and numerous teaching objectives addressing six transition areas. The program also includes a criterion-referenced self-determination transition assessment tool that matches the curricular sections. The Choosing Goals lessons enable students to learn the necessary skills and personal information needed to articulate their interests, skills, limits, and goals across one or more self-selected transition areas. The Self-Directed IEP lessons enable students to learn the leadership skills necessary to manage their IEP meeting and publicly disclose their interests, skills, limits, and goals identified through the Choosing Goals lessons. These lessons teach students 11 steps for leading their own staffing (see Table 2.2). The Taking Action materials enable students to learn how to break their long-range goals into specific goals that can be accomplished in a week. There have been several studies examining the efficacy of the *ChoiceMaker* materials (Allen, Smith, Test, Flowers, & Wood, 2001; Cross, Cooke, Wood, & Test, 1999; Snyder, 2002; Snyder & Shapiro, 1997) documenting positive effects on student self-determination, skills in goal setting and leadership, and student involvement in educational planning.

Whose Future Is It Anyway? A Student-Directed Transition Planning Program

Whose Future Is It Anyway? (WFA; Wehmeyer, Lawrence, et al., 2004)

consists of 36 sessions introducing students to the concept of transition and transition planning and enabling students to self-direct instruction related to

- Self- and disability-awareness
- Making decisions about transition-related outcomes
- Identifying and securing community resources to support transition services
- Writing and evaluating transition goals and objectives

Table 2.2.   Steps for transition planning from the ChoiceMaker program

Step	Activity
1	Begin the meeting by stating the purpose.
2	Introduce everyone.
3	Review past goals and performance.
4	Ask for others' feedback.
5	State your school and transition goals.
6	Ask questions if you do not understand.
7	Deal with differences in opinion.
8	State the support you will need.
9	Summarize your goals.
10	Close meeting by thanking everyone.
11	Work on individualized education program goals all year.

Source: Martin and Marshall (1995).

- Communicating effectively in small groups
- Developing skills to become an effective team member, leader, or self-advocate

The materials are student-directed in that they are written for students as end-users. The level of support needed by students to complete activities varies a great deal. Some students with difficulty reading or writing need one-to-one support to progress through the materials; others can complete the process independently. The materials make every effort to ensure that students retain this control while receiving the support they need to succeed.

Students are encouraged to work on one session per week during the weeks between their previous transition planning meeting and the next scheduled meeting. The final two sessions review the previous sessions and provide a refresher for students as they head into their planning meeting. Wehmeyer and Lawrence (1995) conducted a field test of the process, providing evidence of the impact of the process on student self-determination, self-efficacy for educational planning, and student involvement. More recently, Wehmeyer, Palmer, Lee, Williams-Diehm, and Shogren (2011) conducted a randomized-trial, placebo-control group design to study the impact of intervention with the WFA process on self-determination and transition knowledge and skills, finding that instruction using the WFA process resulted in significant, positive differences in self-determination compared with a placebo-control group and that students who received instruction gained transition knowledge and skills. In a similar way, Lee and colleagues (2010) conducted a randomized-trial study of the impact of the WFA process both with and without the use of technology and determined significant gains in self-determination and transition knowledge and skills as a function of instruction with WFA.

Next S.T.E.P.: Student Transition and Educational Planning

A third student-directed transition-planning program is the *Next S.T.E.P.* curriculum (Halpern, Herr, Wolf, Doren, Johnson, & Lawson, 1997). The curriculum uses video and print materials developed for specific audiences (students, teachers, family members) to help students become motivated to engage in transition planning, self-evaluate transition needs, identify and select transition goals and activities, assume responsibility for conducting their own transition planning meeting, and monitor the implementation of their transition plans.

The curriculum consists of 16 lessons, clustered into four instructional units, designed to be delivered in a 50-minute class period. These lessons include teacher and student materials, videos, guidelines for involving parents and family members, and a process for tracking student progress. Unit 1 (Getting Started) introduces and overviews transition planning. Unit 2 (Self-Exploration and Self-Evaluation) focuses on student self-evaluation, and at the end of this unit, students complete the student form of the *Transition Skills Inventory*, a 72-item rating instrument assessing how well the student is doing in four transition areas: 1) personal life, 2) jobs, 3) education and training, and 4) living on one's own. The student's self-evaluation of these areas is combined with similar evaluations by his or her teacher and a family member to form a basis for future transition-planning activities. Unit 3 (Developing Goals and Activities) addresses transition goal identification in the four areas making up the *Transition Skills Inventory*. Students identify their hopes and dreams, then select from a range of potential goals in each area, narrowing the total set of transition goals to four or five goals that they prefer. In addition, students choose activities that will help them pursue the goals they have selected. Unit 4 (Putting a Plan into Place) includes three lessons that prepare students for their transition planning meeting. The lessons emphasize the implementation of their plan and teach students to ensure that they monitor their progress and, if necessary, make adjustments. Zhang (2001) examined the efficacy of the *Next S.T.E.P.* materials and found implementation significantly affected student self-determination.

The Self-Advocacy Strategy for Education and Transition Planning

Van Reusen, Bos, Schumaker, and Deshler developed a procedure that stresses the importance of self-advocacy to enhance student motivation and that is "designed to enable students to systematically gain a sense of control and influence over their own learning and development" (2002, p. 1). Students progress through a series of lesson plans focusing on seven instructional stages. Stage 1 (Orient and Make Commitments) broadly introduces education and transition planning meetings, the program itself, and how participation can increase student power and control in this process. Stage 2 (Describe) defines and provides detailed information about transition and education meetings and advantages students experience if they participate. In this stage, the I PLAN steps of student participation are introduced. These steps provide a simple algorithm that students can use to chart their participation in planning meetings.

In Stage 3 (Model and Prepare), the teacher models the I PLAN steps so students can see the process in action. Students complete an Inventory, Step 1 in the I PLAN process, resulting in information they can use at their conference. In Stage 4 (Verbal Practice), students are asked questions to make sure they know what to do during each step of the I PLAN strategy and then verbally rehearse each of the steps. In Stage 5 (Group Practice and Feedback), students participate in a simulated group conference (after they have mastered the I PLAN steps). The student receives feedback from the teacher and other students, and the group generates suggestions on where the student might improve. The simulated conference is audio- or videotaped for future reference.

Stage 6 (Individual Practice and Feedback) allows the student to meet independently with the teacher for practice, feedback, and, eventually, mastery. The audio- or videotape from the previous stage is reviewed, and students provide a self-evaluation of their performance. The student and instructor work together to improve areas of self-identified need and engage in another simulated conference that is also audio- or videotaped and used to document improvement and reevaluate performance. Stage 7 (Generalization) is intended to generalize the I PLAN strategy to actual conferences. This stage has three phases: 1) preparing for and conducting the planning conference, 2) preparing for other uses of the strategy, and 3) preparing for subsequent conferences. Van Reusen, Deshler, and Schumaker (1989) and Van Reusen, Bos, Schumaker, and Deshler (2002) have shown that the I PLAN strategy can be successfully implemented with students with disabilities and results in increased motivation and participation.

TAKE CHARGE for the Future

TAKE CHARGE for the Future (Powers , Sowers, Turner, Nesbitt, Knowles, & Ellison, 1996) is a student-directed, collaborative model to promote student involvement in educational and transition planning. The model is an adaptation of a validated approach, referred to as *TAKE CHARGE,* to promote the self-determination of youth with and without disabilities (Powers, Turner, Matuszewski, Wilson, & Phillips, 2001). *TAKE CHARGE* uses four primary components or strategies to promote adolescent development of self-determination: 1) skill facilitation, 2) mentoring, 3) peer support, and 4) parent support. For example, *TAKE CHARGE* introduces youth to three major skills areas needed to take charge in one's life: 1) achievement skills, 2) partnership skills, and 3) coping skills. Youth involved in the *TAKE CHARGE* process are matched with successful adults of the same gender who experience similar challenges, share common interests, and are involved in peer support activities throughout (Powers, Turner, Westwood, Loesch, Brown, & Rowland, 1998). Parent support is provided via information and technical assistance and written materials.

TAKE CHARGE for the Future uses the same set of core strategies to enable learners with disabilities to participate in their planning meeting. Students are provided self-help materials and coaching to identify their transition goals; to organize and conduct transition planning meetings; and to achieve their goals through the application of problem solving, self-regulation, and partnership management strategies. Concurrently, youth participate in self-selected mentorship and peer support activities to increase their transition-focused knowledge and skills. Their parents are also provided with information and support to promote their capacities to encourage their sons' or daughters' active involvement in transition planning. Powers et al. (2001) conducted a control-group study and found that the *TAKE CHARGE* materials had a positive impact on student involvement.

Student-Led IEPs: A Guide for Student Involvement

McGahee, Mason, Wallace, and Jones (2001) developed a guide to student-led IEPs that introduces students to the IEP process, the purpose of an IEP, and suggestions for writing an IEP. Mason, McGahee-Kovac, Johnson, and Stillerman (2002) showed that students who used this process knew more about their IEP and showed enhanced self-confidence and self-advocacy.

Infusing Self-Determination into 18–21 Programs and Postsecondary Education

Students with more severe disabilities will likely receive educational services through the age of 21, either through 18–21 services provided by school districts or through postsecondary education (PSE; Getzel & Wehman, 2005). It is important that high-quality 18–21 and PSE programs ensure a strong focus on self-determination. To that end, Wehmeyer and colleagues have developed and evaluated a multistage model called *Beyond High School* (Figure 2.4) to infuse self-determination into quality 18–21 services and supports and to promote active student involvement (Wehmeyer, Garner, Lawrence, Yeager, & Davis, 2006).

Beyond High School: Stage 1

This first stage of the *Beyond High School* model is designed to enable students to establish short- and long-term goals based on their own preferences, abilities, and interests. First, students are involved in targeted instruction teaching them to self-direct planning and decision making specific to the transition, process. This could be accomplished through multiple informal or formal strategies and methods that prepare students to participate in or direct their educational planning process, such as those discussed previously. Next, students were taught to self-direct the transition goal-setting, action planning, and program implementation process using the *SDLMI*, again, discussed previously. Once students learn this self-regulated learning process, they apply the first part of the *SDLMI* (*What is my goal?*) to identify goals in key transition areas, including employment, independent living, recreation and leisure, and postsecondary education.

Beyond High School: Stage 2

The second stage of the model involves convening a student-directed, **person-centered planning** meeting that brings together other stakeholders in the instructional process to work with students to refine goals, as needed, to support the student as he or she implements the second phase of the *SDLMI* (*What is my plan?*) and to enable the student to provide informed consent with regard to implementation of the instructional program. This meeting is not intended to be the mandated IEP meeting, although these activities certainly can occur at an IEP meeting. Instead, the meeting bears a closer resemblance to person-centered planning process in which stakeholders come together on a more frequent basis to identify hopes and dreams, natural supports, and so forth (Holburn & Vietze, 2002). This meeting varies from traditional person-centered planning meetings in scope, intent, and process. First, it is intended that this is the student's meeting. The teacher or person-centered planning facilitator should support the student, who will use the skills he or she acquired in the first phase of the model to present the goals he or she has generated. The second difference is that these student goals provide the foundation for the meeting's

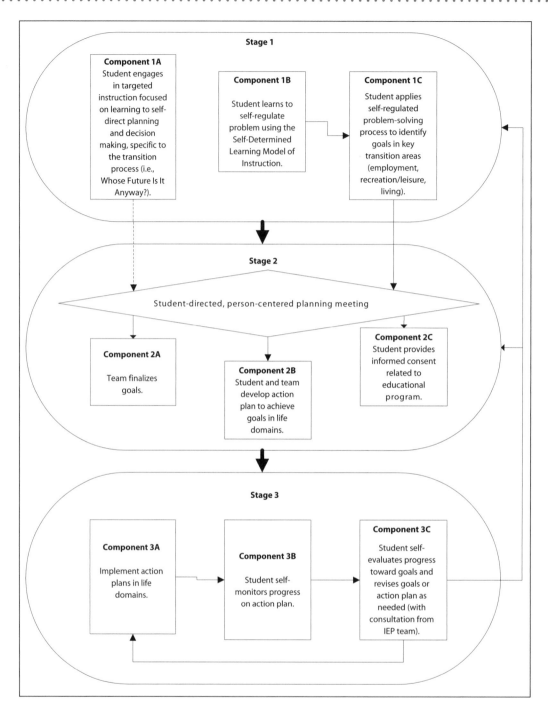

Figure 2.4. Beyond High School 18–21 model to promote self-determination. *Key:* IEP, individualized education program.

purpose and direction. Other stakeholders are encouraged to help the student refine the goals, more clearly define the goals, or identify objectives to reach the goals, but not to criticize or replace the goals. These goals will form only a subset of the total goals on a student's IEP, but the intent is that students have a forum to discuss their goals and gather the support of parents, family members, teachers, and others to make those goals achievable. This is also an opportune time to consider how each stakeholder can support and contribute to the student's efforts to attain those goals.

Beyond High School: Stage 3

During the final stage of the model, the student, with supports identified from the second stage, implements the plan, monitors his or her progress in achieving the goal, and evaluates the success of the plan, making revisions to the goal or the plan as warranted. This is accomplished using the strategies and questions comprising the third phase of the *SDLMI.*

Students involved in the field test of the model were successful at achieving self-set transition goals across multiple domains (Wehmeyer et al., 2006) and increased perceptions of their autonomy after involvement in the process. Anecdotal information provides further evidence of the degree to which students benefited from the process. One student completed the recreation and leisure goal he had set (to contact a volunteer center to find out how to volunteer) and then followed up on that to identify a specific volunteer situation related to his preferences, applied for the position, underwent orientation, and began the volunteer experience. Another student had as her goal to identify a list of questions and then interview a friend to determine if she would make a good roommate. This student and her family had long-term plans for her to room with this friend. In completing this goal, she recognized the need for her friend to interview her and then to discuss their mutual compatibility and did so. This student decided, in the end, that her friend might not be a compatible roommate for her or that there were issues they would need to resolve before that arrangement was made.

Conclusion

Promoting self-determination and student involvement in educational planning has become recommended practice in the education of students with disabilities, particularly in relation to transition planning and services. Students with disabilities who leave school as self-determined young people achieve more positive adult outcomes. Moreover, promoting student self-determination provides, as it were, a gateway to the general education curriculum for students with disabilities and can result in enhanced leadership skills. This chapter overviewed the methods, materials, and strategies to achieve the outcome that students with and without disabilities can become more self-determined. If educators are to achieve the outcomes envisioned by the transition mandates in IDEA, then they will need to ensure that students with disabilities are provided sufficient opportunities to learn these skills and strategies and to use them to play a meaningful role in their educational program, from planning to implementation.

Study Questions

1. Interview a youth with a disability (with support from a parent or teacher if needed) who is in the IEP transition planning process and discuss how self-determination has been infused into the process.

2. Interview two youths with different disabilities about their adult life aspirations and dreams. Compare their views.

3. Interview the parent of a youth with a disability about what he or she has done to promote the child's self-determination and what advice he or she has for other parents.

4. Self-advocacy and leadership are very important skills for young people with disabilities. Give multiple examples of how self-determination instruction facilitates each of these skills.

5. Interview a teacher who uses a self-determination curriculum and discuss how well this curriculum worked to help this student and what, if any, improvements could be made.

Online Resources

The *ChoiceMaker* assessments and materials are available from Sopris Learning:
(http://store.cambiumlearning.com/cs/Satellite?c=CLG_Product_C&childpagename=
Store%2FStore_Layout&cid=1277940957943&pagename=Store_Wrapper&rendermode=
previewnoinsite) and information on the curriculum is available at http://www.ou.edu/
content/education/centers-and-partnerships/zarrow/self-determination-education-
materials/choicemaker-self-determination-materials.html

The *Whose Future Is It Anyway?* materials can be obtained online at no cost:
http://www.ou.edu/content/education/centers-and-partnerships/zarrow/self-
determination-education-materials/whos-future-is-it-anyway.html

Information on the *Next S.T.E.P.* program and assessment battery is available from PRO-ED
Publishing Company: http://www.proedinc.com/customer/productView.aspx?ID=3485

The *Self-Advocacy Strategy* materials are available from Edge Enterprises, Lawrence, KS:
http://www.edgeenterprisesinc.com/products.php?category_id=10&subcategory_id=20

TAKE CHARGE for the Future can be obtained by contacting the Portland State University
Regional Research Institute, Post Office Box 751, Portland State University, Portland, OR
97207-0751

The *Student-Led IEPs: A Guide for Student Involvement* can be obtained online at no cost:
http://www.eric.ed.gov/ERICWebPortal/search/detailmini.jsp?_nfpb=true&_&ERICExtSearch_
SearchValue_0=ED455623&ERICExtSearch_SearchType_0=no&accno=ED455623

The Arc's Self-Determination Scale can be obtained online at no cost:
http://www.ou.edu/content/education/centers-and-partnerships/zarrow/self-
determination-assessment-tools/arc-self-determination-scale.html

The AIR Self-Determination Scale can be obtained online at no cost:
http://www.ou.edu/content/education/centers-and-partnerships/zarrow/self-
determination-assessment-tools/air-self-determination-assessment.html

Information on the Self-Determination Assessment Battery can be obtained online:
http://www.ou.edu/content/education/centers-and-partnerships/zarrow/self-
determination-assessment-tools/field-and-hoffman-self-determination-assessment.html

Families and Young People with Disabilities

Listening to Their Voices

PAMELA TARGETT AND PAUL WEHMAN

3

After completing this chapter, the reader will be able to

- Discuss the research related to student and family involvement in planning the individualized education program (IEP) for transition
- Describe some of the common barriers to active student involvement and participation
- Describe some of the common barriers to active parent involvement and participation
- Explain some strategies to promote active student involvement and participation in the process
- Explain some strategies to promote active parent involvement and participation in the process

Pam, a youth with an **emotional disturbance** explains, "My parents have spent years raising me. I know they want to have their own life. You know what? I do too."

Frank, a young man with **cerebral palsy** relates, "My mom always pushes me to do my best and it will not stop when I leave school. So, the way I see it is, I better get ready for my next big adventure—to get a job so I can get out of the house."

Mr. Stevens says, "I want all doors possible open to my son, Richard, so he can be all that he can and wants to be. Just tell me, do you really think that's too much for a parent to ask for?"

Mrs. Hicks reports, "My daughter, Stella, may have an intellectual disability. In my opinion, she has the right to live and work in the same places as everyone else. This is the United States of America. She will just need some extra support, so planning for the future and these supports is key."

These voices of youth with disabilities and parents are clear and strong. Each one sends a resounding message about a vision for the future of a young person with a disability that is focused on an opportunity for maximizing independence—to live, work, and become a valued member of the community. The student statements indicate the desires of any youth—with or without a disability. The parents' words express their personal views on what they want for their child's future and also echo the voices of students who are not able to "speak their mind" with words, but whose actions show a strong desire to move forward to achieve an adult lifestyle.

However, the rite of passage marking the transition from childhood to adulthood is not always smooth for any young person and can be particularly challenging for some youth with disabilities and their families. But, it does not have to be this way. A results-oriented transition process (Individuals with Disabilities Education Improvement Act [IDEA] 2004, Section 300.43) is designed to address the unique challenges that a youth with a disability may face as he or she comes of age and begins to accept more of the responsibilities associated with adulthood.

Chapter 1 laid the foundation for transition including a review of the law that outlines the what, where, how, and for whose purpose transition planning is taking place. Of particular interest in this chapter are the stipulations in Table 3.1 from IDEA 2004.

As noted in the regulations, the IEP should be based on a student-driven plan for the future. The statute is clear about infusing the IEPs with the student's voice that reflects his or her personal strengths, interests, and preferences. This cannot be overemphasized. A student's IEP that focuses on transition provides a framework that, when followed, should prepare a student with a disability for education, employment, and independent living after completing his or her secondary education. IEP development requires collaboration among the student, family, educators, and (as indicated) adult service providers, or others who can make a meaningful contribution to this effort. Although most professionals in the special education and related fields may agree with this, it is sometimes challenging to find ways to encourage and increase participation of youth with disabilities (especially those with intellectual disabilities) and their parents in the transition planning process. Implementation also requires a unified effort. Without this, youth with disabilities will be destined to be less independent as adult.

Table 3.1. IDEA 2004 regulations related to student role in IEP planning

1. According to paragraph (a) (7) the public agency must invite a student with a disability to attend the student's IEP team meeting if a purpose of the meeting will be the consideration of the postsecondary goals for the student and the transition services needed to help the student reach those goals under § 300.320(b).

2. If the student does not attend the IEP team meeting, the public agency must take other steps to ensure that the student's preferences and interests are considered.

3. To the extent appropriate, with the consent of the parents or a student who has reached the age of majority, in implementing the requirements of paragraph (b) (1) of this section, the public agency must invite a representative of any participating agency likely to be responsible for providing or paying for transition services. (300/D/300.321/[b]).

Key: IDEA, Individuals with Disabilities Education Improvement Act; IEP, individualized education program.

We begin this chapter with a review of the recent literature on parental and student involvement in the transition planning process and recommended practices. This is followed by a discussion of strategies to increase student and parental participation in the process.

Parent and Student Involvement as Key Components of Successful Transition

Perhaps one of the most comprehensive, research-based, and widely accepted frameworks for transition is the Taxonomy for Transition Programming developed by Kohler (Kohler & Field, 2003). The taxonomy specifies five key areas indicative of successful transition-focused programming and outcome-oriented planning process. Of note, family involvement and student-focused planning are two of the key components. A significant body of research shows that both parent and student involvement in the transition-planning process are vital for good adult outcomes. Each perspective is important to consider.

Parent Involvement

Transition to adulthood is an important stage in life for students with disabilities as well as for their parents. Parents are a consistent person in their child's life and play a central role in determining services. In addition, planning for transition offers parents an opportunity to advocate for and link with the services that can help enhance their child's future and their own quality of life. Educators need to understand what works and the challenges parents may face and be prepared to furnish supports to facilitate parent participation in transition planning (Kreider, Caspe, Kennedy, & Weiss, 2007). While the importance of parent involvement is commonly known, the research is limited and the literature focusing on increasing parent and family involvement in the transition process has consisted primarily of conceptual discussions and recommendations about how to encourage parent participation and improve communication among all stakeholders (e.g., providing ongoing communication and collaboration with families, including family resources and community members in planning; Ankeny, Wilkins, & Spain, 2009; Rowe & Test, 2010). Researchers have sought to confirm and quantify the significance of parent involvement, however.

Involvement as a Predictor of Success

Parent and family involvement in the transition-planning process has been found to be a predictor of postsecondary success of young adults with disabilities (Kraemer, McIntyre, & Blacher, 2003; Test, Mazzotti, Mustian, Fowler, Kortering, & Kohler, 2009). For example, Kraemer et al. (2003) found that parent knowledge of adult services and parent involvement in transition planning was significantly correlated to students' overall quality of life. Test, Mazzotti, et al. (2009), on the basis of their literature review of rigorous correlational research in secondary transition, found that family involvement was a significant predictor of postschool success in employment. However, although research has demonstrated a positive correlation between parent involvement in the transition process and improved postschool outcomes for students with disabilities (Kraemer et al., 2003; Test, Mazzotti, et al., 2009), research also has demonstrated that few parents are fully informed about and involved in transition planning.

Levels of Knowledge and Preparedness among Parents

Qualitative studies have indicated that parents have participated in transition planning to some extent and have assumed a variety of roles in transition planning (Geenen, Powers,

& Lopez-Vasquez, 2001; Lindstrom, Doren, Metheny, Johnson, & Zane, 2007). However, other studies have found that many families felt they did not play a role in transition planning (Cooney, 2002; Tarleton & Ward, 2005). For example, Cooney (2002) reported that roles were not established and parents were unsure of how they fit into the transition-planning puzzle and also noted that parents felt powerless because of their lack of knowledge of the service system. In addition, because of lack of knowledge, parents found that navigating the unfamiliar system of transition planning was a very stressful experience. The system of adult agencies and available supports was unknown to many parents and parents claimed to have had an overwhelming sense of uselessness because of unfamiliar transition terms, procedures, and unexpected barriers. Tarleton and Ward (2005) reported that parents expressed feelings of fear and anguish by not knowing their roles in the planning process. Parents felt they needed more knowledge on the following topics: a) the transition process and their role in it, 2) how their child's support needs were going to be met, and 3) local postsecondary choices available to their child. They not only lacked an understanding of their roles but also did not realize what was involved in the transition-planning process.

Findings from data collected by the National Longitudinal Transition Study-2 (NLTS-2; 2007) support the results from these qualitative studies (Cooney, 2002; Tarleton & Ward, 2005), which indicated that families felt unprepared and that minimal training has been offered to parents by the school. Data from the NLTS-2 show that only 11.5% of parents surveyed had attended some types of training on transition planning. Of those parents who had attended, 86.5% found the information obtained helpful.

Challenges of Parents of Youth with Severe Intellectual Disabilities

There is no doubt that parental involvement in transition planning is essential (Powers, Geenen, & Powers, 2009; Ankeny et al., 2009). Neece, Kraemer, and Blacher (2009) pointed out that this is especially critical for youth who have severe intellectual disabilities, and school personnel need to find ways to create more opportunities for parents of children with more significant intellectual disabilities to get involved in their sons' and daughters' transition planning process. Some of the challenges parents face have included balancing expectations, available time and energy, understanding and gaining access to resources and services, and understanding the role of the transition specialist (Wang & Michaels, 2009; Chambers, Hughes, & Carter, 2004; Grigal & Neubert, 2004).

Although recent decades have seen a shift toward providing inclusive, age-appropriate educational opportunities for students with intellectual disabilities, prospects after high school remain bleak for these students, many of whom experience segregation and social isolation (Chambers et al., 2004). In fact, of all students with disabilities, those with intellectual disabilities are the least likely to be involved in job training, paid employment, or education after high school (Braddock, Hemp, & Rizzolo, 2008; Butterworth, Smith, Hall, Migliore, & Winsor, 2008; Simonsen, 2010).

Issues Related to Postsecondary Education

Higher education options are often a component of planning for transition, and for students with intellectual disabilities, a number of specialized postsecondary education (PSE) programs exist, allowing students to continue their education on college campuses. In such specialized PSE programs, students learn academic material, expand social networks, gain employment skills, and develop independence. Although colleges have historically excluded students with intellectual disabilities, PSE programs offer these students an alternative to traditional college admission and participation (Hart, Grigal, & Weir, 2010; Grigal, Hart, & Migliore, 2011).

As more specialized PSE programs become available, families are increasingly considering this option (Hart et al., 2010). Because parents are instrumental in transition planning, understanding their perspectives can improve the approaches taken by educators and service providers. Griffin, McMillin, and Hodapp (2010) investigated the issues that families consider when making decisions regarding PSE for young adults with intellectual disabilities. Survey respondents were 108 family members of transition-aged students with intellectual disabilities. Although respondents were generally positive about specialized PSE programs, they reported that educators' attitudes were less supportive. Respondents identified many barriers that prevent their understanding of PSE options, but a lack of information and guidance was the barrier cited by the most respondents. Of note, when considering PSE options, respondents were most concerned about student safety, and they considered a focus on employment to be the most important program component. The authors reported that more research is needed to investigate the factors critical in developing successful specialized PSE programs for students with intellectual disabilities.

Cultural and Linguistic Diversity

Challenges faced by families of youth with disabilities can be compounded greatly when they are from a different culture or speak a different language (Griffin, 2011). Geenen et al. (2001) investigated the barriers against and strategies for promoting the involvement of culturally and linguistically diverse (CLD) parents in school-based transition planning. They found seven main types of barriers that appear to inhibit or prevent parental involvement in school-based transition planning:

1. Power imbalance
2. Psychological or attitudinal barriers
3. Logistic barriers
4. Information barriers
5. Communication barriers
6. Socioeconomic status and contextual factors
7. Cultural influences

Rueda, Monzo, Shapiro, Gomez, and Blacher (2005) identified several areas in which the orientation of Latina mothers and the service delivery were at odds. The school viewed youth as autonomous individuals, although mothers viewed their children as embedded in the family. Also, the mothers believed that educators devalued and ignored their personal knowledge of their children, whereas the educators promoted the belief that professional expertise was all that mattered. For the mothers in this study, the absence of shared perspective led to confusion, misunderstanding, and isolation. Additional studies conducted and reviewed by Greene (2011) also indicated that CLD families often are not given sufficient opportunities to contribute their perspective.

Landmark, Zhang, and Montoya (2007) indicated that, although CLD parents often did not understand the jargon of special education (e.g., more than one third of parents in that study were not familiar with the phrase *transition planning*), they did possess a great deal of knowledge about their children that was useful for the transition-planning process.

Parental Satisfaction with Transition

The transition from high school to adulthood is a critical life stage that entails many changes. The transition period may be especially stressful for the families of young adults with disabilities, who often experience a sudden change, or decrease, in services. However, little research has examined what constitutes a successful transition.

Neece et al. (2009) examined parent perspectives of transition for 128 young adults with severe intellectual disability—specifically, parent satisfaction with transition. Results suggested that transition satisfaction is related to young adult, family, and environmental characteristics, with environmental characteristics being the strongest predictors of transition satisfaction. Furthermore, transition satisfaction is related to multiple measures of family well-being, indicating the tremendous need for considering the broader family system when one is planning for a young adult's transition.

Eisenman, Tanverdi, Perrington, and Geiman (2009) conducted semistructured interviews with family members of 45 youth with severe intellectual disabilities who were enrolled or had graduated from a transition-focused program that focused on community and social activities. Participants reported youth involvement in a wide variety of typical and specialized activities. Family members primarily provided the supports in the activities in which youth were engaged and these tended to be those in which the family was involved. Families reported that they were mostly satisfied with their community and social situations.

Research indicates that families experience higher levels of satisfaction with services even if they have limited involvement in aspects of service delivery (Neely-Barnes, Graff, Marcenko, & Weber, 2008). Fish (2008) conducted a survey with 51 parents of students receiving special education services. He found that 63% of participants reported their overall IEP experiences as positive. However, his earlier studies and others seem to indicate this is the exception, rather than the norm (Childre & Chambers, 2005; Stoner et al., 2005; Fish, 2006). The NLTS-2 reported that 81% of parents learn about services from their child's school. A lack of information about services and the unavailability of a particular service were barriers parents encountered the most often in their efforts to obtain services for their sons or daughters. For example, parents may not be aware of state vocational rehabilitation services, which provide an array of services and supports focusing on employment, or the eligibility requirements for services, although it should be a core transition resource for youth with disabilities. Parents may want to access a specialized vocational support service for their child, like supported employment, but may find that there are long waiting lists for services or that these do not exist in their community.

Other Difficulties that May Affect Family Participation

Because there is limited empirical research on families specific to the transition period, it is useful to also consider what is known more broadly about the difficulties families of young adults with disabilities face, which in turn may negatively impact participation. Studies reveal that families with youth with disabilities face many challenges. According U.S. Census (2005) figures, approximately 20.9 million American families have at least one member with a disability. Black families and American Indian and Alaska Native families have a much higher incidence of disability among family members. Families with a member who has a disability are more likely to have lower median incomes, higher poverty rates, and a higher dependency on Social Security benefits and public assistance (U.S. Census, 2005). Individuals with disabilities often face barriers that make it difficult to fulfill family roles. In addition, families of people with disabilities face a wide range of barriers to community living and community participation. Examples of these barriers include inaccessible housing and community that make it difficult for a person with a disability to live with his or her family or to participate with his or her family in community activities (National Council on Disability, 2010; Crews & Zavotka, 2006). Anderson, Dumont, Jacobs, and Azzaria (2007) reported on the economic burdens associated with caregiving, which may lead to low-level earnings and limited career options for family members who serve as caregivers. Health care information and treatments that are not designed to address the culture and language barriers faced by families from diverse cultures and backgrounds (Baker, Miller, Dang, Yaangh, & Hansen, 2010) lead to difficulties for some. And perhaps most notably, a lack of effective and coordinated family supports across the lifespan of the family member with a disability (Lamar-Dukes, 2009; Reichman, Corman, & Noonan, 2008; Jokinen & Brown, 2005) can also restrict community life and participation for the caregiver or family members.

Factors that Contribute to Family Resilience

In a recent study, Greeff and van der Walt (2010) identified characteristics and resources that 34 families have that enabled them to adapt successfully and be resilient despite having a child with autism. Resilience factors included higher socioeconomic status; social support; open and predictable patterns of communication; a supportive family environment, including commitment and flexibility; family hardiness; internal and external coping strategies; a positive outlook on life; and family belief systems.

Meadan, Stoner, and Angell (2010) reviewed the literature specific to the stressors and supports for families with children who have autism spectrum disorders (ASDs). They examined 57 journal articles published between 2000 and 2007. Because of limited information on ASDs for a specific subsystem within the family, the authors also included research that focused on families who have a child with a developmental disability. The authors organized their findings into these areas: stress in the marital subsystem, stress in the parental subsystem, stress in the sibling subsystem, and bidirectional relationships between subsystems. Their review revealed the following themes: stress for caregivers and siblings, coping strategies used by family members, preferred methods of support, and the potential of bidirectional influence. A couple of highlights of the review are

a. Related to stressors, the authors found that, although mothers and fathers share parenting roles, mothers usually assumed a greater responsibility in meeting the child's needs.

b. Those who used coping strategies had a reduction in stress and the felt a stronger bond among family members.

Families become resilient when they actively pursue solutions to their problems, look beyond the hardships surrounding their situation, and focus on making the best of the options available to them. This characteristic should also be useful to families throughout the transition process.

Student Involvement

An examination of the literature indicates that student involvement is also vital to effective transition planning (e.g., Thoma & Wehman, 2010). However, to be effective, student involvement must extend beyond the individualization of the student's plan and also include his or her active participation in the process.

Effects of Involvement on Student Self-Determination

Despite researchers, policymakers, and advocates promoting self-determination and active involvement in IEP planning, available data suggest that many students have little involvement in these activities. Findings on the extent to which students are provided opportunities to be involved in IEP development and to receive self-determination instruction have been based on parent and teacher input, with little input provided by students. Agran and Hughes (2008) piloted a tool that asked students with intellectual and other disabilities to provide input on their involvement in IEP development and their opportunities to learn self-determination strategies. Findings revealed that, although the majority of students reported receiving some instruction on one or more self-determination strategies, few students were provided instruction in having an active role in the IEP process. Also, although it has been demonstrated that students can learn the skills leading to enhanced self-determination (Karvonen, Test, Wood, Browder, & Algozzine, 2004), most have had limited opportunities to learn those skills.

An early review of the literature conducted by Test et al. (2004) found limited data to support the link between student involvement in transition planning and enhanced self-determination but recommended additional research in this area. Williams-Diehm, Wehmeyer, Palmer, Soukup, and Garner (2008) conducted a subsequent study that examined the differences in the level of self-determination among groups who had different levels of involvement in their IEP meeting related to transition planning. The study involved 276 students with disabilities from 33 school districts located within five states. Results revealed that students who are more active in their planning meetings were more self-determined.

This has been further supported by other research that indicated that implementing student-led IEPs can lead to positive outcomes in the areas of self-knowledge, self-determination, and self-advocacy (Test et al., 2004). One study examining the effects of a self-directed IEP to teach students the skills needed to lead IEP meetings found an increase in the amount of time that the students started, led, and talked during the meetings (Martin et al., 2006). However, activities to promote self-determination are often not included in transition planning, and, when they are, secondary teachers report spending an average of only 6 hours a month on them (Thoma & Getzel, 2005).

Carter, Owens, Trainor, Sun, and Swedeen (2009) asked teachers and parents to assess the self-determination of 135 youth with severe intellectual disabilities. Teachers reported that youth had limited knowledge about self-determined behavior, ability to perform these behaviors, and confidence regarding the efficacy of their self-determination capacity. However, teachers agreed that opportunities to engage in self-determined behavior were available both at school and at home. Social skill and problem behaviors were significant predictors of teacher ratings and negatively correlated with the rating of a student's self-determination capacities and opportunities.

Youth Leadership and Involvement in Planning

Beyond self-determination, leadership has been explored as a skill to foster in youth with disabilities and to enhance transition. Carter, Swedeen, Walter, Moss, and Hsin (2011) examined the perspectives on youth leadership of 34 young adults with disabilities. Participants identified key attitudes and skills possessed by leaders and addressed the influence these qualities have on others. They also communicated their own experiences and emphasized the importance of early involvement in school and community activities and their relationship with family members, teachers, mentors, and friends. The authors provided some recommendations for fostering youth leadership in the transition period. These included

- Expanding curricular and training opportunities to support youth in developing leadership skills, including involvement in extracurricular clubs, student government, youth development, and other nonacademic activities

- Assisting students with connecting to mentorship programs, receiving informal advice and encouragement from teachers and school personnel, as well as receiving instruction in critical self-determination skills

In addition, a number of studies have found that students who are actively involved in their transition planning are more likely to achieve their goals (Martin, Van Dycke, D'Ottavio, & Nickerson, 2007; Shogren et al., 2007). Students who do not make a connection between their current education program and their future success may be prone to drop out of school or may not be motivated to work on goals (Wagner, Newman, Cameto, Levine, & Marder, 2007; Wehman, 2011a).

Setting and Achieving Appropriate Postsecondary Goals

IDEA requires "appropriate measurable postsecondary goals based upon age-appropriate transition assessments related to training, education, employment, and where appropriate, independent living skills" (Section 614[d][l][A][VIII][aa]), and it requires the active participation of students in their own transition planning (34 C.F.R. 300.32 l[b]) (20 U.S.C. 1414[d][I][B]). And, although federal mandates have resulted in improvements, a significant disparity exists between IDEA regulations and actual implementation or practice. This disparity significantly affects postsecondary outcomes for students with disabilities (Neece et al., 2009), leading to undereducation and underemployment compared with their typically developing peers (Wehman, 2006a).

Grigal et al. (2011) performed a secondary analysis of variables from the NLTS-2 database, which compared students with intellectual disability (ID) to students with other disabilities with regard to postschool transition goals listed on their IEPs/transition IEPs, contacts/referrals made to outside agencies during transition planning, participation of other agencies/organizations in transition planning, and students' postsecondary education and employment outcomes. The authors found that students with ID were less likely to have postsecondary education or competitive employment goals and outcomes and more likely to have sheltered and supported employment goals and outcomes compared with students with other disabilities. Contacts with and participation of external professionals in the IEP/transition planning meetings also differed between the two groups of students.

Gender Differences

There is evidence that young women with disabilities continue to lag behind males on a variety of postsecondary outcomes. Countino, Oswald, and Best (2006) reported that men with disabilities are more likely than their female counterparts to receive a high school diploma, be employed for a greater number of months, and earn more money. Yet, very few studies have attempted to identify the factors that explain and contribute to these gender differences. Rather, the research to date has primarily documented overall group differences between female and male students with disabilities in postsecondary outcomes. Furthermore, there is limited information about how (or even whether) gender disparity is reflected in transition planning and what strategies could be employed to advance the success of young women during the transition planning process.

The few studies that have investigated gender differences in transition suggest that the experiences of females differ from those of males in the following ways. First, the career aspirations of many females with disabilities may be constrained to female-typical, low-earnings jobs (Wagner, Cameto, & Newman, 2003). In reviewing the transition plans of 399 IEPs, Powers and colleagues (2005) found that one third of the employment goals conformed to gender stereotypes. More recently, Hogansen, Powers, Geenan, Gil-Kashiwasara, and Powers (2008) examined the influence of gender on the transition goals and experiences of female students with disabilities. Data were gathered from 146 participants, including young women with disabilities ($n = 67$), parents of young women with disabilities ($n = 34$), and professionals who work with them ($n = 45$). Findings suggested that females with disabilities have unique experiences related to

a. Type of transition goals established for them
b. Factors that shape these transition goals, such as self-perception, mentors, peers, family, and exposure to opportunities
c. Sources of support and impediments to transition to adulthood, such as special education personnel and programs
d. Contextual issues, such as cultural and linguistic diversity

Parents and Student Involvement

Parents and their adolescent children do not always perceive their needs, opportunities, or resources the same way. Thus, some studies have considered youth and parent views or advised both parties. Powers, Geenen, and Powers (2009) explored the similarities and differences in the transition expectations of parents and youth. Independent samples of parents ($n = 270$) of transition-age youth with disabilities and students with disabilities ($n = 242$) were surveyed about the importance of achieving various adult goals, having specific types of transition-related training and skills, and potential barriers to transition. Factor analysis of the data yielded six scales, and significant differences were found between youth and parents on four of these scales, indicating that parents tend to value teacher support more, whereas youth reported higher levels of self-esteem, greater barriers to transition, and more interest in assuming caretaking roles in their future. Parents and students were in agreement, however, around the goals they felt were most important for transition: finishing high school, having health insurance, and having access to a good doctor.

Hetherington et al. (2010) examined the educational transition process experienced by both adolescents with disabilities and their parents. The results of the qualitative study concluded that students rarely were engaged in transition planning and that, when they were engaged, it came too late in their high school careers. Both parties described dissatisfaction in the following areas:

- Inadequate communication from school staff
- Frustration with assumptions made about the student
- Funneling of the student into traditional adult service programs
- A lack of accountability from the schools.

Even those students who reported being engaged in the transition process experienced inadequate transition planning.

In a recent exploratory study, Moon, Simonsen, and Neubert (2011) surveyed community rehabilitation providers (CRPs) to determine their perceptions of the skills, experiences, and information that transitioning youth with developmental disabilities and their families need to access supported employment (SE) services. Supervisors of SE from 12 CRPs across one state provided their perceptions of eligibility requirements for SE services. Results related to the skill requirements and work experiences needed by transitioning youth support previous research findings including the following: paid work experiences, instruction in self-management and advocacy skills, and transition assessments that document employment preferences, interests, and needs. Other findings supported the need for educators to teach transitioning youth and families about getting long-term funding through the state developmental disabilities agency and Medicaid waivers and to prepare families for changes as CRPs continue to phase out facility-based work options and provide only SE. CRP staff strongly encouraged transitioning youth, not families, to communicate their own employment preferences and skills at intake interviews.

Recommended Practices for Providing Quality Transition Services to Families

Quality transition services have been consistently equated with several elements:

- High expectations (Thoma & Wehman, 2010)
- Person-centered or student-directed goals that support postschool employment or education outcomes (Agran & Hughes, 2008; Thoma & Wehman, 2010; Wehman, 2011a)
- Practices that reflect collaboration with external partners, community agencies, and organizations that might be involved in supporting students in their postschool environments (Noonan, Morningstar, & Erickson, 2008)

Over the years, a number of best practices in transition planning have been proven effective. As mentioned earlier, one of the most comprehensive and widely accepted frameworks

Table 3.2.   Practices that promote successful transition

Student involvement	Students actively involved in their transition goal planning are most likely to achieve those goals (Kohler & Field, 2003; Martin, Van Dycke, D'Ottavio, & Nickerson, 2007; Shogren et al., 2007).
Parent and family involvement	Parent engagement in the transition process is as important as adolescent involvement, especially for those with more significant disabilities (Geenen et al., 2001; Neece et al., 2009).
Family/student and school relationships	Both parents and students indicate a desire for individualized and contextualized rather than bureaucratic relationships (Kohler & Field, 2003; Landmark et al., 2007). Culturally and linguistically diverse parents, in particular, desire a more personal relationship that helps them feel less alienated and more valued as a part of the IEP and transition process (Geenen et al., 2001; Geenen et al., 2003; Landmark et al., 2007).
Meaningful curriculum	Curricula that meaningfully focus on vocational and academic pursuits, along with work experiences during the high school years, are frequently missing for high school students with disabilities (Kohler & Field, 2003; Wehman & Kregel, 2011).
Self-determination	Successful postsecondary outcomes also are related to higher levels of self-determination and student leadership in IEP meetings (Agran & Hughes, 2008).
Student-oriented outcome-based goals	Although student-identified, focused transition goals are linked to improved academic and employment outcomes, several researchers have shown that the actual transition services received are minimally related to the goals noted in transition plans (Agran & Hughes, 2008).
Collaboration with vocational rehabilitation	Although collaboration with vocational rehabilitation is consistently called on for transition planning (Wehman, 2011a), high levels of collaboration with vocational rehabilitation or community service providers are not reported (Noonan, Morningstar, & Erickson, 2008).

Key: IEP, individualized education program.

of quality practices comes from the Taxonomy of Transition Programming developed by Kohler and colleagues. As previously noted, this includes student-focused planning (Kohler & Field, 2003) and family involvement (Kohler & Field, 2003), in addition to student development, program structure, and interagency collaboration. Other practices that have been noted in the literature include establishing positive family and student and school relationships, a meaningful curriculum, and student-oriented, outcome-based goals to enhance the transition process (Kochhar-Bryant, & Green, 2009; Wehman, 2011a; Thoma & Wehman, 2010; Wehmeyer, Gragoudas, & Shogren, 2006). Some of the recommended practices are highlighted in Table 3.2. Failure to include any one of these has been associated with poor postschool outcomes (Agran & Hughes, 2008; Powers et al., 2005).

Social interactions with peers are an important aspect of childhood development that is closely linked to emotional well-being and success in school. Carter, Sisco, Chung, and Stanton-Chapman (2010) conducted a comprehensive review of recent intervention studies evaluating strategies to improve the peer interaction outcomes of students with intellectual disabilities and/or autism. The 85 reviewed studies addressed 20 educational practices. Although the overall quality of these studies was high, considerable variation exists in the degree to which specific practices have been adequately evaluated with students across disability categories and grade levels. The authors concluded that additional research is needed to strengthen the depth of evidence for these practices across school levels, school settings, and disability categories.

These and other research-based initiatives have worked in concert with federal special education regulations to improve postschool outcomes for students with disabilities. As a result, the focus on systems change and practices in transition has evolved since the early 1980s. However, although school systems may be in general compliance with policy and regulations, the use of recommended practices is not widespread. For instance, Zhang, Ivester, Chen, and Katsiyannis (2005) concluded that South Carolina schools were doing only "an adequate job." Lubbers, Repetto, and McGorray (2008) reported on the practices in Florida and identified system and policy issues and information and training as key barriers to the transition process. Results also showed a need for future research including a need to examine participation of student and other transition stakeholders in the activities crucial to transition planning.

Today, there remains an undeniable need to continue systems change and implement recommended practices. There is also an irrefutable responsibility to focus on implementation of recommended practices, including ways to enhance student and parent involvement in transition planning. Again and again, studies find that parent involvement is critical to the success of students with disabilities in school, and, yet, we find families are consistently underutilized as partners in the transition-planning process. Next, we turn our attention and take a closer look at some barriers to participation and challenges faced by youth with disabilities and their parents and present some strategies to enhance student and parental involvement.

Barriers to and Strategies for Involvement

Anthony, a young man with a learning disability said

> Yes, I dropped out of school. I was told I had trouble learning. And it was like they think they are telling me something I don't already know. I have been hearing that every day all my life. Anyway, I thought about it and said to myself, *What's in it for me? Why should I stay somewhere to learn something if there's not anything in it for me?* No, I don't regret it yet, but my mom says I will. Anyway, I left, and that's it, and you know what I really think: they were glad when they saw me leave. You know, it was just one less dummy for them to worry about.

Kim, a young lady with an intellectual communication impairment and physical disability reports

> I was never given a real chance to get involved in planning my goals. Yes, I was there at a meeting, but so what? Believe me, I know the real problem. It takes me too long to say anything and people have trouble understanding me; so they think, *why bother?* And, you know, some people even think I am stupid, but it is not true. They don't always know it, but I hear and understand everything they say about me. And, believe me, I get the body language, too.

Mrs. Strickland reports

> I just don't get it! My son's transition plan was nothing more than a checklist of places where he will be referred for services like case management and vocational rehabilitation and county case management services. Now, somebody please tell me: How is referring him to services going to help him get ready for adulthood? He needs to focus his studies on learning to be more independent so hopefully one day he can live in a place of his own with some supports; and what about a job? Shouldn't he have a right to work?

Ms. Kline said

> I can sum up my experiences with a few words: It was just too little, too late! And don't even ask me how I feel now; because, I feel devastated. I did not know that planning could start earlier. When my daughter turned 16, I heard about transition. I think the first time might have been from another parent. Now, tell me this: Why did we have to wait until she was so close to leaving to begin planning for her life after high school? And worse, why did the educational team wait so long? What are we going to do now? What is my daughter going to do? Someone, just help me. Please tell me, what am I going to do?

Ms. Diane reports

> I was not asked to help identify or give input into my daughter's goals and objectives about employment or anything. We just showed up for the planning meeting when we were told to and basically a plan was already in place. The teacher wrote it and explained it to us. Then, all of a sudden, it all came at us really fast. One day she was in school and the next thing you know she had aged out. I don't think her education prepared her for the future. Even now, 2 years after leaving school, she is still sitting around at home spending most of her time watching television with her grandmother.

These remarks illustrate the keen sense of frustration, hopelessness, and despair often felt by students and families when transition planning is ineffective. They also highlight one of the major barriers to meaningful student and parent participation in transition planning: noncompliance with transition planning requirements that have been put in place to ensure their involvement. Furthermore, whenever educators fail to include students and parents in transition planning, there is also a negative ripple effect. Noncompliance with the basic requirements leads to the development of poor-quality goals and objectives, which, in turn, leads to implementing an ineffective IEP—one that does little to prepare the student for his or her life beyond the classroom. This section offers a brief look at some of the requirements that are in place to promote student and family involvement and offers some guidelines on developing high-quality goals. This is followed by a look at some strategies that can be used to increase student and family involvement and participation in the transition-planning process.

Transition-Planning Requirements

Transition planning should begin at age 16; in some states, at age 14. Then, beginning no later than the first IEP in effect after the student turns 16, or younger if determined appropriate by the IEP team, the IEP must include appropriate measurable postsecondary goals based upon age-appropriate transition assessments related to training, education, employment, and, where appropriate, independent living skills; the transition services (including courses of study needed to help the student reach those goals) (34 C.F.R. 300.320[b] and [c]) (20 U.S.C. 1414 [d] [1][A][i][VIII]). It is very important to note that planning can start earlier if deemed appropriate. For example, some students with severe disabilities can particularly benefit from a **functional curriculum** beginning in elementary through their secondary years. Otherwise, the sentiments such as Ms. Kline stated may come true: "It was just too little, too late."

Another issue related to compliance is that schools must invite students to the IEP meetings if transition will be discussed. This is what gives students a voice. It gives them an opportunity to build upon and develop their self-determination and self-advocacy skills. As has been stated earlier in this chapter, student involvement improves outcomes. When this happens, the student should feel that his or her education is meaningful and be less prone to dropping out like Anthony, the young man with the learning disability, or feel a sense of hopelessness associated with not being listened to as expressed by Kim, the young lady with the communication and physical disability.

Effective transition planning takes into account the multiple perspectives of people who know the student well, including parents. Their contribution to this process is extremely important (Hogansen, Powers, Geenen, Gil-Kashiwabara, & Powers, 2008). Parents must be invited and meaningfully involved in the process. Meaningful involvement means educators create a plan with student and family involvement. This way, a scenario such as the one described by Ms. Diane—"We showed up for the meeting and there was already a plan in place"—should not occur.

Table 3.3 highlights what needs to happen to help ensure a proper IEP meeting. It is important that everyone (including parents and students to the degree possible) fully understand what should happen at the meeting in advance. This means educators need to be prepared to offer information in an understandable way and know how to encourage participation in the process. Student and parent education paired with user-friendly reference materials should be made available. Simply sharing information from a web site or handbook may not be enough for some parents. Some will need support to acquire and use the information. Therefore, including resources—for example, a parent education and advocacy group or staff in a national resource center such as http://ideapartnership.org or the National Dissemination Center for Children with

Table 3.3. Legally correct IEP meetings

- Student's parents are meaningfully involved in the IEP process.
- The IEP must be developed by an IEP team, driven by the student.
- The team should include a) the parent or parents, b) a representative of the local educational agency (LEA; e.g., principal), c) a special education teacher, d) at least one general education teacher, and e) an individual who can interpret the instructional implications of the assessment results (this can be someone who is already on the IEP team). Parents or school personnel may also include additional members as long as they have knowledge or special expertise concerning the student.
- The student should be invited.
- Members of the team can be excused from an IEP meeting (all or part) if the parent and school personnel agree that the attendance of the member is not required because the discussion will not be related to his or her area of curriculum or related services.
- An IEP meeting can be held without a member whose area will be under review, as long as a) the parent and LEA consent and b) the member submits, in writing to the parent and team, input into the development of the IEP before the meeting.
- The parent and LEA may agree to use alternative means of conducting meetings, such as through the use of conference calls and video conferences.
- The IEP meeting must be held annually.
- If the parents and LEA decide to modify an IEP following an annual meeting within that school year, they may agree not to convene an actual meeting. Instead, they can elect to develop a written document to amend the student's current IEP (IDEA 2004, 20 U.S.C. § 1414 [d][3][D]).

Key: IEP, individualized education program; IDEA 2004, Individuals with Disabilities Education Improvement Act of 2004; LEA, local education agency.

Disabilities (NICHCY)—on where students and parents can go to ask questions and get additional information on meetings held to develop the IEP related to transition is also recommended.

Some strategies for encouraging participation will be presented later and include things such as interacting with families and students in ways that encourage participation (e.g., using language on a level that the person can understand, complimenting the person, using positive body language, presenting information that is more visual than verbal as needed, making concepts easy to understand by avoiding jargon and using key words, and commenting on good responses).

Quality of Goals

Although compliance with basic transition planning requirements is helpful in enhancing parent and student participation, in reality, it is not enough to ensure an effective plan for transition from school to adulthood. The educational team must also be willing to invest the time needed to develop effective transition goals and objectives on the IEP that reflect the preferences and values of the student with disabilities and his or her family and to move beyond simply meeting the minimum level of state requirement. It is imperative that students' goals on the IEP are high quality. They must be oriented to the future as well as be measurable. To help ensure this during the transition planning process, the student and his or her family must receive instruction from a designated person on the team and, as needed, be guided to express aspirations for the future or for life beyond high school. With a vision of the student's general direction for the future in mind, the team can then move on to translating those desires into goals.

As the U.S. Department of Education has noted, the annual goals must be measurable, written so that the student's "teacher(s) and parents are able to track the child's progress in special education" (U.S. Department of Education, 2006, 34 C.F.R. § Part 300, Appendix C, Question 37). According to IDEA 2004, the IEP must include a statement of appropriate measurable postsecondary goals based upon age-appropriate transition assessments, related to training, education, employment, and, where appropriate, independent living skills, and the transition services (including courses of study) needed to assist the student

Table 3.4. Examples of measurable goals

- Upon graduation from high school, Sherry will successfully complete business courses at ABC Community College to attain the Office Assistant Certificate.
- Before graduation, Ronnie will use a credit card at XYZ grocery store to purchase the items needed to make five simple meals.
- After high school, Andy will improve his social, self-advocacy, and self-care skills by attending instruction at a center-based adult program.
- Before completing high school, Allison will independently ride the bus each work day to her part-time job at a retail store located in the MNO Mall.
- Before graduation, LeAnn will participate in training to improve her work skills by participating in the community-based vocational educational program at the hospital.

in reaching those goals (34 C.F.R. 300.320[b] and [c]; 20 U.S.C. 1414 [d][1][A][i][VIII][aa] and [bb]). The purpose of the annual goal is to: a) project a student's academic or functional progress over a full academic year and b) assess the effectiveness of a student's special education service by measuring his or her progress. If a goal cannot be measured, it is not only useless for the purpose of measuring progress but also legally incorrect. Measurable goals are related to the areas specified in IDEA (2004): education, training, employment, and, where appropriate, independent living are countable and occur after high school (34 C.F.R. 300.320[b]; 20 U.S.C. 1414[d][1][A][i][VIII][aa] and [bb]). Some examples of measurable postsecondary goals related to employment, education/training, and independent living/community participation are provided in Table 3.4.

Writing goals and objectives has been compared with developing a task analysis (Parent & Wehman, 2011). Just as completing each step of a task analysis leads to completing the task on hand, achieving each transition IEP objective leads to accomplishing the annual goal. Conceptualizing goals and objectives this way helps demonstrate the importance of connecting each component to achieve the ultimate outcome.

Wood, Karvonen, Test, Browder, and Algozzine (2004) presented an in-depth set of strategies for promoting student self-determination in IEP planning, including examples of IEP annual goals in this area. For example, for a goal related to increasing a student's leadership in the IEP process, sample activities might include "LeAnn will complete the self-directed IEP lessons by learning 10 steps needed to lead the next meeting. Before the meeting, LeAnn will videotape a role play using the 10 steps needed to lead her own IEP meeting. After the role play, LeAnn will review her performance with the assistance of the teacher and her peers."

Of course it is not enough to have a planning meeting and to put measurable goals in place. Effective implementation also requires basing the selection of interventions and services on peer-reviewed research whenever possible. This precludes choosing services because "this is what we have always done," or "it seems right." It also means that the sentiments of Mrs. Strickland presented at the start of this section should never ring true: "My son's transition plan was nothing more than a checklist of places where he will be referred for services."

If it is necessary to modify an existing IEP after the completion of the annual meeting within the same school year, the parents and school may agree not to convene an actual meeting. Instead they may elect to develop a written document to amend the student's current IEP (IDEA 2004, 20 U.S.C. 1414 [d][3][D]). The planning requirements also note that the school needs to report to parents on the child's progress toward meeting their transition goals.

Beyond mere compliance with the requirements that are in place to promote student and parent participation and involvement and effective goal formulation, teachers should also be familiar with ways to enhance parent and student involvement.

Enhancing Student Participation

Teaching self-determination skills enables students to actively participate in their transition process (Wehmeyer, Gragoudas, & Shogren, 2006; Wehmeyer & Palmer, 2003). Martin et al. (2004) recommended a self-directed IEP, and a follow-up study by these authors promoted the use of contracts for self-regulation (Woods & Martin, 2004). Applying the principles of self-determination to the Student Directed Learning Model as proposed by Agran, King-Sears, Wehmeyer, and Copeland (2003) and/or following some of the tips offered by Bremer, Kachgal, and Schoeller (2003) can help provide a framework for instruction of students in middle and high school.

Several curricula promote self-determination and can be integrated into a student's course of study (see Chapter 2; Wehmeyer et al., 2007a & b; Wehmeyer, Shogren, Zager, Smith, & Simpson, 2010; Wehmeyer, Palmer, Lee, Williams-Diehm, & Shogren, 2011; Wehmeyer, Palmer, Shogren, Williams-Diehm, and Soukup, 2010). Konrad and Test (2004) provided some basic guidelines for including the student in planning the meeting as well as in drafting, revising, and implementing the IEP. In addition, secondary curriculum offers frequent opportunities for students to exercise and develop self-determination skills throughout the day. For instance Konrad, Fowler, Walker, Test, and Wood (2007) recommended that students practice making choices by selecting alternative academic assignments or determining the order in which assignments are completed. Computer-assisted instruction offers another format for teaching goal setting and self-determination (Mazzotti, Wood, Test, & Fowler, 2010).

Some of the skills students need to learn include self-management, self-advocacy, and leadership (Mazzotti et al., 2010; Carter et al., 2011). To succeed in school and in the community, students need to understand their disability, learn and develop their personal strengths, understand their legal rights under IDEA and the Americans with Disabilities Act, and educate themselves about the types of possible supports and accommodations that can enhance their level of independence. Every day, new technology is being developed that not only maximizes independence but also enhances productivity and facilitates participation in academic, employment, recreational, and other adult activities.

Although involving students who are able to able to express themselves seems like common sense to most educators, sometimes even the best teachers become stumped on ways to ensure involvement of those who have more significant disabilities. Thoma and Wehman (2010) provide some ideas on how to more actively involve all students (including those with intellectual disabilities) in the transition planning process.

To further promote self-determination, it is critical that students have an active role in the actual IEP meeting; however, studies have indicated that students too often do not have a meaningful role during the meeting (Martin, Huber Marshall, & Sale, 2004; Martin, VanDyke, Christiansen, Greene et al., 2006). For example, in an examination of who speaks the most during IEP meetings, it was determined that roughly half (51%) of the speaking was done by special education teachers compared with only 3% by students (Martin, VanDyke, Greene, Gardner et al., 2006).

In addition, students report lower levels of understanding the IEP process compared with the other IEP team members (Martin, VanDyke, Greene, Gardner et al., 2006). When students were asked about the nature of the IEP meeting, statistically significant differences were found between the answers of students who did and did not attend the meeting, with students attending the meeting reporting better understanding of the meeting (Martin et al., 2004). This supports that the logical first step toward improving participation is to teach the students about the process. Students who do not participate in the IEP process are often unaware of the importance of what occurs at the planning meeting (Martin, VanDyke, Greene, Gardner et al., 2006; Thoma & Wehman, 2010). Conversely, Morningstar et al. (2010) found that even among students who do not attend the meeting, the more involved students perceived their families to be, the greater the students perceived levels of focus and control, psychological empowerment, hope, and locus of control.

Promoting student involvement in transition planning and the self-determination of youth with disabilities is a recommended practice in secondary and transition services. Increasingly, a critical feature of efforts to promote student access to and involvement with curricular content, including transition-related content, has involved the use of universally designed instructional technologies. Building in support for diverse needs is called "universal design for learning." In learning environments, this approach assumes that students with varying needs will be involved in learning and that the goals, instructional practice, instructional materials, and assessments need to address this diversity. With accessible core materials in place, students can access information by using a variety of assistive technology such as

Input methods and devices

- On-screen keyboard
- Cursor control pointer systems
- Alternative keyboards
- Voice recognition
- Eye-gaze
- Keyboard emulation
- Switches
- Direct switch interface
- Scanning

Output methods and devices

- Visual
- Auditory
- Tactile
- Interfacing
- Combinations

Williams-Diehm, Wehmeyer, Palmer, Soukup, and Garner (2008) examined whether the use of computer software programs would improve outcomes related to self-determination for students receiving instruction in transition planning designed to promote student involvement. They also evaluated the impact, over time, of instruction in transition planning designed to promote student involvement on student self-determination of 194 high school students receiving special education services in multiple disability categories in school districts in six states. About half the students received instruction with the support of cognitively accessible computer software programs designed to support greater independence in decision making and to facilitate exploration related to transition. Results revealed a relationship between student involvement in transition planning and enhanced self-determination and provided evidence of a causal relationship between student involvement combined with technology use and enhanced self-determination.

There are numerous ways educators and transition team members can encourage and promote student involvement in transition planning and IEP meetings. Students can be assisted in preparing for and participating in their transition-related IEP meetings in creative ways. Table 3.5 provides some examples.

Students who are active participants will gain confidence in their abilities. They can also go on to be proud of their accomplishments, learn how to advocate for themselves, and make choices about what they want in life. In addition, there are a number of benefits related to developing leadership skills. Carter, Sweeden, Walter, et al. (2011) examined the

Table 3.5. Tips for preparing and encouraging student participation in IEP transition planning

Ways to prepare the student to be involved in IEP transition planning meeting	• Create student interest and motivation leading up to the event. • Explain how transition planning impacts current life or near future rather than years down the road (e.g., course selection). • Informally assess student's current skill level in self-advocacy, planning, and leading meeting and collect information from former teachers, parents, and other adults in the student's life. • Teach self-advocacy and, as appropriate, assist student in choosing an advocate. • Teach the importance and purpose of postsecondary and annual goals and objectives and rights and responsibilities related to the transition IEP by using a variety of nontraditional approaches and fun activities. • Use appropriate teaching strategies, instructional materials, instructional supports, or specific adaptations for students with moderate-to-severe intellectual disabilities to enhance level of active participation in all aspects of transition planning and implementation and elicit parental support. • Describe roles of participants at meeting. • Assist with identifying guests student wants to invite. • Help identify possible ways to participate and actively lead meeting. • Help design student presentation (e.g., portfolio, videotape, audio clips, scrapbook, poster, collage). • Help identify supports needed to promote active participation. • Develop supports needed to express abilities, desires, goals, and needs. • Provide opportunity to practice with supports in place. (Students with moderate-to-severe intellectual disabilities may require extensive prompting and other types of support throughout meeting to be actively involved.) • Evaluate performance and provide additional instruction or support as indicated. • Include in gathering information about current skills what skills need to be learned and supports needed to facilitate performance. • Instruct student to make invitations. • Support student in sharing what he or she has learned/is learning with parents or others.
Ways for student to actively participate at meeting	• Welcome and introduce participants. • Announce purpose of meeting using own words or student presentation (e.g., PowerPoint). • Inform participants about length of meeting. • Inform participants about where to sit. • Inform participants of restroom location or other announcements. • Highlight accomplishments using student presentation (e.g., handouts, PowerPoint). • Present information on interests, preferences, and desired outcomes for the future. • Choose who should begin a group discussion. • Explain what help is needed and what can help. • Share ideas on goals for the next year. • Share ideas on how to know he or she is moving toward the goals. • Ask others to share ideas at certain times. • Thank everyone for attending the meeting.

Key: IEP, individualized education program.

perspectives of youth leadership development of 34 young adults with disabilities. The key indicators, factors, and benefits of leadership development that were identified in this qualitative study are provided in Table 3.6.

Enhancing Parent Involvement

Parents continue to feel left out of the educational planning process (Cooney, 2002) and indicate a desire for more information to help them actively participate (Tarleton & Ward, 2005), despite the fact that enhancing parents' ability to make informed choices is important to successful transition planning for youth with disabilities. Parent and family involvement in the transition planning process has been found to be a predictor of post-secondary success of young adults with disabilities (Kraemer, McIntyre, & Blacher, 2003; Test, Mazzotti, et al., 2009). Researchers have identified the following issues as particularly important:

a. The need for schools to encourage participation and collaboration with parents

b. Appreciation of the family context with acknowledgment of parental knowledge of their children (Geenen, Powers, Lopez-Vasquez, & Bersani, 2003; Kohler & Field, 2003; Neece et al., 2009)

c. Parent advocacy training to maximize parents' knowledge of both the system and their rights

A number of strategies for increasing or better supporting parental involvement in transition planning also emerged from Geenen et al. (2001) related to promoting involvement of CLD parents in transition planning. These included

a. Positive communication between parent and professionals

b. Preparing for transition at an earlier age

c. Information on school-based transition planning

d. Use of a parent advocate

e. Emotional support for parents

f. Flexibility in meeting formats

Furthermore, effective educational experiences for a student who receives special education services depends upon his or her parents' involvement in educational programming (Stoner et al., 2005), which signifies the need for effective collaboration.

In a recent study, Rowe and Test (2010) examined the effects of a computer-based instructional program on acquisition of parents' knowledge of the transition-planning process. The content of each computer-based training module focused on required components of Indicator 13. Indicator 13 is one of the 20 state performance indicators identified in IDEA (2004) and one of the four indicators related to secondary transition. It is defined as percentage of youth ages 16 and older with an IEP that includes coordinated, measurable, annual IEP goals and transition services that will reasonably enable the student to meet the postsecondary goals (20 U.S.C. 1416[a][3][B]). For example, content covered topics related to requirements of IDEA 2004: postsecondary goals, transition services, and postsecondary transition service providers. Results suggested a functional relation between computer-based instruction and parent knowledge of postsecondary goals, transition

Table 3.6.   Key indicators, factors, and benefits associated with leadership development

Indicators	Factors	Benefits
Attitudes and skills	Key experiences	Personal benefits
• Perseverance	• Extracurricular activities	• Increasing social outlets
• Independence	• Academic rigor	• Diminishing stereotypes
• Positive attitude	• Disability-specific opportunities	• Opening up additional leadership opportunities
• Confidence	• Informal community activities	• Enhancing student-led IEP meeting
• Desire to lead		• Providing youth with greater voice in what happens in the community
• Goal setting	Key relationships	
• Effective communication	• Parents and other family members	Benefits to others
• Social skills	• Teachers and school staff	• Increased accountability
Influence on others		• More job opportunities
• Advocacy/self-advocacy	Mentors	• Greater diversity in workplace and community
	Friends	• More respect for individuals with disabilities
Helping others		
Mentoring youth		• More open and warm welcoming communities
Leading by example		

Source: Carter (2011).
Key: IEP, individualized education program.

services, and postsecondary transition service providers. In addition, the results support the recommendation that transition planning training can provide parents with knowledge needed to become more involved in their child's transition planning and communicate with teachers and other professionals about the needs and supports to help their children achieve their postsecondary goals. Using computer-based instruction, parents gained knowledge and skills that could potentially be used to increase their active participation in transition planning for their child. In addition, computer-based instruction allowed parents to learn content at their own pace in a nonthreatening environment.

In addition to using computer-based instruction, Rowe and Test (2010) offered other suggestions for developing parent training materials that can be derived from the social validity data collected in their study, including

a. Ensuring that the materials were easy for parents to understand

b. Keeping terminology functional or using practical terms (i.e., no educational jargon)

c. Using shorter training sessions

d. Dividing instruction into shorter segments addressing one topic at a time

e. Making complex concepts easier for the learners to understand by dividing the instruction on those topics into several sessions

f. Determining if parents used the information

A final suggestion for practitioners would be to provide training about transition planning to parents of children in the early stages of transition (i.e., age of 13). The authors noted that this would have the potential to enhance the transition-planning process by providing parents in advance with knowledge needed to become more involved in the transition-planning process.

The importance of strengthening the role of the parents and ensuring that families have meaningful opportunities to participate in transition planning and implementation cannot be overemphasized. However, it is not as simple as just issuing an invitation to attend a meeting. Some tips on to help ensure optimal parental involvement are listed in Table 3.7.

Supporting Improved Outcomes

Mary Beth, a student with spinal cord and traumatic brain injury, says of her IEP meeting,

> I was really excited to get involved, especially in planning my presentation for the meeting. My teacher helped me use PowerPoint to create some slides to help me explain things to everyone there. My favorite slide is the one with me standing there with that really cool look on my face and it says, "Does anyone have anything to say about my future?"

Mrs. Penny reports

> Personally, I was taken aback. You know my son has an intellectual disability and I knew he was getting involved because I helped him invite people to the meeting. But, when the meeting started and I saw the portfolio my son and his teachers had put together.… It included so many wonderful things like what we had learned during his personal future planning meeting. There were lists of my son's interests and other things he wanted us to know. During the meeting he was involved, too. I could tell by the look on his face how proud he felt.

There is much that can be done to improve student and parent participation in planning the IEP related to transition, some which was highlighted in the previous section. Here are some other ways to support improved outcomes.

To begin with, personnel must be trained. Over the years, IDEA has developed higher standards and more rigorous compliance requirements; teachers and others involved

Table 3.7.   Strategies to enable and empower parents in transition planning and implementation

- Establish effective communications.
  - Offer a variety of opportunities to communicate ideas, opinion, or concerns (e.g., formal meetings, conferences, team meetings, telephone conversations, informal chats before or after school, e-mail).
  - Ask for preferences for communicating.
  - Ask for ideas on the best way to communicate if it seems the aforementioned methods are not possible or suitable or if an agreed-upon way is not working.
  - Initiate interactions.
  - Arrange for contact across team members (e.g., special education teacher, general education teacher, therapist, counselors, administrators) rather than just the primary teacher.
  - Establish a time of day when you can take calls when the parent can receive your full attention, and if unable to talk (e.g., on another call, something comes up), set up a time to talk within 24 hours.
  - Return calls and e-mails within 24 hours.
  - Be prepared to support parents who do not speak English as their first language by knowing where and how to access interpreter services or other support (e.g., finding a friend of the family or another teacher at the school who speaks both languages).
  - Be familiar with cultural differences and how these may impact communications.
- Inquire about possible barriers to communicate or participate in events (e.g., work, child care, transportation) and, as indicated, be flexible (e.g., offer a variety of times and modes to communicate) and try to find creative ways to overcome.
- Provide information on available resources and instruction on how to access and develop new ones if none exists
  - Self-advocacy
  - Legal rights
  - Emotional resources
  - Internal support
  - External support
  - Financial resources
  - Social Security benefits
  - Community adult service providers
- Take time to follow up with the parent about success in accessing resources and, as needed, help problem solve.
- Be prepared to offer additional skills training (depending on parent need) or other support (offer parent support groups) as the parent begins to tap into and create resources.
- Express high expectations when reporting on student's progress and be sure to focus on abilities, positive attributes, and gains.
- Assist in articulating their child's strengths and needs by asking probing questions.
- Solicit input on ways for the student to get involved in the student-directed IEP process.
- Issue a personal invitation to participate in an event in the classroom or school as opposed to issuing a general invitation to all; ask for input and offer specific options on how he or she might contribute or get involved; make sure there is ample time to respond.
- Ask if special accommodation is needed to enhance participation in meetings or activities (e.g., translators, large print, special time of day).
- If unable to attend a group event (e.g., information night) follow up and extend invitation to meet at a better-scheduled time.
- Express and explain the importance of their contributions and your need and desire to partner.
- Enlist help with preparing the student for the transition IEP planning meeting.
- Offer information and education to help ensure preparation for actively participating in meeting (things to think about; reporting on what student is doing outside school hours; sharing child's strengths, interests, and preferences, and helping translate this into ideas for employment).
- Encourage joint planning (e.g., ask for advice on how to enhance student's learning, provide input into transition goals and objectives); decision making (e.g., prioritizing goals), and problem solving (e.g., ask for advice on resolving behavior issues).
- Offer guidance and instruction if needed on how to reinforce skills learning in the home and community environment; if warranted, help parent set goals for child, self, and others in family.
- (Be prepared to "think outside the box" to come up with new ways to engage with parents. Brainstorm and share ideas and strategies with colleagues.)

Key: IEP, individualized education program.

Table 3.8. Training topics for staff in planning the transition IEP

- Compliance with the Individuals with Disabilities Education Improvement Act of 2004
- Strategies for active student engagement, especially alternate formats or strategies to promote communication
- Strategies for active parental engagement to ensure earlier involvement and playing an active role in shaping his or her son's or daughter's transition IEP
- Positive communications between parents and professionals
- Emotional support strategies for parents
- Student-centered planning strategies
- Developing the characteristics of professionals who make a difference (honest, direct, knowledgeable, caring about youth's future)
- Collaboration (listen, keep an open mind to new ideas, bring resources from programs and community, take risks, make connections with students, parents, and community partners)
- Team building
- Connecting students and parents with community resources (adult services, parent information training centers, other parents and students)

Key: IEP, individualized education program.

in transition must receive training and education not only about compliance but also, perhaps more importantly, information on ways to enhance student and parent engagement. Some examples of topics to include in staff training are listed in Table 3.8.

Training should also focus on higher expectations. One way to get started is to share information on recommended practices. Learning about what other schools are doing is a great way to get first-hand advice and experience on what is working.

Work experience opportunities must be developed for all students. One of the most important things in preparing for the student's future is work, and families are often passionate about their children receiving an opportunity to learn job skills and explore career interests.

The process of transition begins in early childhood when parents are teaching their children to develop independence, decision-making skills, and social skills. During adolescence, the roles of parents get greater as they continue to promote self-determination, offer emotional support, and act as advocates for their maturing sons and daughters. Then, once the student leaves school, parents often become the backup system for limited services, with their support continuing indefinitely over their lifetime. Yet, both students and families remain poorly prepared for life beyond the classroom. To help remedy this situation, teachers should find ways to help make sure students and families are prepared. To begin, this means that early on teachers can refer parents to resources to help them help their child. Some examples of the type of information that parents need early that can have a positive impact on transition later are highlighted in Table 3.9.

In addition, students and their parents need to receive training about rights and the transition process. This should also include detailed information on planning and community resources as well as what to do if needed resources are not readily available or accessible.

Table 3.9. Information parents need early on to support positive transition

- Supporting child's healthy development
- Creating a happy and balanced lifestyle
- Increasing child's independence in and out of the classroom
- Teaching problem solving
- Promoting decision making
- Teaching values
- Teaching social skills and etiquette
- Enhancing child's participation in the community

Conclusion

This chapter described ways to enhance a student's and parent's involvement and participation in the transition process. A review of the literature on student and family involvement and recommended practices in the transition-planning process was provided. This was followed by a discussion of some ways to overcome barriers to meaningful student and parental participation as well as some strategies to improve results.

Study Questions

1. What does the research say about parent involvement in planning the IEP related to transition?
2. What does the research say about student involvement in planning his or her IEP related to transition?
3. Meet with a teacher and a parent to discuss some of the barriers to and strategies for increasing parental involvement and participation in transition planning.
4. What are some strategies to increase a student's involvement and active participation?
5. Interview the head of special education for a school district in your area to discuss what is being done and could be done to improve outcomes.

Online Resources

Parent Educational Advocacy Training Center: http://www.peatc.org/

Council for Exceptional Children: http://www.cec.sped.org/Content/NavigationMenu/AboutCEC/International/StepbyStep/E611.pdf

Beach Center on Families and Disabilities: http://www.beachcenter.org/families/person-centered_planning.aspx

Helping Students Develop Their IEPs: Technical Assistance Guide:
http://www.nichy.org/InformationResources/Documents/NICHCY%20PUBS/ta2.pdf

I'm Determined: http://www.imdetermined.org

Transition Planning
and Support

Individualized Transition Planning

Building the Roadmap to Adulthood

KIRA AUSTIN AND KATHERINE M. WITTIG

4

After completing this chapter, the reader will be able to

- Examine how the values associated with person-centered planning impact transition
- Discuss how a person-centered approach can be used to enhance transition planning
- Explain the role of parents in transition planning
- Describe ways for students to direct their individualized education program (IEP)
- Discuss how to accomplish a person-centered transition IEP
- Explain the importance of community resource mapping

We have noted previously that the combination of parent and family power with individual self-determination is a powerful force for change, yet there must be a roadmap into adulthood. To make this journey to community inclusion with a feeling of self-determination, a well-designed blueprint of transition from school to adulthood needs to be written and implemented. This blueprint must be generated from key stakeholders in the student's life including the student, his or her family and friends, significant educators, and community personnel. This chapter explains how to integrate person-centered planning and transition planning into a meaningful blueprint with the family and student's self-determination as the engine. Four students will be profiled in this chapter: Kristin, Rosa, Ameer, and Tyler.

Goals of Individualized Transition Planning

Students with disabilities at the secondary level participate in postsecondary goal development education, training, employment, and, where appropriate, independent living. These adolescents begin making decisions surrounding sexual and reproductive health, nutrition, fitness, and finances. One of the most important things that adults can do is to assist, guide, and provide structure so that youth learn about themselves in each of these areas. High school general and special educators are essential to this process (Carter, Lane, Pierson, & Stang, 2008). When individualized transition planning is done correctly and comprehensively, students develop statements about their future goals and negotiate with their IEP team members for planned activities that are necessary to accomplish their goals. When it is not done correctly, or if it is not done at all, the student will lack direction and vision, thus resulting in low self-esteem, and low productivity (Wigham, Robertson, Emerson, Hatton, et al., 2008). Furthermore, the students may lack essential skills to enhance their self-determination (Carter et al., 2008).

Individualized transition planning has two goals. The first goal is to identify the postsecondary outcomes desired and expected by students and their families along with the services and supports desired and needed to achieve these outcomes. Cameto (2005) provided National Longitudinal Transition Study-2 (NLTS-2) data on students' post–high school goals as well as the active participants who provide the most effort with transition planning. She indicated that, although 58% of students provide some input to their transition planning, only 12% take a leadership role. In similar manner, Katsiyannis, Zhang, Woodruff, and Dixon (2005) studied transition planning and role of supports for students with intellectual disabilities, finding that approximately 60% of these students in the United States had begun planning at 14 years old. To accomplish desired outcomes, the transition planning process must provide IEP teams with an understanding of what students *want* and *need*, along with jointly created plans or blueprints on *how* to get there. This process is fashioned in a person-centered planning approach, which is the dominant planning model (Holburn & Vietze, 2002; Robertson, Emerson, Hatton, et al., 2006). The second goal is to use data from State Performance Plan Indicators 13 and 14 to drive the way transition services are delivered (Wittig, 2009). The purpose of this chapter is to address the first goal by discussing person-centered practices that may be used by IEP teams to more fully individualize the transition process and outcomes.

We affirm that the student-directed transition IEP is an integral part of self-determination. Commercial and teacher-developed products as well as recent research studies support this. Woods, Sylvester, and Martin (2010) highlighted instruction methods in the Student Directed Transition Planning system. The Virginia Department of Education's self-determination project, I'm Determined (2011), provides templates and teacher lesson plans to improve the student-directed IEP process. Students with intellectual disabilities revealed their understanding of self-determination in Shogren and Broussard's (2011) study. The students were able to describe how setting and working toward goals, choice and control, and advocacy were central themes of self-determination in their lives. Furthermore, they identified personalized supports as key to achieving their goals. Thoma and Wehman (2010) outlined the student-directed IEP process with practical classroom applications.

This chapter emphasizes person-centered planning as a cornerstone of transition planning, because students will direct their IEPs most effectively when supports and input are provided by the important people in their lives: families, teachers, agency personnel, friends, employers, and so on. It is our position that **student-directed transition IEPs** and processes *must* have a person-centered philosophy.

Rosa Rosa is an outgoing and active young woman who is eager to experience living on her own. Rosa also uses a wheelchair for mobility. She would like to move from her parents' home into an accessible apartment within the next 2 years. Rosa and her team envision her living with one other woman from whom she would have 24-hour supports for meals, housekeeping, and daily living care. The transition IEP team agrees that she should be fully independent in her daily self-care routines as long as her bathroom and bedroom are fully accessible. Rosa and her family indicate that, although she likes to spend time in the kitchen, she needs a lot of support to prepare meals. Rosa also notes that she does not enjoy housekeeping tasks and finds many tasks physically challenging.

Person-Centered Planning: Values and Transition

The goal of all person-centered approaches is to learn about people with disabilities in more effective and efficient ways to plan and create supports that can assist them in participating in and experiencing self-directed lives (O'Brien, 2002). Holburn and Vietze (2002) established the goal of person-centered planning to include reducing social isolation, establishing friendships, increasing engagement in preferred activities, developing competence, and promoting respect. A related goal is to place individuals with disabilities in respected positions and even leadership positions during the assessment, planning, and service delivery process. To accomplish these goals, all person-centered approaches share some common values or beliefs. For example, Wehman (2011a) described five basic steps for person-centered transition planning at IEP meetings (Table 4.1).

Person-Centered Approaches Are Driven by the Individual, Family, and Friends

When used to individualize the transition process, person-centered approaches place the student in the driver's seat, which is why the self-determination skills described in the previous chapter become crucial. Person-centered approaches encourage IEP teams to

Table 4.1. Five basic steps in person-centered transition IEP planning meetings

Each team includes the student, family, educators, agencies, and others as appropriate. The team
1. Is convened around that student who assumes the leadership role
2. Reviews transition and other assessment data in the context of the student's interests and preferences, strengths, and challenges
3. Develops IEP goals and services driven by the student's desired postsecondary goals and based on age-appropriate transition assessments
4. Updates the transition IEP annually; implements follow-up activities
5. Hosts a summary of performance meeting in which the student's supports and resources are identified and clarified

Source: Schwartz, Holburn, and Jacobson (2000).
Key: IEP, individualized education program.

Table 4.2.   Person-centered interdependent planning

1. The person and his or her family are informed.
2. The person and his or her family choose services and supports.
3. The person and his or her family choose and attain their goals.
4. The person and his or her family exercise their rights.
5. The person and his or her family have economic resources.
6. The person and his or her family are satisfied with their services.
7. The person and his or her family are satisfied with their life situation.

From Kim, K., & Turnbull, A. (2004). Transition to adulthood for students with severe intellectual disabilities: Shifting toward person-family interdependent planning. *Research and Practice for Persons with Severe Disabilities, 29*(1), 54; reprinted by permission. This article first appeared in *Research and Practice for Persons with Severe Disabilities*. Visit www.tash.org or contact info@tash.org for more information.

define an active, participative role for the student with a disability and the student's family and friends. Kim and Turnbull (2004) expanded the concept of person-centered and family-centered planning to person–family interdependent planning (Table 4.2). As schools continue to grow in diversity, special educators have to become increasingly more culturally sensitive (Xu, Purvis, & Terpstra, 2010). The transition planning process is no different (Valenzuela & Martin, 2005). Research has shown that person-centered approaches have positive aspects that are well received by a variety of ethnicities, cultures, and linguistic backgrounds (Blue-Banning, Turnbull, & Pereira, 2000; Bui & Turnbull, 2003; Hasnain, Sotnik, & Ghiloni, 2003; Trainor, 2007b). Staples and Diliberto (2010) suggest communication systems with parents to promote involvement beyond annual IEP meetings. They promote parent involvement for all age levels to encourage rapport. Wandry and Pleet (2009) offer practical suggestions to promote family involvement in the secondary transition process (Table 4.3).

Person-Centered Approaches
Are Benefits- and Abilities-Focused

Person-centered planning originated in the 1980s with the movement toward social inclusion of people with disabilities (Holburn, 2002). As this approach has gained steam, student outcomes and other internal benefits are being seen. Unlike traditional models, person-centered planning tends to focus on the students' abilities and supports already in place, rather than deficits and supports lacking. Person-centered planning has been shown to improve social networks and family connections and to promote greater engagement in group activities (Holburn, Jacobson, Schwartz, Flory, & Vietze, 2004; Robertson et al., 2006). Wigham and colleagues (2008) conducted a qualitative study that investigated the benefits of person-centered planning for people with disabilities. Informants identified 20 areas of benefit as seen in Table 4.4. Cobb and Alwell suggested that, to make students feel heard and valued at IEP meetings, it is beneficial to "include peer advocates, friends, and mentors as active participants" (2009, p. 78).

Table 4.3.   Promoting student and family participation in the transition-planning process

1. Talk directly to the student and family.
2. Encourage student and family to bring lists of transition goals to the planning meeting.
3. Avoid jargon; ask the student and family to freely express their hopes and dreams.
4. Encourage the student to ask or answer questions; be respectful of processing time.
5. Respect the student's and family's cultural values.
6. Frequently check in with student and family for understanding and consensus.
7. Reconvene meeting if more time is needed.

Source: Wandry and Pleet (2009).

Table 4.4. Benefits of person-centered planning

• Increased activities and opportunities	• Improved social life/social contact
• Fresh look at person and his or her life	• Increased independence
• Participant feels better—confident, happy	• Structure and consistent approach
• Empowerment/control	• Addressed health issues
• Improved choice	• Improved skills
• More people involved in life and planning	• Altered perception of participant
• Improved quality of life (unspecific)	• Increased or improved service receipt
• Facilitates communication	• Community presence
• Gives participant direction	• Changing staff attitudes/motivation
• Improved behavior	• Helps family

From Wigham et al., Journal of Intellectual Disabilities (Vol. 12, No. 2), pp. 143–152, copyright © 2008 by Sage Publications. Adapted by Permission of SAGE.

Tools and Strategies Associated with Person-Centered Transition Approaches

To organize transition services in a person-centered manner, all IEP team members, including students and family members, must be knowledgeable about and skilled in the tools and strategies associated with person-centered approaches. When used together and effectively, these tools and strategies can enhance the quality and quantity of transition outcomes for individuals with disabilities and their families.

To understand the variety of tools and strategies used in person-centered approaches, it is helpful to picture a large toolbox. Within the toolbox, there are a number of odd and unfamiliar tools. Each tool has a different purpose. Once IEP teams become familiar with each tool, many of these tools can be used in a variety of ways to accomplish specific tasks. Others may need to be modified to meet the needs and preferences of individual students and to fit the settings and materials that are idiosyncratic to a particular school, adult services agency, or community. When faced with especially complex and unfamiliar desired transition outcomes and support needs, IEP teams must be competent in the use of many, if not all, of the tools. IEP teams must also not hesitate to think outside the proverbial toolbox to create new tools and strategies as new situations arise. In addition, they must be prepared to use all of them to accomplish systems-change tasks that may be necessary.

At first, the tools and strategies of person-centered approaches will seem strange and unfamiliar. As a result, IEP teams are frequently uncomfortable using person-centered tools and strategies and may try to fit them into a model with which they are more comfortable. As familiarity and experience with each tool increases, IEP teams usually develop an understanding of how the tools work together. In addition, they learn to modify many of the tools to suit their needs and preferences and the needs and preferences of their students.

The person-centered toolbox includes a number of tools and strategies that are common in all person-centered approaches. They may be called various names by different authors of the specific approaches, but, essentially, all person-centered approaches share five common tools and strategies:

1. Assessment tools
2. Planning tools
3. **Collaborative teaming** and action-planning strategies
4. Circles or networks of formal and informal supports
5. **Community resource mapping**

Assessment and Planning Tools

Assessment tools are used to discover the unique preferences, experiences, skills, and support needs of individuals with disabilities. Clark and Patton (2004) created a computerized Transition Planning Inventory. This user-friendly transition assessment may be used by three people along with the student to detail his or her strengths and preferences. It is a valuable instrument to use in the person-centered transition planning process. One of the most frequently used assessment strategies is *mapping*. Specific frameworks exist for developing each assessment map and they can be created in 15–30 minutes. Like all assessment tools, each map will provide a unique type of data about a student's background, preferences, connections to people and places, communication style, medical and health behaviors, hopes, goals, and fears. Maps generally focus on skills or experiences the student has already obtained. Assessment maps do not take the place of traditional assessment tools but instead offer capacity-building data about those students for whom traditional assessment tools typically provide more data on deficits than abilities. Maps can be used by teachers to build the self-determination skills and behaviors of students by guiding them through a self-discovery process.

Maps can also be used as planning tools. They provide IEP teams with a vision of the individual's desired future or goals. Students can create them before participating in their IEP meetings, shared with family members and peers as appropriate for feedback, and then shared at the beginning of the IEP meeting. These maps provide a unique picture of a student's dreams for life after school. Once again, there are specific frameworks for developing planning maps, and each one typically requires 15–30 minutes to create. Planning maps provide IEP teams with an individualized focus for each student and a foundation on which to write and prioritize every IEP goal, objective, and activity.

One example of a planning map would be to assess the lifestyle satisfaction of a person. Consider Kristin, a young woman with an intellectual disability, who developed a map of her life outcomes (Figure 4.1). In this example, Kristin and the people who know her best have identified four phrases to describe the aspects of her life that bring satisfaction: *relationships, community activities, sensory,* and *personal attention.* Kristin and her team then more clearly defined each word or phrase by providing examples of what each means to Kristin, as noted by the bullet points in the square boxes. The ovals are used to identify activities that would enhance the opportunities for Kristin to experience quality-of-life outcomes in those four key areas. When Kristin engages in a variety of experiences, Kristin and her transition team are asked to evaluate what key areas were fulfilled by engaging in that activity. The team would also use the planning map to review how satisfying the activity was and change, alter, or enhance future life experiences. This method of looking at activities and events in Kristin's life is not intended to be free of bias but, rather, to be a focal point of discussion about how a variety of experiences can bring satisfaction to Kristin's life.

Collaborative Teaming and Action-Planning Strategies

Collaborating with other professionals, as well as parents, can be extremely beneficial—not only to facilitate communication but also to benefit the student. Research shows that students whose parents are active participants in their education show better outcomes and lower at-risk behavior (Whitbread, Bruder, Fleming, & Park, 2007). Collaborative teaming and action-planning strategies are used to develop and pursue transition postsecondary and annual IEP goals for the student and to identify interagency linkages, responsibilities, and timelines. Wehman and Wittig (2009) developed suggestions to help teams determine needed members and next steps. Teaming and action-planning strategies are also used to monitor and evaluate progress and to solve problems and create solutions.

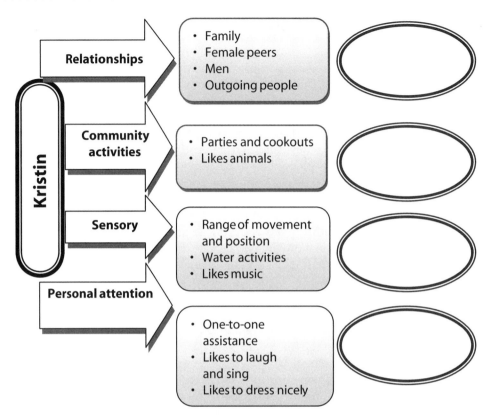

Figure 4.1. Four key areas of life quality and satisfaction as defined by Kristin and her transition team. Activities to enhance satisfaction in the four areas would be entered in the ovals on the right-hand side.

For example, consider Tyler, whose disabilities present challenges. Tyler's transition IEP team collaborated with him to develop action steps for his future.

Tyler Tyler is an 18-year-old man who lives with his adoptive father since the divorce of his adoptive parents. He had been residing with them and his biological sister since removal from the custody of his biological parents at age 4. Tyler was diagnosed with **attention-deficit/hyperactivity disorder**, mild intellectual disabilities, and depressive disorder. Tyler says that school is a "necessary evil," and that he does not enjoy going to class. He is far below grade level academically; his reading and math skills are equivalent to those of the third to fourth grade. He occasionally has discipline problems at school related to skipping classes and smoking. He has held, and lost, a couple of part-time jobs. He rides his bike to school and around his small, suburban neighborhood. Tyler states that he enjoys being outside and playing basketball. Tyler does not see himself going to college but would like to work close to his home. Tyler and his transition IEP team have agreed that Tyler will explore a variety of career options that suit his needs and interests.

Coordinated Circles or Networks of Formal and Informal Supports

A coordinated circle or network of formal and informal supports is created around each transition-age student. To be most effective, each student must have a network that includes several teams, each operating both independently and interdependently. For example, the IEP team provides one team, operating within the mandates of educational legislation. The team is responsible for writing and implementing the IEP according to mandates and policies.

Students may have another team or circle of support consisting of peers, high school friends, and classmates. This circle provides students with comfortable opportunities to refine goals, explore interests and strengths, practice self-determination behaviors and skills, and receive invaluable peer feedback. This circle operates within the culture of high school settings and rituals of adolescence.

Students may have yet another circle of support consisting of parents and other family members, adult mentors, neighbors, church members, co-workers, and employers. This circle provides students with additional opportunities to refine goals, explore interests and strengths, practice self-determination behaviors and skills, and receive equally invaluable feedback from experienced adults. This circle operates within the various cultures of family homes, workplaces, neighborhoods, and other community environments.

The common member across each of these teams is, of course, *the student*. Some students will naturally and easily develop all of these networks, communicate and behave effectively within them, and use all of the opportunities they offer to pursue postsecondary goals. Most students with disabilities, however, need help building their circles, communicating and behaving appropriately within the circles, and using all of the opportunities they offer to pursue their goals. Calabrese et al. (2008) studied the benefits of a specific program that utilized circle theories: "Circle of Friends." They found that networks provided a transformative experience for all participants, regardless of their role, and promoted social inclusion for students with disabilities.

Community-Resource Mapping

Community mapping is an effective professional development activity for all types of teachers who use a contextualized teaching and learning approach. Mapping can acquaint teachers with the target community's culture, resources, transition assets, and needs. Community mapping is best done in small groups of three or four students whenever possible to ensure a variety of perspectives and insights. Crane and Mooney (2005, p. 3) identified community mapping as occurring in four distinct steps:

1. "Premapping," which includes setting a goal and vision
2. "Mapping" local resources
3. "Taking action," which includes action-planning strategies
4. "Maintaining, sustaining, and evaluating mapping efforts"

When educators engage in community mapping, they explore such things as resources, housing, businesses, social services providers, recreational facilities, religious institutions, neighborhood history, and public opinion about local issues. For students and their transition planners, the objective of the exploration is to develop baseline knowledge about the community's current issues and assets that will become an intrinsic part of their transition planning. This experience also allows students and teachers to explore career opportunities that may be relevant to the students' goals and interests.

The challenges facing every IEP team are selecting and modifying the tools, such as community mapping, that are most appropriate for individual students and that the settings and materials are idiosyncratic to a given school, adult services agency, or community. An additional challenge is remaining person-centered when facing the realities of largely systems-centered programs, environments, and processes.

Student-Directed Transition Individualized Education Programs

As mentioned before, person-centered planning and student-directed planning do not have to be separate entities. It is only once a team truly understands and utilizes person-centered planning that the infrastructure is in place to allow a student to successfully direct his or her own transition IEP. Research has shown that student-directed IEPs are becoming an established recommended practice (Martin et al., 2006a; Thoma & Wehman, 2010; Woods et al., 2010). Student-directed IEPs have many student benefits including increased motivation, academic achievement, and self-determination (Thoma & Wehman, 2010). When a student directs his or her own IEP it brings the focus back to the student's desires, goals, and strengths (Martin , Sylvester, & Martin, 2006).

Evidence-Based Practices in Transition Planning

Federal laws and initiatives have placed a high priority on establishing and implementing evidence-based practices into the field of transition planning and services (Powers et al., 2005). Evidence-based practices are practices that have been substantiated through high-quality research to demonstrate a "supporting link between results or outcomes and a practice" (Kohler, 1993, p. 108). Kohler was the first to substantiate recommended practices for transition services. As new research has developed, eight recommended practices are recommended for transition planning and services (Landmark, Ju, & Zhang, 2010):

1. Paid or unpaid work experience
2. Employment preparation
3. Family involvement
4. General education inclusion
5. Social skills training
6. Daily living skills training
7. Self-determination skills training
8. Community or agency collaboration

These domains can be starting points for assessing areas of student strengths and needs. Incorporating multiple, if not all, practices into the student's transition planning and training will produce more effective outcomes.

What Are the Best Steps to Implement Person-Centered Individualized Transition Planning?

In general, person-centered approaches require teams to follow six basic steps that fit within the traditional model used by most IEP team members (Figure 4.2). At the end of a student's high school experience, the final step a transition IEP team will take will be to hold an exit meeting where the student's summary of performance is completed and discussed. The steps are grounded in the values discussed in this chapter and facilitate the use of the tools and strategies that make agencies and transition-planning activities person-centered. The following sections describe the six-step process in sequence and include the activities that are necessary for developing person-centered and individualized statements of transition services within IEPs. Suggestions are also offered regarding responsible personnel and timelines for completion of each step.

Many excellent transition planning manuals are available (e.g., Storms, O'Leary, & Williams, 2000; Thoma & Wehman, 2010; Wehman, 2011b; Wehman & Wittig, 2009). These manuals provide specific and tested guidelines for transition IEPs that can be adapted to the unique needs of individual students in specific communities. This chapter is somewhat unique in that it provides IEP teams with specific examples of how person-centered tools and strategies can be combined with these guidelines to make transition services more person-centered and, ultimately, more individualized.

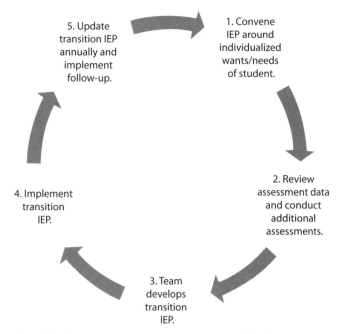

1. Convene IEP around individualized wants/needs of student.

2. Review assessment data and conduct additional assessments.

3. Team develops transition IEP.

4. Implement transition IEP.

5. Update transition IEP annually and implement follow-up.

Figure 4.2.   Best steps to implement person-centered individualized transition planning include a continuous process of assessment, development, data collection, and follow-up. *Key:* IEP, individualized education program.

Step 1: Convene Student-Focused IEP Teams, Individualized Around the Wants and Needs of Each Transition-Age Student

Initiating transition planning for students with disabilities is the responsibility of the **local education agency (LEA)**, because the school is the primary provider of services to youth during the transition-planning years. However, LEAs should not be solely responsible for individualized transition planning; they require the cooperation of local adult services providers, families, and students. Community-wide transition activities should be documented in a local interagency agreement, a critical tool that enables school systems and community core teams to initiate, implement, and monitor interagency transition-planning processes.

Identify All Transition-Age Students

Formal transition planning must begin for all students who receive special education services during the year in which they turn 16. Some states (Virginia, Delaware, and Rhode Island, to name a few) commence transition planning at age 14. Van Dycke, Martin, and Lovett (2006) highlighted incorporating the student in the transition IEP process using a birthday party as the metaphor. Year after year, the student was uninvolved, not invited to his own party. Suddenly in adolescence the student was expected to orchestrate the content for and participate in his IEP meeting. There are many ways to incorporate a student into the IEP process through an open dialogue of the IEP process and goals several years before the transition IEP. A statement of appropriate measurable postsecondary goals based upon age-appropriate transition assessments for the student must be included in the transition IEP. Furthermore, the transition assessments must be related to training, education, employment, and, where appropriate, independent living skills. The transition services (including courses of study) must be identified to help the student reach the postsecondary goals (Individuals with Disabilities Education Improvement Act [IDEA] of 2004, PL 108-446). The IEP team must identify (as appropriate) interagency linkages (e.g., referrals to community service boards, employment providers, or university offices of student affairs) or responsibilities (e.g., job placement activities of **vocational rehabilitation [VR] counselors,** a college course for which a sign language interpreter is needed). Again, the responsibility of establishing these links between agencies is not solely the responsibility of the LEA.

A teacher, social worker, guidance counselor, or other designated personnel typically assumes the role of transition coordinator. The transition coordinator is responsible for compiling the list of transition-age students and overseeing the remaining steps in the transition-planning process. This person operates within the procedures that have been determined by the LEA and the community core team. In many communities, these procedures are documented in a local interagency agreement, which is one tool that can assist collaboration between two agencies. Interagency agreements, also known as memorandums of understanding, that are developed at an operational or local level are often informal in nature, whereas state-level agreements can be highly formalized written documents signed by senior administrators of participating agencies. Good interagency agreements promote actions that directly or indirectly improve personal outcomes for those receiving services and promote systems change.

Identify Appropriate School Service Personnel

School personnel (e.g., teachers, therapists, counselors) who have been involved with the individual student targeted for transition planning should be identified to participate in the individualized transition-planning process. When enlisting school personnel for involvement, the transition coordinator should be careful to solicit input from all staff that has had recent and meaningful contact with the student. However, the number of participants actually attending the transition IEP meeting should be kept to a minimum so that teams are not too large to work productively as a group.

Identify Appropriate Adult Services Agencies

Needed and desired adult services agencies should be contacted when their services can be used best. It is vital for transition coordinators to be knowledgeable about existing local adult service agencies and their functions, resources, and abilities to avoid overloading the agencies when they cannot be active participants. Arrangements should be made (and once again documented in a local interagency agreement) for representatives to participate in the transition-planning process for students in their final 2 years of school. In some cases, it may be desirable to involve representatives before the final 2 years of school; however, transition coordinators should be aware of the very large caseloads of adult services workers and should refrain from requesting earlier involvement unless it is required for certain students. Instead, typically during the early secondary years, adult services providers will assist transition IEP teams best in an informal consultative role and through their participation as community core team members.

During the crucial final transition years, adult services representatives can provide valuable information about the available and most appropriate programs and placements for a particular student as he or she leaves the school program. Adult services areas from which representatives may be drawn include mental health, intellectual disabilities, VR, social services, and other local organizations such as The ARC (formerly Association for Retarded Citizens of the United States) and the United Cerebral Palsy Association. The likelihood that the student will benefit from an agency's participation or will be using its services in the future determines that agency's involvement. When the transition coordinator is knowledgeable regarding the functions and service capabilities of adult services providers and agencies, he or she is better able to identify appropriate agency representatives for participation in transition-planning meetings.

Identify Appropriate Members of the Student's Networks

To truly function as an individualized transition-planning team, the members of the team must, by definition, vary from student to student depending on the vision that the student and his or her family have for the future. When person-centered values and practices are applied to transition planning, one is reminded that students will need to rely on a network of people to make their dreams a reality. Thus, the approaches suggest that people other than paid professionals and service providers be identified. With the help of individual students and their families, transition coordinators must identify these people and define roles for them to play in the transition-planning process. For example, one student may want extended family members to attend all or parts of the transition IEP meeting to support the student's articulation of his or her goals and to describe their roles in supporting the student's accomplishment of the goals. Another student may want an employer or co-workers to attend part of the meeting to support the student's articulation of interests, skills, experiences, and dreams. Yet another student may not want to have a specific person attend the transition IEP meeting because the person has not supported the student's preferences and goals in the past.

Thus, person-centered approaches require that transition coordinators and systems must begin to identify the unique networks around each student, ask the student and family about their comfort with various potential team members, and respond to the student's and family's wants and needs in putting together an individualized transition-planning team. The student and his or her family may find it helpful to develop a relationship map. Figure 4.3 provides an example of some networks you may want to consider when developing a relationship map. Another way to encourage student-directed, self-determined IEP and other transition-planning meetings is to simply ask the student and his or her family to develop a list of people they want and need, define roles for them to play, and invite them to attend the appropriate meetings or parts of meetings. Questions to consider in identifying appropriate members and the roles they might play include

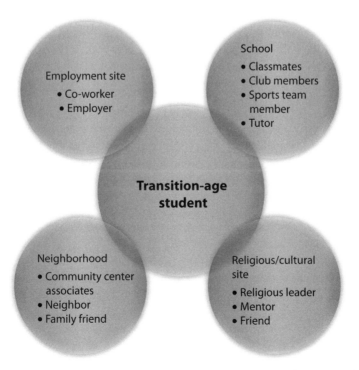

Figure 4.3.   Potential transition-age student networks can be developed from a variety of communities including employment, school, cultural, and neighborhood.

- Who knows you best?
- Whom do you trust and feel comfortable around?
- Whom do you look to for advice and support?
- Whom would you like to help you plan your transition from school to adulthood?
- How can these people best help you (e.g., by giving you letters of recommendation, by helping you create a dream map, by attending your transition IEP meetings and helping you communicate, by sitting in on your meeting and hearing how you will learn best when you go to college)?

At a minimum, the student, his or her family, and a special education teacher must be included as transition IEP team members. Typically, a general education teacher and a vocational educator will also be members. In addition, a VR counselor and one or more representatives from other adult services agencies will be included. As person-centered values and practices begin to be embraced, other family and community members become involved. Table 4.5 identifies key members of the person-centered transition-

Table 4.5.   Roles and responsibilities of transition IEP team members

Team member	Required?	Role/responsibility
Student	Yes	Share personal preferences, interests, skills, goals, wants, and needs (with supports as needed). Ask questions and provide information. Negotiate wants, needs, and goals with professionals and family. Assume responsibility for completing agreed-on goals and objectives.
Parents	Yes	Share student and family's preferences, interests, skills, dreams, support wants, and needs. Negotiate wants, needs, and goals with professionals. Focus the team's planning on the student and family. Provide informal experiences and trainings, if possible. Ask questions and provide information.
Special educators	Yes	Target students eligible for transition planning and coordinate data collection and management. Organize and attend IEP/transition IEP meetings. From student's vision, identify referral needs and ensure that they are made to appropriate adult services agencies. Coordinate the writing and implementation of IEPs/statements of transition services. Ensure that the student's and family's wants, needs, and goals are articulated, understood, and used to drive transition planning.
General educators	Yes	Consult with the IEP team on general education inclusive opportunities, graduation requirements and assessments, and the student's progress and support needs. Help identify and analyze postsecondary education opportunities and needs. Provide instruction in general education classrooms and environments.
Vocational educators	Yes	Consult with the IEP team on vocational opportunities, local employment trends, and specific skills required for jobs. Help identify and analyze community-based vocational training sites. Provide instruction at community-based vocational training sites as necessary. Assist students in creating a vocational resume and portfolio. Provide leadership roles in job placement activities for students during their last years of school.
Vocational rehabilitation counselors	Yes, if paying for or providing service	Serve as a consultant to the team throughout the student's secondary education years. Coordinate the identification and delivery of vocational rehabilitation services (e.g., vocational assessments/evaluations; postsecondary training; job placement, supported employment) through the development of an individualized plan for employment. Provide leadership roles in job placement activities for students during their last years of school.
Adult service providers	No, but encouraged under PCP model	Share responsibility for assessment of student's wants and needs as necessary. Conduct home visits and case management as needed or appropriate. Attend meetings for students in their last years of school or for students at high risk of dropping out. Provide follow-along services once students have been placed in supported living or supported employment programs.
Other family and community members	No, but encouraged under PCP model	Ask questions and provide information and support to the team on various issues that the student and family want to address, such as sexual, wellness, medical, social, financial, or guardianship issues.

Key: IEP, individualized education program; PCP, person-centered planning.

planning team and their roles and responsibilities throughout the transition process. Ameer's transition IEP team used person-centered planning techniques to meet his needs.

Ameer   Ameer is a shy and gentle young man who enjoys spending time alone or with small groups of people. Ameer also has a diagnosis of autism spectrum disorder. Ameer's transition IEP team would like Ameer to be more physically active. After exiting school next year, Ameer plans to move into a two-bedroom apartment. He wants to have his own bedroom, to choose a roommate to share his apartment, and to have a desk with a rocking chair. Currently, Ameer spends a lot of his free time watching television and sleeping. Ameer notes that he enjoys cooking, taking walks, and going to coffee shops. He wants to do these activities when he moves into his new apartment. Ameer and his transition IEP team have agreed that they would like him to experience a variety of activities that allow him to choose some additional preferred leisure options.

Step 2: Review Assessment Data and Conduct Additional Assessment Activities

Transition IEP teams typically have available to them a great deal of educational, psychological, health and medical, behavioral, and vocational data on adolescents with disabilities. Unfortunately, much research focuses on deficits (i.e., what a student cannot do) or problems (i.e., what a student can but should not do). During the transition-planning process, it is essential to move beyond traditional ways of describing and assessing students with disabilities. The time has come to think about students' dreams, their preferences, their gifts and capacities, what they can contribute to their communities, and what they need to accomplish their dreams and make their contributions. For most, if not all, transition-age students, traditional assessment data will need to be supplemented with person-centered assessment tools and strategies in order to respond to these areas.

The goal of all person-centered assessment activities is to get to know individuals with disabilities as people with unique personalities, hopes, dreams, and support needs. Person-centered assessment tools require an initial focus on abilities and a subsequent focus on support wants and needs. Person-centered assessment tools remind transition IEP teams that each student has a set of experiences, networks of people, and a set of preferences that make the student unique. The tools likewise remind transition IEP teams that every adolescent has dreams and fears and that every family has dreams and fears for its own members.

Effective use of person-centered assessment tools requires IEP teams to leave behind preconceived notions of disability labels and test scores. Team members should ask themselves, *What do we need to know about this student that traditional evaluations do not tell us?* Only when teams know a student as an individual should they go back and use traditional assessment tools and data (as necessary) to identify disability labels, test scores, and deficits. But supplementing the data with the results of person-centered assessments is always important.

The crucial task in conducting person-centered assessment activities is to identify the appropriate individuals as members of the assessment team. In traditional, systems-centered agencies and organizations, assessment activities are conducted by a multidisciplinary or interdisciplinary planning team. Individuals with disabilities and their families may be invited to attend these meetings, but they are seldom viewed as equal members of the team or as experts. Extended family, friends, neighbors, co-workers, church members, and other people who serve as natural supports are almost never invited to participate. In contrast, person-centered assessments bring to the table people who 1) know the student well, 2) support or potentially can support the student during the transition process, and 3) are chosen by the student or family to participate in assessment activities. Thus, person-centered assessments are as likely to involve restaurant co-workers, members of softball leagues, and real estate agents as they are school psychologists. Direct support staff, personal care staff, and peer tutors who interact daily with the student are as likely to participate in the assessment process as are physical therapists who see the student weekly or itinerant vision teachers who see the individual biweekly.

To help illustrate the important and unique role that groups of people can play in the life of a student with disabilities, various person-centered planning approaches refer to groups called circles of support or circles of friends (Calabrese , Patterson, Liu, Goodvin, Hummel, & Vance, 2008; Holburn & Vietze, 2002). These individuals are drawn from the student's and family's networks and may play various and highly individualized roles during the transition-planning process. Some may be members of the transition IEP team; many others will not be members. A circle may be initiated by a student, by a family member, by a friend or advocate, by a teacher, by a transition coordinator, or by anyone else who is interested in guiding the assessment and planning activities being conducted by the transition IEP team.

To accomplish person-centered assessment activities, a circle might meet once, twice, quarterly, annually, or on some other as-needed schedule. A circle typically meets at the student's home or other comfortable setting before the team meeting to guide the transition IEP's development and after the team meeting to support its implementation. The tools and strategies used by the teams as well as the meeting schedule are dictated by the unique nature of the student's desired outcomes and by the characteristics of the agencies targeted to serve and support the adolescent as he or she makes the transition from school to adult life. The circle's goal at this step in the transition process is to ensure that the student and other transition IEP members have all the data necessary to write a person-centered and comprehensive transition IEP. Ultimately, once the assessment phase is completed, all circle members will have to make some hard decisions about the time, energy, and other resources they are willing to contribute to assist the adolescent in attaining his or her goals.

Mapping person-centered models offers some unique assessment tools that assist circles and transition IEP teams in thinking about and discovering the student's gifts, capacities, and support needs. Group graphics, also known as mapping, is one of the most unique tools associated with person-centered planning approaches (see previous section on assessment and planning tools). Mapping uses color, symbols, words, and pictures to gather and record information about people. Information is collected using an interactive group process and recorded on large sheets of paper for the entire team to view and discuss. Research has demonstrated that the group process can be a reliable and valid assessment approach that successfully includes students, families, and support personnel in the assessment and planning procedures (Holburn , Jacobson, Schwartz, Flory, & Vietz, 2004; Robertson, Emerson, Hutton, et al., 2007; Wigham, Robertson, Emerson, et al., 2008).

According to each person-centered model, a team begins the assessment process by identifying lists, maps, or graphics representing the student, typically known as a personal profile. Suggested maps to include in a personal profile vary from approach to approach and by the goals, wants, and needs of the individual (Croke & Thompson, 2011; Nelson, 2005). There are a variety of person-centered planning models. Some examples of planning models include Group Action Planning (Blue-Banning, Turnbull, & Pereira, 2000), Opportunity Mapping (Swedeen, Carter, & Molfenter, 2010), Making Action Plans (O'Brien & Pearpoint, 2003), and Planning Alternative Tomorrows with Hope (O'Brien & Pearpoint, 2003). For more explanation of a variety of approaches, see Kilbane and Sanderson (2004) and Blessing (2011). As the transition IEP circles become proficient in using mapping, they can choose specific maps or create their own maps to include in a personal profile on the basis of the wants and needs of the student they are getting to know and the type of services and supports the student wants and needs.

Whatever maps are chosen, circles and transition IEP teams should consider getting to know these things about transition-age students with disabilities:

- People in the student's life, both paid and unpaid
- Where the student spends his or her time

- Things that people see as contributing to the student's positive reputation
- Things that people see as contributing to the student's negative reputation
- Preferences (e.g., things that motivate the student and create happiness)
- Nonpreferences (e.g., things that do not work for the student, that create frustration and unhappiness)
- Personal goals and dreams
- Most important priorities to work on now (2–12 months) and in the future (1–5 years)
- Opportunities (e.g., things or people that can help the student achieve personal goals and dreams)
- Obstacles or barriers (e.g., things or people that are getting in the way of the student's achieving personal goals and dreams)
- Strategies to help the student overcome obstacles or barriers and achieve personal goals and dreams

In sum, circles and teams can create assessment maps before IEP meetings to guide the development of statements of transition services. As an alternative, maps can be created by students as part of classroom self-determination activities provided by teachers. Many of the commercially available self-determination curricula (e.g., *Next S.T.E.P., Steps to Self-Determination, TAKE CHARGE for the Future, Whose Future Is It Anyway?*) use mapping or similar self-discovery activities to encourage teenagers to get to know themselves in order to be more active and informed participants in their transition-planning process.

Regardless of whether assessment maps are created by circles, by transition IEP teams, or by students themselves, students must be encouraged, prepared, and supported in sharing what they have learned about themselves at the beginning of their IEP meetings. Much of the systems-centeredness surrounding the development of IEPs can be minimized by making the student with a disability the focus of assessment activities. For example, consider asking students what assessment information they would like to find out about themselves. Circles and self-determination activities are excellent tools and strategies for making transition planning more person-centered and individualized. When these practices are adopted, together, the student and family, professionals, and community members can let go of old assumptions and begin thinking about adolescents with disabilities in new and different ways. Deficit-finding assessment activities must be eliminated as a part of individualized transition planning. Instead, people with disabilities must be viewed with respect, as people who are capable and prepared to build goals on their strengths, unique talents, and interests.

Step 3: Students and Their Teams Develop Transition IEPs

Developing the actual transition IEP document requires extensive planning and execution by the entire IEP team (Figure 4.4). Many times, the transition IEP is seen as a summative document rather than a formative one. Transition IEPs should be actively discussed and *developed* within the IEP meeting. All transition IEP team members should have input into the creation of this vital planning document. As demonstrated in this chapter, the transition IEP falls in the middle of a transition-planning cycle—not at the beginning or end. Transition planning should be constantly assessed and revised based on the student's skills and needs.

Schedule the Transition Individualized Education Program Meeting

Transition IEP meetings for eligible students should be scheduled so that the student, his or her parents or guardians, school personnel, adult services representatives, and

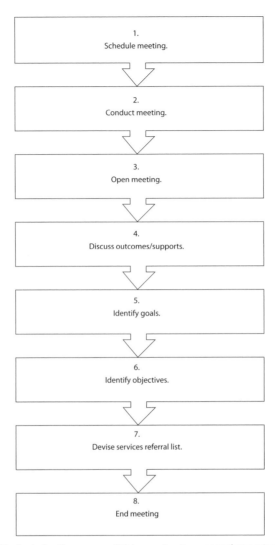

Figure 4.4. Transition individualized education programs (IEPs) are an iterative process that requires multiple steps. To be productive, transition IEP meetings need to be open and goal-focused.

community members can attend. The student should always be included in the scheduling and planning of the transition meeting so that he or she can play an active and informed role in planning his or her future.

Before the transition IEP meeting, the transition coordinator should identify any need for cross-agency sharing of information about transition-age youth and should ensure that release forms can be signed by the appropriate people. These arrangements are essential because the LEA is prohibited from releasing confidential information on students in special education programs without the signature of a parent, a guardian, or the student if the student has reached the age of majority.

Conduct the Transition Individualized Education Program Meeting

Development of the transition IEP should be conducted as the opening component of a student's IEP meeting. In this way, IEP goals and objectives can be written to reflect the individualized postsecondary goals. A transition IEP addresses desired adult outcomes along with the desired services and supports necessary to achieve and maintain these desired goals. In contrast, an IEP identifies skill and behavioral impairments and remediation strategies. An effective transition IEP matches the specific strategies and behavioral objectives of the IEP with desired postsecondary employment, education, training, and independent living goals.

The meeting format outlined and discussed in the following sections is based on a typical transition-planning strategy used in LEAs in many states. Following these procedures will help team members develop transition IEPs that include

1. Clearly defined and expected postsecondary outcomes
2. Selection of desired and appropriate services and supports to achieve those postsecondary outcomes
3. Delineation of skill and behavioral objectives that must be met to arrive at the postsecondary outcomes

Open the Transition Individualized Education Program Meeting

The transition coordinator or the person conducting the meeting should welcome and introduce all meeting participants. An informal atmosphere is recommended so that the student and his or her parents will feel as comfortable as possible. The professionals have the responsibility to encourage honest and open participation from everyone in attendance.

As specified previously, the student or family, with support from other team members as needed, should open the meeting by articulating a future vision statement—a statement of desired outcomes. Consider the case examples of Rosa, Ameer, and Tyler. Both the student and the transition IEP team collaborated to develop a future vision statement that reflected both desires and needs. The articulation of a student's dreams or desired outcomes requires important decisions on the part of an IEP team who is attempting to operate in a more person-centered manner. In particular, team members must ask themselves, *Can we support this student's desired postsecondary outcomes?* And, more specifically, *Do we believe this student can and should accomplish these outcomes?* and *Do we have or are we willing to develop the capacity necessary to support this student's accomplishment of these outcomes?* An important part of the transition-planning meeting during this step is listening to and ensuring understanding of desired and expected outcomes as articulated by the student and family. Following this, the entire transition IEP team must agree to support all of the student's desired postsecondary goals and outcomes, some of them, or none of them and, in some cases, respectfully negotiate with each other until the entire team reaches consensus on a future vision statement. Next, the team must begin to discuss specific outcomes that can be attained through IEP and postsecondary goals, objectives, linkages, and responsibilities.

Generate a Discussion of Desired Outcomes and Available Support Services

Following articulation of the student's future vision or dreams, the remainder of the transition meeting should progress through stages to ensure that delineated goals and objectives are specific enough and person-centered enough to achieve the desired outcomes. A comprehensive transition IEP should address *all* of the student's and family's desired and expected wants and needs. Typically, a comprehensive transition IEP addresses expected outcomes and desired services and supports in vital areas (Table 4.6).

Table 4.6. Vital areas covered in a transition IEP

Employment opportunities	Friendship and socialization needs
Postsecondary education opportunities	Transportation needs
Living opportunities	Health and medical needs
Financial and income needs	Legal and advocacy needs

Key: IEP, individualized education program.

For each outcome area, the team should consider the following five questions:

1. What is the student's dream?

2. What skills or behaviors does the student need to learn to attain this dream?

3. To what locally available programs, services, and supports should referrals be made to support this dream?

4. What responsibilities must education, adult services, and student and family team members assume to make this dream a reality?

5. What program, service, and support gaps and barriers exist that must be addressed by community core teams and/or family- and student-initiated circles of support?

The transition IEP team must acknowledge that schools and adult services may not be able to provide all of the services and supports necessary for the student to attain all desired outcomes. For example, a transition IEP team may support one student's dream of owning his own home but may also recognize a local lack of the services and supports necessary for the student to attain the dream. In this case, the team may agree to support the dream and identify the IEP skills and behavioral goals and objectives the student needs to attain the dream. The team may also identify the interagency linkages necessary to initiate the dream, such as a referral to VR for employment services or a referral to the agency that provides services for individuals with intellectual disabilities for supported living services. Next, the team may suggest that the family assume responsibility for contacting a local bank and nonprofit housing organization to determine availability of affordable housing loans. Last, the team might share the student's future vision statement with the other circles or networks and ask them to review the student's dream and consider expansion of local services and supports to assist the student. Likewise, students' dreams and preferences should be strongly emphasized along with these five questions in the establishment of transition goals for all desired outcome areas.

Thinking about student outcomes is not limited to the individual student. Transition coordinators and other school personnel may have to submit data to their state regarding transition-planning practices and outcomes. The federal Office of Special Education Programs requires states to submit data regarding the long-term outcomes of students with disabilities. Two major areas of data collection include what are called *Indicator 13* and *Indicator 14*. Indicator 13 measures a state's percentage of youth aged 16 years and older with an IEP that includes coordinated, measurable, annual IEP goals and transition services that will reasonably enable the student to meet the postsecondary goals. There also must be evidence that the student was invited to the IEP team meeting where transition services were to be discussed and evidence that, if appropriate, a representative of any participating agency was invited to the IEP team meeting with the prior consent of the parent or student who has reached the age of majority. Indicator 14 measures a state's percentage of youth who had IEPs, who are no longer in secondary school, and who have been competitively employed, enrolled in some type of postsecondary school, or both, within 1 year of leaving high school (IDEA, 2004). It is extremely important for special educators to be aware of federal requirements to ensure that they are implementing them correctly throughout the IEP process.

Identify Postsecondary Goals

Having discussed and agreed on desired outcomes, the IEP team must now consider long-term goals in all desired outcome areas. A goal should include the desired outcome (e.g., full-time employment) and the appropriate service delivery model to achieve the goal (e.g., a supported competitive employment approach). Wehman and Wittig (2009) developed a transition IEP curriculum with more than 50 sample transition IEPs. Each of these IEPs had important postsecondary goals that were seen by teachers and families as crucial in life success. These IEPs reflect real students' goals and provide illustrations of blueprints for success. The typical goal areas included postsecondary career training, employment, education, financial, self-advocacy, independent living, and so forth. Some examples for postsecondary goals to consider include

- Full-time employment with time-limited VR services for job development and job interviewing assistance
- Part-time employment in a group enclave model with two or three co-workers
- Part-time college attendance with an interpreter and note-taking assistance from the college's office of student affairs
- Part-time community college attendance with braille books and audiobooks provided by the college's office of student affairs
- Community living in a supported living apartment program with two roommates and 24-hour supports
- Participation in an integrated recreation program (e.g., beginners' swimming at the YMCA) with support from a local peer-advocate program
- Enrollment in a local health club with facility accessibility and staff in-services provided by a local hospital occupational therapy center
- Community access with training on use of the public transportation system provided by the high school program
- Estate planning with services provided by a pro bono law clinic

Each goal should also include

- The projected date for achievement of the goal, specifying completion before or after graduation
- Delineation of the agencies responsible for attaining this particular goal
- The people primarily responsible for seeing that the goal is achieved by the date set for completion

Determine Objectives and Steps to Accomplish Goals

The IEP team must also identify the objectives and sequence of steps needed to accomplish each postsecondary goal. Typically, objectives should be written for those skills and behaviors that a student needs to learn to attain his or her goals. Thus, mastery of designated objectives is the responsibility of the student. Objectives should be written according to the LEA's policies and procedures on developing IEPs and should include all appropriate components (e.g., level of present performance, modifications or accommodations needed in regular class). Objectives should be concrete, measurable, and attainable. Typically, actions should be identified for all interagency linkages and responsibilities (i.e., those actions to be assumed by students, family members, teachers, adult services providers, and other members of the transition IEP team). This can be done in much the same way as writing a task analysis, the step-by-step delineation of all activities from beginning to end that are necessary for accomplishment of a desired goal. Action steps should also include the responsible team members and time lines for completion.

Devise a Services Referral Checklist

To achieve postsecondary goals, multiple smaller steps may be necessary to ensure a smooth transition. For example, the next step may be to coordinate services and meetings with various service agencies. On the basis of the needed goals and services as identified by the transition IEP team, agency representatives should be designated as responsible for beginning the formal referral and application processes that will initiate the appropriate adult services. Application and referral forms must be completed by each of the adult services representatives who are identified as having a role in the student's postschool life. These may include, for example, representatives from the VR agency, social services, community mental health and intellectual disabilities services, the local Social Security office, the local supported employment program, local recreation center, or a local college or university.

End the Meeting

At the end of the meeting, all participants should sign the transition IEP. The student's case manager, typically the transition coordinator or special educator, should send copies of the transition IEP to all participants as soon as possible. Information describing adult community services should be given to the parents or the student at this time.

Step 4: Implement the Transition Individualized Education Program

Operating under the terms of an interagency agreement, those agencies that are responsible for goals or specific steps in the transition IEP should implement the plans as prescribed. Most of the transition-planning goals will require cross-agency involvement. Some services may be needed immediately, whereas other services may be needed over a period of several school years and may even extend beyond graduation.

Thinking about assessment in new and different ways and creating transition IEPs with goals that reflect the desires and needs of students lay the foundation for agencies to function in a person-centered manner. However, writing person-centered IEPs represents only one component of person-centered planning. Once transition IEP teams have developed personal profiles and have written transition IEPs for students, the teams are then ready to tackle the discussion, planning, and systems-change activities necessary to implement the plans in a truly person-centered manner. At this point, most agencies will have a very *clear* idea of desired consumer outcomes—and most likely, a very *unclear* idea of how the agency can support consumers in attaining their desired outcome.

Agencies that are sincerely invested in person-centered approaches must actively take on the challenging role of assisting consumers in reaching their goals and changing existing consumer support systems. Such a role requires the creation of new relationships with consumers and family members as well as new relationships with community members. This role also requires a revision of existing services and the creation of new service directions. Finally, to be successful, the role requires an effective and coordinated working relationship among all agency personnel including executives, middle managers, and direct support staff.

With the values and tools associated with person-centered planning in place, educators must turn to managing the actual logistics of transition-programming design. For students to attain their dreams, successful implementation of the transition IEP requires the commitment and energy of people in all of the student's various networks. The transition IEP team must implement a set of objectives and activities as specified in the transition IEP. The student must pursue skill and behavioral objectives as specified in the transition IEP.

For many students, a circle of support or circle of friends, either meeting regularly and formally or working informally, will also work on behalf of the student to supplement the efforts of the transition IEP team and the student. Typically, circles will dedicate themselves to activities such as creating assessment maps, helping the student prioritize wants and needs, supporting the student by attending IEP meetings, accompanying the student and family on site visits to interview and choose desired programs, making telephone calls to verify terminology and eligibility procedures, writing letters to appeal decisions or plead cases, providing informal behavioral and skill-training experiences to supplement what is offered in the IEP, and other person-centered activities. The role of the circle is to assist the student in setting goals, developing strategies, and solving problems. The circle members make a commitment to act on behalf of the student and do whatever they can to help the student accomplish his or her goals. As they develop the personal profile, the circle of support should also discuss strategies for working with the IEP team, supporting the goals and activities of the transition IEP, and problem solving any barriers to desired services and supports.

Step 5: Update the Transition Individualized Education Programs Annually and Implement Follow-Up Procedures

As the student nears graduation and completes eligibility for a free and appropriate public education, adult services agencies should increase their involvement with the student. At this point, the school should concentrate on transferring its information and services to these agencies. One of the agency liaisons should be designated to follow up on the progress of the transition IEP as the student exits school. This may mean calling the transition coordinator to check on the status of individual goals or items. Follow-up should occur at least quarterly to ensure completion of all steps and, thus, increase the likelihood of achieving goals. Follow-up may also involve organizing and scheduling another meeting of IEP team participants if goals are not being achieved as planned. Annual or more frequent revisions of the original IEP may be required.

Step 6: Host an Exit Meeting to Discuss Summary of Performance

Toward the end of a student's last year in school, the school liaison and adult services representatives should plan an exit meeting with graduating students and their parents to finalize plans for the transition to adult life. At this time, any final needs relevant to the transition process can be addressed and will be compiled into a summary of performance. The revision of IDEA (2004) included a statute that states: "For a student whose eligibility under this part terminates under circumstances described in clause (i), a local educational agency shall provide the [student] with a summary of the [student]'s academic achievement and functional performance, which shall include recommendations on how to assist the [student] in meeting the [student]'s postsecondary goals" (§ 614[c][5][B][ii]). As the group compiles the summary of performance, they should examine goals that have and have not been achieved by their scheduled completion dates and verify goals that are scheduled for completion shortly after graduation. The team should review the goals that have not been achieved as scheduled and those scheduled for postgraduation for acquisition and relevancy. Achieved outcomes should also be discussed to determine how the student and his or her family are faring with the new activities. The student can use the completed summary of performance to educate future agencies, employers, and/or supports of his or her academic and functional abilities. Table 4.7 provides a sample post–high school checklist for use by the student and transition IEP team.

Table 4.7.   What a student will need post–high school checklist

1. What skills will the student need to access support services on college and university campuses?	
2. Will the student have regular competitive employment opportunities?	___ yes ___ no
3. Will competitive employment programs offer ongoing employment supports?	___ yes ___ no
4. Will various transportation options (e.g., drivers, public buses) be available?	___ yes ___ no
5. Will residential alternatives, such as supported living, group homes, and in-home companions, be available in the community?	___ yes ___ no
6. Will various leisure activities such as cycling club, ballroom dancing, and YMCA membership be available, and will the student be encouraged to check out these recreational options?	___ yes ___ no

From Wehman, P. (2011). *Essentials of transition planning.* Baltimore: Paul H. Brookes Publishing Co.; reprinted by permission.

Conclusion

As is seen in this chapter, there are a number of tools and strategies that transition IEP teams and, specifically, classroom teachers and transition coordinators should consider adopting to more fully individualize the transition-planning process:

- Invite students, their families, and other community members to attend transition IEP meetings and share their stories and experiences as part of the assessment data.
- Devote classroom time to having students pursue self-determination activities, develop maps, and receive peer and family feedback.
- Support students in developing dream maps or future vision statements and presenting their visions at the opening of their transition IEP team meetings.
- Use the future vision statement to drive the identification and prioritization of all IEP goals, objectives, and activities.
- Encourage students and families to identify and use their networks or circles of support throughout the multiyear transition process to supplement transition IEP team actions.
- Encourage other transition IEP team members to recognize the importance of a student's networks and expand responsibility for transition actions to networks of people beyond the traditional IEP team.
- Develop a mechanism to share transition IEP future vision data and summaries of performance with community agencies so that person-centered systems-change activities can be pursued.

Three factors are critical to the successful implementation of a person-centered transition IEP:

1. The involvement of transition IEP members who are knowledgeable about the student, the family, and the availability of local services
2. A process that ensures the identification of all desired outcomes within the least-restrictive service options
3. The ability of community agencies to provide or procure the needed services communities with well-written interagency agreements, a wide array of community service options, and a collaborative plan to address service needs, will produce the best chances of achieving desired outcomes for each student

Study Questions

1. Discuss the values of person-centered planning.
2. Describe various assessment tools and strategies that can be used in person-centered planning.
3. Interview a teacher or transition specialist about nonstandardized transition assessment instruments that can be used in the transition-planning process.
4. Interview a student and family member who have participated in the transition IEP about their experience.
5. Compile a list of adult service team members who should be involved in IEP planning and then contact them to discuss their experiences and advice on how to promote collaboration.

Online Resources

Ansell-Casey Life Skills Assessments evaluates the life skills of youths and young adults. They are completed online and automatically scored: http://www.caseylifeskills.org

Whose Life Is It Anyway? How a teenager, her family and teachers view the transition process: http://www.waisman.wisc.edu/hrtw/wlia.pdf

The Council for Exceptional Children's Division on Career Development and Transition provides resources, fact sheets, and links for secondary transition: http://www.dcdt.org

Transition Coalition provides online information, support, and professional development on topics related to the transition from school to adult life for youth with disabilities: http://www.transitioncoalition.org

National Secondary Transition Technical Assistance Center provides research-based resources for secondary transition planning: http://www.nsttac.org

Virginia's self-determination project provides tutorials as well as reproducibles for the classroom: http://www.imdetermined.org

National Dissemination Center for Children with Disabilities provides a wealth of information about disabilities and resources including person-centered planning and transition planning: http://www.nichcy.org

Cornell University's Person Centered Planning Education Site includes online learning modules: http://www.ilr.cornell.edu/edi/pcp/index.html

A variety of videos demonstrating Making Action Plans and Planning Alternative Tomorrows with Hope used by actual students: http://www.inclusive-solutions.com/pcplanning.asp

Multicultural Transition Planning

Including All Youth with Disabilities

AUDREY A. TRAINOR AND SUNYOUNG KIM

5

After completing this chapter, the reader will be able to

- Define *diversity* in individual, community, and societal contexts of transition
- Recognize the patterns of postschool outcomes across disability, race/ethnicity, and gender
- Understand transition and diversity issues through case application
- Use an ecological lens to examine diverse preferences, strengths, and needs relevant to transition planning and education
- Identify strategies for transition planning and education for diverse youth

This chapter addresses issues in transition education (i.e., planning and instruction) that interface with the range of individual- and community-level variation associated with diversity. First, we explain what diversity means in the context of transition. Second, we examine patterns of postschool outcomes commonly used as indicators of transition success across multiple sociodemographic variables such as race/ethnicity, gender, and disability. Third, we use ecological theory to emphasize the importance of considering the contexts of interactions between individuals in transition and their communities that include education, employment, and daily living. We present cases to illustrate the interactions and contexts that impact individuals' lives in diverse ways throughout the transition process. Throughout this chapter, we have included strategies for improving the postschool outcomes for diverse youth, aligning our work with the results orientation of transition planning and education.

Defining *Diversity*

In the sociopolitical and historical context of the United States, the term *diversity* is complex and takes on many meanings. *Diversity* has largely been used to communicate the importance of considering the range of students' experiences and identities that are often linked to disability, race/ethnicity, gender, socioeconomic background, or language, among myriad other factors (Greene, 2011). Often, the word *diversity* is used synonymously with the word *culture*. Focusing solely on cultural group memberships is limited though, because it fails to account for change and variation. Change and variation make generalizations based on group membership impossible. To avoid the perils of stereotyping, one way to consider culture is to think about the practices associated with cultural communities (Gutierrez & Rogoff, 2003). In this way of thinking, becoming an adult in the United States is associated with a range of practices: leaving compulsory education, finding and maintaining employment, going to college, becoming financially self-supportive, starting a family, and so forth. These practices, however, do not tend to happen in a predictable fashion. Some young adults maintain employment before leaving public schools, whereas others maintain employment and enroll in postsecondary education while contributing to a household family income, and so on.

Prediction based on group membership is not possible, yet examining patterns of postschool outcomes is important so that we develop a repertoire of transition strategies that meets the needs of a diverse group of young adults with disabilities. Used in this broad way, diversity means differences in experiences, opportunities, preferences, strengths, and needs. For example, identifying effective transition practices for youth who live in poverty may include providing detailed information targeted at applying for postsecondary financial aid to parents and young adults who have few collective experiences in seeking financial aid, understanding eligibility and access, or advancing an application. At the same time, we differentiate because we understand that some young adults from low socioeconomic backgrounds may have previous knowledge of these processes or require different support because their parents or other key adults in their lives (e.g., an older sibling) have guided them. Based on existing strategies in transition and inclusive active learning, Tables 5.1 and 5.2 provide ideas for embracing diversity through transition planning and educational activities that can be differentiated to meet individual preferences, strengths, and needs.

Patterns of Postschool Outcomes

Similar to viewing images captured in three-dimensional stereograms, examining postschool outcomes from different angles affords different perspectives and views. Gender-based transition experiences, for example, may differ across disability or racial/ethnic

Table 5.1. Tips for writing transition plans that address diversity

Strategy for improving transition planning	Ideas for action	Embracing diversity in process
Organize a regularly scheduled student-member transition group.	During the transition group meeting, students are grouped according to grade level and their transition plan. The parents review their child's work from transition group as well as provide information as a partner.	• Explicitly acknowledge to students and families values such as self-determination that are embedded in transition programming. • Have students complete an informal assessment of the values they and their families promote during the transition to adulthood. • Map individual-, school-, and community-level values to students' transition goals.
Begin transition planning early— no later than the beginning of high school.	Early planning with the student, family, teachers, and administrators includes informal interviewing, observing in natural settings such as community-based work experiences, and information gathering to create a profile of preferences, strengths, and needs.	• Invite members of civic, business, and faith communities to motivate students by sharing their experiences and paths to transition success. • Hold an annual informational session that outlines transition timeline objectives for common long-range goals such as college enrollment.
Interview youth about their transition goals, beginning early and updating regularly.	Youth interviews should be broad and encompass transition domains of postsecondary education, employment, independent living, and recreation/leisure.	• Have students interview family members to identify employment- or education-related natural supports (e.g., family members who have connections to internships, siblings in college). • Organize peer interview sessions, allowing students to develop the interview guide.
Assist students in the development of transition portfolios.	Portfolios include the student work samples, photos of community involvement, video/audio interviews with family and peers, and awards that illustrate students' identity and relate to long-range goals.	• Provide instruction on using technology to develop an electronic portfolio that interfaces with social networking tools. • Organize a celebratory forum for students to share portfolios with community and family.

Sources: Kellems and Morningstar (2010); Harry, Kalyanpur, and Day (1999).

categories. This point underscores the importance of considering individuals' cultural identities (e.g., socioeconomic background and race/ethnicity) as both plural and fluid. Another important point is that understanding patterns of postschool outcomes requires us to simultaneously consider inter- and intragroup variation. For example, although poverty disproportionately affects Native Americans, not all Native Americans live in poverty. In a similar way, many young adults of Mexican heritage are bilingual; however, some have a range of language and literacy skills in English or Spanish only. In other words, when teachers have knowledge of youths' cultural identities, they begin to understand factors that *influence* rather than *dictate* their experiences.

Lastly, how we identify and serve youth with disabilities may also interfere with our ability to see and understand patterns for at least three reasons. First, the relationship between disability label and outcome is difficult to unpack to examine both societal- and individual-level factors (Trainor, Lindstrom, Simon-Burroughs, Martin, & Sorrells, 2008). This presents a challenge to our efforts to solve problems. Sorting out which barriers are related to the societal response to disability and those related to the disability itself is useful as we generate solutions. For example, are poor postschool outcomes of youth with emotional/behavioral disabilities (EBD) associated with barriers related to limited access to mental health and other related services? And/or, does having an EBD manifest barriers to establishing healthy relationships and prosocial behavior expected in work, postsecondary, and community settings?

Table 5.2. Addressing diversity through inclusive active learning contexts in transition education

Strategy for increasing student engagement	Process and advantage	Embracing diversity in process
Create cooperative learning groups.	Whether heterogeneously or homogeneously constructed, grouping students to collaborate and contribute to collectively problem solve strengthens individuals' social and content learning.	Frame transition goals as common questions or problems in need of solving: For example, have a group of students answer the question, *How can we locate employment opportunities during tough economic times?* by interviewing local experts, creating a community job board, and identifying volunteer and internship opportunities with proximity to school and home. Once information is collected, provide a group platform for sharing.
Engage in informal group discussions.	Students are motivated by opportunities to share reflections and opinions and learn from one another during informal discussions where the risks of penalty or grading are decreased.	Bring together recent graduates with incoming juniors and seniors to discuss tips for applying to and staying in college, beginning the session with faculty involvement, but slowly allowing the returning young adults to lead the conversation and answer questions from current students who may not want to ask their teachers and parents. For example, one discussion might be entitled, "The top-10 steps to identifying a college that is right for you!"
Promote social and content learning through the use of the Internet.	Web-based social networking and informational tools provide students with expanded transition-related resources.	Use web-based social networking tools to help students establish social networks of peers who share information about employment and educational opportunities that are available for youth and young adults. For example, establish a virtual job club with members who have a range of experiences. This club might include a mix of experienced adults who provide online mentorship and check in via e-mail, young adults in college who function as e-mail pals, and transition-aged students who otherwise have limited access to these resources in local contexts.

Source: Montgomery (2001).

Second, some youth are in double jeopardy of failure because they are identified with a disability *and* they face additional discrimination or other obstacles relative to group membership (Blackorby & Wagner, 1996; Skiba, Simmons, Ritter, et al., 2008). For example, are youth with intellectual disabilities (ID) vulnerable to poor postschool outcomes because they face disability-related biases and obstacles? And/or do these barriers reflect those associated with racism and poverty that affect historically marginalized youth who are overrepresented in this disability category?

Third, analyzing postschool outcome data across groups of youth focusing on a combination of racial/ethnic, socioeconomic, gender, and disability backgrounds, and thus more accurately representing a person's lived experiences, is uncommon (Ferri & Connor, 2005). Life experiences cannot be neatly identified according to group membership. For example, do Native American males with learning disabilities (LD) who are from middle and upper socioeconomic backgrounds have more positive postschool outcomes compared with their disability- and racial-group peers from low socioeconomic backgrounds?

Answering these important questions is no simple matter and requires a variety of data and analytic tools that address the role of culture in teaching and learning (Cole, 2010). To begin to understand the state of transition across groups of youth with disabilities, a comprehensive and recent study, the second National Longitudinal Transition Study (NLTS-2) is an important resource. The study comprises longitudinal data across 10 years from more than 10,000 secondary school youth with disabilities who comprise a nationally representative sample (Valdes, Godard, Williamson, et al., 2006). In the following sections, we use the NLTS-2 to examine postsecondary enrollment, employment, and community living across disability and other sociodemographic variables.

Postsecondary Enrollment

Data from the NLTS-2 confirm that youth with disabilities are more likely now than they were in past generations to attend college. Of the disability categories included under the Individuals with Disabilities Education Improvement Act (IDEA, 2004), more than 50% of youth with speech-language (SLI), hearing (HI), visual (VI), orthopedic (OI), other health impairments (OHI) including attention-deficit/hyperactivity disorder, attend some post-secondary institution (Newman, Wagner, Cameto, & Knokey, 2009). This is also true for youth with autism, traumatic brain injury, and deafblindness. Perhaps most confound-ing are the diminished rates of postsecondary enrollment (47%) of youth with LD. Youth with ID and EBD are also among the least likely to enroll in 4-year colleges (Newman, Wagner, Cameto, & Knokey, 2009). See Figure 5.1 for postsecondary enrollment across disabilities. Recent trends in programs designed to reach youth with ID, however, have increased access and enrollment as families and young adults with these disabilities have increased expectations to attend postsecondary institutions (Neubert, Moon, & Grigal, 2004).

Poverty negatively impacts postsecondary enrollment and degree attainment. Consideration of socioeconomic backgrounds reveals that wealthier youth across dis-ability categories are significantly more likely to attend 2-year colleges; however, this difference was not as pronounced at the 4-year college level (Newman et al., 2009). Consid-eration for race among youth with disabilities yielded no significant differences between European Americans, African Americans, and Latinos, when race/ethnicity was a factor considered across disability categories (Newman et al., 2009). Studies that have examined postschool goals and transition education, however, have documented that girls and boys with high-incidence disabilities lack access to general education curricula and effective transition planning and that these barriers can be pronounced for African American and Latino youth, as well as for all youth across racial/ethnic groups from low socioeconomic

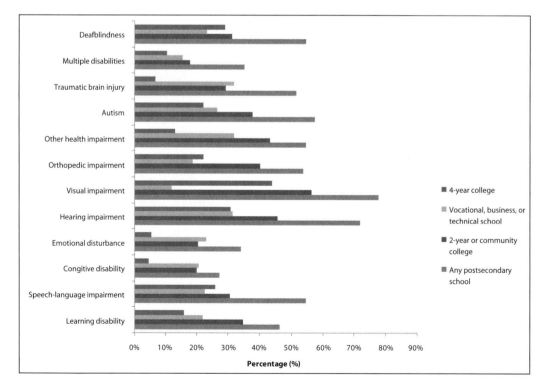

Figure 5.1. Percentage of postsecondary school enrollment since leaving high school, by disability category. (From Newman, L., Wagner, M., Cameto, R., & Knokey, A.M. [2009]. *The post-high school outcomes of youth with disabilities up to 4 years after high school: A report from the National Longitudinal Transition Study-2* [p. 17]. Menlo Park, CA: SRI International; adapted by permission.)

backgrounds (Gil-Kashiwabara, Hogansen, Geenen, Powers, & Powers, 2007; Trainor, 2005, 2007a). Questions about the intersection of disability and race or race and socioeconomic backgrounds across disabilities remain in need of further study (Trainor et al., 2008).

Beyond enrollment, academic program selection, accommodations, and degree attainment are also important details in the transition to postsecondary enrollment. Because disability-related accommodations are based on eligibility and not entitlement at the postsecondary level, it is interesting to note that as many as 55% of young adults who have received services for disabilities in K–12 grades do not consider themselves disabled (Newman et al., 2009). Eligibility documentation required of postsecondary students seeking accommodations for disabilities, however, varies widely and, thus, may be a source of confusion for services providers and students (Madaus, Banerjee, & Hamblet, 2010).

Employment

In general, people with disabilities face many obstacles to full-time employment (Kaye, 2003). The NLTS-2 employment rates illustrate that young adults with disabilities are employed at rates similar to those of their age-peers without disabilities, but their employment status seems to fluctuate at a higher rate (Newman et al., 2009). Employment rates and earnings vary by race/ethnicity (Figure 5.2). Socioeconomic background is another factor that has an impact on employment (Figure 5.3). Unfortunately, youth with disabilities from low socioeconomic backgrounds are less likely to become employed after high school, contributing to a cycle of poverty.

In interview studies, youth from low socioeconomic backgrounds face unique struggles when seeking employment. Job coaches may be focused on placement; however, youth point out that they are unlikely to maintain employment when the jobs do not match their interest, strengths, and needs, even when the income earned is essential to the family budget (Trainor, Carter, Swedeen, Cole, & Smith, 2011). Developing familial and social networks is also particularly important to identifying and maintaining employment opportunities for youth with EBD and other high-incidence disabilities (Lindstrom, Doren, Metheny, Johnson, & Zane, 2007; Potts, 2005). Across disability categories, youth with LD are among the most likely to have a variety of employment experiences (Newman et al., 2009). These early work experiences are considered one of the strongest predictors of

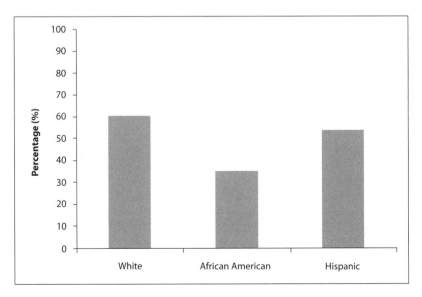

Figure 5.2. Percentage of youth with disabilities with paid employment since leaving high school, by race/ethnicity. (From Newman, L., Wagner, M., Cameto, R., & Knokey, A.M. [2009]. *The post-high school outcomes of youth with disabilities up to 4 years after high school: A report from the National Longitudinal Transition Study-2* [p. 50]. Menlo Park, CA: SRI International; adapted by permission.)

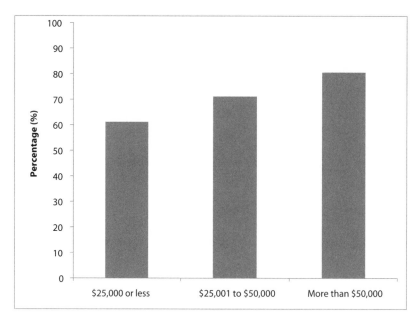

Figure 5.3. Percentage of youth with disabilities with paid employment since leaving high school, by household income. (From Newman, L., Wagner, M., Cameto, R., & Knokey, A.M. [2009]. *The post-high school outcomes of youth with disabilities up to 4 years after high school: A report from the National Longitudinal Transition Study-2* [p. 50]. Menlo Park, CA: SRI International; adapted by permission.)

postschool employment (Benz, Lindstrom, & Yovanoff, 2000). Young adults with significant ID and EBD, however, are less likely to access employment opportunities (Carter, Ditchman, Sun, Trainor, Sweeden, & Trainor, 2010). Poor outcomes are also associated with both Hispanic (Miller & Arango, 2011b) and African American (Miller & Arango, 2011a) individuals who experience traumatic brain injury.

Community Living

Nearly 3 decades ago, Halpern (1985) expanded the conceptual model for transition for people with disabilities beyond its previous, singular focus on employment. Community living is an expansive term that can include the rights and responsibilities of U.S. citizenship (e.g., voting, abiding by laws), everyday chores (e.g., maintaining a home), and social experiences (e.g., making friends, joining clubs, pursuing hobbies). Data from the NLTS-2 contain a wealth of information about community living across disabilities. Unfortunately, between 47% (youth with LD) and 62% (youth with OI) report that they spend the majority of their free time watching TV, a potentially solitary pastime (Newman et al., 2009). Also revealing is that the rate these youth report spending time with friends seems low: only 9% of youth with autism (on the low end of the continuum) and 38% of youth with OI (at the high end of the continuum) report spending free time with friends.

Socioeconomic background is an indicator of diversity that has an impact on free-time activities and experiences such as computer use and Internet access. Whereas 47% of youth with disabilities from high socioeconomic backgrounds report technology use, the same is true for only 26% of their peers from low socioeconomic backgrounds (Newman et al., 2009). Using technology has obvious implications for success in postsecondary and employment settings. To address the digital divide experienced by youth who receive special education, and in particular for youth from historically marginalized groups, teachers can promote and support youths' school-based and public access to technology and instruction across learning environments (Kalyanpur & Kirmani, 2005).

The ability and effort of young adults with disabilities to maintain their rights and responsibilities are also important. Across disabilities, 67% of young adults who have received special education are registered to vote and 25% report that they engage in community service (Newman et al., 2009). Young adults with LD, SLI, VI, and OHI are the most likely to report that they are members of a community group or organization, whereas only 11% of young adults with ID and 20% of those who have a traumatic brain injury are socially connected to their communities in this manner (Newman et al., 2009).

It is regrettable that interactions between the U.S. juvenile and adult justice systems and young adults with disabilities emerge as a critical issue in the field. As many as 31% of youth with disabilities reported involvement in violence (e.g., fighting, carrying a weapon) since high school (Newman et al., 2009). Young adults with EBD are far more likely than their peers with other disabilities to have had this negative experience. Although the NLTS-2 report does not disaggregate arrest rates by race/ethnicity and disability category, the overrepresentation of African American males in the category of EBD make it likely that African American males with disabilities are disproportionately interfacing with the juvenile justice system (Wilder, Ashbaker, Obiakor, & Rotz, 2006). Being bullied or socially ostracized, commonly reported problems associated with special education, is correlated with aggression and delinquency (White & Loeber, 2008). Clearly, rights and responsibilities shape access to further education and career trajectories as youth with detention or incarceration records seek employment and postsecondary financial aid.

Attitudinal, institutional, and societal barriers limit the opportunities both to access high-quality transition education and planning and to pursue postsecondary education and employment goals. Many youth are resilient and achieve postschool success despite these barriers; however, transition specialists must continue to develop awareness and understanding of the barriers and strategies for minimizing their deleterious effects. In the next section, we provide a framework for understanding and action.

Thinking Ecologically: Understanding Culture as Interaction and Process

It is obvious that preparing diverse groups of youth for life after high school cannot rely on simple solutions that equate group membership with experience. Educators must avoid assumptions about disability, gender, race/ethnicity, and so forth as they plan and educate youth, but they must also be aware of potential challenges youth face as a result of marginalization *and* consider preferences, strengths, and needs that are associated with shared experiences and culture. Important to note is the role that communication across groups and individuals potentially plays in all educational experiences. Table 5.3 provides a list of basic steps for improving cross-cultural communication during transition planning and educational activities.

More generally, one useful framework for broadly considering diversity is Bronfenbrenner's ecological theory of development, a theory that has been applied to special education contexts (Garcia & Dominguez, 1997; Gil-Kashiwabara, Hogansen, Geenen, Powers, & Powers, 2007; Trainor, Lindstrom, Simon-Burroughs, Martin, & Sorrells, 2008). Following the brief description of the model, each component is discussed in detail with case study examples that illustrate how diversity can be incorporated into transition planning and instruction.

The Ecological Systems Model

Ecological models encompass five major systems (Bronfenbrenner, 2005). These are depicted in Figure 5.4. The microsystem encompasses all contexts that directly involve an individual; this includes an individual's family context as well as his or her school context. The mesosystem refers to the connections and relationships across microsystems that

Table 5.3. Communicating effectively across communities, families, and individuals

Foundational concept	Communication, both verbal and nonverbal, is a distinctive aspect of community- and society-level identities and contributes to individuals' feelings of belonging and experiences as members of a group. *Intercultural communication* is communication across groups based on any number of characteristics that contribute to identity, including disability, gender, class, and race/ethnicity.
Steps for improving cross-cultural communication	Ideas for action
Increase awareness of the backgrounds of students and their families	Understand the historical, political, and social context of the lives of students and families. For example, if there is a history of disability overidentification, anticipate families' concern when communicating disability-related information and have sufficient evidence to support claims about students' social and academic achievements.
Be sensitive to communication feedback, bracketing defensive reactions	Listen and observe communication from families and students, following or responding to social and verbal cues that indicate (dis)satisfaction and (mis)understanding. For example, if a parent is consistently absent from transition-planning meetings, identify barriers that are preventing the formal exchange of ideas and goals.
Self-assess personal motivation to engage in communication across cultures	Pay attention to personal levels of anxiety, biases and prejudices, and willingness to engage in groups and with individuals whose identities differ from self. For example, gauge and reduce negative feelings by increasing familiarity with others' preferences, strengths, and needs.
Develop effective cross-cultural communication skills	Increase awareness of varied language and communication both of self and of other. For example, note personal communication style variation in teacher–teacher exchanges versus teacher–parent and teacher–student communications, employing appropriate verbal and nonverbal cues that facilitate positive relationships such as greeting parents and older family members using appropriate titles or home languages, if just for a few words in salutation.

Source: Gudykunst (2003).

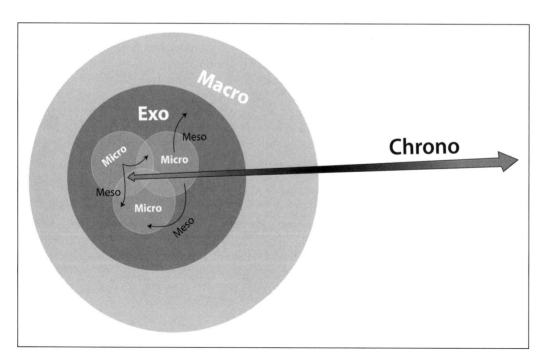

Figure 5.4. Bronfenbrenner's ecological system model explains the correlation of each level of ecological context. The chronosystem contextualizes the other four major systems of the ecological model. (*Sources:* Bronfenbrenner, 1979; Bronfenbrenner, 2005.)

directly involve the individual (e.g., interactions between families and school personnel). The exosystem expands beyond the immediate environment, referring to embedded contexts that connect to the microsystem but do not directly involve the individual (e.g., a parent who is called to active duty in the armed forces must leave the family, potentially affecting the youth's emotional well-being and daily routines). The macrosystem represents the larger culture and includes attitudes, policies, social supports, barriers, and so on about employment and disabilities. The fifth system is the chronosystem and captures the aspect of time, both an individual's lifetime and the social histories of people, as influential to development. As youth with disabilities mature over time, for example, many begin to develop more specific career goals.

Three Transition Cases

The following case studies in transition reflect the complex diversity characteristic of the contemporary U.S. population. Two of the youth might be considered youth "of color" because they are of Latino and Asian heritage; both are bilingual to varying degrees. Mariana, who has LD, is fully bilingual in Spanish and English, and Min-Ho, a young man with autism, comprehends spoken Korean and English but speaks mostly English. All three have diverse strengths and disability-related needs. Socioeconomically, Frank, a European American young man with attention-deficit disorder and emotional disabilities, living in a foster home located in a rural area, struggles more than Mariana and Min-Ho, his middle-class peers. He experiences marginalization associated with poverty, foster care, and having an incarcerated parent. In the remainder of the chapter, we use an ecological systems lens to examine the experiences of Mariana, Frank, and Min-Ho as they transition into adulthood. In doing so, we are able to highlight the complexities of diversity created by the divergence of experiences that create both fortitude and vulnerability.

Mariana   Mariana is a bilingual 18-year-old junior who receives special education for a specific LD in math. She moved to the northeastern United States from Puerto Rico when she was a baby, accompanied by her father, mother, and two older brothers. The family currently resides near friends and extended family members. Her mother died when Mariana was in middle school. Although Mariana and her father live in a large U.S. city, their neighborhood is a tightly knit community and many residents attend the same church for worship throughout the week, recreate together, and access local businesses to meet their daily needs. Mariana's family owns a small business and is actively involved in the community. Mariana's father serves on the local board of Latino-owned businesses, the Latin Business Association.

Mariana receives all of her classes in the general education setting at her school. She works with a special education teacher who functions as her case manager. Mariana's neighborhood high school faces some of the challenges associated with urban education, including failure to make adequate academic progress with a majority of students. Seventy-three percent of the students in Mariana's high school are eligible for free or reduced-cost lunch. The racial/ethnic composition of the student body is 1% Native American, 4% Asian American, 13% European American, 19% Latino, and 63% African American. The racial/ethnic composition of the faculty and administrators at the high school is 2% multiracial/multiple ethnicities, 2% Latino, 14% African American, and 82% European American. Twenty-seven percent of the students use English as a second language; Spanish and Urdu are the most common first languages of this population.

Mariana and her father expect that she will attend a local community college and live at home after high school. Currently, she works in the family business on Saturdays. Mariana does not have a driver's license but she is familiar with public transportation. She has several key friendships with other young women in the neighborhood. Her dream is to pursue a career in marketing or a related field and to help her father and brothers run their family business.

Frank   Frank is a European American 16-year-old who grew up in small town in the Midwest. One year ago, he moved to a group foster home in a rural area near his hometown. Frank was diagnosed with fetal alcohol syndrome (FAS) shortly after birth; later, he was also diagnosed with bipolar disorder and attention-deficit disorder, and has been receiving services for OHI and EBD. Frank has attended seven different schools, including a Head Start program in his hometown, and has been intermittently involved in the juvenile justice system since he was 11 years old. He lives with foster parents who manage a group home for Frank and three other children. Frank's residency at the group home is court-ordered and he has mandatory, regular contact with a probation officer, a social worker, and a court-appointed advocate. Occasionally, Frank's birth mother and maternal grandmother visit him at his foster home. He is expected to be a long-term resident of this group home, living there until he reaches adulthood.

Frank attends an alternative high school that is also a separate special education setting. All 40 students in the school receive special education services and all have been adjudicated for infractions such as truancy, vandalism, and misdemeanor theft. The student and faculty populations are 94% and 100% European American, respectively. The school maintains a vocational preparatory curricular focus, offering several courses and work-study programs in fields such as agriculture, information technology, and construction. Each student is required to complete placements in two unpaid internships and one paid summer employment experience. A transition specialist at the school helps place students in internship settings.

Frank would like to pursue a career in farming. He has worked as a volunteer with a local farmer at the county agricultural cooperative, and he would like to pursue an internship at the large animal hospital close to his home. He relies on his foster parents for transportation as public options are nonexistent and he does not have a driver's license. Frank's interpersonal relationships are a source of difficulty for him; however, he has had mostly positive interactions with his foster family.

Min-Ho   Min-Ho is a 20-year-old Korean American with high-functioning autism. He was born in the United States and currently lives with his parents and typically developing younger sister. He is a part-time community college student where he participates in a vocational training program. His parents came to the United States to study and initially had planned to go back to Korea after his father received his Ph.D. from a university in the southwestern United States; however, the family decided to live in the United States after Min-Ho was diagnosed with autism. When Min-Ho turned 5, his family moved to a city in California with a large Asian immigrant population. Currently, his father has a faculty position at a local college.

Min-Ho attended an inclusive high school, but he spent most of his time in a special education classroom. He took art classes in an inclusive setting and had lunch with typically developing peers. The school's vocational training program provided diverse levels of training for students with disabilities. The program is linked to the county and community colleges and aims to help students with disabilities continue their vocational training after they graduate from high school. Min-Ho and his parents were satisfied with the high school's vocational training program, and they originally planned for him to receive services in high school until age 22. When Min-Ho was 19, however, his younger sister entered the same high school. Family tension increased at this time because the siblings often met in the lunch area and Min-Ho's sister was embarrassed by her brother's atypical behaviors. As a result of the sister's unhappiness, their parents and the school changed Min-Ho's transition plan to reduce further conflicts between family members. Instead of staying at the high school, Min-Ho began attending the vocational program at the community college when he turned 20. As part of his training, he works as an intern at a county service center for 2.5 hours a day.

Min-Ho attends an American church every Sunday. Since he learned how to use public transportation, he meets with the youth group after services and then rides the bus home. Also, he takes classes of interest to him at the community college, including drama and art. He and his parents expect that he will finish the vocational program and get hired as a part-time usher at a theater. His parents have prioritized earning a diploma at the community college as a goal for Min-Ho.

The Individual and the Microsystem

As Figure 5.4 depicts, individuals are a part of multiple micro contexts comprising the individual and other people with whom he has direct contact. These are embedded in immediate settings where experiences and interactions with individuals influence development and learning (Bronfenbrenner, 1979). Our three cases depict the microsystemic variety in which individuals participate. Although all three adolescents interact with family members, their family structures and experiences vary. For example, Frank's interactions with microsystems include a foster care family, the composition of which can change frequently and rapidly (Geenen & Powers, 2006). Gil-Kashiwabara and colleagues (2007) found that youth in foster care had difficulty identifying caring adults who consistently listened and provided support through their transition to adulthood. In addition, changes in foster care placement for Frank may also mean high mobility in school, limiting the social networks of adults who know and understand Frank's goals for the future and the strengths and needs he brings to the transition process. For this reason, Geenen, Powers, and Hogansen (2007) have stressed the importance that individuals in foster care develop self-determination. Teachers, therefore, must acknowledge the strife and uncertainty of family life in foster care and provide opportunities for youth to develop knowledge of self, disability, goal-setting strategies, and other component skills with the same dedication that mathematics and language arts are taught.

Self-determination is an essential aspect of transition for youth with disabilities (Algozzine, Browder, Karvonen, Test, & Wood, 2001); however, its development and opportunities to practice must be responsive to a youth's individuality and cultural identities that shape experience. Those responsible for helping Frank, Mariana, and Min-Ho transition to adulthood must be knowledgeable about self-determination curricula and pedagogy, but they must also be what Gay (2000) calls *culturally responsive teachers*. According to Gay, being culturally responsive includes

1. *Understanding the history and culture of students and families.* Knowledge of marginalization and domination, of the roles that gender, race/ethnicity, and ability have played over time in the lives of people across generations, is an essential step in becoming culturally responsive. This might include reading historical and political accounts, talking with community members, attending local events, and building this exploration into school curricula. For example, Mariana's family settled into a Puerto Rican community in a large urban city. What are the struggles of that community? What are its contributions? How might these shape Mariana's opportunities to pursue a transition to a marketing career? At the microlevel, what role will gender biases and expectations play in her decision to help run the family business? How will having a math disability impact a career in marketing? Educators working with Mariana might immerse themselves in the community, visiting her family business, talking with her father and brothers, and attending local community college recruitment events to gain an understanding of the opportunities that are available to her.

2. *Employing personal and professional self-awareness.* Self-awareness requires knowledge of one's beliefs about race/ethnicity, gender, ability, and so on, as well as knowledge of the values that manifest in professional practice. For example, a transition specialist working with Frank needs to examine both her own biases and expectations for youth in foster care and youth with FAS and the ways in which professional practices (e.g., facilitating an individualized education program [IEP] meeting) promote or hinder Frank's opportunity to practice self-determination. Only when teachers recognize biases, sometimes embodied in phrases like "these kids," or deficit orientations, such as "doesn't stand a chance" or "won't go far," can they begin to self-reflect and to challenge their assumptions. Regarding cultural practices in special education, teachers should be aware, as Martin, Van Dycke, Christensen, and colleagues (2006) have amply documented, that IEP processes often block youths' participation and self-determination

opportunities. At the microlevel, how might teachers prepare Frank to participate and contribute to transition planning? How might they prepare fellow educators who attend Frank's IEP meetings to encourage and honor the student's participation?

3. *Addressing needs and cultivating strengths of the whole child while validating cultural identities.* Transition cuts across domains of learning. At the microlevel, transition educators are concerned not only with domains of knowledge and experience in academic subjects but also with those associated with daily living activities and social skills. Learning and culture are intertwined. For example, Min-Ho's parents emphasized family unity and harmony when they decided that he should move to the local community college program. Whereas teachers who embrace inclusion may have been inclined to focus attention on Min-Ho's sister's attitudes about disability, his parents chose a different approach. A transition specialist working with Min-Ho would need to recognize the multiple layers of Min-Ho's family's cultural practices that include an adult child's deference to parental decision making, a focus on the needs of the whole family, and the pursuit of higher education as a demonstration of accomplishment. Once a transition specialist understands Min-Ho's role and his parents' expectations of him as the eldest son and a youth with a disability, plans should be made to address the strengths and needs in the context of the vocational program at the local community college.

Connections and Relationships Comprising the Mesosystem

As members of an individual's multiple microsystems interact, they form connections and relationships that make up the mesosystem. The strengths and weaknesses of the mesosystem influence a person's development and learning (Bronfenbrenner, 1979, 2005). Our three cases provide examples of mesosystemic variation and the multiple ways that it plays an important role in the transition to adulthood. For example, Mariana is bilingual and, although she speaks English fluently at school, she and her brothers speak Spanish at home with her father and extended family. When Mariana's father attends IEP meetings, interactions include interpreting and negotiating meaning across languages, with and without interpreters and translators. A lack of a systematic approach to conducting special education meetings biculturally and bilingually, however, has resulted in a well-documented pattern of missed opportunities for collaboration and weakened connections that make up the mesosystem (Bailey, Skinner, Rodriguez, Gut, & Correa, 1999; Johnson & Viramontez Anguiano, 2004; Lian & Fontanez-Phelan, 2001; Ramirez, 2003; Greene, 2011). Delgado-Gaitan (2004) asserts that translated forms and interpreters must be available for parents, and she cautions that children cannot fulfill this role for teachers.

The language of communication and its contributions to the ensuing relationships between service providers and families is complex. In Min-Ho's case, for example, his parents are bilingual and do not expect or use translation or interpretation. Their preference to communicate with school personnel in English, however, does not signify that concepts about disability, adulthood, and education translate accurately from English to Korean. In 2001, Park, Turnbull, and Park documented barriers, both those that were intertwined with language and those that were not, of Korean American parents with experiences similar to Min-Ho's mother and father. Based on their research, Park and colleagues stressed the importance of connecting Korean parents to parent advocacy groups, increasing professionals' knowledge of the cultural identities of Korean immigrants, and changing structural barriers such as scheduling and personnel preparation to support more productive mesosystemic interactions.

Similar implications have been documented in studies involving families from other racial/ethnic groups. Garcia, Perez, and Ortiz (2000) documented conceptual discrepancies inherent in home–school communications about disability when Spanish-speaking Mexican mothers acknowledged language delays but did not conceive of these delays as disabling conditions, affecting their approaches to seeking and utilizing special education services. Later, Rueda, Monzo, Shapiro, Gomez, and Blacher (2005) discovered that, despite parental concerns about promoting independent living and employment skills, the lines of communication and accessible information between home and school limited mesosystemic relationships to the extent that transition planning itself was limited. Furthermore, conceptualizations of independence, influenced by cultural identities and processes, have the potential to reflect conflicting ideas between home and school. When lines of communication are open and conflict is acknowledged, according to Harry, Kalyanpur, and Day (1999), a productive discussion that facilitates decision making has the potential to emerge. Transition planning for Min-Ho might necessitate educators' sharing of the advantages and disadvantages of moving from the extended high school program to the community college vocational program, with the acknowledgment that the final decision rests with the family.

The extent to which the mesosystem is affected by the diversity of languages, divergent values, and beliefs about cultural processes such as disability, independence, and/or communication between key stakeholders varies across and within groups of people who share common characteristics. The connections that represent the mesosystem, however, are essential to transition planning and education. These connections also include connections beyond schools and families. For example, access to the general education curricula and college preparatory courses for Mariana may be affected by the mesosystem of relationships between general and special education teachers, particularly in mathematics where Mariana's LD is likely to surface and require teachers' attention. For Frank, connections among social workers, court advocates, and probation officers will likely impact the success or failure he experiences in transitioning out of the juvenile justice system before his reaching the age of majority when incarceration has far more serious implications. When transition-aged youth are involved in the juvenile justice system, mesosystemic links between transition educators and their justice system colleagues is a centrally important link to successfully transitioning to employment (Unruh, Waintrup, Canter, & Smith, 2009). Furthermore, because some of the transition services may be delivered across settings (e.g., foster care home, school, juvenile detention), all members of the team must have the common goal of transition planning (including assessment and delivery of related services) and one central transition specialist to coordinate these activities (Unruh et al., 2009).

The Exosystem: Moving Beyond the Individual and Immediate Contexts

Youth are involved in multiple environments simultaneously. The exosystem represents a more expansive context in which youths' micro- and mesosystemic experiences are embedded. Youths' involvement in the exosystem is typically indirect and lacks their active participation. Nevertheless, youths' lives are affected by activities across the exosystem. For example, many community colleges and universities have recently begun to add programming and courses for young adults with autism or other developmental disabilities (Hart, Grigal, & Weir, 2010). Although neither Min-Ho nor his parents played an active role in advocating the development of these opportunities, the creation of the programs has opened doors for him and other students with disabilities to transition into adulthood by enrolling in college and being engaged in postsecondary life. The development of these programs is representative of a paradigmatic shift away from post–high school referrals of young adults with autism and developmental disabilities to segregated, nonwork environments; concern for a history of limited outcomes for young adults with these disabilities; and strengthened links between postsecondary education and competitive employment for workers with and without disabilities (Grigal, Hart, & Migliore, 2011).

As the ongoing development and increased access to postsecondary education expands beyond disability-specific programming, colleges and universities are also responding to students who share Frank's experiences in foster care, a system of services embedded in a broader context. According to Sim, Emerson, O'Brien, Pecora, and Silva (2008) mental health services and financial aid assistance are two areas in which young adults who have been in foster care often identify need for assistance while enrolled in postsecondary settings. At the exosystemic level, opportunities for Frank and others are being made available through the establishment of programs such as the postsecondary education programs embedded in Casey Family Programs and the Orphan Foundation of America (Sim et al., 2008). The job of the transition educator, then, is to gain awareness of these opportunities and share the information with Frank and the adult advocates in his life so that they can plan accordingly.

Both Mariana and Frank have also had experiences losing parents. The death of Mariana's mother likely influenced her life in numerous and somewhat immeasurable ways. As a single parent and small business owner, Mariana's father may not be available to attend special education or extracurricular events held at the school, many of which follow a scheduling framework that reflects the traditional school day and academic year. Mariana is affected by the decisions that are made by teachers in her father's absence; however, she is not a key player in scheduling for either the business or the school. Community-based school models have been introduced as a systemic solution to barriers often faced by families in urban locales who have multiple demands on their time and involvement in educational decision making for their children. For example, the school that Mariana attends might consider adapting a school–community collaborative approach, striving to incorporate stakeholders' leadership and involvement in schools that are open centers of activity designed to meet the breadth of needs of members of the community (Center for Mental Health in Schools, 2011). This includes supporting atypical scheduling (e.g., holding parent conferences in the evening) and integrating health care and other services on site.

The loss of Frank's mother, first to addiction and then to the justice system, has affected Frank in direct and indirect ways. Microsystemically, having FAS directly impacts Frank's experiences. Mesosystemic interactions between Frank's mother and the foster care system result in regulated visits and interactions between his foster home and his birth parent. At the exosystemic level, more complex and indirect implications begin to surface. The stipulations of Frank's mother's illness and incarceration may mean that she experiences withdrawal and depression or a diminished opportunity to seek independence and gainful employment. Although these experiences are primarily associated with his mother, they may manifest in limited opportunities for her to develop a healthy relationship with Frank.

Educators cannot be expected to solve all problems or remove all barriers that youth experience. Returning to Gay's (2000) description of culturally responsive teaching, however, is a productive way to approach teaching and learning in preparation for positive transition outcomes. For example, understanding Frank's life as a child of an incarcerated parent should inform his teachers about his transition-related needs. In addition, Frank has a career goal of becoming a farmer. His teachers may consider a mentoring approach to expand Frank's access to social networks of adults that also align with his goals to pursue an agricultural vocation. Specific steps to establishing school-based mentoring approaches for youth who have been incarcerated, as well as a resource list for implementation, are outlined by Waller, Houchins, and Nomvete (2010).

The Cultural, Historical, Political, and Social Layers of the Macrosystem

The macrosystem is inclusive of the micro-, meso-, and exosystemic contexts and interactions. The complexity of the macrosystem is evidenced by the number of processes and the contextual variables that interact and result in overarching perceptions and experiences that influence development and outcomes (Bronfenbrenner, 2005). For all youth with disabilities in the United States, disability policy and its place in our labor history, and more specifically the employment of youth, is important to consider when we think about the experiences of young adults like Mariana, Frank, and Min-Ho. In the not-so-distant past, for example, youth with disabilities were not included in public education. The focus of current educational policy on access to the general education curriculum establishes a clear focus on academics, potentially reducing the availability of transition and vocational educational opportunities (Kochhar-Bryant & Bassett, 2002). Similarly, expectations and regulations of youth employment have changed over time and have influenced vocational programming, legislation, and policy that support its development. See Figure 5.5 for depiction of selected related movements.

A contemporary and specific concern related to our diverse society involves consideration of immigrant youth and their access to disability services and employment in school and as they transition to adulthood. The numbers of school-aged immigrants have rapidly increased over the past 2 decades, currently composing nearly 20% of U.S. children (Capps et al., 2005). In secondary schools, the number of immigrant students increased by 72% during the 1990s. English learners may fall into one of several protected groups identified in the No Child Left Behind Act of 2001 (PL 107-110; i.e., limited English-proficient, racial/ethnic minorities, students from low-income backgrounds, and students who receive special education). Still, one challenge of transition for all youth with disabilities is leaving a system of entitlement and entering a system of eligibility. This transition can be more difficult for immigrant youth with disabilities because eligibility for some adult services is tied to proof of citizenship. For example, a 1982 U.S. Supreme Court ruling protects the educational rights of immigrant students regardless of documentation of citizenship, making schooling an entitlement (Green, 2003). Secondary school–based services to which youth with disabilities are entitled, however, may suddenly become unavailable in early

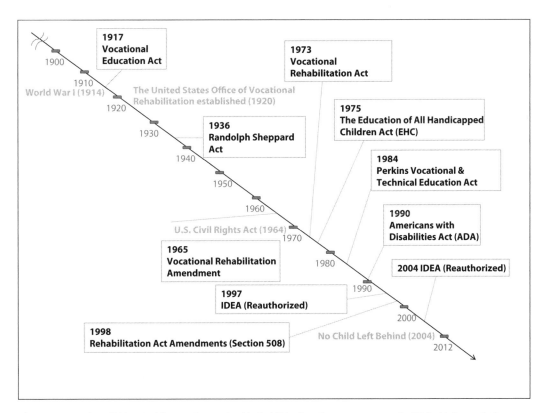

Figure 5.5. Timeline of U.S. major labor acts for people with disabilities. Boxed terms represent major U.S. legislation, and other terms indicate historical events or moments.

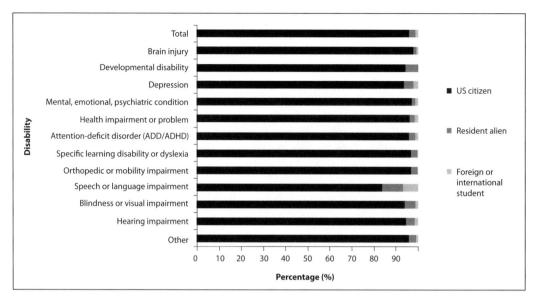

Figure 5.6. Percentage distribution of undergraduate students by citizenship and disability. (From U.S. Department of Education, National Center for Education Statistics. [2009]. Percentage distribution of undergraduate students by citizenship and disability: Preliminary condition or impairment. In *2007–2008 National Postsecondary Student Aid Survey [Ed.]*: Author.)

adulthood where services access may be based on eligibility related to disability identification, need, and the documentation of citizenship, among other criteria.

Historically, access to postsecondary education for their children has been a key factor in immigrants' decisions to come the United States. Increasing access to postsecondary education for youth with and without disabilities is also a goal of federal policy. For youth with disabilities, transitioning to postsecondary school may require the continuation of accommodations and modifications. Figure 5.6 depicts the U.S. undergraduate enrollment of students with disabilities and their citizenship status. For youth with disabilities who are also undocumented residents of the United States, barriers to admissions and eligibility for financial aid are difficult to overcome. The DREAM Act (Development, Relief and Education for Alien Minors) has been proposed to provide eligible undocumented immigrant school-aged youth who are not U.S. citizens but have been the country for several years with conditional permanent residency (Connolly, 2005). After an undocumented youth is qualified as a conditional permanent resident under certain criteria (e.g., arrived in the United States before age 16, has "good moral character," and has admission to an institution of higher education or has earned a high school credential), he or she has access to federal benefits such as attending postsecondary institutions for in-state tuition rates, nationwide (Lopez, 2007). At the federal level, this legislative proposal was originally introduced in 2001, reintroduced in 2009, and has yet to be ratified; however, individual states such as California have implemented versions of this legislation with varying degrees of success at the state level (Flores, 2010).

Teachers may or may not know of the citizenship status of their immigrant students. Because the 1982 U.S. Supreme Court decision determined that all youth are entitled to an education regardless of citizenship, it is not appropriate for school personnel to ask parents or youth for related documentation. Regardless, parents and youth who are undocumented and living and/or working in the United States are at risk of deportation and are not likely to freely share their related concerns with school personnel. In transition planning, however, it may be necessary to be sensitive to this issue based on information shared by families. Transition to employment and access to postsecondary and other disability-related services may be greatly altered by citizenship documentation and an open discussion of the necessary facts may not be possible. For youth with disabilities that significantly affect their physical or mental health and daily life functioning, the loss of related services in adulthood is potentially devastating, particularly because many undocumented families are living in poverty and cannot access such services for a fee.

As Harry and Klingner (2006) have documented, stereotypical beliefs about disadvantage color educators' views of a child's present and future educational experiences. In Mariana's case, for example, teachers must first learn about her ethnicity and understand that, despite her linguistic heritage, she is a U.S. citizen, and so are her family members. Second, bilingualism should be acknowledged as a one of her strengths. When transition teachers learn that her father has served on the board of a major local business organization, transition planning should also connect Mariana to internship and social networking opportunities with help from her father, particularly because her career goals are business-oriented. Again, validating students' heritage and maintaining high expectations are foundational to culturally responsive teaching. Similarly, Min-Ho's teachers should make efforts to bridge the cultural capital associated with applying, entering, and completing college with Min-Ho's father's career in higher education. It is likely that Min-Ho has been to his father's campus and office and understands some of the social rules and conventions common to postsecondary settings. In terms of social networking, Min-Ho's father may also have access to knowledge of precollege programming and peer mentors who would be available to work with his son. Unfortunately, connections to existing caches of families' cultural and social capital are sometimes overlooked because of a lack of transition-related information and planning or because teachers employ stereotypical thinking (Trainor, 2005, 2007a, 2008).

The Chronosystem and the Importance of Time

According to Bronfenbrenner (2005), examining time as the fifth system in the ecological model is important because time provides a lens for the examination of both developmental and generational maturation. This is an underexplored concept in educational research in general (Bronfenbrenner, 2005) and specifically in the study of transition of youth with disabilities into adulthood. Other than the NLTS-2, few longitudinal studies have been conducted with youth and their families with disabilities that examine transition; hence, this is an area in need of researchers' attention. Practitioners, however, share anecdotal information about how their students' career development goals and transition objectives change over time. The IDEA (2004) also stresses the importance of conceptualizing transition as an ongoing approach that requires frequent assessment and goal adjustment with a focus on outcomes. Some of the same techniques to culturally responsive teaching discussed earlier in this chapter could be applied when one is considering the passing of time as a factor in transition planning and education. For example, because self-determination is one of the most promising practices for transitioning youth from foster care to adulthood, Frank should be given incremental instruction and opportunities to practice as he matures and develops through high school. Because he may experience few adult connections and periods of time characterized by mobility and decreased close supervision from adults who know him well, opportunities to practice and outcomes of his attempts to be self-determining should be closely monitored over time and correspond to the demands of his ecological system, including the chronology of his development.

Strategies for Transition Planning and Education in a Diverse Society

In some ways, responding to the strengths and needs of diverse youth with disabilities who are entering adulthood mirrors evidence-based practices in transition education. Test, Fowler, Richter, and colleagues (2009) have identified such practices as providing structured, extended transition programming, community-based instruction, student and family involvement in transition planning, and student-focused transition education. At the same time, however, consideration for the complex diversity embedded in individual- and community-level experiences is essential. We have advocated the use of an ecological systems model, which facilitates an examination of transition-related experiences, opportunities, needs, and strengths from multiple angles. In addition, an ecological systems model underscores the specific junctures at which a culturally responsive approach is necessary. The following strategies, though not an exhaustive list, are jumping-off points for researchers and practitioners to consider as we strive toward positive postschool outcomes for all youth, including those from historically marginalized backgrounds:

1. Maintain high expectations for youth across groups, regardless of the perceived risks associated with sociodemographic characteristics.

2. Support high expectations by sharing the necessary information about both education- and employment-related postschool options. Sharing this information early and with both youth and their family members is essential to defining a trajectory toward goal attainment.

3. Practice reflexivity when working with youth from historically marginalized groups, questioning the use of stereotype and the unexpected or unintended application of biases. Preservice education programs frequently employ a journaling or working group approach to increasing reflexive practices.

4. Dedicate time and effort to understand the personal and cultural identities and processes that youth, their families, and educational systems contribute to transition education processes. This includes familiarizing oneself with general histories and experiences of groups and/or getting to know individuals' personal histories and experiences. In addition, maintaining awareness of and compliance with education policy is important.

5. Consider the multisystemic and ecological nature of transition as a set of interactions and processes that are embedded in individual, interactional, societal, and sociopolitical and historical contexts that influence outcomes. This includes observing and interviewing youth, family, and community members about their transition expectations and experiences and facilitating interactions on multiple levels.

6. Foster positive interactions across the ecosystem by increasing youth and family access to information (both material/factual, as well as implicit/intangible; i.e., cultural capital) and people (i.e., social capital). This includes strengthening the trusting relationships across settings. For example, consistently checking in with youth and families following transition-planning discussions increases trust and strengthens conduits of information and social networks.

7. Embrace the diversity youth bring to the transition processes by validating their identities and experiences *and* by having ongoing discussions about the critical choices they make as they enter adulthood.

8. Employ transition practices that are known to facilitate the development of cultural and social capital as part of timely, consistent transition education processes with a focus on postschool outcomes. Increasing cultural capital includes providing information about adult service providers such as state vocational rehabilitation agencies, college preparatory courses, financial aid, independent living support services, and adult health care programs.

Conclusion: Diversity as Strength

As noted throughout this chapter, diversity is a complex concept and one that has been used to express a multitude of ideas. Whereas early educational approaches to multiculturalism embraced the notion that teachers would use different instructional tools or approaches when working with specific groups of learners and their families, the contemporary education context requires us as educators to meet the needs of people of many different backgrounds simultaneously. Rarely does a teacher or transition specialist work with groups of youth from identical backgrounds, preferences, strengths, and needs. Given this reality, diversity can be taken at face value to mean ranges of difference. Embracing diversity in transition planning requires seeing these differences as strengths and opportunities for learning on the parts of both school personnel and families.

Study Questions

1. What does *diversity* mean in context of transition?
2. What are the patterns of postsecondary outcomes (e.g., postsecondary enrollment, employment, and community living) of youth with disabilities?
3. What are two strategies teachers can use to become more culturally responsive?
4. Describe the five major systems of the ecological model.
5. Select one of the case study students and discuss which aspects of his or her identity could be incorporated into transition planning and education.
6. Explain how one of the strategies for successful transition planning and education for diverse youth could be applied to the existing cases.

Online Resources

The National Center for Culturally Responsive Educational Systems, now called the Equity Alliance at Arizona State University, has extensive resources for teachers who are interested in expanding their knowledge, skills, and practices in the area of culturally responsive teaching: http://www.nccrest.org/index.html and http://www.equityallianceatasu.org/

The American Association for Affirmative Action has many resources on diversity, careers, and equality: http://www.affirmativeaction.org/

Virginia Commonwealth University, Project Empowerment: Improving Minority Disability Research Capacity: http://www.vcu-projectempowerment.org

Information About Scholarships to Postsecondary Education Specific to Race/Ethnicity

For Latino youth: The Hispanic Scholarship Fund: http://www.hsf.net/

For African American youth: The United Negro College Fund: http://www.uncf.org/

For Native American youth: The American Indian College Fund: http://www.collegefund.org/students_and_alumni/content/special_scholarships

For Asian youth: The Asian American Legal Defense and Education Fund: https://www.aaldef.org

Transition Planning and Community Resources

Bringing It All Together

VALERIE BROOKE, W. GRANT REVELL,
JENNIFER McDONOUGH, AND HOWARD GREEN

After completing this chapter, the reader will be able to

- Identify at least six community agencies that support youth in transition
- Describe the critical elements in community-based transition
- Describe the important role of interagency planning in transition
- Discuss the importance of benefits planning as a component of transition planning
- Understand the potential support available through community programs in the areas of case management, employment services, and funding
- Describe the role of business and industry in transition

This chapter addresses transition planning from a community perspective. It builds on the overview from earlier chapters of the governing legislation and the critical issues involved in high-quality transition planning, particularly a specific focus on self-determination and strategies to promote student involvement. Vital to the success of all transition planning is the involvement of key community agencies and organizations. This school-to-community connection must be made to ensure such outcomes as postsecondary training, educational outcomes, employment opportunities, residential services, and leisure recreational possibilities. Specifically, this chapter presents the vast array of community partners potentially involved in the transition-planning process and the roles, functions, and benefits of each partnership.

Community Organizations: Service Structures and Outcomes

High-quality transition planning requires that a major emphasis be placed on strong community participation in the transition process (Wehman, 2011a). Yet, all too frequently, individual transition plans fail to effectively involve community resources. A major reason for this inconsistency is that many educators, students, and family members of individuals with disabilities do not recognize that most adult services are eligibility driven. In comparison, special education is an entitled service, and local school systems are the single agency that coordinates education services. This single-point-of-service coordination does not exist in adult services. Instead, postsecondary education, counseling, rehabilitation, therapy, residential services, and recreational services all have their own individual eligibility system that must be met before acceptance into an individual program. Different laws and policies govern each of these programs. As a consequence, students with disabilities and their family members must develop a strong understanding of these community programs to ensure a smooth transition that reflects student-driven outcomes.

In assisting students with transition planning, it is important to look at resources within the school and to also target community agencies and organizations that can provide support (Brooke, Revell, & Wehman, 2010). Each of these organizations will play a unique and vital role in the successful transition from school to work and independence in the community. Successful youth with disabilities will receive services and support from a variety of public and private programs. However, the exact mix of programs will vary depending upon the needs of each student, his or her family's economic resources, and each program's eligibility requirements (Wittenburg, Golden, & Fishman, 2002).

Planning for transition must involve the entire community. An extensive analysis of the community must be completed to ensure that all programs and services are identified. Community organizations that are important transition resources include Community Work Incentive Coordinators (CWICs), the federally funded state vocational rehabilitation (VR) program, community rehabilitation service providers, social services, community colleges, Social Security Administration (SSA), **Centers for Independent Living**, One-Stop Career Centers, community service boards, and local businesses (Inge & Moon, 2011). Each of these community agencies brings its own unique set of services and supports to students with disabilities as they plan for and consider preparing for a productive life in the community. Many have entrance eligibility and prerequisite criteria necessary to gain acceptance to these programs and services (Smith & DiLeo, 2011). Table 6.1 identifies a variety of typical community organizations and the purpose of each organization. The role and function of the agencies listed in Table 6.1 and how these agencies can support successful transition are discussed in detail in this chapter.

Table 6.1. Community organizations that support youth in transition

Community organizations/agencies	Role and functions
Local rehabilitation services	Determines eligibility; provides assessments, guidance and counseling, and job placement services under an individual plan for employment
Community rehabilitation providers/ employment service organizations	Provides assessments, counseling, job placement, and follow-up services
Social services	Assists with housing, financial, health, and transportation issues
Community colleges and technical schools	Provides assistance with application, financial aid, and information on accessibility during attendance
Social Security Administration	Provides financial assistance with Supplemental Security Income as well as other work-related benefits (e.g., Plan to Achieve Self-Support, impairment-related work expense)
Centers for independent living	Provides information for self-advocacy and understanding one's rights, as well as training programs dealing with money management, sexuality, leisure activities, and socialization
One-Stop Career Centers	Assists students with career and vocational counseling; also, can help with occupational training and job placement
Local community service boards	Provides case management services and assistance for counseling, family planning, nutrition, health care, and transportation
Local businesses	Business representatives can assist with mock interviews, job-seeking skills, career information, and work experience opportunities
Community work incentive coordinators	Provides financial analysis and information on work incentives and disability benefit programs operated under the Social Security Administration

There are several other local resources that could be accessed in a particular locality. The programs listed in Table 6.1 provide a snapshot of the typical options that are available to provide assistance in the transition-planning process. It is important to involve these community agencies early in the process so the entire transition team can learn and become familiar with the resources that are available from the specific agencies (Wehman, Brooke, & Revell, 2007). Without continual involvement, planning, and collaboration from key community agencies, the potential for a successful transition from secondary education to the community will be greatly diminished for students with disabilities.

Critical Elements in Community-Based Transition

A meaningful transition includes postsecondary educational opportunities such as admission to a community college program or employment in real work. It also includes moving toward postsecondary residential independence and individual competence in community living. Transition does not simply mean being placed onto a waiting list or having a referral made on one's behalf. Clearly identified community-based outcomes such as work or school are essential. Table 6.2 presents a series of six critical elements necessary for a successful **community-based transition,** which includes

1. Students and parents as stakeholders
2. **Functional community-referenced skills**
3. Connections with adult services and VR
4. Work before graduation
5. Business alliances with schools
6. College opportunities

Each of the six elements presented in Table 6.2 has corresponding community-based outcomes.

Table 6.2. Critical elements in community-based transition

Six critical elements	Community-based outcome
1. Parents and students as stakeholders	Parents and students are proactive during transition years both in the school and in the community to achieve adult outcomes that match the student's interest and desire.
2. Need for functional community-referenced skills	A functional curriculum fosters the development of skills and experiences that a student will need to perform independently or with supports in the workforce, residential services, and community environments.
3. Need for connections with adult services and vocational rehabilitation	Effective collaborations between vocational rehabilitation and other adult services will yield planning and 'potentially' outcomes across such adult areas of functioning to include employment, transportation, recreation, and residential.
4. Need for work before graduation	Participating in community-based work and employment before graduation helps a student gain valuable skills that employers are looking for.
5. Need for business alliances with the schools	Employers provide a student-learning situation where students are able to connect the information gained from the workforce and what they are learning in a classroom situation.
6. Need for college opportunities	Involvement of colleges and universities will increase postsecondary opportunities and reduce ambiguity regarding the availability and delivery of services.

Parents and Students as Stakeholders

As noted in Chapters 2 and 3, students and families play a critical role. Parents must take a proactive role in the planning for their children during secondary school and adult years. Students and families must be the focal point of services (O'Brien, 2007). If this principle is ignored, service providers will begin to plan curricula and services around what they think is necessary rather than what students and families consider important. Families must not only participate in the educational planning but also be involved in the community for their children to have viable living and work opportunities. The responsibility for locating a community or 4-year college with learning disability services cannot fall exclusively on the school counselor—parents need to be involved.

Functional Community-Referenced Skills

Students need to acquire community-referenced skills while they are in high school. This tenet has been frequently described by researchers (Davidsen & Streagle, 2011; Moon, Simonsen, & Neubert, 2011; Wehman & Kregel, 2004) and is discussed in considerably more detail in Chapter 16 on design of community-based training programs for students with intellectual disabilities. In fact, most researchers have concluded that these skills are critical for students, especially those with severe disabilities, to effectively make the transition to adult living. A functional curriculum fosters instruction that focuses on developing needed skills and experiences based on objectives drawn from career exploration and individual assessment. It emphasizes the most important activities that the student will need to perform independently or with supports in vocational, residential, and community environments (O'Brien, 2007; Scott, 2007).

Selecting the most necessary skills in which an individual student needs instruction involves the student, teacher, and others who either know the student well or know the environments well in which the student will most likely participate after leaving school (O'Brien, 2007; Michaels, 2007). Continued use of an individualized functional curriculum provides the opportunity for the student to make incremental improvements in job-related skill areas, mobility about the community, and the ability to interact appropriately in a variety of circumstances with the public and with co-workers without disabilities.

Connections with Adult Services and Vocational Rehabilitation

Helping youth with disabilities successfully negotiate the transition from school to work and community life requires innovative, effective, and enduring partnerships among a variety of key stakeholders. The VR system is identified consistently as a fundamental partner in any collaborative transition effort because of its ability to help youth develop vocational skills, obtain employment, and advance the opportunity to live independently. Systematic efforts must be undertaken to address the barriers that historically have prevented school and VR staff from working together effectively on behalf of youth with disabilities and their families.

Many researchers have promoted the benefits of collaboration between the schools and VR (Benz, Lindstrom, & Yovanoff, 2000; Carter, Owens, Sweeden, et al., 2009), yet these arrangements remain far from commonplace and are limited largely to the basic referral of students to VR. The two general barriers to school and VR collaboration cited most often include 1) poor or inaccurate perceptions of VR by school staff, youth, and parents, and of schools and youth in transition by VR staff; and 2) nonexistent or ineffective procedures to structure collaboration by school and VR staff across the referral, eligibility determination, planning, and service delivery process.

Developing effective school and VR collaborations appears especially problematic for youth with learning disabilities or emotional disabilities and for youth who reside in rural communities. The transition-planning team is responsible for establishing and maintaining relationships with adult services and funding agencies, a job that is easier said than done. Little doubt exists that all students and their families would like to know that a planning team is available at school or within the community that will take care of all matters that affect transportation, accessibility, community recreation, and nondiscriminatory employment—important goals that all transition models should embrace. (See later in this chapter for some of the ways to create these interagency agreements that allow planning teams to be more effective and less restrained by bureaucracy.)

Work Before Graduation

The availability of paid community employment after graduation is a major outcome that must be established in all communities (Luecking, 2009a; Johnson, Thurlow, & Stout, 2007). This was discussed and recommended by Wehman (2002b) in his testimony to the President's Commission on Excellence in Special Education. Full employment for all people with disabilities who want to work must be a national goal (as illustrated by the Employment First efforts across the United States and further illustrated in Chapter 13). This goal will not be attained unless the schools actively promote employment, ideally while the student is still in school. Local planning teams must be involved in planning for job placement because few rehabilitation counselors will have the resources or the time to place every student.

The Partnership for 21st Century Skills report titled *Are They Really Ready to Work?* (Casner-Lotto & Barrington, 2006) addressed the importance of work before graduation when an employer community stated that, although basic reading comprehension, math, and writing skills continue to be important, soft skills such as professionalism and work ethic, communication, teamwork, collaboration, and critical thinking/problem solving were even more important in today's workplace. One of the best ways to build these skills among students with disabilities is in real work settings. Participation in community-based work helps the student with a disability to build work and work-related skills and also to explore a variety of work settings as a tool in career awareness and exploration. **Community-based work experiences** can involve unpaid activities in a variety of job areas (Luecking, 2009b). This type of training can take the form of vocational exploration, **vocational assessment**, or vocational training (Inge & Moon, 2006).

Community-based work experiences can also include a variety of paid activities including work experience and on-the-job training. The Bridges Model, developed by the Marriott Corporation (Luecking, Fabian, & Tilson, 2004), is an excellent example of a formal community-based work experience program in which students are placed in 4- to 6-month paid internships in positions matched to their interests and skills. The range of community-based options available provides the student who has a disability with exposure to real-work settings and experience in interacting with a variety of people and situations. These community work experiences that ultimately lead to competitive employment is perhaps the best way to eliminate or greatly reduce the need for "employment readiness" adult service options and ultimately increase the employment rate of people with disabilities (Niemiec, Lavin, & Owens, 2009).

Business Alliances with Schools

Education and business need to learn how to work together and how to understand each other to create successful school-to-work partnerships (McMahon et al., 2004). To get business involved with education, a starting point is necessary—a place of access that makes it possible for employers to understand the experiences of the children and young adults who will one day become employees in the workforce. Employers can become involved with the school-to-work system in many different ways (Luecking, 2009a). Opportunities can range from minimal investment to intense, long-range involvement. The key is to ask *What is most important to this employer?* and to be flexible in opportunities for the employer's involvement

The National Employer Leadership Council (2001) gathered data on businesses involved in alliances with schools from various reports. Overall, the council found that business involvement is growing and producing positive changes:

1. Expansion of the curriculum
2. Increases in development of training and internships
3. Rise in having guest speakers in the classroom

Other areas of business participation included mentoring (one-to-one and e-mentoring), workplace tours, job shadowing, internships, career days/fairs, speakers bureaus, cooperative education, and youth **apprenticeships** (Hood & Rubin, 2004).

College Opportunities

Involvement in colleges and universities has been limited for young people with disabilities but this is all changing (Getzel, 2005). The National Longitudinal Transition Study-2 (NLTS-2; 2007) reported that students in secondary education have begun taking a more rigorous academic coursework. This change is reflected with postsecondary education appearing as a goal for four out of five secondary students in special education (Wagner, Newman, Cameto, & Levine, 2005). Movement into postsecondary institutions of higher education is critical. Several strategies should be implemented and are presented in Table 6.3.

At present, too much ambiguity exists in availability and delivery of services, which limits the access of students with disabilities to services and accommodations. One promising discussion includes college representatives becoming contributors to the

Table 6.3.   Critical factors affecting movement into postsecondary education

Strategy 1	Greater efforts should be made to educate faculty, staff, and other students regarding disabilities, accommodations, services, and the legal rights of students with disabilities.
Strategy 2	Appropriate action should be taken against instructors or professors who repeatedly refuse to make course or examination modifications and other accommodations for students with identified disabilities.
Strategy 3	Postsecondary schools should initiate more creative measures to advertise disability-related services to prospective students in need.
Strategy 4	Support groups and clubs, if not organized in particular schools, should be encouraged and supported by postsecondary schools.
Strategy 5	Students with disabilities should be included in formulating disability-related policies and services.
Strategy 6	Consistency should be developed both within and among postsecondary schools regarding the types of services and accommodations that are available to students with disabilities.

individualized education program (IEP) transition team and ultimately leading to an increase in **dual enrollment** and disability supports services (Grigal & Hart, 2010a; Lindstrom, Flannery, Benz, Olszewski, & Slovic, 2009). Because of the importance of this topic, an entire chapter has been dedicated to it (see Chapter 15).

Interagency Planning in Community Transition

For interagency cooperation to occur and tangible goals for individuals with disabilities to be achieved, state and local community leaders must follow federal examples of leadership. Terms for cooperation must be designed and written for local-level agencies, and staff and participating agency resources must be committed to accomplishing transition-related outcomes. Plans must be developed and implemented to provide for regular and frequent face-to-face interaction of interagency teams at the service delivery level (Crane, Gramlich, & Peterson, 2004).

Interagency Cooperation at the State Level

For state-level interagency collaboration to bring about changes in local-level activities, the leaders must have a strong and visible commitment to common missions. This sense of mission is necessary in order to focus the activities of an organization. For most agencies serving individuals with disabilities, the mission is service provision.

The purpose of providing educational programming to children and youth with disabilities is to maximize their independence as adults. Education should prepare children and youth for adulthood. In contrast, adult services providers do not begin their service provision to individuals with disabilities until these individuals are adults. The goal of service provision is the same for schools and adult services providers; it is their deadlines for accomplishing the goal that differ. To use time more efficiently, adult services providers look for more immediate and varied means to accomplish their goal. Because their missions are the same but different approaches are being used by these agencies, the methods of each agency should be examined and efforts should be coordinated. Gaining a better understanding of how and why the different agencies operate as they do will improve efficiency and reduce instances of duplicated services.

One example of duplication is the repetition of expensive diagnostic evaluations because one state agency does not accept the records of another state agency or because an agency is required to conduct its own evaluations as a part of eligibility determination. Yet, some agencies continue to complete diagnostic evaluations in advance, assuming they will meet the receiving agency's eligibility requirements. This duplication, however, is senseless. Individuals who have received services while in public school special education programs must have been determined eligible for those services because of a disability; procedures for eligibility determination are carefully prescribed in the regulations specified by the Individuals with Disabilities Education Improvement Act (IDEA) of 2004 (PL 108-446). The existence of an IEP, as required by law for each student with disabilities, should therefore be sufficient documentation that there is a disability and that the individual is eligible for adult services for individuals with disabilities.

Programs with similar service provision goals for people with disabilities include the vocational education program (Workforce Investment Act of 1998, PL 105-220) and developmental disabilities programs. Unlike educational services, however, these are eligibility programs, not **entitlement** programs, which means that there is no guarantee of service. To demonstrate how these service providers are similar in mission, it is necessary to restate or reexamine each agency's mission and to recognize common goals. This process is also a useful tool for initiating interagency cooperation. Once a common mission is identified across agencies, the purpose of formalizing interagency collaboration and efficient provision of services becomes clear and logical.

After recognizing that interagency cooperation is advantageous, the leader at the state level must work with agencies to commit staff and resources to initiating the transition process. For example, designating middle-level management personnel to develop interagency activities is a logical starting point. Management liaisons from the different agencies must come together as a core team to examine the need for interagency cooperation by conducting state- and local-level needs assessments to define necessary changes.

One approach to assisting state-level transition coordinators has been advanced by Stodden, Brown, Galloway, Myrazek, and Noy (2004) with an instrument called The Essential Tool. The purpose of The Essential Tool is to assist state-level transition coordinators and others responsible for forming, conducting, and evaluating the performance of interagency transition teams that are focused upon the school and postschool needs of youth with disabilities. This tool helps state-level interagency team facilitators learn and measure the effectiveness, for example, of key team-building factors such as purpose of the transition team, how to solve problems regarding typical transition issues encountered within the team, and how the team fits into state, district, and local systems. The Essential Tool is designed to guide the coordination efforts of people working at the grassroots level up through the state government. The Essential Tool will assist state interagency transition teams to operate in an efficient and successful manner and will ultimately help guide agency work toward the primary purpose of an interagency transition team: to improve postschool outcomes for youth with disabilities who are transitioning from secondary school to adult living.

Negotiating the array of adult services and programs can be "at best" disjointed and "at worst" completely overwhelming. If youth with disabilities and their families are ultimately going to achieve a smooth transition from school to the full community, strong relationships need to be built. Several states serve as models for evidence-based models of interagency transition teams, which include Arizona, Connecticut, Colorado, and Pennsylvania (Stodden et al., 2004). Although all of the community resources presented here are important, there are three relationships where transition teams need to concentrate their efforts:

1. **Social Security** benefits planning
2. VR and community rehabilitation agencies
3. Relationships with business

These relationships will reduce gaps in services and support families as they face the many financial challenges that are presented when transitioning into adulthood (Davies, Rupp, & Wittenburg, 2009). The remainder of this chapter provides in-depth information on why these three partners are so important and some illustrations of models of success.

Social Security Work Incentives: Removing Barriers to Work

Since the early 1990s, several exciting legislative reforms have occurred aimed at assisting people with disabilities in accessing competitive employment. Yet, none of these reforms holds more promise than The Ticket to Work and Work Incentives Improvement Act of 1999 (TWWIIA; PL 106-170). The TWWIIA contains several different components and strategies aimed at removing barriers to employment and creating greater choice for individuals with disabilities, but the most significant component for youth in transition is the national **Benefits Planning, Assistance, and Outreach (BPAO)** initiative. Lack of understanding of the complex requirements for accessing Social Security work incentives and Medicaid benefits available under the Social Security Act is a major barrier contributing to the unemployment of youth with disabilities. The BPAO program, contained in Section 121 of the TWWIIA, addresses this barrier. Section 1149 of the Social Security Act, as added by section 121 of the TWWIIA, required the Commissioner of Social Security to establish a community-based work incentives planning and assistance program. This SSA program is called the Work Incentives Planning and Assistance (WIPA) Program.

The goal of the WIPA Program, composed of approximately 102 projects nationally, is to disseminate accurate information to beneficiaries with disabilities on work incentives programs and issues related to such programs to assist them in their employment. In addition, the program provides the availability of protection and advocacy services to beneficiaries with disabilities, including beneficiaries participating in the Ticket to Work and Self-Sufficiency Program established under section 1148, the **Supplemental Security Income** (SSI) program established under section 1619, and other programs that are designed to encourage beneficiaries with disabilities to seek, maintain, and regain employment. The WIPA Program is an important part of SSA's employment strategy for beneficiaries with disabilities. One of SSA's goals in implementing TWWIIA was to help achieve a substantial increase in the number of beneficiaries with disabilities who return to work and achieve greater self-sufficiency. The WIPA is achieving positive outcomes toward SSA's goal of improving employment outcomes and reducing dependence on benefits for beneficiaries with a disability while also generating cost savings for SSA (Kregel, 2012). As a result, each SSA disability benefits recipient is better able to make informed choices about work. These services are available to all individuals receiving SSI and/or Title II disability benefits who are between the ages of 14 and 64 years.

During the transition-planning process, students and families often express concerns about the potential impact of earnings from competitive employment on their existing federal benefits (Fraker & Rangarajan, 2009). Generally, these concerns are related to a potential loss of Social Security income benefits and/or medical benefits. The CWICs employed by a WIPA program provide a resource through which individuals receiving a Social Security benefit can access benefits counseling to determine the impact of employment on the specific benefits they receive. These highly trained specialists provide informational resources as well as conduct intensive benefits analysis that is specific to each individual's unique circumstances. Once this benefits analysis is complete, the individual with a disability is able to make an informed decision regarding employment. The results of this analysis identify the true impact of employment on the person's SSA benefits and on other federal benefit programs. Because there are unique work incentives that are available to students, a local WIPA program should be contacted for all students with disabilities who receive a SSI or a **Social Security Disability Insurance (SSDI)** benefit and are interested in employment. The following is a summary description of key Social Security benefits and work incentives that are potential resources for youth with disabilities in the transition process.

Supplemental Security Income Program Basics

A CWIC working with students who are receiving or who may be eligible for SSI can help students and their families to clearly understand four key points about this program:

1. Students will always have more money working than by not working when they receive SSI.

2. There are several "work incentives" that may help SSI recipients to pay for items that are necessary in order to work.

3. There is a special work incentive targeted to students that makes employment highly desirable while attending school.

4. Students can keep Medicaid until they earn as much as nearly $40,000 annually in some states.

To understand how all of these features of the benefits program work, CWICs would first introduce the basics of the SSA's SSI program. This program is designed to supplement any income a person with a disability may already have to meet the minimum needs for food and shelter expenses such as rent and utilities.

A person can be eligible for SSI if he or she is a U.S. citizen or is able to meet the necessary requirements for noncitizens under the law. In addition, he or she must have a disability serious enough that it substantially limits the individual from engaging in the activities that other students often perform. Furthermore, to gain eligibility for SSI, the individual must have a limited income and very few resources. The bottom line is that the more income and resources an individual has, the less the benefit will be. Because SSI has income criteria for eligibility, if there is too much income, the individual will not be eligible for a benefit.

The first question that teachers, students with disabilities, and families typically ask is when a person should apply for SSI. An individual with a disability can apply for SSI at any time. It is important to know that, if SSA turns down an application, the family should keep that record and, if circumstances change, a new application can be submitted (Hemmeter, Jauff, & Wittenburg, 2009). There are a variety of ways to apply. Applications can be made by contacting the local SSA office by phone, calling the SSA toll-free number at (800) 772-1213, downloading the application from their web site at http://www.ssa.gov, or by making an appointment at the local SSA office. There is a variety of paperwork that SSA will request at the time of application, so being prepared can save everyone a lot of time. The applicant will need to provide

- *Medical history*: names and address of physicians, medical and/or treatment facilities where services have been provided, as well as records of treatment
- *Educational history*: names and addresses of schools attended, records, and the most recent teacher and/or school counselor
- *VR*: names and addresses of VR services, records, and the most recent VR counselor contact information
- *Employment history*: name and addresses of current and previous places of employment and summary of work history tasks
- *Legal records*: birth certificate, adoption papers, marriage certificates, divorce papers, or immigration or naturalization papers
- *Financial records*: recent tax bill, property statements, rental agreements, proof of utilities, proof of food expenses, insurance policies, and recent bank/credit union statements to include checking and savings accounts
- *Resource and assets records*: car registration, bank book, insurance policies, and so on
- *Parents/family financial history*: only needed when person is aged younger than 18 years

When SSA makes a decision about whether an individual qualifies for SSI, it will send a letter to directly inform the new beneficiary. If eligible, the first monthly check will include the 3–6 months that the applicant waited during the application process. This check can be automatically deposited into a personal bank account. If SSA has found that the individual is not eligible for a benefit, an explanation will be provided. It is important to know that this SSA finding can be appealed, and the letter from SSA will include information on how to initiate an appeal process.

Impact of Employment on Supplemental Security Income Benefits

The SSA wants beneficiaries to attempt employment and provides multiple opportunities for this to occur without the beneficiary losing his or her cash benefit. The CWIC with the local WIPA program can carefully analyze how employment will impact SSI, Medicaid, and other federal benefits. The CWIC will explain the multiple employment supports and

SSA work incentives that are available to the SSI recipients. Taking advantage of these work incentives will allow a beneficiary to continue to receive his or her SSI check and/ or Medicaid while maintaining employment. The SSI incentives that will be reviewed here include the following: **1619 (a) and (b)**, **Earned Income Exclusion**, **Student Earned Income Exclusion (SEIE)**, **impairment-related work expense (IRWE)**, **Blind Work Expense (BWE)**, **Plan to Achieve Self-Support (PASS)**, and Expedited Reinstatement (Easy Back On).

1619 (a) and (b)

The SSA has a law that protects individuals receiving SSI and Medicaid who want to attempt work. Once a person is employed, SSA will count less than half of gross wages when they calculate the amount of the SSI cash benefit. As long as the individual still qualifies for even one penny of the SSI benefit when the calculation is performed, then he or she is protected under the first part of the law known as 1619 (a). Essentially, this means that the SSI beneficiary will always have more money by working than if he or she were solely dependent upon the SSI benefit. The SSA simply reduces the SSI check by about $1.00 for every $2.00 earned, and Medicaid continues for as long as the beneficiary remains in 1619 (a).

If the individual continues on his or her career path and earns so much income that the SSI check ultimately gets reduced to $0.00, protection is available under the second portion of the law known as 1619 (b). This guarantees that SSA will keep a beneficiary's file open in case employment hours are reduced or if there is a loss of employment. Furthermore, 1619 (b) protects Medicaid eligibility for all SSI recipients, even those living in states where an individual's income level may be too high to receive a Medicaid benefit. These individuals can't have more than $2,000 in resources but they can earn more than $25,000 to $30,000 in most states and not worry about losing Medicaid (these numbers are subject to change, however; check with SSA for the most current information). Recipients who choose to accept medical insurance coverage provided by their employer are still covered by 1619 (b).

Earned Income Exclusion

As further proof that SSA wants SSI recipients to attempt employment, SSA disregards most of the income that was earned when they calculate the amount of the SSI check. The first $65.00 of wages in any month is not counted and, if there is no other income, SSA excludes $85.00 rather than $65.00. Once this calculation is completed, SSA will then only count half of the remaining wages. Therefore, if Travis was receiving a $674 monthly SSI check and then went to work for St. Mary's Hospital earning $600 a month as a materials management clerk, the following calculation would be performed to determine total monthly income.

Earned Income Exclusion Example

Travis is working as a materials management clerk earning $600.00 per month and receiving a $545 per month SSI benefit from SSA.

$600.00 (wages)

$- 85.00$ (exclusion)

$515.00/2 = $257.50 (wages counted by SSA)

$674.00 (amount of SSI check if there are no wages)

$- 257.50$ (wages counted by SSA from employment)

$416.50

New Monthly Amounts

$600.00 (wages from clerk job)

$+416.50$ (amount of SSI check)

$1,016.50 **Total monthly income plus no loss of Medicaid**

Student Earned Income Exclusion

This particular work incentive is designed exclusively for people younger than 22 years who are attending school. To qualify, one of the following must apply to the student's individual situation:

1. Attending college for at least 8 hours per week
2. Attending junior or senior high school at least 12 hours per week
3. Attending a vocational training program for least 12 hours a week (intern program for at least 15 hours per week)

Less time may be needed in these programs if it is the result of student illness. If a student qualifies for this incentive, he or she can go to work and SSA will count even less of total earnings when calculating the SSI benefit. In some cases, families are using this incentive for saving for postsecondary education (Miller, O'Mara, & Getzel, 2009).

In the case of Travis, a CWIC would help him and his family to understand that, while he was in school and earning $600 in wages, an SEIE would apply and SSA would not count any of his wages from his job at St. Mary's Hospital. Therefore, without the job at the hospital, Travis would simply be receiving a SSI monthly check for $674. Applying the SEIE, Travis continues to receive the $674 from SSI, along with $600 in earnings from employment, resulting in a total monthly income of $1,274.00.

Student Earned Income Exclusion Example

Travis works as a materials management clerk earning $600.00 per month and receives a $674 per month SSI benefit from SSA.

$600.00 (wages from job)

_ +674.00 (amount of SSI check)

$1,274.00 **Total monthly income plus no loss of Medicaid**

A CWIC would further explain that, if Travis decided to work full time in the summer (June through August) while he was on school break, the SEIE would make it possible for him to keep his earnings from his paycheck while maintaining his SSI check of $674.00. So, if Travis earns $1,000 a month from his summer job, his total monthly income, including his SSI check of $674, would be $1,674. Clearly, Travis is doing much better working than if he was just receiving an SSI check.

Impairment-Related Work Expense

Another SSA work incentive known as IRWE can be used to pay for items that are necessary to work and are incurred because of the individual's disability. The benefits counselor would explain that this work support can be used in any month while work is occurring for the total length of employment tenure. A "credit" is given for expenses if they meet the following rules. The item or service must directly assist the individual to maintain employment and is needed because of a physical or mental impairment. In addition, the item or service must be purchased by the SSA beneficiary and be "reasonable" according to a standard cost in the community.

A CWIC is not able to approve an individual for an IRWE; only an SSA claims representative is able to make this determination. It will be the SSA claims representative who determines if the four previously mentioned criteria apply. Examples of items or services that some people have had approved as IRWE expenses include specialized transportation, assistive technology, medications to control a disability, attendant care, and job coach services. Talking with a CWIC before employment can assist in identifying possible expenses that may qualify for an IRWE.

In the case of Travis, who is earning $600.00 each month from his job at St. Mary's Hospital, he is paying $200 each month from his wages to receive door-to-door transportation because of his disability. Once a SSA claims representative approves Travis's transportation cost as an IRWE, this ultimately will have a positive effect on his total monthly income, allowing Travis to recover half of the expense that he pays for transportation.

Blind Work Expense

BWE is limited to those individuals who receive SSI and who are blind. Unique to this population, SSA deducts all work expenses, whether or not they are attributable to an individual's disability. A CWIC would be able to demonstrate how students who are blind are able to receive a higher SSI check when they go to work than other people on SSI. Similar to the IRWE, to receive a BWE, the work expenses must have been paid for by the individual beneficiary and the expense must be deemed reasonable by SSA. The BWE will continue throughout an individual's tenure of employment and as long as the employment expense is still present. Unlike the IRWE, the BWE includes a much broader range of work expenses including, but not limited to, taxes, union dues, parking fees, transportation, assistive technology, reader services, meals eaten during work, and guide dog expenses.

Plan for Achieving Self-Support

Most CWICs would describe SSA's PASS as a tremendously flexible work incentive. This particular incentive allows an SSI recipient to save money to pay for expenses that are necessary to reach a stated career goal. For example, if a certification, degree, or car is necessary to achieve a career goal, then a PASS could be written to help pay for the expense. The development of a PASS and how it excludes earned income, unearned income, and/or resources allows a beneficiary to use financial resources now or in the future for approved expenses related to a career goal.

For a PASS to be approved, it must meet the criteria presented in Table 6.4. Each of the nine steps found in the table must be achieved. A CWIC can assist an SSA beneficiary in the development of a PASS, but it is the sole responsibility of SSA to approve the PASS. Typical expenditures that have been approved by SSA for a PASS include equipment, supplies, operating capital and inventory required for starting a business, supported employment services, costs associated with advanced education or vocational education, dues and publications for academic or professional purposes, child care, attendant care, and uniforms. The development of a PASS can be a complex process; some of the frequently asked questions regarding PASS are presented in Table 6.4.

In the past, teachers, VR counselors, advocates, social workers, and employment support personnel have included benefits planning as part of their existing job responsibilities. However, because this was typically an add-on job duty to an ever-expanding job description, students and adults with disabilities would often get inaccurate information regarding the impact of work on their Social Security benefit as well as the other federal benefit programs. Clearly, work incentive counseling is critically important at the onset of employment, but it can also be extremely valuable in combination with other services, over a sustained period of time, to support more individuals' move toward financial independence (Kregel & O'Mara, 2011). For true reform to take place, our country is in need of practitioners dedicated to providing high-quality benefits planning to SSA recipients with disabilities. SSA truly understood that concern and created the WIPA program. To find the location of WIPA programs across the country, go to https://secure.ssa.gov/apps10/oesp/providers.nsf/bystate. Youth with disabilities in transition and their families who have a clear understanding of the impact of earnings on benefits are well prepared to make decisions about employment and to select appropriate community programs and services.

Table 6.4.   Frequently asked questions regarding Plans to Achieve Self-Support (PASS)

Questions and responses

Who can have a PASS?

Anyone who receives supplemental security income (SSI) or could be eligible for SSI can have a PASS plan. PASS plans are designed to help individuals set aside income or resources for a specified time period for a work goal. The intent of the PASS program is to assist persons in achieving self-sufficiency and reducing their dependency on Social Security Administration (SSA) benefits.

Who can help set up a PASS?

Anyone can help set up a PASS plan, including Benefits Planning, Assistance, and Outreach project personnel (benefits planners), teachers, rehabilitation counselors, consultants and advocates, and SSA personnel. SSA PASS specialists and employment support representatives will play a very major role in both the application process and the review process. Both PASS specialists and employment support representatives can be reached via 1-800 phone lines and are located around the country in regional and local SSA offices. Specific locations and contact information can be found through the SSA web site at http://www.ssa.gov/work.

Can students younger than 18 years establish a PASS to assist with the transition process?

Students younger than 18 years can establish a PASS if they have earned or unearned income or resources of their own or have deemed income or resources from an ineligible parent to be set aside.

Does an individual need to be determined eligible for SSI before establishing a PASS?

The two processes typically occur simultaneously for persons interested in establishing a PASS who are currently not eligible for SSI. These individuals will have to go through the SSA application process to determine eligibility before the PASS resulting in the SSI cash benefit being issued. Individuals already receiving SSI have already established eligibility, so this step is not necessary.

Can wages be excluded under a PASS in determining SSI eligibility?

One of the eligibility criteria for the SSI eligibility determinations is that the individual is either currently not working or, if working, earning less than substantial gainful activity (SGA). Although income or resources that are set aside in a PASS are not counted in the SSI eligibility determination process, wages that are set aside in the PASS cannot be deducted from gross wages for SGA determination.

How are a PASS and an impairment-related work expense (IRWE) different?

The PASS work incentive allows an individual who is receiving SSI or could be found eligible for SSI to set aside income and/or resources for a specified period of time to purchase items and/or services necessary to achieve a work goal. The IRWE work incentive allows individuals to deduct certain impairment-related items and/or services that are necessary to maintain employment from their gross earnings on an ongoing basis as needed.

Is it possible to use a PASS and an IRWE at the same time?

It is possible and allowable to have a PASS and also use an IRWE at the same time for ongoing expenses not included in the PASS. For concurrent beneficiaries, it is also possible to use the exact same expense as a PASS for the purpose of SSI and simultaneously claim it as an IRWE for the purpose of the Social Security Disability Insurance, assuming that the expense meets the requirements of the two work incentives. In addition, during the SSI eligibility process, an individual could use an IRWE that is also included as a PASS expense to reduce gross monthly countable income below SGA. Only during SSI eligibility determination may the same expense be counted as an IRWE and included in the PASS simultaneously.

Would an individual be penalized if he or she did not reach his or her work goal at the end of the PASS?

Individuals would not be penalized if they did not reach their work goal at the end of their PASS if they

- Followed their PASS steps to reach their work goal as established and/or revised
- Spent the set-aside income and/or resources as outlined in the PASS
- Kept records of the expenditures including receipts and actively sought employment at the end of the PASS

What are the steps for writing a successful PASS?

A PASS plan must

- Be individualized and designed for a specific individual
- Be in writing on the established form (SSA-545)
- Have clearly stated career goal that is feasible for the individual to obtain
- Include a timeframe for when the career goal will be reached
- Show the expenses that will be incurred to reach the career goal and which expenses will be paid for with funds set aside in the PASS
- Document the resources that will be used to pay for the expense related to the career goal; these resources cannot be from an SSI benefit
- Show income and/or resources will be set aside to pay for the expenses; for example, an individual bank account
- Be submitted to SSA for approval before the PASS can be initiated
- Be reviewed by SSA on a regular basis to update progress

From Module 3, Part A Competency Unit 7-Plan to Achieve Self-Support (PASS). In L. Miller, S. O'Mara, & J. Kregel (Eds.), *WIPA national training curriculum: Promoting employment of SSA beneficiaries with disabilities 2012 edition* (pp. 109–147). Richmond: WIPA National Training Center at Virginia Commonwealth University; reprinted by permission.

Transition and Community Training, Employment, and Support Programs

The Rehabilitation Act Amendments of 1998 (PL 105-220) define *transition services* as follows:

- A coordinated set of activities for a student designed within an outcome-oriented process that promotes movement from school to post-school activities, including postsecondary education, vocational training, integrated employment (including supported employment), continuing and adult education, adult services, independent living, or community participation.

- The coordinated set of activities must be based upon the individual student's needs, taking into account the student's preferences and interests, and must include instruction, community experiences, the development of employment and other post-school adult living objectives, and, if appropriate, acquisition of daily living skills and functional vocational evaluation.

- Transition services must promote or facilitate the achievement of the employment outcome identified in the student's individualized plan for employment.

(Federal Register, January 17, 2001, p. 4389)

In relation to the adult service community, this definition of transition services emphasizes an outcome-oriented process focused on postsecondary education and vocational training, employment, independent living, community participation, and/or other adult services as needed by each transitioning youth. This range of potential services encompasses a variety of programs with distinct roles, eligibility criteria, service guidelines, and funding requirements. Youth with disability in the transition process from school to the community do have potential access to a variety of community training, employment, and support programs (Certo et al., 2008). These programs offer an array of case management assistance, employment services, and funding possibilities. However, these programs operate under a wide assortment of federal, state, and local laws, regulations, policies, and service arrangements. The key to a successful transition outcome is person-centered planning (O'Brien, 2007; Scott, 2007; Michaels, 2007) and early involvement with these programs during the planning process. Here are a set of key steps to follow in blending these resources into individualized transition plans:

- Become fully educated regarding the resources and services in your community that provide community training, employment, and support programs specific to youth in transition.

- Identify the primary community agencies that are critical to the success of each individual's transition plan.

- Identify the primary case management/service coordination resource among these community agencies. This role might be taken on by different agencies for different youth in transition depending on the nature of their disability, core service needs, and/or local eligibility requirements. Early transition planning can help to establish these key relationships with community agencies and establish the primary- and secondary-level participation needed by each to support a successful employment outcome.

In approaching agencies and programs in the adult service system, it is most helpful if youth with disabilities in transition and their families understand the core general role and function of each agency in the following areas:

1. Service coordination, including case management services

2. Direct service provision

3. Potential for accessing funds to use in acquiring services

The following description of the role of programs and agencies in the adult service community in supporting transition is framed around these three areas.

State Vocational Rehabilitation Services

Individuals with disabilities may qualify for publicly funded VR services if the individual's disability presents a barrier to obtaining competitive employment or maintaining employment. The Rehabilitation Act of 1973, as amended, provides states with federal grants to operate comprehensive programs of VR services for individuals with disabilities. VR is a federal–state cooperative program that exists in all 50 states, the District of Columbia, and the U.S. territories.

A rehabilitation counselor will process an application for services and make a determination of eligibility for VR services. Eligibility is based on the presence of a disability that presents a barrier to employment and an expectation that the provision of VR services will help the individual achieve an employment outcome. VR services can provide an array of services and supports before and after graduation. Once eligibility has been determined, an individualized plan for employment (IPE) must be developed in connection with the completion of high school. Driven by the IPE, and specifically the work goal of the individual with a disability, a host of services and supports is then made available. Rehabilitation counselors are an excellent resource for schools as they plan for the transition of students with disabilities.

Case Management through Vocational Rehabilitation

Each applicant for VR services is assigned a rehabilitation counselor. This counselor is responsible for determining eligibility for VR services and for assisting the individual in completing the IPE. The counselor is positioned to provide information and referral on a variety of community services and can incorporate a variety of services into the IPE if those services specifically support the identified employment outcome. Case management through VR continues until case closure occurs. Case closure can occur after a minimum of 90 days of employment in a job consistent with the employment objective established in the IPE. Case closure can also occur if the individual is not making progress toward achieving an employment outcome.

Employment and Related Services
Available through Vocational Rehabilitation

There are a variety of services potentially available through a VR agency. These services include, but are not limited to

1. Assessment for determining eligibility for VR services
2. Vocational counseling, guidance, and referral services
3. Physical and mental restoration services
4. Vocational and other training, including on-the-job training
5. Maintenance services such as meals and housing
6. Interpreter services for individuals who are hearing impaired
7. Reading services for individuals with a visual disability
8. Personal assistance services, including training in managing a personal assistant
9. Rehabilitation technology services
10. Job placement services and supported employment services.

A VR agency directly provides services such as counseling and guidance and job placement assistance, and it will usually arrange with other community providers to acquire services such as rehabilitation technology, physical and mental restoration (medical services that may remove or substantially reduce or stabilize the disabling effects of a physical or mental condition), and supported employment. The ability of a VR agency to reach out into the community for individualized services is one of the key potential strengths of the VR system.

Funding Available through Vocational Rehabilitation

VR counselors have access to case service funds that can be used to purchase services from authorized vendors. If the service supports the employment goal established on the IPE, VR funds can be used to purchase services such as postsecondary education and training, supported employment, transportation, tools and uniforms, and a variety of other services. VR counselors are also usually very familiar with other funding sources that can be used to complement VR funding. The critical consideration in advocating for VR funding of a service is that the service clearly supports the employment goal and is not available from another funding source.

VR counselors can serve as an information resource about community services for transition teams during the earlier planning stages in the transition process. As the youth with a disability nears completion of his or her secondary education program, the rehabilitation counselor should become actively involved with the youth so that an IPE is in place before the student exits the school program. VR agencies are well positioned to serve as the service coordination hub for employment-oriented community services for eligible youth with disabilities transitioning from secondary-level programs.

Case Study Examples of Transition Services through Vocational Rehabilitation Agencies

Here are two brief examples of applications of services through VR for planning and implementing transition services to youth with disabilities.

Joanne   Joanne is 19 and has been receiving special education services within her secondary-level education program on the basis of the presence of a moderate intellectual disability. She is participating in a work-study program arranged through her school where she has gained work experience in a variety of areas. She has demonstrated particular interests and abilities in working in an office setting doing a variety of clerical aide activities such as assembling documents, filing, mail delivery, and copying. Joanne learns best when given consistent one-to-one training with repeated practice opportunities. To achieve her transition goal of employment in an office setting, she will need assistance with job placement to identify a setting that matches well to her abilities and interests, an extended initial period of on-site training in the expectations and routines of her job, and ongoing periodic follow-up contact to monitor her stability in the job. The state VR counselor serving Joanne's school and transition program takes her application for services and finds that she is eligible for VR services. The counselor develops with her an IPE that identifies resources in her community for the needed job development and job site training services. These services will be purchased through VR case service funds. The counselor also identifies an additional resource that will pay for the ongoing periodic follow-up services that will continue after VR case closure once Joanne demonstrates that she is stable in her job performance.

Brandon   Brandon is 21 and experiences multiple mobility, dexterity, and communication impairments resulting from cerebral palsy. He has demonstrated interests and abilities in the web site design area. He is interested in working in a marketing situation using his computer and web site design skills. Brandon applies and is found eligible for VR services. His IPE includes a 1-year period of training in a postsecondary web site design program, personal assistant services, transportation services, and equipment purchases for required computer hardware and software for use in his training. Once his training is completed, he will receive job placement assistance and continued personal assistant services. VR funding will pay for his training, transportation, and equipment, and it will arrange for job placement assistance once he completes his training. The VR counselor also will assist in identifying an alternative source of funding outside VR funds for Brandon for personal assistance services.

For both Joanne and Brandon, VR provides the key resource in the transition plan for each to achieve his and her individual employment goal. VR is a critically important transition resource.

Community Rehabilitation Providers

A typical community will often have multiple community rehabilitation service providers with an agency mission of assisting people with disabilities to obtain and maintain competitive employment. In general, providers will offer services as a free-standing employment service organization or as a component of a segregated center-based program. Cimera (2011) cautions users of segregated centers, sometimes referred to as sheltered workshops, because skills learned in a sheltered workshop may not improve the employability of the job seeker and, in addition, may make competitive employment more costly.

Many of these service providers work closely with the state VR service agency. Specific services offered by providers will vary with many offering counseling, assessments, benefits counseling, job placement, and supported employment services designed to assist students to live independently in the community. Community rehabilitation programs providing employment-related services for individuals with a disability can operate as for-profit or as nonprofit businesses. However, it is important to note that these programs do usually provide services based on contract or fee-for-service arrangements. Therefore, access to their services will frequently require a funding authorization from an agency such as VR.

Case Management Services through Community Rehabilitation Providers

The employment support staff for community rehabilitation providers is usually called employment consultants/specialists, job coaches, or other closely related job titles linking their work closely to employment outcomes. Some community rehabilitation providers have contracts with their local developmental disabilities agency, for example, to provide case management services. Usually, case management–type assistance involving identification of potential resources in the community and coordination with other service providers is provided in response to individual support needs critical to employment success. For example, an employment consultant might seek out benefits counseling assistance, child care options, mental health services, or other supports needed for an individual with a disability who needs this type of assistance. The case management role of community rehabilitation providers is most frequently time-limited and situational with staff coordinating its services with the funding agency such as VR and/or addressing individual support needs critical to employment success.

Employment and Related Services Available through Community Rehabilitation Programs

Community rehabilitation programs provide a variety of employment-related services such as helping the youth with a disability explore potential job and career options through situational assessments at competitive job sites and through job tryouts. A variety of job preparation, job development, and job placement services are also provided. These services might include practicing job interviews, job seeking skills classes, résumé preparation, guided job searches, and negotiations with employers. For example, an employer has a job with multiple job duties. Some of these duties match well to the abilities of the job applicant with a disability; other features of the job responsibilities are a poor match for the applicant. The employment consultant, with the permission of the applicant, might work with the employer to negotiate a job carved out of the original job description that is a good match for the individual with a disability (Griffin, Hammis, Geary, & Sullivan, 2008). Once the job match is completed, the employment consultant can assist with training at the job site, help the worker with a disability adjust to job demands, and provide ongoing support as needed to help maintain the job. Also, the employment consultant can potentially assist with job change.

Funding Available Through Community Rehabilitation Programs

Because they usually work under contract/fee arrangements to cover the cost for their services, community rehabilitation programs are usually not a primary source of funding. However, these programs are frequently quite familiar with the funding resources in a community and can assist in identifying funding resources. Community programs combine the funding received through contracts/fees with funding available to an individual consumer, such as the Social Security PASS plan described earlier in this chapter. Successful community rehabilitation programs create a diversified funding base that brings together a variety of funding options (Hall, Freeze, Butterworth, & Hoff, 2011).

Community rehabilitation programs are a very important resource for youth in transition. The programs can offer specialized services that match well to the needs of individuals with specific types of disabilities, with specific training and support needs and/or more time-intensive, prescriptive service requirements that are beyond the capacity of public agencies serving large number of people. Youth with disabilities and their families need to review information on the providers in their community before committing to a specific program. This review should potentially include personal interviews with the representatives of the programs. Funding agencies such as VR agencies should have information on the outcomes achieved by these programs, including satisfaction reports from their consumers (O'Brien, Revell, & West, 2003). Before selecting a community rehabilitation program, the following questions should be researched:

1. What are the general characteristics of the program (e.g., location, contact information, program model, and availability of transportation to the program)?
2. What kinds of jobs do consumers get?
3. How stable and supportive is job coaching staff likely to be?
4. What level of hours, pay, and benefits can a consumer expect?
5. How likely is a consumer to get a job and how long will it take to get one?
6. How satisfied were other consumers with the services of the provider?

Case Study Example of Services Provided through a Community Rehabilitation Program

Here is an example of an application of services through a community rehabilitation program to transition planning for a youth with a disability.

Micah Micah is 21 and has received special education services while in school on the basis of an autism spectrum disorder. He has difficulty mainly in the areas of socialization and communication, particularly in new and unfamiliar situations. He performs well with supervision and close guidance in situations where he can remain active and interact with a limited number of people. With the support of funding arranged through VR, an employment specialist from a local community rehabilitation program is hired to provide job development and job placement services for Micah. There is a retirement community in his neighborhood that has a large in-house laundry facility. There is a position in the laundry area that matches well to Micah's abilities and interests. The employment specialist accompanies him for a job interview and arranges for a "working interview" for Micah where he is given the opportunity to demonstrate his ability to do the required job tasks as an alternative to a predominantly verbal interview. Micah is hired. His employment support plan includes the employment specialist spending an extended period of time with him at the job site learning the required job duties and also assisting him in becoming comfortable in his work and social interactions with co-workers.

Community rehabilitation programs can be a primary source of employment and related training and support for a variety of transitioning youth with disabilities who benefit from job placement, job site training, and ongoing support services.

State Developmental Disability Agency/ Local Community Service Boards/Agencies

Services in the intellectual disability/developmental disabilities areas operate under a variety of different names. In some communities, these services are managed by local community service boards. Some states operate these services under direct state supervision of local agencies. These local boards and/or state-directed programs frequently also serve individuals with disabilities based on mental health and/or substance abuse issues. Eligibility for these services is usually on the basis of the presence of a disability that meets specific state guidelines, and these eligibility criteria will vary from state to state (Braddock, Hemp, & Rizzolo, 2008). The services from these local community service board/agencies are a core potential resource for youth with disabilities in transition who meet the eligibility guidelines.

Case Management Services Available through Local Community Services Boards/Agencies

Case managers within the local community through the mental health/developmental disabilities/substance abuse services system are frequently excellent resources for the transition-planning process. In general, case managers are available to serve as a coordination hub with very specific knowledge of services for the youth as well as for family members. Case managers will be knowledgeable about resources for community housing and supported living, for example, and can help the youth and family identify and access a variety of services funded through the **Home and Community Based Services Medicaid Waiver** that is discussed shortly in this chapter. Case managers can attend transition meetings, both as resources for information and referral and also to help plan for specific transition support services needed by an individual.

Employment-Related Services Available through Community Service Boards/Agencies

These programs can provide an array of services that include counseling, family planning, training, nutrition, personal health care, and consultation. Many community service boards operate or contract for community housing and supported living programs, a critical need for many youth with significant disabilities in transition as they seek to live separate from their families (or, in fact, do not have the option of living with family). For individuals with a mental health–related disability, these programs are the primary source of public mental health clinical and support services, including medication management and therapeutic counseling. There is substantial evidence that the integration of mental health and employment services increases the expectation for successful employment outcomes for individuals with a severe mental illness (Bond, Drake, & Becker, 2008). Therefore, it is critically important that transition plans and services include close coordination with the local mental health agency for youth in transition with mental health–related issues.

Funding Available Through Community Service Boards/Agencies

Depending on state and sometimes local laws and policies, the populations served by individual community service boards/agencies can vary widely. Some serve a wide range of individuals with a disability; others serve a much more limited population. Unlike state VR agencies discussed earlier, community service boards/agencies are not operated under a specific set of federal laws. The disability-related service areas these agencies serve can include, but potentially are not limited to, mental health, developmental disabilities, and/or substance abuse services. Therefore, because public funding is frequently categorical in nature and targeted to specific disability groups, the funding resources available through community service boards/agencies can vary widely from state to state and across communities. It is critically important that youth with disabilities in transition, their families, and key stakeholders take the time to become fully informed regarding the target populations and related funding resources and priorities.

Community service boards/agencies have access to a variety of funding resources. Funding is frequently available to assist with the acquisition of housing and supported living services, as well as employment supports. A primary funding source is the Home and Community Based Services Medicaid Waiver. The purpose of this waiver is to provide services in the community for individuals who, without these services, because of the significant nature of their disability and resulting support needs, would need to live in an institutional setting. However, funding for the waiver is drawn from federal funds matched with state dollars (Braddock et al., 2008). Transition-aged youth living in states experiencing difficulties in fully funding needed waiver services with the required state match face the potential of waiting lists, limited services, and/or narrowly defined target populations that result in gaps and limitations in services.

Case Study Example of Services Provided through State and Local Community Service Boards/Agencies

Here are two examples of applications of services through state and local community service boards/agencies to transition planning for a youth with a disability.

Denise   Denise is 22 and has a significant intellectual disability. She has had very limited community and work experience while in school and does not have a specific area of identified vocational interest as she nears the completion of her secondary program. Denise is eligible for services funded through the Home and Community Based Medicaid Waiver program because, without these services, she is at risk for placement in an institutional setting. Her transition plan emphasizes the need for her to have an extended period of community exploration and experience, potentially including job site observations and job tryouts as a community-based assessment process for employment. The state developmental disabilities program and the local community services board will arrange for her to live in a supported living situation and will coordinate a program of community exploration designed for her to have an opportunity to "discover" (Griffin et al., 2008) her vocational interests and abilities.

Joseph   Joseph is 19 and has received special education services on the basis of an emotional disability. He has periodic episodes of severe depression. His transition team, in working with Joseph and his family on his transition plan, has noted a number of needed support services if he is to live and work successfully in the community. He needs continued mental health treatment services and assistance with medication management. He needs job placement assistance and ongoing support and encouragement once he is placed in employment. He will also need supported living assistance if he is to reach his goal of living independent of his family. Joseph's transition team seeks assistance in these support need areas from the state mental health program and its community treatment program. The community mental health program has an integrated treatment and employment program for which he is eligible. His transition plan includes assistance from the state VR program and services through his local mental health community services program for supported living and an integrated mental health treatment and employment program.

These examples demonstrate how state developmental disabilities/mental health agencies and community boards can assist in providing employment and related resources for eligible transitioning youth with disabilities.

Centers for Independent Living

Centers for independent living (CILs) are a valuable potential resource for local transition teams (Wehmeyer & Gragoudas, 2004). These programs can provide a wealth of information for students and their families. CIL staff can assist in helping students to build their advocacy skills as well as to understand their rights. Most CILs provide general information about resources in the community and will also offer classes in areas such as financial management, socialization, sexuality, leisure activities, peer counseling, and self-advocacy.

Case Management Services Available Through Centers for Independent Living

CILs place an emphasis on hiring staff who are persons with a disability (Usiak, Stone, House, & Montgomery, 2004). These staff have personal insights into the challenges and opportunities in the local community involved in living and working with a disability. The staff offers information and referral assistance, peer counseling, and self-advocacy training, as well as crisis intervention assistance. CILs frequently serve as a community hub for information, services, and support for individuals with disabilities and can help significantly in transition planning and in implementing transition plans.

Employment Services Available Through Centers for Independent Living

Employment services available through CILs can vary substantially from program to program. The service most frequently available is training on job-seeking skills. Some CILs do provide direct employment supports in helping consumers locate jobs. CILs place a premium on self-advocacy and independence, so a part of the peer-counseling service is to help job applicants represent themselves effectively to employers. The peer education might also involve information and guidance on how to approach self-disclosure to an employer about the presence of a disability, particularly in situations where there is a need to negotiate a job accommodation.

Funding Available Through Centers for Independent Living

Many CILs receive federal funds appropriated through the Rehabilitation Act that include purchase of service dollars that can be used to acquire goods or services for individuals. These independent living services funds are usually very limited but are a potential resource that should be explored. The CILs also have targeted state or local dollars that can sometimes be used for services such as transportation, personal assistance services (at home and/or in the workplace), and training. As a community service hub, a major strength of CILs related to funding is the strong partnership arrangements these programs have with other community service agencies. Frequently the CIL can help an individual with a disability obtain funding support from these partner agencies.

Case Study Example of Services Provided Through a Center for Independent Living

Here is an example of services provided through a CIL to a youth with a disability transitioning from school into the community.

Ed   Ed is 21 and has a significant physical disability caused by spina bifida. His mobility is limited in terms of his transferring independently into and out of his wheelchair. He requires assistance in a number of personal care areas. He has received personal care assistance during his school program. Ed currently lives at his parents' home and has a personal goal of living on his own. The CIL offers a variety of programs that are key to Ed developing the skills needed for him to live and work in the community. The CIL offers an independent living skills program, peer counseling, and training in managing a personal assistant. The CIL works closely with a supported living apartment program where Ed could have his own apartment but still receive assistance needed for him to live there successfully. The CIL also works closely with the local VR office that can assist Ed in achieving his employment goals.

Ed's example demonstrates how a CIL can assist in providing community living and related resources for eligible transitioning youth with disabilities.

One-Stop Career Centers

The Workforce Investment Act of 1998 created One-Stop Career Centers as a key employment resource in the community. The One-Stop Career Centers have core services that are available to anyone in a community who needs help in locating employment. These core services mainly involve access through self-directed job searches to an information center that contains information on available job openings in the community. For those individuals who meet the criteria for eligibility for more intense service through the One-Stop Career Center, a variety of more individualized services are available. Youth and young adults with disabilities are targeted for services through One-Stop Career Centers, which can play a significant role in the delivery of transition services. The One-Stop Career Centers can be a tremendous resource for both students and the school's transition team in developing a plan for transition. One-Stop Career Centers have an exciting information and referral mechanism through which they can connect their customers with disabilities to a large variety of community resources. Specifically, youth with disabilities can take advantage of their career guidance program and competitive employment services.

Case Management Services Available Through One-Stop Career Centers

One-Stop Career Center staff includes plan managers who can assist in planning employment-related services through the One-Stop Career Center and can also reach out into the community to help identify and acquire other needed transition services. Some One-Stop Career Centers have "program navigators" to help individuals with a disability match up with the most appropriate service within the One-Stop Career Center and the community. The One-Stop Career Center, by design, frequently serves as a home base for many community partners who colocate staff within the One-Stop Career Center setting. VR and social services are two of the partner agencies that participate in the One-Stop Career Center program and offer additional case management support for eligible participants.

Employment Services Available Through One-Stop Career Centers

One-Stop Career Centers have job listings identifying available employment opportunities. Information from interest inventories can help guide a job search. For individuals who need accommodations to access job information through, for example, computerized job search resources, One-Stop Career Center workstations are frequently equipped with accessibility kits that accommodate a variety of disabling conditions. One-Stop Career Centers offer job clubs where an individual looking for employment can get the support and information from peers and a group facilitator. Some One-Stop Career Centers have more **customized employment** resource staff that will represent the job interests of an individual with a disability to a potential employer and help negotiate a job opportunity (Targett, Young, Revell, Williams, & Wehman, 2007). Additional employment services of potential value to youth in transition include paid and unpaid work experiences, occupational skills training, job placement, and follow-up services after employment to help with job retention and career development.

Funding Available through One-Stop Career Centers

For individuals eligible for intensive Workforce Investment Services through the One-Stop Career Center, funding can include access to individual training accounts (ITAs). On an individual prescriptive basis, the ITA funds can be used to purchase services such as training, adapted equipment, or supported employment. The main funding strength of a One-Stop Career Center is its direct links with the other community agencies that fund employment services, such as VR and community service boards/agencies.

Case Study Example of Services Provided through a One-Stop Career Center

Here is an example of how a One-Stop Career Center can assist in providing employment and related resources for eligible transitioning youth with disabilities.

Reggie   Reggie is 17 and is receiving special education services on the basis of a severe learning disability. He has participated in a variety of in-school career awareness and career exploration activities. His local One-Stop Career Center offers a Summer Youth Work Experience Program where he can work in a paid position for 30 hours a week for 8 weeks. The One-Stop Career Center also has a work-study program during the regular school year for which Reggie is eligible. His IEP and transition plan include his participation in the Summer Youth Work Experience Program and also the work-study program as he completes his secondary-level education program. Reggie's plan also includes application to the VR agency to assist his transition from the school program to the adult community when he completes his secondary-level education program.

This example demonstrates how One-Stop Career Centers can be a primary source of career awareness, career exploration, training, and employment support for a variety of transitioning youth with disabilities in their transition process.

Strong Alliances Between Schools and Businesses

As previously discussed, the business community is a natural partner for school programs interested in assisting transition-aged students with job shadowing, mentoring, work-study programs, internships, and competitive employment. However, business is frequently either overlooked or taken for granted in the transition process. School programs and business need to do a better job of establishing strong collaborative relationships. Businesses should see a partnership with a local school program as a rich source of potential labor and, therefore, should consider it a good investment of time to nurture these relationships. Schools, conversely, must also understand that they are creating a value to community employers and be willing to commit the necessary resources that will yield productive relationships. This type of relationship building, where school personnel are actively marketing their potential labor source to the local business community, will mean a drastic departure from current practices.

With the growing demands for labor in this country and the dwindling number of available workers, school programs must be prepared to initiate this new marketing approach to business. The Hudson Institute predicts that the supply of labor in the country will not catch up until 2050 and there is a need to actively recruit from untapped labor pools (Kotlikoff & Burns, 2005). New public–private partnerships with the schools can answer this labor shortage if school programs will actively participate in the community, collect data about the business community needs, and employ this newly acquired information to satisfy these personnel shortages (Wehman, Brooke, & Green, 2004).

The key to this marketing approach is satisfying the needs of business through an exchange process in which each party receives some value from the relationship. Often, school programs do not see themselves as adding value to the business community. Yet, many businesses already recognize their labor shortage needs and are actively looking for interested school programs and rehabilitation agencies for assistance. Business is telling the public sector that they want to know more about the issues facing people with disabilities as they relate to employment. Business also wants to know how rehabilitation programs can benefit their business operation (Luecking, 2009a). They want to know what value rehabilitation and school programs bring to the relationship and how that will affect the bottom line for the business.

School programs need to develop a clear and simple message to business regarding the value they bring to the business relationship. It is important to develop a full range of services that can be provided to the business community and to market how they benefit business. Like any relationship, a business partnership needs to be nurtured to grow and stay healthy. The qualities that make most relationships successful apply to any business partnership that a school forms. These qualities include trustworthiness, honesty, commitment, perseverance, and reliability. It is in the best interest for all involved (i.e., school agency, employer, and students) that the school program lives up to promises and commitments made to the business community. For example, a school program should not promise an employer a qualified worker if no one is available who can meet the employer's needs. In the same respect, it would not be appropriate to promise a student a job with a specific employer if a job opening does not exist (Wehman et al., 2004).

School professionals cannot be complacent. Teachers, transition coordinators, and other school personnel need to learn more about current trends in employment and the latest assistive technology. It is important to join business-led organizations and become active members of the community. They must ask for business assistance and demonstrate that they have something of value for the employer.

Business Partnerships that Are Working

Partnerships with the business community are essential. There are many examples of excellent working public–private partnerships throughout the country. These partnerships have been established because both parties were able to build a trusting relationship with each other. Businesses will realize the value of this approach that leads to a win–win situation for employers, students, and school programs. The following corporate example describes one partnership that continues to yield great jobs for students with significant disabilities, a competent workforce for the business, and an outstanding employment-training site for students who may be interested in this particular career path.

Ten years ago, Erin Riehle, clinical director of the Emergency Department at Cincinnati Children's Hospital, had a revelation. She had been struggling to solve a problem to improve the efficiency of the emergency department. Restocking supplies was a problem because of a high rate of staff turnover. One day, Riehle noted that the hospital had adopted a policy that stated, "Healthcare organizations must lead their communities in increasing employment opportunities for qualified persons with disabilities and advocate on behalf of their employment to other organizations" (American College of Healthcare Executives policy [1995], adopted by Cincinnati Children's Hospital [1998]). With this in mind, she began to think about alternative staffing solutions by training and hiring individuals with disabilities, and, soon afterward, Project SEARCH® came to be (see also Chapter 7). The goal would be to provide employment for individuals whose disability had been a significant barrier to employment, such as people with multiple disabilities and severe learning disabilities. Two collaborating partners were identified: the Great Oaks Institute of Technology and Career Development and the Hamilton Country Board of Mental Retardation and Developmental Disabilities (MR/DD). Great Oaks served

36 school districts and prepared more than 6,000 youth in full- and part-time programs per year. Hamilton County MR/DD Board provided countywide educational and residential services to adults and children with intellectual disabilities and other developmental disabilities and served more than 10,000 individuals.

The partners dedicated personnel to this effort who were responsible for learning about the workplace, culture, and job responsibilities; the partners also committed to providing training and support services to participants.

"The key to our program is having the professionals from the Great Oaks Institute of Technical and Career Development and Hamilton County MR/DD Board working on site," Riehle explained. "All of the employees report to their department supervisors, like traditional employees. But [they] also have follow-along support services to aid the employee in resolving problems and adapting to change, among other things."

The employees work in a wide range of positions, such as sterilization technician, lab courier, and clinical support staff. "Our program uses a business model," explained Riehle. "We provide a single conduit for organizing and delivering employment services, in collaboration with the community, and deliver them in an effective and accountable way as an integrated part of the work site. It is an appealing model to employers, and it works."

There have been other employers and programs working collaboratively with local schools to offer students with disabilities opportunities to learn valuable work skill sets. One such business is Walgreens drug stores, which has gained a national reputation for its hiring initiatives in its distribution centers. Even before Walgreens gained national attention it was working with many local schools to offer internships opportunities in its local stores. One example is located in Topeka, Kansas. In 2006, eight Topeka-area Walgreens stores partnered with area public schools to offer students with disabilities an opportunity to work in their stores as a part of their school curriculum. This community work experience has made it possible to place many graduates into jobs at Walgreens as well as other employment opportunities with local businesses in Topeka. Walgreens shared its social skills curriculum, which they use for their prehires, and that information has been embedded into the public school curriculum. One key aspect of the program was the community-based instruction/work experience program agreement signed by both the Topeka Public Schools and Walgreens. This agreement now serves as a model for collaboration.

Another employer making headlines and developing a deliberate process to hiring individuals with disabilities is Lowe's home improvement store. Since January 2009, Lowe's distribution center in Pittston, Pennsylvania, partnered with the ARC of Luzerne County to provide training for staff and build a pipeline of candidates with disabilities, which included many local graduates from the schools to work at Lowe's. Lowe's and the ARC of Luzerne County are working with the Luzerne Intermediate Unit and associated school districts to provide students with disabilities the opportunity to train for potential full-time employment upon exiting school. Pam Zotynia, executive director for the ARC, said

> the students spend a semester at Lowe's [engaged in paid part-time employment, learning a variety of jobs within the company.] She said the Luzerne Intermediate Unit provides job mentors on site, as well as transportation for the students. "Once the students complete the program successfully, they become eligible for employment," Zotynia said. "They can either begin work immediately, or bank the eligibility until they complete school. They will then leave school with a job in place. We run three or four classes per school year." (O'Boyle, 2011)

Students must be 18 years or older, have the ability to lift 70 lbs., successfully pass a drug screening test, and successfully pass a criminal background check. Lowe's has created similar programs initiatives in all of the Lowe's distribution centers. To fill the jobs at Lowe's, it is critical to have local schools as a partner, providing a continuum of quality student graduates as part of the pipeline (O'Boyle, 2011).

Workforce issues and the need to hire good workers has become a major focal point for businesses. This concern is not just a business concern. It has direct impact for

Table 6.5.   Examples of collaborative activities for building business partnerships

- Meet with community business people to clarify the role you want business to play in the transition process.
- Seek the advice of business regarding curriculum-training programs, marketing materials, and other items that are targeted toward the business community.
- Get business involvement in joint newsletter articles regarding success stories.
- Request that business sit on focus groups to identify program strengths and weaknesses.
- Seek a commitment from business to participate in career exploration activities at school.
- Share information regarding disability-specific issues such as the Americans with Disabilities Act.
- Schedule joint speaking opportunities to such community groups as the Lions Club, Rotary Club, local chamber of commerce, and the local Society for Human Resource Management (SHRM) chapter.
- Seek opportunities for students to do tours and information interviews at the work sites.
- Request possible internships and mentors for students involved in transition.
- Develop opportunities for businesses to recruit and interview students with disabilities.

educational systems across the country. By coming together at a local level, businesses and schools have the opportunity to build a partnership that has direct economic benefits for both parties. If school transition programs expect business to work with them, it is important for schools to recognize the need for an ongoing collaborative partnership. There are many ways a business can interact with youth with disabilities while they are still attending schools. Table 6.5 provides a range of ideas that schools could utilize to build business partnerships. Businesses are concerned about the educational and economic issues in the communities where they conduct their work. To grow and make a profit, they need young people coming out of the schools ready to engage in work activities that will meet their skill demands. Being involved with a school-to-work transition program allows the business to invest first-hand in making sure that youth with disabilities will meet their labor demands.

Conclusion

This chapter has emphasized that effective transition planning involving movement from secondary education into the community involves integrating the input and resources of a variety of key partners. First, youth with disabilities and their families and key stakeholders need to be fully educated on the impact of employment on disability benefits. The WIPA projects now in place across the country provide a critically important resource for obtaining benefits-related information and assistance. Second, there are a variety of community training and employment support programs that can serve as resources in planning and providing transition services. These services vary considerably across states and communities. Early involvement with these services will help a youth in transition become known to the case management, employment services, and funding support resources most needed to support his or her plan. Finally, successful employment outcomes depend on employer involvement. Work experiences and job internships while a youth with a disability is completing his or her secondary program expands job and career awareness and helps target postsecondary training and employment interests. Access to information about benefits, involvement of key community programs, and employer participation in the transition process are the cornerstones of effective community involvement in the transition of youth with disabilities from school to living and working in the community.

Study Questions

1. Describe the major roles of at least six community programs in supporting transition.
2. Describe the six critical elements in community-based transition.
3. Explain the importance of benefits planning as a component of community-based transition.

4. Identify and describe at least four work incentives offered through the SSA available to recipients of SSI.

5. Describe and discuss the case management, employment services, and funding opportunities offered by at least three community service agencies for youth in transition.

6. Identify five questions that should be researched before selecting a community rehabilitation program.

7. Describe six examples of collaborative activities for building business partnerships in support of youth with disabilities in transition.

Online Resources

Social Security Online – The Work Site: Service Provider Directory: https://secure.ssa.gov/apps10/oesp/providers.nsf/bystate

National Center on Workforce and Disability: http://www.onestops.info/i.php?i=1

Institute for Community Inclusion, University of Massachusetts, Boston: http://www.communityinclusion.org/index.php

Dartmouth Psychiatric Research Center: http://prc.dartmouth.edu/

Job Accommodation Network: http://askjan.org/

Individualized Career Planning: http://ruralinstitute.umt.edu/transition/art_careerplanningmod.asp

Transition Service Delivery in the Schools

Full Inclusion into Schools

7

Strategies for Collaborative Instruction

KIM SPENCE-COCHRAN,
CYNTHIA E. PEARL, AND ZACHARY WALKER

After completing this chapter, the reader will be able to

- Describe the historical perspective on the movement to integrate or merge general and special education resources, personnel, methods, and curriculum
- Defend the arguments and the critical issues related to the implementation of inclusion
- Discuss the importance of working collaboratively with students, families, and a variety of professionals to facilitate successful inclusion
- Recognize practical strategies for achieving successful inclusion in school and community settings
- Recognize crucial transitional supports to facilitate inclusion across the age span
- Support a personal position on the issues surrounding inclusion

National Commitment to Inclusion

Volumes have been written on the issues surrounding the inclusion of students with disabilities in school and community settings. Authors have discussed at length why students should be included, which students should be included, where students should be included, and how students should be included (Kauffman & Hallahan, 2011; Landmark, Ju, & Zhang, 2010; Smith, 2006). Foreman, Arthur-Kelly, Pascoe, and King (2004) identified the range of perceptions that have been aired by various stakeholders as falling between two polarized positions—those who contend that all children should be educated together with the necessary resources or services provided in the general education classroom and those who argue that an appropriate educational experience for some students, particularly those with complex and severe disabilities, is only possible with the infrastructure of a special school or unit.

Despite varied opinions on the best educational placements for students with disabilities, there is general agreement that our highest aspiration should be the inclusion of students in integrated school and community settings, to the fullest extent possible, with the appropriate individualized supports necessary for a successful educational experience. This is the position supported in the Individuals with Disabilities Education Improvement Act (IDEA) of 2004 (PL 108-446), the most recent reauthorization of IDEA. IDEA 2004 renewed our commitment to provide a free appropriate public education (FAPE) for students with disabilities and moved beyond questions of why and where students should be included to focus attention on how, as a nation, we can come closer to attaining the goal of full inclusion for individuals with disabilities not only in school settings but also in their communities and, ultimately, in the world of work.

The need to facilitate inclusion across the age span is highlighted by data indicating that people between the ages of 16 and 64 years are less likely to be employed if they have a disability. The Bureau of Labor Statistics (2011) released disability employment statistics revealing that, in 2010, only 18.6% of people with disabilities were in the labor force compared with 63.5% of persons with no disability. Furthermore, the unemployment rate for those with disabilities was 14.8%, compared with 9.4% for persons with no disability. In an effort to address barriers to employment, IDEA 2004 requires that a plan for transition to postsecondary activities be in place beginning no later than the first individualized education program (IEP) to be in effect when the child is 16.

As noted in Chapter 1, Kohler and Field (2003) promoted an even more comprehensive approach identified as transition-focused education. This perspective recognizes that transition planning should be viewed not as an additional activity to be introduced when students with disabilities reach age 16 but, rather, as a foundation from which educational programs and activities are developed. Long-range planning for transition should provide students with disabilities with opportunities to learn alongside peers without disabilities throughout their schooling. In inclusive settings, they can begin to develop academic, social, and functional skills necessary for eventual independence and participation in society. These skills are further developed when inclusion in school settings is paired with community-based instruction (CBI) aimed at the acquisition of independent living and job-related skills (Lawrence-Brown, 2004). Ryndak, Ward, Alper, Mongomery, Wilson, and Storch (2010) compared outcomes for two persons with significant disabilities, one who received services in self-contained special education and one who received services in inclusive general education settings. They noted better adult outcomes related to community living and work, social interactions, participation in naturally occurring activities, and natural support networks for the individual who received services in inclusive settings. The findings of Ryndak et al. support the assertion of Certo, Mautz, Pumpian, Sax, Smalley, Wade, and colleagues who maintained, "It is difficult to imagine that students with significant support needs, who have been fully included through high school, and their families, will continue to accept less than full inclusion into typical adult life

Table 7.1. Areas for research

1. Do learners with disabilities in inclusion programs make better academic gains than their peers who are in noninclusion programs or who spend less time in general education contact?
2. Do learners with disabilities enrolled in inclusion programs demonstrate better social competence and more positive peer and adult relationships than their peers in more restrictive programs?
3. Do typically developing and achieving peers have a more positive or less positive perceptions of students with disabilities as a consequence of the inclusion of students with disabilities in general education programs?
4. Are postschool outcomes such as employment, incarceration, social service, and mental health contacts improved by students' inclusion in general education?

Source: Kauffman, Nelson, Simpson, and Mock (2011).

after graduation" (2003, p. 3). Overall research is scant and does not indicate that one type of placement is most likely to lead to academic or social benefits (Kauffman, Mock, Tankersley, & Landrum, 2008). Some recommendations for areas to research offered by Kauffman, Nelson, et al. (2011) are noted in Table 7.1.

The cases that follow describe the high school experiences of two students with disabilities and illustrate how our progress toward full inclusion must be measured on a student-by-student basis (Ryndak, et al., 2010). Unfortunately, it seems that for every student like Ryan, whose educational experience illustrates how far we have come toward the inclusion of students with disabilities in schools and communities, there is another student like Helen to demonstrate how little has changed over the years. Even though these two students are within the same school district, their daily educational experiences are completely different. After reading about Ryan and Helen, reflect on the questions in Table 7.2.

. . . .

Ryan in School   At 14 years of age, Ryan was formally adopted by his foster family. At the age of 4, he was removed from his home by child protective services and then spent the next 10 years of his life in specialized foster care because his mother was unable to adequately care for him. Ryan's foster parents received special training on assisting and managing Ryan's autism and juvenile diabetes in addition to securing a variety of local and statewide supports to provide him with the best possible inclusive living and school situation. Despite an extensive history of physically aggressive behavior and difficulty managing his diabetes, Ryan was fully included at his neighborhood elementary and middle school at the urging of his foster parents. He went on to high school after being formally adopted by his foster parents and received a regular diploma when he graduated from his home-zoned school. Multiple supports were provided to facilitate his successful inclusion in general education classrooms. While attending school, Ryan received specialized language instruction, occupational therapy, social skills instruction, and medical support from highly qualified personnel every week. At the request of several support agencies, Ryan's peers were prepared to provide supports when he encountered difficulty with his health or behavioral issues in any school setting. A comprehensive behavior plan was in place to assist and instruct him during times of frustration, as well as to provide the staff with support while maintaining safety. Ryan uses a computer to communicate with others because he is nonverbal and became very proficient with computers before exiting high school. After school and on weekends he participated with the swim team and attended various athletic events at the school. Ryan rode the regular school bus to and from school, receiving assistance from designated staff or peers when necessary.

. . . .

Ryan Today   Ryan currently works in a commercial nursery within his community. He works 20–35 hours per week watering plants, replanting, and "cleaning" plants and utilizes the public transportation system or his bicycle to get himself to and from work each day. Ryan has successfully worked at the nursery in a supported employment situation for the past 4 years. He is supported in a variety of jobs by several young adults he met in general education classes in high school. Ryan's adoptive parents alternate taking him to private language sessions and social skills instructional groups each week in an effort to improve his overall ability to communicate and socialize with others, which he appears to greatly enjoy. Ryan continues to live with his adoptive parents, though he lives on his own for the most part within a "mother-in-law"–style suite attached to the back of his parents' home. Ryan has expressed a genuine desire to work full time at the nursery and appears to have the skills to do this should the opportunity arise.

A Historical Perspective on Inclusion

On May 17, 1954, the historic *Brown v. Board of Education* decision struck down the "separate but equal" doctrine that had prevailed for 58 years. Chief Justice Warren concluded, "We come then to the question presented: Does segregation of children in public schools solely on the basis of race, even though the physical facilities and other 'tangible' factors may be equal, deprive the children of the minority group of equal educational opportunities? We believe that it does." The *Brown* decision was the catalyst that led to the broadening of education for all people. Actions initiated by families, advocacy organizations, and civil rights lawyers culminated in two historic decisions, *Pennsylvania Association for Retarded Citizens (PARC) v. Commonwealth of Pennsylvania* (1972) and *Mills v. Board of Education of the District of Columbia* (1972). The Commonwealth of Pennsylvania and the District of Columbia were ordered to

1. Provide FAPE to all students with disabilities
2. Educate students with disabilities in the same schools and basically the same programs as students without disabilities
3. Put into place certain procedural safeguards so that students with disabilities can challenge schools that do not live up to the court's orders

Three years later, the **Education for All Handicapped Children Act (EHC)** of 1975 (PL 94-142) was enacted, guaranteeing the right of students with disabilities to FAPE and providing federal money to assist states in paying for special education. Before the enactment of EHC, only one in five children with disabilities was educated in U.S. schools and many states had laws specifically excluding children identified as deaf, blind, emotionally disturbed, or mentally retarded (U.S. Department of Education [U.S. DOE], Office of Special Education and Rehabilitative Services [OSERS], 2010). Since the 1970s, key amendments to EHC, now codified as IDEA, have expanded on its support for equality of access and quality programs and services for children with disabilities. Via legislation, Congress has clearly and consistently supported the intention that educational outcomes for individuals with disabilities mirror those of their peers without disabilities. IDEA has provided the major impetus to the movement of students with disabilities away from segregated settings. The concept of **least restrictive environment (LRE)** is central to IDEA. Federal law states

> To the maximum extent appropriate, children with disabilities, including those children in public and private institutions or other care facilities, are educated with children who are not disabled, and special classes, separate schooling, or other removal of children with disabilities from the regular educational environment occurs only when the nature or severity of the disability is such that education in regular classes with the use of supplementary aids and services cannot be achieved satisfactorily (IDEA 2004 [Part B, Sec 612 (a) (5)]).

Philosophical Approaches to Inclusion

Although few dispute the moral and ethical basis of the LRE concept, its implementation has been the focus of continued debate (Kauffman & Hallahan, 2011; Landmark, Ju, & Zhang, 2010). Three widely recognized terms—*mainstreaming, inclusion,* and *full inclusion*—refer to different approaches to the placement of students with special needs in general education classrooms. In the 1970s and 1980s, the placement of students with special needs in general education classrooms was referred to as *mainstreaming.* This term was largely replaced when the terms *full inclusion* and *inclusion* became popular following the IDEA of 1990 (PL 101-476) mandates for increased participation of general education.

Helen in School   Helen spent her entire educational career in self-contained special education classrooms with the blessing and encouragement of her school district. She is diagnosed as having a moderate cognitive impairment, having entered school at the age of 3 to receive prekindergarten services in a specialized classroom for students with developmental delays. Helen attended schools where inclusive practices were encouraged and realized for many students with mild disabilities but did not receive any services or supports in this regard. Despite many requests by Helen's parents to allow her the "most-appropriate" and "least-restrictive" classroom placements, Helen was educated with a handful of students for the majority of her time at public school. This meant that all of her daily instruction, including her lunch, was provided within one classroom, with a very small group of other students with significant disabilities. When Helen became angry or frustrated or did not desire to complete the repetitive worksheets she was often provided by paraprofessionals, she often engaged in self-injurious behavior. Despite having a teaching assistant specifically assigned to her for the majority of her school career, Helen's school records reflect little documented progress over the years. Her IEP goals included objectives that were repeated for several years because of lack of mastery. There were few opportunities for Helen to interact with her typical peers during the school day because of the nature of the segregated classes she attended. For all 6 years she attended high school, Helen rode a special education school bus with an assigned attendant.

Helen Today   Helen exited high school in June 2009, just shy of her 22nd birthday. She "graduated" with a special diploma, very few functional skills of independence, and no vocational training or experience despite having expressed a good deal of interest in becoming a child care worker. Despite her involvement with vocational rehabilitation consisting of attendance at a sheltered workshop two times per week, Helen currently spends most days watching television, playing with her doll collection, or with paid staff who supervise her while her parents are working. She is not working, nor has she applied for any job or educational programs since graduating from high school. Her parents have expressed frustration at the "system" for failing to provide Helen with an appropriate education that would have actually prepared her to work and/or participate in her community. Helen asserts that she would very much like to work with young children but has expressed to numerous support staff that she does not have any idea how to achieve this goal. She continues to live in her parents' home, relying completely on her family and paid support staff for support in all aspects of her life.

Mainstreaming refers to the selective placement of special education students in one or more regular education classes. These placements are based on the assumption that students with disabilities have earned opportunities to participate in the mainstream by demonstrating the ability to "keep up" with the other students. Essentially, mainstreaming refers to a part-time placement of students with disabilities in general class settings

Table 7.2.   Reflecting on the educational experiences of Ryan and Helen

Questions for reflection

After reading about the educational experiences of Ryan and Helen, reflect on the following questions:
1. Why are the educational placements of these students so markedly different?
2. What is your opinion regarding the marked differences in the experiences of these two students?
3. What are the supports that facilitate Ryan's inclusion in school and classroom activities?
4. Do you think it would be possible to include Helen at the same intensity as Ryan?
5. Education benefit is an important consideration in the placements of students with moderate and severe disabilities. What are the benefits of Ryan's full inclusion?
6. Which of these students do you think is more likely to be employed in an integrated setting following graduation from high school? Why?

and is associated with the belief that, although these students visit the mainstream, they remain the responsibility of special education. Although many professionals have adopted the term *inclusion* in referring to this practice, the basic philosophy of mainstreaming is still prevalent in the field.

Inclusion is conceptually similar to mainstreaming, albeit a critical difference between the two definitions exists. This difference represents a significant paradigm shift requiring only that the child will benefit from being in a general education class with no demands that he or she "keep up" with other students.

In the case of inclusion, although a student may leave the classroom for special education services, that student remains the responsibility of the general educator. The inclusion model enlarges the role of general education but also acknowledges the need to maintain a continuum of special education services. Educational programs may be provided in settings ranging from fully segregated, such as hospital and homebound services and special schools, to full-time placement in general education. The degree to which a student with a disability is included should be specifically and effectively tailored to meet his or her individual needs.

Those who advocate for *full inclusion*, including TASH and Schools Are for Everyone (SAFE), reject IDEA's "maximum extent appropriate" caveat and consequently do not acknowledge the need for a continuum of services. Supporters of full inclusion maintain instead that full-time placement in a general education classroom is appropriate for all students including those with moderate to severe disabilities (Ryndak, Jackson, & Billingsley, 2000). In a full inclusion model, special education is imported into the general education setting. Support is provided in the regular classroom and students do not leave for special education services. Ryan is an example of a student who was fully included. He did not leave the classroom to receive special education services. Language therapy, occupational therapy, social skills instruction, and health management skills were provided in his general education classroom.

In reviewing the evolution of the term *inclusion* and looking to the future, Kochhar, West, and Taymans (2000) predicted that schools will continue to review inclusion practices in an effort to assess the quality and effectiveness of educational programs for students with disabilities. They identified the trend for 2000 and beyond as *full participation* and *meaningful educational benefit.* These terms represent an approach that emphasizes not only maximum opportunity for inclusion but also positive outcomes for students with disabilities. This trend is in keeping with the focus in the No Child Left Behind Act (NCLB) of 2001 (PL 107-110) on accountability for results and proven educational methods. Under NCLB, states are currently working to close the achievement gap to ensure that all students achieve academic proficiency.

Special Education Service Delivery

Despite a lack of consensus on the issue of inclusion (Kauffman, Nelson, Simpson, & Mock, 2011), increasing numbers of children with disabilities have moved and continue to move away from segregated schools and classrooms to general education settings. According to the U.S. DOE (2011, July 11) Data Accountability Center, Office of Special Education Programs (OSEP), state-reported data revealed that, in fall 2010, 61% of students with disabilities ages 6–21 served under IDEA spent 80% or more of the school day in the regular education class. In comparison, 10 years earlier, in fall 2000, only 46% of students with disabilities spent 80% or more of the school day in regular classrooms (U.S. DOE, OSERS, 2003).

Although there is much to celebrate in the increasing inclusion of students with disabilities in general education settings, concerns have emerged in regard to specific populations of students with disabilities based on age, race/ethnicity, and disability label.

According to the U.S. DOE, OSEP (2010), progress toward less-restrictive settings is seen across all age groups, though younger students are more likely than older students to be served in the regular classroom. Data for fall 2005 revealed that 2.1% of students ages 6–11 years, 4.8% of students ages 12–17 years, and 12.8% of students ages 18–21 years served under IDEA were educated in separate environments. Percentages of students educated outside the regular class also varied for different racial/ethnic groups. For example, 43.9% of black (not Hispanic) students ages 6–21 years spent the majority of the school day in the regular education class compared with 59.1% of White (not Hispanic) students with disabilities. Furthermore, students with high-incidence disabilities were more likely to be served in the general education classroom than were those with low-incidence disabilities. The placements of students with multiple disabilities and intellectual disabilities run counter to the trend toward less-restrictive environments found in other disability categories. Helen's placement in self-contained special education classrooms in elementary and middle school, followed by placement in segregated classes in high school, is a prime example of this difference. Although her placements were highly restricted by educational options compared with Ryan's, they are actually very similar to those of other students with cognitive impairments, the majority of whom spend 60% or more of the school day in educational environments outside the regular class. According to Kauffman and Landrum

> IDEA requires different education for students who need it because of their disability. The need for education, including the place in which students with disabilities are to receive their education, is to be decided on an individual basis….The student is to be separated for special instruction only to the extent necessary to make his or her education appropriate. (2009, p. 182).

The question, then, is whether or not 60% or more of the school day outside the regular class is "necessary."

Preparing for Successful Inclusion

Successful implementation of inclusion requires that school administrators and teachers make changes in the ways in which they assign students to classrooms, schedule classes, set up teams, allocate resources, design curriculum, deliver instruction, and assess student progress. However, it is important to recognize that real change is deeply embedded in the systemic structure of an organization; it goes beyond reallocation of resources and implementation of new teaching methods (e.g., Smith, 2006). Though programs and materials support change, it is primarily about the beliefs and actions of individuals. As schools take on the challenges of inclusion, those working for change must recognize that it is a process that occurs slowly and requires that all stakeholders make a long-term commitment to provide ongoing support and address problems as they emerge.

How Do We Best Assess?

The first step in preparing for successful inclusion is to assess school and personnel readiness for the changes ahead. Increasing the quantity and quality of inclusive education in schools requires comprehensive and collaborative efforts for systemwide planning, implementation, and ongoing evaluation. Kochhar and colleagues (2000) identified several areas for evaluation including readiness

1.   For student evaluation and assessment
2.   Of the educational environment
3.   Of the physical and support services environment

4. Of the attitudinal culture and environment

5. For school and community involvement

6. For individualized planning and student and parent involvement

7. For professional development and teacher in-service training

8. Of the leadership and resources

9. For data collection, evaluation, and continuous improvement

In addition, the school should embrace beliefs central to this process such as (Kauffman & Hung, 2009)

- All students can learn.

- Special education is a service, not a placement option.

- All students may require supports in the classroom depending on individual needs.

- Most important of all, there must be more concern for what the students learn than for where they learn it.

Administrative Support

Administrative support has been identified as a meaningful variable associated with successful inclusion for all levels of students with disabilities (Eisenman, Pleet, Wandry, & McGinley, 2011; Mastropieri & Scruggs, 2001). Despite an overall increase in the numbers of students with disabilities being included in general education settings, a variety of barriers continue to hamper the successful inclusion of students with disabilities including negative teacher attitudes, lack of special educational knowledge, poor collaboration skills, and difficulties managing schedules (Worrell, 2008). Kennedy and Fisher (2001) found that teachers were more willing to consider alternate service delivery models when administrators created an atmosphere that was supportive of inclusive education. Administrative involvement can ensure that the inclusion planning team consists of willing and capable participants who are representative of all of the key stakeholders, including general and special education teachers, resource and related services personnel, and families (Carter & Hughes, 2006; Worrell, 2008). Administrators also play an important role in addressing many of the issues that arise with inclusion such as the allocation of resources, teaching assignments, student assignment, scheduling of classes and planning time, and assignment of paraprofessionals.

Identifying Opportunities for Inclusion

IDEA 2004 requires the education of students with disabilities in the general education curriculum to the greatest extent possible and has ushered in an unparalleled period of inclusive opportunities for students with various disabilities. As noted in Chapter 1, researchers have determined that individuals with disabilities who are included in the general education curriculum are more likely to experience better postschool outcomes (Landmark, Ju, & Zhang, 2010), particularly for students graduating with a standard diploma, which appears to be a strong predictor of successful employment (Dukes & Lamar-Dukes, 2009; Landmark et al., 2010).

Dorn and Fuchs (2004) identified four questions to consider when identifying appropriate settings for students with disabilities:

1. Where can the student learn specific skills?

2. Where does the student feel better?

3. Where can the student socialize?

4. Where do current skills of teachers fit the needs of the student?

The general education classroom is often the most appropriate answer to these questions; however, in considering these questions, it is important to bear in mind that inclusion opportunities are not limited to the general education classroom. All too often, students with disabilities are excluded from school activities for reasons of convenience. Students eat lunch in their classrooms or, in some cases, with the school nurse simply because the logistics of arranging for a student to eat in the school cafeteria poses difficulties that require additional planning and special supports. Even though schools are prohibited from excluding students with disabilities from extracurricular activities, they are less likely to participate without the added encouragement and support of school staff and peers.

It cannot be overstated: When one is identifying inclusion opportunities, it is important to recognize that inclusion is not about a place. Zigmond, Magiera, and Matta (2003), reflecting on a review of 35 years of efficacy research on the settings in which special education services are delivered, noted that location is not what makes the difference, but rather what occurs in the educational setting. Physical placement of a student with a disability in an inclusive setting does not guarantee that that student will be included. Dorn and Fuchs observed situations in which students with developmental disabilities were given very different tasks and in which teachers were not assisted in dealing with difficult behavior problems. They noted that, in such circumstances, "these children served primarily as classroom mascots and problems, not peers" (2004, p. 64).

To be fully included, the student with a disability must have access to the natural supports available to all students (Ryndak, Ward, Alper, Storch, & Montgomery, 2010). This includes access to general education peers who are not specifically designated as peer tutors or buddies. A substantial body of research suggests that the excessive physical proximity of paraprofessionals can have negative social effects. Paraprofessional training to increase awareness of practices that may isolate students with disabilities from their peers and to teach strategies to facilitate peer interactions is needed (Causton-Theoharis & Malmgren, 2005; Ryndak, Ward, Alper, & Storch et al., 2010). Although Ryan had the extra support of highly trained inclusive staff and peers who were specially trained to assist him in times of need, it was also important that he was provided with opportunities to interact and develop relationships with peers independently.

Effective Teaching Skills

Performance mandates of the NCLB Act of 2001 and IDEA 2004 have demanded ever-greater access to the general curriculum for all students, including those with disabilities. Inclusive classrooms and the elevated expectations for all students have a profound impact on preservice teacher preparation. In a study of preservice teachers' perceptions of teaching students with exceptional needs, Shippen, Crites, Houchins, Ramsey, and Simon (2005) looked at current teacher-preparation programs and their failure to address perceived problems in inclusive education, specifically the area of collaboration. Based on the findings of their study, Shippen and colleagues (2005) concluded that dual training in general and special education may indeed produce educators who are more willing and more capable to deal with their students' diverse learning needs.

Brownell, Ross, Colon, and McCallum (2005) reported that a critical element, among others, of effective teacher-education programs is collaboration. Collaboration is widely recognized as a prerequisite for inclusive education. Successful inclusive schools have a unified educational system with general and special educators collaborating to provide effective programs and services for all students (Burstein, Sears, Wilcoxen, Cabello, & Spagna, 2004).

A more recent national exploratory study focused on training efforts used to prepare preservice teachers for inclusion as well as on perceptions of the level and effectiveness of preservice teacher training in inclusion. Harvey, Yssel, Bauserman, and Merbler (2010) obtained information about preservice teacher preparation for inclusive classrooms from a national sample of faculty members in special education, elementary and secondary education, and curriculum and instruction at teacher education institutions. Faculty perceptions of training efforts used to prepare preservice teachers for inclusion were assessed through electronic survey methods.

The survey instrument used a five-point, Likert-type scale and open-ended questions focused on program elements and perceived effectiveness of inclusion and collaboration. Results indicated a high level of agreement among respondents regarding training efforts and program effectiveness. The study identified issues with current practices, program coordination or collaboration efforts, and training needed for preservice educators. Respondents to the study reported several positives in current practice in the area of teacher preparation at the preservice level concerning inclusion. There was significant agreement that institutions of higher education were offering coursework to preservice teacher-education majors regarding exceptional children and/or special education across all departments or program areas and that students were taking introductory courses in this area. In addition, respondents indicated that field experiences offered opportunities for preservice teachers to collaborate across disciplines and majors. Respondents also noted that opportunities were provided for preservice teacher educators to work with diverse learners through their departments or programs and that students have other opportunities (e.g., service learning, professional-development schools, charter schools) made available to them. The authors also found promising practices and potential opportunities for growth concerning collaboration across teacher-education majors. Respondents seemed in agreement that their departments strongly encourage cross-articulation in teacher-education programs.

The Council for Exceptional Children worked in collaboration with the Interstate New Teacher Assessment and Support Consortium (INTASC; 2001) to develop a comprehensive set of standards for general and special educators. The INTASC Special Education Committee based their work on the premise that "all teachers are responsible for providing an appropriate education to students with disabilities" (2001, p. 1). In 2001, INTASC released *Model Standards for Licensing General and Special Education Teachers of Students with Disabilities*. Forty-nine standards for general educators were identified to represent appropriate and pedagogically sound teaching practices essential to the provision of equal access to quality learning for students with disabilities. Particular emphasis was placed on abilities in Table 7.3. The reader is referred to the Council for Exceptional Children web site for additional information (http://www.cec.sped.org/AM/Template.cfm?Section= About_CEC).

Collaborative Teaming

Of the 10 essential general educator abilities identified by INTASC, the seventh ability, "work collaboratively with special education teachers," is pivotal to the accomplishment

Table 7.3. Standards related to teaching practices

1. Set realistically high expectations for students with disabilities.
2. Demonstrate knowledge and understanding of disability legislation and special education policies and procedures.
3. Demonstrate knowledge of the general characteristics of the most frequently occurring disabilities.
4. Demonstrate basic understanding of ways that disabilities impact learning and development.
5. Make accommodations, modifications, and/or adaptations to the general curriculum.
6. Use a variety of instructional strategies and technologies.
7. Work collaboratively with special education teachers.
8. Promote positive social relationships among students with disabilities and their age-appropriate peers in the learning community.
9. Foster independent engagement, self-motivation, and independent learning.
10. Incorporate accommodations and alternate assessments into the ongoing assessment process of students with disabilities.

Source: Interstate New Teacher Assessment and Support Consortium (2001).

of the other nine. Few general education teachers feel prepared to integrate students with disabilities in their classrooms (Kamens, 2007). Although there is a critical need for general educator preparation to work with students with disabilities (Ansell, 2004; Boudah et al., 2000; Coombs-Richardson & Mead, 2001; Snell & Janney, 2005), even highly skilled general educators require the support of other professionals to work effectively with students with disabilities in general education classrooms (Carter & Hughes, 2006). The LRE provisions in IDEA support the "use of supplementary aids and services" in order that "education in regular classes" may be "achieved satisfactorily" (IDEA 2004 [Part B, Sec 612 (a) (5)]). Services that focus on general and special educator collaboration are often critical to the success of students with disabilities in inclusive settings.

In its most recent edition of *What Every Special Educator Must Know*, the Council for Exceptional Children identified *collaboration* as one of 10 standard domain areas for special educators, noting, "Special educators are viewed as specialists by a myriad of people who actively seek their collaboration to effectively include and teach individuals with exceptional learning needs" (2008, p. 30). Special educators participate in a variety of collaborative structures in an effort to increase instructional options for students with disabilities in general education settings. Consultative models with the special educator as consultant and the general educator as "consultee" were widely used in the 1970s and 1980s. However, the role of the special educator as expert was not well received by many general educators (Pugach & Johnson, 1989). According to Friend and Cook (2003), effective models emphasize four defining characteristics of collaboration:

1. It is voluntary.
2. It requires parity among participants.
3. It is based on mutual goals.
4. It depends on shared responsibility for participation and decision making.

Providing Supports in General Education Classrooms

Collaborative efforts should emphasize curriculum and instructional practices that are responsive to students with varied educational needs. Administrators, general educators, special educators, and families must work together to develop individualized supports tailored to the specific needs of students with disabilities. Fisher, Sax, and Pumpian (1999) identified formalized supports for students with disabilities in general education classes in three major areas: 1) personal supports, 2) curriculum accommodations and modifications, and 3) assistive and instructional technology.

Personal Supports

A variety of **personal supports** may be employed to increase the participation of students with disabilities in general education classrooms. Specialized support staff including special educators, related services personnel, paraprofessionals, and peers can be used on a full-time, part-time, or as-needed basis to assist students in inclusive settings. Ryan is an example of a student who required a high level of personal support to function successfully in the general education classroom. Highly qualified support staff and trained peers were available to help him as needed throughout the school day. Helen also required a high level of support, yet, sadly, it was not offered to her despite her clear need for behavioral programming, functional skill development, and communication supports. The difference in outcomes between Ryan and Helen is notable given that both should have been offered the same level of supports in an effort to successfully transition at the conclusion of their school experience; what is most disturbing when one is comparing these two case studies is the vast difference in their community inclusion and participation.

Special educators may provide support to students in general education classrooms through **consultation**, support facilitation, or **co-teaching** service delivery models. Consultation between the general and the special educator can help to identify instructional and curricular accommodations and modifications to be implemented by the general education teacher. As a **support facilitator**, the special educator provides the appropriate level and frequency of in-class support or engages others, including paraprofessionals and peers, to provide additional support in the general education classroom. Peer-mediated instruction, partner learning, and cooperative group learning provide academic support for students with disabilities in general education settings (Carter & Kennedy, 2006). Increasingly, special educators and related services providers are leaving resource settings to work with students in inclusive settings. Co-teaching is a model that has steadily gained popularity as a way to increase access to the general education curriculum for students with disabilities. The special education teacher provides additional support in the classroom and supplements the content area knowledge of the general education teacher with knowledge and expertise related to teaching students with disabilities (Rea, McLaughlin, & Walther-Thomas, 2002). This expertise includes an understanding of how disabilities affect academic performance as well as knowledge of specific instructional practices, accommodations, and enhancements to increase access to the general education curriculum for students with disabilities. The need for consultation, support facilitation, or co-teaching varies across students and across activities. To avoid the problems associated with under- or overutilization of these supports, the implementation of personal supports must be tailored to the individual needs of the student.

Curriculum Accommodations and Modifications

When students with more significant disabilities are working toward different goals (IEP goals or alternate learning outcomes) than their peers in the general education classroom, the practice is often referred to as a *modification*, whereas changes in teaching methods and materials for students working toward the same goals and standards as the rest of the students in the general education classroom are frequently referred to as *accommodations*. Because students learn in different ways, a "one-size-fits-all" instructional approach presents barriers to learning for some children (McPherson, 2009). Proven teaching methods that promote the achievement of individuals with wide differences in abilities within general education classrooms have been identified.

Universal design for learning (UDL) is based on multiple and flexible methods of presentation, expression, and engagement (Rose & Meyer, 2002; Center for Applied Special Technology, 2010). Originally from the field of architecture, the Center for Universal Design at North Carolina State University defined UDL as "the design of products and environments to be usable by all people to the greatest extent possible without the need for adaptation or specialized design" (Center for Universal Design, 1997, para. 1). McPherson (2009) explains that, specific to learning, UDL research is grounded in the premise that all children can learn if instruction is *designed* to trigger the neurological networks that control the learning process. These networks are defined as follows (Rose & Meyer, 2002, p. 11):

- Recognition networks receive and analyze information (the *what* of learning).
- Strategic networks plan and execute actions (the *how* of learning).
- Affective goals evaluate priorities (the *why* of learning).

UDL is based on the premise that thoughtfully designing lessons beforehand and appealing to the learning networks of all learners is more effective than modifying and accommodating lessons later. The term *universal* indicates these are not disability-specific practices but rather recommended practice for all students. Therefore, it is recommended these methods be promoted for all classrooms. UDL instruction can develop self-determination and pride in accomplishment and increase the degree to which students feel connected to their learning (Center for Applied Special Technology, 2010).

Tomlinson (e.g., 1999, 2001, 2003) also proposes the use of **differentiated instruction** as a way to reach all learners through effective lesson planning and delivery. Differentiated instruction addresses the needs of diverse learners and emphasizes a variety of elements including (Tomlinson, 2001, p. 4)

1. Content that includes concepts, principles, and skills students must learn
2. Process that includes a variety of instructional groupings
3. Products that include ongoing formal and informal assessments

Differentiating content is an element that allows students with a wide range of abilities to be included in a single general education classroom. Lawrence-Brown (2004) identified several ways to differentiate content based on individual needs, including

1. Goal adaptations (only parts of the general curriculum are included in the student's instructional goals)
2. Prioritized instruction (student participates in general curriculum "while accomplishing very different content or curriculum goals" King-Sears, 2001, p. 75)
3. Authentic instruction (additional goals for students with severe disabilities are addressed by changing the emphasis and presentation of large-group lessons)

Assistive and Instructional Technology

IDEA 2004 mandates, "On a case-by-case basis, the use of school-purchased assistive technology devices in a child's home or in other settings is required if the child's IEP Team determines that the child needs access to those devices in order to receive FAPE." IDEA further delineates the required school-aged technology intervention for students with disabilities as "any service that assists a child with a disability in the selection, acquisition, or use of an assistive technology device" (IDEA, 2004).

A variety of evidence-based recommended practices have emerged with respect to inclusionary practices with **assistive and instructional technology** over the past decade. These types of instructional methods include **video modeling** (VM), video self-modeling (VSM), and point-of-view video modeling (PVM; Shukla-Mehta, Miller, & Callahan, 2010). According to Bellini and Akullian, "Video modeling is a technique that involves demonstration of desired behaviors through video representation of the behavior" (2007, p. 266). Essentially, VM consists of showing a student a brief video clip or "model" of someone performing a targeted skill or behavior for instructional purpose. The video clip is prepared by instructional or intervention staff in an effort to specifically illustrate the essential behavior a student needs to attain. VSM is an application of VM in which the individual learns by imitating video clips showing his or her own successful performance of targeted behaviors (Ayres & Langone, 2007).

In contrast to VM and VSM and other forms of video-based instruction, PVM is defined by Shukla-Mehta et al. as "the process of videotaping elements of the environment or activity context from the visual perspective or vantage point of the student who needs to acquire and/or master the target responses" (2010, p. 24). Essentially, a videographer records steps for completing an activity or behavior by actually shooting video that would simulate what the student would be seeing while he or she engaged in an activity or transition—making sure to keep the focus at the eye level and perspective of the student. Positive outcomes for people with a variety of disabilities have been well-documented across the age span and spectrum for a variety of targeted dependent variables related to social, communication, functional living, and vocational skills (Apple, Billingsley, & Schwartz, 2005; Ayres & Langone, 2007; Ayres, Maguire, & McClimon, 2009; Bernad-Ripoll, 2007). Moreover, research suggests that video-based instruction is effective for teaching functional skills in a consistent manner without the need for repetitive lessons or time spent in or on alternate locations (Ayres & Langone, 2007; Bellini & Akullian, 2007; Chiak & Schrader, 2008; Shipley-Benamou, Lutzker, & Taubman, 2002) and teachers can produce permanent products for intervention, saving time and resources, and capitalizing on a consistent mode of instruction. VM proved a very effective tool for Ryan's support staff and was often used to provide him with targeted social skills. His speech-language pathologist trained his entire school-based team, including his support peers, on how to use VM and VSM in an effort to work with Ryan in a proactive manner.

The use of self-prompting devices by students with disabilities holds great promise for increasing an individual's independence while decreasing his or her reliance on teachers and/or instructional staff (Davies, Stock, Holloway, & Weyhmeyer, 2010; Mechling, 2007; Mechling, Gast, & Seid, 2009; Mechling & Seid, 2011; Spence-Cochran & Pearl, 2009). **Self-prompting technology** includes any device or system capable of prompting a person through a task analysis, set of directions, or task to complete a designated task, assignment, or job without additional prompting by teachers or instructional staff. Palmtop personal computers are portable handheld systems that employ features of a touch screen for input and multimedia capabilities including the capability of producing text, sound, digital photographs, and video clips (Mechling, 2007; Mechling & Seid, 2011) that can be and have been used as prompting devices.

Transition and Inclusion

During transition, students leave the ranks of high school programs to actively join local adult communities. The metaphor of a vehicle is often used to describe the metamorphosis that takes place during this period (Nuehring & Sitlington, 2003) and is frequently described as a car reaching an intended destination. The provision of inclusive activities within the community during transition preparation and implementation should be considered in order to plan appropriate instruction, systems of support, and activities for all students with disabilities.

Test, Fowler, White, Richter, and Walker noted that "one of the more significant transitions in a person's life is being graduated from high school and pursuing a productive adulthood" (2009, p. 16). Although inclusion in general education is an important goal for students with disabilities, there is a critical need to prepare these exiting high school students for transition and the world of work (Conley, 2003; Frank & Sitlington, 2000; Kiernan, 2000; Kraemer, McIntyre, & Blacher, 2003; Neubert, Moon, & Grigal, 2002; Nuehring & Sitlington, 2003) within environments similar to those where they may seek future employment. As discussed in previous chapters, and the historical perspective of this chapter, educational advocates and reformers continue to push for comprehensive inclusive transition programs that will prepare all students for life beyond school. Most are in agreement that creative new approaches are necessary to blend federal and state accountability standards with individual students' needs (Bassett & Kochhar-Bryant, 2006; Mazzotti et al., 2009; Test, Fowler, Richter, White, et al., 2009).

Facilitating Functional Instruction

Historically, instructional programs for students with moderate to severe disabilities included a multitude of nonfunctional tasks (Bassett & Kochhar-Bryant, 2006; Iovannone, Dunlap, Huber, & Kincaid, 2003), such as inappropriate paper-and-pencil assignments and a lack of community focus. Instruction over objectives poorly suited to individual needs was most often provided within segregated settings. In addition, the instruction provided within these noninclusive settings was at skill or developmental levels that were not appropriate for individual students. With the increased acceptance of the normalization movement in the late 1970s (Perske, 2004), questions began to surface regarding the efficacy of merely providing instruction within segregated school-based environments to students with severe disabilities. Educators and parents expressed concerns about nonfunctional skills identified as irrelevant to individuals with severe disabilities and recommended independent functioning within communities as a main priority and goal for instruction. Because of these global concerns, many educators began to focus on the development of chronological, age-appropriate skills within the inclusive environments that students would be living and working in as adults (Neubert et al., 2002; Nietupski et al., 1988; Nuehring & Sitlington, 2003; Perske, 2004; Sternberg, 1994). Although functional curriculum is important when one is preparing students with disabilities for the world of work, it is often challenging for general education teachers to provide appropriate functional curriculum within their classrooms. Careful team planning and collaboration between special and regular educators is necessary to ensure that student goals are meaningfully addressed and that the mastery of necessary postsecondary skills may be achieved. For many teachers, the creation of functionally based curricula blended with general curricula that adheres to a particular state's standard is incredibly challenging. Parrish and Stodden recommend a process of **backward design planning** to achieve this goal:

> As defined by the American Federation of Teachers, traditionally planned instruction begins with the teacher: a) choosing a lesson from the curriculum, b) following the order of presentation outlined in the curriculum, c) deciding instructional activities, d) evaluating level of mastery with a grade or feedback, and e) proceeding to the next lesson (Jamentz, 2003). Standards-based instruction is developed through a backward design planning process which includes: a) identifying the standards and the desired learning outcomes, b) determining acceptable evidences of progress toward the standard, and c) developing instructional plans and learning experiences that aid a student's progress toward the statewide standard. (2009, p. 47)

One method of providing specialized instruction during general education classes is through the use of an **infused skills grid**. An infused skills grid clearly illustrates where identified skills will be taught during a student's day and which team members have identified particular skills for targeted instruction.

Standards-Based Transition Planning for Inclusion

Inclusive education is understood as an approach aiming to meet the educational needs of all children, youth, and adults, and emphasizing students who are subjected to marginalization and exclusion such as those with disabilities. Inclusive practice includes the premise that special educators and general educators will collaborate to meet the standards required by legislation. With increased academic accountability now required in all states for students with a large range of disabilities, school districts, administrators, and teachers are struggling to design appropriate lesson plans for students with moderate to severe disabilities aligned with their corresponding state standards. As a result of IDEIA 2004 and NCLB, states are now required to demonstrate and use instructional programs and practices grounded in scientifically based research to address the transition needs of all students with disabilities (Mazzotti et al., 2009; Test, Fowler, Richter, White, et al., 2009). These requirements place a heavy emphasis on teachers to work together to find solutions for all students while still meeting state standards.

One of the main challenges with designing standards-based instruction for a large group of students with varying abilities is the fact that many of the standards are overly broad and in many instances are vague with respect to the specific or core concepts of the content (Luft, Brown, & Sutherin, 2007; Patton & Trainor, 2002). To address this issue, Bassett and Kochhar-Bryant outlined several of the key features of standards-based lesson planning necessary for appropriate transition programming, planning, and instruction:

> Applying ideas to standards begins with standards and then develops appropriate curriculum around them. Because educators must be constantly aware of meeting academic content standards, instruction becomes focused on linking standards to instruction and assessment. The process lends itself nicely to creative and integrated pedagogy that can reflect life skills and contextual learning experiences, challenging academic content, and authentic assessment. (2006, p. 13)

It is critically important that transition planning and instruction be relevant to the individual students by addressing their interests, needs, preferences, and strengths (Luft, Brown, & Sutherin, 2007). To do this, transition teachers and support staff should prioritize their students' instructional needs in an effort to determine which skills are necessary for life-long applicability and inclusion opportunities (Luft, Brown, & Sutherin, 2007; Wiggins & McTighe, 2005) within their respective communities.

Community-Based Instruction for Inclusion

Although students with severe and moderate disabilities receive educational benefit from interacting with their peers without disabilities during school and classroom activities and instruction, they also benefit from inclusive opportunities within the community. Specialized vocational instruction is especially critical for students with significant disabilities (Noyes & Sax, 2004; Nuehring & Sitlington, 2003; Pearman et al., 2004). Traditionally, vocational instruction has been conducted inside simulated classroom settings or sheltered workshops. Alternatively, CBI is a more inclusive approach to vocational instruction because it provides students with opportunities to receive vocational instruction within the communities in which they are likely to seek gainful employment (Noyes & Sax, 2004; Nuehring & Sitlington, 2003; Mazzotti et al. 2009; Parrish & Stodden, 2009). The element of CBI, in the real world, is particularly important for students with disabilities because of their difficulty in generalizing instruction between settings and functional instruction (Post & Storey, 2002; Ryan, Hughes, Katsiyannis, McDaniel, & Sprinkle, 2011).

When an increase of CBI and inclusive transition programming for students with all types of disabilities occurred during the late 1980s, researchers intently began to study best practices for students with moderate to severe disabilities. Several studies outline the characteristics noted in Table 7.4 as necessary to successful inclusive transition planning for positive student outcomes.

Table 7.4. Characteristics to successful inclusive transition planning

- Early planning
- Interagency collaboration
- Individualized transition planning
- Focus on integration
- Community-relevant curriculum
- Community-based training
- Business linkages
- Job placement
- Ongoing staff development and program evaluation, including identifying specific individuals involved, identifying the role of each person involved, and identifying the time that services should begin

Sources: Garcia-Villamisar, Ross, & Wehman (2000); Mazzotti, Rowe, Kelley, Test, Fowler, Kohler, & Kortering (2009); Morgan, Gerity, & Ellerd (2000); Neubert, Moon, & Grigal (2002); Parrish & Stodden (2009); Ryan, Hughes, Katsiyannis, McDaniel, & Sprinkle (2011); and Land, Ju, & Zhang (2010).

The importance of CBI is delineated by the reality that most students with moderate to severe disabilities have great difficulty generalizing skills learned within their classroom to actual job sites within the community (Brooke, Revell, & Wehman, 2009; Wehman & Kregel, 2011). Numerous studies indicate the need for students with severe cognitive issues to be educated within the settings they will likely become employed in after high school (National Longitudinal Transition Study-2, 2007; Brooke, Revell, & Wehman, 2009) demonstrating evidence of a specific need to design instructional practices for these students that will meet the expectations and realities of specific postschool settings or work.

Inclusive Community Programming

Today, more and more programs are emerging that promote inclusive educational programming designed to prepare students for postsecondary employment. For example, Project SEARCH® (see Chapter 6) has evolved since 1996, when it started at Cincinnati Children's Hospital into a comprehensive program model with more than 150 sites in 39 states and four countries. More and more individuals are finding work in nontraditional occupations for individuals with disabilities in places such as banks, zoos, municipalities, museums, and research centers.

Notably, Project SEARCH offers an alternative for older students with significant disabilities who have traditionally received services in self-contained settings on high school campuses through age 21. These students rotate through three on-site internships during their last year in school. Through these targeted internships, students acquire competitive, marketable, and transferable skills enabling them to apply for related positions upon completion of the program. Students also have an opportunity to build communication, teamwork, and problem-solving skills important to their overall development as a young worker.

Project SEARCH at Quest

Project SEARCH in Orlando, Florida, has the distinction of being the first program to open more than one work site at the same time. In Fall 2010, Quest, Inc., a nonprofit organization that provides a comprehensive family of services to people with disabilities, opened sites at the Rosen Shingle Creek, the nation's first hospitality site to host a Project SEARCH program; the Florida Hospital East Orlando; and Winter Park Memorial Hospital. Each site represents a collaborative effort involving Quest, Orange County Public Schools, the respective business partner, Vocational Rehabilitation Services, the Agency for Persons with Disabilities, and families. According to Barbara Moses, Quest Works' director of employment services, "The goal is to mirror a real job as much as possible. The focus from day one is on getting a job!" She projects 60%–70% employment for the first group of participants. Moses noted that Project SEARCH differs from traditional community-based vocational education experiences in a number of ways:

1. It is a full-day program.
2. Students are treated like employees.
3. The intern has to be committed to work.
4. There is no allowance for absenteeism.
5. Interns independently travel to work each day. In other words, there is no yellow school bus.

Edward Edward, a 19-year-old Hispanic man with an intellectual disability, was selected for an internship at Florida Hospital beginning in fall 2010. He was born in New Mexico and moved to Orlando when he was 13 years old. He currently lives with his mother, stepfather, and younger sister. Edward has received a variety of special education services since he started kindergarten and graduated from high school with a special diploma. He was referred to Project SEARCH through his community-based vocational education teacher. When he was interviewed for the program, he appeared to be very quiet and did not ask many questions. However, over the course of the school year, those who worked with him saw his self-esteem grow and his ability to communicate improve. Less than 2 months into the program, Edward's supervisor chose to feature him in an article about the program for the Florida Hospital newsletter. His supervisor also suggested a change in Edward's schedule so that he would be available at the shift change in the department because this would allow him to learn a lot of tasks that he would not otherwise experience. Edward interned with environmental services and the emergency department; laundry, floor maintenance, and stocking and completing IV kits were

among the many tasks he performed. When he completed his rotations, he asked to return to environmental services. In April 2011, Edward was hired as a utility technician within the environmental services department. He began work at 35 hours per week and at $9.00 an hour. Edward had the following to say about his experience with Project SEARCH: "I love my job and working with Dave. I get to learn new things as I go on. I get to know the job better than I did the day I started. I get to help my mom now that I have a job."

Conclusion

According to Davies, Stock, Holloway, and Wehmeyer, "Community inclusion is a valued goal for most people with intellectual and developmental disabilities and their families" (2010, p. 454). Most would agree that this sentiment is shared by individuals affected by all types of disabling conditions and those parents, families, teachers, and providers who care about them, advocate for them, and strive to provide relevant and appropriate inclusive transition planning to support the richest possible quality of life for all people. We are indeed fortunate in the 21st century to have the guidance of federal legislation that supports and emphasizes the meaningful inclusion of all students within their communities in an effort to prepare them for work, living, leisure, and the world beyond. Lieberman cautioned:

> We cannot drag regular educators kicking and screaming into a merger with special education.… This proposed merger is a myth, unless regular educators, for reasons far removed from "it's best for children," decide that such a merger is in their own best interests. This is something that we will never be able to point out to them. They will have to come to it in their own way, on their own terms, in their own time. How about a few millennia? (1985, p. 513)

Fortunately, progress since the 1980s has not borne out Lieberman's prediction. It has not been "a few millennia" and yet increasingly the perceptions of educators reflect the emerging consensus that most, if not all, students with disabilities should spend the school day in general education classrooms. The essential flaw in Lieberman's reasoning is the assumption that the reasons why a merger of special and general education is "best for children" could possibly be "far removed" from the "best interests" of teachers. Such a merger will occur when it is fully understood by all stakeholders that the reasons why inclusion is "best for children" are inextricably entwined with the reasons why it is best for teachers. Inclusion is "best for children" when it provides students with access to the general education curriculum and opportunities to interact in meaningful ways with peers without disabilities within general education settings and when it is individually planned, specialized, intensive, goal-directed, research-based, and guided by student performance (Heward, 2003). Inclusion is in the "best interests" of teachers when professional development and follow up is provided, when it is carefully planned and evaluated on an ongoing basis, and when it involves differentiation and parity in general and special educator roles and responsibilities.

Half a century has passed since the *Brown v. Board of Education* decision. Parents and educators have gone forward to meet the challenges of full implementation of IDEA. As a group, the majority of children with disabilities are now being educated with peers without disabilities in general education classrooms in neighborhood schools (U.S. DOE, OSERS, 2010). Ryan's educational experience illustrates the progress that has been made. Unfortunately, Helen's case offers a reminder that the stigma of categorical segregation persists. Each reauthorization of IDEA has required a renewed effort to build on past successes to ensure that all students with disabilities, including those with severe disabilities, are taught in the LREs. This will require highly qualified general and special education teachers who are skilled in individualized approaches that allow students with disabilities to gain access to the same educational environments and curriculum as students without disabilities. It will also require teachers with a vision of the future who use sound instructional programming to afford students opportunities to engage in vocational preparatory activities that will adequately prepare them to successfully work and function within their communities. In summary, it will require educators with an expanded view of IDEA's "to the maximum extent appropriate" as it applies to the inclusion of students with disabilities.

Addressing the need for systems change and the community integration of individuals with severe disabilities, Brown and York stated, "It seems that we now have an opportunity to create humane, tolerant, developmentally sound, and existentially relevant social and emotional environments that can replace oppressive, rejecting, undignifying, and intolerant systems so long in operation" (1974, p. 10). These words exemplify a modern need to change systems that continue to relegate individuals with severe disabilities to segregated settings. Moreover, they lend credence to a belief system that encourages the inclusion of all individuals within a community and offer hope to those wishing to conduct their lives in a dignified and meaningful manner.

Study Questions

1. List three barriers to inclusion and outline a plan for overcoming each.

2. Imagine that you have been given the responsibility of explaining to a group of classroom teachers why inclusion is occurring and how it might be accomplished. What would you say?

3. What do you think might be the major argument against merging special and general education? What are the key arguments for the merger of special and general education?

4. Ask a friend, roommate, or fellow student if he or she would have a friendly discussion or debate with you about what Walter Lippmann said more than a half century ago. He stated:

   If a child fails in school and then fails in life, the schools cannot sit back and say: you see how accurately I predicted this. Unless we are to admit that education is essentially impotent, we have to throw back the child's failure at the school, and describe it as a failure not by the child but by the schools. (Quoted in Block & Dworkin, 1976, p. 17)

5. One of the best ways to learn about people with disabilities is to interact with and get to know them. Thus, one activity to further your knowledge about students with disabilities and inclusion might be to volunteer to serve as a buddy or on a circle of friends for a student with disabilities. Many public schools have recently started this or are considering

it. Ask your instructor, a teacher you know, or someone else connected with the schools if it would be possible for you to do something like this.

6. How would you feel about being put into a special class in which all the children had disabilities?

7. What do you think the major agenda items might be for a schoolwide inclusion task force?

8. How do you think the parents of children without disabilities would feel about children with severe disabilities being in their child's general classes? Present your brief oral arguments for both sides of this opinion.

9. Research the major changes made to IDEA in its most recent reauthorization. How do those changes relate to the issue of inclusion?

10. Develop a statement that articulates your position on the inclusion of students with disabilities in general education.

Online Resources

Virginia Commonwealth University and Virginia Department of Education Inclusive Practice Guide: http://www.vcu.edu/ttac/inclusive_practice/

American Institutes for Research Access Center: http://www.k8accesscenter.org/index.php/category/co-teaching

IRIS Center for Faculty Enhancement: http://iris.peabody.vanderbilt.edu/agc/chalcycle.htm

Inclusion Press International and the Marsha Forest Centre: http://www.inclusion.com/

Inclusion Network: http://inclusionnetwork.ning.com/main

High-Stakes Accountability and Students with Disabilities

The Past and What's to Come

MARGARET J. McLAUGHLIN

After completing this chapter, the reader will be able to

- Explain the history of current standards-based policies
- Describe the rationale for including students with disabilities in state assessment and accountability systems
- Compare and contrast the benefits and the challenges of including youth with disabilities in the reforms
- Discuss the next generation of reforms and the potential impact on federal special education policy

8

Michael and Melissa Michael and Melissa are two experienced special education teachers. They have taught together at Elmore High School for the past 17 years and they think they are pretty good at what they do. Together with 27 other special education teachers, Michael and Melissa share responsibility for educating about 250 students in grades 9–12. Melissa alone manages transition plans for about 55 students in vocational and career education. Some of her students require extensive support and spend half of their school day at job sites in the community and in school. Michael teaches English, social studies, math, and history to special education students. He also provides support to students with individualized education programs (IEPs) who come to his room to learn study skills, take tests, and get help with class assignments during one period a day. These two teachers are proud of the good relationships they have with their students and their students' families. They are also proud of their students' accomplishments. For example, in past years, Michael would focus on helping his students not only to get enough credits to graduate but also to get jobs; Melissa had focused on transitioning her students to jobs in the community and preparing them to live on their own.

Things began to change for both Michael and Melissa more than a decade ago. First, they learned that the special education students they teach will no longer be able to graduate unless they success-fully pass an end-of-course examination in general education courses in English, algebra, and geometry as well as basic science. Melissa learned that her students with intellectual disabilities would also have to pass an alternate assessment in the academic content. Then they learned that Michael was no longer considered "qualified" to teach core subject matter courses to special education students and that "his" students must be taught by teachers who are certified to teach English, math, and science. Michael began to coteach in general education math and science classrooms, sometimes supporting as many as 15 students in content classes they must pass to graduate. Melissa is frustrated. She wonders why she must spend so much time on **alternate assessments** when "her" students should be learning job skills. At the same time, she is excited about new opportunities for her students to go to college. Michael just wants his students to stay in school, and fears that the pressures of the academic courses may push more of them out.

Melissa and Michael are like many secondary special education teachers today who are trying to understand and negotiate the continual pressure of higher standards, assessments, and accountability. They see the graduation requirements increasing and they also see an increasing need for their students to go on to postsecondary education, but they are not sure of their role in all of this. Many of their students and their families are confused and anxious about the future. They look to Michael and Melissa to help them pass the mandatory exams, find a job, and make it to the next phase of adulthood. These are just a few of the pressures felt by special education teachers across the United States. Despite the 10 years of reform, special education teachers are confused and exasperated about their role in all of this. They do not see how many of the students they teach will ever be able to meet the increasingly rigorous graduation exams. What is more, they question whether many of these students should be wasting their time sitting in these classes when they could be getting career or vocational training or learning more fundamental skills. They are trying to reconcile the students' rights to have specially designed instruction and educational supports with the one-size-fits-all notion of standards. Although all special education teachers are struggling to understand the new requirements, in some ways, secondary-level teachers face even more challenges as they attempt to reconcile two core policy goals. The first goal is to ensure that each individual student with a disability makes a successful transition to postsecondary employment, education, and life, and the second demands that every student has the same opportunity to learn challenging content.

In this chapter, we describe the characteristics of the reforms that are dominating today's schools. We also explain the foundations of these reforms as well as the issues schools face in implementing these policies with students with disabilities. Finally, we discuss considerations for aligning accountability requirements with important transition goals.

What Are the New Reform Policies?

The education of students with disabilities in U.S. schools today is shaped by two very powerful laws: the 2004 Individuals with Disabilities Education Improvement Act (IDEA; PL 105-17) and the Elementary and Secondary Education Act (ESEA; PL 89-10; also currently known as the No Child Left Behind Act NCLB), 2001, PL 107-110). The basic provisions contained in IDEA have been in federal law since 1975 and guarantee each eligible child with a disability a free appropriate public education (FAPE) in the least restrictive environment (LRE). Some major changes were made to the IDEA in 1997 (PL 105-17) to begin to align this law with the larger standards-driven reforms under way in the United States, and these were extended and strengthened in the 2004 amendments. The NCLB is the 2001 reauthorization of the 1965 ESEA. This law has been a major presence in schools since 1965, but, as we discuss further in this chapter, changes made in the 1994 and 2001 to ESEA began to drastically reshape federal (and state) education policies for all students. In the following sections, I provide an overview of the current policies of both ESEA and IDEA, preceded by a brief history of the evolution of these policies.

The Rise of Accountability in U.S. Schools

As previously noted, current reform policies being enacted in U.S. schools had their origins in changes made to ESEA in the past decade, which in turn evolved from individual states' education policies that began in the 1980s. In 1994, Congress reauthorized the ESEA and renamed it the Improving America's Schools Act (IASA; 1994; PL 103-382). The IASA required that, for states to receive Title I funds, they were to develop challenging content and performance standards in reading and math and adopt yearly assessments to determine how well all children were meeting the states' performance standards. However, unlike previous mandates that allowed states to use a variety of assessments and required no real accountability for results, the IASA required states to develop and implement one statewide assessment and accountability system that covered all students and schools. The IASA stipulated that *all* students should participate in the state assessments, and that the results for all students must be publicly reported. In defining "all," the IASA specifically referred to students with disabilities as well as students with limited English proficiency (34 C.F.R. § 111[b] [3] [F]).

To align policies for students with disabilities with the IASA and the reforms that were occurring within general education, several new provisions were added to the 1997 amendments of the IDEA. Language was incorporated that required students with disabilities to have access to the general education curriculum and participate in the state and local assessment systems with accommodations and/or alternate assessments if needed.

Although the 1997 IDEA implied that students with disabilities should participate in accountability by requiring their participation in assessments and reporting of scores, the IDEA did not specifically mandate their inclusion in accountability systems (Thurlow, 2004). The IDEA referred to the IEP as the method of accountability and did not require that any agency or person be held accountable if a child does not achieve the goals and objectives listed on the IEP (34 C.F.R. § 300.350 [b]). The IDEA also did not require states to reward or sanction schools based on the outcomes for students with disabilities. This lack of accountability was cited as a significant problem by a National Academy of Sciences committee (McDonnell, McLaughlin, & Morison), which noted that the IEP was a form of "private" (1997; p. 151) accountability and was inconsistent with the move toward public reporting of student achievement and of holding schools or individual students accountable for that achievement.

In fact, as states implemented their assessment and accountability systems throughout the latter part of the 1990s, students with disabilities were erratically and inconsistently included. For example, in some states, the scores of students with disabilities who received an assessment accommodation were not reported at all or were not included in the accountability formula. Few states reported the assessment results of all of their students with disabilities and even fewer states had implemented and reported student performance on alternate assessments. In 2001, the reauthorization of ESEA, referred to as the No Child Left Behind Act, changed all of that.

The No Child Left Behind Act

In 2001, Congress made sweeping changes to ESEA. Building on the 1994 requirements, Congress mandated new accountability requirements and renamed the law. The law mandates that states hold individual schools accountable for ensuring that all students reach proficiency on state standards in reading, math, and science by 2014. To do that, states must administer assessments annually in reading/language arts, math, and science to students in grades 3–8 and at least once in grades 10–12. State assessments were required to be aligned with state standards in the three areas and to establish, at minimum, "Basic," "Proficient," and "Advanced" levels of performance. The primary purpose of these assessments is to determine the yearly progress of students and hold schools, districts, and states accountable for helping all students master the content standards (Hanushek & Raymond, 2002; Linn, 2001). The NCLB requires states to use one other measure in addition to assessments (e.g., attendance, graduation rates) to measure a school's performance; accountability is based primarily on assessment results.

Assessment of Students with Disabilities under No Child Left Behind

The NCLB parallels IDEA in specifying that students with disabilities receive assessment accommodations, and, for students who cannot participate in the state assessment, states must provide an alternate assessment. Alternate assessments may be based on the regular achievement standards or on modified or alternate achievement standards. In 2003, the U.S. Department of Education released regulations that allowed school districts to measure the achievement of students with the most significant disabilities using alternate *achievement* standards in reading, math, and science (34 C.F.R. § 200.1[d]) and can count not more than 1% of these students as proficient in the calculation of adequate yearly progress (AYP; 34 C.F.R. §200.13[c][1][i]). Individual states are allowed to define alternate achievement standards as long as they are aligned with the state's academic content standards, promote access to the general curriculum, and reflect professional judgment of the highest achievement standards possible (34 C.F.R. § 200.1[d]).

In 2005, a second exception was introduced. Often referred to as the 2% rule, schools were allowed to test additional students other than those with significant cognitive disabilities using alternate assessments tied to modified standards. As with the previous exception, school districts were allowed to count no more than 2% of the passing scores on these assessments toward their AYP calculations (34 C.F.R. § 200). In 2007, additional regulations were introduced that gave states the option to offer an alternate assessment based on modified standards. This is not a requirement under NCLB, and, as of late 2009, only eight states had developed and implemented this type of assessment (Albus, Lazarus, Thurlow, & Cormier, 2009). Of particular note, however, is that both alternate and modified assessments are to be aligned with a state's academic content standards. Thus, students with disabilities are required to have the opportunity to learn the same content as their peers without disabilities.

Accountability under No Child Left Behind

One of the key provisions in NCLB is that schools be accountable for the performance of all of their students as well as for the performance of specific subgroups such as

Table 8.1.   What happens to schools that do not make AYP?

- Year 1: School choice, 2-year improvement plan, professional development
- Year 2: Supplemental educational services to low-income students
- Year 3: Additional local education agency intervention
- Year 4: Additional restructure plan
- Year 5: Implement restructure plan

State determines whether consequences apply to all schools or only Title 1 schools.

Key: AYP, adequate yearly progress.

students who receive special education services. The key accountability tool that is used in NCLB is AYP. For a school to make AYP, it requires that student performance be calculated separately by grade and subgroups in mathematics, reading/language arts, and science. AYP combines the percentage of students who score at "proficient" and "advanced" levels, and requires that 95% of the students be assessed. High schools must also meet the state graduation standard. The goal of achieving AYP is to ensure that 100% of each subgroup of students reaches the state standard of proficient by 2014. This requires that states set annual goals for the percentage of students in each subgroup that must reach "proficient" or "advanced." Obviously, the percentage increases each year and schools are required to meet each year's goals.

Schools that do not make AYP for any year or for any subgroup are subject to a mandatory sequence of increasingly serious consequences (Table 8.1). Any school (specifically those receiving Title I funds) that does not meet AYP goals for 2 consecutive years must be identified for "school improvement." Schools under improvement must devise a school improvement plan that addresses strategies to improve performance and incorporates a mentoring and professional development program. These schools must provide parents with written notice regarding the schools' identification and must offer students the option to transfer to another school. Choice schools for students with disabilities do not have to be the same as choice schools for nondisabled students, but they must be able to offer the special education and related services that the student requires.

If a school fails to meet AYP goals for 3 years, the school must continue offering choice to students as well as supplemental services, which can be tutoring or other services offered in addition to instruction provided during school hours. After 4 consecutive years of failing to make AYP for any one subgroup, districts and states can take "corrective action" with a school and can institute a "restructuring plan" that may include replacing staff, implementing a new curriculum, or changing the internal organization of the school. After 5 consecutive years of failing to make AYP, local education agencies (LEAs) must prepare a plan to reopen the school as a charter school, replace all or most of the school staff, or turn the operation of the school over to the State Educational Agency. In the years after NCLB was enacted, a trend of schools not making AYP solely because of the performance of students with disabilities began to develop (Center on Education Policy [CEP], 2009b).

Other No Child Left Behind Requirements

Title II of NCLB required that states ensure that their teachers are "highly qualified" by 2005–2006 (34 C.F.R. § 200.55[a]). To be considered highly qualified under NCLB, teachers must have a bachelor's degree, full state certification or licensure, and be able to demonstrate that they are knowledgeable about each subject they teach. Teachers in middle and high school must prove that they know the subject they teach by either having a graduate degree or major in the subject they teach, having credits equivalent to a major, passing a state-developed test, or possessing advanced certification from the state. Some of these requirements have been eased for teachers in rural areas as well as multisubject teachers.

The 2004 Individuals with Disabilities Education Improvement Act

The 2004 reauthorization of IDEA continued to align the educational provisions of the law with the requirements of NCLB. For example, new definitions were added that refer to core academic subjects and highly qualified teachers as being consistent with the definitions in NCLB. Furthermore, provisions related to assessment or general education curriculum cross-reference the NCLB. Continuing the emphasis of the 1997 amendments, the IEP requirements require

- [Consideration of] how the disability affects the child's involvement and progress in the general education curriculum
- Measurable annual goals including academic and functional goals designed to enable the child to be involved and progress in the general education curriculum
- A statement of any individual accommodations that will be necessary to measure the academic achievement and functional performance of the child on state- and district-wide assessments; if the IEP team determines that the child will take an alternate assessment on a specific state or district assessment, the IEP must include a statement that explains why the child cannot participate in the regular assessment and indicate why the particular alternate assessment selected is appropriate for the child
- Requires at least one regular education teacher contribute to the IEP if the child is or may be participating in the regular education curriculum

Other provisions require that states report the assessment results of students with disabilities in the manner required by NCLB. States must also establish performance goals that will be publicly reported and that must include assessment results, dropout rates, and graduation rates.

Highly Qualified Special Educators

Of particular interest to special educators is the definition in IDEA of a highly qualified special education teacher. Consistent with NCLB, any public elementary or secondary school special education teacher must have obtained full state certification as a special educator or passed a state's licensure exam allowing him or her to teach and hold at least a B.A. degree. Then, special education teachers must meet the same requirements as all other public school teachers, such as being able to demonstrate that they are knowledgeable about each subject they teach. Special education middle and high school teachers must prove that they know the subject they teach in the same manner described previously under the NCLB.

Special education teachers who are teaching core academic subjects to students who are held to alternate achievement standards as defined under the NCLB must meet the basic certification requirement specified previously and also have knowledge of the subject matter appropriate to the student's level of instruction. The IDEA and NCLB require that each state determine the level of competency and how that will be demonstrated.

The Next Phase of the Standards Movement

For anyone who imagined that the standards movement would pass, it is not over. Several recent developments attest to this. These include a major step toward the standardization of standards. However, before reviewing the latest developments, it is important to note that the reauthorization of ESEA is on the horizon and there will likely be a number of changes. First, there is strong support for changing the way that schools are held accountable. There is strong likelihood that the accountability metric (i.e., AYP) will be altered and that consequences will focus on improving the lowest performing schools. For students with disabilities, it is very likely that the "2% rule" that allows students to be measured against "modified achievement standards" will be discontinued. And, more interesting is the possibility that some provisions that are currently in the IDEA, such as response to intervention, early intervention services, and positive behavioral interventions, will be incorporated into ESEA and pertain to all children covered under that law as well as students with disabilities. However, these are all speculative at this point.

Regarding standards, currently, each of the 50 states has established its own standards. However, there is now a movement to create one common set of state standards.

Common Core State Standards

The Kindergarten–12 Common Core State Standards were introduced in June 2010 by the Council of Chief State School Officers (CCSSO) and the National Governors Association Center for Best Practices (NGA Center; Common Core State Standards Initiative, 2010b). The standards, which were developed by the two organizations after extensive feedback from various stakeholders in education, consist of expectations for students in all grade levels in the subject areas of English/language arts and mathematics. These new standards build upon the college- and career-readiness standards, also developed by CCSSO and the NGA Center, and provide the research-based, more rigorous approach that the organizations believe will better prepare students for higher education and their careers. As of January 2011, 41 states as well as the District of Columbia and the U.S. Virgin Islands adopted the Common Core.

The CCSSO and NGA Center believe that the Common Core State Standards give students with disabilities "an historic opportunity to improve access to rigorous academic content" (Common Core State Standards Initiative, 2010a, para. 2). The organizations recommend that schools provide additional supports to students with disabilities during instruction, including accommodations, assistive technology, and methods informed by the principles of Universal Design for Learning, so that access to the general curriculum and opportunities for success under the new standards can be maximized.

Common Assessments

Consistent with the model of standards-driven reform, assessments of student performance must be aligned with the established standards. The Race to the Top Fund was introduced in 2009 as a competitive grant program funded by the American Recovery and Reinvestment Act of 2009 (ARRA; PL 111-5) as a means to encourage educational reform by awarding states additional federal funding for developing plans to increase student achievement (U.S. Department of Education, 2009). One of the selection criteria upon which state applications are evaluated is development and implementation of "common, high-quality assessments" (2009; p. 19,507) as part of a multistate consortium. In addition, states that show evidence of participation in a consortium that includes more than half of the states in the country will receive the highest number of points possible for this criterion (34 C.F.R. Subtitle B, Chapter II, 2009). As of April 2010, 26 states had joined to form the Partnership for Assessment of Readiness for College and Careers (PARCC) consortium, which is focused on developing summative assessments, and 31 states joined the SMARTER Balanced Assessment Consortium (SBAC), which is focused on formative assessments (Maryland State Department of Education, 2010; U.S. Department of Education, 2010b). In September 2010, the U.S. Department of Education announced that, as part of the Race to the Top competition, it would award PARCC $170 million and SBAC $160 million to develop assessments for the states in their respective consortiums (U.S. Department of Education, 2010b). The department expects the new assessments to be implemented during the 2014–2015 school year, and both consortiums are taking steps to ensure that these assessments will be appropriate for students with disabilities.

Evolving Accountability

Despite the notion that student assessment should inform school improvement, assessments have been used primarily to comply with the accountability and reporting requirements of ESEA and IDEA and have come to be perceived as tools for imposing negative consequences (Data Quality Campaign, 2009). There are several reasons for this, including the inadequacy of the assessments to provide the precision necessary to make changes at the classroom or school level. In addition, traditional approaches to student assessment largely consisted of a snapshot approach: assessments are administered at one point during a school year and the results may not even be available for use during the current year. Results are used only to determine how students, schools, and districts are performing at that point in time with a cohort of students referred to as the status approach (Data Quality Campaign, 2008). When used with specific performance targets such as those defined by AYP, the results are useful for determining whether students are proficient at that point in time. However, tracking individual student progress over time offers greater precision and some believe greater fairness to schools as it allows for schools to show growth, even if students fail to meet a preset target. To implement growth models, states must have student-based data systems that allow longitudinal tracking of performance.

Longitudinal data systems, which collect detailed information on students and staff that can be linked together over time, provide a detailed description of an individual student's educational history from the onset of schooling through graduation and even beyond high school into postsecondary education and employment. Longitudinal data systems have the potential to be a repository of data that can be used to follow students' progress as they move from grade to grade, to determine whether they are progressing toward college and career readiness, to identify students who are at risk for failure, to calculate the "value added" by specific schools and programs, to evaluate trends over time, and to identify consistently high performing schools (Achieve, Inc., 2006).

In contrast to the current accountability mechanisms required by NCLB, which utilize snapshot data to determine whether a minimum number of students within states, school districts, and schools attain proficiency on annual assessments, longitudinal data systems allow for accountability based upon the "value added" by teachers (Harris, 2009). As noted earlier, the accountability mechanisms in NCLB have been widely criticized because they fail to address wide variations in student performance attributable to nonschool factors. Factors such as family and community demographics are strong predictors of student achievement and these are not adequately considered in the current status model of accountability (Harris, 2009).

A pilot program utilizing growth-based accountability models was announced by the U.S. Department of Education in 2005. Rather than relying on the traditional accountability approach where schools are held accountable for the number of students who are proficient on state exams in any given year, the growth models track individual student achievement from year to year and schools are given credit for improvements in student achievement over time. In 2005–2006, two states, Tennessee and North Carolina, received approval to participate in the pilot program and, since then, an additional 13 states received approval by the 2009–2010 school year.

Student-Level Accountability

Policies that have focused on measuring the aggregate performance of students at school and system levels have been the most predominant since the 1990s, but states and districts have also been increasing standards and accountability at the student level, notably through new graduation requirements and exams. States began using exams to make decisions about graduation in the late 1960s and early 1970s (Johnson, Thurlow, & Stout, 2007), but these tests were designed to make sure that all students achieved a basic level of education in core academic subjects. North Carolina, New York, and Florida were among the first states to administer minimum competency exams during the early years (CEP,

2009a). The use of these exams, which specifically tested literacy and numeracy skills, gained momentum in the 1970s and 1980s and were relatively common in states in the early 1990s (Lerner, 1991).

The current national picture of student-level accountability has changed drastically. As of November 2009, 24 states required students to pass exit exams before they receive a high school diploma (CEP, 2009a). Sixteen of these states added this requirement within the past 9 years (CEP, 2009a). Arkansas began withholding diplomas for students who did not pass the Arkansas Comprehensive Assessment Program in 2010, and, in 2012, Oklahoma will no longer grant diplomas to students who do not pass the Oklahoma End-of-Instruction Exams (CEP, 2009a). Of the 26 states that currently require or plan to implement exit exams as a requirement for graduation, 19 offer alternate pathways to graduation for general education students and 22 states allow students with disabilities to pursue alternative methods. The requirements for students to demonstrate mastery of high school–level knowledge in an alternate manner vary widely from state to state, but alternative assessments, portfolio assessments, and waivers are popular options (CEP, 2009a).

Graduation Requirements and Students with Disabilities

As the minimum competency movement grew, so did the questions about including students with disabilities in the exams (Johnson et al., 2007). Without explicit federal policy, states were left to decide whether students with disabilities would be required to fulfill the test requirement. Some states chose to exclude students with disabilities from these tests altogether. Others decided to establish different standards for these students, modify the testing procedures, use a student's IEP as the standard for graduation, or allow no modifications at all. Although states are now required by law to include students with disabilities in statewide assessments, there is no federal policy that mandates specific graduation requirements. Accordingly, graduation requirements, including implementation of these requirements for students with disabilities, vary widely from state to state and even between school districts within a given state (Johnson et al., 2007). Many states offered multiple diploma options tied to the different types of academic standards and performance on state assessments. Students with disabilities tend to be especially affected by this trend, as they can be awarded a certificate of attendance or other nonstandard diploma when they are unable to meet traditional graduation requirements. These nonstandard diplomas can lead to consequences after high school when students attempt to obtain a job or pursue further education (Johnson et al., 2007; Thurlow & Johnson, 2000). The extent of the use of such exit documents may in fact change as states must define and report only "regular diplomas."

Standardizing Graduation Rates

While states have been increasing the requirements for obtaining a high school diploma, there has also been a movement to standardize how graduation rates are calculated. In 2005, the NGA Center convened a Task Force on State High School Graduation Data to make recommendations on how states could develop a graduation measure that was comparable across states and based on high-quality data. The result was a recommendation, agreed to by all 50 governors, to calculate a high school graduation rate based on this formula:

$$\frac{\text{On-time graduates by Year X}}{[(\text{first-time 9th graders in Year X} - 4) + (\text{transfers in}) - (\text{transfers out})]} \text{ (NGA Center, 2005)}$$

This graduation rate is applied to students who receive a standard diploma, not a certificate of completion or attendance or a general equivalency diploma (GED). Before a state can apply this formula, it must have the ability to identify first-time ninth graders, which generally implies that the state can track each student's enrollment and participation status from year to year.

On October 29, 2008, the U.S. Department of Education amended Section 200.19 of the Title I regulations of ESEA, as amended by NCLB of 2001. The amendments change the "other academic indicators" that states use in defining AYP including new requirements for calculating graduation rate, which is the other academic indicator for high school. The regulations require states to calculate graduation rates in a mandated uniform way referred to as the adjusted cohort rate. This is defined in regulations as the "four-year adjusted cohort graduation rate" as the number of students who graduate in 4 years with a regular high school diploma divided by the number of students who entered high school 4 years earlier (adjusting for transfers in and out, émigrés, and deceased students. Students who graduate in 4 years include students who earn a regular high school diploma at the end of their fourth year, before the end of their fourth year, and, if a state chooses, during a summer session immediately following their fourth year (U.S. Department of Education, 2008). For a school or district to make AYP, it must meet or exceed the state's graduation rate goal or demonstrate continuous and substantial improvement from the previous year toward meeting that goal for each student subgroup, including those with disabilities. Each state must submit the following for peer review and approval by the U.S. Department of Education:

- A single graduation rate goal that represents the rate the state expects all high schools in the state to meet
- Annual graduation rate targets that reflect continuous and substantial improvement from the previous year toward meeting or exceeding that goal, (34 C.F.R. § 200.19)

Graduation rates for each subgroup calculated with the previously mentioned formula will be reported as part of the AYP decisions beginning in school year 2011–2012.

Legal Issues Surrounding High School Assessment of Students With Disabilities

Requiring that students pass an assessment to receive a high school diploma has implications for all students. However, exit exams or assessments raise a number of policy and legal issues for students with disabilities, including the economic and educational consequences of credentials that students are awarded, the stigmatizing effect of the denial of a diploma, the need for adequate notification and appropriate instruction, and the provision of reasonable accommodations and alternate assessments (Karger & Pullin, 2002).

Legal challenges have included constitutional claims brought under the due process and equal protection clauses of the 14th Amendment of the U.S. Constitution and claims under disability statutes, including

- The mandate for FAPE
- The requirement that a sole criterion not determine an appropriate educational program
- The need to provide reasonable accommodations and/or alternate assessments
- The decision to provide alternate exit documents in place of a regular diploma

Karger and Pullin (2002) cited the following three cases as the legal basis for high school assessments and students with disabilities. ***Debra P. v. Turlington*** **(1981)** is the leading case concerning high school exit examinations. Although this case did not specifically address students with disabilities, it established a model for student challenges to exit exams, including those made by students with disabilities. In this case, the U.S. Court of Appeals for the Fifth Circuit held that the state could not deprive students of a high school diploma on the basis of an exit exam unless the state could prove that the students received adequate notice about the test, that the test was fundamentally fair, and that it covered material actually taught in the classroom.

The first court case pertaining to students with disabilities and exit exams was **Board of Education v. Ambach** (1981) in New York State. In *Ambach*, the New York state trial court held that, in general, the state had the power to adopt standards requiring the passing of an exit exam for receipt of a diploma and that the denial of diplomas to students with disabilities was not a violation per se of the Education for All Handicapped Children Act (EHC; PL 94-142; the forerunner of IDEA) or Section 504. In **Brookhart v. Illinois State Department of Education** (1983), the U.S. Court of Appeals for the Seventh Circuit also found that requiring students with disabilities to pass an exam as a prerequisite for receipt of a diploma was not a violation per se of the EHC or Section 504. However, the *Brookhart* court also found that the students' due process rights were violated because they received only a year and a half period of notice before the test requirement was imposed.

According to Karger and Pullin (2002), there are a number of issues pertaining to exit exams and students with disabilities. For one, the denial of a diploma to students with disabilities has a negative effect on future educational and occupational attainment and can thwart the underlying goals of IDEA and the Americans with Disabilities Act (ADA; PL 101-336), which are to help students with disabilities lead active and productive adult lives in the community. Second, decisions about how an individual student with a disability participates in a state or local assessment program must be made by the student's IEP team. Third, students with disabilities and their families must receive adequate notification of the testing requirement and the date of the test to enable their IEPs to be adjusted and to ensure that they receive appropriate instruction in the material that will be tested. Procedural due process requires states to provide students with adequate notice of testing requirements that are prerequisites for receipt of a diploma. But courts have not set specific time periods that constitute adequate notice, and the sufficiency of notice for a testing requirement will depend upon the curriculum and instructional opportunities provided to prepare students for the test as well as whether there are opportunities for retesting and remediation.

In short, students with disabilities must be afforded the opportunity to learn the material covered on exit exams. Furthermore, an important measure of the fairness of an exit exam is whether curriculum and instruction provided to a student are aligned with what the test measures. As challenges to exit exams continue, states will have the burden of presenting substantial evidence that the students have actually had the opportunity to learn the material on which an exam is based.

Students with disabilities must also receive appropriate accommodations on exit exams. IDEA and NCLB require the participation of students with disabilities in state- and district-wide assessments such as exit exams, with *appropriate accommodations* where necessary. Similarly, Title II of the ADA and Section 504 require states and school districts to provide students with disabilities with reasonable accommodations on exit exams. Increasingly, the use of accommodations on assessments is being decided in court. In **Chapman v. California Department of Education** (2002), the judge ruled that the California High School Exit Exam violated the rights of students with disabilities under federal law because students were not allowed to use calculators and other accommodations on the assessment. Similar legal challenges in Oregon (*A.S.K. v. Oregon Department of Education,* 1999) and Alaska (*Noon v. Alaska State Board of Education,* 2004) were settled out of court, with the states in both cases agreeing both to expand the accommodations students are allowed to use and provide alternate tests for the high school exit exams. Finally, if an exit exam is not appropriate for a student with a disability, even with accommodations, the student must receive an alternate assessment.

Teacher Policy

Teachers are among the most important resources necessary for providing high-quality education for all students and increasing standards for teachers have been addressed in federal policy. Currently, NCLB and IDEA require teachers of core academic subjects to be "highly qualified," meaning they must hold a minimum of a bachelor's degree in the subject they teach or the credits equivalent to a major in the subject, have full state certification, and be able to demonstrate subject matter competency (Yell, 2006). However, research indicates that teacher's educational attainment, as well as other characteristics that are the basis for teacher compensation (e.g., experience), are weak predictors of teacher effectiveness (Hanushek, 1997). As a consequence, accountability, as well as teacher compensation, based on teachers' impact on student achievement, has begun to gain momentum as a policy alternative for promoting teacher quality and, consequently, student achievement. This approach to accountability and teacher compensation utilizes longitudinal data systems to determine the "value added" by teachers—their contribution to their students' achievement. As a result of this potential to use value-added models to determine teachers' contributions to student achievement, there is renewed interest in teacher merit pay policies, as well as using teacher value added as a component of teacher tenure decisions (Harris, 2009; Koedel & Betts, 2009).

Value-added accountability is viewed as a more effective and efficient way to improve teacher quality than current policies that reward teacher credentials and experience (Harris, 2009). Current policies emphasize educational attainment and experience (i.e., tenure), factors that have a weak relationship with teacher effectiveness (Hanushek, 1997). A value-added system shifts the focus away from credentials and experience and toward student achievement. However, teacher merit pay based upon value-added models is not without limitations (Harris, 2009; Koedel & Betts, 2009). For example, one criticism of value-added models is the difficulty in isolating the value added by individual teachers, separating it from other factors influencing student achievement including school administration, teamwork among teachers, and the cumulative nature of education (Harris, 2009). In addition, value-added models are often criticized for their reliance upon quantitative measures as these tend to be more reliable and stable over time compared with the less precise and qualitative measures of teacher performance (Gordon, Kane, & Staiger, 2006; Harris, 2009).

The Challenge and Opportunity for Students with Disabilities

One of the first questions many special educators ask is, *Why do we continue with these reforms; are they working?* Arguably, progress can be viewed through a different lens. In terms of inclusive policy, it is important to remember that, in the 1980s, as the state and federal governments embarked on the standards-based reforms, students with disabilities were not even an afterthought. However, families and advocates feared that the benefits, such as increased focus on helping every child progress and increased resources, that would come from having standards and accountability would be lost to students with disabilities. Thus, there was a consistent push to make sure these students were included in these policies. Have they benefitted? It is difficult to judge.

One of the most important indicators might be the progress made in closing the achievement gap between students with disabilities and other subgroups. Measuring this has been complicated by the changing state and federal policies that govern how students with disabilities were to be included in various assessments. For instance, as late as the mid-1990s, it was common for states to have policies stating that students with disabilities were to be included in their standards and assessment but at the same time allowing IEP teams to make decisions regarding if or how specific standards would be interpreted for an individual student (McLaughlin & Thurlow, 2003). Further, until the late 1990s, students with disabilities were routinely excluded from the National Assessment of Educational Progress (NAEP) and state and local assessments. Yet, the most recent NAEP data (National Center for Education Statistics, 2010a) indicate that the average fourth-grade reading score for students with disabilities increased significantly from 1998 to 2009; however, the mean scores have remained relatively flat since 2005 and a gap of about 35 points continues between the achievements of students with and without disabilities. For eighth-grade reading, there has been no significant increase in average scores since 1998 and the gap has remained at about 36 points. The average mathematics score for students with disabilities in the 2009 NAEP assessment was higher than in previous years, and the gap between these students and those without disabilities was only 21 points. Eighth-grade math scores for students with disabilities were also higher than all previous years, but there was a 58-point gap between the average scores for students with and those without disabilities.

Aggregate information on the performance of students with disabilities on state assessments is difficult to obtain because, in part, of the variation among state standards, tests, and accommodation policies. McLaughlin, Krezmien, and Zablocki (2009) analyzed 2005–2006 school year assessment data compiled by the National Center on Educational Outcomes from state reports submitted to the U.S. Department of Education, which used a common approach to classify students into three performance levels: basic, proficient, and advanced. The McLaughlin et al. (2009) analyses of these data indicated that less than 40% of third-grade students with disabilities scored at or above proficiency on state reading assessments and just over 40% scored at or above proficiency on state math assessments. The data also indicated a decreasing percentage of students scoring at or above proficiency as grade level increased.

There has been a number of limitations to assessing and reporting the performance of students with disabilities. These include issues with accommodation policies and test design (see, e.g., Cormier, Altman, Shyyan, & Thurlow, 2010). In addition, the population of students who receive special education changes from year to year, making it difficult to draw conclusions about changes in the aggregate achievement of students with disabilities over time. Individual students move in and out of the subgroup and the assumption is that the higher-performing students will no longer receive special education and students with greater academic and functional learning needs will remain or enter the subgroup. In addition, NAEP does not offer an alternate assessment and, therefore, some students with more severe disabilities are excluded. As a consequence, the NAEP data represent a higher-functioning group of students than the national population of students with disabilities.

Educational Attainment and Economic Implications

Another way to judge the impact of reforms on students with disabilities is by examining educational attainment. Obtaining a high school diploma and a postsecondary degree or certificate has an important economic impact on individuals. Recent data from the Bureau of Labor Statistics (BLS) indicate that, among individuals aged 25 years and older, the average weekly earnings of those with no high school diploma was about 47% less than the earnings of individuals with high school diplomas and GEDs. Although there is only about a 15% difference in average weekly wages between high school graduates and those with some college or an associate degree, the wage gap only gets larger as individuals obtain more education (NCES, 2010b).

There is a substantial body of research documenting the poor educational and post-school outcomes of students who have received special education (Blackorby & Wagner, 1996; Levine & Edgar, 1994; Newman, Wagner, Cameto, & Knokey, 2009; Wagner, Newman, Cameto, Garza, & Levine, 2005). For instance, the nationally representative National Longitudinal Transition Study-2 (NLTS-2), which is following more than 11,000 youth with disabilities, has reported that 32% of students with disabilities in the sample who left high school in 2003 did not receive a diploma (Wagner et al., 2005). About 42% of these students had enrolled in some type of postsecondary education or training, compared with 51% of students in the general population (Wagner et al., 2005). Among the group enrolled, 6% had enrolled in business, vocational, or technical schools; 13.1% in 2-year colleges; and

7.6% in a 4-year college or university. In comparison, 12% of the youth within the same age ranges in the general population were enrolled in 2-year colleges and 28% in 4-year institutions (Wagner et al., 2005). However, in terms of employment, the NLTS-2 found that about 40% of the youth in the sample who had left school were employed at the time of the first follow up, which was substantially less than the 63% employment rate among students without disabilities in the same age group. However, employment varied by type of disability as well as by whether the student had received a high school diploma. A recent Current Population Survey, a monthly survey of households conducted by the Bureau of the Census, indicated a 72% employment rate for individuals without a disability aged 20–24 years compared with 44% for the same-aged individuals with a disability (U.S. Department of Labor, 2010). These employment outcomes have not improved significantly over time.

A 2001 report of the Urban Institute (Loprest & Maag, 2001) analyzed data from the Disability Supplement of the National Interview Survey to examine employment of persons with disabilities. They found that the main reason given by these individuals for not working was lack of appropriate jobs (53%), whereas 22% reported lack of adequate training and skills as the reason they could not find a job. A separate survey of private and public sector employers (Bruyere, 2000) found that lack of experience (49% of private sector and 53% of public sector) and lack of required skills/training (39% of private sector and 45% of public sector) were the top barriers to employment and advancement of persons with disabilities.

Clearly, we know that education is a powerful mediator of adult income. Beyond the association with high school diplomas or postsecondary credentials, studies have found a significant positive association between reading assessment scores in adolescence and young adult outcomes, including educational attainment (Daniel et al., 2006; Lee, Daniels, Puig, Newgent, & Nam, 2008), employment (Caspi, Wright, Moffitt, & Silva, 1998), and wages (Neal & Johnson, 1996; Murnane, Willett, & Levy, 1995).

Researchers have similar findings with respect to mathematics. For instance, basic math skills, such as numeracy (i.e., number representation and ability to employ mathematical techniques), are associated with effective navigation of life events such as health care and making emergency medical decisions (Reyna & Brainerd, 2007). Math course-taking has been shown to be associated with the likelihood of attaining a postsecondary degree and subsequent earnings (Rose & Betts, 2001). Using math course–taking data from the High School and Beyond Study, Rose and Betts found that in 1982 there was an earnings gap of $11,000 between students whose highest level of math was vocational math versus students whose highest-level class was calculus. According to the NLTS-2, youth with disabilities take and complete more mathematics coursework at the high school level than they did 2 decades ago (Wagner, Newman, Cameto, Levine, & Marder, 2003). However, the percentage of youth with disabilities taking mathematics courses markedly decreased in the last 2 years of high school when advanced mathematics courses are typically taken.

A recent study of students with disabilities in the Educational Longitudinal Study (Wilson, 2008) examined the effect of the high school curriculum on math achievement among students with IEPs. Specifically, the study explored the effects of being enrolled in a high school that offered a limited but rigorous sequence of math courses compared with a high school that offered a "cafeteria" math curriculum of lower-level remedial math classes. The study used multilevel models that controlled for gender, race/ethnicity, and family socioeconomic status (SES), and results indicated that being enrolled in a school with the more constrained curriculum was associated with an average increase in math achievement of about 30%. In other words, a curriculum structure where most students take the same level of math coursework and that level of coursework includes advanced level math is associated with higher average math achievement for students with and without disabilities. The findings of this study suggest that the structure of curriculum matters in the math achievement and course-taking choices of students with disabilities. Thus, schools that adopt high standards for all students may limit the curricular options but may in fact help students with disabilities choose courses that can have an impact on their ability to access postsecondary education as well as their success in those environments.

Acquisition of key educational skills gives the individual a relative advantage with cumulative returns in education (i.e., achievement in later grades, ultimate educational attainment, and adult wages). Thus, decisions that restrict a student's opportunity to learn challenging subject matter content known to advantage them in the future are both inequitable and economically unsound. Yet, at the same time, we must acknowledge that the data concerning students with disabilities, though indicating some progress toward increasing academic achievement and educational attainments, also suggest that the impacts on adult economic attainment are yet to be fully realized.

The conflicts between standards and individualized decision making reflect differing beliefs about equity. As noted by Brighouse and Swift (2008), it is not unusual for different values to conflict in policy discussions, nor is it unusual to conclude that one value is more important than the other. However, they argue that, in some instances, one has to make a judgment of whether Policy Y, which we believe to be so critical (e.g., IEPs with individually referenced outcomes), has a moral priority over Policy X (e.g., IEPs that are based on common standards). That is, does Y always trump X, or only in some instances? For example, under what conditions might a parent of a student with a disability argue for individualized outcomes? Would a parent argue for lower standards for graduation if his or her child's diploma was not at risk? Would some educational outcomes matter more to some groups of students with disabilities? One cannot argue for individualizing outcomes only when it is convenient or beneficial. However, we must be explicit about if or when a comparative or relational concept of equity is called for and when certain inequities are tolerable. We must also be realistic about the challenges to including students with disabilities in the standards movement. For instance, despite progress related to assessment, issues remain with assessment design, specifically related to assessment accommodations, and issues over how scores are reported and/or progress is determined (Almond, Lehr, Thurlow, & Quenemoen, 2002; McLaughlin & Thurlow, 2003).

Perhaps the most prominent issue surrounding the assessment of students with disabilities is the use of accommodations. As noted earlier, several federal laws, including ADA, Section 504, and IDEA, all guarantee students with disabilities the right to assessment accommodations. IDEA gives the IEP team the right to decide which accommodations are necessary for a student to participate in the classroom and in assessments. The issue is how to treat the scores of assessments when students have used certain accommodations, such as having the reading test read to a student.

Advocates, parents, and legal groups have claimed that it is a violation of students' rights to withhold any accommodation listed on the students' IEP. Others have argued that, if certain accommodations are used, the scores are invalidated, and under NCLB, the student's score becomes a zero or is classified as nonproficient, which jeopardizes a school's performance. However, courts and the Office of Civil Rights have tended to find that accommodations that have an impact on the integrity of the test by altering what is being measured (e.g., reading aloud a reading test) are not required by law, have not been considered appropriate accommodations, and do not have to be "counted" (Karger & Pullin, 2002). Some of these issues may be solved as test developers move toward universal design for learning and incorporating accommodations in tests.

Standards and Free Appropriate Public Education

A consistent criticism of the standards as applied to students with disabilities is how the notion of common standards aligns with the entitlement to FAPE. As defined in the IDEA, students with disabilities are entitled to an appropriate education, which is to be individually tailored to a student's unique needs and expected to confer benefit. For many special educators, the concept of common standards flies in the face of this core entitlement. However, in response to the standards movement, states and local districts have moved toward standards-based IEPs. An IEP that is based on standards is one in which individual educational goals are directly linked to a state's grade-level content standards and assessments (Nolet & McLaughlin, 2005; Holbrook, 2007). These IEPs are designed to allow each child to receive an individually designed plan of services and supports, but the goals are focused on the attainment of state content and achievement standards. These IEPs may seem counter to the principle of individualization and to subvert the procedural rights for determining what constitutes FAPE for a student. Yet, standards-based IEPs can ensure access to the same curricula and opportunity to learn content that has been established for all other students. These IEPs can both meet the procedural standards as specified in the IDEA and provide real and meaningful educational benefit.

Nevertheless, a concern consistently voiced by special educators is that the focus on standards has diverted attention from other critical needs (McLaughlin, Henderson, & Rhim, 1997; Nagle, 2004). In particular, special education teachers report being caught between the competing priorities (McLaughlin et al., 1997; Nagle, 2004) of teaching to the standards and trying to teach important life skills. The standards that are assessed are overwhelmingly academic as are the resulting curricular frameworks, goals, and school improvement efforts. Finally, the notion of standards-based IEPs is viewed by some teachers as undermining their professional opinion and judgment in determining what an individual student needs to learn. This has been a particular issue for IEP teams, which have traditionally had the right to determine what constitutes an "appropriate" education for a student with a disability and 'in some cases' even determine the "curriculum" for a student.

On the positive side, both content and achievement standards provide important guidelines and benchmarks for measuring student progress and setting performance targets. Research conducted at the state and district levels has revealed that special education administrators and policymakers are seeing some positive impacts from the new accountability reforms (Nagle, 2004). In interviews with state and local special education administrators, teachers, and parents conducted in eight districts, increased expectations for students with disabilities was identified as the most positive and valued outcome of including these students in the standards-based reforms. Parents and special educators agreed that expectations for students with disabilities had been too low and that both special and general education teachers tended to underestimate the abilities of students with disabilities. As one policymaker noted, "I think historically that we underestimate the ability of children with disabilities. We usually set up our instructional program around those expectations. What we want to do is force people to reconsider their expectations and allow children to have opportunities they haven't had before" (Nagle, 2004, p. 15).

Conclusion

How students with disabilities will fare within a standards-based educational model remains a work in progress. We are definitely witnessing some positive effects, but a number of challenges remain. Some of these challenges may be addressed in the near future through new assessment and curricular designs that are based on the principles of universal design for learning (UDL) (Johnson & Thurlow, 2003). Other adjustments to current policies, such as the use of individual student versus cohort progress monitoring, may also help deal with some of the issues inherent in annual accountability goals. But, special education will need to reconcile what constitutes an "appropriate" education for a student with a disability with universal standards. Special education programs and practices and standards represent a convergence of two social forces. One is the rights-based movement that provides equal protection and access to individuals with disabilities, whereas the standards movement is a response to society's beliefs about the importance of education as a social tool and a remedy for inequality of social and economic opportunity. It is clear that standards can lead to greater access to rigorous courses and higher expectations, which have been shown to make a difference in both school and postschool outcomes. Research related to the IEP and special education has suggested that, historically, schools have held low expectations and have had no accountability for students with disabilities (McDonnell et al., 1997; McLaughlin & Thurlow, 2003). This suggests that the differences in access and outcomes between students with and without IEPs may result from an individualization mandate as seen in the IEP but yet is vulnerable to preconceived and historic notions about students with disabilities (McLaughlin, 2010). Without standards that guide the process, how are we to know if a student is being treated equitably?

For us to meet the true intent of what constitutes an "appropriate" education for any given student with a disability, we must be able to have an objective measure against which we can compare a student's progress and to judge the adequacy of his or her education. Nonetheless, the practical issue of what is meant by "standards" in the context of an individualized education cannot be ignored. Whether it is feasible or even wise to endorse one *common* set of achievement standards is open to discussion. What is certain is that we need to reconcile what we understand about educating students with disabilities with a standards model if we are to ever achieve the goal of a "free appropriate public education" for every student with a disability.

Study Questions

1. Do an online search to learn more about NCLB and IDEA to further examine how these help students with disabilities.

2. Discuss whether the reforms are working.

3. How does IDEA support accountability for students with disabilities?

4. Interview a professional responsible for hiring special education teachers about what is a "highly qualified" special education teacher; then compare and contrast what is learned with the information presented in this chapter.

5. There are a number of legal issues concerning requiring students with disabilities to pass one or more assessments to receive a high school diploma; discuss the benefits and consequences of these policies.

6. Use the Internet to investigate various types of alternate assessments.

7. Meet with the head of special education services for a school district to discuss the major issues surrounding the inclusion of students with disabilities in the types of high-stakes accountability that is in place in today's schools.

Online Resources

National Center on Educational Outcomes: http://www.cehd.umn.edu/NCEO/

IDEA Resources and Information on the Law: http://idea.ed.gov/

The National Alternate Assessment Center: http://www.naacpartners.org/

Good Sources for Updates on Current Policies Related to Standards, Assessments, and Accountability

The department of education web site for your state: Look for assessments, standards, accountability.

The Council for Exceptional Children: http://www.cec.sped.org/am/template.cfm?section=Home

The National Association of State Directors of Special Education: http://www.nasdse.org/

Council of Chief State School Officers: http://www.ccsso.org/

Secondary Curriculum and Transition

9

EMILY C. BOUCK

After completing this chapter, the reader will be able to

- Describe issues facing secondary curriculum
- Differentiate between a functional and an academic approach to secondary curriculum and the benefits and limitations of each approach
- Examine what the research says about secondary curriculum
- Discuss the factors guiding and affecting secondary curriculum decision making for students with disabilities
- Apply a framework for curriculum decision making for secondary students with disabilities

Issues Facing Secondary Curriculum

States, policymakers, researchers, schools, teachers, and parents are continually asking and discussing what to teach students in high school in the United States. Secondary curriculum for students in general is a topic currently debated around the country; yet, concern over secondary curriculum is not new. Discussions of reform for secondary education regarding *what* is taught (i.e., curriculum) in the United States have existed for the past several decades. In the 1980s, the National Commission on Excellence in Education, in *A Nation at Risk* (1983), focused on beefing up the academic requirements of high school because of concern that American graduates were falling behind their international counterparts. The recommendations included requiring students to take 4 years of English/language arts instruction; 3 years of mathematics, science, and social studies courses and encouraging higher standards (Olson, 2003; Corcoran & Silander, 2009; Lee & Ready, 2009; Rouse & Kemple, 2009; Yell & Dragsow, 2005). Another round of education reform occurred in the 1990s with the reauthorization of the Elementary and Secondary Education Act (ESEA; 1965; PL 89-10)—called the Improving America's Schools Act (IASA; 1994; PL 103-382)—which focused on schools following rigorous academic standards, assessing all students, and holding schools accountable for student outcomes (Yell & Dragsow, 2005). The start of the new century brought another round of educational reform following the implementation of No Child Left Behind Act (NCLB; 2001; PL 107-110)—the latest reauthorization of the ESEA. Although all aspects of the NCLB law are pertinent to secondary education, perhaps most relevant with respect to secondary curriculum are the issue of accountability (i.e., *all* students taking an assessment every year in reading, math, and science in grades 3–8 and once again in high school) and the goal to graduate all students from high school (Yell & Dragsow, 2005).

During this most recent wave of educational reform, additional high-stakes testing—particularly high school exit exams—also appeared on the scene. Exit exams typically require a student to pass a test, or set of tests, to graduate from high school; failure can result in a certificate of attendance rather than a diploma (Reardon, Arshan, Atteberry, & Kurlaender, 2010). The most recent data suggested that approximately three fourths of high school students in the United States are affected by high-stakes exit exams (Center on Education Policy [CEP], 2010). As of 2010, 28 states implemented exit exams for high school students, of which 25 base receipt of a diploma on passing the test (CEP, 2010).

Despite decades of reform pushing for more rigorous high school learning environments, data suggested that schools repeatedly failed to implement the higher standards. For example, in 1998, just over half of the states reported that students needed four credits in language arts and three in social studies to receive a high school diploma ($n = 26$), and only 14 required three credits in mathematics and science (National Center for Education Statistics, 2001). As of 2007, 37 states required 4 years of language arts, 31 at least 3 years of social studies, 27 at least 3 years of mathematics, but still less than half ($n = 23$) demanded 3 or more years of science (U.S. Department of Education [U.S. DOE], 2007b). Although progress has been made (i.e., average number of high school credits earned increased from 21.7 in 1982 to 25.8 in 2004), continued conversations and reform efforts suggest additional room for improvement (U.S. DOE, 2007b). Furthermore, although dropout rates decreased over the past several decades (from 14.1% of all students aged 16–24 in 1980 to 8% in 2008), double-digit rates still exist in some ethnicity categories (e.g., 18.3% of Hispanic students and 14.6% of American Indian/Alaska Native; National Center for Education Statistics, 2010a).

Secondary Curriculum and Students with Disabilities

The previously noted issues facing secondary education clearly have implications for curriculum. Furthermore, the issues affect all students, including now students with disabilities who historically were excluded from accountability systems and considerations of rigorous high school curriculum. Students with all types of disabilities served under the Individuals with Disabilities Education Improvement Act (IDEA; 2004; PL 105-17) and Section 504 plans are now being held to high standards in high school, including exit exams to earn an diploma, participation in state accountability systems, and attention to a more rigorous academic curriculum focus (e.g., some states requiring *all* students to take and pass advanced algebra; Bouck & Wasburn-Moses, 2010; Mack, 2010; Yell & Drasgow, 2005). Hence, special educators and general educators must stop and give greater consideration to the secondary curriculum for students with disabilities. In other words, over the past decade, more teachers, researchers, and policymakers have been asking *what* do and should secondary students with disabilities learn in school, and these conversations are likely to continue.

The participation of students with disabilities in a state's accountability system, the focus on access and participation in the general education curriculum, and the requirement of passing high school exit exams hold implications with respect to curriculum for these students. All three suggest that students are best served in a general education setting with a general education curriculum or, at minimum, curriculum aligned to the state content areas standards. With the connection between these high-stakes assessments and curriculum, an underlying key idea is that alternative curricula—such as a functional curriculum—is no longer a viable option. It is unfair to ask a student to take the general large-scale assessment or an exit exam to earn a diploma if that student has not been exposed to the curriculum covered on those tests (i.e., the general education academically oriented curriculum; Bouck, 2009b). In a similar way, it is unfair to expect schools to meet NCLB's adequate yearly progress (AYP) or the requirement of 100% graduation rates if students are not provided an opportunity to learn the curriculum on which they will be assessed. Although federal policy acknowledged that not all students with disabilities should take the general large-scale assessment (Branstad et al., 2002; Burling, 2007; Council for Exceptional Children [CEC], n.d.; NCLB, 2001; U.S. DOE, 2007a) and some states who employ an exit exam allow for student waivers—such as students with disabilities (Kober et al., 2006; Krentz, Thurlow, Shyyan, & Scott, 2005)—many students with disabilities still participate in these high-stakes tests based on academic standards and the general education curriculum. All these issues, combined with the history of debate over what and where to teach students with disabilities, resulted in a divide in the field, the sides boiling down to a more academic focus and curriculum versus a functional curriculum.

Types of Curriculum

What is curriculum? Curriculum, in the literal sense, means "running course," which has been interpreted today to be a series of experiences or courses (Morrison, 1993). Ultimately, what most people think of curriculum is the *what* of schooling. However, curriculum can refer to the materials used in classes (e.g., textbooks) or the expected outcomes of learning and the resources to achieve those outcomes (McDonnell, Wilcox, & Hardman, 1991; Nolet & McLaughlin, 2000). Within the realm of special education, the conceptualization of curriculum can even be broader, such as the total school experience (Doll, 1989), what one learns or is taught (Kavale, 1990; Pugach & Warger, 1993), or even an individualized education program (IEP; Sands, Adams, & Stout, 1995). Curriculum, as discussed throughout this chapter, is operationally defined in the general sense of "the *what* of school." It is not narrowly considered as a textbook or even a model but, rather, as the content of the teaching and learning of students with disabilities.

Multiple options exist for curriculum at the secondary level for students with disabilities, which inevitably relate to the instructional environment where students receive services. Bigge (1988) outlined five main approaches or options for special education curriculum:

1. Identical curriculum, which uses general education curriculum and implements the same standards but with special services or accommodations
2. Parallel curriculum, which also uses the general education curriculum but reduces the complexity
3. Lower grade–level curriculum
4. Practical academic curriculum, which utilizes different but related curriculum to achieve the general curriculum
5. Life management curriculum (functional)

More than a decade later, Pugach and Warger (2001) narrowly situated special education curriculum into two options: 1) functional for students with more low-incidence disabilities and 2) remediation for students with more high-incidence disabilities. Since Bigge and even Pugach and Warger conceptualized curriculum, a number of political and societal shifts have occurred (e.g., IDEA, 2004; NCLB, 2001) and conversations in general education and special education have morphed into "teaching to the standards" (Alwell & Cobb, 2009a; Browder, Spooner, Wakeman, Trela, & Baker, 2006). The standards-based movement has monopolized the educational reform of all students, including students with disabilities.

Standards—academic/content standards—are "general statements of what students should know or be able to do when they complete each grade level or by the end of their overall school program" (Spooner & Browder, 2006, p. 2). Standards exist for the core content areas by grade level (i.e., language arts/English, mathematics, social studies, science) and are to drive the curriculum for the grade-level content. In the past, national standards have not existed; rather, national professional organizations developed grade-level standards (e.g., the National Council of Teachers of Mathematics). States independently adopted and implemented their own core content standards, often reflecting the national professional organizations). Yet, 2010 resulted in a majority of states adopting the Common Core State Standards for all students; see http://www.corestandards.org (Council of Chief State School Officers [CCSSO] and the National Governors Association Center for Best Practices [NGA Center], 2010). As of January 2011, 41 states as well as the District of Columbia and the U.S. Virgin Islands adopted the Common Core (Common Core, n.d.). The Common Core addresses standards for students in grades K–12; focuses on college and career readiness (CCSSO & NGA, 2010); and exists along two domains: 1) literacy, including English/language arts and "literacy in history, social studies, science, and technical subjects" and 2) mathematics.

Beyond fueling what to teach, standards drive the assessments states use to measure AYP (i.e., the accountability system under NCLB, 2001), which indirectly has implications for curriculum. With the requirement that all students must participate in yearly assessments in grades 3–8 and once again in high school (IDEA, 2004; NCLB, 2001), four options exist for students with disabilities to participate in a state's accountability system (Yell & Dragsow, 2005). The most common method of participation is through the **general large-scale assessment** system aligned to the state's general education standards, and, for students with disabilities, this level of participation can occur with or without accommodations.

However, in the creation of the accountability system, it was acknowledged that not all students may be successful with the general large-scale assessments, even with state-approved accommodations, and, hence, each state offers an approved alternate assessment (U.S. DOE, 2003; Perner, 2007). Alternate assessments are defined as "an assessment designed for a small group of students with disabilities who are unable to participate in the regular state assessment, even with appropriate accommodations" (U.S. DOE, 2003, p. 68,699). Alternate assessments are typically reserved for students with severe disabilities and were initially established for 1% of the student body to take and have scores count toward a school's AYP (Branstad et al., 2002; NCLB, 2001; Perner, 2007; Yell & Drasgow,

2005). Although more than 1% of students can take an alternate assessment based on alternate achievement standards, the scores of students who exceed 1% of the school's population count as zeros toward AYP (Yell & Drasgow, 2005).

The U.S. DOE acknowledged the limiting nature of only 1% of students who take an alternate assessment counting toward AYP. They specifically noted the exclusion of students with disabilities for whom the general large-scale assessment is still not appropriate, but who exist outside the small percentage allotted to count toward AYP. Thus, the U.S. DOE determined "a small group of students with disabilities" (2007a, p. 17,748) would be allowed to use modified achievement standards and take alternate assessments based on these modified achievement standards (Burling, 2007; CEC, n.d.; Lazarus, Thurlow, Christensen, & Cromier, 2007). This change reflected an additional 2% of students with disabilities who may take an alternate assessment and have scores count toward a school's AYP. Former U.S. DOE Secretary Margaret Spelling indicated that this 2% would capture students classified beyond severe disabilities, such as students with mild intellectual disabilities, severe emotional–behavior disabilities, and so forth. However, states and IEP teams are left to determine student eligibility for the 2% as well as decisions about the actual assessments (Burling; retrieved September 14, 2011, from CEC, http://www.cec.sped.org/am/template.cfm?section=Home).

Curricular Options

As previously discussed in this chapter, there is divide in secondary education curriculum for students with disabilities. Guy, Sitlington, Larsen, and Frank (2009) situated the two perspectives as preparation for adult life and traditional academics. Another way to think about the perceived dichotomy over what to teach (functional versus academics) is to view the two positions as existing in a more general representation that education should be relevant and education should train the mind. One of the fundamental concerns regarding the two curricula involves sacrificing one for the other. One side is concerned about secondary students' access to functional/life skills, given the emphasis on standards-based or general education curriculum. However, the opponents raise the opposite concern—students with disabilities receiving a functional curriculum to the detriment of receiving an academic/standards-based curriculum to prepare them for postsecondary opportunities.

Functional Curriculum

A functional curriculum, also known as a life skills curriculum, is a type of curriculum focused on teaching students the necessary skills to function in adult life (Wehman & Kregel, 2011). A functional curriculum can be defined in a multitude of ways, but its central tenet remains the same—to prepare students with the skills necessary for daily living after school—and often includes the following components: functional academics, vocational education, community access, daily living skills, financial skills, independent living skills, transportation skills, social/relationship skills, and self-determination (Wehman & Kregel, 2004). In essence, a functional curriculum involves teaching chronologically age-appropriate skills needed to function in one's daily life (e.g., grocery shopping, navigating public transportation, personal hygiene).

A functional curricular approach to teaching students with disabilities can manifest itself in a variety of ways. A range of commercially available functional curriculum models exist; the majority target students with moderate to severe disabilities; however, packaged functional curriculum models also exist for students with more high-incidence disabilities (see Table 9.1 for examples of functional curriculum models, their alignment with functional curriculum components [Patton, Cronin, & Jairrels, 1997] and adult life subdomains [Cronin & Patton, 1993] as well as a basic description). The reviewed functional curriculum models are diverse, with varying degrees of functional components (Patton, Cronin,

Table 9.1. Functional curriculum models for students with disabilities

Curriculum model	Cost	Functional curriculum components[a] (n = 11)	Adult life subdomains[b] (n = 26)	Description
A Functional Curriculum for Teaching Students with Disabilities (Bender, Valletutti, Baglin, & Hoffnung, 1996)	$125.00	7	9.5	A series of three manuals that provides teacher and family interventions for four age ranges (early childhood, primary, intermediate, and secondary school)
Adaptive Living Skills Curriculum (Anderson, Bruinlinks, Morreau, & Gilman, 1991)	$457.50	6	12	A four-book curriculum for young children through adults focused on personal living skills, home living skills, community living skills, and employment skills
Community-Based Curriculum (Falvey, 1989)	$30.00	9	14	A book focused on community-based instruction for students with severe disabilities, which provides both functional and age-appropriate skills in inclusive settings
Everyday Life Skills (American Guidance Service, 2001)	$114.97 (without extras) $519.93 (with extras)	6	15	A textbook—complete with student and teacher editions—focused on preparing students for life after school, including career development as well as independent living (e.g., home skills, personal skills)
Functional Curriculum for Elementary, Middle, and Secondary Age Students with Special Needs (Wehman & Kregel, 3rd ed., 2011)	$52.00	10	17	A user-friendly edited book providing and connecting a functional curriculum throughout the grade levels to create a comprehensive program
Functional Independence Skills Handbook (Killion, 2003)	$62.00	9	6	A curriculum and assessment program designed for students with developmental disabilities focused on promoting independence (e.g., cognitive skills, vocational skills, social skills)
Impact: A Functional Curriculum Handbook (Neel & Billingsley, 1989)	Out of print	2.5	.5	An out-of-print book focused on providing functional skills for students with moderate and severe disabilities
Life Centered Career Education (Brolin, 2004)	$519.93			An educational system for students with all types of disabilities produced by the Council for Exceptional Children focused on three main components: daily living skills, personal–social skills, and occupational guidance and preparation
Life Skills Activities for Secondary Students with Special Needs (Mannix, 1995)	$29.95	9	11.5	A book for teachers or parents with exercises that can be photocopied for use with students within six domains: self-awareness, people skills, academic and school skills, practical living skills, vocational skills, and problem-solving skills
Life Skills Instruction for All Students with Special Needs (Cronin & Patton, 1993)	$39.00	9.5	23	A guide to assist teachers with integrating aspects of functional curriculum into their teaching and/or curriculum
The Syracuse Community-Referenced Curriculum Guide (Ford et al., 1989)	$59.00	8.5	15.5	A guide focused on students with moderate and severe disabilities; provides research to support inclusion of specific functional curriculum components but is organized like a textbook for educators

Source: Bouck (2009).

[a]Aspects of a functional curriculum are functional academics, vocational education, daily living, social/relationships, independent living, community access or skills, transportation, financial skills, self-determination, leisure and recreation, and communication skills (Patton, Cronin, & Jairrels, 1997).

[b]The six domains of adulthood are employment/education, home and family, leisure pursuits, personal responsibilities and relationships, community involvement, and physical/emotional health. The 26 subdomains fell within the six domains and included aspects such as goal setting, family life, general job skills, and travel (Cronin & Patton, 1993). All these curriculum models were reviewed in Bouck (2009a) for the target population of secondary students with mild intellectual disabilities.

& Jairrels, 1997) and adult life subdomains (Cronin & Patton, 1993) addressed. They also represent different structures to presenting a "curriculum," such as a textbook for teachers (*Community-Based Curriculum*, Falvey, 1989; *The Syracuse Community-Referenced Curriculum Guide*, Ford et al., 1989) to a book of worksheets for students to complete (*Life Skills Activities for Secondary Students with Special Needs*, Mannix, 1995) to a reference guide to assist teachers in developing their own functional curriculum (*Life Skills Instruction for all Students with Special Needs*, Cronin & Patton, 1993). In essence, the noted functional curriculum models represent options for teachers to consider and evaluate in light of competing demands (e.g., cost, depth versus breadth of components, scripted versus supplementary; Bouck, 2009a).

However, a curriculum model is not the only medium in which teachers can access and implement a functional curriculum. In fact, commercially available models may be restrictive (e.g., above-grade-level reading, worksheets, or a teacher-based textbook reference) and fail to meet the needs of a range of learners (see Bouck, 2009a, for an analysis of functional curriculum models for secondary students with mild intellectual disabilities). Teachers can also develop a functional curriculum by creating their own materials, using real-life tasks, involving community resources, and utilizing technology (Wehman & Kregel, 2004). Yet, this decision must be weighed with respect to time, access to resources, and federal policy regarding evidence-based practices or ones supported by scientifically based research (NCLB, 2001; U.S. DOE, 2002).

Typically, a functional curriculum is viewed differently from a general education curriculum in that it is not driven by a scope and sequence but is a more individualized model. Thus, a teacher could essentially select the skills an individual student—or at times a class of students—needed and teach those, essentially creating what Browder and colleagues (2004) referred to as a "catalog" (p. 212). Besides the individualized nature of "selecting" or "developing" a functional curriculum, one also approaches the implementation of a functional curriculum with a longitudinal trajectory in that skills can and should build upon one another (Collins, Kleinert, & Land, 2006).

Although historically one might associate a functional curriculum—or life skills instruction—with students with more moderate or severe disabilities (e.g., intellectual disabilities), this approach is not restricted to such students. In fact, students with more high-incidence disabilities—or all students in general—can benefit from receiving individualized aspects of a functional curriculum (e.g., how to balance a checkbook). Furthermore, a functional curriculum is not restricted to being taught in a pullout special education class. Although it can be a single course of individually tailored life skills or an entire program, life skills instruction can also be infused into content instruction in the general education setting.

Use of a functional or life skills curriculum experienced a decrease in recent decades. Although a functional curriculum was once the most popular curricular approach for educating students with disabilities—particularly students with more moderate and severe disabilities—an academically oriented curriculum focused on standards replaced its stature (Alwell & Cobb, 2009a; Bouck, 2004; Browder, Spooner, et al., 2006; Nietupski, Hamre-Nietupski, Curtin, & Shrikanth, 1997). It is logical to associate the decreased attention to a functional curriculum with some of the aforementioned reforms and changes in education, such as the increased focus on accountability and all students participating in a school's accountability system (IDEA, 2004; NCLB, 2001); a political shift toward inclusive education and access and participation in the general education curriculum (IDEA, 2004; NCLB, 2001); and states requiring subject area competency from students, as measured on tests, to receive a diploma (Reardon et al., 2010).

Academic or Standards-Based Curriculum

An **academic or standards-based curriculum** is the teaching of academic content to students with disabilities. When one typically thinks of academic content, one thinks of the general education curriculum and the *standard* or *typical* curriculum students without disabilities receive in high school: English/language arts, mathematics, science, and social studies, to name the core content areas. Although an academic curriculum refers to academic content regardless of setting, it often conjures up an association with inclusive education, although that view is limiting (Browder, Wakeman, & Jimenez, 2006). The connotation of the term *academically oriented* or *standards-based* curriculum is multifaceted, referring to the general education curriculum with or without accommodations in the general education setting as well as instruction that addresses state standards to occur in a variety of settings (i.e., general education, special education, community-based).

For some students, an academic or standards-based curriculum means taking geometry in the general education setting with accommodations. The geometry class is taught by a general education mathematics teacher and aligned to the state's geometry standards. However, for other students, the academic or standards-based curriculum can mean learning to dial a cell phone and provide information about one's location when lost; the instruction is occurring in the community but the ideas being taught can relate to science standards (e.g., physical science) (Courtade, Spooner, & Browder, 2007; Taber, Alberto, Hughes, & Seltzer, 2002; Taber, Alberto, Seltzer, & Hughes, 2003).

Stated differently, an academic or standards-based curriculum can be the general education curriculum with no accommodations (i.e., consisting of the same curriculum for students without disabilities [Wehmeyer, Lattin, & Agran, 2001]) or the general education curriculum with accommodations, which Wehmeyer et al. referred to as "curricular adaptation" (2001, p. 334). In the past, common accommodations for students with disabilities included books on tape or materials read aloud, use of a calculator, and preferential seating (McGahee-Kovac, 2002).

A third option is a general education curriculum but with modification or augmentation. There is no one set way to adapt the general education curriculum to meet a student's needs. Each teacher, each student, and each classroom is unique and adaptations must be specific to the situation.

Here is an example of how a science teacher might go about considering modifications to the general education curriculum. First, the teacher would briefly identify the curricular goal for most learners (e.g., *By the end of this class, most students will be able to define and explain the relevance of concepts for describing reality [space, time, relativity, and quantum physics] from Chapter 6 in their textbook*). Next, the teacher would briefly identify the instructional plan for most learners: (e.g., *I will ask the students to read the chapter, identify the four key concepts, and write a short paragraph describing each concept they have chosen*). Next, the learners who require adaptation would be identified (e.g., Brian and LeAnn). Afterward, the teacher would consider a number of different adaptations and choose one to adapt what or how he or she teaches to accommodate Brian and LeAnn in the classroom for this lesson. For example, Brian will be allowed 2 extra days to complete the task or LeAnn's goal will be different and set to being to write the key concept words only or just listening to the words and descriptions. There could also be a modification in the evaluation, such as, while most students write essays at the end of the unit, the adapted strategy would be for Brian to take an objective test with additional time.

It is also important for educators to remember that the curriculum does not always need to be modified. For instance, by providing multilevel instruction, teachers may find that adapting a lesson may not always be necessary (Giangreco, Cloninger, & Iverson, 1998). Differentiating instruction and providing multiple ways to evaluate students allows more flexibility for students to meet the standards and requirements of the class, or the curriculum can be made more accessible through accommodations (e.g., using a tape recorder) or supports (e.g., paraprofessionals). It is also important to note that a student's support needs may change from one class to the next. Therefore, supports should be used when the instructional or social activity warrants the need for assistance rather than the disability label.

Another view on academic or standards-based curriculum is to employ a more hybrid model in which curriculum is linked to the content standards but perhaps has a look and feel of incorporating traditionally associated life skills. For example, Browder & Cooper-Duffy (2003) discussed how teaching students functional academics could be aligned to academic content standards, such as functional mathematics and functional reading. In another example, Courtade and colleagues (2007) discussed how functional skills such as first aid were connected to science content standards. Furthermore, curriculum alignment to general education grade-level content standards may also be achieved by employing programs or frameworks, such as *Academic Curriculum Framework* (PCI Education, n.d.), which aligns curriculum to standards across the education spectrum (e.g., K–12+) for students with more moderate and severe disabilities (Tilly & Haney, 2010).

What Does the Evidence-Based Research Say About Secondary Curriculum?

Beyond the perceived dichotomy of professional options regarding what curriculum secondary students with disabilities should receive in school lies the question of what curriculum is evidence-based or, in other words, what the research says regarding the impact of the two curriculum approaches. This is particularly so given the definition of evidence-based education according to the U.S. DOE: "the integration of professional wisdom with the best available empirical evidence in making decisions about how to deliver instruction" (2002, slide 3). NCLB (2001) ushered in an era of evidence-based practices, meaning educators need to consider and implement practices—including curriculum—that have scientific or empirical data to support their effectiveness as well as to consider the consensus gained through professional experiences.

Overall, the evidence is limited regarding secondary curriculum for students with disabilities, in part because of limited research comparing different types of curriculum as well as the impact of curriculum on outcomes. Over the past several decades, a decreased focus on functional curricula occurred in research, literature, and practice (Nietupski et al., 1997), and, despite significant discussion regarding an academically based curriculum for students with disabilities, a lack of research exists on the impact of providing students with disabilities access to academic content, particularly when one is considering a) the relationship between receipt of academic content and postschool outcomes and b) academic content instruction geared toward students with more low-incidence disabilities (Agran, Cavin, Wehmeyer, & Palmer, 2006; Browder, Spooner, et al., 2006; Nietupski et al., 1997). Further complicating the discussion of evidence-based curricula is difficulty isolating curriculum at the secondary level from instructional setting, despite the difference between *what* and *where*; setting influences curriculum in that being in the general education setting is associated with receiving academic instruction aligned to content standards (Wehmeyer, Lattin, Lapp-Rincker, & Agran, 2003; Soukup, Wehmeyer, Bashinski, & Bovaird, 2007).

In addition to considering the limited existing research, one should examine current practice. The most recent data available examining secondary education at a national level—the National Longitudinal Transition Study-2 (NLTS-2)—suggested that the secondary programming for students with disabilities in general is similar to that of their peers without disabilities in terms of the focus on academic content (i.e., more than 90% taking a language arts and mathematics class and more than 80% a science and social studies class; Wagner, 2003). In contrast, just over one third of all students with disabilities report taking a class devoted to life skills or study skills (Wagner, 2003). In terms of the instructional environment of courses, Wagner indicated that, in general, for students with disabilities, there was a relatively even divide between mathematics and language arts instruction taking place in the general education and special education setting; however, more science and social studies courses were taken in the general education setting than in the special education setting. For life skills instruction, the most common instructional environment was the special education setting. When broken down by disability categories, most of the categories still have a large percentage of students taking academic courses, although the lowest frequency occurs for students with more severe and/or low-incidence disabilities (i.e., deafblindness, multiple disabilities, and autism spectrum disorder). In contrast, students with intellectual disabilities, multiple disabilities, autism spectrum disorder, and deafblindness report the highest rates of life skills or social skills instruction (Wagner, 2003).

Regardless of the current landscape and the political ebbs and flows of curriculum (see Browder et al., 2003, for a historical review of curriculum), within the existing literature, there is support for both functional curriculum and an academic-focused curriculum, suggesting that the dichotomy can be less two-sided and viewed more as a continuum with curricular decisions at the secondary level based on the individual needs of individual students. Or, in other words, secondary curriculum should be viewed as a continuum of supports personalized for each individual student rather than as an either/or debate.

Functional Curriculum

Within the limited literature, Alwell and Cobb (2009a) reviewed research on a functional curriculum and outcomes of secondary students with disabilities between 1984 and 2002. From the 50 studies reviewed, the authors suggested that students benefit from receiving a functional curriculum; however, they noted a few caveats. For one, the majority of the research was conducted with students with more moderate and severe disabilities; little research actually examined the receipt of a functional curriculum on the outcomes for students with more mild or high-incidence disabilities. Furthermore, a functional curriculum was loosely defined, in that their review examined functional or life skills interventions, which ranged in duration from a single session to many months, as well as included a wide variety of functional curriculum components (e.g., money and purchasing, safety, leisure, meal preparation and cleaning, and personal care). Finally, no research related to life skills was conducted outside a special education setting. Although Alwell and Cobb (2009a) indicated that life skill interventions "worked," more research is needed to confidently say that functional curriculum is an *evidence-based* practice for students with disabilities. However, within the focus on students with severe disabilities, Ayres, Lowrey, Douglas, and Sievers (2011) provided a nonexhaustive review of literature supporting functional skills instruction and argued for the benefits this curriculum provided in terms of independent living.

In the author's own work targeting one particular population—secondary students with mild intellectual disabilities—she argued for a functional curriculum but found little empirical support (Bouck, 2004). For example, in a systematic review of the literature on use of a functional curriculum for secondary students with mild intellectual disabilities, Bouck and Flanagan (2010) found only seven published articles between 1994 and 2008. Although the studies showed improvement in the functional areas targeted, none of the studies examined the relationship between learning skills or receipt of the curricular component and outcomes in life outside school (e.g., employment, independent living). In another disability category—students with emotional–behavior disorders—researchers called for expanding the secondary curriculum for this population to include functional curriculum elements rather than just a focus on academics (Lane & Carter, 2006). In particular, Lane and Carter (2006) advocated a greater focus on work and vocational educational opportunities and suggested that research supports the association between success in postschool and work experiences (Johnson, Stodden, Emanuel, Luecking, & Mack, 2002; Lane & Carter, 2006). Although many arguments are made regarding the need and importance between acquiring life skills and a) one's quality of life or b) postschool outcomes, little empirical support exists for the claims (Alwell & Cobb, 2009a).

Within the limited research, earlier work by Benz and colleagues (Benz, Lindstrom, & Latta, 1999; Benz, Lindstrom, & Yovanoff, 2000) provided support for functional curricular components added to secondary education for students with more mild disabilities. The authors examined the Youth Transition Program (YTP)—a program aligned with components of a functional curriculum (i.e., self-determination; instruction in functional academics, vocational, independent living, and personal–social content areas; paid work experiences)—which provided services for special education students in their last 2 years of high school. Students in the YTP improved their rates of graduation, demonstrated increased rates of engagement in postsecondary education or productive work, and reported higher average hourly wages, higher average weekly wages, and higher maintenance of employment.

Less positive is current research by Bouck in which the NLTS-2 was examined to understand the relationship between receipt of life skills curriculum in high school by students with mild intellectual disabilities and postschool outcomes (i.e., employment, postsecondary education, independent living). Bouck and Joshi (in press) found no statistically significant relationship between receipt of a life skills curriculum in school and more positive postschool outcomes. In converse, more positive postschool outcomes were also not associated with receiving an academic curriculum; curriculum was not related to outcomes. The same results were found for students with moderate–severe intellectual disabilities—no relationship between curriculum and postschool outcomes (Bouck, in press).

Academic/Standards-Based Curriculum

Given the vast array of ways to situate an academic or standards-based curriculum, the literature regarding the evidence base of this approach is also quite diverse. In terms of students with more low-incidence disabilities, Collins, Evans, Creech-Galloway, Karl, & Miller (2007) found that students with moderate disabilities were successful at acquiring academic content (e.g., core content sight words) in a general education environment; however, the authors cautioned that functional sight words still needed to be taught at the secondary level. In considering students with more high-incidence disabilities, Scruggs, Mastropieri, Berkeley, and Graetz (2009) reported that evidence-based practices existed for educating students with disabilities at the secondary level in an academic curriculum when specific content area instruction strategies were used, such as mnemonic instruction, learning strategies, advanced organizers, study aids, and computer-assisted instruction. The results found by Scruggs et al. (2009) suggested that promising practices exist for students with disabilities not only to access academic instruction but also to be successful in content area instruction.

Whereas a multitude of research could be found supporting an academic curriculum resulting in improved acquisition of a targeted skill—similar to that that can be found for a functional curriculum—few findings connect academic curriculum to positive postschool outcomes, which is an important aspect of evidence-based curriculum at the secondary level. Yes, it is important that increased alignment between curriculum taught to students with more severe disabilities and content standards results in an increased opportunity to learn the core content areas, such as mathematics, language arts, and science (Browder et al., 2003), as well as a positive association between teacher instruction (i.e., enacted curriculum) aligned to state standards and student achievement in content areas such as mathematics (Gamoran, Porter, Smithson, & White, 1997; Kurtz, Elliott, Wehby, & Smithson, 2010). But what does the evidence suggest for after school when students receive a more academic or standards-based curriculum at the secondary level?

In a systematic review of the literature, Test, Mazzotti, et al. (2009) indicated that inclusion in general education was a predictor for postschool outcomes, including postsecondary attendance, employment, and independent living. For example, Baer et al. (2003) found students with disabilities in general education content cores were more likely to attend postsecondary education. The connection between access to academic curriculum and increased outcomes—particularly postsecondary education—was found by Flexer, Daviso, Baer, Queen, and Meindl (2011). Yet, the relationship was also affected by type of disabilities. In other words, Flexer et al. (2011) found that state policy and school structure affected students with intellectual and other developmental disabilities with regard to achieving participation in postsecondary education (i.e., these students failed to pass state high school exit exams or were provided less access to courses leading to postsecondary education attendance).

Similar to the caveat found by Flexer et al. (2011)—the link between academic curriculum and postschool outcomes affected by disability—not all associations between this curricular approach and outcomes were positive. For example, Goodman, Hazelkorn, Bucholz, Duffy, and Kitta (2011) found negative—albeit most likely unintended—consequences for students with high-incidence disabilities with an increased academic curriculum in school. The authors indicated that, as a result of high school exit exams, students with disabilities were increasingly receiving an academic curriculum with a decreased emphasis on life skills or vocational education, which were coinciding with a decrease in graduation rates for this population of students.

Guidelines for Teachers in Curriculum Design

In light of the competing agendas of a functional versus an academic curriculum, how does one decide what gets taught? In other words, what guidelines exist for teachers in determining secondary curriculum for students with disabilities? In the larger sense, secondary curriculum—the *what*—is guided by a variety of factors. Researchers have suggested that a multitude of factors affect curriculum with ranges from four to 11 competing forces (Bouck, 2006, 2008; Milner, 2003; Morrison, 1993). Central to the varying perspectives regarding curriculum choices are factors such as federal policies (e.g., IDEA, 2004; NCLB, 2001), state standards, school factors (e.g., geographical location, size), curriculum/

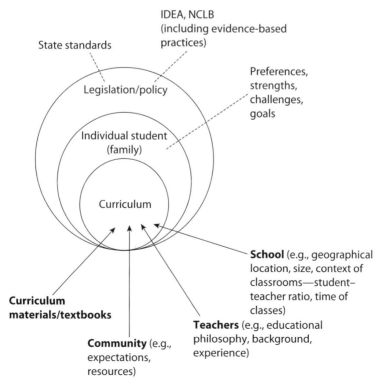

Figure 9.1. Factors and forces of consideration in secondary curriculum decision making. (*Source:* Bouck, 2008.)

textbook factors, community factors (e.g., resources), and teacher factors (e.g., educational philosophy, background, experience). (See Figure 9.1 for a depiction of the factors that affect curriculum decision making for secondary students with disabilities and the competing forces teachers must consider when making a decision.) To make a decision on a curriculum, teachers need to consider the larger perspectives of local (i.e., school, school district), state, and federal policies and practices while working within the context of their situation (e.g., their own capabilities and beliefs, available resources) and while simultaneously being responsible for the students and the families they serve in terms of needs and preferences.

When one is considering the secondary curriculum of students with disabilities, regardless of the larger models, the most important facet—typically not as conceptualized when one is considering curriculum in general—is individual students and their preferences, strengths, challenges, and goals (Wehman, 2011a). Because a hallmark of special education is *individualized* instruction, considerations of curriculum for secondary students with disabilities naturally include the individual and personal nature of each student. Hence, fundamental questions when deciding *what* to teach (i.e., curriculum) include a) *Where does that individual student want to be after high school?* and b) *What outcomes or goals does the student want to achieve when he or she leaves high school?* (Figure 9.2). Stated differently, curriculum decision making can rest on the answers to the following questions: *How, when, and where will the youth use this knowledge in their lives both now and in the future?* Or, when considering a student's point of view, *Will I need it?* An important consideration is that, for secondary students with disabilities, curriculum does not mean a textbook or a model, but the instruction—individualized program—they receive. Curriculum decision making then becomes a focus on what a student needs to achieve his or her goals relative to life after school, which can be a combination of functional curriculum and an academic or standards-based curriculum.

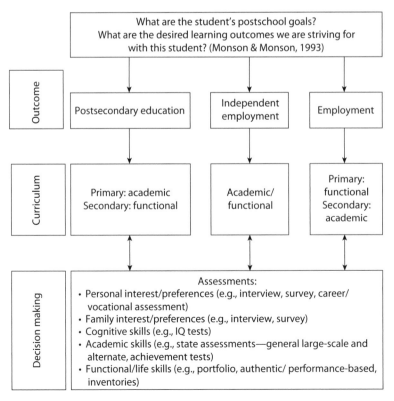

Figure 9.2. Guidelines for secondary curriculum decision making

Beth and Cara Beth and Cara are both 11th-grade students with a disability currently attending the same local high school; they are both enrolled in the same advanced algebra class that is required to obtain a diploma in the state they live in. Both have been actively engaged in their transition plans and have a clear idea of what they want to do after high school. Beth is planning to take the upcoming SATs and is looking into applying to colleges. She is aware that she will need some accommodations to be successful on the SAT as well as in college and that she will need to advocate for herself in her college courses. Cara does not plan on attending college; Cara would like to enroll in a cosmetology program after high school. Cara currently has a work placement in a local salon. For Beth, enrollment in advanced algebra is a logical and necessary part of her curriculum as she plans on attending college. Although Beth struggles in the course, she seeks the necessary assistance and, with accommodations, is maintaining around a B average. However, for Cara, the decision to take advanced algebra can be questioned. She struggles significantly in the math course even with accommodations, and there is concern that she will not pass the course; Cara barely passed algebra. Cara would prefer to focus on mathematics skills that will suit her after school (i.e., financial skills), but she really wants a high school diploma.

It is also important to note that, for some students with disabilities, family involvement plays a critical role in addressing what curriculum is essential. In other words, a curriculum decision-making framework needs to address not only consideration of the student's postschool goals but also the family's (e.g., parents') postschool goals and desired learning outcomes. The priorities of families for outcomes and, hence, secondary curriculum—second to those of the individual student—are still key factors in curriculum decision making. The priorities of students and their families may be the same or they may be different; however, after a student's voice, the voices of families should be critical in the curriculum determination at the secondary level.

The second important factor in deciding what to teach a secondary student with a disability is the legislation or educational policy of the time. Policy surrounds a student's postschool goals and will have an impact on the achievement of the desired outcomes. Today, curriculum decisions are affected by the two large educational policies: the ESEA, which was reauthorized in 2001 and then known as NCLB, and the 2004 reauthorization of IDEA, called the Individuals with Disabilities Education Improvement Act. The 2004 reauthorization of IDEA aligned IDEA with NCLB, and both focused on academic achievement and improving outcomes for students. Hence, a fundamental question when one is making curriculum decisions is how a student's postschool plans align with the current policies guiding education. For example, if a student wants to attend postsecondary education, he or she needs a high school diploma and to have met the high school graduation requirements of the state where he or she resides. For some states, this can mean taking and passing a minimum number of core content area courses (i.e., mathematics, science, social studies, language arts) and/or passing an exit exam (Olson, 2003; Corcoran & Silander, 2009; Kober et al., 2006; Krentz et al., 2005; Lee & Ready, 2009; Rouse & Kemple, 2009).

Mrs. Smith Mrs. Smith is a high school special education teacher. She is creating recommendations for the curriculum for her students for their upcoming IEP meetings. Today, she is considering three students: Tony, Jill, and Seth. Mrs. Smith begins her curriculum decision-making process by asking each student what are his or her postschool goals, or, in other words, what they want to do after they graduate from high school. She also makes the same inquiries to each student's parents. Mrs. Smith knows that it is important to consider the desired outcomes for an individual before any curriculum planning. Both Tony and his parents indicate a desire for him to attend postsecondary education, such as 4-year college. Currently, Tony is interested in pursuing a degree in computer technology. Jill, conversely, wants to gain independent employment—although she is not sure in what area—after school as well as to live outside of her parents' house after she graduates. Her parents support her goal of employment but are cautious of her plans to live independently. Seth, conversely, would like to pursue a trade, such as becoming an auto mechanic.

Now that Mrs. Smith understands the desired postschool goals for each student, she can start to formulate an appropriate curriculum that will assist them in meeting their goals. For example, Mrs. Smith must consider what larger policy surrounds each student's desired goals as well as what the school and community have to offer. For example, Mrs. Smith knows that, for Tony to attend college and major in computer technology, he will need to earn a diploma from high school as well as pass the state's high school exit exam. Based on this information as well as the assessments Mrs. Smith and others have conducted (e.g., cognitive skills, academic skills, aptitude assessments, life skills inventories), Mrs. Smith recommends that Tony receive a general education curriculum in general education settings with accommodations. She also recommends that he receive some resource room support as well as a course on study skills. Mrs. Smith also knows that she will work with Tony on some aspects of life skills, such as social skills.

Mrs. Smith recommends that Jill receive a mixture of academic and functional life skills curricula. She believes Jill can find success in the general education setting with general education curriculum with heavy resource room support and knows Jill will need a diploma for her to gain competitive employment after school. Yet, Mrs. Smith also respects Jill's desire to live independently and enrolls her in a functional life skills class that is tailored to the individual life skills each student is working on. Based on the assessments given to Jill, Mrs. Smith creates a life skills program for Jill that involves exploring aspects of independent living, such as cooking and cleaning as well as navigating public transportation. Mrs. Smith works extensively with Jill's parents to implement these skills at home.

For Seth, Mrs. Smith recommends a vocational education program, complete with spending half his day at the county vocational education program and the other half of his school days split between general education classes to earn a standard diploma and classes that will support Seth in obtaining employment (e.g., filling out job applications) and living independently (e.g., finding housing, banking).

Hence, one suggestion is to start curriculum decision making with the presumption that all students are general education students first (Branstad et al., 2002) and consider an academically oriented focus with academic courses occurring in a general education environment. General education courses are typically aligned with state standards and, hence, with state assessments. Yet, a general education curriculum in the general education setting is not the gold standard, nor is it the best option or least restrictive environment, but is merely a starting point for consideration. Next, as illustrated in Figure 9.3, teachers should give various considerations to different curricular options that fit with the student in light of context and policy/legislative mandates. A key idea in Figure 9.3's presentation of a framework for secondary curriculum decision making is that no one option is privileged; any result is acceptable as long as it meets the transition needs of the student with a disability pending his or her desired outcomes.

Conclusion

In determining secondary curriculum for students with disabilities, the focus should not be on one or the other (functional versus academic) but on the needs of the student and how much and what to use with each curriculum. Students with disabilities at the secondary level are best served by considering curriculum to be a continuum and allowing decisions of curriculum to be made for individual students based on what is needed for their success in reaching their postschool goals. The idea of a continuum is, of course, not new. More than a decade ago, the CEC's Division on Career Development for Exceptional Individuals argued that "all students, including those with disabilities, should participate in secondary education programs that integrate academic and occupational curricula" (Eisenman, 2000, p. 105). In a similar way, Benz and Kochhar (1996) argued that, too often, students must choose between an academic focus and a functional life skills focus for their curriculum, rather than programs that integrate the two.

The curriculum divide does not need to be as polarizing as people are led to be believe. For students with more low-incidence disabilities, a natural connection between an aca-

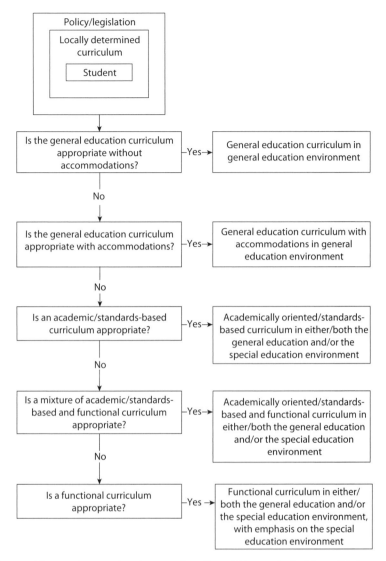

Figure 9.3.   A framework for secondary curriculum decision making. (*Source:* Wehmeyer, Lattin, & Agran, 2001.)

demically oriented curriculum and functional life skills may already exist. For example, in systematic reviews conducted by Browder and colleagues (Browder, Spooner, Ahlgrim-Delzell, Harris, & Wakeman, 2008; Browder, Wakeman, Spooner, Alhgrim-Delzell, & Algozzine, 2006; Courtade et al., 2007), many of the examples given regarding the connection in the literature between content area standards (e.g., science) and the focus of leading national professional organizations (e.g., reading—National Reading Panel; mathematics—National Council of Teachers of Mathematics [NCTM]) can be associated with functional life skills. For example, in the review of science for students with significant intellectual disabilities, Courtade et al. (2007) indicated that research on teaching students to use cell phones and identify their location in the community related to the physical science content standard (Taber et al., 2002, 2003). In a similar way, the acquisition of sight words on warning labels addressed the content standard of science in personal and social perspectives (Collins & Griffen, 1996; Collins & Stinson, 1995). In the review of mathematics instruction for students with significant intellectual disabilities, teaching students the more functional mathematics elements of money and time related to the NCTM content standard of measurement (Browder, Spooner, Ahlgrim-Delzell, Wakeman,

Table 9.2. Examples of academically oriented and functionally oriented curriculum elements

Content area	Academically oriented	Functionally oriented
Language arts	• Reading a novel • Drama class (Ward, Van De Mark, Ryndak, 2006)	• Completing job applications or looking through help-wanted ads • Sight words for leisure/recreation activities
Mathematics	• Algebra I • Use a calculator to solve problems (Collins, Kleinert, & Land, 2006)	• Banking skills, including how to write a check, deposit money, and balance an account • Cooking or baking requiring measuring of ingredients
Social studies	• Government (e.g., learning about rights and responsibilities of individuals such are registering to vote) • Registering to vote	• Navigating one's community, including walking, driving, or taking public transportation independently • Self-determination/self-advocacy
Science	• Biology • Sort foods by their nutrient level and plan a balanced meal (Spooner, Di Biase, & Courtade-Little, 2006)	• Weather/seasons relative to clothing selections • Learning what to do when one is sick (health)

& Harris, 2008). Although the focus on measurement should decrease in high school, according the NCTM, and the direct connection between the concepts of money and time and the expectations for the measurement content standard for grades 9–12 are weak, teachers can still integrate standards-based instruction with these concepts, such as working with students to use make appropriate decisions about units needed for solving problems involving measurement (e.g., the coin units needed to make change while running a school store; NCTM, 2000).

Functional can be academic and academic can be functional (see Collins, Hager, & Galloway, 2011; Courtade et al., 2007; Table 9.2). Curriculum decision making should be less about one or the other and more about what each student needs to be successful in his or her postschool goals (Ayres et al., 2011). Secondary curriculum can and should be a vital part of transition for students with disabilities if the right approach is taken—secondary curriculum as one of the vehicles for successful transition of students to postschool outcomes, whatever those are on an individual level.

In summary, the curriculum decision making for secondary students with disabilities should be done on an individual student basis. And guiding the individualized decision making should be considerations of the student's preferences, strengths, challenges, and desired goals after school (Figure 9.2). Of course, curriculum decision making does not occur in a vacuum, and educators needs to be aware of the policy or legislative influence surrounding curriculum decision making and the influence they themselves as well as the school and community bring to the decision (Figure 9.1). Related, curriculum decision making should be based on providing *all* students with disabilities evidence-based education, meaning that empirical evidence and professional wisdom are considered (U.S. DOE, 2002). With that said, the field is charged with increasing research regarding the connection between curriculum and outcomes and working to build consensus on appropriate secondary curriculum to assist educators with curriculum decision making.

Josh   Josh, currently a 10th-grade student, receives all his content-area instruction in a special education setting. His special education teacher, Mr. Jones, has Josh doing instructional activities that are aligned to content-area standards (e.g., mathematics, science, language arts) and that are also functional in nature. For example, in science class, Josh is learning basic first aid procedures. The instruction is simultaneously aligned with the science content standard of science in personal and social perspectives; it is also functional in nature (Courtade et al., 2007). Josh's curriculum is addressing both the standards-based instruction as well as life skills that can benefit him after school. In a similar way, Josh's current language arts instruction involves reading an age-appropriate novel that is similar to one that may be used in a high school general education language arts class. Josh is listening to the story and working to identify sight words from his community-based instruction work experiences as well as leisure and recreation activities.

Study Questions

1. What should guide secondary curriculum decision making for students with disabilities?

2. How do a functional curriculum and an academic/standards-based curriculum compare and contrast? Where do the two approaches overlap?

3. How do the issues facing secondary education have an impact on decisions made regarding curriculum for secondary students with disabilities?

4. Describe functional and academic approaches to teaching the core content areas (i.e., mathematics, English/language arts, science, and social studies) to secondary students with varying disabilities (e.g., learning disabilities, moderate intellectual disabilities).

5. Interview a teacher about what factors should be considered when recommending curriculum for secondary students with disabilities and compare it with the information presented here.

Online Resources

National Center to Inform Policy and Practice in Special Education Professional Development: http://ncipp.education.ufl.edu//index.php

Regional Resource Center Program for Special Education: http://www.rrcprogram.org/content/view/136/193/

National Alliance for Secondary Education and Transition: http://nasetalliance.org/

RTI Action Network: http://www.rtinetwork.org/

Technical Assistance on Transition and the Rehabilitation Act: http://www.pacer.org/tatra/

Assessment and Teaching for Transition

10

COLLEEN A. THOMA,
KIMBERLY BOYD, AND KIRA AUSTIN

After completing this chapter, the reader will be able to

- Understand the concept of access to the general education curriculum

- Define universal design for learning and universal design for transition

- Use a universal design for transition approach for instructional planning and delivery to link academic and transition education

- Explain at least three strategies that classroom teachers can use to assess student learning

- Identify research- and evidence-based strategies for secondary and transition education

To this point, this book has been devoted to planning for transition, working with other agencies, and designing transition individualized education programs (transition IEPs). Very little attention has been focused on individualized instruction for transition or what the teacher should do in the classroom. The previous chapters focused on what to teach; the purpose of this chapter is to discuss how to deliver instruction and, specifically, the strategies and supports that enhance the likelihood of positive transition outcomes for students with disabilities from an instructional perspective. The expectation is that the information provided will help you organize your own efforts to more effectively meet the needs of a student like Susan.

....

Susan   Susan is a high school sophomore with a plan for going to college after she graduates. However, there are a number of challenges that could have an impact on her ability to meet this goal. First, Susan receives special education services, qualifying for those services as a student with an intellectual disability who requires intermittent supports. She is completely included in general education classes for academic instruction, but she is struggling with her reading skills in those content classes. Second, although the teachers in those general education classes are supportive of having Susan in their classes, they are asking for additional support to identify teaching strategies that would meet her needs but not be overwhelming to implement. Third, Susan needs to have a comprehensive transition assessment to identify concrete transition outcomes. As her parents have pointed out, everyone is supportive of Susan's plan to go to college, but her struggles with reading will be an even greater challenge in that setting. They would like to see her have a clearer idea of a career choice to determine whether college is the right path for her. But, as the special educator responsible for Susan's education, you wonder how you will meet all her needs while still ensuring that she receives the academic instruction that will give her the best chance of achieving her dream: acceptance into college.

....

Susan's story highlights the key struggle that teachers of students with disabilities face in secondary education settings: how to balance the demands of ensuring access to the general education curriculum while still addressing the preparation of students for the transition to life after high school. For students like Susan who plan to go on to pursue their education in postsecondary settings, the need to provide a solid academic foundation (Hitchings, Retish, & Horvath, 2005) is coupled with the need to improve their self-determination skills so they can advocate for accommodations, supports, and services so they can be successful once they are there (Field, Sarver, & Shaw, 2003; Getzel & Thoma, 2008). And, as the trend for providing opportunities for more students with disabilities to pursue postsecondary education experiences continues to grow (Thoma, Lakin, Carlson, Domzal, Austin, & Boyd, 2011), the challenge for the field of special education to address both academic and transition goals will also increase.

The guidelines for enhancing the likelihood of positive transition outcomes from an instructional perspective have changed a great deal since Will (1983) first called for a concerted effort to prepare students with disabilities for a transition to work. Educational reforms brought about by the No Child Left Behind Act of 2001 (NCLB; PL 107-110) and the Individuals with Disabilities Education Improvement Act of 2004 (IDEA; PL 108-446) required a new emphasis in education on accountability and standards-based education. The job of teaching students with disabilities required greater expertise in delivering academic content, collaborating with general education teachers, and organizing supports, services, and accommodations in settings other than a self-contained classroom. These changes did not eliminate the need to also focus on outcomes and the postschool goals of individual students. Instead, teaching those skills now must be tied to the general education curriculum, fusing the two rather than taking an either/or approach (Thoma, Bartholomew, & Scott, 2009). Therefore, this chapter addresses the following questions:

1. What are educational strategies for teaching academic content that have been demonstrated to be effective for students with disabilities?

2. What assessment strategies provide direction for secondary transition education?

3. How can teachers tie transition outcomes to educational standards?

4. What are some principles to follow when choosing alternatives and/or augmentations to the general education curriculum?

5. How should an educator use individualized accommodations, supports, and services, including **paraprofessional** support, to best meet student needs?

Teaching Academic Content to Secondary Students with Disabilities

For many years, the education of students with disabilities, particularly students with significant disabilities, had very little relationship with the curriculum to which students without disabilities were exposed. Instead, a team defined what was appropriate for an individual child's annual goals. These annual goals were based on information collected from a series of assessments and were focused on deficits and not necessarily tied to what everyone else in that grade was learning. This made progress difficult to monitor and made the inclusion of students with disabilities more difficult to achieve. Teachers might ask why that would be important—why would we care if including students with disabilities in general education classrooms was not possible? Inclusive education is an evidence-based practice that is linked to improved academic outcomes for students with and without disabilities (Jackson, Ryndak, & Wehmeyer, 2009). Cole, Waldron, and Majd (2004) indicated that students without disabilities who received their education in inclusive classrooms made significantly greater academic progress in mathematics and reading. In addition, students with disabilities made academic progress in inclusive settings, particularly those students with learning disabilities and mild cognitive disabilities.

The IDEA Amendments of 1997 (PL 105-17) changed the process of developing educational programs from a purely individualized approach. This law required that students with disabilities have access to the general education curriculum, the first time that it was necessary that IEPs be developed with an explicit connection to the standards to which all other students are held. Access to the general education curriculum does not refer to where the education was provided but to making the necessary adaptations and modifications to ensure that students with disabilities can participate in the educational activities and assessments regardless of where the instruction is provided (Dymond, Renzaglia, Gilson, & Slagor, 2007). When IDEA was reauthorized in 2004, the law strengthened its focus on access to the general education curriculum, bringing the law even further into line with the NCLB legislation.

NCLB addressed the education of all children in the United States, with an emphasis on ensuring that all states develop academic standards and test students on their progress in learning those standards (Yell, Drasgow, & Lowrey, 2005). It also indirectly increased the responsibility for teachers to connect IEP goals for students with disabilities to the general education curriculum. Teachers need to demonstrate that students with disabilities are making adequate yearly progress (AYP) and, eventually, that they are able to meet the same standards as students without disabilities (by 2013–2014).

The General Education Curriculum

Wehmeyer (2002) recommended that teachers begin their individualization of a student's curriculum by starting with the general education curriculum (Nolet & McLaughlin, 2005). The general education curriculum refers to both the formal curriculum (what is taught explicitly) as well as the informal curriculum (what is learned through peer interactions) of the school. Ensuring that students with disabilities have access to the general education curriculum should include both informal and formal aspects of the curriculum. How can teachers learn to modify the general education curriculum so that each student with a disability can learn? When the instructional strategies for teaching and assessing student progress in the general education curriculum follow the principles of universal design for learning, there is a greater likelihood that students with and without disabilities will be able to benefit from receiving their education in the general education classroom and that adaptations and modifications will not become overwhelming for the general education teacher (Wehmeyer, 2006b). Good teaching of all students is the foundation for meeting the academic and transition needs of students with disabilities like Susan.

Universal Design for Learning

Universal design for learning provides teachers with an alternative approach to meeting the learning needs of all students. The premise of UDL is the provision of education designed for all learners, regardless of ability, through the flexible application of technology tools, instructional networks, and manipulation of digital content (Spooner, Dymond, Smith, & Kennedy, 2006). Universal design for learning has its root in architecture, where it was introduced to design public spaces, buildings, and everyday items that are accessible for individuals with and without disabilities. In the late 1990s, universal design was applied to school instruction. This was the beginning of some exciting research at the Center for Applied Special Technology (CAST). CAST's web site provides information on the latest research on UDL and examples of how to incorporate this approach into classroom instruction (see the resources list at the end of this chapter).

The UDL approach is based on research designed to understand how the brain learns and how some people learn differently (Bowe, 2000). This research demonstrates the success of using a mixture of technologies to enable students with diverse learning needs achieve academically (Spooner et al., 2006). Instruction and assessment designed by using a UDL approach has three primary characteristics (CAST, 2010):

1. "Multiple means of representation," which gives students various ways to acquire information and knowledge (materials and instructional delivery)

2. "Multiple means of expression," which provides students with alternatives to demonstrate what they know (assessment)

3. "Multiple means of engagement," which focuses on students' interests to offer appropriate challenges and increased motivation and engagement

Figure 10.1 provides a visual representation of the three characteristics of UDL, with examples of strategies that fit into each category.

Teaching Strategies from General Education

More and more of the research in the field of special education now is based on strategies that come from the general education field, providing evidence that many of the same strategies work to teach all students (Wehmeyer, 2006b). This development in the field provides further support for continuing to hold high expectations for students with disabilities and for the use of a UDL approach for teaching academic content. Table 10.1 provides an overview of some of these research-based strategies published in special education journals between 2007 and 2012. A few of the most widely used strategies are described in detail subsequently, including the use of technology, **text enhancement strategies, cognitive and metacognitive strategies**, and student self-determination and/or student-directed learning. Examples of how they could be used to enhance Susan's access to the general education curriculum are also provided. Teachers are encouraged to explore other strategies independently by going directly to the source listed in the table or using some of the online resources located at the end of this chapter.

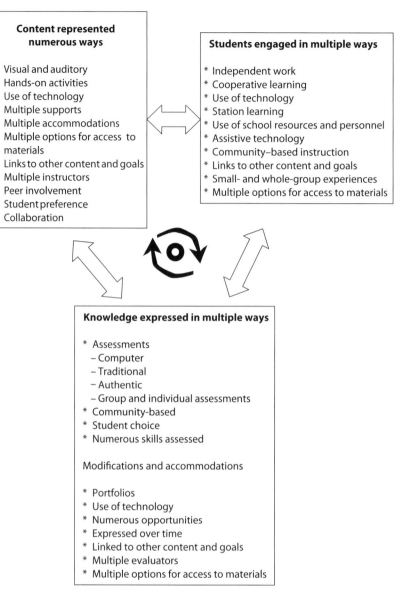

Content represented numerous ways

* Visual and auditory
* Hands-on activities
* Use of technology
* Multiple supports
* Multiple accommodations
* Multiple options for access to materials
* Links to other content and goals
* Multiple instructors
* Peer involvement
* Student preference
* Collaboration

Students engaged in multiple ways

* Independent work
* Cooperative learning
* Use of technology
* Station learning
* Use of school resources and personnel
* Assistive technology
* Community–based instruction
* Links to other content and goals
* Small- and whole-group experiences
* Multiple options for access to materials

Knowledge expressed in multiple ways

* Assessments
  – Computer
  – Traditional
  – Authentic
  – Group and individual assessments
* Community-based
* Student choice
* Numerous skills assessed

Modifications and accommodations

* Portfolios
* Use of technology
* Numerous opportunities
* Expressed over time
* Linked to other content and goals
* Multiple evaluators
* Multiple options for access to materials

Figure 10.1. Universal Design for Learning. (From Thoma, C.A., Bartholomew, C.C., & Scott, L.A. [2009]. *Universal design for transition: A roadmap for planning and instruction.* Baltimore: Paul H. Brookes Publishing Co.; reprinted by permission.)

Using Technology

Using technology to support the instruction of academic content offers two advantages. First, it encourages students to use tools that they will ultimately need to function in an increasingly technology-enhanced world. The speed in which technology tools are developed, used, and then discarded for the latest advancement cannot be overexaggerated. Most current high school students cannot remember a world without text messaging, iPods, and Google searches, whereas most of their teachers are often more familiar with phone calls, CDs, and e-mail. So, not only has the use of technology in instructional delivery been shown to increase student learning, but it also prepares them for the transition to adult life where using these technologies (in their latest versions) will be necessary. Second, students typically find the use of the latest technology motivating, so it addresses the "multiple means of engagement" component of a UDL approach, supporting the

Table 10.1. Summary of strategies for teaching academic content to students with disabilities

Academic content area	Strategy	Description	Resource
All or multiple content	Use of technology: video modeling	Videotaping is used to enhance student skill performance, to help remember steps of a process, or to increase engagement in learning through project-based learning	Hammond, Whatley, Ayres, and Gast (2010)
	Mnemonics	Linking new information with existing knowledge through visual and/or auditory cues	Jitendra and Gajria (2011)
	Response to intervention	Framework for providing high-quality instruction and tiered interventions to students struggling to learn content in multiple or single areas	Mellard, Stern, and Woods (2011); Chun and Witt (2008)
	Self-modeling	Use of static-picture prompting to facilitate self-monitoring	Cihak, Wright, and Ayres (2010)
	Graphic organizers	Includes use of pictures, charts, tables, or other visual cues to help students organize their time, stay on task, or perform skills	Spriggs, Gast, and Ayres (2007)
	Self-determined learning model of instruction	Used to promote active engagement in general education classroom and access to general education curriculum	Agran, Wehmeyer, Cavin, and Palmer (2010)
	Instructional rubrics	Used to increase class engagement and achievement of lesson objectives	Lee and Lee (2009)
	Differential treatment intensity	Communication interventions in multiple settings	Warren, Fey, and Yoder (2007)
English/ language literacy	Response to intervention	Tier 2 and 3 strategies identified	Denton (2010)
	Explicit instruction cycle	Used to teach word identification to students with reading difficulties	Denton and Al Otaiba (2011)
	Text enhancement strategies	Used to enhance reading in content areas; text enhancement strategies include graphic organizers, story maps, study guides, and computer-assisted learning	Jitendra and Gajria (2011)
	Cognitive and metacognitive strategies	These strategies help students develop higher level operations, building on what they already can do; examples include recognizing text structure, questioning, summarization, identifying main ideas, and cognitive mapping	Jitendra and Gajria (2011)
	Multiple strategies	Multiple strategies combine features of text enhancement strategies and metacognitive strategies; examples include reciprocal teaching, POSSE (predict, organize, search, summarize, evaluate), and SQ3R (survey, question, read, recite, review)	Jitendra and Gajria (2011)
	Increasing intensity of reading instruction	Strategies and considerations for increasing the intensity of teacher-led instruction as well as key factors used to plan for intense instruction	Allor, Champlin, Gifford, and Mathes (2010)
Math	Systematic instruction	Systematic instruction used to teach problem solving in algebraic equations to students with moderate intellectual disabilities	Jimenez, Browder, and Courtade (2008)
	Simultaneous prompting	Used to teach decimal subtraction	Rao and Kane (2009)
	Response cards	Used to teach math concepts	Horn (2010)
	Pentop computers	Used to teach multiplication	Bouck, Bassette, Taber-Doughty, Flanagan, and Szwed (2009)
Social studies	Universal design for transition (UDT)	Improved performance on academic as well as engagement in lesson using UDT	Scott, Thoma, et al. (2011)
Transition/ community-based skills	Parent teaching	Use of simultaneous prompting by parents in community settings	Tekin-Iftar (2008); Rowe and Test (2010)
		Chained tasks	Dogue and Banda (2009)
	Constant time delay	Used to teach students to use public bus	Mechling and O'Brien (2010)
	Computer-based video instruction	Used to teach multiple transition goals	Walker, Uphold, Richter, and Test (2010)
	Community-based instruction		

emotional component of learning. And, as a bonus, increased student engagement in the learning activities is associated with increased academic achievement.

Some of the most common technologies used to teach academic content include

- Use of digital cameras to take pictures for student schedules, student-directed learning activities and lessons, and other step-by-step skills such as participating in group work, project-based learning, and writing summaries of books

- Use of video recording technology to teach step-by-step activities, to complete projects, to develop summaries of historical events or stories, or to supplement written assignments

- Use of web-based resources to enhance instruction of science, math, social studies, and other academic content; web-based resources can include virtual reality, manipulatives, and video and/or audio clips

- Use of smartphone technology to provide individual access to web-based content, to participate in immediate response activities (quizzes and/or question surveys), and to communicate with partners on projects

- Use of software programs that help with organizing schedules, work, and/or projects such as Google Docs, Inspiration, and Microsoft Word templates

Susan's teachers met to discuss her struggles with reading academic content and identified strategies that could be incorporated into her classes, building on her strengths. Mr. Frank, Susan's teacher for social studies, uses a variety of technology in his instruction and found that Susan does best when she is able to use audio-based translations of her reading material, when she is able to use graphic organizers to prepare her written assignments, and when he uses various strategies to ensure that students remain actively engaged in class lectures. The use of response cards (Cavanaugh, Heward, & Donelson, 1996; Horn, 2010) to check for understanding of a key concept was helpful for Susan as well as for the other students (with and without disabilities) in the class. Response card use requires that students write the answer to a question posed by the teacher to check for understanding of a key concept. Students hold up their answer so the teacher can see it and make a decision about whether to move on with the lesson or to clarify.

Text Enhancement Strategies

Reading and literacy skills were particularly challenging for Susan, as they can be for many students with and without disabilities. For this reason, there are a number of strategies developed that teachers can use to support student learning in this area. One group of strategies is known as "text enhancement strategies" (Jitendra & Gajria, 2011), which are designed to increase students' comprehension and retention of critical content. Examples include *graphic organizers* that can be used to visually depict relationships between ideas (DiCecco & Gleason, 2002); *advance organizers* that provide an outline of the major components of a lesson (Getzel & Wehman, 2005); *story maps* that diagram grammar elements in narrative texts (Boulineau, Fore, Hagan-Burke, & Burke, 2004); and *mnemonic illustrations* that link unfamiliar information with information in the students' existing knowledge base (Scruggs, Mastropieri, Berkeley, & Marshak, 2010). These are only some examples of the many different ways that teachers can work collaboratively to support students in reading in content areas. Figure 10.2 provides some examples of common graphic organizers that can support the implementation of a UDL approach to instruction.

Susan's teachers use advance organizers for each lesson that includes a majority of lecture and/or reading from text to implement. In addition, they have used graphic organizers to help her with notetaking and have used them in constructing test questions designed to assess her basic understanding of concepts without assessing her overall writing skills.

Cognitive and Metacognitive Strategies

Cognitive and metacognitive strategies can also help students with and without dis-abilities learn from text (Jitendra & Gajria, 2011). They list some of the strategies that have been found to be effective in various research studies, including "recognizing text structure, cognitive mapping, questioning, identifying main ideas, and summarization" (Jitendra & Gajria, 2011, p. 5). Other strategies are more complex and combine elements of these singular strategies. They include "Reciprocal Teaching and its variants such as Collaborative Strategic Reading (CSR) and POSSE (Predict, Organize, Search, Summarize, Evaluate), as well as SQ3R (Survey, Question, Read, Recite, Review)" (Jitendra & Gajria, 2011, p. 6).

Susan's teachers have introduced her to the SQ3R process in her study skills class and her academic teachers use the steps to help her identify critical content from her course readings. This was a process she could use in multiple academic classes and one they hope will help her with the even larger reading requirements of college.

Self-Determination, Student-Directed Learning

Self-determination has been recognized as one way to increase access to the general edu-cation curriculum for students with disabilities (Spooner, Dymond, Smith, & Kennedy, 2006). Self-determination refers to "volitional actions that enable one to act as the primary

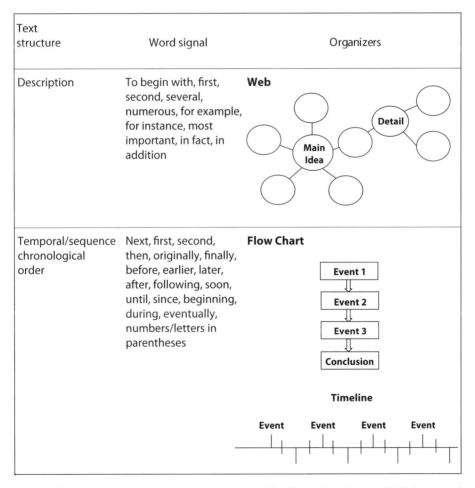

Figure 10.2. Graphic organizers based on text structure. Adapted from Fisher, D., Frey, N., and Lapp, D. (2009), *Brain research, teacher modeling, and comprehension instruction* (pp. 97–98), Newark, DE: International Reading Association, as it appeared in Jitendra, A.K. & Gajria, M. (2011), Reading comprehension instruction for students with learning disabilities, *Focus on Exceptional Children, 43*(8), 1–16. www.reading.org Copyright © 2009 by the International Reading Association.

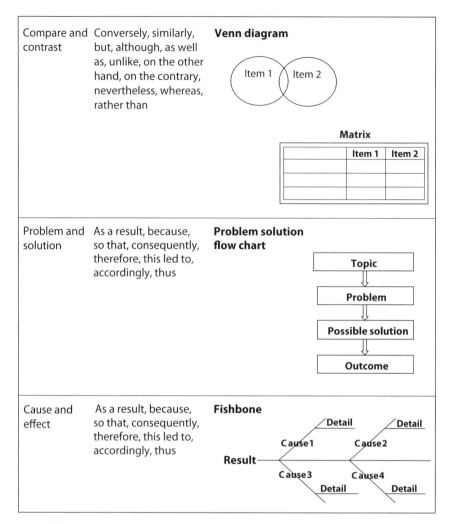

Figure 10.2.   *(continued)*

causal agent in one's life and to maintain or improve one's quality of life" (Wehmeyer, 2005, p. 117). There is a set of interrelated component elements that together help individuals become causal agents in their own lives. These elements include choice making, decision making, problem solving, goal setting and attainment, self-management, self-advocacy and leadership, self-awareness, and self-knowledge as well as perceptions of control and efficacy (Wehmeyer, 2005). Learning and using these skills in the classroom can help students with meeting their academic goals; in particular, the use of problem-solving strategies has been widely demonstrated in the research literature to result in increased academic performance (Agran, Wehmeyer, Cavin, & Palmer, 2010; Cote, Pierce, Higgins, Miller, Tandy, & Sparks, 2010). The Self-Determined Learning Model of Instruction provides a framework that teachers can use to structure student use of a problem-solving approach to accomplish a number of academic, transition, community living, and social–behavioral goals. It involves three phases and each phase has a set of questions the student uses to identify the problem, develop a goal, and evaluate progress in meeting the goal. Figure 10.3 provides an example of a worksheet developed by Susan's teachers and used by Susan to improve her ability to advocate for accommodations she needs in her academic classes and which she can use in college.

Name: Susan	Date: March 1, 2012
Phase I: What is my goal?	

Set a goal

1. What do I want to learn? *How does my disability affect my ability to learn? To hold a job?* *What supports work to help overcome/minimize the impact of my disability in school? At work?* *How can I advocate for the supports I need?*	3. What must change for me to learn what I don't know? *I need to find out more about my disability and my strengths and weaknesses/needs.* *I need to determine my ability to do my work.* *I must learn more about my own strengths and preferences.* *I need help with matching my strengths/preferences and needs with available supports.*
2. What do I know about the goal now? *I know that I struggle with reading.* *I know that I am easily distracted.* *I know that I get extra time on tests and assignments.*	4. What can I do to make this happen? *I can work with my teacher to identify steps to determine the impact of the disability on my learning and work goals.* *I can research possible supports through the Internet, teachers, and other resources that my school identifies.*

Phase II: What is my plan?	

Take action

1. What can I do to learn what I don't know? *I will meet with my teacher to develop a plan of action.* *I will meet with the school psychologist to identify an assessment of the impact of my disability.* *I will list the things that I struggle with in school and at work.* *I will list the things that have worked to overcome the things with which I struggle.* *I will meet with an assistive technology specialist to determine if there are other supports/technologies that I should try to better meet my needs.*	3. What can I do to overcome these barriers? *I can work really hard on accomplishing these goals.* *I can schedule meetings with the key people as far in advance as possible.* *I can learn my rights and how to advocate for what I need.*
2. What could keep me from taking action? *I might not find web sites that have enough information to help me make a decision.* *People might not have time to meet with me.* *The school psychologist might not be able to administer additional assessments.*	4. When will I take action? *I will use my study hall time this week to organize my meetings.* *I will take the online assessment on Friday during my technology lab.* *I will schedule meetings with the school psychologist, the assistive technology specialist, and my teacher within the next 2 weeks.*

Figure 10.3.   Student worksheet for the Self-Determined Learning Model of Instruction. (From Thoma, C.A., Bartholomew, C.C., & Scott, L.A. [2009]. *Universal design for transition: A roadmap for planning and instruction* [pp. 37–39]. Baltimore: Paul H. Brookes Publishing Co.; adapted by permission).

Phase III: What have I learned?	
Adjust goal or plan	
1. What actions have I taken? I met with the school psychologist, who shared assessment information from previous years. He did not conduct additional assessments. I met with the assistive technology specialist, who identified some additional technological resources that I could try. I completed the online learning assessment.	3. What has changed about what I didn't know? *I know additional resources that can help.*
2. What barriers have been removed? *I can talk about my learning style/ preferences.*	4. Do I know what I want to know? *I want to learn some of the technologies that were identified by the assistive technology specialist.*

Figure 10.3.   *(continued)*

Universal Design for Transition

Thoma, Bartholomew, and Scott applied the components of UDL to elements of effective transition planning to develop a strategy teachers can use to "bridge the perceived discrepancies preparing students to meet academic standards and their transition outcomes" (2009, p. 6). This approach, **universal design for transition (UDT),** incorporates the three components of UDL and adds the following components (Thoma, Bartholomew, & Scott, 2009):

- Multiple transition/life domains
- Multiple means of assessment
- Student self-determination
- Multiple resources/perspectives

Three of these components are explained in the following section, except for student self-determination, which was covered earlier in this chapter as well as in Chapter 2 of this book.

Multiple Life Domains

Successful transition planning should focus on preparing students for a full life, addressing their goals for employment, community living, recreation and leisure, postsecondary education, independence, and community integration. Teachers can incorporate these goals into academic instruction by considering the academic skills that are necessary for their attainment and using those as real-world, authentic tasks in instructional delivery and assessment. For example, Susan's English teacher uses a variety of real-world activities to teach and reinforce grammar and expository writing skills, including writing cover letters for employment purposes, writing college admissions essays, writing letters of complaint to a landlord or manufacturer, and writing in a journal.

Transition Assessment

Transition planning and services depend, to a large extent, on the quality of transition assessment: of identifying the goals students have for their adult lives and the supports, services, and instruction necessary to help students achieve those life goals (Morningstar

& Liss, 2008). There are a number of different transition instruments and approaches available, but it is clear from the literature that there is no one-size-fits-all assessment instruction available for transition planning. Instead, a combination of assessment approaches and targeting the individual purpose of the assessment to choose the specific assessment(s) that will yield useful information is best (Sax & Thoma, 2002). Hughes and Carter (2002) developed a transition assessment model that helps guide teachers through that decision-making process. That process consists of eight steps:

1. Determine the purpose of the assessment.
2. Identify relevant behaviors and environments.
3. Verify Steps 1 and 2 with input from students and important others.
4. Choose appropriate assessment procedures.
5. Modify procedures as needed.
6. Conduct the assessment.
7. Use assessment findings to identify transition goals and objectives.
8. Develop curricular plans to achieve goals.

However, to implement Hughes and Carter's transition assessment processes, teachers need to know the range of different assessment approaches and instruments that have been developed to assess student skills and identify their transition goals for the future. Assessments can be divided into three different categories: formal (standardized assessments), informal (teacher-made surveys or curriculum-based measures), and alternative (performance-based assessments such as portfolios or demonstrations of mastery; Karan, DonAroma, Bruder, & Roberts, 2010). Each type of assessment has strengths and weaknesses, necessitating thoughtful consideration of the purpose of the assessment, the time it takes to complete, and the willingness of the student and others to participate in the process.

For example, standardized assessments typically require that students or someone who knows the student will answer questions in writing or verbally. This requires an ability to read and understand the question and enough self-knowledge (or knowledge of the student if the answers are being provided by another person) to accurately report a preference, interest, or ability. Conversely a performance-based assessment does not rely on self-reporting but, rather, on a demonstration of the skill. This increases the accuracy of the assessment results, but the drawback is that it often takes much longer to conduct. Teachers should become familiar with a range of assessment options and use the ones that yield the best results in the context of the needs of the student, the time required, and available supports for administration of the assessment. The online resources located at the end of this chapter include a few web sites that list assessment instruments and their features and/or requirements. These resources should provide a good starting point for those who need additional ideas or examples of transition assessment strategies. And, for those who are working with students who have multiple transition assessment needs, Figure 10.4 provides a tool that teachers can use to organize their transition assessment process and summarize the results.

Susan's goals for her adult life included going to college, but her transition team had a number of questions about her ability to make a successful transition to postsecondary education. These questions were the focus of their plan for her transition assessment for the year. First, they wondered about her ability to self-advocate for the accommodations and supports she would need. Did she know what worked, and why, so that she could advocate for those as needed? In addition, the team did not know if she wanted to live in a dorm or commute, and whether she would need any supports to be able to do either of those. Those three purposes—to determine Susan's ability to advocate for accommodations she needed, her ability to live on her own, and her ability to use public

Goals and standards ....

1. *Students will develop foundational understanding of hurricanes and related natural disasters.*
2. *Students will learn the importance of tracking hurricanes. They will learn the intensity scales of hurricanes and how to prepare for these disasters.*

Transition center: Multiple transition domains ....

1. *Preparation, critical-thinking, and problem-solving skills needed to get ready for a natural disaster*
2. *Learning to work as part of a team, working together to solve problems by performing group-related work during the lesson*
3. *Employment: careers in weather, disaster relief, disaster preparation*
4. *Community living: preparing the home and community for disasters and/or severe weather; volunteering to help others who are victims of natural disasters*

Self-determination ....

1. *After exposing all students to the basic information, provide opportunities for students to choose their own learning goals, using the Self-Determined Learning Model of Instruction (Wehmeyer, Palmer, Agran, Mithaug, & Martin, 2000).*
   a. *Two students indicate a desire to live on their own in the community.*
   b. *One student desires a career in a field where responding to emergencies is a main requirement (police officer).*
   c. *Three other students indicate that they would like to help others.*

Multiple representation ....

1. *Read-aloud book presentation (or electronic book with read-aloud software program) and guest speaker*
2. *Computer research activity and video presentation of hurricane disasters*
3. *Classroom discussion and brainstorming*

Multiple engagement ....

1. *Group practice activities (e.g., read-aloud and book activity)*
2. *Technology-driven activities, (e.g., video clips and Internet research)*
3. *Self-Determined Learning Model of Instruction (Wehmeyer et al., 2000) with individualized focus for learning, assessment, and strategies*

Multiple expressions ....

1. *Group brainstorming and class discussions*
2. *Jeopardy review game*
3. *Hands-on classroom-based tracking activity with hurricane tracking chart*

Reflection/evaluation ....

1. *Were students able to comprehend how serious hurricanes are?*
2. *Will students be able to link the academic goal to life domains after they leave the classroom?*
3. *What are the next steps needed to continue this lesson?*

Figure 10.4. Sample Universal design for transition (UDT) planning sheet. (From Thoma, C.A., Bartholomew, C., Tamura, R., Scott, L., & Terpstra, J. [2008, April]. UDT: Applying a universal design approach to link transition and academics. Preconference workshop at the Council for Exceptional Children Conference, Boston; adapted by permission.)

transportation to get to and from college—became the focus of her transition assessment that year. Her teachers used a variety of methods to collect relevant information, using a self-determination assessment instrument (the ARC Self-Determination Scale) to determine her ability to advocate, a performance-based assessment to determine her ability to use public transportation, and a survey completed with support from Susan's parents to determine her ability to live on her own in a dorm.

Multiple Resources/Perspectives

Preparing students for all they need for a successful transition to adult life is a huge responsibility for any one person to assume. Rather than thinking that this task should be assumed by the teacher, a more reasonable and effective approach is to use a true collaborative teaming approach, where each member of the team shares responsibility for working together to achieve the common goal: a student's goals for a preferred adult lifestyle. There are a number of examples of transition stakeholders working together, sharing resources, and blending funding to ensure that student goals are met (e.g., Certo, Sax, Pumpian, Mautz, Smalley, Wade, & Noyes, 2002). In addition, many of the strategies and assessments that were once accomplished during the school day are now being implemented with parent support during after-school hours, on weekends, and/or over the summer months. In fact, parents of students with disabilities from diverse cultural and linguistic backgrounds may prefer to take the lead in some transition-planning activities (Landmark, Zhang, & Montoya, 2007; Trainor, 2005) and the literature from the field increasingly includes examples of parents implementing strategies such as community-based instruction (Tekin-Ifkar, 2008), teaching self-determination (Rowe & Test, 2010), and process training (Crites & Dunn, 2004).

Of course, for some students, a UDT approach may not be enough to meet all their transition-planning needs. Wehmeyer (2006b) likewise reported that a UDL approach to academic instruction might not be sufficient to ensure student academic achievement. In these instances, the general education curriculum may need to be further augmented, or, for some students, alternatives might be deemed necessary. The rest of this chapter addresses strategies for further individualizing student educational plans. More details can be found in subsequent chapters of this book or by consulting some of the resources at the end of this chapter.

Has Assistive Technology Been Considered?

A first step in considering individual adaptations to ensure access to the general education curriculum (Wehmeyer, 2002) is to consider any assistive technology (AT) that might be necessary for an individual student with a disability. Considering AT is a different process from using a UDL approach in that it requires that the needs of an individual student be considered as opposed to choosing multiple means of teaching to a group. Of course, individualized AT could conceivably include technology that is offered to all students in a particular lesson.

AT can include either devices or services. IDEA 2004 defines *assistive technology devices and services* as follows:

- Assistive technology device means any item, piece of equipment, or product system, whether acquired commercially off the shelf, modified or customized, that is used to increase, maintain, or improve the functional capabilities of a child with a disability. (§ 1401, PP1)

- Assistive technology service means any service that directly assists a child with a disability in the selection, acquisition, or use of an assistive technology device. (§ 1401, PP2)

AT can have a variety of applications in the classroom and can meet a variety of needs. To benefit from their education, some students with disabilities may require AT for mobility and others may require AT for communication so that they can demonstrate what they have learned. There are many ways to describe AT, but most describe it by its degree of complexity and its primary use. *Low tech* refers to devices that are passive or simple, with few moving parts (Mann & Lane, 1991), such as picture communication boards, pointers, and switches. *High tech* refers to devices that are complex and typically contain electronic components (Inge & Shepherd, 1995), such as voice output communication aids, electronic wheelchairs, universal remote controls, and computers. Typically, the complexity of AT devices can be conceptualized as a continuum from low or no tech to high tech.

Considering AT for the transition-age student needs to go beyond those devices and services that can meet purely academic goals. Instead, devices and services also need to help students move toward their transition goals and, therefore, must take into account the needs they have related to work, postsecondary education, recreation and leisure, socialization, community living, and/or personal care. Considering this requires that teachers and transition-planning team members know both the students' needs as well as the needs of the environment in which they will need to use the device or service. The Matching Person and Technology process (Craddock & Scherer, 2002) provides guidelines for taking into consideration not only individual student preferences about technology but also the demands of the environment. For instance, Maria was a young woman whose ability to communicate verbally was very limited. An AT assessment was conducted and a laptop system with voice output was chosen for her. Maria had the intelligence to use the system, but not the desire. She hated the slowness of the computer and the impersonal nature of this means of communication. Maria preferred to attempt to use her limited speech and have an interpreter who knows her well translate when others did not understand. She was quick to voice this opinion, yet, until this model was used with her, assessments continued to point to a higher technology system that would spend more time sitting in a closet than on her desk at school. Table 10.2 outlines the steps in this approach.

Maria's IEP team conducted an AT evaluation for her and found that her continued struggles with reading and writing could be addressed through the use of software programs such as Write:OutLoud and Dragon Naturally Speaking. These programs provide an opportunity for Maria to use the spoken word for computer input and output. In addition to these software programs, Maria's computer was equipped with headphones and a microphone to help her use the features of the software more effectively.

Alteration of or Adaptation to the General Curriculum

Wehmeyer defined **curriculum adaptation** as "any effort to modify the representation or presentation of the curriculum or to modify the student's engagement with the curriculum to enhance access and progress" (2002, p. 52). Many of the same strategies or techniques that could be used in a universally designed curriculum could also be used to adapt the general education curriculum specifically for one student. The difference between the two is that the techniques for adaptation are used to meet the needs of a small number of students (sometimes just one student with a disability) and are not available to all students.

Like UDL, curriculum adaptations can include modifications to instructional materials, the delivery of instruction, the manner in which a student engages in instruction, or

Table 10.2.   Matching person and technology components of assistive technology usability

Device evaluation:	Assistive technology (AT) meets the individual's functional need.
Milieu:	Determination of environments in which it will be used
Person:	Discussion of preferences and needs
AT:	Delineation of desired functions and features
Device selection:	AT has appeal and is obtainable.
Milieu:	Good device/environment fit exists
Person:	Accepts AT use and is psychologically ready for use
AT:	Product is acceptable in terms of cost, delivery date, aesthetics, and usefulness
Device use:	AT performance and achievement of the functional goal
Milieu:	Environmental accommodations in place, AT performs adequately in different environments
Person:	Satisfaction with use
AT:	Has the desired durability and operability

From Craddock, G., & Scherer, M. (2002). Assessing individual needs for assistive technology. In C.L. Sax & C.A. Thoma (Eds.), Transition assessment: Wise practices for quality lives. (p. 100). Baltimore: Paul H. Brookes Publishing Co.; reprinted by permission.

the process of assessing what a student has learned (Nolet & McLaughlin, 2005). Because many instructional materials are print-based, adaptations to these materials can include books on tape, braille, computer-based work, interactive whiteboards, DVDs, iPads, and book readers such as the Kindle.

Teachers generally deliver instruction verbally through lectures or in written format on whiteboards, PowerPoint presentations, or worksheets. Changes in instructional delivery can make learning more functional through the use of community-based instruction (CBI), hands-on or discovery learning, and authentic learning. For example, instead of teaching algebra through the use of worksheets and textbook-based homework, students can use formulas to determine how much paint they need to buy to paint one room in their house. In addition, they can determine how much money they will need to earn to afford a lifestyle of their choosing, using equations to factor in taxes, insurance, and other payroll deductions. Choosing appropriate adaptations for the transition-age student with disabilities requires examining the where, what, how, and when components of instruction (Cawley, Foley, & Doan, 2003; Downing & Eichinger, 2003; Downing & Peckham-Hardin, 2007).

Adaptations to What to Teach

Instructional objectives must focus on skills that the student will need to function as an adult in his or her preferred setting (Wehmeyer, 2002). Therefore, the choice of objectives must start with a backward planning process, starting with where the student wants to be (the outcomes of transition planning) and comparing that with where he or she is now. That difference, or discrepancy, provides a focus for planning the individualized curriculum for that student, providing a clear roadmap for where the student is currently and where he or she wants to be, and then developing concrete steps to get him or her there.

The activities and skills that are most conducive to independent performance in postsecondary education, vocational, residential, and community environments must guide the selection of transition IEP objectives. For instance, if a student wants to live alone after high school, then skills related to safety, home ownership, and independence would be the most important to learn. Conversely, if a student wants to continue to live at home with his or her family, independence in living might not be as important as academic skills because going to college is what is most important to him or her. Transition planning must be an open dialogue between the student and family and the school personnel.

In addition to keeping student and family ideas in mind when choosing transition IEP goals and objectives, teachers must be familiar with college entrance requirements because students with mild disabilities frequently plan to attend college (Wehman & Getzel, 2005). The process of determining objectives cannot be conducted exclusively by the teacher but requires ongoing collaboration with the student and family. In fact, for a transition IEP team to use a self-determined approach, the student must be the starting point in the plan.

Accommodations for Standardized Testing

Students with disabilities who receive special education services in the school setting may need to use accommodations for standardized tests. These accommodations allow students to demonstrate their knowledge without their disability being a major factor in their scores or outcomes. Research has shown that, when some accommodations are provided in both the daily learning environment and the testing environment, the accommodations have a greater impact on student achievement on standardized testing (Bottsford-Miller, Thurlow, Stout, & Quenemoen, 2006).

It is important to note the difference between instructional accommodations and testing accommodations. Instructional accommodations are changes or modifications made to the specific curriculum or daily instruction and the various ways of collecting student responses (National Dissemination Center for Children with Disabilities, n.d.). For example, a student who has fine-motor problems and is unable to write legibly for lengthy assignments may need to use a word processor to type assignments. Testing accommodations are often viewed as adaptations that "allow students to participate in state or district assessments in a way that assess abilities rather than disabilities" (Lehr & Thurlow, 2003, p. 2). An example of a testing accommodation would be allowing a student who demonstrates high distractibility to have extended time or unlimited time on an assessment that is normally timed for the general population.

IDEA 2004 requires that all students with disabilities participate in state- and/or district-wide standardized assessments. It also requires that students who access the general education curriculum be assessed in the same manner as their nondisabled peers in the same course. This is where accommodations and modifications become an important part of the services that students with disabilities receive. It is also imperative that the IEP team incorporate the appropriate accommodations into the student's IEP for both classroom and testing situations. If the accommodation has not been listed as an accommodation within the IEP for a testing situation, the student will not be allowed to use it. If a student is being exposed to an accommodation the day of testing, he or she may be unfamiliar with how to use it and it may be more of a distraction than a help. This is another reason why it is important that the student use his or her accommodations in the classroom as well as during a testing situation. Almost all states have policies regarding student's use of accommodations in the classroom setting as well as in a testing situation (Lazarus, Thurlow, Lail, Eisenbraun, & Kato, 2006). When the IEP team decides what is appropriate or not, they must consider the student's strengths, weaknesses, and daily routines, along with his or her disability (Luke & Schwartz, 2007). It is important for the student to be included in the decision as to what accommodations are necessary. This allows the students to have ownership in the services they receive and the decisions that impact their education and future and increases their self-determination and advocacy skills.

There are various ways that accommodations can be provided for the presentation of the assessment, the timing of the assessment, the way a student responds to the assessment, and the setting in which the assessment is given. See Table 10.3 for some common examples.

Table 10.3.   Common assessment accommodations

Presentation (how directions or content of assessment are delivered)	• Oral administration (adult reading or audiotaped version) • Large print or the use of magnification devices • Braille • Clarification or repeat of directions • Use of hands-on manipulatives • Formula sheets or calculators
Timing (the amount of time given to a student to complete an assessment)	• Extended time or untimed • The use of breaks • Multiple test sessions or multiple test days
Response (alternate methods of responding to assessments and showing an understanding of content)	• Use of a word processor • Use of a scribe • Use of a brailler • Use of spell check • Pointing • Use of communication device • Mark in test booklet as opposed to transferring an answer to an exam page
Setting (where an assessment is administered or changes in the testing environment)	• Small group testing • Individualized testing • Separate room testing • The use of noise buffers • Location with minimal distractions • Specific seating or proximity seating

From Cox, M.L., Herner, J.G., Demczyk, M.J., & Nieberding, J.J. Remedial and Special Education (Vol. 12, No. 6), pp. 346–354, copyright © 2006 by Sage Publications. Adapted by Permission of SAGE. *Additional source:* Luke and Schwartz (2007).

Progress monitoring is another important piece of the puzzle when it comes to accommodations and standardized testing. Too often, the IEP team provides a student with access to various accommodations and no one ever follows up to see if the accommodations are being used, or if they are even helpful to the student (Luke & Schwartz, 2007). Teachers and IEP case managers can easily monitor accommodations' usefulness through a variety of methods: classroom assignments, curriculum-based tests and quizzes, previously released standardized assessments that are similar to the assessments on which students will use accommodations, and so on.

Overall, it is important to remember that accommodations should be chosen on the basis of the student's strengths and weaknesses and that not all accommodations work for all students, even those who have similar disabilities. The student should have a voice in the decision about what accommodations are appropriate and what are not; after all, the student is the one who decides whether he or she will use the accommodation. Teachers and IEP case managers should monitor how often a student uses accommodations, how comfortable he or she are with using them, and if he or she are familiar and comfortable using them in a testing situation. Accommodations can be a great tool in helping to level the proverbial playing field; however, the students must be familiar with the tools that they are given to do so.

Paraprofessional Support

Another example of individualized support that might be useful to consider for students with disabilities is paraprofessional support (Downing & Peckham-Hardin, 2007). With the reauthorization of NCLB of 2001 and IDEA 2004, greater emphasis has been placed on ensuring that paraprofessionals are providing high-quality services to special education students. Under the direction of teachers, paraprofessionals are now performing **functional assessments,** observing and documenting data, implementing behavior management systems, and instructing students in small groups (Riggs & Mueller, 2001; Carter, O'Rourke, Sisco, & Pelsue, 2009; Downing, Ryndak & Clark, 2000).

Teachers serve as the immediate supervisors of paraprofessionals, often serving in multiple roles. Teachers serve as liaisons, trainers, and collaborators to paraprofessionals. To create a successful classroom environment, teachers need to ensure that they are effectively communicating to paraprofessionals their role, the classroom expectations, and useful teaching strategies (Wallace, Shin, Bartholomay, & Stahl, 2001). Teachers also need to provide direct modeling of how to use targeted instructional strategies and reach desired outcomes. French (2001) found that many teachers do not plan with their paraprofessionals, and when instructions were provided, the rationale for the lesson was provided only half the time. Teachers should provide clear direction for lesson plans and, ideally, hold team meetings at least weekly.

With low wages, turnover among paraprofessionals is high (Tillery, Werts, Roark, & Harris, 2003; Ghere & York-Barr, 2007). To retain experienced and dedicated paraprofessionals, teachers need to demonstrate respect, show appreciation, and acknowledge contributions to the team (Giangreco, Edelman, & Broer, 2001). Causton-Theoharis, Giangreco, Doyle, and Vadasy (2007) provide guidance for teachers in the form of five easy strategies to incorporate paraprofessionals in instruction (Table 10.4). Teachers are encouraged to clearly delineate the responsibilities of paraprofessionals, identifying some independent responsibilities within the classroom such as taking attendance or allowing students to go to the restroom. However, paraprofessionals should not be planning lessons, writing IEPs, or left to work with students without direction.

Although small, there are a growing number of studies that have focused on training paraprofessionals to increase student achievement (Causton-Theoharis & Malmgren, 2005; Forbush & Morgan, 2004; Keller, Bucholz, & Brady, 2007; Leblanc, Ricciardi, & Luiselli, 2005; Quilty, 2007). These studies have demonstrated that paraprofessionals can have a

Table 10.4.   General recommended practices for working with paraprofessionals

Practice categories	Methods for incorporating this practice
Welcoming and acknowledging paraprofessionals	• Provide space for the belongings of the paraprofessional. • Place a plant or coffee cup on the desk of the paraprofessional at the beginning of the year. • Include the name of the paraprofessional on the classroom door. • Introduce the paraprofessional as part of the teaching team, not as a specific student's helper. • Share routine tasks that communicate authority (e.g., taking attendance, writing on the white board, doing hot lunch count). • Write specific thank you notes periodically.
Orienting paraprofessionals	• Provide a thorough school tour and introduce the paraprofessional to important people (e.g., office personnel, librarian). • Orient the paraprofessional to the location of supplies and the technology within the school and classroom. • Review school and classroom policies, procedures, and rules each year. • Provide access to individualized education programs and teach paraprofessionals how to read and interpret the documents.

Planning for paraprofessionals	• Provide a daily and, weekly schedule. Include who the paraprofessional will be supporting, what the paraprofessional will be doing, and when he or she will be doing it.
	• Include the following in daily plans:
	  – Goals/objectives for an activity
	  – Role of the paraprofessional
	  – What the paraprofessional should do
	  – Support level
	  – Modifications/adaptations
	• Review each plan.
	• Teach, model, support, and provide feedback.

Communicating with paraprofessionals	• Clarify roles and responsibilities. • Develop shared expectations and mechanisms for communication (e.g., daily notebook, check-in point at the start and end of each day, weekly meetings for planning and communication). • Be open to the perspectives and ideas of the paraprofessional. • Use active listening skills.

From Causton-Theoharis, J.N., Giangreco, M.F., Doyle, M.B., & Vadasy, P.F. (2007). Paraprofessionals: The "sous-chefs" of literacy instruction. *Teaching Exceptional Children, 40*(1), 56–62; reprinted by permission.

profound impact on students and the level of instruction provided. To fully utilize your instructional team, it is important to clearly inform paraprofessionals of the importance of transition skills training. Find ways to explain to paraprofessionals that CBI is not a field trip but, rather, an alternative learning environment. Paraprofessionals need prompting and fading strategies modeled, practiced, and reinforced. Paraprofessionals can be invaluable during CBI by providing prompting, collecting data, and building community relations. One of the most commonly used data collection methods in the community is the use of a task analysis (TA). A TA breaks down complex jobs or processes into smaller steps that can be taught in sequence. A teacher would first develop a TA and then train the paraprofessional how to complete the task in the TA sequence. Finally, the teacher would instruct the paraprofessional how to collect and monitor data on each step of the TA.

Peer Tutoring

One of the substantiated recommended practices in transition is the inclusion of students with disabilities into general education classrooms (Landmark, Ju, & Zhang, 2010). In the secondary setting, curricular demands often make it more difficult for students with disabilities to be included in core curriculum courses with their same-age peers. As inclusive efforts are growing, teachers need to increase teaching practices that can meet a wide variety of learner needs (Spooner, Dymond, Smith, & Kennedy, 2006).

Structured peer tutoring is a teaching strategy that has been shown to be a research-based practice. Peer tutoring has been used in classrooms for decades; however, it did not truly establish itself as an effective practice until the late 1980s. Peer tutoring can improve the learning of students with and without disabilities (Mastropieri et al., 2001; Mastropieri, Scruggs, Spencer, & Fontana, 2003; Stenhoff & Lignugaris, 2007). The literature demonstrates that peer tutoring systems have the benefits of improved academics (e.g. reading, math computation, safety skills), positive work behaviors (on-task, motivation), and improved social interactions (Mastropieri et al., 2006; Okilwa & Shelby, 2010).

It is theorized that peer tutoring is effective because it provides more opportunities for individual responding and has high peer motivation (Stenoff & Lignugaris, 2007). Peer tutoring or supports have been shown to help students even with the most significant needs increase access to the general curriculum and social interactions (Carter, Cushing, Clark, & Kennedy, 2005; Carter & Kennedy, 2006). Carter, Sisco, Melekoglu, and Kurkowki (2007) found that social interactions for students with significant disabilities were significantly increased when paired with peer supports rather than a paraprofessional.

Heron, Villareal, Yao, Christianson, and Heron (2006) clearly defined the differences between incidental peer tutoring and structured peer tutoring. An example of incidental peer tutoring would be when Student A is struggling to finish an assignment so the teacher assigns Student B to help Student A. Structured peer tutoring differs in that it is "built around active student response (ASR), opportunity to respond (OTR), feedback, and reinforcement" (Heron et al., 2006, p. 28). Peer tutoring systems purposefully train the tutor and tutee in the procedures of peer tutoring.

To begin implementing peer tutoring into your classroom, it is helpful to think about Miller, Barbetta, and Heron's (1994) procedure for developing a program. They titled it START Tutoring to encourage teachers to

S - Select a tutoring format
T - Train the tutors
A - Arrange the environment
R - Run the program
T - Test for effectiveness

There are several different peer tutoring formats that can be used in the classroom that are effective. The four most commonly used models include class-wide peer tutoring, reciprocal relationship, cross-age matching, and reverse-role tutoring. Okilwa and Shelby (2010) clearly described the differences between the models and provided examples (Table 10.5).

Structured peer tutoring includes training the tutors and assessment. Students can be trained to tutor through role-playing, scripted instruction, and videotape scenarios

Table 10.5.   Models of peer tutoring

Model	Description
Classwide peer tutoring	All students in the class are paired into tutor–tutee dyads who work together on tasks structured by the teacher with a standard error-correction procedure. Each dyad is assigned to one of two competing teams to earn points, with the winning team determined daily or weekly (Greenwood, Delquadri, & Hall, 1989)
Reciprocal relationship	The peer-assisted learning strategies (PALS) is a variation of class-wide peer tutoring and includes partner reading, paragraph summarization, and prediction (Fuchs, Fuchs, & Kazdan, 1999). The unique aspect of PALS is that the tutor–tutee dyads switch roles (Hughes & Frederick, 2006).
Cross-age matching	The tutor–tutee dyads are students with different ages and grades. Older students in higher grades are matched with younger students in lower grades (Heron, Welsch, & Goddard, 2003).
Other	In reverse-role tutoring, students with mild disabilities tutor younger students with or without disabilities in group-oriented work to accomplish an outcome (Utley, Mortweet, & Greenwood, 1997).

(Heron et al., 2006). Assessments can be collected through a variety of means including dyads completing checklists, mini quizzes, or individual projects. Teachers should then use the assessments to determine future teaching strategies, tutor dyad relations, and curriculum instruction.

Community-Based Instruction

CBI is a valuable tool for teaching academics, life skills, and employment skills in a natural environment and the real life setting (Hamill, 2002; Wheeler, 2006; Wehman, 2011a). The experiences that students have in community-based settings allow students not only to gain knowledge but also to gain the necessary skills and supports that are needed upon entering the postsecondary world (Walker, Uphold, Richter, & Test, 2010). As a society, we look to the educational systems to help produce persons who can function independently in their adult life. Unfortunately, this goal is often overlooked for persons with disabilities. Within the educational system, we must prepare persons with disabilities to function independently, to the best of their ability. Many of the skills needed to function independently can be taught through CBI. Walker, Richter, Uphold, and Test (2010) noted Fabian, Lent, and Willis' (1998) statement regarding CBI being one of the many variables that leads to successful postsecondary outcomes. Because of the positive outcomes that CBI has shown, it is important for practitioners to begin CBI early (elementary years) and continue increasing the difficulty and variables of instruction across middle and high school years. The connection across grade levels is imperative; the decisions that are made in elementary school affect the decisions in middle school and high school and, in turn, students' adult life (deFur, 2003; Walker et al., 2010).

In elementary school, practitioners can use CBI to teach social skills, safety skills, and career awareness. Social skills and safety skills can be taught outside the classroom on the playground (Walker et al., 2010) during recess, on the school bus to and from school, and on monthly field trips to the swimming pool, movies, museums, and so forth. In middle school, practitioners can use CBI to build on previously learned social skills and safety skills and begin the basics of employment skills and independent living skills. As in elementary school, social skills and safety skills can continue to be incorporated into activities both outside and inside the classroom. Employment skills and independent living skills should become the primary focus at this level. Independent living skills can also be targeted, including budgeting through the use of a community bank, grocery shopping at the local grocery store, and holiday gift shopping at the local mall. These lessons should begin with instruction inside the classroom involving exposure to grocery ads and comparison shopping, the use of coupons, organizing items to buy with a list, and so forth.

In high school, CBI should build on the experiences of elementary and middle school at a more advanced level. At this point, the instruction should become more focused on the student's interests and should no longer be a "one-size-fits-all" curriculum. Career exploration should be a large part of the focus for both classroom and CBI. Students should have community placements in businesses that align with their interests. For example, a student who is interested in attending college and becoming a veterinarian could spend some time working or volunteering at a veterinarian's office or a pet store. A student who has an interest in obtaining a job as a child care worker immediately after graduating high school could work or volunteer at a local day care center.

Some important points to remember when implementing CBI are (Wheeler, 2006)

- Begin CBI with a specific goal or outcome in mind
- Activities and community setting must be age-appropriate for the students participating
- All training (work skills, life skills, recreation skills, and so on) should be taught in real world/natural environments

- Once skills have been mastered in one setting, assess the student in another setting to see if the skill has generalized
- Students are integrated with their nondisabled peers/co-workers in all settings, including community-based settings
- Students are assessed and evaluated under real life/natural conditions
- Students have documentation of their strengths and weaknesses in each community placement that could be shown to and discussed with a potential employer

What Resources Should Teachers Use for Curriculum Development?

After an initial transition IEP is designed, the teacher should obtain direct input from the student and family, members of the community, and others who are interested and concerned about this student's future. The teacher's primary responsibility is to teach those skills that the student will need for a successful future. This does not mean that the teacher purchases a variety of curricula and then teaches all the skills on those curricula, hoping to teach something that the student may be able to use. On the contrary, this "shotgun" approach should be abandoned for a targeted approach that identifies the most essential skills for independence in adulthood. This process is more time-consuming and requires greater thought than simple identification of objectives from a set curriculum or checklist. The teacher must have the intelligence, creativity, and, above all, diligence to work closely with the family in narrowing down those skills that are most necessary and realistic. The strategy for developing a functional curriculum based on the general education curriculum involves identifying and prioritizing key activities. Table 10.6 describes these points and should be followed by teachers who are designing transition programs.

Using Universal Design for Transition to Plan Instruction

This last section of the chapter helps teachers organize their efforts in designing instruction that addresses both academic and transition goals and outcomes. When making the link between academic standards and transition and/or functional goals, Thoma, Bartholomew, and Scott recommend that teachers consider the following:

- What are the overall goals?
- What skills are needed for transition?
- What academic content will support most (or all) students' goals (e.g., math, English)?

Table 10.6.   Establishment of priority activities for instruction

Step	Activity
1.	With the student and his or her family, evaluate the student's performance in each of the domain categories and identify desired future environments in which the student will function.
2.	Identify activities and skills relevant to the student's current environment and skills necessary to function in projected future environments.
3.	Review all relevant current and future activities and indicate those activities that occur in two or more domains and that are age-appropriate.
4.	List these activities from most to least frequent in occurrence.
5.	From this list, identify activities that are crucial for the student's safety. Next, identify activities critical for functioning independently in the desired future environments.
6.	Select for immediate instruction:
	Activities essential to the student's safety within current environments
	Activities that the student must perform frequently in order to function independently within his or her current and identified future environments
7.	Select remaining objectives from the list of activities (see Step 4).

- How does this academic content link to life after high school?
- How can we demonstrate this link in the transition goals and objectives?
- What resources are available to assist us in teaching these skills?
- What resources are available to support students in demonstrating their understanding of these skills? (2009, p. 15)

Figure 10.5 provides an example of a planning form used to organize a teacher's lesson linking a science unit on hurricanes with transition goals for safety, self-determination, and community living.

Susan's teacher met with Susan and her transition-planning team to identify her primary goals for the year. Because Susan still expressed a desire to go to college, her

Self-check:

Academic connection/ information	Transition assessments	Administered by	Assessment format	Environment	Results
English class: writing professionally	Employment	Ms. White	Writing cover letters and résumés for employment	Classroom/ homework	Needs additional help with this task. Explore the use of technology tools to help organize efforts.
Science class; project	Exploration of jobs in science areas	Mr. Scott	Project using Self-Determined Learning Model of Instruction to organize work for project	Classroom/ Internet searches	Earned A in project; identified two employment areas of interest to explore further: health care work and lab assistant.
Science end-of-course assessment	Content knowledge to assess possibility of going on to postsecondary education	Mr. Scott	State assessment exam	Classroom	Passed exam.

Self-check:

- 🕑 Student preferences/interests considered
- 🕑 Multiple and/or appropriate environments
- 🕑 Multiple means of expression/representation/engagement
- 🕑 Academic links
- 🕑 Multiple evaluators
- 🕑 Multiple opportunities

Transition domain (circle as many as apply): self-determination, employment, community living, transportation, postsecondary education, recreation/leisure, other:_____

Figure 10.5. Transition assessment checklist. (From Thoma, C.A., Bartholomew, C., Tamura, R., Scott, L., & Terpstra, J. [2008, April]. *UDT: Applying a universal design approach to link transition and academics*. Preconference workshop at the Council for Exceptional Children conference, Boston; adapted by permission.)

transition plan focused primarily on her needs with that in mind. Besides passing her classes and earning a regular high school diploma, Susan's goals included improving her reading and writing skills; conducting transition assessments to identify her strengths and needs related to self-determination, dorm living, computer skills, and use of public transportation; and increasing her self-advocacy skills. The English, social studies, and science teachers all indicated a willingness to try to incorporate those transition skills and assessments into their classes, believing that they would be appropriate activities for all students to use the skills learned in the classes. Her English teacher identified writing opportunities as well as reading skills as priorities. Her social studies teacher indicated that they had a field trip scheduled where they could do an initial assessment of Susan's public transportation skills. And her science teacher indicated that the problem-solving approach that was the basis of the Self-Determined Learning Model of Instruction would be useful for the inquiry-based instructional unit. Once Susan learned to use the approach, Susan's parents would work to help her learn to generalize the approach to other situations. In addition, Susan would be participating in a summer program at a local college, which would include an opportunity to live in a dorm and work with a counselor to identify information about her needs related to independence in that setting. Susan was happy with the plan for the coming year, and her team members felt that the goals included were doable while still ensuring that ample focus was on teaching academic material.

Conclusion

This chapter covered a range of different strategies and approaches that can be used by teachers to meet their responsibility of preparing students with disabilities for successful adult lives by providing instruction that meets their need for academic and transition skill acquisition and development. It clearly is not an easy task, and this chapter merely provides a starting point to focus teacher efforts and identify valuable resources that can be used to individualize one's own development as an exceptional teacher. Subsequent chapters in this book also help provide further direction in teachers' efforts to improve transition outcomes for students with disabilities.

Study Questions

1. Explain why technology is such an important piece of the puzzle when it comes to instruction and transition. Include three examples to support your answer.

2. Explain why backward planning is a useful strategy when deciding what transition skills to teach for a specific student's transition goals.

3. Describe how you, as an educator, can help build and maintain an enjoyable working relationship with the paraprofessional(s) in your classroom. Include three examples to support your answer.

4. Think of a student that you currently work with or have worked with in the past. Complete the planning form from Figure 10.4, linking a math lesson with transition goals for budgeting, banking, and purchasing family groceries.

Online Resources

Abledata: http://www.abledata.com

Center for Applied Special Technologies: http://www.cast.org

Microsoft Accessibility: http://www.microsoft.com/enable

Self-Determination Synthesis Project: http://www.uncc.edu/sdsp

Enderle-Severson Transition Rating Scale: http://www.estr.net/scale/pdf/sampleReport.pdf

America's Career InfoNet: http://www.acinet.org/acinet/

WebQuest: http://webquest.org

College Preparation Resources for Students

DO IT Center, University of Washington: http://www.washington.edu/doit?Resources/college_prep.html

Jump Start Coalition: http://www.jumpstartcoalition.org

Teaching Social Skills and Promoting Supportive Relationships

11

ERIK W. CARTER AND CAROLYN HUGHES

After completing this chapter, the reader will be able to

- Understand the importance of teaching social skills
- Discuss some of the challenges youth encounter in social-related domains
- Describe three primary approaches to enhancing social skills and participation of youth
- Explain the benefits of peer support programs, key designs, and implementation considerations
- Describe the range of interventions teachers might draw upon to improve social competence, participation, and relationships of their students with disabilities

Most conversations about life in middle school, high school, and college—whether among current students or adults reflecting back on their experiences years later—inevitably turn to friendships and the activities in which youth participate with one another. The social skills students develop, the relationships they form, and the supports they access can be instrumental in shaping their success and enhancing quality of life throughout adolescence and into adulthood. For transition-age youth who have disabilities—many of whom struggle with respect to social interaction—providing targeted instruction and creating supportive opportunities are a critical focus of secondary education and transition services. This chapter addresses the social dimension of the lives of youth and young adults with disabilities, focusing on promising and evidence-based strategies for increasing the social participation, skills, supports, and outcomes of youth as they transition to life after high school.

Importance of Social Skills and Relationships in the Lives of Youth

Decades of research addressing the social lives of adolescents converge upon a simple, but important, theme: Social relationships really do matter (Rubin, Bukowski, & Laursen, 2009). Through interactions with their peers, teachers, family members, and other caring adults, students can develop a repertoire of social, communication, and collateral skills that can contribute to success and a sense of belonging in the workplace, on campus, and in the community. Youths' attitudes and aspirations for the future are shaped through their conversations and time spent with others. Moreover, these relationships can enable youth to make critical connections and build social capital. Indeed, all of the reasons why positive relationships are considered important in the life of *any* young person apply to students with disabilities. At the same time, there are compelling reasons to place additional emphasis on building social competence and connections among youth with disabilities in transition.

Social Competence Enhances Participation and Increases Opportunities

The extent to which students learn, use, and generalize critical social and communication skills can impact both participation and success in a wide range of school, work, and community settings. For example, secondary general and special educators identify a constellation of social-related skills (e.g., cooperation, self-control, assertion skills) considered essential to success in their classrooms (Lane, Pierson, & Givner, 2004). The degree to which students learn and use these skills effectively can have an impact on their learning and influence their access to general education classrooms. In the workplace, employers consistently identify communicating effectively, working well with others (e.g., co-workers, customers, supervisors), and responding well to feedback as critical "soft skills" that can impact hiring, promotion, and retention (Chadsey, 2008). Students who can develop these skills may be more likely to find and maintain employment (Carter, Trainor, Ditchman, Swedeen, & Owens, 2011). Finally, greater social competence can also enhance participation, social acceptance, and sense of belonging in an array of recreational, volunteer, and other shared activities in the community (King et al., 2003).

Quality of Life and Supports that Come Through Friendships

Adolescence is a developmental period during which peer relationships take on particular importance. As students progress through middle and high school, the influence and importance of peer affiliations become especially prominent in the lives of all students with disabilities. The extent to which students develop positive and supportive relationships with peers and others can contribute substantively to their overall well-being and quality of life (Rubin, Bukowski, & Laursen, 2009). For example, students with durable, positive peer relationships also gain access to range of instrumental, emotional, academic, and personal supports that can help them as they launch into adulthood. When these relationships are absent for students, they may experience loneliness, anxiety, and other mental health challenges (Prinstein & Dodge, 2008).

Contributions to Outcomes in and After High School

Increasing students' social competence also may have a long-term impact on students' success well beyond high school (Alwell & Cobb, 2009b). There is mounting evidence to suggest that the quality of students' relationships with peers and caring adults can have a direct impact on learning, and vice versa. In other words, relationships can enhance access to rigorous, relevant education experiences, and shared learning experiences can set the stage for the development of key relationships. Furthermore, Test, Mazzotti, et al. (2009) reviewed studies that have shown a strong association between greater social competence, increased postsecondary educational participation, and improved employment outcomes after leaving high school. In addition, possessing greater social skills and fewer challenging behaviors may be associated with increased self-determination (Carter, Trainor, Owens, Swedeen, & Sun, 2010).

Challenges Encountered by Youth with Disabilities

In light of these multiple factors, it is not surprising that most transition frameworks place particular emphasis on promoting social competence, participation, and relationships (Hughes & Carter, 2012; Kohler & Field, 2003; National Alliance for Secondary Education and Transition, 2005). Indeed, Halpern's (1985) early transition model placed social and interpersonal networks as one of three primary pillars of community adjustment. Yet, many youth and young adults with disabilities encounter substantial challenges in these social-related domains.

Social Skills Limitations

The absence of well-developed social skills can limit access to inclusive classrooms, workplaces, and community activities. Although social skills limitations can be a defining feature of special education categories such as autism, emotional–behavioral disorders, and intellectual disabilities, students with other disabilities may also have needs in these areas. Some students may benefit from learning skills that would enhance collaborative work with others in a classroom or workplace, allay anxiety or uncertainty in social situations, or facilitate the development of new friendships. For other students, the social, communication, and behavioral challenges they encounter may be more substantial, hindering their involvement in the range of interactions that occur in school and community settings (Carter & Hughes, 2006).

Limited Inclusion and Access to General Education

Although access to inclusive school, work, and community activities can promote the development of skills and dispositions that enhance social competence, many students with disabilities have limited involvement in these settings during the transition years (Wagner, Cadwallader, & Marder, 2003). Enrollment in general education classes often becomes more restricted as students with disabilities enter secondary school, particularly students with more extensive support needs (e.g., intellectual disabilities, autism, multiple disabilities). Extracurricular involvement—which typically fosters social connections around shared interests and strengths—can be fairly limited for youth with disabilities compared with the participation of peers without disabilities. And many adolescents with disabilities are not participating in after-school or summer jobs that can promote career-related social skill development. As a result, many students with disabilities are not involved in already existing and naturally occurring opportunities for learning new skills and developing important relationships (Carter, Hughes, Guth, & Copeland, 2005; Hughes et al., 2011).

Elusiveness of Friendships and Supportive Peer Relationships

The confluence of social-related challenges experienced by many youth with disabilities and diminished involvement in the array of activities that make up everyday high school life means that the relationships and social involvement many young people look forward to during adolescence remain rare for secondary students with disabilities. Findings from the National Longitudinal Transition Study-2—which provides a comprehensive and representative portrait of the secondary experiences of youth with disabilities—suggest that many adolescents with disabilities lack the social skills and connections that can contribute substantially to adolescent well-being (Wagner, Newman, & Cameto, 2004; Wagner, Cadwallader, & Marder, 2003). In this study, parents were asked a series of questions about the social participation and relationships of their children with disabilities. Table 11.1 displays their responses to three of these questions. These findings illustrate the necessity of attending more fully to the social dimension of adolescents' lives within comprehensive transition services and supports.

Promising and Evidence-Based Intervention Approaches

Since the early 2000s, there has been a growing interest among policymakers, researchers, and practitioners in identifying effective and feasible avenues for improving the quality

Table 11.1.   Percentage of youth participating in each activity, as reported by parents

Disability category	Never visits with friends[a]	Rarely or never receives telephone calls from friends[b]	Not invited to other youths' social activities during the past year[c]
Autism	44.3%	83.5%	50.6%
Deafblindness	26.7%	64.4%	34.6%
Emotional disturbance	10.7%	25.5%	17.1%
Hearing impairment	8.4%	41.3%	11.9%
Intellectual disabilities	16.4%	41.5%	24.8%
Learning disabilities	6.9%	18.8%	11.3%
Multiple disabilities	30.0%	62.7%	43.5%
Orthopedic impairment	20.0%	46.6%	29.7%
Other health impairment	5.8%	23.3%	11.8%
Speech–language impairment	8.8%	22.0%	10.9%
Traumatic brain injury	7.8%	34.0%	19.6%
Visual impairment	14.6%	33.0%	21.9%

From Wagner, M., Cadwallader, T., & Marder, C. (2003). *Life outside the classroom for youth with disabilities.* Menlo Park, CA: SRI International; reprinted by permission.

[a]Parents were asked, "During the past 12 months, about how many days a week did [youth] usually get together with friends, outside of school and organized activities or groups?"

[b]Parents were asked, "During the past 12 months, how often have his/her friends called on the phone?"

[c]Parents were asked, "During the past 12 months, has he/she been invited by other students to social activities, like over to their home or to a party?"

and impact of transition education for youth with disabilities. Many studies have examined innovative approaches for increasing secondary students' social competence and participation. As a result, much is now known about how to enhance the social-related outcomes of youth and young adults with disabilities across a range of school and community settings (Alwell & Cobb, 2009b; Carter, Sisco, Chung, & Stanton-Chapman, 2010; Snell et al., 2010). Moreover, many of these approaches are considered by secondary general educators, special educators, and paraprofessionals to be acceptable and feasible to use with their students (Carter & Pesko, 2008). In this section, we briefly describe three primary approaches to enhancing the social skills, supports, and participation of adolescents with disabilities.

Student-Focused Strategies

As noted elsewhere in this chapter, many students with disabilities experience social and/or communication challenges that can hinder their involvement, acceptance, and success within classrooms, clubs, workplaces, and other community activities (Wagner, Cadwallader, & Marder, 2003). Student-focused intervention strategies address these potential barriers by teaching students specific skills and dispositions that can increase or improve the quality of their social interactions with others. In other words, these strategies focus on providing instruction to increase students' social and communicative competence as the primary avenue for enhancing participation and positive relationships.

A number of different student-focused strategies have evidence of promise for increasing students' interactions or social competence (Table 11.2). Social skills training may be among the most widely used intervention approaches for adolescents (Cook, Gresham, et al., 2008; Tse, Strulovitch, Tagalakis, Meng, & Fombonne, 2007). This approach involves providing explicit instruction in discrete skills (e.g., initiating conversations, conversational turn-taking) or clusters of skills (e.g., cooperation skills, assertion skills) to individuals or groups of students to facilitate interpersonal interactions. This training can address a broad set of existing skills generally considered to be important to success in the classroom, workplace, or other community settings, or it may target specific skills with which a particular student struggles. For students with complex communication challenges, it may be necessary to introduce new augmentative or alternative communication systems or teach students to use elements of their existing systems more effectively (Hughes et al., 2000). For example, a student might be shown how to use a communication book to start and sustain a conversation with co-workers, communicate choices to a fellow teammate using an iPad, or request directions using a computerized system with dynamic display.

Javier   Javier had held several after-school and summer jobs in the past, but none had been a particularly successful experience. He often encountered difficulties interacting successfully with customers, accepting feedback from his supervisor, or getting along with co-workers. Javier's special education case manager encouraged him to take advantage of the courses and other activities offered within the school's career–technical program. For example, in one of his courses, instruction addressed the interpersonal skills essential to successfully finding and maintaining a job. In another, he had opportunities to hear from different guest speakers who addressed the specific skills they look for in new employees. Finally, he and several other students with learning disabilities met weekly during study hall as part of a "job club." Led by a special education teacher, this group talked about their experiences in the workplace and the teacher shared specific strategies for finding success on the job.

Table 11.2.   Examples of educational practices evaluated for secondary students with disabilities

Student-focused practices	
Social skills training	Providing explicit instruction in social and communication skills to students
Conversational turn-taking	Providing systematic instruction and conversational structures to facilitate balanced turn-taking by conversational partners
Augmentative and alternative communication use	Introducing aided or unaided communication systems (e.g., pictures, communication books, electronic systems) to students and providing instruction in their use
Collateral skills instruction	Teaching students with disabilities other skills (e.g., game playing, computer skills) that are not explicitly social in order to enhance participation in recreational or other activities
Self-management strategies	Teaching students with disabilities to self-manage their own social behaviors by using goal setting, self-prompting, self-monitoring, self-evaluation, and/or other self-directed strategies

Peer-focused practices	
Peer awareness training	Providing activities to promote greater awareness or understanding of disabilities among peers
Peer interaction training	Providing direct social skills training to equip peers without disabilities to become effective communication partners, interaction facilitators, and/or social skill instructors
Peer tutoring	Assigning a peer without disabilities to provide academic or other task-oriented support to a student with disabilities within tutor–learner pairs
Peer networks	Establishing structured social groups around a student to promote social and communication outcomes within the classroom and/or across the school day
Peer support arrangements	Arranging for one or more peers without disabilities to provide regular social and learning support to a student with disabilities, with needed feedback and assistance from adults

Support-focused practices	
Educational placement	Enrolling students with disabilities in general education classes with appropriate supports (e.g., active collaboration among educators, curricular adaptations and classroom modifications, individual supports)
Interactive activities	Designing interactive activities to promote social opportunities between students with and without disabilities
Instructional groupings	Small-group cooperative arrangements to promote collaborative and interdependent interactions among group members
Environmental modifications	Modifying aspects of classrooms or workplaces to promote the greater participation of students with disabilities
Adult facilitation	Adult-provided prompts or facilitation strategies to promote social interactions among students with and without disabilities

From Carter, E.W., Sisco, L.G., Chung, Y., & Stanton-Chapman, T. (2010). Peer interactions of students with intellectual disabilities and/or autism: A map of the intervention literature. *Research and Practice for Persons with Severe Disabilities, 35,* 63–79; adapted by permission. This article first appeared in *Research and Practice for Persons with Severe Disabilities.* Visit www.tash.org or contact info@tash.org for more information.

Two additional strategies have also shown promise for improving the social outcomes of youth and young adults with disabilities. Teaching students to self-manage their own social behavior can promote greater independence and encourage broad use of newly learned skills across settings. For example, students can be taught self-directed strategies such as goal setting, self-instruction, self-monitoring, and self-evaluation for actively managing their own social interactions (Hughes et al., 2004). Teaching students collateral skills that enable them to participate more meaningfully in shared activities with peers, co-workers, and others may also be beneficial. Social interactions typically happen within the context of an ongoing activity, such as eating lunch together, participating in a recreational or leisure activity, or working in a cooperative learning group. When students do not possess the related skills needed to participate in joint activities alongside their peers, they inadvertently miss out on many of the social opportunities that take place in these activities. When students are taught these participation skills, they encounter more opportunities to meet and develop relationships with others.

Peer-Focused Strategies

Although many students with disabilities may benefit from social skills instruction and other student-focused intervention strategies, other prominent barriers to social participation may need to be addressed concurrently. Sometimes, classmates, co-workers, or other participants in community activities may initially express hesitation or uncertainty about how to interact with someone who has a disability or communicates in atypical ways (McDougall, DeWit, King, Miller, & Killip, 2004; Siperstein, Norins, & Mohler, 2007). In other cases, peers may have interest in spending time with and getting to know a student with disabilities but are reluctant to do so when specialized staff (e.g., paraprofessionals, job coaches, teachers) are always present (Carter, Sisco, Brown, Brickham, & Al-Khabbaz, 2008). Peer-focused interventions are intended to equip others in a setting with the skills, opportunities, and confidence to interact socially with a student with a disability. For transition-age youth and young adults, an array of people might be considered to be peers, including classmates, team members, friends, co-workers, and other individuals with whom they spend substantial amounts of time.

Peer-focused interventions often incorporate awareness elements designed to provide others with accurate and relevant information about certain disabilities broadly (e.g., autism, intellectual disabilities, mental health issues) or about an individual student specifically. For example, awareness training might focus on teaching classmates about autism and the ways in which this disability impacts students' learning and relationships or explaining to co-workers the different accommodations that will be used by a student with a visual impairment in the workplace. In some cases, it is useful to share more personalized information about how a particular student communicates his or her own needs, choices, and preferences to others; participates in everyday activities; and benefits from specific supports from his or her peers. Both of these approaches are aimed at dispelling myths about or negative attitudes toward disabilities and presume that lack of accurate knowledge is a salient barrier to social acceptance and participation. In addition to participating in awareness activities, peers may also benefit from learning specific strategies for interacting with students with disabilities (Haring & Breen, 1992). For example, peers who work closely with the student may be taught how to phrase questions to elicit responses, encourage communication system use, or provide constructive feedback. This guidance can be especially helpful for peers who are unsure how best to initiate and sustain conversations with students experiencing communication challenges.

Watertown High School   A group of youth and teachers at Watertown High School wanted to foster a school culture in which every student felt valued and engaged in the life of the school. Recognizing that many students with significant disabilities were disconnected from the array of social and learning opportunities offered in and beyond the classroom, they decided to take several steps to promote greater awareness and acceptance. They held a screening of the movie *Including Samuel* (http://www.includingsamuel.com) to launch conversations about inclusion, followed with discussion by a panel of young adults with disabilities. Students worked together to spearhead a campaign at their school to end the use of disparaging words and promote the inclusion of students with intellectual disabilities (http://www.r-word.org). And teachers in the English and social studies departments found ways to address disability in readings and discussion as part of National Inclusive Schools Week.

Peer-mediated intervention strategies reflect more sustained approaches to enhancing social engagement for students with disabilities. Although many variations exist, these approaches typically involve one or more students without disabilities in providing social and/or learning support to their peer with disabilities, while receiving ongoing assistance from adults in the setting (e.g., teachers, paraprofessionals, supervisors, job coaches; Carter & Kennedy, 2006). When these strategies emphasize helping students with disabilities learn academic content or other new skills, they often are referred to as peer tutoring or peer-assisted learning strategies (Harper & Maheady, 2007). Such approaches may be ideally suited for inclusive secondary or postsecondary classrooms. Peer networks typically are implemented when the focus is primarily on fostering friendships and arranging shared recreational/leisure activities. For example, a group of students who have interests and/or classes in common with a student with an intellectual disability might be assisted in forming a social group that gets together regularly during school or outside of school. Blended approaches—that emphasize both instructional and friendship elements—are sometimes referred to as peer (or co-worker) support arrangements (Carter, Moss, Hoffman, Chung, & Sisco, 2011).

Support-Focused Strategies

Even as students with disabilities develop social and communication skills and peers receive information and training, aspects of school, work, and community settings may still limit the opportunities students with disabilities have to interact and develop relationships with their peers. For example, general education participation in secondary schools often becomes more restricted as the curriculum becomes increasingly challenging, providing fewer opportunities for students with and without disabilities to meet and get to know one another. Moreover, students with disabilities may spend an increasing proportion of their school day in off-campus work and community settings. Even when students with and without disabilities are in the same classrooms, they may have few regular opportunities to work collaboratively (Carter, Hughes, et al., 2005; Hughes et al., 1999). Support-based strategies focus on the efforts of adults to create socially supportive environments in which peer interactions are actively encouraged and social skill development is supported.

Spencer   Freshman biology class was the highlight of Spencer's day. Ms. Pike, a relatively new general educator at the school, intentionally designed her class to be highly collaborative. Students regularly worked in cooperative learning groups of four or five students and regularly participated in hands-on lab activities together. Because Spencer had complex communication challenges and used a high-tech communication device, Ms. Pike and a paraprofessional assigned to this inclusive classroom made sure that activities were interactive and appropriately modified so that Spencer could participate in meaningful ways. As the students worked together throughout the semester, the paraprofessional was strategic about finding ways to encourage interactions between Spencer and his peers.

Increasing access to general education classrooms can increase students' opportunities for interaction with a wider range of peers than in self-contained classrooms. However, changes in educational placement alone may be insufficient for substantially improving social outcomes. The use of cooperative learning groups or other interactive learning and social activities have been shown to encourage interdependence and provide students with more frequent opportunities to interact with others (Cushing, Kennedy, Shukla, Davis, & Meyer, 1997). In a similar way, the introduction of carefully designed modifications and accommodations can promote greater involvement and contributions of youth with disabilities in ongoing activities. For some youth, school staff or job coaches can also play an important facilitative role by actively encouraging interactions among their students and others and reinforcing prosocial behaviors (Causton-Theoharis, 2009). For other youth, the constant presence of an adult (e.g., paraprofessionals, job coaches, related service providers) may inadvertently hinder a student's interactions with classmates or co-workers. In these situations, fading adult direct support may actually facilitate social participation.

Developing a Peer Support Program

Promoting positive relationships for and building social competence among youth with disabilities requires intentional efforts on the part of school staff and others. Many schools turn to formalized peer support programs as an avenue for strengthening the social and communication skills of students with disabilities, creating more welcoming school cultures, and expanding the quality of opportunities students with and without disabilities have to get to know and spend time with one another. Although these programs can be referred to by a variety of names (e.g., peer buddy programs, peer partner clubs, peer mentoring programs, Best Buddies) and each adopts somewhat varied approaches, they share in common an emphasis on establishing regularly occurring opportunities for students with and without disabilities to spend time together while receiving needed support from adults (Hughes & Carter, 2008; Janney & Snell, 2006). These programs have been widely implemented in numerous high schools throughout the country and evaluated in numerous studies. Indeed, approximately 40% of secondary schools nationally offer some type of peer support program for students (Wagner, Newman, Cameto, Levine, & Marder, 2003). In this section, we address the possible benefits of structured peer support programs and describe key considerations when designing and implementing such programs. This information is drawn from both a review of the literature and our own experience implementing peer buddy programs in numerous high schools (Hughes & Carter, 2008).

Benefits of Peer Support Programs

Although informal or individualized efforts to address social-related goals throughout the school day can be instrumental to students' social success, there are benefits to also establishing more structured contexts within which students with and without disabilities can spend time together. First, many peers recognize the pivotal role they can play in promoting belonging and modeling acceptance for their classmates with disabilities, but they may not necessarily know how and where to put this commitment into action (Copeland et al., 2004). Peer support programs provide an avenue for these students to become change agents in their school and get involved in the lives of their classmates with significant disabilities. Second, as the real experts in social norms and expected peer behaviors, peers without disabilities can be especially effective at modeling appropriate social and communication skills. Third, peer support programs address prevalent barriers to the development of peer relationships in secondary schools by organizing activities in schools that may not otherwise be inclusive, providing participating students with information about how to interact with and support one another, and making assistance available from school staff as needed. Fourth, involvement in these programs can offer tangible benefits for all participating students. Students with disabilities gain additional opportunities to learn and practice important social and academic-related skills through interactions with their peers, become less reliant on school staff for support, and gain access to a broader range of social and learning activities that make up everyday high school life (Carter & Kennedy, 2006). In a similar way, students without disabilities have reported improved attitudes toward and raised expectations of their peers with disabilities, deeper appreciation of diversity, new commitment to advocacy, and new friendships (Copeland et al., 2004; Hughes et al., 2001).

Laying the Groundwork

A strong foundation is critical to ensuring that a new peer support program flourishes and accomplishes its articulated goals (Hughes & Carter, 2008). Although programs are sometimes initiated at the behest of a single teacher, an important initial step is to build a strong base of support among teachers, school leaders, other school staff, and families who will be involved in or affected by the program. For example, administrators can be instrumental in allocating needed resources to and advocating among school staff for the program; school counselors often recommend students with and without disabilities who would benefit from involvement; special educators and/or paraprofessionals are involved in orienting peers to their roles and supporting students as they work together; and parents can be critical partners in supporting interactions that take place beyond the school campus. When key stakeholders are firmly committed to the program's goals and willing to invest in getting the program off the ground, success will generally follow.

Generating Interest

Initially, a program can be launched by a small group of teachers and focus on just a few students. To expand and involve greater numbers of students, steps should be taken to promote the program to the broader school community and enlist the support of additional school staff. Presentations at departmental or school-wide faculty meetings can provide an efficient way to describe the program and its benefits for participating students, offer multiple avenues for teachers to become involved (e.g., recommending students for participation, supporting students and peer supports in their classrooms or clubs, sharing information about the program with students), solicit suggestions for strengthening the program, and answer any questions. Other approaches for building support for and promoting awareness of the program can include writing articles for inclusion in school and parent–teacher organization newsletters, distributing program information sheets to staff, or having informal conversations with individual teachers in whose classes or clubs students with disabilities are enrolled.

Program Configuration

In addition to building these strong partnerships, decisions must be made about how the school's peer support program initially will be configured. Programs can look quite different from one school to another as program elements are tailored to match a school's vision, culture, and goals for all students. For example, some schools offer course credit to participating students with and without disabilities, typically under the umbrella of service-learning or elective requirements (Hughes & Carter, 2008). Because many high school students have limited flexibility in their course schedules or are involved in off-campus or after-school activities, a structured course creates daily, on-campus opportunities for participating students to spend time with one another. Early conversations with school administrators should address procedures for introducing a new course offering or integrating peer support program elements into existing courses. When offered as a stand-alone course, peer support programs typically incorporate written assignments (e.g., journals, end-of-semester papers), attendance expectations, and other graded activities. Other schools have developed inclusive social-oriented clubs aimed at connecting students with and without disabilities outside the classroom (see "Extracurricular Activities"). Finally, schools may instead adopt a more individualized approach in which peer supports are arranged for particular students at specific times throughout the week (e.g., lunch, after-school activities, specific general education classrooms; Haring & Breen, 1992). Each configuration requires advance consideration of whether and how additional school staff will be involved, which students will be encouraged to participate, and what resources will be needed to sustain and grow the program.

Identifying Participating Students

Once the initial format of a program is determined, attention can shift to identifying students with and without disabilities in the school who would benefit from participation. Peer support programs may be appropriate for students with disabilities who have

a. Educational goals focused on improving the quantity or quality of interactions with peers

b. Few friendships with same-age peers

c. Substantial social and/or communication skills challenges

d. A need for additional support to participate meaningfully within inclusive classrooms, extracurricular programming, and other school-sponsored activities

Although peer support programs most often are developed for students with significant disabilities (e.g., autism, intellectual disabilities, multiple disabilities), students with high-incidence disabilities may also benefit from involvement in these programs.

Selection Considerations

The impact of any program will be inextricably linked to the students who participate as peer supports. Therefore, it is important to consider carefully those qualities and characteristics that participating peers without disabilities should possess. Although there is no fixed set of skills and previous experiences that every student must exhibit to be effective in providing support, it may be beneficial to consider peers who are close in age to the students with disabilities with whom they will work, have shown previous interest in getting to know their classmates with disabilities, have consistent attendance, hold interests in common with participating students with disabilities, demonstrate a willingness to learn new skills, and exhibit appropriate interpersonal skills. Although many teachers tend to encourage students who are academically high performing, female, and are/or already have positive attitudes to participate, research suggests that a much broader spectrum of students may benefit from involvement in peer-mediated interventions. For example, students who themselves are struggling academically or who have high-incidence disabilities have been shown to benefit from involvement in these interventions as peer supports (Carter & Kennedy, 2006).

Extending Invitations

A number of different avenues exist through which educators can invite students to participate in peer support programs, each of which has its own strengths and drawbacks (Carter, Cushing, & Kennedy, 2009; Hughes & Carter, 2008).

- *Invitations from teachers and other school staff.* Many students are first introduced to peer support programs through the invitation of teachers who know them well. General educators, special educators, paraprofessionals, guidance counselors, coaches, and other school staff typically know of particular students who exhibit the qualities of an effective peer support. Personal invitations are an especially effective way to discuss opportunities for involvement with students who may not have known about or initially considered participating in the program.

- *Presentations about the program.* Teachers—sometimes in collaboration with participating peer supports—can make brief presentations about the program to service-oriented student organizations (e.g., Future Teachers of America, Key Club), in classes (e.g., civics, health, literature) when disability-related issues are addressed, at school-wide assemblies, or in elective and related classes. In addition to recruiting students, these approaches increase awareness about the program among the entire school staff, who are essential partners in the educational inclusion of youth with disabilities.

- *Broad announcements.* Peer support programs can also be advertised through the same approaches used by other school clubs and programs, such as hallway displays (e.g., posters, bulletin boards), articles in student publications, tables at freshman orientation events, a program description in the student handbook, and daily school announcements. These broad approaches ensure that every student in a school has the opportunity to participate in and benefit from such a program.

- *Inclusive classrooms and school activities.* Often, peer supports are needed to support participation within specific classrooms, extracurricular activities, or other school contexts (e.g., lunch, breaks, before or after school). Peers can be invited from within these settings by approaching specific students; making a brief, but general, announcement; or asking lead staff (e.g., classroom teachers, club sponsors) for their recommendations.

- *Current peer supports.* After a program is up and running, participating peers typically carry out a large portion of recruitment efforts. Because most students report compelling personal benefits from their involvement, they often are strong advocates for their friends and classmates to also become involved. Encouraging currently involved students to invite their friends to participate in program activities expands the network of students from the same peer groups.

- *Asking students with disabilities.* Like all students, youth with significant disabilities may have clear preferences about the peers with whom they want to spend time and get to know. Therefore, it is important to seek students' preferences when one is considering potential peer support matches. When a student has complex communication challenges, creative strategies may be needed to discern his or her preferences.

Although a menu of recruitment options exist, the particular approaches used to recruit students should align with the program's goals and structure, available resources and time, and culture of the school.

Selecting Students

When multiple peers express interest in becoming involved in the program, it can be helpful to implement screening strategies. For example, some teachers hold informal interviews with students to assess their motivation for and fit with the peer support program. (See Table 11.3 for potential screening questions.) Other teachers ask students to complete a brief written application, asking about their interest in the program, current course schedule, and involvement in other school activities or to provide recommendations from school staff who know them well.

Equipping Students to Support One Another

Before enrolling students in a peer support program, participating teachers should establish a clear set of procedures and expectations for participating students with and without disabilities (Table 11.4). Although specific roles and responsibilities can vary from program to program, teams should determine the primary focus of peer supports' interactions with

Table 11.3. Example interview questions for potential peer supports

How did you first learn about this opportunity?

What leads you to want to become involved?

How well do you know the students with disabilities with whom you will be spending time?

What are some of your expectations for your involvement?

Have you had similar experiences in the past?

What qualities do you think make for an effective peer support?

In which other extracurricular and community activities are you involved?

What experiences have you had that you feel would make you a good peer support?

Are there aspects of the opportunity that you want to know more about?

What do you hope to gain as a result of your involvement in this experience?

From Carter, E.W., Cushing, L.S., & Kennedy, C.H. (2009). *Peer support strategies: Improving all students' social lives and learning.* Baltimore: Paul H. Brookes Publishing Co.; adapted by permission.

Table 11.4. Facilitation strategies that can be used by educators, paraprofessionals, and job coaches

- Modeling ways for students with and without disabilities to initiate, maintain, and extend conversations with each other
- Demonstrating to peers how to converse with someone who uses an augmentative and alternative communication system
- Highlighting interests, strengths, and experiences shared among students
- Teaching critical social interaction skills (e.g., initiating a conversation, greeting classmates, requesting help, refusing support) and encouraging their regular use
- Redirecting peers' questions and comments away from the adult and to the student with disabilities (and vice versa)
- Interpreting the communicative intent of challenging or nonverbal (e.g., expressions, gestures, signs) behaviors and suggesting appropriate responses to those behaviors
- Highlighting students' strengths and contributions to small-group and other projects
- Assigning classroom responsibilities requiring frequent interaction, such as small-group assignments, cooperative projects, or activities that involve joint responsibilities
- Relocating students so they work together and remain in close physical and social proximity to one another
- Asking other peers to provide occasional support as needed

From Carter, E.W. (2011). Supporting peer relationships. In SNELL, MARTHA E.; BROWN, FREDDA, INSTRUCTION OF STUDENTS WITH SEVERE DISABILITIES, 7th Edition, © 2011, pp. 446-447. Adapted by permission of Pearson Education, Inc., Upper Saddle River, NJ.

their classmates with disabilities (e.g., providing academic and/or social support), the contexts within which interactions will take place (e.g., classrooms, clubs, cafeterias, and/or community-based locations), and whether and how students will be matched with one another. In addition to clarifying how information will be exchanged among participating educators, paraprofessionals, and other school staff (e.g., school counselors, administrators), the manner in which these expectations will be communicated with participating students should also be determined.

Although some students will naturally work well with one another right from the outset, most students will benefit from receiving some initial information and guidance related to their new roles. Therefore, peer support programs typically incorporate an initial orientation session for peers (Bond & Castagnera, 2006; Longwill & Kleinert, 1998). Often held before or after school, during a free period, or over lunch, these sessions offer an important vehicle through which new expectations are communicated to peers. Moreover, these sessions can increase students' confidence and competence as they provide social and/or academic support.

Teachers will have initial ideas about the settings and activities within which students with and without disabilities will interact with and support one another. Therefore, the information and strategies that are addressed during orientation sessions should be tailored to prepare students well for those specific contexts. At the same time, there are some common issues that may be beneficial to address with participating students. For example, students may benefit from learning about (Carter, Cushing, & Kennedy, 2009; Hughes & Carter, 2008)

- The rationale for involving peers in providing support to their classmates with disabilities
- Basic information regarding their partner's interests, hobbies, talents, and school involvement
- The broad educational and/or social goals of their partner
- The importance of maintaining confidentiality and respecting privacy
- Basic support strategies and instructional procedures (e.g., modeling, prompting, providing effective feedback)
- Ways to interact with students who use specialized technology or augmentative or alternative communication systems
- Strategies for motivating and encouraging their partners

- Ideas for promoting greater participation and increasing interactions with other peers
- When to seek assistance from teachers or paraprofessionals
- Any additional responsibilities and expectations specific to their roles

These initial orientation sessions set the tone for how students will interact with one another throughout the year. By communicating high expectations and emphasizing reciprocal relationships, teachers can play a key role in helping new relationships launch well.

Supporting Students to Interact and Learn Together

When students with and without disabilities first begin working together, they will benefit from having access to ongoing support and encouragement from school staff. Indeed, active monitoring and regular feedback by school staff can be instrumental to students' early success. Therefore, teachers should establish regular times to observe as students work together, share constructive feedback and recommendations, and solicit suggestions for improving the program. These observations should focus on identifying what is working well and determining areas in which students would benefit from additional clarification, information, and/or support.

Students will also benefit from receiving clear guidance on how to support their partner with disabilities in the school or community settings in which they will be participating. The supports students provide to one another are usually very individualized, ranging from intermittent to ongoing, from very informal to highly directed. For example, peers may provide supports aimed at fostering social interactions (e.g., starting conversations, making introductions to other classmates or co-workers, talking about common interests during a break), communication (e.g., modeling setting-specific social skills, reinforcing communication device use), active engagement (e.g., sharing class materials, teaching self-directed learning strategies), and/or learning (e.g., reviewing homework, completing group assignments, discussing key concepts, mastering job-related responsibilities). The supports should be determined on the basis of the needs of the participating students with disabilities and the school or community settings in which they are involved together.

Although orientation sessions are typically held toward the beginning of the school year, students may benefit from meeting periodically with teachers—as well as other peer supports—as they accrue experience working with their partners. Students with disabilities and their peers often encounter new challenges as the semester progresses and new activities, projects, and classes are introduced. Providing students with regular opportunities to talk about their experiences, discuss their concerns, and problem-solve challenges can be important to sustaining their involvement. For example, our peer buddy program developed and distributed handbooks containing written resources (e.g., information about specific disabilities, readings about key issues in the lives of people with disabilities, ideas for shared activities, relevant program forms) that participating students can draw upon as needed throughout the semester (Hughes & Carter, 2008). Teachers may also ask students to keep reflection journals or complete written assignments as a vehicle for sharing their perspectives on the impact of the experience.

Sustaining and Expanding a Program

As with any school-based transition program, it is essential to thoughtfully reflect on the extent to which a peer support program is meeting the goals it was initially designed to accomplish. Investing time evaluating the impact of a program on participating students and the broader school community can inform efforts to further refine and strengthen the program. Moreover, documenting the ways in which students are benefiting from their involvement can provide additional support for expanding the program to other settings or additional students. Multiple approaches can be incorporated into evaluation efforts, including surveying or interviewing students with and without disabilities who are involved in the program, observing students as they interact with one another in classrooms and other activities, soliciting feedback from participating school staff, having conversations with family members, and examining changes in the school and community participation of students with disabilities.

As initial success is demonstrated, attention can shift toward broadening the reach of the program. Establishing a program advisory board composed of multiple stakeholders (e.g., general and special educators, school counselors, paraprofessionals, club sponsors, parents) can provide much-needed support, feedback, and guidance as expansion efforts are undertaken (Hughes & Carter, 2008). This group might meet one time per semester to discuss strategies for strengthening student recruitment efforts, revising the program handbook, expanding inclusive opportunities at the school, and/or supporting the development of relationships that extend beyond the school day.

Promoting Social Skills and Relationships Across Settings

In addition to the connections available through formal peer support programs, educators and other school staff can take active steps to promote their students' social development and participation across the range of settings in which transition-age students typically spend their days.

Inclusive Classrooms

Although general education classes typically provide frequent opportunities for students with and without disabilities to meet, interact, and work with one another, ensuring that students with disabilities benefit maximally from these opportunities can be challenging. Some students will benefit from explicit instruction on social skills that enhance their ability to work well within cooperative groups, interact effectively with teachers, or request help from peers. Teaching students strategies to self-direct their own social behavior and learning (e.g., self-instruction, self-monitoring) can also promote greater independence and encourage generalized use of important social skills (Carter, Lane, Crnobori, Bruhn, & Oakes, 2011; Hughes et al., 2000, 2004). At the same time, educators and paraprofessionals can embed regular opportunities for students to work with one another through cooperative learning groups, peer-assisted learning strategies, and small-group projects.

For students with more significant disabilities, classroom-based peer support arrangements offer a viable and effective approach for encouraging students to work more closely with their peers during ongoing classroom activities. As with broader peer support programs, peer support arrangements in inclusive classrooms also require identifying students with and without disabilities who might benefit from working together, orienting students to their roles and responsibilities, structuring ongoing opportunities for students to sit next to and interact with one another, and providing regular feedback and support to students as they work together. In addition to exchanging myriad social and academic supports (Table 11.5), students benefit from additional opportunities to meet and get to know additional classmates.

Extracurricular and Noninstructional Activities

Although students spend the majority of the school day in classrooms, much of adolescents' social lives and connections focus on the times when students travel the hallways between classes, visit their lockers, hang out before and after school, or eat lunch together.

Table 11.5. Examples of supports students with and without disabilities might provide one another in inclusive classrooms

Academic-related supports
- Helping check the accuracy of assignments
- Sharing or assisting in taking notes
- Sharing class materials other than notes
- Paraphrasing lectures or class discussions
- Prompting the student to answer a question or idea
- Explaining a key concept or how to solve a problem
- Writing down answers given orally or using augmentative and alternative communication systems
- Providing instruction on completing tasks
- Reviewing class content to ensure understanding
- Helping the student participate in group activity
- Encouraging the student for academic successes
- Reading aloud a section of a book or assignment
- Redirecting the student when he or she is off-task
- Helping the student keep organized

Social-related supports
- Encouraging the student to interact with other classmates
- Drawing other classmates into conversations with the student
- Explicitly teaching specific social-related skills
- Prompting use of an aided communication device
- Reinforcing social or communication attempts
- Providing emotional support or giving advice

Other supports
- Helping the student self-manage his or her own behavior
- Explaining and/or demonstrating specific classroom rules
- Explaining the class schedule and upcoming activities

From Efficacy and social validity of peer support interventions for high school students with severe disabilities by Carter, E.W., Moss, C.K., Hoffman, A., Chung, Y., & Sisco, L.G., *Exceptional Children*, in press. Copyright 2012 by The Council for Exceptional Children. Reprinted with permission.

These relatively unstructured segments of school can be rich with social opportunities for some students but times of considerable isolation for others (Hughes et al., 1999). Organizing informal gatherings of students during lunch, breaks, or other times of day can encourage new relationships and promote a sense of belonging among students (Hughes & Carter, 2008). For example, lunch groups can be arranged by a teacher, who initially invites a core group of students with and without disabilities to participate. As students get to know one another, they assume increasing responsibility for sustaining the group and inviting new members.

Extracurricular clubs and other school-sponsored activities also provide a natural venue for promoting social connections within inclusive settings. Because most activities are structured around a core set of shared activities (e.g., fine arts, hobbies, social activism), students are more likely to meet and spend time with peers who share similar interests. To promote meaningful participation in inclusive extracurricular activities, Carter, Swedeen, Moss, and Pesko (2010) recommend that IEP planning teams work to

a. Identify existing opportunities that align with students' interests and strengths

b. Teach students the skills and information they need to participate in meaningful ways

c. Prepare peers and program leaders to support the involvement of students with disabilities

d. Collaborate with family members to address logistical issues such as transportation and fees

e. Evaluate the extent to which students' participation is contributing to desired outcomes

Community and Workplace Settings

Even when students spend a substantial portion of their time off campus in work or community contexts, peers can still be involved in providing social-related instruction and support to students with disabilities. For example, students with disabilities can access support from peer mentors to learn work-related tasks at community-based sites (Westerlund, Granucci, Gamache, & Clark, 2006), from peers with disabilities who are participating in job or self-advocacy clubs (Lindstrom, Benz, & Johnson, 1996), or from peer supports during off-campus field trips, service activities, or other learning opportunities. Arranging for peers and co-workers to provide certain support may actually be less stigmatizing for some youth than always having service providers present.

College Campuses

As postsecondary education becomes a viable option for increasing numbers of students with significant disabilities, ensuring youth are prepared socially for learning and life on a college campus can be an important focus of transition education. Students may benefit from social skills instruction addressing the social expectations, pressures, and opportunities students will encounter on campus (Grigal & Hart, 2010b; Zager & Alpern, 2010). For students with intellectual and developmental disabilities, established friendship and mentorship programs such as Best Buddies can provide some of the supports and connections youth need to participate fully and flourish socially in college.

Designing Quality Instruction and Effective Supports

The previous sections of this chapter addressed the range of student-, peer-, and support-focused interventions that transition teachers might draw upon to improve the social competence, participation, and relationships of their students with disabilities. However, one hallmark feature of special education and transition services is its emphasis on individualization. The social-related skills, experiences, and supports that will be instrumental for one student may look quite different from those that should be emphasized for another. Likewise, the social expectations that any particular student encounters can vary from one setting to the next. Therefore, it is important to carefully align intervention efforts with students' individualized needs in particular transition contexts (Hughes & Carter, 2002). In short, these determinations can be made by obtaining answers to a series of key questions:

- What skills and relationships contribute to success and satisfaction in a particular school, work, or community setting?
- Which of these skills and relationships will the student with disabilities need help developing?
- Should interventions focus on providing instruction, developing supports, or both?
- Do intervention efforts lead to noticeable improvements in the student's social outcomes and participation?

Identifying Important Skills and Relationships

As students with disabilities progress through middle and high school, they encounter an increasingly diverse range of instructional settings. For example, high school students may take as many as eight different academic, vocational, or elective classes in a given semester; become involved in any number of extracurricular clubs, sports, fine arts, or service activities; receive community-based instruction for part of their day; and/or hold an after-school or on-campus job. As the range of contexts within which students spend their days expands, so too does the array of social-related expectations they will encounter. Although certain social skills have broad relevance across different school and community settings, there may also be setting-specific skills that are essential for students to learn. Likewise, the range of individuals with whom youth are expected to successfully interact and develop relationships (e.g., service providers, work supervisors, co-workers, customers, and community members) also broadens as time spent outside the classroom increases.

Identifying those skills and relationships that are especially salient to success in the specific school, work, or community settings in which a student is currently involved—or in which the student will eventually participate after leaving high school—is an essential step when one is designing socially valid interventions (Hughes et al., 1998). By determining which particular skills and relationships are most valued by key people in a given setting, instruction and support can be focused on those areas most likely to enhance a student's participation. Consideration of these issues can also help teachers avoid losing valuable instructional time focusing on teaching skills that are not critical for students to possess.

Several strategies can be used to identify those skills and relationships important in a particular setting. The research literature includes a number of studies in which key social-related competencies already have been validated by teachers, employers, peers, and others (e.g., Hughes et al., 1998; Lane et al., 2004). Such studies can provide teachers with some insight into the types of social skills that may be highly valued in certain settings. For example, Lane, Wehby, and Cooley (2006) surveyed more than 700 general and special educators and found that teachers ascribed different levels of importance to classroom social behavior depending on the type of setting (i.e., general versus special education), school level (i.e., elementary versus secondary), and type of school in which they taught (i.e., high-risk versus low-risk school). Likewise, Carter and Wehby (2003) asked local employers to evaluate the importance of 30 social-related behaviors (e.g., accepting constructive criticism from a supervisor, asking a co-worker for assistance when needed, offering compliments to others) to success on the job for adolescents employed at their business. Although findings from studies such as these can be instructive, it is still necessary to verify such findings locally in the settings in which students are participating. Conversations with key individuals within these settings can confirm which of these (or other) skills are most directly linked to success. For example, a teacher might interview a shift supervisor to identify which customer service skills are highly valued at a local restaurant, a coach about the collaboration skills that enhance participation on a sports team, or a volunteer coordinator about the interpersonal skills that are required for a long-term community service project. In addition, spending time directly observing in these classroom and community settings can provide teachers with first-hand insights into the types of skills and relationships that can contribute to a student's success (Hughes et al., 1998).

Assessing the Social-Related Needs of Students

The transition mandates within the Individuals with Disabilities Education Improvement Act Amendments of 2004 (PL 105-17) place strong emphasis on the important role of assessment in secondary education. Aligning instruction and delivery with students' needs is an essential element of designing effective and efficient intervention strategies. As with other transition domains, social-related interventions should focus on building students' capacities in ways that will enhance their attainment of short- and long-term goals.

Formal Approaches

A number of formal assessments can be used to evaluate the social-related strengths and needs of secondary students (e.g., Bullis & Davis, 1996; Gresham & Elliott, 2008). Such tools can provide insights into how a student's social skills and challenging behaviors compare with those of other similar-age peers or to certain expected criteria. Because teachers, family members, and others who interact with a student may hold divergent views regarding his or her social competence, it is helpful to solicit multiple perspectives when gathering assessment information (Carter, Trainor, Sun, & Owens, 2009; Renk & Phares, 2004).

Informal Approaches

Informal assessments, however, can be developed or tailored to provide more targeted and contextualized information about specific social-related skills that may be important to a student's success in a particular setting (Black & Ornelles, 2001; Hughes & Carter, 2002). Because the appropriateness of social behavior is heavily dependent on context, it is important to consider assessment findings alongside key skills identified in the previous step. Observing students as they participate in everyday school and community activities provides perhaps the most direct assessment of the extent to which students possess the skills that promote participation and relationships that enhance belonging. Such observations might focus on the quantity and quality of interactions with peers, co-workers, supervisors, or other key participants as well as on identifying potential social supports that may be drawn upon by the student. When such observations are not feasible, interviews with others who participate in or lead specific school and community activities can provide informative perspectives on the degree to which students are meeting the social expectations associated with a setting. In addition, conversations with youth themselves can provide important information about the source of students' social difficulties and the skills and relationships they want to develop. Checklists, rating scales, and questionnaires can be distributed to individuals who know the student well to solicit their feedback on behaviors and relationships that may be difficult to observe directly. Finally, social network assessments can be used to ascertain whether youth have access to needed social supports and to identify those relationships that students would benefit from developing and/or deepening (Kef & Dekovic, 2004; Kennedy, 2004).

Providing Instruction and/or Developing Social Supports

The social-related needs of youth with disabilities are often multifaceted, and myriad barriers to the development of supportive peer relationships can exist in schools and communities. As a result, many students will benefit from comprehensive intervention approaches that combine multiple elements of these student-, peer-, and support-focused strategies. Although social and communication skill instruction holds strong potential to improve the quantity and quality of students' interactions, few interactions are likely to occur if peers are hesitant to start a conversation or infrequent interaction opportunities exist. Likewise, even when students with disabilities are actively involved in inclusive classrooms, workplaces, and other settings rich with social opportunities, interactions can be limited if students are not taught essential social and communication skills (Hughes et al., 1999, 2000). Focusing on any single area to the exclusion of others risks neglecting the important contributions that social competence, peers, and context can collectively make to social development and satisfactory relationships.

Research indicates that social skills instruction and the provision of social-related supports are most effective when carefully matched to a student's individualized needs and taught in actual settings (Alwell & Cobb, 2009b; Carter & Hughes, 2007). Although many packaged social skills training interventions are designed to address the range of social-related challenges adolescents with disabilities might encounter, this breadth may not adequately address a particular student's most pressing areas of instructional need. Therefore, intervention efforts should be directed toward the convergence of valued skills and student's individualized needs.

Evaluating Students' Progress and Outcomes

Regularly collecting data is critical to determining whether educational interventions and supports are having the intended impact. Many of the approaches used to assess the social-related needs of students can be drawn upon to document their progress. For example, formal and informal assessments can be administered again to gauge progress, observations can focus on changes in the students' interactions with others, and interviews can be conducted with others in a setting to capture whether and how intervention efforts might be strengthened.

Conclusion

The relationships youth have with their peers and others can provide an important source of support and satisfaction as they transition to adulthood. Moreover, the social and communication skills students demonstrate can have an impact on their participation and success in a host of school and community activities. This chapter synthesized evidence-based and promising practices for enhancing the social competence and social lives of youth and young adults with disabilities. For practitioners committed to meeting the multifaceted needs of these youth, addressing the social dimension of the lives of students with disabilities is an essential element of comprehensive transition programming.

Study Questions

1. What are three categories of approaches to social-related intervention? How are these approaches similar and different in their focus and approach?

2. Describe the types of supports students with and without disabilities provide one another within peer support programs and other peer-focused interventions. How might these supports differ across school and community settings?

3. In what ways might students without disabilities benefit from involvement in the interventions described in this chapter?

4. What steps are involved in establishing and sustaining a peer support program in a high school?

5. What approaches should be used to assess the social-related intervention needs of youth with disabilities?

Online Resources

LD Online: http://www.ldonline.org/article/Teaching_Social_Skills_to_Kids_Who_Don't_Yet_Have_Them

National Association of School Psychologists resources:
http://www.nasponline.org/resources/factsheets/socialskills_fs.aspx

Teacher Vision: Popular resources on social skills:
http://www.teachervision.fen.com/interpersonal-skills/resource/55817.html?detoured=1

Center for Implementing Technology in Education: Multimedia instruction on social skills:
http://www.cited.org/index.aspx?page_id=154

IV

Work and Life in the Community

Using Technology from School to Adulthood

Unleashing the Power

AMY J. ARMSTRONG, TONY GENTRY,
AND PAUL WEHMAN

12

After completing this chapter, the reader will be able to

- Examine the impact assistive technology (AT) may have on the quality of life of individuals with disabilities

- Recognize types of AT that enable access to computers and cell phones and how it can be used as a cognitive–behavioral aid

- Describe the roles of the consumer and the AT professional in choosing AT devices and services

- Discuss the benefits of a team-oriented approach to selecting AT devices and services

- Discuss the terms AT abandonment and discontinuance

- Become familiar with factors associated with AT device discontinuance

- Evaluate the holistic nature associated with using AT applications in multiple environments

Impact of Assistive Technology on Quality of Life

From the moment an alarm clock wakes us in the morning, our lives are filled with technology intended to make life easier, richer, and more convenient. Eyeglasses, microwave ovens, cars, computers, cell phones, and TV sets are just some of the technologies that surround us. It is a very small step from our device-driven milieu to the world of AT, which is defined by the federal Assistive Technology Act (ATA; PL 108-364) as "any item, piece of equipment or product system, whether acquired commercially off the shelf, modified, or customized, that is used to increase, maintain, or improve functional capabilities of individuals with disabilities" (2004, p. 4). We think of AT as a collection of devices designed specifically for people with physiological impairments, intended to help level the playing field with people who do not have disabilities; but, in fact, all technologies—from a pencil and paper to a robot—are assistive and address everyday functional challenges that we all face.

As defined by the ATA, AT may be seen as an additional tool set designed specifically for people with disabilities—such as wheelchairs and prosthetic limbs—or as an overlay of devices that allow access to all of the other technologies that fill our lives. This type of AT may include specialized switches for computer access, voice-controlled cell phones, electronic aids to daily living, and behavioral management applications on a personal digital assistant (PDA), among many others. However we define them, the lines between everyday technologies and ATs are rapidly blurring. In practice, people use a mix of technologies; as service providers, it is important to recognize this fact and consider how best to encourage a wide-ranging exploration and adoption of appropriate technologies to address functional challenges for all of the people we serve.

The absence of technology to the individual without a disability becomes a nuisance that affects *perceived* quality of life. The absence of technology to an individual with a disability is a blow to one's quality of life that can increase dependence. Thus, the acquisition of appropriate AT by a person with a disability increases independence, inclusion, employability, and often access to environments such as college classrooms (Roberts & Stodden, 2005). Radabaugh states that: "For Americans without disabilities, technology makes things easier. For Americans with disabilities, technology makes things possible" (n.d., p. 1).

The convenience distinction is apparent when speaking of AT and individuals with disabilities (users). It is *not* convenience in the sense of comforts and amenities, but convenience in the sense of freedom and accessibility. AT, although perhaps not completely leveling the playing field for many users, does close the gap by increasing quality of life possibilities. Users typically experience greater physical accessibility and accessibility to integrated employment (Morgan, 2003; Morgan & Ellerd, 2005) as well as enhancement of their social skills (Simpson, Langone, & Ayres, 2004).

Anna   Anna is an 18-year-old student who experienced a moderate traumatic brain injury in a fall from a cheerleading pyramid as a high school senior. She missed the second semester of her senior year undergoing physical rehabilitation, so she is taking courses at a local junior college in order to graduate. Anna must now deal with a visual field deficit that makes reading difficult, a tremor in her dominant right hand, and attention difficulties that make schoolwork a challenge.

Anna's junior college guidance counselor referred her to a speech therapist who set up special software on her laptop computer to assist with schoolwork. An application called *Soundnote* records lectures and attaches them to Anna's scribbled notes. At home, Anna can quickly move through her lecture notes and review exactly what the teacher said. Because her visual deficit and tremor make typing challenging, Anna relies heavily on the word prediction and spell checking accessibility features of her computer, especially when typing long papers. She drags onscreen text to one side of her computer screen, so it stays within her visual field. Instead of thumb-tapping, she uses a smartphone-based speech-to-text program called *Shoutout* to record and send text messages to friends.

On weekends, Anna has begun working part-time at a local library. At this job, she wears prism glasses that have been custom-fitted by a neurooptometrist. The glasses adjust her visual field so she can negotiate the library stacks safely and find books there. For Anna to overcome her tremor when checking out books, her **occupational therapist (OT)** has taught her to use a weighted pen and to support her elbow on a table. The OT also recommended a number of task organization applications for her Android smartphone. "Remember the Milk" is both a to-do list and reminder application that helps her schedule activities and stay on task during her day. She has included alarms for her medications, work breaks, and homework, and has learned to add in things that she used to remember easily, such as meet-ups with friends. Anna does not see these tools as "assistive technology." She says, "Everybody uses things like this every day. It's just part of the air we all breathe, and if it helps, why not?"

AT may be used in all aspects of a person's life—at home, school, work, and in social and recreational settings. Technology can be extremely empowering, resulting in enhanced participation and access. For example, adaptive driving equipment on a van can make transportation to the workplace possible. Mobility equipment, such as a power scooter, can make employment a reality. Devices that assist in daily living skills such as food preparation and hygiene impact independent living. Using these devices to maximize independent living is a necessary first step to community inclusion and employability. With this interdependence acknowledged, this chapter focuses on AT from the user's perspective in the arena of employment. AT most often refers to low- and high-technology devices and related services that support an individual with a disability, thereby increasing independence. The chapter also provides specific examples of computer applications and handheld devices.

The promise of technology has never been greater, and its impact is enormous. The challenge is not only to harness the promise of technology but also to anticipate the advances in technology that will create new opportunities to develop and adapt devices to guide and direct individuals with disabilities through their daily activities. Medical technology will allow individuals to live longer. Internet technology will make information readily and quickly available. Internet-based distance learning will make training and education available for everyone, anywhere, at any time, and at low cost.

Advances in technology also offer concerns. As the Internet is increasingly viewed as a repository of information and a social network linking users worldwide, a lack of access limits opportunities for learning, employment, and social interaction. It is extremely important to monitor advances in technology to ensure that they are accessible to all people, whatever their abilities. Everyone who works to support people with disabilities and their families must remain sensitive to technology gaps and avoid presumptions about ready access to technological advances. Among the emerging issues related to advances in technology are

- The designers of emerging technologies must take into account universal design for learning principles that guarantee access to their products by the widest possible user base, whatever their functional abilities.

- Clinicians and educators must scramble to keep up with new technologies to provide appropriate AT for the people they serve.

- Rapid evolution of technologies leads to product obsolescence that can leave users without the financial means or wherewithal to maintain, upgrade, or replace currently used AT.

- Enormous gaps exist between the rich and the poor in access to AT, and this gap is especially glaring in developing nations.

- Insurance companies, school systems, and other third-party payers are often slow to recognize and provide emerging AT.

- Increased use of database technology threatens many people's sense of personal privacy.

- Advances in medical technology raise questions about our standards for their application with people with intellectual and developmental disabilities and the relative value of human lives.

- As a relatively "small market," developing and adapting technology for the needs of people with intellectual and developmental disabilities may need more than just the incentives of the "marketplace."

Employment and Assistive Technology

A critical aspect of transition from school to adult life is locating and retaining competitive employment. The U.S. Bureau of Labor Statistics (2009) reports that total employment is projected to increase by 15.3 million, or 10.1%, during the 2008–2018 period. However, in spite of this growth, according to the Kessler Foundation and National Organization of Disability report:

> [T]he environment for hiring people with disabilities needs a great deal of improvement. Although corporations recognize that hiring employees with disabilities is important and, for the most part, do not perceive the costs of hiring people with disabilities to be prohibitive, most are not hiring many people with disabilities and few are proactively making efforts to improve the employment environment for them. (2010, p. 6)

Often, for an individual with a disability, a primary barrier to becoming and staying employed is access to, and availability of, AT. Such technology strives to level the playing field in terms of integration and production at the worksite (Carey, Potts, Bryen, & Shankar, 2004). For people with physical disabilities, the term *jobsite enabling* is used to describe the process of bringing together AT and other factors such as specialized training, ongoing support, and advocacy in the workplace (Targett & Wehman, 2003). Jobsite enabling may involve the negotiation of job duties or requirements, environmental modification, the use of co-workers and personal assistants, or any combination of these and other factors. Therefore, it is imperative to note that, albeit important, AT is merely one of many factors involved in placing an individual in a work environment where he or she can become successfully employed.

Identifying appropriate physical or social solutions (Carey, Potts, et al., 2004) is paramount and may include raising a desk or table for a worker with a power wheelchair, changing auditory signals such as a fire alarm to a visual cue of a flashing light or a tactile cue of a vibration, adjusting the slant of a computer keyboard, adding a guiding mechanism onto the paper tray of a copier or braille next to the copier buttons or adding a keyboard guide, providing a grounded desktop stamper with a lever for dating invoices received, using jigs for counting items, using a carrying unit for supplies, using existing equipment such as a head pointer to type or a writing splint, using a lap board to carry supplies, using print magnification devices, using a telecommunications device for the deaf, or using a shoulder telephone rest. Vocational training and effective use of AT go hand in hand. Training increases a person's knowledge; however, AT gives people the opportunity to practically use that knowledge.

Before seeking employment, the individual with a disability and professionals working with him or her should have some concept of needed technology. That is, need(s) can be anticipated. Such anticipation is useful when one is looking at specific jobs and tasks or closely examining the educational requirements in a 2- or 4-year college classroom (Sharpe, Johnson, Izzo, & Murray, 2005). Sharpe et al. used a structured interview approach in which 139 postsecondary graduates were asked to identify instructional accommodations and ATs provided to them in secondary and postsecondary settings. Findings of this study showed that, generally, instructional accommodations and ATs are provided at much higher rates at the postsecondary level. With regard to users of AT, the majority of graduates indicated that they gained access to and learned to use the technology by themselves or with the help of family members. The user of AT must constantly represent his or her respective need(s) and suggestions for possible worksite solutions. To do this, it is helpful to become familiar with legislation, advocacy skills, technology options, and strategies for using a team approach to acquire AT. Evaluating AT needs in order to procure devices and services is discussed later in the chapter.

Computer and Assistive Technology Utilization

Computers have been touted as a "great equalizer" for competitive employment (National Council on Disability, 2009). They play an ever-increasing role in our daily lives for activities such as work, socialization, research, communication, and daily living activities. Competence in the use of computers (i.e., information technology skills) is a prerequisite for postsecondary education as well as most occupations to include food service and auto repair to engineering, medicine, and law among others (Izzo, McArrell, Yurick, & Murray, 2010). It is hard to imagine a student graduating from college today without basic computer competence. In addition, the U.S. Department of Labor reports that 13–19 million Americans now telecommute at some level in a wide array of positions such as typists, database management, sales, marketing, and accountants (West & Anderson, 2005). Many of these positions require some degree of computer and telephone utilization. Telecommuting may help reduce potential barriers such as inaccessible worksites, transportation, and need for personal care assistance by allowing individuals to work from their home.

Unfortunately, people with disabilities are less likely to own cell phones (Tobias, 2003) and computers and are likely to have less access to the Internet than people without disabilities (Kaye, 2000).

A recent Pew report (Fox, 2011) states that one in four American adults live with a disability that interferes with activities of daily living. Fifty-four percent of adults living with a disability use the Internet, compared with 81% of adults who report no disability. Two percent of American adults indicate that they have a disability or illness that makes it harder or impossible for them to use the Internet (Fox, 2011). It seems that, although people with disabilities have the most to gain from new technologies and computer use, they have among the lowest utilization rates. The Pew report (Fox, 2011) indicates that 43% of Americans say that people who do not have the Internet at home are at a major disadvantage when it comes to finding out about job opportunities or learning career skills. The potential benefits of computers and the Internet to those within the disability community are a long way from being adequately realized because of lower rates of access and utilization (Mechling & Ortega-Hurndon, 2007).

Reported barriers may include funding issues, lack of awareness of accessibility adaptations, a shortage of AT professionals qualified to provide AT and train consumers, and the constant evolution of computer products, which makes devices and adaptations quickly obsolete (Burgstahler & Comden, 2011). Many web sites do not follow Internet accessibility guidelines, making job search and employment-related web searches challenging. For all of these reasons, people with disabilities may find fewer computer-related job opportunities than others, despite the fact that technologies exist to make computers and cell phones accessible for people with disabilities.

Assistive Technologies for Computer and Cell Phone Access

For people with sensory, motor, intellectual, or cognitive disability, access to computers may require adaptation. The cost of AT for computer access ranges from very little to thousands of dollars, depending on individual needs and budget constraints; however, the long-term benefit of such expenditures may be significant in terms of employment opportunity and retention (Roberts & Stodden, 2005; Sharpe et al., 2005). As cell phones, PDAs, and tablet computers become more powerful, portable, and ubiquitous, their importance to community integration and success at work grows. For people with disabilities, however, access to portable communication and computing devices poses both opportunities and challenges. For instance, videophonic capabilities on many smartphones allow instant audiovisual communication between worker and employer at a distance, but a worker with a mobility impairment may find this feature inaccessible because of the design characteristics of current devices.

Fortunately, since their creation, computers have incorporated accessibility features (and new hardware and software adaptations are introduced each year) so that people with disabilities can utilize these tools at school and at work. In a similar way, cell phones have begun to incorporate universal design for learning principles that may include options such as voice control and talking screens. The burgeoning variety of smartphone applications that support work-related activities such as communication, wayfinding, task management, image and document sharing, and behavioral adaptation allows for robust computer functionality in a user's pocket at home or in the community.

Computers, cell phones, PDAs, and tablets offer a wealth of onboard accessibility tools (Table 12.1). These may include screen readers, speech-to-text translators, screen magnification, vibrating or flashing alarms, virtual keyboards, "sticky key" and "slow key" keystroke and mouse controls, and input access for switches and adapted keyboards. Computer accessibility features are managed through the Control Panel on Windows PCs and through the Preferences Menu on Apple devices. Apple iPhone, iPod Touch, and iPad accessibility features are reached in the Settings menu (see Figure 12.1).

Computers and portable devices, word processing, electronic book, and e-mail programs may include word completion, spell check, instant dictionaries, and other

Table 12.1. Assistive technologies for computer and cell phone access and utilization

Impairment	Solution	PC/Mac technology	Cell phone technology
Impaired vision	Screen magnification; white-on-black text	Basic feature in PC and Mac accessibility set; ZoomText fully featured software	Basic feature in Apple iPhone/iPod Touch/iPad accessibility set; Electro-Optix magnifier overlay
Blind	Text-to-speech screen reader, identifies onscreen objects and speaks description or reads text	Basic feature in PC and Mac accessibility set; EdBrowse fully featured software (free); JAWS advanced-feature software	VoiceOver screen reader is a basic feature in Apple iPhone/iPod Touch/iPad accessibility set; various open-source Android screen readers
Blind	Braille reading/writing	Bluetooth or USB braille keyboard linked to accessibility feature set of Mac or PC; braille text translator software	Bluetooth-enabled braille terminal linked to Apple iPhone/iPod Touch/iPad; various open-source Android braille drivers; MoneyReader application for devices with cameras

(continued)

Table 12.1. *(continued)*

Impairment	Solution	PC/Mac technology	Cell phone technology
Deaf	Text messaging; videophone calls for signing; video relay service; vibrating reminder alarms; flashing screen messages	E-mail; instant messaging; Mac iChat, Facetime, or Skype videophone signing; video relay service; onscreen pop-up calendar reminder	Text-messaging; Apple FaceTime or Skype videophone face-to-face signing; video relay service (deaf to hearing calls); vibrating reminder alarms for cell phone
Impaired speech	Text-to-speech products; augmentative communication tools	Text reader is basic feature in PC and Mac accessibility set; Proloquo for Mac is a fully featured augmentative communication software	Applications for Apple and Android devices include Proloquo2Go, Voice4u, Speakit!, TalkAssist
Impaired mobility	Options for adapted mouse; alternative keyboard; mouthstick; head/eye-gaze/sip-n-puff/muscle twitch/voice-controlled screen cursor and mouse	Trackball mouse, button switch, Mouthstick, keyguard, and accessibility options on Mac or PC Naturalpoint SmartNav head tracking system; LC Technologies, Inc. Eyegaze Edge eye-control mouse; Lipsync L4 sip-n-puff mouse; Nuance Dragon Naturally Speaking voice control	Vocalize! voice-control cell phone with wheelchair setup kit; voice-control features on many basic cell phones (requires button or screen tap to initiate feature); Dragon Dictate or Vlingo applications for text messaging and web search

Figure 12.1. Three popular computer mouse access options for people with mobility impairments: A) Quadmouse with chin, lip, or tongue control; B) NaturalPoint SmartNav with head movement control; and C) Jouse 2 Joystick Sip-n-Puff with mouth-controlled drag-and-drop.

content-enabling features (Hartmann, Post, & Gardner, 2010). Communication features such as text messaging and videophonic chat work well for many people with hearing impairment, as do voice mail, speech-to-text generators, and talking screens among people with visual impairment.

Computer add-on technologies for text input include expanded or oversized keyboards, such as BigKeys and IntelliKeys, along with customized keyguard overlays. Mouse substitutes include trackballs, joysticks, and touch screens. The head pointers and mouth sticks often used by people with severe motoric impairment have recently been supplemented by electronic head pointers (such as the SmartNav and TrackerPro), eye-gaze mouse controls (such as Advanced Multimedia Devices, Inc.'s My Tobii and LC Technologies International, Inc.'s Eyegaze Edge), and sip-and-puff switches (such as the Quad-Joy) linked to onscreen virtual keyboards (Kurtz, 2011). Efforts are under way to expand add-on capabilities to portable devices. Switches such as R.J. Cooper's BIG iPod Remote allow button switch control of iPod music players, and the Vocalize! system allows voice control of cell phone functions (for any phone that supports the Bluetooth "hands-free" profile) without requiring the tap of any button. The iPhone's latest accessibility feature, Assistive Touch, allows individuals with motor control challenges (i.e., limited fine motor skills or dexterity) to access features without requiring hand or multiple finger movements (Pogue, 2011). An individual can create and define his or her own gestures to include a palette of two, three, four, or five fingers. The preferred gesture is then saved so that users may zoom in or out of web pages, photos, maps, and so forth (Pogue, 2011). The iPhone is now usable for people with vision, hearing, and kinetic impairments. Keyguard overlays for onscreen phone and tablet keyboards are useful for people with dexterity or visual impairments. Downloadable applications for PDAs, cell phones, and tablets allow users to build customized and highly portable toolkits of supportive technologies. These include money readers, Global Positioning System (GPS) maps, person locators, augmentative communication products, automated behavioral management coaches, and multifeatured reminder and task management planners, among others. Many of these applications are free or inexpensive and, in some cases, have supplanted bulky, exorbitantly priced, free-standing products.

The use of Internet browsers and e-mail programs can prove daunting for many people with intellectual or cognitive impairments. Products such as AbleLink's Web Trek and Endeavor Email provide a simplified, icon-based computer interface that can be customized for individual needs. With the right set of onboard and add-on features, nearly everyone can access computers and cell phones. Unfortunately, however, many people with disabilities are unaware of these tools or do not know how they work (Dell, Newton, & Petroff, 2008).

Because each person's needs and preferences vary, and because the range of computer and telephone AT features is so large, a computer and cell phone accommodation evaluation by an OT or another AT practitioner is recommended to properly fit the right technology to each user.

Computer accommodation evaluations can assist individuals with disabilities to gain access to computers for educational, vocational, and other activities of daily living needs. This evaluation process should be designed to identify effective ATs and software for full computer accessibility. Appropriate computer evaluation includes computer access capabilities, computer/hardware options, workstation evaluations, and school-/office-related tasks (e.g., page turning, faxing, copying).

Adam: iPod Touch as a Cognitive–Behavioral Aid Adam is a 20-year-old with autism, who understands speech and written language, but is largely nonverbal. He has been working with a job coach at a local hospital, where his primary job duty is to stock 20 emergency crash carts on the intensive care unit. This is an important job, because these carts store all of the essential materials needed to help a person who "crashes" and is at risk of sudden death. If a needed item is missing, a patient may die.

Adam very much wants to manage his workday independently, but a lack of organizational and memory skills makes this especially challenging. Fortunately, his job coach has provided him with an Apple iPod Touch, which provides exactly the support he needs to do his job.

A calendar reminder alarm on Adam's iPod Touch helps him wake up and complete his morning routine in time to catch a bus to work. Utilizing an application called Picture Scheduler, the job coach has programmed in a wake-up reminder alarm linked to a checklist of pictorial prompts for each step of Adam's morning routine (hygiene, breakfast, making lunch, and locking up the house on the way out the door). Reminder messages programmed into the device's Clock application help him clock in and out of work, go to breaks at appropriate times, and take his medications. The job coach has downloaded a PowerPoint-based video that shows photographs of each drawer of a crash cart, including with each photograph a list of items needed for the drawer. Adam can play the video, pausing at each step of the process, to make sure he completes his job successfully. As he completes filling a crash cart, Adam opens an application called Visules, which provides a checklist for all 20 carts. He taps the screen to check off each cart he has stocked, and shares this information with the job coach at the end of the day.

The hospital has recently installed an open wireless Internet connection. This allows Adam's job coach to check in on Adam remotely during the workday, utilizing the FaceTime videophone application. Adam can pan his work area with the iPod Touch videocamera to show his job coach where he is and what he is doing. Adam also makes use of a speech generation application called Voice4u, which he has programmed to include a customized library of spoken phrases appropriate for communication with fellow workers and supervisors. By tapping an onscreen icon, the iPod Touch speaks for him when needed.

The job coach has arranged icons on the iTouch screen so that the five applications described here are instantly available on the home screen. Other applications have been moved to a second screen for Adam to access after work. These include games, puzzles, a music library, and an Internet search browser, among others. Adam wears his iPod Touch on a belt clip, with the speaker volume turned up, so he can hear reminder alarms and alerts for Facetime calls. In this way, he can work with his hands free, while still having immediate access to the iPod Touch throughout the workday.

Handheld Technologies for Cognitive–Behavioral Support

Since the early 2000s, as handheld computers, PDAs, and cell phones have become smaller, more powerful, and more multifeatured, their potential for use as cognitive–behavioral aids has grown immensely. Whereas, in the early 2000s, the burgeoning population of people with cognitive impairment was the least likely group to use any sort of AT (LoPresti, Mihailidis, & Kirsch, 2004), that situation is rapidly changing as people discover the advantages of having what amounts to a pocket-sized behavioral coach on hand at all times.

People with cognitive–behavioral impairment typically list a range of functional challenges in performing everyday life tasks (Gentry, 2009):

1. Remembering to take medications

2. Remembering to perform chores

3. Completing complex tasks

4. Multitasking

5. Transitioning between tasks

6. Negotiating interpersonal situations

7. Managing frustrations arising from everyday life

Fortunately, PDAs may be leveraged to address each of these difficulties, providing a portable reminder and organization system to help people manage life tasks. In addition, downloadable applications (apps) now afford users a variety of inexpensive tools for augmentative communication, task sequencing, wayfinding, videophonic mentoring, and vocational support (Hammond, Whatley, Ayres, & Gast, 2010; Mechling & Seid, 2011).

PDAs and smartphones, however, are not a solution for every potential user. At this writing, though single-button switches have been developed to allow music playing on some devices, to access other programs, users must have the dexterity to manipulate on-screen keyboards and program icons. Though some devices incorporate accessibility features, such as talking screens and magnification, users with visual or hearing impairment are at a disadvantage in accessing these devices. Users must also recognize the need for cognitive assistance and choose to use them consistently. Occupational therapists can assist in assessing each user's needs, making an appropriate fit of device to person, and training both user and caregiver. Let us now examine some of the ways that handheld devices may be used as cognitive–behavioral supports.

Reminder Messages   The reminder function of PDAs has been well-researched among populations ranging from brain injury (Morris & Reinson, 2010; Gentry, Wallace, Kvarfordt, & Bodisch-Lynch, 2008) and autism (Ferguson, Miles, & Hagiwara, 2005; Gentry, Wallace, Kvarfordt, & Bodisch-Lynch, 2010) to multiple sclerosis (Gentry, 2008) and schizophrenia (Sablier, Stip, & Franck, 2009). In all cases, users are taught the steps of entering reminder alarms into PDA-based calendar programs, which provide auditory and visual message alerts ahead of scheduled tasks. (In some cases, caregivers record the reminder messages, and users need only respond to the reminders as they occur.) It is generally best to start with just three or four daily reminders programmed on a single scheduling application, in order to help the user become acclimated to the device. As users demonstrate that they can respond to the electronic reminders, additional items may be added. This strategy has been shown to help people with cognitive impairment independently manage medication regimens, schoolwork, home routines, and work tasks.

Practically every cell phone sold now comes with a calendar program that includes reminder alarms, as do PDAs and computer tablets, but these programs vary widely in their features and accessibility. Add-on scheduling applications may offer simplified interfaces, choices of alert sounds, and other extra features (e.g., an iTunes application, Picture Scheduler, allows the creation of a reminder message linked to a video. This means that a reminder to brush teeth would open a video of the user brushing his or her teeth, providing additional task support). As with other AT, selecting the right scheduling application for each individual user is an important element of the assessment process.

Organization and Task Sequencing   There are many ways that PDAs may support task sequencing of complex activities. Typical strategies may include

1. Making activity list sequences, using a typed PDA "to-do" list application
2. Recording step-by-step audio prompts, using a PDA voice memo application
3. Creating a PowerPoint slide show with photographs and typed captions, converting the slide show into a movie, and uploading the movie to a PDA (this is a relatively simple process, using recent versions of Microsoft Office)
4. If the device has a videocamera (as many smartphones, PDAs, and tablets now do), recording a video showing the person successfully performing the task (see "The Power of Video Modeling" in the next section)

In each of these cases, the user can preview the task sequence before performing an activity, play-and-pause the prompt during an activity, as needed, or review the PDA-based sequence after activity completion to make sure the task was performed completely and correctly. As with reminder messages, there are many add-on applications designed to provide additional options for task sequencing, including item check-offs, links to reminder alarms, and simplified interfaces.

The Power of Video Modeling   Video modeling is the most thoroughly researched of all cognitive–behavioral ATs (Bellini & Akullian, 2007; Ayres & Langone, 2005) and has been shown to be effective in supporting home, school, and vocational skills; social behaviors; communication; and wayfinding for people with autism and other conditions. Many PDAs, tablets, and smartphones include videocameras and video playback software, making the creation and use of video prompts inexpensive, straightforward, and user-friendly. Videos created on free-standing videocameras can be readily converted for download to any device that includes movie playback software. In creating a prompting video, it is important to remember that the video may be played back on a palm-sized device. For this reason, close-up shots with good lighting prove easier to follow. Using a camera tripod reduces playback shakiness. Some users may benefit from voice-over audio prompts or captions to supplement the video; these may be added in the editing process.

Some researchers recommend including the end user in a behavioral video, self-modeling successful task performance. This may require filming a multistep activity several times to edit together a seamless video that shows successful task completion. Users may preview, play-and-pause, or review these videos, as needed. In addition to providing task-sequencing support, videos may show a user following a path through a workplace or in the community, describing or enacting a social strategy, or providing "self-talk" encouragement and advice. In some cases, it is helpful to videotape a caregiver or sibling offering these prompts. There are a number of add-on applications available, as well, that allow the download of generic videos that demonstrate successful completion of everyday tasks and social interactions.

Videophonic Coaching   Vocational coaches have long yearned for a device that would allow a remote window into a client's workday. With the advent of Internet-based videophone capabilities on many smartphones and PDAs, that feature is now available. Users of videocamera-equipped Apple devices can video chat using Apple's *FaceTime* application. People with other videocamera-equipped devices can download free applications, such as Skype or Fring, to video chat. In this way, employers and job coaches can speak face to face with workers, offering advice and troubleshooting without having to be onsite. Workers tend to like this approach, which allows a sense of independence while also allowing immediate audiovisual access to an employer or job coach, as needed. Research is under way to explore how videophonic coaching can best be used.

Behavioral Management and Social Skills   Homemade videos played on portable devices, as noted previously, offer a promising just-in-time strategy for self-talk advice, social skill modeling, and behavioral coaching. A growing number of self-coaching behavioral applications are available, as well, allowing a user to rate levels of fear, anxiety, depression, insomnia, anger, or worry and automatically access adaptive behavioral strategies based on those ratings. Other applications—designed for clinicians—allow the recording of observed behavioral challenges and the graphing of behavior patterns across time. Many portable devices allow multiplayer gaming and text messaging that can promote social interaction.

Utilities and Accessibility Features   Handheld devices make all sorts of vocational applications available, ranging from pocket calculators to carpenter's clinometers. Typical onboard accessibility features may include automated text-to-speech generation, spell checking and word prediction, screen magnification, talking screens, and voice-controlled web searching and text messaging. Speech generation products range from simple "type to talk" applications to fully featured augmentative communication tools, which allow customized interfaces, pictographic icons, voice choices, and the creation of individualized phrase libraries.

Home and Office Applications   Portable devices are easily configured as word processors, often with the addition of a Bluetooth-enabled external keyboard and an add-on word processing software. Applications are available to help users keep track of homework, day-to-day finances, address lists, and maps. Smartphones allow communication options ranging from plain old phone calls to text messaging, document sharing, and videophonic conferencing. Most handheld devices are designed to easily link to a personal computer, allowing the sharing of office documents across platforms.

Simplifying and Protecting the Device   In configuring a PDA, tablet, or smartphone as an AT for cognitive–behavioral challenges, it is important to simplify the screen interface, so that users will not become confused or frustrated when using the device. Most devices now allow screen icons to be compressed into onscreen folders, hidden, or resized, as needed, so that a user's vocational applications can be readily separated from recreational applications that may crowd the screen and prove distracting during the workday. As powerful as these tools are, they are also quite fragile, susceptible to water, impact, heat, and cold. It is important to choose a protective case that also allows the user to carry the device hands-free (such as a belt clip, armband, or lanyard). Sometimes, the addition of a Bluetooth-enabled pocket speaker is recommended, especially if the device is being used as a speech generator or to play back video in noisy work environments where earbuds are not allowed. Users may need to be trained to care for their device, keeping it charged and safe from harm (an instructional video can be helpful).

Keeping Up with Change   Computer tablets, PDAs, and smartphones are evolving rapidly, as are their uses as cognitive–behavioral aids. It is important to learn how to use these tools, to stay abreast of research and product development, and to share experiences with colleagues to make best use of these powerful tools. In addition, providers must remember that a PDA may be just as important to a person with cognitive–behavioral challenges as a motorized wheelchair is to a person with mobility challenges (failing to take medications on time, for instance, may lead to hospitalization). It is the provider's responsibility to carefully assess user–device fit; configure a device, as needed; provide training that enables a person to successfully manage the device to improve functional performance; and offer follow-along and trouble-shooting assistance as a user's needs change, and as devices and applications evolve. Several online resources are available at the end of this chapter to assist providers with their continued education to stay current.

Acquiring and Using Assistive Technology

As stated previously, the potential costs of AT must also be taken into consideration. Coverage for such items may be available through insurance, federal or state employment programs, school systems (if the individual is a student), and/or from personal resources. Local, state, and federal government programs (including possible grant support), along with private companies, may offer loans to subsidize the costs incurred by individuals. Still, these subsidies may not be available or may not be enough to establish the necessary accommodations. Relevant considerations for the provider and the individual AT user include the use of a team approach, facilitating user empowerment, determining needs and preferences, and, finally, evaluating AT.

The Team Approach

In the past, if someone needed AT, a professional would spend a brief amount of time with the person, make a decision about what was needed ("assessment"), place an order, and, finally, drop a device off without training or follow-up. Sanctioned dependency instituted by professionals in the guise of protection, accepted by people with disabilities for lack of another option, is outdated and unacceptable. Individual choice and advocacy now empower this process.

In a team approach, the user of technology is the central driving force. He or she leads the process and his or her input and opinion determines the final solution. After all, it is the individual who will develop an intimate relationship with the device(s) chosen. If the solution does not work for the individual, then the device will most likely be abandoned.

Often, abandonment occurs when the user does not drive the team process. The individual may not know how to advocate for himself or herself because he or she has not had the opportunity or experience, or he or she may allow professionals to make the final determination. Allowing others to make critical decisions has often been a lifelong learned behavior. Professionals who cross the path of an individual who does not have the skills of self-advocacy must encourage and teach leadership skills. Wherever that person comes in contact or interacts with the educational, rehabilitation, and/or medical systems, those professionals must begin to educate the user on taking control of his or her own treatment and of getting his or her own AT. A person with a disability learning to take control of the technology process requires reciprocation. It is a combination of the professional teaching the user and the user teaching the professional. It is mutual mentoring, face-to-face, one-to-one.

The professional facilitates opportunities for decision making and assertive communication. Professional mentoring may include teaching the user how to

- Gather information
- Communicate effectively
- Make decisions based on data, preference, and need
- Navigate the system
- Choose a support network

In kind, the user may provide the professional

- Feedback on ability to teach self-advocacy skills
- Individualized insights on specific needs and preferences
- Local community contacts
- Opportunity for a true team effort
- Opportunity for professional growth

If the individual has difficulty communicating or has a cognitive disability, then the role of the professional and/or advocate is especially critical.

Empowerment, Effectiveness, and Efficiency

Empowerment, effectiveness, and efficiency highlight a team approach. Individuals from a variety of backgrounds and experiences come together to assist the individual in evaluating and identifying the most useful solution. Team members vary depending on the individual and information needs. A team approach is *effective* because it contributes a multitude of expertise and knowledge. Communication and activities are clear, constructive, and outcome oriented. A team approach is *efficient* because team members may have delineated responsibilities that decrease the likelihood of duplication and incompletion and increase the likelihood of procurement in a timely manner (Rust & Smith, 2005).

There is no shortage of the human services professions that may be drawn from, and they have been used for many years as "experts" in their respective fields. However, professionals now assume a role of consultant, providing practical and competent suggestions. A team approach involves *empowerment* when the user actively participates and influences the direction of the process in concert with professionals.

Cindy   Cindy, an elementary school teacher with severe arthritis, identified a work task need and conducted her own research to prepare for determining an appropriate solution with her team. Cindy expressed an interest in using a computer to help her with her lesson plans and other written work. She is exploring all possibilities including modified computer keyboards, software that assists with simultaneous keystrokes, wrist supports, and voice recognition systems. With this information, she expects to obtain a complete computer evaluation before deciding which AT products work best for her. To help achieve her goal, she will chair the team, having identified her need and many possible solutions. Other team members include her physician, an OT, a computer consultant/evaluator, her employer, and a vendor.

The User's Role

As stated earlier, the user is seen as the "expert" based on his or her needs, comfort level, and preferences. With a customer-driven approach, teams will *always* include the individual with a disability. The user must be involved in the development of his or her own team or support network. Professionals may assist in the development of the team or support network, if requested to do so or if the individual requires assistance.

The team is in place to support and consult with the individual. The rapport with the team should be open, direct, and creative. As the word *team* implies, members are working in concert for the common goal of community inclusion with maximum accessibility to all opportunities offered.

The AT user must ask himself or herself

- Did I assist in the selection of team members?
- Do I have decision-making responsibilities? Am I willing and ready to take on this role?
- Do I have input into the direction of my AT needs and preferences?
- Do I have or want a mentor who can assist me in developing advocacy skills or advocating on my behalf?

The user may have a mentor. If so, the user and the mentor are one unit and may ask these questions in tandem. The user must always ask questions and not rely on one single professional for technology solutions. The team approach strengthens individualized outcomes. See Table 12.2 for examples of additional team members.

Table 12.2.   Assistive technology team members

Team member	Role
Employment specialist	Assists with job accommodation needs to enhance job performance; may assist with funding issues
Vendors	Offer knowledge on available technology, services, and repairs (usually high-end technology)
Rehabilitation engineer	Assists in development or modification of devices, accommodations, or job redesign
Occupational therapist	Assesses performance in daily living tasks, positioning, and mobility; recommends activities, devices, and adaptations to environment
Recreational therapist	Identifies and assesses social/recreational needs and preferences
Physical therapist	Assesses work capacity—physical strengths and limitations, analysis of workstation; recommends mobility needs, workstation design, and modifications
Employer	May assist with job accommodation needs, input, and approval of workstation modifications
Speech-language pathologist	Assesses language and speech capabilities and recommends specialized communication aids
Educator	Shares knowledge of individual based on experience within school system– or community-based instruction sites; provides insight into matching assistive technology to continuing education that may enhance long-term employment opportunities and advancement
Family members	Share knowledge of individual and environments; advocate on behalf of user; demonstrate willingness to acquire knowledge of the device in order to provide in-home support
Rehabilitation counselor	Assists with funding issues and logistics of services to be provided in effort to reduce barriers to employment

(continued)

Table 12.2.   *(continued)*

Team member	Role
Physician	Provides input on medical issues and cognitive and physical abilities of individual; addresses health concerns; provides prescriptions and letters of medical necessity when needed for evaluations and durable medical equipment
Social worker/case manager	May act as coordinator of holistic/community services
Computer consultant	Evaluates computer needs and recommends adaptive computer equipment and training

Often, there is a distinction between a team and a support network. The team's primary role is to assist in the identification and acquisition of technology. The support network's primary role occurs once the technology is acquired. They assist with the successful implementation and use of the equipment or device. The support network may be ongoing and consist of specific team members as well as family members.

Choice Based on Needs and Preferences

AT provides individuals with physical, sensory, and cognitive disabilities with the ability to compensate for functional limitations. In the maze of rehabilitation technology, one can easily become lost. There are so many possibilities in terms of individual need, preference, and potential options. Any acquisition of AT is preceded by a need. A person with a disability wants to be able to perform a specific task; his or her disability may prohibit or limit him or her from doing so. The individual, family member, or professional begins to brainstorm about a device that would assist the individual in performing the task. It may be something as simple as getting a cup off a shelf or as complex as using a computer to perform job functions. Mull and Sitlington (2003) summarized findings regarding the use of technology in helping students with learning disabilities succeed in postsecondary education settings. The primary purposes of this article were to

1. Identify the specific technology recommendations found in the literature
2. Identify issues related to using these recommendations in the transition to postsecondary education
3. Provide recommendations for planning for the transition to postsecondary education

In addition, Stodden, Conway, and Chang (2003) highlighted the importance of access to postsecondary education for individuals with disabilities and barriers to this access that revolve around the provision of supports, including the provision of technology. The researchers indicated a number of barriers to transition, which included differences in classrooms, a lack of supports, and a focus on factors like compliance with the law and costs rather than on a student's needs and potential outcomes. They also stressed ways to improve transition and access to technology, such as carryover and use of high school supports and technology into postsecondary school and providing more information to students about their rights in those settings. They also stated the need to view technology and supports as an investment in a student's future.

One must keep in mind that high-tech solutions may not always be needed. When arriving at some technology solutions, one does not have to choose complex; simple may work exceedingly well. That is, when problem solving, look to the low-tech technology before moving onto the more involved or elaborate. This strategy, of course, is dependent on the individual and his or her respective need. If, for instance, communication or mobility is the issue of concern, then one may require a higher tech device such as a Liberator for communication or a powered wheelchair for mobility.

Modified equipment or homemade solutions often meet an accessibility need. The use of switches, Velcro, or grips on existing items often solves an inaccessibility problem. These low-tech solutions usually fit well into the work environment and will not cause stigma. Creativity is the key to simple, low-tech solutions. Conrad's situation is an example of a core work task accommodation using a low-tech device (see case study later in this chapter).

Regardless of whether a device or equipment is low- or high-tech, choice and effectiveness remain the central concerns. The user must be comfortable with the AT, and it must satisfy the need. When one makes a major purchase, one may have many options. If an individual is purchasing a sofa, then he or she may sit on many to determine the comfort and fit into his or her home. The user should determine if there are alternatives or options available to a specific device. If the user has been excluded from the process, or if his or her input has been minimized, the longevity and usefulness of the intended solution is in jeopardy. A user must be vested in the technology and must be trained on how to use the technology; if not, the closet door will open wide.

Jeffrey   Jeffrey is a 20-year-old college student studying landscape architecture. He has been very active in determining his needs and preferences regarding AT. Jeffrey has used a motorized tilt-in-space wheelchair for the past 4 years, since a dive into a swimming pool broke his neck at the C-5 spinal level after sophomore year of high school. Jeffrey has full head, neck, and shoulder strength and can flex his elbows, but otherwise, he has no active arm movement or any other active movement below his neck. He drives the wheelchair by using a joystick and is able to roll directly into his adapted van, which has a side-door lift ramp and lockdown tabs for his chair in place of a driver's seat. The van is equipped with bilateral hand controls (the right control replaces the steering wheel and the left replaces the gas and brake pedals), and Jeffrey has learned to drive well by using these adaptations. Jeffrey purchased the van with a partial grant from his state's department of rehabilitative services and a low-interest loan from an AT loan funding organization.

Jeffrey has equipped his wheelchair to be a fully equipped mobile office. His laptop computer is attached to the wheelchair with a swing-away support post, and his smartphone is Velcro-strapped to the post. He connects to both via voice control, utilizing a Bluetooth earpiece with a built-in microphone. The laptop is operated by using Nuance's Dragon Dictation voice-control software, and the cell phone accepts voice commands for calls, text messages, and web searches with the Vlingo application. Jeffrey's cell phone also serves as his GPS mapping device when he is driving and as an always-on Internet hot spot for his computer. Phone prompts remind him to tilt his chair for pressure reliefs periodically.

In the classroom, Jeffrey switches to a mouth stick for typing notes, supplementing his typed notes by recording lectures with the *SoundNote* application. This software allows him to tap a note at home and fast-forward the recorded lecture to that topic, making studying easier. On days when Jeffrey is working in the field with his mentor, his part-time home health aide switches out the wheels on his chair for wider, all-terrain wheels and attaches a gooseneck camera post to the chair. This allows Jeffrey to negotiate rough terrain and photograph sites. All of the software needed for site design is on his computer. This offers Jeffrey a real advantage in his future work. Unlike most other landscape architects, he will be able to complete meetings, site visits, and planning on location, immediately sharing his work via the Internet without ever having to use a central office.

Evaluating Assistive Technology

The process of matching AT to a particular user's needs and wants involves a step-by-step assessment process, which may include professionals from disciplines such as OT, rehabilitation counseling, speech and language pathology, physical therapy, special education, and rehabilitation engineering, among others. Professionals with special expertise in AT may have an Assistive Technology Practitioner certification, which is earned through the Rehabilitation Engineering and Assistive Technology Association of North America (refer to Table 12.2). Several strategies assist in the evaluation process, including assessment of

1. A user's skills, functional abilities, and interests
2. The environment(s) where AT may be used (with an eye toward environmental adaptation, where possible)
3. Tasks and activities that a user needs or wants to perform and that may benefit from AT

Rehabilitation professionals have an arsenal of assessment tools focused on measuring physical, cognitive, and emotive abilities. Person-centered assessment tools focused on measuring a person's goals and desires are less common. The Canadian Occupational Performance Measure is one such tool, designed as a structured interview that includes discussion of a person's activities of daily living, school, work, and recreational goals and produces an individualized performance and satisfaction score for activities in each category. Such a tool allows people to shape their own performance goals in keeping with their skills and abilities.

When one is considering the use of AT, assessing the environment in which the device or modification will be used is critical. Sometimes an inexpensive environmental modification can obviate the need for AT (e.g., improved lighting in a work area can make the area safer for all workers while improving access for workers with visual acuity impairments). At the same time, AT must fit the environment where it is to be used. To ensure that the optimal "fit" occurs, a team approach is valuable. Again, the user and the employer provide primary input in the direction of this process. Team members may vary according to the user's needs and the work environment. An office jobsite evaluation team may include an OT, a rehabilitation engineer, a computer consultant, a rehabilitation counselor, and/or a building maintenance specialist. To provide an optimal AT solution, it is important to examine the tasks and activities that AT will support and to try out promising ATs in performing those duties. When using AT on the job, the user and team must identify the essential functions of the job and barriers to accomplishing those tasks.

Functional analysis, which involves observing and trouble-shooting with the user as he or she utilizes a recommended AT to perform his or her common tasks or activities in the actual home, community, or work environment, culminates the assessment process. By considering skills, goals, the environment, and required tasks and activities, as well as the respective user's input regarding needs and preferences, the assessment team can be sure to provide a customized and appropriate AT for each user.

Assessment is only the first step in AT provision, however, as it is equally important to take the time to train a user how to operate and maintain the device successfully and problem solve with the user strategies for optimizing task performance. One would not dream of buying a car unless one had the opportunity to drive it down the street, kick the tires, and haggle with the salesperson. Yet, people with disabilities often get both high- and low-technology devices chosen for them, without an opportunity to try them out in the environment or to be fully trained in their use and maintenance. If one is unable to try it out and to be trained on using the device, then it can be very discouraging and, ultimately, expensive. The user must also keep in mind that what has worked for one person may in fact be a poor solution for another. Individualized services and devices will be furthered by trying out the proposed solution.

Conrad   Conrad has right-side hemiplegia and is receiving supported employment services in a small town. A recycling company opened in town recently, and Conrad was hired to crush beverage cans. The volume of cans was such that Conrad would do this activity for the majority of his shift, along with one other co-worker. While wearing gloves, co-workers would crush the cans with their hands and then toss them into a bin. A fellow employee rigged a new device in which Conrad places a can on the bottom holder of the rig, pulls a lever, and crushes the can. With this device, Conrad's production is almost as high as that of his co-workers. Conrad's experience is a good example of creating a device by using a "tinkerer" within the community. Not all devices created need to be developed by professional experts. Users can educate themselves as to who in their community may be helpful with AT solutions.

If possible, the user should borrow or rent the device. Use it at home, at work, or in the community before making a purchasing commitment. Test the device's capabilities, limitations, and comfort. The device should look good, feel good, and, many times, create a greater feeling of self-esteem or capability. One user recently ordered a chair that she felt was big, black, and bulky. The chair did not make her feel good, even though it was functional. Another individual who uses forearm crutches has several pairs that represent different functions and settings—bright neon for informal days, a classy bronze for business days, and so forth. If the user of AT feels good about his or her ownership of the device, then he or she will use it to its fullest. If it makes the individual more independent, then it is the right equipment to own.

AT providers must recognize that it is not enough to provide a thorough assessment, assist in device acquisition, and provide training in its use. It is important to provide follow-along support to accommodate changing skills, abilities, needs, tasks, and environments over time. Follow-along support is also essential when AT malfunctions or a new, better product becomes available. Many people require AT permanently, and ongoing collaboration with an AT practitioner is just as important as an ongoing relationship with a doctor or therapist in ensuring optimal functional performance and satisfaction over time.

Clara   Clara experiences limb–girdle muscular dystrophy, resulting in weakness to the limb musculature. A rehabilitation engineer evaluated Clara's work environment and proposed several changes to increase access and function. Her employer was very supportive. Clara's desk became an L-shaped countertop attached to the wall. This space houses a computer, telephone, and file holders. Clara uses a head-set attached to her phone so that she does not need to hold the receiver for an extended length of time. Open-ended file folder organizers were mounted within her reach on the wall. A file cabinet was purchased that had drawers that could be lifted open and slid back so that they are always open. Clara's power wheelchair also raises and lowers electronically to increase her access to the files. She uses voice-activated software to reduce the need to use a keyboard for her data entry computer-based tasks. Clara believes the new design is functional, simple, and professional looking. Her work environment suits her needs and preferences, as does her power wheelchair.

Tech Discontinuance: The Assistive Technology Closet

As mentioned earlier, if the solution does not work for the individual, then the AT device most likely will not be used. Lauer, Longenecker-Rust, and Smith (2006) researched this phenomenon and the factors that influence nonuse. They contend that the term *abandonment* should be replaced with the term *discontinuance*. *Abandonment* has a connotation of irresponsibility on the part of the user, the industry, and service providers, as well as a negative meaning. There may be times in which it is a positive discontinuance, such as improvement or healing. The authors define *discontinuance* as the process by which a person ceases to use AT devices after a period of time. This term has a neutral connotation and alludes to the cessation of use across time. (Lauer et al., 2006) Factors associated with nonuse include social aspects, personal factors, health status, economic factors, and physical environment.

Technology discontinuance is widespread and very expensive. Devices may no longer be used because they just do not work for the respective user (Lauer, Longenecker-Rust, & Smith, 2006). Discontinuance may happen for a variety of reasons—no evaluation, incompetent evaluation, little or no user input, or no training or support. Thus, negative discontinuance may involve faulty devices and/or inadequate services. The results of this type of discontinuance are twofold, neither of which is desirable. First, the situation the intended user is attempting to alter is not changed. For example, if an augmentative communication device is purchased but is discarded because it is too cumbersome on the job, then the person is still without alternative speech. In this situation, perhaps a simpler communication board or other solution is more appropriate. Second, inappropriate devices can be costly. No one wins when the device is discontinued because of negative factors—not the person with the disability nor the individual who purchased the device.

There are other, rarely recognized, reasons for nonuse. One reason is timing and acceptance by the user. A person with a disability must be ready to accept the need and the usage of the device; otherwise, he or she will reject or find excuses for not using it. A second reason is funding. For example, often, third-party payers will pay for a manual wheelchair but not a power chair. So, the user gets the manual chair and then cannot propel it adequately. The chair goes into the closet to gather dust while the person with the mobility difficulties either stays at home or waits a very long time for funding for the wheelchair he or she needed in the first place.

Devices that end up in the "AT closet" present a challenge. They need to be recycled, but there is little funding. Third-party payers rarely pay for a used item. In the future, some method of consistent redistribution needs to be developed to assist in combating technology discontinuance.

Selecting a Vendor

The informed user can make a case for using a specific vendor. Selecting a vendor should not be based solely on the product or device chosen. Choosing the ideal product is, of course, a critical component. However, the relationship with the user and the device is only the beginning. The user must "look down the road." There may come a day when the equipment or device needs repairs. This can be a user's worst nightmare, depending on the function the device serves in the user's life. High-end technology, such as power wheelchairs and augmentative communication, may be difficult to live without, no matter how temporary. When selecting a vendor, ask

- What services do you offer?
- Do you provide a trial period?
- What will you do for me if this breaks down (e.g., loan equipment)?
- What is your turn-around time for repairs?
- How much do you charge for services and repairs?

Service costs can be enormous. As in any business, customer responsiveness and satisfaction should be a priority for the vendor. If the vendor does not offer to loan a comparable device, or if he or she does not respond with a knowledge of the necessity to get repairs done quickly, then the choice may be made easier for the user.

Training may be a part of the vendor agreement and purchase contingent on receiving immediate and quality training. If a vendor lists services in promotional materials, then the user should look for training, repair, and loans as an indicator of whether he or she will do business with the respective vendor.

The loan aspect is critical to the user who would not have mobility, communication, accessibility, or integration otherwise. Being proactive with anticipated needs and repairs will serve the user well in selecting a vendor. With high-end technology, the user, vendor, and device may have a relationship for life. As with all relationships, it should not be entered into lightly.

Funding Issues

Anyone who uses AT knows that funding is often a challenge and a barrier. However, most work accommodations cost very little. According to the Job Accommodation Network (n.d.), employers report that approximately 56% of accommodations cost nothing, and, of those accommodations that did have a cost, the typical one-time expenditure by employers was $500 or less. As with identifying technology solutions, creativity and perseverance may be the key to success. An individual may be able to make use of a variety of funding options, including Department of Rehabilitation Services, Medicaid, education, private insurance, Social Security Administration, Veterans Administration, and independent living programs. Each of these sources has eligibility requirements and specific procedures. Public school systems may be required to purchase AT if it is a part of the student's individualized education program. Employers may be required to purchase reasonable accommodations per the Americans with Disabilities Act (PL 101-336). The user and service providers must be aware of legislation that impacts AT such as the Individuals with Disabilities Education Act (1990; PL 101-476), the Americans with Disabilities Act, and the Technology-Related Assistance for Individuals with Disabilities Act of 1988 (The Tech Act; PL 100-407), including subsequent amendments.

Nontraditional funding sources may include service, civic, or religious organizations. Federally funded AT projects exist in each U.S. state and territory. These projects maintain current information on AT resources in a respective state. These state AT projects should be the starting point for individuals seeking financial assistance to purchase AT devices. AbleData (n.d.) maintains information on traditional as well as alternative funding sources for AT that include federal, nonprofit, corporate, foundation, and other private entities. Funding sources may focus on specific categories of AT such as mobility aids, speech and communication aids, and visual aids.

Carey, DelSordo, and Goldman (2004) noted that literature on gaining access to AT services and AT funding, as well as literature on gaining access to loans (e.g., mortgages, car loans), has indicated that people from minority populations tend to experience less access to and benefit from these programs. Given these trends, the question they ask is, "To what extent does race affect access to AT through alternative financing programs?" Using a national database of 10 participating states, they explored the impact of race on which people apply for—and succeed in obtaining—alternative financing. The authors then provided an in-depth discussion of Pennsylvania's model outreach program designed to increase access to and use of alternative financing by members of the African American, Latino, and Southeast Asian communities in the commonwealth. This paper does an excellent job of showing the challenges of funding AT for minority populations. It is often possible to blend funding sources (i.e., to use different sources for different devices and services, to use a variety of sources to fund one device or service). The user must become informed about all available funding sources and their respective stipulations. This knowledge provides a "leg up" in the acquisition of AT. Do not rely completely on professionals for this information as their knowledge may vary. Doing one's own research will truly enhance the possibilities.

Several steps are involved in locating funding (Wallace & Neal, 1993; Virginia Assistive Technology System, 2001). The user must

- Be prepared
- Prove a need
- Match the need with the device or service
- Research prices, providers, and alternatives
- Choose and contact funding sources (identify a specific contact person)
- Be determined and persistent
- Do all of the necessary paperwork
- Keep detailed, written records
- If denied, appeal
- If denied again, move on to another funding option

The Americans with Disabilities Act of 1990 has created another potential funding option through employers. This, of course, is true as long as the solution is deemed a reasonable accommodation and does not present an undue hardship to the employer. Acquiring funding is a tedious process, one that requires preparation, organization, and perseverance. The user must go in with the attitude that this may take patience, thought, and time.

Maximizing Independence in All Aspects

As mentioned earlier, AT must be used to maximize independent living before it is used to enhance employment opportunities. It can be an important part of the daily living routine of a person with a disability or his or her caregiver. The user needs to be comfortable with his or her activities in the home and community before exploring job opportunities. In simple terms, housing, food, hygiene, medical care, and transportation needs have to be addressed first. Many times, optimal independent living can be achieved by filling these needs with AT services.

Examples of AT devices used for independent living are bath and dressing aids, food preparation aids, lifts, augmentative communication devices, wheelchairs, and low-tech items such as reachers, rubber jar openers, grips, and so forth. Individuals may also require home modifications and specialized transportation.

Addressing independent living issues first will contribute to success in the arena of employment. However, not all individuals with disabilities may need to address independent living on the same level, depending on need(s). Devices used in other areas of life may be used on the jobsite as well.

Susan Susan is currently in a special education program for students with significant intellectual and physical disabilities. Because she is 20 years old, her teacher is concerned about transition from school to work and has referred Susan to a special program designed to work with students who have similar disabilities. Team staff identified a job at the local university library stamping identification numbers on the spines of new books. After Susan's physical strengths and limitations were assessed, the following characteristics were identified:

- Susan uses a wheelchair for mobility and requires personal assistance for movement from one place to another.
- She has limited movements in both arms because of hypertonicity throughout her head, trunk, and limbs.
- Lateral wheelchair supports and a seat belt are necessary to assist Susan in sitting upright in her chair. She also requires foot support and straps.
- Susan can raise her right arm at the shoulder joint so that her forearm is parallel to and 6 inches above her wheelchair lap tray.

- She does not have any functional mobility in her fingers, which are usually tightly fisted into the palms of both hands.
- She is visually attentive and can turn her head from side to side.
- Susan is labeled as having a significant intellectual disability.

Because she has multiple physical characteristics that could have an impact on her performance, it was obvious that Susan would need AT to complete the job of stamping books with the library identification number. The team worked closely with a rehabilitation engineer, and a spring-loaded device was designed to assist Susan in completing the task. The first step in the job required personal assistance from a co-worker or project staff member to load the equipment with 10 books for stamping. At that point, Susan was responsible for pressing a switch to drop a book into position. She then would touch another plate that held the heat stamp to apply heat to the spine of the book. Susan kept this in place for 10 seconds, finally touching another switch to move the book off the work surface. Intensive systematic instruction was provided by a trainer to assist Susan in learning her job.

Looking to the Future

Not only do service providers need to stay current with AT devices and services, but so too should the end user to the best of his or her ability. Needs change, technology changes, and goals change. The user must be a visionary and look to the future, anticipating physical, medical, and/or career changes. Low-tech solutions do not necessarily require a prophetic approach because they are creative, simple, and often inexpensive. However, high-end devices, because of funding issues and expense, will require a future-oriented vision. Funding sources may have timeframes in which, once a device is acquired, they will not pay for another similar device or equipment for a certain period. Thus, it is important for the user to know his or her insurance coverage. The team approach will assist an individual with planning for the future.

Conclusion

AT closes the gap between inaccessibility and accessibility. Technology on the worksite continues to be an exciting, integrating opportunity for many individuals with disabilities. The user must be as prepared, as relentless, and as questioning as possible to arrive at appropriate solutions. Technology continues to advance and change at a rapid pace, with all members of today's society becoming dependent on and benefiting from its use. However, challenges exist that may impede the community inclusion of people with disabilities including lack of access and utilization of available technologies, funding AT devices and services, and staying current of advances. Individual advocacy and research in procuring AT on the worksite, as well as other areas of daily living, will continue to increase the independence of individuals with disabilities. It is a matter of convenience in terms of freedom, full inclusion, and, ultimately, quality of life.

Study Questions

1. Meet with an adult with a disability to discuss how AT affected the user's quality of life.
2. Interview a rehabilitation engineer and/or an OT to discuss the role of the consumer in choosing AT and how professionals can assist.
3. Who may serve on the AT team and what are the benefits to using this approach?
4. Why is it necessary to evaluate the use of AT devices across a variety of life settings?
5. Use the Internet to further investigate how AT may be funded for youth and adults.

6.   What is *jobsite enabling* and how can it impact employment?

7.   Use the Internet to conduct research on the latest advances in technology and future directions for adults with orthopedic and other health impairment and traumatic brain injury.

Online Resources

Internet Resources

State Assistive Technology Projects (Assistive Technology Act of 1998): http://resnaprojects.org/nattap/scripts/nattapcontacts.pl

The Alliance for Technology Access: http://www.ataccess.org/

Job Accommodation Network: http://askjan.org/

AbleData: Assistive technology resource and vendor catalog: http://abledata.com

DO IT Center, University of Washington: http://uw.edu/doit/

Enablemart: Assistive technology resource and vendor catalog: http://www.enablemart.com

Trace Center: Essentials for cross-disability accessible cell phones: making mainstream market phones more usable by more people: http://trace.wisc.edu/docs/2010-phone-essentials/

Associations

Assistive Technology Industry Association: http://atia.org

Closing the Gap: http://www.closingthegap.com

Rehabilitation Engineering and Assistive Technology Society of North America: http://www.resna.org

Assistive Technologies Discussed in Text

BIG iPod Remote: http://www.rjcooper.com/ipod/index.html

BigKeys: http://www.bigkeys.com/or http://www.rjcooper.com

Endeavor Email: http://www.ablelinktech.com

Eyegaze Edge: http://www.eyegaze.com/content/assistive-technology/

IntelliKeys: http://www.intellitools.com

myTobii: http://www.tobii.com/en/assistive-technology/north-america/products/hardware/mytobii-p10/

QuadJoy: http://www.quadjoy.com/

SmartNav: http://www.naturalpoint.com/smartnav/

TrackerPro: http://www.madentec.com/products/tracker-pro.php

Vocalize!: http://www.broadenedhorizons.com/vocalize.htm

Web Trek: http://www.ablelinktech.com

Securing Meaningful Work in the Community

Vocational Internships, Placements, and Careers

PAUL WEHMAN AND VALERIE BROOKE

13

After completing this chapter, the reader will be able to

- Give four reasons why work is valuable
- Understand vocational integration and the importance of the Employment First philosophy
- Understand the value of internships and mentoring, especially Project SEARCH®
- Present six models of vocational placement and give examples of each
- Know what supported employment (SE) is and what customized employment is and how they differ from sheltered work
- Discuss the five strategies associated with systems change

Teri Teri is a 20-year-old student with severe intellectual disabilities and autism who lives with her family and still attends her local high school. She has limited expressive language and communicates primarily through her body language and willingness to participate in activities. Teri participated in a community-based vocational education program and then received SE services to assist her with gaining and maintaining a job. As a result, she has worked part-time at a restaurant as a food preparation assistant for more than 1 year while still in school. Her job duties include making salads and preparing potatoes for baking. She also assists her co-workers with cleaning the workstation by taking dirty pans to the sink area. It is notable that her job was created by negotiating specific duties from a food preparation worker's job description. Teri works approximately 20 hours a week and every other Saturday as part of her school curriculum and earns $7.00 per hour. Transportation is provided to and from work by the school during the week and by her parents on the weekends.

Teri is supported at work by her co-workers, managers, assistive technology (AT), and her job coach. For example, her co-workers assist her with clocking in and out; putting on and taking off her hair net, apron, and gloves; setting up and replenishing her work supplies; and going on break. The assigned co-worker provides verbal and physical assistance throughout her workday as needed. Technological assistance such as described in Chapter 7 has also been incorporated into the routine. For instance, the manager ordered a magnetic scanning card, which eliminated the need to manually enter her employee number into a computer to clock in and out. An audio prompting/praising system was also developed to provide her with consistent intervention and to decrease her dependence on co-worker prompts. The job coach provided upfront assistance with developing the job and then provided one-to-one jobsite training using systematic instruction and helped identify and facilitate co-worker support. Now, the job coach is on site only once or twice a week.

There are thousands of people like Teri in this country who are looking for a job that can lead to a career. As most children leave middle school and enter high school, their thoughts turn to college, jobs, careers, and, essentially, what they are going to do with their lives. For young people with disabilities, the questions are as follows: Is there an internship that I can find that will help me? Can I get off a waiting list and into a vocational training program? Will Vocational Rehabilitation find me eligible for services? Can I get a job that pays more than minimum wage? Will I be stuck in the same job for the rest of my life? Will I have to go to an adult activity center or a sheltered workshop? These questions have increased in number and urgency since more and more students have been educated with classmates without disabilities, making them even more aware of the possibilities of postsecondary education and career opportunities (see Chapter 7).

Good jobs in America are not easy to come by. As this is written, the United States is struggling to emerge from the greatest financial crisis in 70 years, with unemployment rates exceeding 9% and underemployment higher than 18% (U.S. Department of Labor, June 3, 2011a). This is a country that wants people to work, expects people to work, and even defines who people are by their type and amount of work.

So, what lays ahead for Teri and what possibilities are there, especially in these difficult times? What jobs will be available for her? In education, rehabilitation, and other postsecondary agencies, there is an increasingly strong feeling that vocational services should make transition-age students a priority—a feeling that has been intensified by the large investment in resources for special education entitlement programs. Certo and his colleagues (2008) have called for a national model of "seamless transition" for students from school to work. They observe

> Despite the various mandates and funding mechanisms, the low employment rate of people with severe intellectual disabilities and the consequent social and economic marginalization are significant social problems (Migliore & Butterworth, 2008). Securing and maintaining employment continue to be the areas that result in the largest negative discrepancy between those with severe intellectual disabilities and those without. Eight percent of those with several intellectual disabilities were employed, in comparison with 81% of those without

disabilities. More recent data show these figures are essentially unchanged. (National Organization on Disability, 2004, p. 87)

This chapter is about inclusive employment options, careers, and new models for providing vocational services in order to empower young people to enter the work force meaningfully.

What Is Possible: Setting Options for Work

Transitioning from school into segregated **day programs and sheltered workshops** cannot be an acceptable end point for young people with disabilities (Bates-Harris & Decker, 2011; Gore, 2011; Kiernan, Mank, & Wehman, 2011; Rogan & Rinne, 2011). Although segregated day programs may be the only placement option for some, most students with disabilities aspire to competitive employment as their first career option and work to achieve that (Luecking, 2009a; Wehman, Inge, Revell, & Brooke, 2007). Teachers must help these aspirations become realities. If people with disabilities do not view themselves positively and have high vocational aspirations, then the expectations of advocates, family members, friends, and others working on their behalf will reflect that position.

Despite national and state policies promoting integrated employment, the majority of adults with intellectual or developmental disabilities (71%) are served in facility-based programs or nonfacility community programs (Braddock et al., 2010). Migliore, Mank, Grossi, and Rogan (2007) focused on whether or not this gap between policy and practice is in part attributable to the lack of interest of adults with intellectual disabilities and their families for employment outside facility-based programs. The overwhelming response of workshop clients was clear: "We want competitive employment." Results were based on the answers given by 210 adults with intellectual disabilities in 19 sheltered workshops, their respective families or caregivers ($n = 185$), and staff members in these workshops ($n = 224$).

Migliore et al. (2007) reported that the majority of respondents would either like employment outside sheltered workshops or at least consider it an option. Moreover, the majority of respondents believed that adults with intellectual disabilities can perform outside workshops, if support is made available if needed. It is noteworthy that the preference for employment outside of workshops is not associated with the severity of the disability.

Barriers to Employment Competence

Unfortunately, numerous barriers exist in attaining employment competence for people with disabilities. These barriers are societal, programmatic, attitudinal, and physical. Even more critical is the barrier of poverty. Many people with disabilities are poor; they do not have enough money to afford housing, utilities, transportation, or even food (Fremstad, 2009; Parrish, Rose, & Andrews, 2010; Hughes & Avoke, 2010). Without these basic human needs being met, it is next to impossible for someone to embark on a job search.

> Despite more than 40 years of legislation to improve the outcomes of children and youth with disabilities and those growing up in poverty, vast numbers of adults with severe disabilities are unemployed or underemployed and living in poverty. One of the factors maintaining the problem is our failure to acknowledge the prevalence and complexity of poverty and its relation to disability and employment. Disability is both a cause and an effect of poverty, affecting employment and quality of life of people with severe disabilities. (Hughes & Avoke, 2010, p. 5)

Power and Influence

Another major barrier that must be considered for people with disabilities is their collective inexperience with gaining control over key events in their lives. The American culture is rooted in a set of values that are strongly tied to power, control, and influence. Bookstores, newspapers, and magazine articles are filled with feel-good stories about self-made millionaires, powerful CEOs of large corporations, and gifted athletes from humble backgrounds signing multimillion-dollar contracts. Americans have a great fondness for these stories because they are about people who take control of their lives, accept risks, make difficult decisions, set goals, and, most important, become successful.

Historically, individuals with disabilities have been denied access to the very events that would provide them with the opportunity to take risks, make decisions, and ultimately experience these highly prized American values of power, control, and influence. Furthermore, because of a lack of economic resources or a loss of specific skills, many people with disabilities are vulnerable and depend on a human services system in which they are stereotyped and stigmatized. Among medical and human services professionals, people with disabilities are viewed as recipients of services with very little to contribute. As a consequence, systems are created and service practices are institutionalized that contribute to the disempowerment and dependency of people with disabilities.

Health Care Benefits and Social Security Administration Policies

Usually, the most imposing barrier to employment for people with disabilities is the potential loss of income assistance and health care through programs administered by the Social Security Administration (SSA) and the Centers for Medicare and Medicaid Services (CMS). The two major SSA disability programs are Supplemental Security Income (SSI) and Social Security Disability Insurance (SSDI). Although the two have different eligibility criteria, under both programs, individuals with disabilities must prove themselves to be incapable of engaging in substantial gainful activity (SGA), currently determined as earnings of more than $600 per month, to be eligible for benefits (Kregel & O'Mara, 2011).

For many individuals with disabilities, full-time employment with health benefits is not an option because of low levels of job skills, local labor market conditions, limitations in stamina or endurance, or the need to commit substantial amounts of time to personal care needs or treatments. Yet, if they obtain part-time employment, they risk losing cash and other benefits, particularly medical coverage under Medicaid (in most states linked to eligibility for SSI) or Medicare (linked to eligibility for SSDI). This economic disincentive persuades most beneficiaries to limit their earnings to less than SGA or, more commonly, not to enter the labor market at all despite the fact that those utilizing Medicaid waivers can do well in the work (Miller, O'Mara, & Kregel, 2012).

Employer Reluctance to Hire

Businesses rarely admit the real reasons that keep them from hiring people with disabilities (Hartnett, Stuart, Thurman, Loy, & Batiste, 2011). However, looking behind the excuses given, it is possible that the primary reasons are concern, fear, or anxiety that people with disabilities cannot work successfully and a general lack of knowledge about what employment looks like for people with disabilities. Luecking (2011) notes that words, concepts, and descriptors, such as *vocational assessment, supported employment, individualized education program, discovery,* and other terms in common usage by disability employment programs and professionals are not understood by employers, who consistently report that interaction with disability employment programs is characterized by both unfamiliar terminology and a lack of understanding of business protocol. In an interesting recent study, Kaye, Jans, and Jones (2011) surveyed human resource professionals to find out the reasons for this reluctance. Table 13.1 lists those reasons for employers' reluctance to hire people with disabilities. The principal barriers to employing workers with disabilities are lack of awareness of disability and accommodation issues, concern over costs, and fear of legal liability. With regard to strategies employers might use to increase hiring and retention, respondents identified increased training and centralized disability and accommodation expertise and mechanisms. Public policy approaches preferred by respondents included no-cost external problem solving, subsidized accommodations, tax breaks, and mediation in lieu of formal complaints or lawsuits.

Transportation

The lack of available, affordable transportation is a barrier to employment that cuts across virtually all disability groups (Moon, Luedtke, & Halloran-Tornquist, 2010). For many individuals with disabilities, such as those with epilepsy, visual impairments, intellectual disabilities, or severe physical impairments, driving is restricted by law or by individual limitations. Financial constraints may prohibit automobile ownership for individuals with

Table 13.1. Proposed reasons for employers not hiring people with disabilities, ranked by the proportion of respondents expressing agreement

Reason	In agreement[a]	Strongly agree	Strongly disagree
1 They are worried about the cost of providing reasonable accommodations so that workers with disabilities can do their jobs.	81.4	30.1	2.9
2. They do not know how to handle the needs of a worker with a disability on the job.	80.9	25.4	4.1
3. They are afraid they will not be able to discipline or fire a worker with a disability for poor performance because of potential lawsuits.	80.2	23.4	4.8
4. They cannot ask about a job applicant's disability, making it hard to assess whether the person can do the job.	73.3	20.3	4.9
5. They are concerned about the extra time that supervisors or co-workers will need to spend to assist workers with disabilities.	70.9	14.8	3.8
6. They are worried about other costs, such as increased health insurance or worker's compensation premiums.	69.9	22.8	4.2
7. They are afraid the workers with disabilities will not work up to the same standards as other employees.	68.5	12.1	5.4
8. They rarely see people with disabilities applying for jobs.	66.3	12.5	8.0
9. They believe that people with disabilities cannot do the basic functions of the jobs they apply for.	55.8	8.1	8.9
10. They discriminate against job applicants with disabilities.	53.3	12.8	12.6
11. They are concerned about attitudes of co-workers toward the person with a disability.	46.7	7.1	8.8
12. They find that job applicants with disabilities do not have the necessary skills and experience.	41.8	6.2	12.3
13. They think of workers with disabilities as "problem employees."	40.9	5.9	12.3
14. They find that job applicants with disabilities do not present themselves well in interviews.	31.5	3.9	12.4

[a]Response was "strongly agree" or "agree."
Note: Response categories were "strongly agree," "agree," and "strongly disagree." Responses of "don't know" are treated as missing and not included in the percentages.
Reprinted with kind permission from Springer Science+Business Media: *Journal of Occupational Rehabilitation,* Why don't employers hire and retain workers with disabilities?, Vol. 21, 2011, pp. 526–536, H.S. Kaye, L.H. Jans, & E.C. Jones, Table 1.

other disabilities, such as psychosocial impairments, who are unemployed. In either case, the result is that many individuals with disabilities must rely on either public transportation or alternative modes of transportation to enter the job market.

Unfortunately, Nick's situation is not unusual. People with disabilities are frequently without the transportation services and supports that they need to be included into the workforce and community.

Nick   At 5 p.m., Nick exited from the office building where he was employed as a customer service representative and began to wait for his ride home. It was a hot summer day and Nick tried to keep cool under the shade of a tree.

When Nick was 12, he was in a motor vehicle accident that left him with a **spinal cord injury** and mild brain injury. His life changed dramatically that day, and now he depends on others to help him with activities of daily living, such as bathing, dressing, cooking, and eating. Over the years, Nick made great progress. Last year, he moved out of his parents' home into an apartment. A health care assistant visits him each morning and evening to assist with the things he is not able to accomplish alone. As Nick waited for his ride, he reflected on how well things were going. One month ago, he was offered a position at an insulation supplier. After 6 years of looking for a suitable work opportunity, he finally found an employer who was willing to hire him. The job offered decent wages and good benefits, which would give him the chance to be more self-sufficient and no longer depend on the public assistance he received.

Nick watched as his co-workers, many of whom were friends, left the building and drove away. It was becoming hotter, and it started to rain. Nick stared at the watch mounted on the arm of his wheelchair. It read 6:15 p.m.—he had been waiting for longer than an hour. A security guard patrolling the parking lot stopped and asked Nick if he needed help. He requested that the guard call the paratransit service that was supposed to pick him up. As the guard was calling, the van pulled up to the building. Nick was wheeled to the lift by the van driver, who offered no apology for his late arrival. Nick felt very angry about being subjected to the incompetence of others and frustrated because this was his only option. He was further saddened and frightened by the fact that he might have been left outside in the heat for a prolonged period of time. The next day, Nick had to go to the local emergency room because he felt very ill, and he was eventually diagnosed with heat stroke. He missed work but was able to return in a week.

Establishing a National Employment Agenda[1]

Since the Great Recession of 2008, more and more people in the United States, especially those with disabilities, find themselves unemployed or significantly underemployed (Fogg, Harrison, & McMahon, 2010). Job security is more difficult than ever to count upon and new graduates from high school, trade school, and college are finding employment more difficult than ever. Fogg, Harrison, and McMahon noted

> Recent data from the U.S. Bureau of Labor Statistics allows assessment of the impact of the Great Recession on working age persons with disabilities in America. Differences which favor those without disabilities were detected in the labor market activity rate, the official unemployment rate, and in the desire for work among those who have quit the workforce. These differences persist among subgroups based upon age and educational attainment. (2010, p. 193)

Hence, since the early 2000s, we have gone from a very fertile job-producing economy to one that is struggling to provide jobs. Where do persons with disabilities fit into this new labor market?

To overcome these huge barriers, we have to examine the issues from two perspectives. The first one is looking at these barriers from a large societal perspective, one that

---

[1]This section draws heavily on Unger, D. (2001). *National study of employers' experiences with workers with disabilities and their knowledge and utilization of accommodations* (doctoral dissertation). Richmond, VA: Virginia Commonwealth University.

will require substantial federal investments and many more public–private partnerships between the government and the business sectors. As important as these changes in policy will be for the future, they are beyond the scope of this book, which is specifically directed to the second perspective—that is, the teacher, the transition coordinator, and the counselor or parent. What tools do these frontline providers and end users of vocational services need to make transition a reality? How can we help persons with disabilities and the professionals engaged in working with them find strategies and models to maximize their strengths and minimize their weaknesses?

In this chapter, we examine approaches that have shown themselves repeatedly over time to be effective. Each of these approaches draws upon the concept of **discovery** (Griffin, Hammis, & Geary, 2007). Discovery is an assessment process that seeks to answer the questions, "Who is this person?" and "What are the ideal conditions of employment?" The outcomes of this process are multiple employment directions to pursue that are not based upon an occupational title or job description, but rather upon the individual's vocational interests and skills, which form the basis for developing a job for the person in his or her community. From this approach, a strengths-based model building on an individual's capacities is revealed. In effect, employment support is viewed as knowledge creation (O'Brien & Callahan, 2010). Bolles (2009) in *What Color Is Your Parachute?* suggested that people think "outside the box" when looking at job prospects, building upon unique skills and talents rather than traditional job trends.

O'Brien and Callahan (2010) in this creative mode of thinking noted that, although there have been especially unfavorable labor conditions and financial limitations for job programs in recent years, there is another way of looking at identifying employment opportunities. In Table 13.2, they offer up an Employment System Matrix, which constructs the solution of the employment challenge as a mechanism that builds off the individuals' strengths identified through discovery, which then allows the job search to be wider and more flexible including the option of creating new opportunities. Later in

Table 13.2. The employment system matrix

Actions by/with job seekers	Natural support + reasonable accommodation and technology	Support to ordinary processes	Negotiation of personalized conditions and contributions
Decide to work	• Job seeker makes his or her own decision to work without assistance/support.	• Job seeker gets encouragement and support from family and allies to consider employment.	• Job seeker and allies are explained customized employment and assured that work will reflect the person.
Identify focus: job or interests, conditions, and contributions	• Job seeker reflects on local job market and personal interests and considers good match.	• Job seeker receives typical assessment for employment and is assisted to identify job match.	• Job seeker receives facilitated discovery to assist in identifying conditions, interests, and contributions.
Get the job	• Job seeker uses personal connections and those of allies to make employer contacts.	• Job seeker is assisted by a job developer to find open jobs that match interests.	• Job seeker is represented by a job developer to negotiate a custom fit with personal conditions, interests, and contributions in relation to employer needs/benefits.
Succeed on the job	• New employee receives supports as typically offered to all workers, including reasonable accommodation.	• New employee and employer receive support from a job coach to perform the job responsibilities of the position filled.	• New employee and employer receive support from a job coach to perform the duties of the customized job description.

From O'Brien, J., & Callahan, M. (2010). Employment support as knowledge creation. *Research and Practice for Persons with Severe Disabilities, 35*(1–2), 1–8; reprinted by permission. This article first appeared in *Research and Practice for Persons with Severe Disabilities*. Visit www.tash.org or contact info@tash.org for more information.

the chapter, we discuss the numerous models and vehicles available for this system to be implemented.

Employment First

Citizens with disabilities in the labor force have a positive financial impact on our economy, generating income that is ultimately returned in the form of tax revenues and purchase of goods and services. Despite this knowledge, citizens with disabilities continue to have the high rates of unemployment. Employment rates for individuals with and without disabilities differ considerably. The Bureau of Labor Statistics (2010b) reported that, in July 2010, 18% of individuals with disabilities ages 16 years and older (excluding institutionalized populations) were employed versus 64% of individuals without disabilities.

Author of the Americans with Disabilities Act (PL 101-336), the Honorable Tony Coelho, stated, "A lot of people focus on our disability and ignore our ability, and all we want is the right to be fired, because if you give us the right to be fired, then you have to give us the right to be hired" (2003). Citizens with disabilities do not necessarily want to be fired, but they do want to be treated equally in the labor force.

In recent years, there has been a growing grassroots movement to establish **Employment First** initiatives in the United States (Tennessee, 2002; Kansas, 2011; Washington, 2004; California, 2005; Indiana, 2005; Minnesota, 2006; Virginia, 2011). This concept is built upon the notion that competitive employment should be the first choice for all persons with disabilities (Wehman, Revell, & Brooke, 2003; Wehman, 2006b). The Association for Persons in Supported Employment (APSE), the Employment Network, has endorsed the concept of statewide Employment First initiatives as a recommended practice. It has also been expanded dramatically with the work of Butterworth (Butterworth & Callahan, 2010) who has spearheaded the Supported Employment Leadership Network. Many states are working with their state APSE chapter and state government to secure input from all stakeholders.

Establishing Employment First Initiatives

Although no universal definition of *Employment First* exists, the policies, practices, and strategies focus on integrated, community-based employment as the desired outcome for individuals with disabilities. Employment First strategies generally consist of a clear set of guiding principles, policies, and practices disseminated through state statute, regulation, or operational procedures that identify employment in integrated, community-based businesses as the priority for state funding. Kiernan, Hoff, Freeze, and Mank (2011) identified 15 principles that are associated with an Employment First agenda. A number of state initiatives have also taken steps to clarify what *Employment First* means. In Minnesota, for example, Employment First means "expecting, encouraging, providing, creating, and rewarding integrated employment in the workforce as the first and preferred option of youth and adults with disabilities" (Minnesota's Employment First Manifesto, 2007).

Recommendations for Implementing Employment First

Employment First is about raising expectations. The real engine of social change is not money but, rather, expectations. Of course, adequate public resources are required to obtain high-quality education and integrated-employment outcomes. However, without high expectations, individuals with disabilities and their families often settle for programs or services that do not encourage them to participate fully in the mainstream of community life.

Build a "Coalition of the Willing" Collaboration with multiple stakeholders, such as individuals with disabilities, educators, business, rehabilitation agencies, state agencies, disability organizations, and families, is an initial step. Although it is difficult to get everyone on board, this should not become a barrier to your local efforts. It is far more important to have "doers" on the team than representatives from influential organizations who do not contribute solutions to move Employment First forward. In building a strong coalition, start with people who have the interest, passion, time, and energy to work on the real issues. Intentionally leave any naysayers standing on the outside because you cannot afford the distractions or negative energy.

Clarify "Employment" and "Employment First"   It is important to establish a clear and uncompromising definition of "employment." For most Employment First initiatives, this means a focus on real jobs, real wages, and real business settings. It also means the launch of self-employment and **microenterprises.** It is critical for everyone to be working from the same set of assumptions. Who can be against people with disabilities having an equal opportunity to get a good job, use their talents and skills, earn competitive wages, increase their self-support, and contribute to prosperity of their communities?

Emphasize Real Systems-Change Policies   Our country spends millions of dollars on secondary education, adult community services, Social Security disability benefits, transportation, and comprehensive health care of Americans with disabilities. Unfortunately, many of these resources do not encourage or reward integrated, community-based employment. Resolving our national unemployment problem will require a shift in policies and "rebalancing" of many existing resources.

The most successful initiatives, therefore, recognize that the core charge is to thoughtfully and methodically address policies that encourage and support integrated employment outcomes. This vision for change needs to be reflected in all appropriate public policies impacting education as well as adult health, disability, and human services. To the extent possible, public policies need to be unmistakably clear about expectations as well as provide for flexibility to rebalance existing resources. Of course, this means moving aggressively to develop new policies, amend existing ones, and reallocate funding to promote an Employment First approach.

Focus on the Positives   The most successful alliances focus on what they are for—not what they are against. This is an example of taking the high road. When local initiatives remain focused on the one, simple idea and stay true to "everybody means everybody," arguments are neutralized. In sum, the most successful alliances work hard to build momentum that others want to join.

Vocational Options: What Are the Choices?

When most students are in high school, the thought process eventually comes around to, *What am I going to do when I graduate?* Some will go to technical school, some will go college, some get jobs, and some will have no idea what they are doing. Young people with disabilities are no different. So what are the vocational options? Since the mid-1990s, inclusive work opportunities in integrated employment arrangements have become the highest goal and vocational option of choice (Flippo & Gardner, 2011; Hall, Butterworth, Winsor, Gilmore, & Metzel, 2007; Luecking, 2009b; Rusch & Braddock, 2004; Wehman, Inge, Revell, & Brooke, 2007). There is an increasing recognition that individuals with disabilities want competitive employment (Migliore et al., 2007) and want to be heavily involved in planning their own futures (see Chapter 2). The following sections review different vocational options that are available in some communities in the United States.

In Figure 13.1, we list the numerous types of vocational options that are increasingly available to young people with disabilities as they exit school. College is a major option as well, but in this chapter, we focus only on work. (See Chapter 15 for information about postsecondary education options.) The figure provides a range of choices, and what follows in a large part of this chapter is a description of these choices. It is very important to

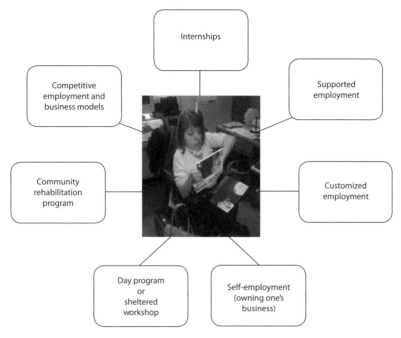

Figure 13.1. Vocational choices for young people with disaiblties.

note that many communities do *not* offer all of these choices, and in some communities, the choices are not well developed. It is also important to note that some of these choices have richer, higher-quality outcomes associated with them such as real work compared with sheltered work.

Day Programs and Sheltered Workshops

In the United States, approximately 6,000 adult activity centers or day programs serve people with mental, physical, and emotional disabilities (Braddock, Rizzolo, & Hemp, 2010). These programs are sponsored by The Adult Resources Center (ARC), United Cerebral Palsy, local churches, and other community organizations. Usually, these programs offer skill training, prevocational training, make-work vocational activities, field trips, recreation, and other types of special education–related curricula that people with severe cognitive disabilities are assumed to require.

Migliore, Mank, Grossi, and Rogan (2007, 2008) observed several definitions and labels that have developed over time to indicate what is referred to as workshops. Examples include the following: sheltered workshops, workshops, industries, industrial workshops, affirmative industries, training workshops, vocational workshops, and rehabilitation workshops. The core attributes of workshops can be identified by looking at

a. What activities are being offered
b. What work environment is taking place
c. What wages are being paid

For instance, because of their conditions, adults with disabilities in workshops are always subordinated to staff members. In addition, adults with disabilities in sheltered workshops are typically paid less than the minimum wage in accordance with a special certificate issued by the Department of Labor.

In fact, there are few positive endorsements for the large-scale maintenance of adult day programs, and Congress has publically questioned the value of these programs (U.S. Senate, October 20, 2005). Most agree that they should be shut down or phased out and that

funds should be transferred to providing support to people in more productive and dignified community pursuits (e.g., Mank, 2008; Walker & Rogan, 2007). Dale DiLeo (2007), in
arguably one of the most poignant books of the decade on segregation, called for an end to
workshop day programs and institutions. He wrote the following:

> I once worked in place where the rules were the rules, and all of us staff were very young. It
> was in 1975, very early in my career, and the place was a residential facility for children with
> autism. Most of the residents were challenging. Some were aggressive; others would hurt
> themselves.
>
> Management decided that three residents in particular must live in the secure room at
> night. The room was a small space, about 8 by 10 feet, not much bigger than a walk-in closet.
> It was largely taken up with two sets of bunk beds. There was no other furniture. There was
> also no "overnight staff," just the owners of the facility, who had a bedroom and lived in the
> residence. In truth, I doubted that they looked in on any of the residents in this home very
> often. So to secure the room of the three most challenging residents, the outside of the door
> was locked, closed with an eye-hook and latch from the outside.
>
> Was this a breach of every safeguard, fire policy, and human rights policy I now know?
> Of course. But because we were all right out of college and had no real training in the realities
> of this business, we accepted the explanation we were given by those in charge—that this was
> for the residents' own protection: the only solution for people so severely disturbed.
>
> But it gets worse. This room had a radiator controlled by a thermostat in the hall. In
> summer it was stifling on its own. But in winter, overnight, with the door closed and the heat
> on, that room would get really hot. More troubling still, since the door was locked, there was
> a portable toilet inside. Combine the heat with the smell, the room was simply unbearable.
> Opening that door each morning was difficult, and one could only imagine what spending
> the night inside was like.
>
> This was called Raymond's Room.
>
> Raymond was the room's most permanent resident. Other students were assigned
> there from time to time, but Raymond never moved from his room. He was the resident who
> couldn't be trusted, and he had been in this room so long it was now named after him. (DiLeo,
> 2007, pp. 1–2)

So, from a moral and ethical perspective, large questions have been raised about the
legitimacy of sheltered workshops and day programs. These discussions have continued
at state and federal levels (NDRN, 2012).

In addition, there are cost-effective issues related to sheltered work versus SE in the
community. Kregel, Dean, Wehman (2002) presented an in-depth comparison of sheltered
work versus SE and found that SE yielded better wage outcomes than sheltered work.
Similarly, Cimera (2008) investigated the cost trends of supported and sheltered employees with intellectual disabilities as they completed one "employment cycle" (i.e., from the
point they entered their programs to the point when they changed their jobs, left their program, or otherwise stopped receiving services). Data indicated that the cumulative costs
generated by supported employees were much lower than the cumulative costs generated
by sheltered employees ($6,618 versus $19,388). In a more recent study, Cimera (2011) examined the vocational outcomes of the two cohorts of supported employees—4,904 supported employees who participated in sheltered workshops and 4,904 supported employees
that did not participate in sheltered workshops. Individuals in these groups were matched
on the basis of their diagnosis, the presence of secondary conditions, and their gender.
It was found that supported employees from the nonsheltered workshop group were just
as likely to be employed as supported employees from sheltered workshops (60.4% versus
59.6%). Furthermore, nonsheltered workshop–supported employees earned significantly
more ($137.20 versus $118.55 per week), worked more hours (24.78 versus 22.44), and cost
less to serve ($4,542.65 versus $7,894.63).

Popular media are also shining a spotlight on segregated or sheltered employment.
For example, in the *Orlando Weekly*, Gore noted

> On any given weekday, in a small warehouse tucked into a wooded area off of Jimmy Huger
> Circle in Daytona Beach, a couple dozen people work at what may be the last of America's

manual-assembly jobs. Two wiry men pull stringy pieces of yellow nylon out of white cords that are destined for a buoy commissioned by the U.S. military. In the rear of the room, a bespectacled young woman sits at a table where she feeds a large spool of copper wire into a modified guillotine paper cutter and cuts the wire into 2-inch pieces that are later dipped in flux, soldered and used as electrical connectors by a utility company. Most of the workers in the warehouse, however, are assembling "tangs"—metal widgets slightly larger than a fingernail that serve as attachment points for the guy-wires that stabilize telephone poles. This unusually post-industrial workshop is even more intriguing when you consider that all of the workers here have an intellectual or developmental disability of some sort, and for their 5 hours of daily labor, some will earn far less than $100 in their biweekly paychecks. That's because the state minimum wage of $7.31 per hour does not apply here; rather, workers are paid by the piece, such as 1.8 cents per tank or 5–7 cents per stripped buoy cord. Because of their disabilities, few of them work fast enough to pull in a wage remotely comparable to their able-bodied peers. (2011, p. 17).

The value and continued funding of this questionable vocational option will continue to be under scrutiny as national organizations such as APSE, The Alliance for Full Participation, and the Employment Network promote Employment First initiatives.

Sam   Sam has autism and his parents are looking forward to his enrollment in a workshop even though his teachers and others feel that he should pursue competitive employment using SE services. But Sam's parents moved ahead and made arrangements for Sam to go to the facility to learn work skills each morning during his last year of school. They do not understand that this undermines his chance to work in the community and what he learns will not generalize to another workplace.

At the facility, along with others, Sam boxes ink pens for a manufacturer located in town. He is responsible for packing 50 boxes per hour. He is paid $1.00 for every box packed. The pens are then sold to a local vendor. Sam's co-workers also have disabilities such as mental retardation or physical disabilities. Most are nonverbal, so he is not learning social skills. Sam does not receive any fringe benefits, has no room for advancement, and there is only limited likelihood that he will be able to pursue work in his community. Sam cannot be expected to generalize any skills that he has learned into a newer, faster-paced competitive environment because he has not been trained.

Community Rehabilitation Programs

Community rehabilitation programs (CRPs) are usually more comprehensive in work services offered and provide multiple employment options available than the traditional day program or sheltered workshop. These tend to be quite large programs with some day program aspects, some sheltered work enclaves such as group vocational placements in the community, as well as some competitive employment and supported employment programs. These facilities are multidimensional and offer many services. Some programs are quite progressive and look to downsize and expand into the community, CRPs can play a major leadership role with their ample expertise if their focus is predominantly on integrated employment and real jobs for real people in the community (Brookes-Lane, Hutcheson, & Revell, 2005).

Sam and his parents (see case study) chose the local sheltered workshop, which will lead to a path of segregated employment and, subsequently, a dependent vocational lifestyle. Service providers, advocates, special education teachers, and families must ask themselves whether they have made the right choice when people like Sam are placed in segregated facilities. Is this the best we can do for people with significant disabilities like Sam in America? Is this the best that Sam can hope for? What kind of employment and career future will Sam have with making boxes all of his life? And, is this a self-fulfilling prophecy, meaning, is this what Sam and his parents have come to expect of him?

CRPs emerged in large numbers as individuals with developmental disabilities began to leave state residential facilities, or state institutions, in the 1970s (Stancliffe & Lakin,

2005). Deinstitutionalization was the result of court decisions and new laws that eventually led to more than 6,000 to 7,000 CRPs and day programs nationally (Braddock, Rizzolo & Hemp, 2010). These programs known as "extended employment programs" are also referred to as sheltered workshops/employment or facility-based programs. The Vocational Rehabilitation (VR) program regulations define "extended employment" as "work in a non-integrated or sheltered setting for a public or private nonprofit agency or organization that provides compensation in accordance with the Fair Labor Standards Act" (34 C.F.R. 361.5[b][19]). Individuals with more significant support needs typically are referred to adult activity centers, and those with perceived potential for work are assigned to extended employment programs.

Internships: Another Way to Success

There is another way to employment success, and this is the use of carefully planned internships (Luecking, 2009b; Rutkowski, Daston, Van Kuiken, & Riehle, 2006). They can be short, long, summer-length, and so forth, but they all have one thing in common: They provide real life experiences for individuals searching for their best skill path. Carter, Austin, and Trainor (2011b) recently observed in their study of National Longitudinal Transition Study-2 (NLTS-2) follow-up data with students with intellectual disabilities that the early work experiences of a nationally representative sample of youth with severe disabilities (i.e., intellectual disabilities, autism, multiple disabilities) were highly instrumental in leading to employment. Using data from the NLTS-2, they explored the extent to which various student-, family-, school-, and community-level factors were associated with paid work experiences during high school. Findings highlighted the elusiveness of early work experiences for many youth with severe disabilities and called attention to malleable factors that may play a role in shaping employment success during high school. Recommendations for research and practice were highlighted.

One such program is the Project SEARCH high school program (http://www.project search.us/), which provides a unique school-to-work transition model for young people with significant disabilities with a strong emphasis on internship rotations for the entire school year (Luecking, Riehle, & Donovan, 2004; Rutkowski, Daston, Van Kuiken, & Riehle, 2006; Wehman, McDonough, Molinelli, Schall, Riehle, & Ham, 2011). The program combines real-life work experience, training in employability and independent living skills, and placement assistance through an active collaboration of the education system, employers, and the VR system. The hallmark of the Project SEARCH model is complete immersion in the workplace. Students spend their entire school day at the workplace, for a full school year. Within the workplace students receive a seamless combination of classroom instruction, career exploration, and on-the-job training and support through internships or worksite rotations.

Project SEARCH is a business-led transition model where schools create collaborative partnerships with local large businesses such as hospitals, bank centers, or government centers. Such businesses afford students in transition to adult life the opportunity to work in internships across their senior year of high school. Students attend their individualized program at the business instead of school. Table 13.3 presents a sample list of the skills taught during this instructional time.

Critical Project SEARCH Components

There are components of the Project SEARCH model that set it apart from intensive community-based instruction that many high school programs provide to transition-aged students. They include setting a goal of 90% community-based employment at a competitive wage, rotation through internships that equate to career training, and shared case management between school and adult services agencies. Each of these critical components is discussed briefly:

Table 13.3. A sample list of skills taught during morning instructional time in a Project SEARCH® classroom

- Identifying job skill strengths, preferences, and interests
- Communicating with supervisors and co-workers
- Dressing and behaving professionally
- Communicating with customers or clients
- Practicing specific work skills
- Accepting constructive criticism related to work tasks
- Asking for and taking a break
- Calling in sick, late, or requesting time off
- Preparing a resumé
- Attending a job interview

1. *Programwide Employment Goals*—Each Project SEARCH replication site sets, and *actively pursues,* competitive employment at a prevailing wage for each participant in the program. This is *the primary goal* of the program.

2. *Internship Model*—The most critical aspect of Project SEARCH programs is the internship rotation. Students rotate through three, 10- to 12-week internships across the school year. These internships usually comprise a set of skills the student requires to attain employment in a career of his or her choice. For example, if a student expresses an interest in data processing, that student may rotate through three internships that teach different aspects of that career. In a hospital program, such a student might complete an internship creating address files of donors to the hospital, followed by an internship in diabetes management to create a database with addresses of doctors, with a final internship inputting invoice totals into a spreadsheet in the accounts payable office.

3. *Collaboration*—The third important component of Project SEARCH is collaboration among agencies that serve students with disabilities in transition to adulthood. The essential collaborative partners include school staff, host business liaisons, rehabilitative services agency staff, developmental and/or intellectual disabilities agency staff, employment services organization staff, transition students, and their families.

Jason   Jason's first internship was with the coronary care unit at a community hospital, which is a small, eight-room unit. His job was to remove soiled linen bags, stock medical supplies, and restock lab trays. A sedentary portion of his job was to stamp patient flow sheets (charts). Jason needed little support learning his job skills. As originally presented, this internship would require Jason to set his own schedule and determine his own work priorities. At the same time, his greatest challenge was his work ethic and concern for work quality. He rushed through his work so that he could read or watch television in the break room. To institute good work habits, Jason was not allowed to bring a book to his internship and his job coach created a structured schedule that provided periods for him to complete his duties. In addition, his job coach developed a structured schedule that met the requirements of the unit and provided a consistent structure to Jason's day.

Jason's second internship was with Biomedical Durable Equipment. Employees in this department work on teams of two and they circulate systematically throughout the hospital to clean and distribute IV pumps. Jason built a close relationship with his partner and enjoyed saying hi to everyone he passed throughout the hospital. He learned how to properly clean IV pumps, as well as the IV poles to which they are attached. Jason frequently had to be reminded to take his time to clean thoroughly. Jason always counted how many items he cleaned on a shift and was proud to announce this number daily to his job coach and employer. He did not face challenges with job tasks, but by the nature of the job, his break times were limited. Over time during this internship, his endurance improved.

Following his graduation from Project SEARCH, Jason was hired to work 24 hours a week in the intensive care unit where he earns $9.14 per hour. He performs many of the same tasks similar to those he was responsible for as an intern. He works closely with his job coach on consistently stocking the carts properly, completing all of them in a day, and following his schedule. Jason has an iPod Touch, which contains a checklist of supplies for bedside carts, photos of properly stocked carts, and reminder alarms. Jason's job coach has created several schedules, and daily logs to hold him accountable for the work that he completes and the way that he spends his time.

The Marriott Bridges Internship Program

Another well-known internship program is the Marriott Bridges Internship Program, which was developed by the Marriott Foundation for People with Disabilities. The program, which operates in a number of major urban centers across the country, matches the interests and abilities of young people with the workforce needs of employers, creating and supporting strong employment relationships that work to the benefit of all (www.bridgestowork.org). The core elements of Bridges include

1. Initial career counseling and job search
2. Placement in a paid position with training and support available to ensure job success
3. Postplacement follow-up support and tracking of participants to enable and measure vocational growth

The students who participate are primarily referred by teachers and transition personnel. Serving the entire spectrum of special education students, the program has boasted a typical placement rate of 68%–90%, regardless of the primary disability, gender, and race of the participants (Fabian, 2007).

The success of Bridges highlights the advantages of pairing paid work experiences with other educational activities. First, youth are achieving an employment rate that notably exceeds typical employment rates of transitioning students. Second, with a high percentage of long-term employment, it is apparent that exposure to youth with disabilities—along with the competent support of Bridges professionals—enables employers to gain access to an untapped workforce.

Competitive Employment and Business Models

Competitive employment is defined as work in the competitive labor market that is performed on a full-time or part-time basis in an integrated setting and for which the individual is compensated at or above minimum wage, but not less than the customary wage and levels of benefits paid by the employer for the same or similar work performed by individuals who are not disabled. Some individuals with disabilities require support to gain competitive employment and others do not. Some businesses are set up to support workers too, which minimizes the need for support from other sources. This section takes a look at job placement, networking, and business partnerships as well as how mentoring may be used once an individual is hired.

Job Placement

Some people with disabilities secure work in their communities through job placement services offered by the state VR agency or purchased from a private vendor of such a service. For example, VR counselors are located in most cities in the United States. However, rehabilitation counselors are often challenged with heavy caseloads and their subsequent inability to handle the most challenging cases. In such instance, the service may be purchased from another source. Job placement typically involves having a VR professional personally represent the individual with a disability to a potential employer. If a possible job opportunity is identified, then this is discussed with the job seeker and the application process proceeds from there in hopes that the person is hired. After the individual goes to work, the VR professional follows up with the employer and the new hire to for an established period of time (e.g., 30 days).

Networking

Another approach to securing work is to tap into the job seeker's family-and-friend network (Luecking & Tilson, 2009). This simply involves identifying people (i.e., personal connections) who can introduce the job seeker and/or VR professional to potential employers. These employers are then contacted and asked to take time to share their thoughts on job possibilities for the job seeker within their business. If this is not possible, referral to other contacts is requested, which expands the job seeker's network. Tapping into the family-and-friend network reflects an increasing reliance on people in the community—that is, employers, friends, and other individuals who are not involved in the VR system who are willing to try to find jobs for people with disabilities.

Creating partnerships with businesses for the long term is another approach that can lead to employment for individuals with disabilities.

Business Models and Partnership

Today, there is a clear trend toward community rehabilitation programs and services having a greater involvement in and partnership with the business community. Today, those charged with assisting students with transitioning to work are increasingly defining their work as consulting with business and meeting their unique needs as a way to build lasting relationships. Employers are finding that support strategies for individuals with disabilities are not an isolated set of strategies but are largely the same strategies used to enhance productivity and increase job tenure among all workers. To stay competitive, businesses must seek ways to tap nontraditional labor pools. Workforce diversity needs to be viewed as a competitive advantage and a business opportunity (Chubb Group, 2011).

Businesses can better achieve their diversity goals, become more profitable, and grow by hiring qualified workers with disabilities but will need more reliable information on the recommended practices for hiring and retaining individuals with disabilities. There is limited research available that details effective employer practices that facilitate employment outcomes for individuals with disabilities. Table 13.4 presents some of the most pressing employer needs for evidence-based guidance.

There are examples of successful employer practices from small and large businesses that understand the "business case" for hiring, retaining, and advancing individuals with disabilities (McMahon et al., 2004). However, there is an urgent need to quantify, document, and translate knowledge on such employer practices that have resulted in quality employment outcomes.

Diversity Inc. has developed a list of the top-10 companies for people with disabilities

Table 13.4. Employer practices: What does business need?

Need to find qualified workers with disabilities.

Need to know how to effectively recruit workers with disabilities. (There is emerging evidence that indicates a preferred vendor is an exemplary evidence-based practice.)

Need to know the best interview protocol(s). (How can employers communicate with individuals who have limited language skills?)

Need to know information on accommodating workers with disabilities as well as universal design for all workers.

Need to know what staffing support systems are most effective.

Need to know how health care reform will affect employees with disabilities.

Need training on how to implement evidence-based employer practices.

Need to determine an effective way to measure success.

based on the company having active recruitment programs for people with disabilities, having a strong employee resource group for people with disabilities, and having certain work/life benefits, such as flex time, telecommuting, caregiving assistance, and leaves of absence (Frankel, 2009). See Table 13.5 for some exemplary employers.

Wallace   Wallace is 19 and is diagnosed with multiple learning disabilities and neurological impairments. He has auditory and visual learning problems that make it difficult to read. He also has problems with memory and often does not follow through with instructions. Wallace was referred to a state VR counselor by his individualized education program team. His rehabilitation counselor spent several hours providing guidance about future vocational options. To be specific, the counselor wanted to learn more about what Wallace liked most about work and what his ideal job would be.

Wallace's dad is an attorney. Wallace wants to work in a similar environment, a big building downtown. Therefore, a decision is made to look for work in a law firm or other big business downtown. One firm in town had a job opening for a law library clerk. This job entailed copying legal documents and reshelving books. The supervisor trained Wallace for a number of weeks. Wallace was able to learn how to perform the job successfully without specialized onsite help in about 3 months.

The firm initially gave Wallace 20 hours of work per week, questioning his ability to learn and perform the job. Today, he works 40 hours per week. The major reasons for the success on the job include: 1) Wallace's personal interests were given careful consideration, 2) his father's background in the field had a positive family influence, and 3) the counselor communicated frequently with the employer to verify Wallace's progress and offered assistance if needed.

Self-Employment: The Resource Ownership Choice

People with the most significant disabilities traditionally have been overlooked as candidates for self-employment. However, support systems can help many people operate their own businesses, limited partnerships, or businesses within businesses (Griffin & Hammis, 2003; Ispen, Arnold, & Colling, 2005). The key to success is support, which gives the entrepreneur a chance to compete in the open market.

The myriad supports necessary for a small business owner typically include accounting services, business planning, access to capital (e.g., loans), marketing consultation, and training in product or service production. The same needs are evident for individuals with disabilities, but sometimes the manner in which the needs must be met is different. For instance, a typical entrepreneur has a credit history that a bank officer can review in structuring a start-up loan. In many cases, small business hopefuls with disabilities have little credit available and few savings because of long-term reliance on Social Security benefits. Support from rehabilitation personnel may be necessary to gain access to VR resources, to determine useful assistive or universal technology, to apply for local low-interest loan funds, or to develop a Plan for Achieving Self-Support (PASS) through Social Security in order to self-finance. In Figure 13.2 is the story of Keith, who created his own company near Atlanta, Georgia.

Supported Employment: Three Decades Later

SE emphasizes the benefits of having opportunities for real, integrated work as a primary option (Butterworth & Callahan, 2010; Hall et al., 2007; Wehman, Brooke, & Revell, 2007). All parties involved benefit from competitive employment. Such employment provides the individual with a disability a real job, benefits, and the dignity that arises from gainful employment. SE has been found to be highly effective for VR clients to gain employment (e.g., University of Wisconsin–Stoughton Study, March 2011). Both VR services and SE were found to have a strong impact on employment quality. VR services were found to improve quality of employment outcomes and SE was found to be associated with higher quality of employment outcomes in terms of average weekly earnings, average hours worked per

Table 13.5. Business models that promote employment for persons with disabilities

Business	Emerging employer practices
Cincinnati Children's Hospital – Project SEARCH®—New Freedom Initiative Award in November 2004 from the U.S. Department of Labor	• Major diversity initiative in their hiring practices • Business model of meaningful employment and education for individuals with significant barriers to employment • Full benefits in a wide range of positions that require mastering complex functions
Walgreens—Ranked #2 in *CAREERS* & the *disABLED Magazine* readers' survey (http://www.eop.com/awards-CD.php)	• Accommodations/technology for efficient workplace • Diversity on work teams • Universal design • Hiring practices that are disability-friendly • Collaboration with community partners
Bank of America—Ranked as #14 by Riley (2006) as a disability-forward company; ranked as #14 in 2009 list of Top 50 Companies for Diversity (Diversity Inc., 2009).	• Use of embedded employment specialists • America/Works program • Outreach and recruiting efforts—persons with disabilities, individuals on welfare, homeless veterans, youth at risk, the working poor, and low-income seniors
Marriott Bridges—Ranked as #31 by Riley (2006) as a disability-forward company; ranked as #4 in 2009 Top 50 Companies for Diversity (Diversity Inc., 2009).	• Transition from school to work • Positive working environment for people with disabilities • Ethnic diversity • Disability-friendly hiring practices and support for job retention
Cascade Engineering—Employer of the Year Award in 2002 by Goodwill, Inc.	• Diversity culture • Community partnerships • Disability-friendly hiring practices • Job retention • Return to work
Best Buy Co., Inc.—2008 New Freedom Initiative Award	• Employee business network/INCLUDE (award recognizing employee business network) • Supportive services and accommodations for people with disabilities • Company-sponsored health plan • Strategic partnerships with disability organizations
Imperial Irrigation District	• Interactive process for accommodation • Supervisor participation • Return to work for job retention
AMC	• Collaboration with community partners • Inclusive workplace • Internship opportunities

week, and access to employer-based health insurance.

With SE, the employer gets a good employee and receives specialized support for job acquisition and retention. The family is able to see the newly employed family member in a fully competent role in the workplace. Finally, taxpayers spend less money than they would to support the individual in a segregated day program. However, several questions remain: Why do the vast majority of individuals with intellectual, physical, psychiatric, and sensory disabilities remain in segregated day treatment programs? What values are service providers and advocates operating under?

The answers to these questions lie partially in the inability of advocates and people with disabilities to adequately coordinate their collective efforts to increase employment opportunities. Adult service systems using segregated services remain deeply entrenched as they have for decades. Changing this way of providing services is extremely difficult, particularly in times of reduced funding resulting from a recessionary economy. Hence, there is an overwhelming necessity to market the positive attributes of SE intended to

A chance trip to Home Depot with one of his customized employment team members led to the job of Keith Woodall's dreams. Woodall, 33, had recently been laid off from his job as a dishwasher and was passing time at NewDirection, a day center for people with developmental disabilities in Douglasville, GA.

"We were picking up wood at Home Depot for our woodworking class, and Keith saw some construction workers picking up supplies, and he said, 'I would like to do that kind of work—a man's work,'" recounted Wanda Standridge, who leads Woodall's customized employment team as the disability navigator.

"NewDirection had just moved from a warehouse to a new business park," explained Nancy Brooks-Lane, who also serves on Woodall's team, to the Cobb-Douglas Community Service Board. "Wanda contacted the construction company that built their new building and asked them if they would consider Keith for a job."

While working with that company, Woodall, who has Down syndrome, met Troy Aquila. When Aquila decided to start his own construction company, Troy Aquila Construction, he hired Woodall.

As an added incentive to Woodall's employment, his customized employment team used $10,000 from a U.S. Department of Labor grant to purchase a piece of earth-moving equipment (i.e., Bobcat) his employer could use. The plan was for Woodall to rent the Bobcat to other construction companies when his company was not using it, helping him earn extra money.

"We found out if Keith rented the Bobcat out, it would have a negative consequence on his benefits because it would be unearned income," team member Doug Crandell of the Cobb-Douglas Community Service Board said. "So, now, Troy rents it out for him and pays Keith a bonus for it."

The customized employment team negotiated the terms of Woodall's employment with Aquila, who agreed to pay for the insurance and maintenance on the Bobcat and to train Woodall to use it, though his main responsibility is to help get sewer pipes to the right location. "Troy is a wonderful natural support for Keith," Brooks-Lane said.

Woodall enjoys his job. "My dad does the same thing as me and Troy," he said. "I like working with Troy." Woodall works up to 20 hours a week, and Aquila drives him to and from the construction site. The two have developed a friendship beyond typical employer–employee as a result of working together.

"Hiring Keith was the greatest thing I've ever done. I didn't know I'd get so close to him," Aquila said. Although the Bobcat is a nice addition to his company, Woodall's contributions are far more important to Aquila. "Keith will work for me forever even if he didn't have the Bobcat."

Figure 13.2. Resource ownership and job carving give a man the job of his dreams. (From Buxton, V. [2004]. Customized employment makes dreams come true, *Making a Difference 4*[5], 18–21. Atlanta, GA: Governor's Council on Developmental Disabilities; reprinted by permission.)

serve people with significant disabilities. Table 13.6 provides a brief description of nine values that have guided SE efforts since the early 1980s.

These values mirror the themes discussed at the beginning of this chapter that have been increasingly reflected in rehabilitation legislation. Presumption of employment, person-centered control, wages, supports, interdependence, and social connections within the community: These are the underlying values that should be reflected in a quality employment program for people with significant disabilities. It is only with a clear vision and an articulated set of core values that individual organizational members are able to consistently make decisions and conduct business in a manner that 'over time' stays true to the mission of the organization.

Table 13.6.   Supported employment values

Values	Values clarification
Presumption of employment	Everyone, regardless of the level or the type of disability, has the capability and right to a job.
Competitive employment	Employment must occur within the local labor market in regular community businesses.
Self-determination and control	People with disabilities must choose and regulate their own employment supports and services, which will ultimately lead to career satisfaction.
Commensurate wages and benefits	People with disabilities should earn wages and benefits equal to that of co-workers performing the same or similar jobs.
Focus on capacity and capabilities	People with disabilities should be viewed in terms of their abilities, strengths, and interests rather than their disabilities.
Importance of relationships	Community relationships both at, and away from, work lead to mutual respect and acceptance.
Power of supports	People with disabilities need to determine their personal goals and receive assistance in assembling the supports necessary to achieve their ambitions.
Systems change	Traditional systems must be changed to support self-determination, which is vital to the integrity of supported employment.
Importance of community	People need to be connected to the formal and informal networks of a community for acceptance, growth, and development.

Charlie   During the early 1970s, Charlie spent his days sitting in a church basement stringing beads and doing other simple craft activities. When he went to work in the late 1970s, he had a case file with evaluation report language that stated: "Charlie is a nice fellow, but realistically he has no potential for employment." He was the initial person that the authors' group at Virginia Commonwealth University successfully placed into competitive employment. After working for 23 years, Charlie retired with benefits from his job at the University of Richmond. Long before the Rehabilitation Act (PL 93-112) openly embraced employment for people with significant disabilities, Charlie was establishing his career. Yet, the longevity of his career stands as a testament to the power of choice, benefits of accepting risks, advantages of family, and long-term supports.

The story of his move from that basement to the University of Richmond is historic. First, Charlie is a man of small stature with very little muscle tone. Although he had some receptive language, he had no expressive language. Charlie was fortunate to have access to the public schools. However, his educational program was limited, and his parents were never given any hope that competitive employment was a possibility. As a consequence, while in school, Charlie had limited home-based work experiences and no industrial work experiences.

Second, the University of Richmond had no previous experience supervising employees with significant disabilities. Furthermore, the University had no community employers to give testimonials of people with disabilities achieving employment success. At that time, most people with significant intellectual, psychiatric, and/or physical disabilities were going to adult activity centers or sheltered workshops, not to jobs in the competitive workforce. These segregated centers were so popular in the late 1970s and alternative options were so limited that individuals were placed on long waiting lists in hopes that someday they would be accepted. Finally, the extreme incentives to employment during this period in history required people with disabilities to risk complete loss of all government benefits if they decided to pursue competitive employment. Charlie overcame impressive odds to enjoy the benefits of competitive employment and SE provided the necessary supports to ensure success.

Target Population

Although SE has been in place for more than 3 decades, people and organizations still struggle with who should receive services. The federal legislation is clear that SE is for individuals with the most significant disabilities who

- Are in need of ongoing supports
- Have no or an interrupted work history
- Have an intermittent employment record

There has been confusion over the term *significant disability*, because different programs and services define these terms in multiple ways. For example, could someone with a master's degree have a significant psychiatric disability? The answer is yes, and much of this confusion has been simplified in the past few years with adult service organizations such as mental health/intellectual disability and VR agencies accepting proof of a significant disability from Special Education Services and/or SSA's Disability Determination.

Still, issues persist when one is considering an individual's intermittent work history. An example is an individual who works for 3–4 months, is not successful, drops out of the employment market, and then comes back several months later. For some individuals, this pattern repeats over and over. Essentially, the individual is good at selling himself or herself but is unable to keep a job. This pattern defines what is meant by an intermittent work history. Individuals with this work history are appropriate for SE, because they need support in selecting a job and identifying the right combination of **workplace supports.**

Integrated Work Settings

At times, lines have been blurred when attempting to define a competitive employment work setting. Determining what constitutes an integrated work setting can be difficult when an SE program secures employment for multiple people. For example, an agency decides to move the individuals who are working on a hospital kit assembly contract out of its segregated facility into the company that is contracting for the service. The 14 individuals with disabilities assigned to produce the hospital kits are located in the community business, but they are in an area away from the other employees without disabilities in terms of physical proximity, break schedules, and room assignment. This should not be considered an integrated work setting. If negotiations with an employer result in redesigning a position that isolates the employee with a disability, such as scheduling breaks differently from those of other employees, then integration is not occurring.

The legislative intent was for SE services to be provided in business settings where people with disabilities are working and interacting with co-workers who are not associated with an SE program. From the beginning, SE was intended to occur in typical, competitive employment work settings. An integrated work setting has a number of distinct characteristics:

- Work occurs in community businesses that are not owned and operated by agencies that are funded to support individuals with disabilities.

- Supervision and opportunities for social interaction are available from workers without disabilities rather than from paid service providers.

- Ratio of individuals with disabilities to co-workers without disabilities reflects the national norms.

Competitive Employment

There also has been some confusion related to what is meant by *competitive employment*. This confusion often occurs when organizations approach businesses and attempt to "sell" an employer or offer ideas that are not in the potential employee's best interest, generally done to secure a quick placement. *Competitive employment* is defined as

- Full-time or part-time consistent with the individual's choices

- Commensurate wages—at or above minimum wage

- Benefits commensurate with those of co-workers in the same business setting

The definition of what constitutes competitive employment has changed over time. In the initial legislation, the 1986 Rehabilitation Act Amendments (PL 105-220), competitive employment was defined as a job that involved 20 hours or more of employment. The reference to a specific number of hours of employment for SE was dropped when the regulations were amended in the early 1990s. It was hoped that, by dropping the hour regulation, the number of individuals with the most significant disabilities in the workplace would increase. In fact, the opposite had happened. It is easier to obtain a 5-hour-a-week job versus a 30- or 40-hour-a-week position. In addition, when the hour regulation was dropped, there was also the expectation that an individualized plan would be developed to gradually increase total hours worked. All too often, this has not occurred.

Competitive employment also involves payment of commensurate wages at or above minimum wage. Negotiating employment at subminimum wages for any individual with a disability is unacceptable. This belief is based on the ability of SE programs to effectively match an individual's interests, preferences, and support needs to the labor needs of community businesses. Organizations have to be clear on their values. If 'over time' an individual is unable to perform the essential functions of his or her job, the preferable option would be to secure a better job match within the same or another business setting rather than consider the payment of subminimum wages.

Long-Term Support Services

The final component of the SE definition is the concept of continuous support services, which is referred to as long-term supports. Long-term supports is the component of the

SE definition that makes this service unique among a variety of service models. This requires an ongoing commitment from the SE service provider to the employee with disabilities throughout his or her job tenure. Long-term support services include the provision of specialized support or assistance to the employee with a disability either at or off the job site at least 2 times per month for as long as the person remains employed. Once the employee has become stabilized on the job, the employment specialist continues to provide, at a minimum, twice-monthly contacts. The number and focus of these contacts are individually tailored to the needs of the employee. The services can occur at or away from the job site. Exactly how services are delivered will be directed by the employee. Many individuals with psychiatric disabilities and brain injuries, who are independent in performing their job duties, seem to struggle with employer or co-worker relationships. These individuals often request that support services be provided away from the job site to reduce the stigma of having an employment specialist. Ultimately, the employee will drive this process with the employment specialist respecting the individual's concerns and wishes.

Regardless of where long-term supports are delivered, they are presented to the employee and employer in a two-step sequential process: time-limited and extended services. Both are addressed in the legislation. The time-limited phase generally ends with a 60-day assessment of the employee's job stability and satisfaction. Once this initial hurdle is cleared, there is a general ongoing assessment of the initial employment situation with a primary focus of assisting the individual to maintain or advance his or her career, which may or may not occur in the business setting.

Customized Employment: Building on the Supported Employment Choice

Customized employment is a process for individualizing the employment relationship between a job seeker or an employee and an employer in ways that meet the needs of both. It is based on a match between the unique strengths, needs, and interests of the job candidate with a disability and the identified business needs of the employer or the self-employment business chosen by the candidate. This is a business deal (Griffin, Hammis, & Geary, 2007; Targett, Young, Revell, Williams, & Wehman, 2007).

Customized employment starts with the development of an employment plan based on an individualized determination of the strengths, needs, and interests of the job candidate with a disability. Once the candidate's goals are established, one or more potential employers are identified.

Is customized employment real employment? Yes—customized employment is real work. It is based on identifying tasks that an employer needs done to effectively conduct his or her business and matching those to the job candidate's abilities and interests. The 21st-century workplace cannot be thought of in the same terms as that of the preceding century. The emerging global economy is creating jobs that cannot be accomplished under the old 9-to-5 model or that do not necessarily need to be performed in the employer's workplace. Furthermore, workers are demanding more autonomy, more freedom, and more customization of the terms and conditions of their employment. The world of work is changing to merge the demands of the new workplace and the needs of the workforce. One approach that has emerged is customized employment.

What is a customized job? A **customized job** is a set of tasks that differ from the employer's standard job descriptions but are based on tasks that are found within that workplace. A customized proposal unties the tasks that exist in a workplace and makes them available to be rearranged in a customized job description. For example, the customized job may include only a subset of the tasks from one of the employer's job descriptions or a mix of tasks taken from several existing job descriptions. It may include new tasks that are not currently being performed but that fill a need for the employer. The customizing process often causes the employer to think of existing tasks in a new way.

For self-employment, the customized job would be based on tasks to be performed by the individual in the business, including any accommodations or disability-related assistance the individual may need.

How are customized job descriptions developed? There are several ways to customize a job description (U.S. Department of Labor, Office of Disability Employment Policy, n.d.):

1. **Carving a job**—creation of a job description based on tasks derived from a single traditional job in an employment setting. The carved job description contains one or more, but not all, of the tasks from the original job description.

   Example: The individual assessment showed that the individual has skills to do filing and he has a strong desire to be a police officer. To meet both the individual's needs and employer's needs, a carved job was negotiated within a county sheriff's department that incorporates tasks of organizing and filing misdemeanor arrest reports and traffic citations.

2. **Negotiated job description**—A negotiated job description is one in which all the tasks of the work setting (tasks contained in more than one job description) are available for selection to form a new, individualized job description.

   Example: After working in a crew doing evening janitorial work, a worker told his crew director that he wanted a job where he could wear nice clothes, did not have to clean after other people, and could work around other people. He liked people but never got to see them in his current job. A job working in a department store was negotiated for the individual that combined duties from several departments. Only one part of the job involves maintenance and support activities. Additional duties involve helping the advertising department put up and take down the huge number of weekly ads, helping the furniture department manager rearrange the furniture department, uncrating merchandise in the electronics department, and loading merchandise in cars for people at the stockroom pick up.

3. **Created job description**—a created job description is negotiated from unmet needs in the employer's workplace. This leads to a new job description based on unmet needs of the employment setting or based on the self-employment business chosen by the individual.

   Example: An individual who is a wheelchair user enjoys people and wants to perform delivery tasks. A branch office manager of an insurance company was receiving frequent complaints that faxes were not being delivered to agents in a timely manner by the fax room clerk. Agents needed the faxes pulled from the fax machine and hand-delivered promptly. The job description for the clerk in the fax room involved copying, mailroom responsibilities, and handling the fax machine. Carrying out those responsibilities did not leave time to hand-deliver the faxes. The individual was able to meet this genuine employer need through a created job description for delivering the faxes.

So, what does customized employment mean to young people with a variety of challenging disabilities? This is yet one more powerful tool to help get individuals with serious disabilities into the workplace. Let us look at how this approach might be implemented in one community. Consider the groundbreaking work done by Citron et al. (2008), who

> Described and analyzed a 7-year systems-change effort focused on developing customized employment opportunities through a CRP that provides supports to persons with mental illness, developmental disabilities, and addictive diseases in Georgia. By using case studies and qualitative data, the path to real and effective organizational improvement in the area of customized employment outcomes was explored. Seven points of analysis on systematic organizational development emerged from the data review:

1. Staff development
2. Community partnerships
3. Diversified funding
4. Sustainability
5. Shift in managerial approaches and supervision
6. Changes in human resource processes
7. Expanding the customized employment to diverse populations (i.e., offenders, youth, welfare to work)

This examination illustrates the need for

- Best-practice staff training
- Person-centered and community-based vocational assessments
- Customer-directed personal budgets
- Flexible funding
- Focus on evidence-based customized employment outcomes as performance indicators
- Values-based human resource processes
- CRP executive leadership involvement with staff and customers to break down barriers and achieve organizational momentum for outcome-driven change

Workplace Supports

All workers, not just individuals with disabilities, require different types, levels, and intensity of supports in their workplaces. Businesses provide supports to their employees and offer them a wealth of resources during the normal course of business. However, some employers may need additional assistance in creating workplace cultures that are supportive of individuals with disabilities. The goal is to work with employers so that businesses can increase their capacity to support workers with disabilities. The following sections list some of the key issues in implementing workplace supports.

What Are Workplace Supports?

Workplace supports typically exist in a business and are available to all employees. They may include 'but are not limited to' such things as a co-worker mentor who assists an employee in learning the job, a supervisor who monitors work performance, a co-worker who assists the new worker in developing social networks, or making maximum use of orientation training. This also could include other company-sponsored training events, programs, and benefits such as an employee assistance program. Workplace supports also may be specifically designed to assist a particular employee with his or her job performance.

What Are Examples of Workplace Supports that May Already Exist in a Business?

Three major categories of workplace supports that may already exist in a business are environmental, procedural, and natural. *Environmental supports* are defined as physical structures, surroundings, or objects present in the business that make the job site more accessible for current or future employees. For example, automatic door openers may be available when one is entering the building or signage on the walls may help employees successfully navigate from one department to another. *Procedural supports* are actions or activities that employers provide to assist potential or current employees with performing their jobs and job-related functions. For instance, flextime may be offered to allow employees to work within the hours that are more conducive to their personal lives. *Natural supports* exist in any workplace and are informal supports that are typically available to any employee. This might include workers sharing rides to and from work or a senior staff member helping a new co-worker get the job done when he or she needs extra assistance.

Can Individuals with Disabilities Gain Access to Workplace Supports on Their Own?

The person with the disability may already know or have some ideas of what he or she needs. At other times, the individual may need guidance. Taking advantage of the support resources that are available in a workplace may not automatically occur for many individuals with disabilities.

Even if a resource exists, the individual may not know how to gain access to or benefit from its use. He or she may be unaware of the potential support, how to choose among the support alternatives that are available, or how to gain access to a desired resource. In addition, a company may have varying levels of resource options. For instance, one company may have an intensive orientation and training program whereas another has none. The existing workplace supports within any company must be analyzed to determine if they meet the needs of the individual with a disability who has been hired.

Are Workplace Supports the Same Thing as Reasonable Accommodations?

Workplace supports and *reasonable accommodations* are sometimes used synonymously; however, there are differences. Some employers may be more open to hearing about "workplace supports" because "reasonable accommodation" may conjure up unwarranted fears about complying with the law and costs associated with accommodations. Under the Americans with Disabilities Act, employers must provide reasonable accommodations to a qualified individual with a disability. A qualified individual with a disability is someone who can perform the essential functions of a job with or without reasonable accommodations. Many businesses will have a policy in place on how a request for accommodation should be handled.

Some examples of workplace supports that might be useful to an employee with a disability include having a co-worker prompt him or her to take a break, having an employment specialist provide additional job skills training, creating a quiet work area, giving an employee a written list of job duties to perform at the start of each shift, replacing a manual stapler with an electronic one, or allowing a change in the usual work schedule. Support needs vary from person to person. Thus, it should not come as a surprise that workplace supports must be tailored to the particular situation on hand. What works for one employee in one workplace will not necessarily be effective for someone else in another business.

Natural Supports in the Workplace: Ways to Enhance All Integrated Employment Choices

Natural supports reflect an increased recognition of the ability of employers to accept and accommodate a diverse array of employees, the potential role of family members in locating jobs, and the willingness and ability of co-workers to provide training, assistance, and support. Two of the most popular examples of natural supports are the employer or supervisor as a training mentor and the co-worker as a support. By using naturally occurring supports, it may reduce the cost of SE for some (Cimera, 2007b). The PACER Center in Minneapolis, Minnesota, developed an excellent table for how to be an advocate for natural supports (Table 13.7).

Employer or Supervisor as Training Mentor

For a number of individuals with severe disabilities, the immediate employer or supervisor will be the best trainer for a number of reasons. In some cases, the job is simply too complex or specialized for a job coach to grasp without an extended learning period. Sometimes, companies simply prefer to use their own personnel for training. Other companies are committed to affirmative action hiring but do not wish to have noncompany personnel on the premises.

A particular benefit of this approach is that the employer/supervisor feels additionally empowered to handle difficulties that may arise on the job. A job coach or rehabilitation counselor still may be involved in the initial framing of the training, assist with a behavior management plan, or be available for troubleshooting, but the primary responsibility is assumed by the supervisor or employer.

Co-worker Assistance

The co-worker assistance approach is increasingly being documented in the research literature as a critical component in job retention (Chadsey, 2008). The co-worker's roles include trainer, observer, and advocate for the individual within the workplace, including the education of other staff about a person's specific cognitive assets and

Table 13.7.   Advocating for natural supports

If you are an employer	If you are a parent	If you are a teacher	If you are an adult employment provider
Be open to include people with moderate and severe disabilities; focus on people's strengths.	Advocate in general for inclusion of natural supports in your own workplace or in other organizations to which you belong.	Involve the employer in training, supervising, and supporting students at work sites.	Use your resources as a supplement to, not a substitute for, employers' resources.
Build your capacity for Work Force 2000 and increased diversity.	Do regular career planning for your son or daughter to provide information on skills, interests, preferences, and support needs to help when it comes time to choose the right job.	Prepare students for employment and community life, not the adult service system. Focus on communication skills, adaptive technology, and supports each person needs to participate in the community.	Keep in mind that your expectations shape employers' attitudes and that companies have the will and skill to hire and support workers with moderate and severe disabilities.
Promote hiring people with disabilities among other employers.	Be part of the network for job leads or job support for a person with a disability.	Develop a network for job leads and support. Involve members of a student's broader community in planning meetings.	Change your job development process to always include employers in identifying workplace supports.
Be involved in job search and support networks for persons with disabilities whom you know.	Help your son or daughter find a job by approaching employers yourself.		

impairments. This typically leads to co-workers who are more cooperative and supportive of the person.

Mentoring

Using mentors to enhance employee success once hired is a popular trend in corporate America that deserves a more thorough mention. Businesses see how both formal and informal mentoring can reduce learning time for new employees, increase career advancement opportunities, and prepare new leaders (Getzel & Briel, 2008b). More specifically, work-based mentoring programs can help young adults by imparting crucial job-specific, social, and personal skills; enriching and expanding the youth's social connections; and positively impacting self-esteem and optimism for the future. Work-based mentors often counsel individuals beyond purely job-specific issues, which may include tips on organizational skills or how to set priorities. In addition, mentors can share resources, provide a new perspective, and ask thought-provoking questions (Heckman, Brown, & Roberts, 2007).

College students with disabilities face similar issues as all students exiting college seeking a professional job. However, students with disabilities also need

a. Direct exposure to the variety of career opportunities potentially available to them
b. An understanding of their disability and how it may influence career choice and work performance
c. An awareness of their rights and responsibilities in the workplace
d. The risks and benefits of disclosing disability status to employers
e. An understanding of which accommodations improve work performance and how to effectively request them from an employer

Students with disabilities graduate from college without the chance for on-the-job experiences, and have a difficult time selecting a job that matches their preferences and abilities.

In a recent business mentoring study (Getzel & Briel, 2008a), 25 college students with disabilities in their junior or senior years were matched with a working professional in the career choice of the student. This work-based mentoring program provided a minimum of 4 hours per month for at least two semesters of contact between the student and the mentor at the work site. Students developed a relationship with the professional and engaged in worksite experiences, asked questions and exchanged ideas, and emerged with a clearer sense of their career choice. Students set specific goals with their mentors for their time together. The four primary areas that served as the focus for activities in the mentoring relationship included career counseling, job shadowing opportunities, job placement assistance, and conflict resolution/problem solving in a workplace environment.

Results from the mentoring study reflected positive outcomes for participating students. When student participants were given choices, the two primary areas of focus for a majority of the participants involved career counseling and job placement assistance activities. Students expressed the importance of mentors to assist in exploring career options and clarifying their career goals. Being able to meet at the work site, be a part of the workplace culture, or use professional work materials provided a better understanding of the work environment and the skills required in their field of study. Mentors provided students with relevant resources through topic-related books, professional handbooks, printed materials, and organization web sites to assist them in further researching their career interests. Student participants were provided opportunities to discuss the demands of the work environment and their disability in a nonthreatening atmosphere.

Conclusion

This chapter describes available vocational placements and models as well as the values associated with responsive, high-quality employment programs and employers. Case studies of young people with disabilities working in the different vocational arrangements and internships illustrate the strengths and weaknesses of each model. The range of vocational models in place for people with disabilities is increasing; however, there must be a greater focus on career development and better outcomes for young people with severe disabilities. The national and local emphasis on pushing an Employment First agenda is making a difference for students with disabilities. Students with disabilities are waiting to begin their careers and contribute to the business community. They are waiting to earn a living and to be seen as productive citizens. With educators who are willing to believe in them and ready to work in partnership with business and other community resources such as state VR and community employment providers, new doors will continue to open for these youth and pervasive unemployment will become a thing of the past.

Study Questions

1. Describe the major barriers to vocational competence for students with disabilities and how to overcome them.
2. How do employers perceive people with disabilities in the workplace?
3. Why is transportation critical when one is considering employment? Describe options when people with disabilities do not have access to public transportation.
4. List five vocational options for students with disabilities and the advantages and disadvantages of each.
5. Describe the recommended practices that encompass SE.
6. Give examples of customized employment.
7. Provide an illustration of mentoring.
8. Describe the different roles of the employment specialists in SE.
9. Explain how natural supports can help workers with disabilities maintain their employment.
10. Describe the major issues to consider when one is implementing workplace support.
11. What can be done to help more people work in community-based employment?

Online Resources

Worksupport: http://www.worksupport.com

Office of Disability Employment Policy: http://www.dol.gov/odep/

Institute for Community Inclusion: http://www.communityinclusion.org/

TransCen Inc.: http://www.transcen.org/about.html

National Center on Secondary Education and Transition Institute on Community Integration: http://www.ncset.org/

Developing Jobs for Young People with Disabilities

14

PAMELA TARGETT AND CARY GRIFFIN

After completing this chapter, the reader will be able to

- Define job development
- Describe what resources an employment specialist may have to offer to bring additional value to a business
- Identify some typical employer concerns associated with hiring individuals with disabilities and indicate how an employment specialist would address these
- Formulate questions an employment specialist might ask an employer to learn more about business operations
- Formulate a description of a job seeker to share with potential employers
- Understand the need for **workplace and job analysis**
- Describe how to carve or create jobs for youth with disabilities

Public schools are charged with providing a free and appropriate education that puts a young person on a path of prosperity. But the sad reality is that, for many students with severe disabilities, it is a path to unemployment or at best underemployment in facility-based programs to work in congregate settings or as part of a mobile work crew. In a national study on vocational outcomes for adults with developmental disabilities, Migliore and Butterworth (2008) reported that only 18% were employed in integrated community-based jobs, 41% were in facility-based programs, 9% worked in congregate or mobile work crews, and the remaining 33% were in nonwork programs. These and other statistics on employment outcomes paint the ugly truth—whereas most working-age adults in the United States are employed or can expect to find paid jobs, most adults with intellectual disabilities spend their days in sheltered workshops, day centers, and nonpaid community activities (Butterworth, Smith, Hall, Migliore, & Winsor, 2009; Winsor & Butterworth, 2008). In actuality, there are signs that efforts to support real work for real pay are stalling (O'Brien & Callahan, 2010). The unemployment problem is further amplified when one considers that the lack of work means an increased likelihood of poverty, welfare, government entitlements, and no tax revenues (Cimera, 2011; Fremstad, 2009).

With this shameful picture, one would be remiss not to ask the obvious question— What is the problem? Why is it that, after years of promoting evidence-based practices in transition to work and reform through legislation, the majority of youth with disabilities are either underemployed or unemployed upon leaving school? Why do individuals with severe disabilities not have the opportunity to experience employment and enjoy the quality of life that all people aspire to attain? Some are quick to point a finger at employers and blame it on bias, others blame a poor economy and high rates of unemployment, and then, of course, there are the schools' problems, which range from depleted budgets to a shortage of qualified teachers—and the list could go on and on. Given the gamut of problems and the possibility of even larger forces at work (i.e., societal prejudices, government scapegoating, family fears, and greediness of organizations operating workshops and day centers), one then has to wonder what, if anything, can be done to improve employment for youth with disabilities?

To begin, we must be honest with ourselves. It is a terrible dilemma, stimulated by a lack of sincere attention that leads to inaction on the part of many. Accepting the truth is the first step. Then, there is no longer a need to try to place blame on others, and, instead, we can get on with the real hard work ahead of us by renewing a commitment to focus on the solutions to this problem and becoming accountable. This means being responsible. Blaming provides an artificial solution to an often-complex problem. Whereas accountability recognizes that we all make mistakes or fall short on commitments, becoming aware of our past errors or shortfalls and viewing them as opportunities for learning and growth then enable us to be more successful in the future.

School's Role in Improving Outcomes

Describing all that needs to happen is beyond the scope of this chapter, or, for that matter, beyond the authors' expertise. However, it does not take a rocket scientist to see that all stakeholders need to stop hiding from the problem and tackle it head on. And, with that goal in mind, we begin by offering some brief guidance to the schools on how to do this.

If we are truly sincere about the responsibility to improve postschool outcomes for youth with disabilities, we need absolute commitment and far-reaching action. Schools must comply with federal transition mandates and responsibility of the school for the achievement of students' postschool outcomes must be expanded (Hughes & Avoke, 2010; Rusch, Hughes, Agran, Martin, & Johnson, 2009; Wehman, 2011a). For youth with disabilities who are leaving school, competitive work before exiting is the best way to negate these poor employment outcomes (Luecking, 2009; Wehman, 2011a). Some testimony and research support that, for students with severe disabilities, achieving employment before leaving school is mandatory (Rusch et al., 2009; Wehman, 2011a). Going to work not only teaches these students valuable skills but also helps them begin to build confidence and a work history that can put them on a career path (Luecking, 2009; Wehman, 2011a).

Schools must profess that all students can and should work in their communities earning regular pay and declare that "all means ALL" (Niemiec, Lavin, & Owens, 2009). Schools must understand the power of supports and understand how these can be used to assist students with pursuing and maintaining real work for real pay. With a pro-work or work-first philosophy in place, schools will recognize that all students with disabilities have personal strengths and abilities that allow them to make a meaningful contribution to the workforce (Inge et al., 2009; Inge & Moon, 2011).

Schools that are determined to face the problem head on can also gain insight into how to advance employment for youth by adopting an employment-first agenda. Some state initiatives have taken steps to clarify what this means. The goal is to move toward an educational and workforce system that identifies, markets, and employs assets and strengths of one person at a time.

There is no doubt that schools on all levels are in the position to lead the development of this initiative and keep the momentum going to reshape the future by being persistently present. Schools can begin by locating the willing and begin to build coalitions (e.g., business, families, vocational rehabilitation, state agencies, disability organizations) to help shape the transformation of state and local support systems (Niemiec et al., 2009; Lindstrom, Flannery, Benz, Olszewski, & Slovic, 2009).

Improving employment outcomes for youth will disabilities also requires involvement and buy-in from parents (Niemiec et al., 2009; Wehman, 2011a). Parents need to be engaged early on individualized education program (IEP) planning to help plan for their sons' and daughters' adulthoods; the catch phrase "too little too late" related to the age when transition planning starts for some students should no longer resonate. It will also call for education about Social Security benefits (Hemmeter, Jauff, & Wittenburg, 2009) and strategies that promote transition of youth to work (Fraker & Rangarajan, 2009; Davies, Rupp, & Wittenburg, 2009).

Furthermore, schools need to find ways to challenge students with disabilities to rise above the status quo to have a career, live in the community, and control their lives to the greatest extent possible. To accomplish this, some students will need no or limited assistance, whereas others will require much more intensive, extensive, and individualized supports—which may include the supports necessary to gain and maintain employment in their communities.

Assisting students with more significant support needs or severe disabilities requires skilled, motivated, and dedicated staff (e.g., transition specialist, special educators, vocational specialist) to support each student with finding his or her way toward achieving the "American Dream." The professionals charged with this most important work must be competent. Competency requires the attitude, knowledge, and skills needed to get the job done.

And that brings us to the major focus of the chapter—how to develop jobs to assist youth with the most significant disabilities with gaining employment in their communities. This crucial activity is known as *job development*.

Guiding Points

While reading this chapter, the reader should keep the following points in mind. First, although everyone on a student's transition team can provide input and assist with developing a job, someone must be responsible for ensuring that the student actually goes to work. Who is responsible will vary from school to school and state to state. Some schools may be rich in resources and have an employment specialist in-house, whereas others may be very limited and teachers may be expected to conduct such activities. Others may be progressive and have vocational education personnel involved in locating work for all students regardless of their ability. And still others may have the state's vocational rehabilitation agency actively engaged in this process, especially during the student's last year of school. As illustrated, variability can be quite extensive. Thus, for purposes here, the chapter addresses issues from the perspective that the school has *employment specialists* on staff who are responsible for ensuring that those students with the most severe disabilities (i.e., those who need supported employment) will gain and maintain employment before exiting school.

Second, when a business contact is made, it should be done with a specific student in mind and never on behalf of groups of people. Job development should be driven by a student's interest, abilities, and support needs. The goal is not to find just any job, but one that allows the student to build on and maximize his or her personal strengths. However, this is a guiding principle and not a hard and fast rule because other student job seekers may come to mind after an employment specialist learns more about a particular organization's needs. But, as a general rule of thumb, an employment specialist should have a specific job seeker in mind when approaching an employer.

Third, to locate meaningful work, employment specialists must look beyond available options and conduct a creative job search. In a traditional job search, employers attract a large number of applicants, screen them, and then pick the best of the pool to interview. In job development, the goal is to avoid the competition by developing relationships with businesses and developing employment opportunities. Instead of looking for jobs in a traditional way (e.g., using the Internet to search for job postings, mailing résumés to employers, answering advertisements announcing vacancies), the creative search involves asking for leads from people known or just met as well as calling and visiting employers whether there is a job opening or not.

Fourth, instead of initiating employer relations with the sole intent to locate a job for a specific student, employment specialists should have some other things to offer to businesses and consider ways to develop strategic partnerships. For example, the employment specialist may give the employer educational materials. Then, in return, the specialist may ask if students can tour the workplace or request a referral to another business, particularly when an opportunity to develop a job is not probable in the foreseeable future.

This chapter begins by defining job development. Then a description of supported employment and a brief review of job development literature follows. Next, information about what an employment specialist needs to know to engage business and develop jobs is provided. Finally, the chapter takes a look at the concept of job carving or job creation, a job development strategy that should have employers saying "yes" to hiring young people who just happen to have disabilities.

Job Development Defined

Job development is the process of creating a work opportunity on behalf of a job seeker with a disability that is achieved by earning an opportunity to connect with an employer to learn about business needs and then moving on to get a commitment to meet and possibly hire a job seeker. As noted in the definition, oftentimes, jobs are created or negotiated for the student. This is because some students do not qualify for existing positions and/or need a work opportunity that is developed in way that highlights the use of their specific vocational skills and talents while bringing value to the business.

These are often individuals with disabilities who require advocacy-level services like supported employment. Then, once a position is established, he or she may need help with preemployment activities such as completing applications and other paperwork or testing. Once hired, he or she may require additional on-the-job support from an employment specialist for either a time-limited period or the duration of the job (i.e., supported employment). The approach described is not intended for those youth with disabilities who require guidance and counseling or perhaps instruction to locate work opportunities, negotiate a job, or request accommodations. Instead the job development activities described in this chapter are intended for students with more severe disabilities, and may be offered by the school's in-house personnel or could be purchased from an outside vocational rehabilitation (VR) provider by either the school or the state's department of VR services.

Supported Employment

In supported employment, a staff person, known as an *employment specialist* or a *job coach*, assists a person with a severe disability with gaining and maintaining work in the community. A brief description of the individualized approach follows (Wehman, 2011a).

Before initiating job development, the employment specialist should not only have some general knowledge of the business community but also have a good understanding of the job seeker's abilities, desires, and support needs. Person-centered and functional assessment activities are conducted to help identify student interests, abilities, and support needs.

Some students with disabilities will qualify for existing positions because they are able to perform the essential job functions (major duties) either with or without reasonable accommodation. However, other students may not be able to perform the primary job tasks or myriad duties. Under these circumstances, a position that benefits business is specifically "developed" or created for the student. For instance, some duties from one or more existing staff positions are identified, combined, and then reassigned to create a new job, or someone may be hired to perform work that has often been overlooked or causes the company to accrue overtime expenditures.

Consider a busy real estate office with eight realtors. Each one is responsible for keeping a computerized database up to date and mailing out customer newsletters. These and perhaps other tasks could be taken and combined to form a part-time job. This frees up the realtors to spend more time in the community with their potential buyers and sellers.

A job may also be created by reassigning work that is not getting done to one employee. For example, the wait staff at a five-star establishment rarely have time to polish the silverware. When the staff do polish the silverware, overtime wages are usually paid. A position may be created by hiring someone who is solely responsible for polishing the silverware. Creating this job helps the restaurant sustain its image as a posh place to dine and cuts cost associated with paying overtime.

No matter how the job is developed, after becoming employed, the newly hired student receives individualized on-the-job supports. For example, the employment specialist may provide the new employee with one-to-one skills training (e.g., using systematic instructional techniques) that extends beyond that offered by the employer while ensuring that the work is getting done. Or, in some instances, the specialist may help the employee select and learn how to use assistive technology (AT; e.g., key guard, reaching device) or compensatory memory strategies (e.g., picture book, checklist).

Throughout this process, performance data are collected to evaluate the worker's performance. As the employee learns the job and is able to meet the employer's standards, the employment specialist begins to fade from the job site until eventually he or she is no longer present on a regular basis. However, the specialist continues to offer periodic follow-up services throughout the individual's employment.

These ongoing job retention services are increased as needed. For example, if the employee receives a promotion or is assigned new job duties, then one-to-one skills training may be reinitiated, or if the person cannot solve work-related problems (e.g., unreliable transportation services, difficulty getting along with others), then assistance may be provided.

Review of Literature

Much has happened over the years and because of the hard work of quality programs, individuals with significant disabilities do go to work in their communities instead of workshops and day programs. Here is a brief look at some of the more recent literature that relate to job development.

Getting to know the job seeker is critical for optimizing the job match (Morgan, 2011; Targett & Wehman, 2009; Phillips et al., 2009). The literature recommends using a functional or practical approach to get to know the person by spending time together in the community, talking to those who know the person best, and observing the student during vocational situational assessments (Inge & Moon, 2011; Wehman & Kregel 2012. Recently, Morgan and Horrocks (2011) found that video assessment to identify high- and low-preference jobs may to some extent correspond with subsequent job performance. However, the study results were variable and the sample was small ($n = 3$), so much more evidence would be needed before considering this practice in the classroom. In addition, this activity should not be seen as a substitute for community-based job exploration. Morgan (2011) looked at inter-rater reliability of a job-matching assessment instrument. He found, among other things, that, even when stakeholders discuss the degree of match among different jobs, they may not produce a job placement decision with a high level of reliability.

Employers look for candidates connected to the network of acquaintances rather than advertising (Levinson & Perry, 2009; Luecking & Tilson, 2009; Luecking, 2009; Luecking, Fabian, & Tilson, 2004; Griffin, Hammis, & Geary, 2007). Tapping into the hidden job market (jobs that are not advertised or not known) is essential. Creating and negotiating a job description is an effective approach to assist individuals with locating work that matches the job seeker's skills while meeting an employer's needs (Inge & Moon, 2011; Luecking, 2009). Understanding the needs of the business is key (Luecking, 2009; Levinson & Perry, 2009; Wehman, 2011a). Maintaining a connection with the new hire and employer is another strategy to smooth the transition and enhance retention. The reader should note that the employment specialist takes on this role (on-the-job support and long-term follow along) in a supported employment approach.

There is more: Employers who have previous contact with individuals with disabilities tend to hold more favorable attitudes toward workers with disabilities than those who have not (Unger, 2002). Carter, Swedeen, and Trainor (2009) found employment outcomes for youth with significant disabilities were improved by bringing key stakeholders together to generate solutions to common challenges in their community. Intentional planning, linking planning to the big picture, creative thinking, and identifying supports and resources are effective strategies to connect youth with significant disabilities with summer work and community experiences (Carter, Swedeen, & Trainor, 2009). Employers have been more positive about work with employees who have psychiatric and intellectual disabilities when appropriate supports are provided (Fabian, 2004; Morgan & Alexander, 2005). Employers point to quality services and perceived support from an employment specialist as a critical factor in making a hiring decision (Unger, 2002). And, businesses' hiring decisions are influenced more by the perceived contribution the individual can make to the organization than by the disability. This means that, when value can be added to the organization, business is more apt to hire (Luecking, 2008). A recent study by Harnett, Stuart, Thurman, Loy, and Batiste (2011) showed that employers benefited from hiring, retaining, and accommodating individuals with disabilities. Benefits derived by employers included the ability to retain quality employees, increased company profitability, and avoidance of the cost associated with hiring and training a new employee.

In addition, providing accommodations in order to retain employees was shown to improve the organizational culture and climate as well as to foster a sense among all employees that employers recognize both the value of the individual as a human and the inherent social benefits of creating and sustaining an inclusive workplace.

Understanding the public view on employment of people with disabilities can also inform job development practices. Burge, Ouelette-Kuntz, and Lysaght (2007) conducted a survey on public perception regarding work inclusion of individuals with intellectual disabilities. A majority or 680 respondents believed that hiring individuals with intellectual disabilities would not negatively affect the image of the workplace. In a national public survey, Siperstein, Romano, Mohler, and Parker (2006) extended previous studies focused on the attitudes of employers by assessing consumer attitudes toward companies that hire employees with disabilities. Specifically, the survey examined how consumers feel about people with disabilities in the workplace and how consumers view companies that employ individuals with disabilities. Findings indicated that 75% of the participants had positive direct experience with people with disabilities in the workplace. Ninety-two percent of consumers felt more favorably toward companies that hire employees with disabilities, and 87% said they would prefer to give their business to such companies. From this review, it should be apparent that a great deal of success of employment depends on the competency and commitment of employment specialists. As Luecking (2008) so aptly pointed out, when employment specialists are competent, job seekers get jobs. If they are not, the barriers to work can become overwhelming.

Until recently, little has been known about to what extent employment specialists follow recommended practices. Migliore, Cohen-Hall, Butterworth, and Winsor (2010) surveyed 163 employment specialists from 74 programs in 28 states about practices related to getting to the job seekers, finding job openings, engaging employers to hire, and facilitating transition to a job. The employment specialists reported that practices that they utilized conflicted with recommended practices as cited in the literature. Possible reasons for this include

- Certain practices are unnecessary for the job seeker served (i.e., job carving may not be needed for someone with less significant disability, individuals who can self-represent need less or no representation)
- Not familiar with recommended practices and strategies
- Time constraints
- Billing standards conflict with strategies

The authors recommended implementing job development based on activities in the literature and further research on evidence-based practices.

In another recent study, Post et al. (2010) presented case studies illustrating successful collaborations between supported employment providers and human resource managers. Some of the practical suggestions on how providers and human resource departments could work together were offered and are summarized in Table 14.1. The authors concluded that a willingness to listen and collaborate was essential to success.

Table 14.1. Strategies on how providers and human resource departments could work together

- Do some preliminary research on the business; this shows interest and will help prepare intelligent questions.
- Start with the top human resource administrator for the initial contact.
- Select an initial contact method depending on business type (e.g., personal contact versus letter followed by a call).
- Have letters of recommendation and information on benefits available.
- Pitch the abilities of individuals served.
- Tie disability into wider diversity issues such as efforts both in and out of the workplace to promote hiring.
- Advocate universal design principles.

Research Implications

Implications from the research include that businesses must be viewed as another "customer" of services. Employment specialists must recognize that it is critical to meet the needs of businesses just as they meet with needs of people with disabilities. If businesses are not well served, individuals with disabilities are not well served.

Second, employment specialists must not only be well versed in supports for individuals with disabilities but also know how to develop employer partnerships and manage relationships. Employment specialists need to know how to build trust and negotiate among other things to build new and maintain existing business relations.

Third, employment specialists must be prepared to do business with business. For example, an employment specialist needs to be able to speak to business representatives in an intelligent and engaging manner.

Fourth, when developing job opportunities, employment specialists need to maximize interactions in order to learn more about the nature of a particular business and its operational needs. Only then can they make recommendations or offer solutions about customizing a job or explain how hiring a specific individual with a disability can help meet a business' needs. This requires the ability to listen to learn about needs and translate those into work opportunities for the individuals employment specialists serve. It also requires risk removal. The biggest barriers may be the unspoken risks that the employer perceives. This means employment specialists need to be able to identify and eliminate risks.

Finally, employment specialists must be honest and ethical in everything they do. Hiding concerns or overestimating performance of a particular employment candidate can lead to failure. So the employment specialist must be able to project the job seekers' assets and be prepared to speak about the aspects of support. This is not to say that every job developed will be successful, but it does mean the employment specialist's word will mean something. Being trustworthy will take an employment specialist far in forging lasting relationships with the business community. The remainder of this chapter focuses on conducting a creative job search using a supported employment approach.

Getting Prepared

To conduct a creative job search, employment specialists must know what they have to offer businesses; be able to respond to employer questions and address any perceived risks or concerns; understand the preferences, abilities, and support needs of the job seeker; know how to request next steps; and conduct a work and job analysis. Without this knowledge, employment specialists will not be able to talk intelligently to employers or exude the confidence needed to move toward the primary goal—a job offer! The employment specialist must also embrace a demand-side approach to job development.

Demand-Side Approach to Job Development

Facilitating employment searches with people with disabilities, particularly those who require extensive support, requires a complete understanding of an employer's circumstances. So how do employment specialists engage employers? Luecking (2009) calls for adopting a demand-side approach to job development, which requires an employment specialist to work with employers to identify operational needs and ways to address them. In this long-overdue approach, according to Luecking, the success of linking job seekers with work is as much about meeting employers' needs as it is about serving job seekers.

The advantages are that it augments methodology to assist individuals who have unique and often complex job assistance needs and it offers a way to engage employers other than traditional attempts to "sell" disability employment. In a larger sense, the adoption of demand-side job development methodology, such as attentive consultation, responsive service, and focus on company need, will enable job developers to expand their employer partnerships. When this approach is adopted, the possibilities to create unique and lasting partnerships with employers are considerable.

Luecking (2008) goes on to note that recent examinations of employer views on disability overwhelmingly suggest that, in spite of continuing misperceptions among many employers, there is ample evidence that disability in and of itself does not trigger inherently negative employer responses. Furthermore, exposure to disability usually yields improved employer views of disability. Key reasons, then, for persistently low rates of employment for individuals with disability are not attributable to inherent or pervasive unemployability or to ingrained negative employer attitudes. Rather, explanations for this circumstance may be found in how well prepared workplaces are to support the employees with disabilities. Demand-side job development offers VR another tool in its arsenal to enhance and expand employer partnerships and thus prepare the workplace for people with disabilities.

More recently, Certo and Luecking (2011) offered some tested and true job development strategies and described some emerging ones that can minimize the effects of rising national unemployment prospects for individuals with disabilities. First, employers must be viewed as partners. Three ways for employment specialists to discover employer needs that may lead to job opportunities are

1. Get your face in the place: Conduct informational interviews and negotiate for mutual benefit.

2. Find ways to customize (i.e., create, carve, restructure) jobs. As was mentioned earlier, this has been shown to benefit the employer and the employee.

3. Network. Use your connections to create and sustain relationships in the business community.

With all of these things, the employment specialist must understand that company needs, not altruism, drive employer hiring decisions.

Business Services and Benefits

The employment specialist needs to understand the school's mission related to employment of students with disabilities and how support services will be provided as this information will be necessary when interacting with business. The employment specialist should take inventory of what he or she knows and what he or she needs to learn. Table 14.2 offers questions to consider when evaluating this current level of knowledge. By taking the time to investigate the answer to these and other questions in advance, the

Table 14.2. Questions for an employment specialist to ask to evaluate level of knowledge about the school

- What is the history of the school?
- How is service delivery set up?
- What are the mission and goals of the service?
- What is the school's performance record in assisting students with gaining and maintaining work?
- What processes or procedures are involved in service delivery?
- How are support services such as supported employment or assistive technology funded?
- What services should the student with a disability expect?
- How does an employment specialist get to know the job seeker?
- What services can a business expect from an employment specialist?
- How does an employment specialist learn more about a business' needs?
- What are employment specialists currently doing to partner with businesses in the community?
- What do those employers have to say about past experiences?

employment specialist will be better prepared to develop a message to an employer and answer questions.

During initial talks with an employer, an employment specialist will also need to be able to describe what resources, skills, and opportunities he or she has to offer that will motivate the employer to develop a working relationship. This means the employer needs to understand what value can be brought to the business and the potential benefits associated with working with an employment specialist. It is important to note that, at some point in time, an employment specialist will also need to convey how a specific particular job seeker will bring value to the business and this topic will be discussed. However, for now, the focus is on answering this question: Why should a business consider working with an employment specialist to meet its needs?

To help further his or her understanding, the employment specialist may want to consider some highlights provided from a technical report titled "A Survey of Employer Perspectives on Employment and People with Disabilities" published in late 2008 by the Office of Disability Employment Policy (Domzal, Houtenville, & Sharma, 2008). The information is based on a survey of 3,797 company representatives. Although this survey was not specific to employment of individuals with significant support needs and more research is needed in this area, the information can help further one's thinking about ways to bring value to business.

Information on the first two points—job performance and productivity—are cited more often by small and medium-sized businesses, whereas large businesses are more persuaded by information based on research and statistics. In addition, the survey asked companies that do not actively recruit people with disabilities about the type of information that would persuade them to recruit people with disabilities. Information about performance, productivity, and the bottom line was considered to be the most persuasive information, whereas information about costs was the least persuasive.

In the survey, all companies were asked, "I am now going to describe several factors in hiring people with disabilities that we often hear from employers. How much of a challenge are the following factors to an employment specialist company in hiring people with disabilities? I would like an employment specialist to say whether it is a major challenge, somewhat of a challenge, or not a challenge."

The work also reported the percentage of companies that cited a particular factor as a major challenge or somewhat of a challenge. The percentages and rankings were provided for each factor for all companies and by company size. When one looks across company size, the rankings suggest that health care costs, workers compensation costs, and fear of litigation are more challenging for small and medium-sized companies than for large companies. Also it should be noted that not knowing how much accommodations will cost is considered more of a hiring challenge than the actual cost of accommodation, which suggests that aversion to risk may be a challenge that needs to be addressed in the cost of accommodation literature.

Companies were also asked about strategies that would be helpful in hiring people with disabilities. Regardless of company size, the top-five strategies to facilitate hiring were very similar across company size: employer tax credits, disability awareness training, visible top management commitment, mentoring, and assistive technology. The relative rankings of the other strategies varied by company size, with tax credits most important to small and medium companies and visible top management commitment most important to large companies. Small companies were also more likely to cite flexible work schedules as a strategy to facilitate hiring. And, regardless of company size, a centralized accommodations fund and reassignment were the least-cited strategies. The larger the company size, the more likely a given strategy was cited. This information can be used to help employment specialists think about the type of service or resources to offer to employers. For example, Table 14.3 offers some ideas about the services and resources that an employment specialist may have or will want to offer to employers to build a relationship.

Table 14.3.   Ideas on what to offer employers to help build a relationship

- Develop a profile of hiring needs.
- Develop up-to-date, accurate, and well-written job descriptions.
- Act as intermediary to assist company with locating workers.
- Offer training for management and staff on disability and employment-related issues.
- Offer on-site consultation and technical assistance to workers with disabilities and management.
- Work with top management to develop or refine corporate commitment and strategies to hire, retain, and promote workers with disabilities.
- Have access to pool of applicants with disabilities.
- Do an analysis to determine how applicants' skills can meet business needs, which include
    - Referral of applicants
    - Recommendations on job design to match applicant's skills to best meet company needs
    - A description of how new hire will be able to perform the work and information on costs associated with hiring (if applicable)
- Offer job coaching services to support employer's orientation and on-the-job training program.
- Provide information on topics like the following:
    - No-cost accommodations
    - Costs associated with hiring
    - Disability awareness (specific and nonspecific)
    - Tax incentives and credits
    - List of employer liaisons in education and training programs
- Provide a monthly e-zine (a newsletter sent out by e-mail that would include information of interest to employers on disability and employment-related topics).

It is also important to note that one of the greatest values an employment specialist will bring to the business relates to the contributions that will be made by the job seeker. Naturally, this is extremely important. Some of the other benefits that may be associated with the resources and services an employment specialist may offer are listed in Table 14.4. When an employment specialist is talking to business, it is important to find ways to bring value to the business. This may extend beyond what the job seeker will offer to the business and will help the employment specialist develop a relationship with the business that, if all goes well, will earn him or her an opportunity to take the next step and learn more about a business' needs.

Although the primary goal of job development is to develop a job for a student, sometimes work is not immediately available. In such instances, employment specialists should be familiar with some other things employers could offer. For example, perhaps they can serve on an advisory committee, provide expertise and insight about their industry, give feedback or advice on marketing materials and ways to approach employers, or allow student job seekers to tour the business. Whenever a job offer is not on the immediate horizon, employment specialists should consider these and other ways to develop business partnerships.

Employment specialists should keep in mind that not learning about an immediate work opportunity still leaves the door open for building relationships. If an organization is not interested or unwilling to hire at the time, then employment specialists should at least leave the employer with a positive first impression in case they want to reach them at a later date. In this instance, the employer is not necessarily saying that he or she will

Table 14.4.   Possible benefits that an employment specialist may offer to employers

- Strategic positioning for future workforce needs
- Reduce turnover
- Reduce cost associated with new employee hiring and training
- Enhance organization's efficiency and productivity
- Financial benefits for gaining consumers with disabilities and others to buy or use company's products or services

never consider this, but is saying not right now. Time may be needed to build rapport and gain the trust necessary to form a working relationship that eventually leads to employment opportunities.

To engage with business, an employment specialist must be prepared. So far, this chapter has identified what an employment specialist needs to know and has described some of the services and resources an employment specialist may be able to offer to help encourage a business to develop a working relationship.

An employment specialist also needs to know how to address every perceived risk or concern an employer may have before meeting. If not, the employer may hesitate, stall, or refuse to consider hiring a student at the time.

Employer Questions and Concerns

Potential employers will want to know what value a student can bring to the business. In addition, they will need to know what types of specialized services are available to assist the business when applicable. Thus, employment specialists should know the nature of the services represented and be well versed in how to respond to potential employer questions or concerns without hesitation (Targett & Wehman, 2009). Employers will be more open to listening to employment specialists who can answer their questions with confidence. Reviewing some typical employer questions and formulating possible responses in advance will not only put employment specialists at ease but also help them respond without hesitation.

In addition, employers want to know that what an employment specialist says will work. This means an employment specialist needs to consider the question, "What is the perceived risk?" from the employer's perspective in advance. An employment specialist also needs to be able to address all concerns. Often, whenever an employment specialist is able to do so, the reward will be an opportunity to move forward and learn more about the business operations and needs, which in turn will give an employment specialist the chance to investigate ways to develop a job. Fortunately, typical employer concerns are known which include: *Will this work? What will others think? Will I lose or spend too much money?* An employment specialist needs to take time to think about how to respond to each concern.

Will this work? This fear is based on the risk that the service an employment specialist describes will not function as it is supposed to and/or the person hired will not be able to get the job done. One way to address this early on is for the employment specialist to let the employer know that he or she represents individuals with a wide range of skills (even though an employment specialist may be there with one person in particular in mind) and interests and allowing an employment specialist to learn about needs will make sure good recommendations are made. Also, the employment specialist should let the employer know that he or she, too, is concerned with recommending someone who could be a good match for the job and who should be able to get the job done with the right supports in place. An employment specialist may also want to share references from other businesses or articles about businesses that have used an employment specialist or a similar service.

What will others think? This fear is based on losing face or status with one's peers. Some employers may also be concerned about what customers or other workers might think. Once again, an employment specialist may be able to provide information on other businesses he or she has worked with or could speak in general about hiring initiatives among companies such as Walgreens, Lowe's, and others. This too may be a good time to recite some of the findings such as the fact that a study (Siperstein et al., 2006) found that people prefer to give their businesses to companies that hire individuals with disabilities. Asking about personal experiences and mentioning opportunities to receive press may also be useful.

Will I lose or spend too much money? Typically, job coaching services or on-the-jobsite training services like those offered in a supported employment approach are provided at no cost to the employer and usually are paid for by the school or the state's department of VR services. Also, indicating examples of no-tech or low-tech solutions should also be useful. These are inexpensive ways to support a worker such as rearranging the work area so a new hire can access materials or developing a checklist for the person to use to help monitor performance and change in schedule.

The Job Accommodation Network offers an array of information on these inexpensive work supports. An explanation about the role of the employment specialist after the person is hired may also need to be reiterated. The employer should know that additional on-the-jobsite training is available to the new hire and, while he or she is learning the job, the specialist would help make sure the work is completed to the employer's standards. The employer should also know that an employment specialist wants the best for both parties and, if for some reason the job was not working out, an employment specialist would support an employer's decision to let a worker go and would then work with the person to locate more suitable work.

In summary, in addition to creating enough value in the employer's mind, an employment specialist also has to eliminate or alleviate perceived risks. Whenever there is a stall, it likely means there is an employer fear or concern that has not been addressed. Addressing perceived risks should also help an employment specialist develop rapport with a potential employer. As with the development of any relationship, trust and understanding need to be established by both parties before things can develop. If the employment specialist invests the time up front, hopefully, there will be opportunities for numerous students with disabilities.

Asking Questions to Identify Business Needs

In addition to what has been described, the employment specialist should also spend a little time investigating a business and preparing a list of questions before meeting with an employer. This will save time and help make sure an employment specialist gets relevant information. Table 14.5 offers a list of some questions that could be asked to learn more about a business and its needs.

Closely listening to the employers' responses to these and other questions should give the employment specialist information to begin to address a particular employer's unique issues and needs. And, keep in mind, an employment specialist should also know something about the business before he or she walks in the door.

Getting to Know the Job Seeker

Sooner or later, an employment specialist will need to describe a specific job seeker to an employer. Therefore, an employment specialist must take time to get to know the person. How this is done will vary from one organization to the next. Recommended practices would dictate that an employment specialist get to know the person by using

Table 14.5.   Questions for an employment specialist to ask businesses

- Tell me about this business.
- What exactly is the nature of the business service or product?
- How does the business do what it does?
- How is business, and does the business foresee any trends that will affect an employment specialist's industry?
- What does the business need from its employees?
- What does the business pride itself on?
- What are the greatest areas of growth in the business?
- What circumstances or factors are affecting the business' hiring needs?

person-centered functional approaches to assessment. This means an employment specialist spends time with the person in community settings to get to know him or her. This not only allows time to build rapport but also allows an employment specialist to see the person's abilities first hand.

In addition, depending on the individual's ability to express himself or herself, an employment specialist should spend time talking to him or her and/or those who care about and know the person best. These talks would help an employment specialist gain insight into the person's typical daily routines, strengths, abilities, interests, potential support needs, and possible work supports. At the end of these activities, an employment specialist should have a good grasp of who the person is. This important information will guide job development. Some questions that an employment specialist should be able to answer are listed in Table 14.6.

An employment specialist can also use a number of person-centered planning strategies to gain this information. Person-centered planning is a team process in which a person with a disability and his or her chosen support network meet and discuss their vision for a positive future. This technique has also been used to look specifically at work. The end result is a plan that will guide future action to help the person gain and maintain employment.

Introducing the Job Seeker

An employment specialist should also take time to develop a brief introduction of the person to an employer. This could be paired with a presentation portfolio that includes pictures or a video of the student in action during his or her work experience or while out and about in the community and letters of reference or other work-related material. Some guidelines that an employment specialist can use to create an introduction to the student are offered in Table 14.7.

Asking for the Next Step

At some point in talks with employers, an employment specialist will need to be prepared to ask for what he or she wants. For instance, an employment specialist might also ask for a tour as a way to learn more about the business operations and possible needs.

Also, depending on the circumstances, there may be the opportunity to present a particular job seeker's attributes. Each situation will be different. Sometimes, the first

Table 14.6. Get to know the student as a job seeker

- What does the student do during a typical day?
- What does the student do without support?
- What activities require support and what type or level?
- Which activities does the student prefer?
- Does the student have any special interests?
- Which activities does the student not prefer?
- What do those who know the student best have to say about his or her abilities, interests, and potential support needs?
- What type or level of support can those closest to the student offer related to making initial contact with potential employers?
- What type of tasks might the student prefer to do in a work setting?
- At what type of tasks might the student be good at in a work setting?
- What schedule would be preferred?
- Are there any environmental or other characteristics associated with work that should be taken under consideration when developing a job?
- What are some examples of the type of supports that the student requires once hired (e.g., additional on-the-job site skills training, modified work schedule, assistive technology)

Table 14.7.   Guidelines for developing a student introduction

- What are a few of the student's positive attributes (e.g., dependable, on time, able to get along with others, detail-oriented, enthusiastic)?
- What are some examples of the student's work experiences or skills (e.g., tried out task in a retail store, bagged groceries)? Also include a reference (e.g., "Ms. Jenkins will be happy to serve as a reference").
- What does the student like to do for fun or what does he or she enjoy (e.g., he is a Redskins fan and watches the game with his dad; she likes to garden in the summer; she swims at the gym three times a week)?
- What are the student's support needs in context of work performance (e.g., he uses pictorial checklist to learn new tasks and we will make this available and teach him how to use it; she uses a removable key guard to type; or it may take him longer to learn some new things so we will offer a job coach to complement an employment specialist training)?

meeting will lead to another meeting to learn more about the business by spending time in departments or touring the business; at other times, this could occur on the spot and the next meeting may lead to meeting a particular student who wants to apply for a job. Or sometimes, at the end of the first meeting, the employer may choose not to move forward at this time.

Now, in the instance that an employer does not want to move forward, an employment specialist does not have to leave empty handed. This is when an employment specialist may ask the employer for a referral to another business or ask for a time period to wait before touching base again. The employment specialist may ask if the employer would be willing to let some of the job seekers the employment specialist represents come on site to learn more about the particular industry.

Employment specialists should also keep in mind that a first step may be to bring value to the business by offering one of the things discussed earlier such as providing training or signing them up for a monthly e-zine on disability and employment-related issues. Then again, on some occasions, an employment specialist may find that he or she and an employer are not getting anywhere fast or an employment specialist may find that the business indeed may not hold opportunity for anyone he or she represents anytime in the near future. An employment specialist may just thank the employer for his or her time and move on from there or mark his or her calendar to follow up sometime in the future.

Whenever an employer is agreeable, the next step is for the employment specialist to spend some time learning about the employer's operations and the types of work being performed. The information obtained can then be used to determine if there may be a good employment fit for a student either in an existing position or by creating a job that meets the employer's needs and highlights the abilities of the worker. The time spent learning more about the business is referred to as a workplace and job analysis. Before meeting with an employer, the employment specialist needs to be familiar with how to do this.

Conducting a Workplace and Job Analysis

Performing a workplace and job analysis is not difficult, but it is important to understand a way to go about it. Typically, during this time, the employment specialist examines operations. Notes are taken on the work setting and environment, specific job tasks, work pace, and production standards. This time also offers a chance to get a feel for the workplace culture and the natural cues and supports that exist in a business.

Here are some factors an employment specialist should review related to the work culture:

- Structure of organization—levels of supervision and management or leadership style
- Tones of interactions—are they friendly and supportive or curt
- Social activities both at and away from work—where people break, what kind of humor goes on in the workplace, whether there is teasing and joking

- The dress code and required grooming
- New employee initiation

It also helps to note the natural cues in the workplace. The natural cue is the clue to do something. For instance, a clock rings indicating a time to break; or co-workers leave the work area to go to lunch; or when a machine stops, it is time to get more supplies. Or perhaps a co-worker provides instruction on how to solve a problem or complete a new task. Environments have all kinds of signals built into them and an employment specialist needs to note these.

An employment specialist will also want take a look at the natural supports. For example, what is involved in the employer's new hire orientation and training program? An employment specialist will always want to maximize the use of natural or the existing supports in the workplace and build upon these as required and as time goes on specifically with the new worker in mind.

During a workplace and job analysis, an employment specialist will also want to learn more about the specific job tasks within an organization. There are some different ways to go about getting this information. For instance, an employment specialist may review job descriptions and make observations of workers in the workplace. The goal is to get a clear picture of the job to understand what the employee does and what the employer expects.

Employment specialists must keep in mind that, sometimes, depending on the nature of the business and the job seeker's abilities and support needs, an existing position that will be a good fit for a candidate may be found. However, at other times, an employment specialist will need to get creative and explore the possibilities of developing a job description for a particular job seeker with an employer. This has been described as job carving, creation, or restructuring. The remainder of the chapter examines this approach in more detail.

Creating a Job

Sometimes, when an employment specialist is either touring or analyzing a workplace and job, he or she may see an opportunity to discuss the possibility of creating a new job. The new job could support a new department that was recently added, but has not determined all of their human resource needs, or it could be taken from other positions in which the employees are either overworked (as indicated by paying of overtime or high turnover) or in job tasks that are simply not being completed because of the percentage of time the employee spends doing the most essential or important job function.

Oftentimes, inquisitive questions about the business can encourage ideas and incite informal conversations about the possibilities of creating a job. Questions to ask the employer include: In what areas do you pay overtime? Are there any job tasks that are not being completed on a regular basis?

Whenever an employment specialist is analyzing job descriptions, he or she should pay particular attention to the "other duties as assigned by supervisor," which typically include the nonroutine activities. This is one place where an employment specialist may find some clues about a way to develop a job for a particular student.

Also, it should be kept in mind that, just because a job description exists, does not mean that it is accurate. Having an opportunity to observe workers will help clarify the information and can also provide clues about a possible way to develop a job for a particular job seeker. The truth is that typically the employees have the best understanding of what they do. So, whenever possible, an employment specialist should informally solicit input from them to try and find out what is working and what is not. Again, this may provide ideas on how to develop a job.

Sometimes, a job description will include a percentage of time associated with a task that may or may not be accurate. For instance, a description may indicate that an employee spends 50% of his or her work day stocking shelves; however, observation and informal chats with the employee and/or supervisor indicate that 80% of time is usually expended performing that task. This, too, may point toward the possibility of developing a job for a student.

If an employment specialist discovers that a job description has 10 or more duties, which is a lot of duties, this could point to the fact that, indeed, some things are not getting done or maybe indicates that some employees are overworked. Once again, this may point to an opportunity to develop a job.

An effective workplace and job analysis need not be long or detailed. What is needed will vary depending on the nature of the business and the employment specialist's experience.

The employment specialist should keep in mind that some students will not qualify for a specific job, which is also an incentive to find ways to develop or create a new job. When a new job is created, a new job description will be written that uniquely fits the new hire's skills and qualifications.

Whenever an employment specialist is creating a job, he or she will need to work with the employer to develop a proposed job description. When broaching the subject with the employer, an employment specialist will need to be prepared to make the case for the new position. This means an employment specialist must have the details and explain why this makes good business sense. Once again, the bottom line is that the employer will have to see some value in the proposed job description. For example, perhaps some workers are overworked and the new position will help the company be more productive and success-ful. Or, perhaps some important task is not completed on a regular basis but needs ongo-ing attention or perhaps, in some instances, a new service could be added that will bring value to the business.

Some benefit will have to become apparent. For example, a problem will have to be solved or some cost savings or time benefits will need to be realized. The advantages will have to become evident. Sometimes, this will be apparent early on, and at other times, it takes longer; each situation is different.

When creating a job, an employment specialist should promote the employer's needs, not his or her own or that of the students. Once again, consideration should be given to the following: Can the employer save money? Can new customers be brought in? Can turno-ver be reduced? With the focus on the employer's needs, the employment specialist should be able to capture his or her attention. Some examples of job creation follow.

The employment specialist should note that it is important to identify the individual in the organization who has the power to create a position or who has the hiring authority in department, such as a manager or supervisor. Although sometimes it is appropriate to start at the human resources department, employment specialists should keep in mind that the goal is to tap into the hidden job market in order to identify jobs that have not been advertised yet and opportunities to create new positions.

In summary, the best way to learn about the workplace and the work that needs to be accomplished is for the employment specialist to spend time there. Brief, unobtrusive observations coupled with informational interviews with managers and workers will pro-vide a wealth of information about whether a job can be developed. And, although this activity is not always completed in advance of referring someone for an interview, it is extremely highly recommended. For some job seekers, it is absolutely mandatory, as this offers the first step toward exploring the possibilities of restructuring or creating a job.

Illustrations of Successful Job Carving

A few examples of job carving from Griffin and Targett (2006) follow to illustrate the strat-egies or approaches employed in developing work experiences and employment options for individuals with severe disabilities.

Business Efficiency and Productivity Strategy

The business efficiency and productivity strategy can be utilized with a variety of service and manufacturing operations. The business efficiency and productivity strategy, which might seem beneficial to all employers, is not always workable. In a variety of bureaucracies, such as government offices, university departments, and some social services entities, increased efficiency does not have a cash payoff and, therefore, is difficult to engineer.

Shelly Shelly, a 17-year-old student with a behavior disorder and mild cognitive impairment, has good interactive and communication skills, can orient well to landmarks, can match and sort items by color, and enjoys walking. The job developer observed that university department administrative assistants left their desks at various times in the morning and again in the afternoon to pick up incoming mail and to deliver outgoing mail at the campus post office. The job developer recorded this activity and estimated that approximately 15 administrative assistants spent more than half an hour per day walking to and from the post office. The developer then checked with university personnel to determine the average salary of a department administrative assistant, broke that down into an hourly wage, and multiplied that by half an hour.

The activity of the 15 staff members was costing the university approximately $20,000 per year. The employment specialist reasoned that a 4- or 5-hour-a-day job could be created for the individual with disabilities at $6.00 per hour, plus benefits and vacation, for less than $8,000 per year. This would save the university $12,000 in lost productivity and quell complaints by the administrative assistants who did not enjoy having to leave their other assigned duties twice each day.

This information was well received by the university vice president. The efficiency increase would benefit staff morale and improve service to faculty and college students; however, the personnel system was such that all available positions were filled, and funding for new positions was restricted by the state legislature. No new positions could be added without significant maneuvering, which would be inconvenient, time consuming, and potentially politically hazardous for the vice president. In short, the rigid employment systems of some bureaucracies may dictate that other approaches or long-term efforts are required to break into these markets. Employment specialists should be advised that sometimes things do not work out even after a lot of effort goes into analyzing employer needs. On the bright side, employment specialists should also remember the receptivity of the employer and try to get referrals to other businesses or consider reanalyzing needs at a future date.

Consultative/Employment Service Strategy

The consultative/employment service strategy can be utilized with a variety of businesses, especially those that have high personnel turnover or seasonal market fluctuations. Jobs typically having high turnover may not be choice jobs for anyone, however. These positions should not be utilized as dumping grounds for people with severe disabilities and may indeed result in heightened anxiety about work demands, job loss, and employment expectations. These jobs should be approached with common sense and the understanding that such positions can be great first jobs or seasonal jobs and a step on the career ladder. Again, it is important to note the corporate culture and work environment of businesses that appear to have high personnel turnover.

Motel There was a motel that had a high turnover rate of certain staff, but after a few days of on-site observation, a core group of stable employees became apparent. This group of housekeepers had long-term employment records and shared a highly ritualized culture that was hard to infiltrate. Admission was gained by showing work stamina and a strong sense of insider humor and by contributing to the purchase of donuts, soda, and snacks for team members to share. Failure to understand the culture and take slow, decisive action to fit in led quickly to exclusion. New employees who failed to perceive these rites were left to fend for themselves. In this situation, many workers simply moved on to the next job. A good job developer recognizes these worksite traits and develops strategies to make consumers accepted members of the work force, thus protecting the job and the individual.

In the consultative/employer service strategy, research is performed to find business trends conducive to job development (Griffin, Hammis, Geary, & Sullivan, 2008). In keeping with the motel example, research was performed in a western city to assist in the creation of a service niche. The research included the identification of motels near the homes of individuals seeking first and second jobs in housekeeping departments. Calls were made to the owners of a dozen small to moderate-size motels. Almost all of the owners were willing to discuss their turnover, recruitment, and training issues. From these discussions, it was determined that the average moderate-size motel in this area employed five housekeepers, one of whom was the head housekeeper with additional duties, responsibilities, and pay. The average work week for the housekeepers was 40 hours in 6 days, and the average pay was $6.50 per hour with varying benefits. Head housekeepers made $8.00–$10.00 per hour. Average annual turnover was approximately 200% with a range of 80%–300%. Turnover varied by city and motel, necessitating case-specific research.

When the housekeeping department terminates the employment of a staff member, the manager or the head housekeeper performs the work or sees that the duties are covered. Head housekeepers get the first option to work extra hours for overtime pay in many cases. Usually, overtime is split between the head housekeeper and the other housekeepers. In any case, the managers or owners view this as a possible time for reduced work quality, poorer consumer service, and additional cost. The search for another housekeeper is vital and is initiated through classified advertisements, a pool of former employees, or word of mouth to friends of the other housekeepers.

Once a new employee is identified, a week is often required for training on company standards. This pulls the head housekeeper away from typical duties and requires more overtime expenditures. When recruitment and training are completed, the expense to the employer can range from $500 to $2,000, largely in hidden costs. If the motel employs five housekeepers and has an average turnover rate of 200%, then the employer stands to lose as much as $20,000 per year in hiring and training costs. The job developer must create a problem-solving relationship with the motel manager or owner and approach the discussion of these costs over time. A rush to accomplish this can cause the owner to feel incompetent or angry, inhibiting employment opportunities.

A job developer can approach the manager with a possible employment service strategy, including hiring, screening, training, and follow up. Charging for this service, on the basis of an analysis of what the employer stands to save by hiring one or two people through the service agency, is also a reasonable business activity. When people get something for nothing, their dedication to it is minimal, and if the provider agency does not value the employment services it offers, then ongoing service accountability to the employer is diminished. Good employment services are worth paying for, and the addition of a market-based price may raise the expectations and accomplishments of all involved parties.

Another strategy is to perform an analysis of housekeeper routines and carve out unproductive or duplicative efforts to make all workers more productive. This also reduces the inconvenience associated with a team member quitting. Such carved duties at a motel might include stripping beds, emptying trash cans, stocking supply carts, and replenishing towels in towel carts. All of these activities save time and make the workers more productive.

Making people more productive can have the short-range effect of lowering weekly paychecks, however. This event can lead to trouble for the new employee if he or she is viewed by the others as the cause of their misfortune. If this situation occurs, then a strategy should be developed with the employer. Perhaps increased productivity dictates that the next vacancy not be filled, thus guaranteeing full employment for those remaining while securing the need for the newly created assisting position.

Many businesses and offices of all types face similar circumstances and can benefit from consolidating activities into a new core job or jobs. Grease Monkey, a quick oil-change franchise company, has carved a number of duties to speed production and smooth operations. Consumers at Grease Monkey are greeted by an attendant who takes vital information on the service desired. Quickly, an employee begins to vacuum the carpets, while another cleans windows. The vehicle is pulled inside a work bay, and one employee, stationed in the grease pit, drains the oil and lubricates the chassis. Topside, employees check tire pressure, fill fluid reservoirs, and add new oil. The whole process takes less than 15 minutes and costs a little less than typically slower service at a local garage. The labor costs for Grease Monkey can be higher than other companies in the oil-change business because Grease Monkey has as many as four employees working on one car; however, consumer satisfaction, resulting from convenient service hours, short wait periods, and quality service, brings an increase in highly profitable repeat business.

Employment specialists looking for summer employment for students can also find the consultative/employment service strategy useful. One possible avenue to creating employment is to simply walk around the community and note all of the odd jobs that the city or county government has overlooked. This might include painting sign posts or buildings, cleaning and mowing vacant lots, watering flower beds in the city park, or performing maintenance on city vehicles and equipment or tasks predictably overlooked by city officials during the summer because of the activity of road repair, the impact of tourism in some locales, and the shortage of staff because of vacation schedules. By approaching the city manager, the mayor, or the public works director and explaining that there is a waiting work force, temporary summer employment can be created. These jobs represent valuable evaluation and experiential opportunities for transition-age students, teachers, and new job coaches. Towns and cities often use summer employment programs operated by entities such as the local Workforce Investment Act or One-Stop Career Center vendor. Supervision, training, and wage assistance are available and should be utilized by schools, families, employers, and adult services providers.

Interactive Duties Strategy

The interactive duties strategy shares aspects with other strategies but is presented to show how job restructuring can lead to the creation of natural or typical supports.

Welding Shop   A welding shop operation was observed and inventoried to determine a possible job match for an individual with severe intellectual disability. The shop employed four welders who performed all duties associated with business, except accounting, which was handled by an outside agency. To create a naturally supportive environment and minimize job coach presence, the inventory of daily activities facilitated the identification of tasks that could be carved for this individual to perform. This also included duties that normally would be accomplished by two welders working together. The sales approach here emphasized that now, instead of having two welders, who each earn $12.00 per hour, perform tasks, one welder and the newly hired assistant, who earns less, can perform the same job at reduced cost and greater efficiency.

This example can be modified to fit many industries. Table 14.8 illustrates the tasks that are performed routinely, possible carved tasks, and the duties that can be performed by the assistant with other workers or performed in the presence of co-workers. The interactive duties strategy decreases job coach presence and stigma, emphasizes natural supervision and co-worker involvement, and reduces consumer reliance on service systems.

White-collar employment also offers diverse opportunities to create employment.

Business Office   In one case, an inventory was performed of an office administrative assistant's duties and interactions. Core duties included answering telephones, word processing, preparing bulk mailings, filing, desktop publishing, bookkeeping, ordering supplies, photocopying documents, running errands, and coordinating company travel logistics. As the business grew, juggling all of these duties became increasingly difficult.

Table 14.8. Job carving at a welder's shop

Welder's inventory (nonsequential)	Carved tasks	Interactive and shared tasks
Clock in	Yes	Yes
Drink coffee and talk	Yes	Yes
Get work orders	Yes	Yes
Design and troubleshoot	No	No
Weld	No	Maybe
Change welding tanks	Yes	Yes
Sort scraps	Yes	Maybe
Carry scraps to recycling or trash bin	Yes	Sometimes
Clean work area	Yes	Yes
Clean facility	Yes	Maybe
Label stock and supplies	Yes	Yes
Check in and stock deliveries	Yes	Yes
Talk with customers	No	Maybe
Lunch/breaks: talk and joke	Yes	Yes
Check out; ride home	Yes	Yes

The job developer identified a student interested in office work, contacted several employers, performed job duty inventories by observing and interviewing clerical staff, and approached one of the employers with an efficiency plan. The business manager, consumer, administrative assistant, and job developer created a clerical assistant position that is supervised by the administrative assistant. The individual in this position performs filing, preparing bulk mail, and photocopying. The job is part time, working with a variety of professionals who are well connected in their community, and all of the work is performed with or near co-workers without disabilities. No job coach is necessary on site because of management's commitment to use co-workers in the mentoring process. The employer saw immediate improvement in work quality, consumer service, and office efficiency. The administrative assistant got a helping hand and lessened his work stress.

Some other examples of job carving are in Table 14.9. To get employers thinking about these ideas, employment specialists may want to ask questions like those provided in Table 14.10.

Another variation on job carving and job creation is resource ownership (Griffin et al., 2008). The competitive labor market operates on the principle of exploitation. That is, employers hire people with skills, talents, and attributes that are saleable in the greater marketplace. For instance, a mechanic hired at a local garage is expected to bring talent and tools that allow the owner to charge customers a fair price for repair work. The mechanic is paid less than the value of the work, and the owner keeps the remainder to pay operational costs and for profit. Someone with a college education in computer science costing $40,000 or so is hired because of the apparent value of that education. The assumption is that the education benefits the employer through better and marketable ideas and

Table 14.9. Job carving methods and examples

Brief description	Example
Reduce overtime expenditures	Receptionist has to stay overtime or work weekends to make marketing packets; new part-time job is created for employee to make packets.
Reassignment of functions to allow focus on expertise	Well-paid paralegals have to spend valuable time copying materials in law library; new position is created for employee to make copies.
Offer a new service	Sandwich shop creates a new job to offer new service to its customers (i.e., deliver foods to business buildings in nearby walking radius during lunch hours).
Get task done	During "down time," wait staff at large hotel are supposed to polish silver used for events; but it is not maintained on an ongoing basis; job is created for employee to polish silver so it is ready to use.

Table 14.10. Questions to get employers thinking about job creation

1. Are there any job tasks performed by one or more employees that might improve overall efficiency when combined to create a job opportunity for someone else?
2. Are there any areas where you are paying employees overtime?
3. Are there any tasks that never seem to be completed in a timely fashion because other employees are too busy to get around to doing them?
4. Would you be willing to hire someone to do a portion of a job if it would improve the other employees' productivity?
5. Are there new services you would like to add to your business?

Source: Hagner and DiLeo (1996).

skills, such as computer repair or programming. Without these skills and attributes, such as a college education or mechanics' tools, the individuals are less likely to retain these particular jobs.

Transition-age students with the most significant disabilities often leave school without skills and talents immediately obvious to employers. Most have a limited résumé consisting of unpaid work experiences in stereotypical jobs such as janitorial work, stocking shelves, and pet care. Such experiences do not motivate the worker and teach that work is not rewarding (Griffin et al., 2008). Ownership of exploitable goods can change this outcome.

A note of caution is important here. The purchase of equipment is not solely based on the employer's wishes. The equipment or other resource must fit the job seeker's vocational interests and desires and be used predominantly by the individual. Buying resources for the employer that are not used by the worker in a job of his or her choice betrays the principles of inclusion and respect.

Beth Beth is a young lady living in the rural South. She has an interest in computers and children. She is graduating with a Certificate of Attendance, cannot read or write very well, and has few options except the local sheltered workshop. Her team considers her interests and proposes that she operate a computer center in a child care center. Unfortunately, no employer will hire her. Her challenges outweigh her talents. The team uses a local Workforce Investment grant through the U.S. Department of Labor and assistance from Vocational Rehabilitation (VR) to purchase intuitive children's software and a complete computer and printer tutoring set up. The prospective employer solicits parents who desire individualized computer lessons for their children and signs up 27 students. The employer charges an additional fee for the computer tutoring that Beth provides, thereby creating a new position at the child care center. An agreement is developed that stipulates that Beth's equipment remains in her possession until its useable life is exhausted (about 3 years) and then the employer will pay to replace and upgrade it. With one small investment and a bit of person-centered planning, a job was created that highlights Beth's gifts and that increased the profitability of the host business (Griffin et al., 2008).

Edward Edward left school early because of his extreme behaviors. He was clear, however, that he wanted to work detailing cars. Unfortunately, no jobs were readily available in his local community until a job development visit to a local detailing operation revealed that the employer did not own a carpet steam shampooer. Upon meeting Edward, the employer agreed to hire him and train him in the entire detailing process as long as Edward purchased a $2,000 carpet steamer. Edward now works daily at the business, makes a wage typical to others employed there, and is on a career path that includes training in all aspects of the business. Two thousand dollars is a minor sum to be paid considering what was spent on his education and what the public tax burden would be if no job was secured upon graduation. The sources for such funds include the school's appropriation for educating Edward, VR, a Plan for Achieving Self-Support (PASS) through Social Security, family funds, Workforce Investment Act dollars, and so forth.

Conclusion

Job development will lead to an opportunity for an employment specialist to spend time with an employer. This offers a chance to make a great impression and communicate how hiring a student can bring value to the business. Therefore, to do the best job possible, an employment specialist must be prepared. An employment specialist must be able to speak intelligently to business about the nature of the request. In addition, the employment specialist must also know the individual job seeker who is being represented. An employment specialist needs to know each individual's interests, abilities, and potential support needs. An employment specialist cannot develop a job for someone without this information.

The use of an approach such as job carving to create viable work opportunities for people with more significant disabilities cannot be overemphasized. It is crucial that those charged with this mission learn how to use this powerful technique to develop jobs.

Study Questions

1. What is the definition of job development and who can it benefit?
2. What is involved in a supported employment approach?
3. Meet with an employer to discuss what we know from the research and get his or her advice on best ways to approach job creation.
4. What does an employment specialist need to know in advance of meeting with a business to investigate the possibility of developing a job for a student?
5. Meet with an employer (not human resources) to ask about employer concerns associated with hiring individuals with disabilities. How can these be addressed?
6. What are some questions that an employment specialist might ask an employer to learn more about business operations and needs?
7. What is the purpose of a workplace and job analysis?
8. Interview professionals who have successfully assisted youth with disabilities with going to work and investigate some ways they have created jobs.

Online Resources

Job Accommodation Network: http://askjan.org/

Rehabilitation Research and Training Center: http://www.worksupport.com

Disability Resources, United States Department of Labor: http://www.dol.gov/dol/topic/disability/jobsearch.htm

Office of Disability Employment Policy: http://www.dol.gov/odep/

National Collaborative on Workforce and Disability for Youth: http://www.ncwd-youth.info/

Pursuing Postsecondary Education Opportunities for Individuals with Disabilities

15

ELIZABETH EVANS GETZEL AND LORI W. BRIEL

After completing this chapter, the reader will be able to

- Discuss the challenges involved in gaining access to postsecondary education for people with disabilities, including specific transition issues
- Describe the skills needed by students for a successful transition to college
- Discuss the importance of accommodations and instructional and assistive technology devices in a college environment
- Discuss the expanding postsecondary education options for students with intellectual disabilities

There are several decisions involved when one is planning and preparing for the transition to college; this is true for all students, including students with disabilities. Every student involved in the transition to college needs to consider the size and location of the college, the majors or degrees offered, campus activities including student organizations and clubs, diversity of the student body, and availability of financial aid or scholarships. Students with disabilities faced with these same decisions must also determine the availability of support services and the documentation requirements to receive accommodations, campus accessibility, and other services and supports offered in addition to academic supports.

This chapter highlights important components for students with disabilities considering postsecondary education. To help students with disabilities prepare for their transition to higher education, information and resources are provided for five primary areas of consideration when creating a planning process. These include exploring postsecondary educational settings, preparing academically for college, identifying financial aid resources, developing essential skills for college, and applying strategies to remain in college.

New Postsecondary Education Opportunities for Students with Intellectual Disabilities

Much of the resources and information contained in this chapter can apply to students with intellectual disabilities (ID) when considering college as a postschool goal. At this time, there are a number of colleges and universities around the country that are providing educational experiences for students with more significant disabilities (Grigal & Hart, 2010a). Much of the planning and preparation materials and information provided here can be used by students with ID, their families, and individualized education program (IEP) teams when exploring postsecondary experiences. The Higher Education Opportunity Act of 2008 (PL 110-315) expanded the opportunities for students with disabilities to access postsecondary education programs. The act provides expanded access for students with ID to federal financial aid including Pell Grants, Supplemental Educational Opportunity Grants, and Federal Work-Study Programs (Lee & Will, 2010). These financial aid opportunities are available to students with ID enrolled in a postsecondary setting taking courses for credit, audit, or in non–credit-bearing, non–degree-seeking programs. For students with ID to access financial aid opportunities, the postsecondary institution must offer a comprehensive transition and postsecondary education program and students must meet the definition of ID as described in the Act (Lee & Will, 2010).

When one is considering postsecondary education opportunities for students with ID, it is important to understand the variety of options that are available. Hart and colleagues (2006) identified three types of models that are being used by postsecondary programs. The first is a **mixed/hybrid model** that is designed to offer social and academic experiences (for credit or audit) on campus with students without disabilities. Students with ID or other developmental disabilities typically spend some portion of their time with other students with disabilities to cover life skills or other transition programs. The second model, the **substantially separate model**, is where students with significant disabilities are on campus, but primarily take classes with other students with significant disabilities. Interacting with other college students without disabilities occurs mainly through social activities on campus. The third model, which is the most inclusive model, is the **inclusive individual support model**. This model is highly individualized in the services and supports provided and how classes are accessed on campus; essentially, students with ID or other developmental disabilities enroll in classes (for credit or audit) based on the course offerings in the college catalog.

Although these models differ in their approach in supporting students with ID or other developmental disabilities and the coordination of services, they do share common goals. These goals include offering transition services to students in a college setting to assist in obtaining jobs; opportunities to participate in social activities with other college students without disabilities; and promoting a higher degree of independence and self-confidence (Zaft, Hart, & Zimbrich, 2004). In addition, young adults participating in postsecondary education experiences were 26% more likely to leave vocational rehabilitation with paid employment and were able to earn a 73% higher weekly income (Migliore, Butterworth, & Hart, 2009).

Dual-Enrollment Opportunities for Students with Disabilities

Dual-enrollment opportunities can assist students with or without disabilities in preparing for the academic rigor in college and in earning college credit while still in high school (Karp & Hughes, 2008). Dual-enrollment classes are a collaboration between high schools and colleges enabling high school students to attend college-level classes, usually during their junior or senior year. National data collected during 2002–2003 revealed that 5% of all high school students have participated in a dual-enrollment program, primarily taking courses at 2-year postsecondary institutions (Golann & Hughes, 2008). Students participating in dual-enrollment classes can be on a college campus with postsecondary education students or at a high school with other high school students taught by a college instructor. Either way, students enrolled in the class must meet the requirements to earn college credit (Karp & Hughes, 2008).

Previously, dual-enrollment (also called concurrent enrollment) was for students (with or without disabilities) taking college preparation classes (Karp & Hughes, 2008). However, taking college courses while still in high school is expanding to provide college academics to other student populations (Grigal & Hart, 2010a; Karp & Hughes, 2008). These students include youth enrolled in career and technical education classes, low-achieving students, and students with ID (Grigal & Hart, 2010a; Golann & Hughes, 2008). Some of the benefits of participating in dual-enrollment programs include "increasing the academic rigor of high school curriculum, helping low-performing students meet high academic standards, providing more academic opportunities and electives, and reducing high school dropout rates and increasing student aspirations" (Golann & Hughes, 2008, p. 3). There is some evidence that students taking courses through dual-enrollment are more likely to pursue college after high school graduation and are able to persist once in college (Karp & Hughes, 2008). However, more research is needed on the effectiveness or impact of dual-enrollment in general for high school students and also including students with ID who are increasingly participating in dual or concurrent programs (Grigal & Hart, 2010a; Karp & Hughes, 2008).

Postsecondary Transition Considerations

Preparation for postsecondary education includes learning those skills necessary to deal with both the academic and the social challenges presented by college. Educators, family members, and students may assume that, if a student is academically capable of participating in higher education settings, then systematic preparation for college is not needed (Getzel, Briel, & Kregel, 2000; Getzel, McManus, & Briel, 2004; Kochhar-Bryant, Bassett, & Webb, 2009; Shaw, Madaus, & Dukes, 2010). Unfortunately, without effective planning and preparation, students with disabilities can become overwhelmed and unable to adapt to a postsecondary environment (Hughes, 2009). Therefore, the transition to college must begin early in students' educational experiences. Pre–high school activities could include taking challenging courses in English, math, science, history, or foreign language. Exploring course options among high school programs is also important so students can learn more about their academic and career interests. In addition, students need to work on developing strong study skills and learning strategies (Kochhar-Bryant et al., 2009; Getzel, 2008; Shaw et al., 2010).

Although many postsecondary education programs are increasing in the attention and support given to students with disabilities, success in these settings, for the most part, remains dependent on the individual qualities of the student (Kochhar-Bryant et al., 2009; Brinckerhoff, McGuire & Shaw, 2002; Getzel, 2008; Shaw et al., 2010). Students need to be aware of their new rights and responsibilities in postsecondary education (U.S. Department of Education, Office of Civil Rights, 2007). Understanding these rights and responsibilities is particularly important because college students with disabilities are now responsible for documentation of a disability, assessment information, programming, advocacy, decision making, and transition planning (Brinckerhoff et al., 2002; Getzel, 2008; Getzel et al., 2004; Webb, Patterson, Syverud, & Seabrooks-Blackmore, 2008). Unfortunately, the stigma attached to identifying oneself as needing special services or supports remains an issue and can drive some students to elect not to disclose their disabilities in order to avoid being labeled as needing specialized services (Getzel, 2005, 2008; Hadley, 2006; Kochhar-Bryant et al., 2009; Shaw et al., 2010). In too many instances, students who fail to identify themselves as having disabilities are often unable to gain access to many of the supports designed to get them closer to having equal (rather than special) access to education (Getzel, 2008; Getzel et al., 2004; Getzel & Thoma, 2008; Troiano, Liefeld, & Trachtenberg, 2010). The following sections provide critical information needed by students with disabilities and their IEP teams to consider when planning for college.

Exploring Postsecondary Educational Settings

It is important for students to explore a variety of postsecondary education options to determine what best meets their educational and training needs. When assessing a college or university, it is important to look comprehensively at the programs, college environment, and general feel of the campus and, then, to look specifically at the disability-related supports and services needed. The Internet provides a wealth of information through specific college web sites or general web sites on colleges that provide specialized programs for students with disabilities. Shaw and colleagues (2010) believe such web sites as Collegenet.com and Collegeview.com can assist students with disabilities to view programs, where the college is located geographically, course offerings, tuition fees, financial aid, and other information. Resource books that compile information on colleges and universities are available in bookstores, state departments of education, or other organizations. All aspects of the college experience should be explored during the process of selecting a college; however, it is important to understand the requirements in specific majors that students are interested in pursuing. Remember, preparing for the transition to college is one step in the process; staying in college and completing a degree or certificate program is the ultimate goal of thorough transition planning. For example, students with disabilities may be accepted to a college without taking a foreign language, but then face challenges meeting the college's foreign language requirement for graduation (Madaus, 2003; Shaw et al., 2010). It cannot be assumed that courses, such as a foreign language or math, will be substituted at the college level. It is critical to understand the policies and procedures for course substitutions and degree requirements for earning a college diploma.

Virtual tours are helpful when one is deciding what colleges to visit, preparing for an onsite visit, or serving as a campus visit when time or finances are limited (Shaw et al., 2010). If a campus tour is possible, visiting potential schools to learn about the academic program offerings, the services and supports provided to all students, and those services specifically for students with disabilities can greatly assist in the decision-making process. Before visiting a campus, students should contact the office that is responsible for determining accommodations for students with disabilities; often, these offices are called **Services for Students with Disabilities** or Disability Support Services. Talking with this office about the process for receiving accommodations once enrolled is a critical step in getting the services and supports needed. When requesting a meeting, students should ask to also speak with a current college student with a disability. Talking with someone already enrolled at the college can provide tremendous insight on what to expect when entering a college campus. According to Wilson, Getzel, and Brown (2000), some suggested areas to consider when visiting a program or reviewing information include

1. Campus climate: Is the campus atmosphere generally accepting of students with differences in learning styles? Are students considered in the planning process and encouraged to participate fully in a variety of campus-life activities?

2. Program philosophy: Is there a specialized area of emphasis associated with the services? Is there an emphasis on learning strategies, remediation, or social skills?

3. Awareness and support: Are the school administration and faculty aware of the needs of students with disabilities and the accommodations that will help meet these needs? Is there good communication among all parties on whom the student will rely for support?

4. Academic adjustment: How are academic accommodations coordinated? Are there specialized accommodations such as note takers, real-time captioning, and readers/scribes for examinations?

5. Waivers and substitutions: What are the procedures for waivers and substitutions, and is assistance available with these procedures? What kind of documentation is required? What is the probability that waivers and/or substitutions are granted?

6. Course load and graduation time: Do students with disabilities generally take longer to complete the requirements for graduation? Is priority registration available for students with disabilities?

7. Tutorial support: Is tutorial support scheduled or on an as-needed basis? Is tutoring provided by peers or professional staff? What is the student–tutor ratio? Does the staff receive continual professional development?

as well as student support activities or groups: Are there ongoing groups that meet to talk about issues or concerns related to their experiences on campus? Are there specific activities that are designed to assist students with disabilities to network with other students on campus? Are there student leadership/mentoring programs to help students feel connected with other students with disabilities on campus? Is there a campus disability advocacy or advisory group that students can join to provide input concerning issues on campus?

Preparing Academically for College

Students with disabilities must be able to demonstrate that they meet the academic requirements to enter postsecondary education programs. It is critical that students are enrolled in college preparatory classes during high school to build a foundation of knowledge to not only enter college but also meet the academic demands once in college (Getzel, 2008; McGuire, 2010; Brinckerhoff et al., 2002). Students interested in pursuing postsecondary education options after high school need to be taking courses in the general curriculum or in the most-inclusive classroom settings (Kochhar-Bryant et al., 2009). General curriculum classes, including college preparatory classes, build learner independence, assist students with disabilities to become familiar with lecture presentations, and develop test-taking skills (Kochhar-Bryant et al., 2009).

Use of Technology

Today, students' lives are filled with technology that gives them mobile access to information and resources around the clock. Both secondary and postsecondary education systems strive to use the learning sciences and modern technology to create engaging, relevant, and personalized learning experiences for all learners that will reflect the reality of their futures (U.S. Department of Education, Office of Educational Technology, 2010). In one study, a majority of college freshmen and seniors reported regular use of course management systems, presentation software, and the college or university library web site (Smith & Caruso, 2010). Also noted in the study were the increased numbers of college students (62.7%) owning and using hand-held devices that access the Internet daily, and 40% reported posting video to video web sites and updating wikis (Smith & Caruso, 2010). Students with disabilities need to understand and have access to technology the same as their classmates without disabilities.

Advances in technology have also increased access to tools for all students that can assist in learning. Significant growth in both assistive and instructional technology provides an important link to promoting access to information and learning for students with disabilities (Michaels, Pollack Prezant, Morabito, & Jackson, 2002). Students with disabilities need opportunities to try out and customize various technologies to compensate for challenges presented by their disabilities while still in high school or *before* entering a higher education program (Briel & Getzel, 2009; Burgstahler, 2005; see also Chapter 12). Yet, many students with disabilities are entering postsecondary programs unaware of existing technologies that can assist them in college (Getzel, 2008; Shaw et al., 2010). Understanding what technology is available is a significant need that can make a tremendous difference in students' ability to perform effectively in college. In postsecondary settings, the use of technology benefits students by providing access to previously unavailable academic and social opportunities, providing alternative methods of responding, increasing learner independence, and increasing the ability to cope, compensate, and accept their disability (Bryant, Bryant, & Reith, 2002).

Introducing students to the use of technology and software that assists them in organizing textbook materials or the development of a paper; text-to-speech software for reading, writing, and taking exams; or hand-held technologies to assist in time management is essential. Students who begin working with devices while in high school or earlier are able to determine what technologies are most effective and can explore postsecondary programs to determine which devices can be used to gain access to information (McManus, Smith, & Jones, 2010). Students with disabilities along with their IEP team can collaborate with technology specialists in their school districts to identify and customize software or devices that meet individual learning needs. The use of technology that enables success in higher education increases the likelihood of improved career outcomes (Burgstahler, 2005; Fichten et al., 2001; Getzel, 2008; Kim-Rupnow & Burgstahler, 2004).

Preparing for Standardized Admission Testing

Before applying for college, students with disabilities will need to take a standardized admission examination—the SAT and/or the ACT. In many ways, it is advantageous for students to take the PSAT or PLAN practice test in their sophomore year to get feedback on skills needed for college study and to project future scores. Educators, guidance counselors, students, and families can then use this information to adjust the student's curriculum and guide course selection in high school (Banerjee & Brinckerhoff, 2010). In addition, the PSAT provides opportunities to enter the National Merit Scholarship Corporation program and allows online access to college and career planning tools (College Board, 2011).

If a student is going to request accommodations for the examination, then ample time is needed before the date of the test to request these accommodations. SAT and ACT have very specific rules for qualifying for accommodations (Fuller & Wehman, 2003). It is important that students and family members work closely with the high school staff to provide the necessary information to request testing accommodations. Since 2003, the SAT and ACT do not indicate if an examination was taken using accommodations. In addition, as of 2009, all students, including students with disabilities, can select which score will be sent to the college or university, enabling students to determine the highest score they would like to submit (Banerjee & Brinckerhoff, 2010). Students with disabilities will need to determine with the assistance of instructors or other education professionals their personal test-taking strategies (Banerjee & Brinckerhoff, 2010; Fuller & Wehman, 2003).

Identifying Financial Aid Resources

A large number of students seeking a college education will need additional financial resources beyond what their families can provide (Heath Resource Center, 2010). There are four types of financial aid that students with disabilities can consider including (Rioux-Bailey, 2004)

a. Grants (funds that usually do not need to be repaid)

b. Loans (funds that are borrowed to cover costs and are repaid over time)

c. Work study (employment that helps students earn money to cover costs)

d. Scholarships (e.g., awards based on specific criteria such as academic achievement, career goals)

Students with disabilities and their family members will need to explore what types of financial assistance are available, whether it is disability-related expenses or general college expenses that need to be covered. Financial assistance may be needed to help cover the cost of tuition, room and board, transportation, or other college-related expenses.

Researching financial aid resources from both public and private entities takes time, so starting early in the planning process is essential. Often, there are changes in financial aid resources because of legislation, eligibility requirements, or policies (Heath Resource Center, 2010), so it is important to ensure that students and their families are reviewing the most current information available. It is recommended that students with disabilities and their families complete the Free Application for Federal Student Aid, which is located online or available through the student's guidance office or the school's career center. Other potential resources for students with disabilities may be available from the state Vocational Rehabilitation Agency or from the Social Security Administration (Miller, O'Mara, & Getzel, 2009). Students should review several sources of information to determine what financial aid, grants, or scholarships might be available (Heath Resource Center, 2010).

Developing Essential Skills Needed for College

Self-Determination Skills

A growing consideration in transition planning is supporting the development and use of student self-determination skills (Morningstar et al., 2010). Self-determination is a set of personal or interpersonal skills that include (Getzel, 2008; Getzel & Thoma, 2006; Thoma & Wehmeyer, 2005)

a. Acceptance of a disability and how it impacts learning

b. Awareness of what support services are needed

c. Knowing how to describe one's disability and the need for specific supports to services providers

d. Having the determination to overcome obstacles that may be presented

The development of self-determination skills should begin in the early years of school for students with disabilities, but often, these skills are not included in the academic experience of students with disabilities until middle or secondary school. Strategies and tools are needed to assist students with disabilities to understand who they are both academically and personally, to become an integral part in their IEP planning process, and to discover their own "voice" in this process. One tool that can assist students in acquiring self-determination skills is the *One Pager,* which provides opportunities for students to describe their strengths, interests, preferences, and needs. Students can prepare and distribute this document before their IEP meetings. A second tool is the *My Good Day Plan.* This activity allows students to describe what happens on a good day, identify positive behaviors, assess if it is happening, problem solve what actions are needed to reach goals, and identify who can assist in this process. Both of these tools along with numerous resources for educators, families, and students with disabilities can be found at http://www.imdetermined. org. See Chapter 2 for more information on self-determination and transition planning.

In the past, students with disabilities were often unaware of the goals established in their IEPs or saw little connection to their education and future goals (Thoma, Saddler, Purvis, & Scott, 2010). Active participation in the IEP process is essential in developing self-determination skills, directing the meeting itself, and helping establish the goals and required services (Thoma & Wehman, 2010; Wehman & Wittig, 2009). The IEP process offers students the opportunity to practice applying skills of self-advocacy and choice in a safe environment, and it provides an opportunity for them to develop an awareness of their strengths and needs (Thoma & Wehman, 2010). Each of these is essential to developing self-determination. Many times, well-intentioned educators and family members protect youth with disabilities from making mistakes and refrain from discussing the details and impact of the student's disability (Bremer, Kachgal, & Schoeller, 2003). Exercising personal choice options allows students to know themselves, understand their disability, and understand how it may affect academic learning, relationships, employment, and participation in the community (Getzel, 2005, 2008; Thoma & Wehman, 2010; Thoma & Wehmeyer, 2005).

Self-Management Skills

By far, abilities in self-management are the most critical skills that all students attending postsecondary programs need. These skills include time management, organizational skills, and study skills. Students with disabilities often report the need for organizational skills, time management, and goal setting as needed when in college (Getzel & Thoma, 2006; Getzel & Thoma, 2008; Finn, Getzel, & McManus, 2008). Larger projects, assignments, and academic loads combined with reduced daily structure challenge all college students to organize their day, break down assignments, and monitor the work flow. Students often struggle with trying to manage their academic studies with the variety of social opportunities on campus. Self-management skills such as time management become a lifeline to success and a critical skill to help students balance their academic studies and social activities (Getzel, 2008; Getzel & Thoma, 2006).

Strategies for managing time in postsecondary programs focus on techniques that encourage students with disabilities to monitor their study habits and to understand the types of resources or supports they will need to meet their course load requirements (Webb et al., 2008). Some suggested strategies that students with disabilities can use to self-monitor their time-management skills in college include (Dillion, 1997; Getzel, 2008; Kochhar-Bryant et al., 2009; Shaw et al., 2010)

a.　Creating a semester schedule, assessing and planning their work load each week, adjusting their plan daily, and evaluating their schedule regularly

b.　Locating a place to study that is suitable to their learning style and using this location on a consistent basis

c.　Locating tutoring services on campus, if needed

d. Studying an average of 2–4 hours daily and reviewing the syllabus and taking advantage of faculty office hours to get their questions answered about course content or assignments

Setting Career Goals

Setting career goals is an important component of transition planning because students with disabilities entering postsecondary education must be aware of the career-related programs and activities on campus to assist them in preparing for a profession. All too often, students have limited career development or meaningful work experiences to assist them in choosing a career (Briel & Getzel, 2005; Carter, Trainor, Cakiroghu, Swedeen, & Owens, 2010; Getzel & Briel, 2008b; Roessler, Hennessey, & Rumril, 2007). These students may be uncertain about their strengths and limitations and how these fit with different career choices (Briel & Getzel, 2005; Getzel, 2008; Getzel & Briel, 2008b). It is critical for students with disabilities to prepare for the global marketplace in light of recent estimates showing that 29% of youth with disabilities between the ages of 20 and 24 are employed compared with 61% of their counterparts without disabilities (U.S. Department of Labor, 2011).

There are several ways to begin exploring career goals. Keep in mind that approximately 80% of all college students change their majors at least once and 50% change more than once (Hughes, 2004). Currently, with the continuing increases in the cost of attending postsecondary education, students with disabilities need to gain exposure to the variety of career options available and the skills that are required. A beginning step to assist a student with a disability, who may be unable to articulate his or her general career interests, is taking an interest inventory or other career assessment instruments. Students with disabilities can begin to identify their career goals and what is needed to reach them by considering current and future school, employment, and living goals, as well as existing strengths and areas to work on; skills needed to reach those goals, including necessary coursework; and action required to make post–high school dreams a reality. (Greene & Kochhar-Bryant, 2003).

Promoting participation in volunteer work, extracurricular school activities, or jobs held while in high school are methods to discover and define potential interests. Family, friends, and education professionals can be very helpful in identifying further strengths. Discussing any experiences that may have influenced the student's interests is also very important. Together with the student, determine several career areas to research. Students need to find out what the academic requirements are for specific careers and what are the typical daily skills and proficiencies that would be expected for an employee (Getzel & Briel, 2008b). Encouraging students to gain access to career information online, use interactive software to communicate with individuals in a specific field, and talk with family and friends about their jobs, their likes, and their dislikes are just a few ways to gather information. These opportunities will assist students in better determining their postschool goals and what type of postsecondary educational setting can best meet their needs.

Students with disabilities have similar challenges as their nondisabled peers as they seek careers in professional fields; however, there are some unique differences in the career development needs of students with disabilities. These differences include (Briel & Wehman, 2005; Gerber & Price, 2003; Getzel & Briel, 2008b; Hennessey, Richard, Cook, Unger, & Rumril, 2006; Michaels & Barr, 2002)

a. Direct exposure to the variety of potential career opportunities

b. Knowledge of how one's disability can influence career choices and work performance

c. Awareness of their rights and responsibilities in the workplace

d. Understanding the potential risks and benefits of disclosing a disability to employers

e. Knowledge of which accommodations improve performance and how to request them from an employer

Programs exist on college campuses to assist all students in building career-related skills for employment. These programs may include job clubs, employment workshops, and work experience programs including internships, job shadow opportunities, and informational interviews, mentors, and career counseling (Getzel & Briel, 2008b). These experiences provide opportunities for students with disabilities to practice and obtain information not only on the skills needed for a career but also on the work-related qualities that are often referred to as "soft skills" (Gerber & Price, 2003; Getzel & Briel, 2008b; National Association of Counselors and Employers, 2004). For example, exhibiting effective communication, interpersonal, and teamwork skills and demonstrating motivation, initiative, and a strong work ethic are desirable qualities for employees in a majority of careers. When choosing a postsecondary setting, students should assess the degree to which career exploration and development activities are supported. Does the school or career center offer internship or work co-opportunities? What student organizations are available to develop teamwork and leadership skills? Are there service-learning courses available that connect students with agencies in the community where the content or skills learned in the course benefit people served by the agency? Hands-on work experiences not only confirm and define a career direction but also help students with disabilities to identify support needs and better prepare for the competitive job market upon graduation (Briel & Getzel, 2005; Getzel & Briel, 2008b).

Applying Strategies to Remain in College

Connecting with Supports and Services at College

Colleges and universities vary in the types of supports and services provided to students with disabilities. Typically, some of the most commonly requested supports by students include e-text or books on CD/DVD, notetakers in class, extended time on tests, distraction-free environments for test taking, use of calculators, and priority registration (Deschamps, 2004; Janiga & Costenbader, 2002; Kochhar-Bryant et al., 2009; Getzel & Wehman, 2005; Shaw et al., 2010; Thomas, 2000). Students also need to explore services that are available on campus for all students (e.g., counseling services, writing or math labs, study skills or time management classes offered either through a counseling center or other entities on campus). There is a full range of services on campus to assist all students to successfully meet their academic coursework, and students with disabilities should take advantage of these services along with any specialized services they are receiving.

One of the biggest differences between high school and college concerns the receipt of services for students with disabilities. Most college campuses have a specific office or a designated individual to handle the request for accommodations or specialized supports for students with disabilities. Students must be prepared to make disclosure decisions. Disclosing a disability is optional in both the postsecondary setting and the employment arena. Often, students entering college are not fully prepared to disclose their disability or lack understanding of the services available on campus and how to access them (Getzel, 2005, 2008; Kochhar-Bryant et al., 2009; Shaw et al., 2010). Unlike their experience in secondary education, students in postsecondary education must self-identify to request accommodations and supports from the college; yet, nationally, more than half (55%) of students identified as having a disability in high school do not consider themselves as having a disability when entering postsecondary programs (Newman, Wagner, Cameto, & Knokey, 2009). Another 8% of youth know they have a disability but decide not to disclose (Newman et al., 2009). Nearly two thirds of college students with disabilities begin their experience without disclosing their disabilities and face the challenges of managing course work without accommodations.

Disclosing a disability at the college level to receive accommodations can be very confusing to young adults because of the significant differences between secondary and postsecondary education services and supports. One of the major differences between secondary and postsecondary education is the differences in the laws that pertain to receiving services and supports. What this means is that, if a student needs special education, the student is entitled to these services through federal regulations under the Individuals with Disabilities Education Improvement Act (IDEA; 2004; PL 105-17). In college, young adults are responsible for providing documentation of their disabilities to determine if they are eligible for accommodations provided by the university or college. If a student is eligible for accommodations in college, the accommodations are based on ensuring access to materials, information, and programs on campus (Eckes & Ochoa, 2005). The Americans with Disabilities Act Amendments Act (2008; PL 110-325) and Section 504 of the Rehabilitation Act (1973; PL 93-112) are the laws that cover higher education institutions. These laws have provisions to ensure that institutions a) cannot discriminate, and b) provide access to education (Eckes & Ochoa, 2005; Shaw et al., 2010). Because the IEP is no longer a legal document in college, students are fully responsible for self-disclosing disabilities and providing documentation on the impact of their disabilities. Unfortunately, many families and students are unaware of these changes until after the student enrolls in a college program (Getzel, 2005, 2008; Kochhar-Bryant et al., 2009).

Another document that is provided by secondary education is the Summary of Performance (SOP), which is provided to students with disabilities upon their exit from school. The SOP is an IDEA 2004 requirement that local education agencies must provide to students with disabilities as they transition from high school into the community. The summary must address three areas—academic achievement, functional performance, and recommendations on how to assist students in reaching postsecondary goals (Getzel, Deschamps, & Thoma, 2010). It is important that the SOP is developed in user-friendly language because the intent of the information is for it to be used by students with disabilities as they transition to the workplace, postsecondary education or training, and the community (Martin, Van Dycke, D'Ottavio, & Nickerson, 2007). It should be emphasized that not all colleges and universities accept the SOP as documentation of a disability for purposes of receiving accommodations. Like the IEP, the SOP can be used by postsecondary programs to provide insight on the strengths and accommodations needs of students. It will be necessary to discuss the use of the information contained in the IEP or SOP with the office on campus that provides accommodations. This discussion should take place before students with disabilities enter the college campus. It is critical that students with disabilities and their families understand the differences between college and secondary education and how to access accommodations in college. This information is essential and needs to begin early in the planning process.

Colleges and universities have documentation policies or procedures in place to determine eligibility, and it is important for students to inquire about the documentation process on each college campus they are exploring. Table 15.1 provides a series of

Table 15.1.   Questions to ask concerning services and supports

What specific documentation does your campus require to be eligible for services?

What types of support services are typically provided to students (e.g., learning disability, attention-deficit/ hyperactivity disorder, low vision)?

Is new documentation required every year to remain eligible for services?

What is the process for gaining access to these support services?

How are faculty notified of a student's academic accommodations?

From Deschamps, A. (2004). Traveling the road from high school to college: Tips for the journey. *Transition Times, 9*(1), 1–2; adapted by permission.

questions (Deschamps, 2004) that can be used by students with disabilities and families as they explore colleges and universities. Knowing about the services and supports before applying for college can assist students to gain access to what is needed before academic problems occur.

Shannon   Shannon is a 22-year-old freshman enrolled in an urban university. She recently acquired a mild traumatic brain injury and has little understanding of how her injury affects her life. Shannon elected to live on campus in the dormitory. She is not certain about her career goal, but thought she wanted to become a journalist and planned to major in English.

During Shannon's first semester, she discovered difficulties writing notes in class and finishing her tests in the time allotted. It was also a challenge for her to remember the information presented in lectures and to write college-level papers. Her time-management skills were inconsistent. After completing her first semester, Shannon was placed on academic probation.

These were not problems Shannon encountered while in high school so she was not sure why she was not doing well. Shannon scheduled an appointment with her advisor who told her about the Services for Students with Disabilities (SSD) office on campus. She was hesitant to go to this office but decided to find out how they could help. After reviewing her documentation, the SSD office determined that Shannon was eligible for accommodations such as a notetaker, extended time on tests, testing in a limited distraction room, and priority registration. The SSD office gave Shannon her letters of accommodation to give to each of her professors. In addition, they suggested technology that could help her such as a smart pen that captures audio and links it to the written notes, which made reviewing and remembering her notes much easier.

The SSD Office also connected Shannon to several campus and community services. She learned about the university writing center and about regularly scheduled miniworkshops on topics such as test-taking strategies and time management skills. She also was informed about the university career center and decided to complete some interest assessment instruments and see what volunteer opportunities were available on campus. Finally, Shannon was given information about the vocational rehabilitation office to help her with choosing a career that would maximize her strengths.

Building a Network of Supports

College students with disabilities were asked to identify the self-determination skills that were essential for high school students to possess to be successful in college (Finn, Getzel, & McManus, 2008; Getzel & Thoma, 2006). Students felt that forming ongoing relationships with college personnel and classmates was very important. It was recommended that students establish positive associations with their instructors (e.g., greeting instructor by name, participating in class, engaging in occasional short conversations after class). Also, getting to know staff members in the office that provides services and supports for students with disabilities was suggested. By establishing rapport with at least one student in each class, students can assist each other to understand the course content, confirm due dates for assignments, or review for a test. In addition, being aware and willing to use campus support services such as the writing lab, supplemental instruction sessions, and peer tutoring was considered a great advantage.

It is also important for students to develop a network of supports in postsecondary environments because of the changing role that family members will play in their lives. Entering college, perhaps one that is away from home, is a major change and adjustment for all families. This is especially true for families of students with disabilities who have served as their children's advocates throughout their educational experience. There are many legal differences in what information can be shared with families and the delivery of services and supports between postsecondary education and secondary education. It is important that students with disabilities and their families work together to better understand these differences and to begin working on shifting the responsibility of managing one's education more to the student before exiting secondary education.

Enrolling in a postsecondary program involves a series of decisions that include identifying academic programs that can meet the personal, educational, and career goals of students with disabilities (Briel & Getzel, 2009; Getzel, 2005, 2008; Kochhar-Bryant et al., 2009; Shaw et al., 2010). Once students have made their decision and have started their advanced degree program, they must be prepared to face new challenges as they adjust to a different environment and educational process. College students with disabilities are in an environment in which classes meet less frequently, the services and supports they need are their responsibility to obtain, and there is typically less student–instructor contact (Getzel, 2005; Kochhar-Bryant et al., 2009; Shaw et al., 2010). Although much adjustment depends on a number of factors that are difficult to plan for, students with disabilities can increase their chances of successfully adjusting to college life if they are adequately prepared for this transition.

Conclusion

For individuals with disabilities, an advanced degree from a university, community college, or technical school can significantly increase their vocational options and financial success. Individuals need to make a series of decisions about which program best meets their academic and personal needs based on information gathered from a number of resources. Students with disabilities who are able to successfully enter and complete postsecondary education will have an increased chance of fulfilling their long-term employment potential in careers of their choice.

Study Questions

1. Describe ways to help young people with disabilities prepare to enter college and supports that can be helpful for them to be successful once they enter college.

2. Meet with a guidance counselor to discuss some of the areas to consider when students with disabilities are in the process of selecting a postsecondary institution to attend.

3. Identify essential skills that are necessary for a successful transition to college.

4. What changes in postsecondary education have occurred enabling students with intellectual disabilities to access these programs?

5. Meet with a disability services office representative to discuss strategies that assist students with disabilities to remain in college.

Online Resources

Going to College—A Resource for Teens with Disabilities: http://www.going-to-college.org

Virginia College Quest—A Guide to College Success for Students with Disabilities: http://www.vacollegequest.org

I'm Determined—The Virginia Department of Education Self-Determination Project: http://www.imdetermined.org

Heath Resource Center at the National Youth Transitions Center—An Online Clearinghouse on Postsecondary Education for Individuals with Disabilities: http://www.heath.gwu.edu

Think College!—College Options for People with Intellectual Disabilities: http://www.thinkcollege.net

Dare to Dream for Adults (worksheet on exploring colleges on pp. 76–79): http://www.fldoe.org/ese/pdf/dream_adults.pdf

V

Designing and Implementing Plans for Transition

Applications for Youth with Intellectual Disabilities

16

PAUL WEHMAN AND LaRON SCOTT

After completing this chapter, the reader will be able to

- Describe how youth with intellectual disabilities learn transition skills
- Describe the obstacles that parents, students, and schools face when trying to provide education for youth with intellectual disabilities
- Identify the main aspects of the definition of intellectual disabilities
- Describe how universal design for learning has an impact on learning strategies
- Discuss the benefits of using community-based instruction
- Discuss the relevance of minority overrepresentation in the schools
- Discuss the best ways the education team can plan for transition
- Understand the emerging research on literacy for youth with intellectual disabilities
- Understand how employment can positively affect outcomes for transition-age youth with intellectual disabilities

Jamie   Jamie is a 20-year-old who recently graduate from high school after spending 1 additional year working toward a modified diploma, with which he was unsuccessful. Despite not accomplishing the goal of a modified diploma, Jamie found some academic success in his last year of high school. He spent more time practicing and building his math calculation skills and improving his work readiness skills. Jamie is described as a brave and charismatic adult with a mild intellectual disability. Despite some minor discipline issues in school, he was popular with both his peers and school staff.

He and his father live together and both aspire for Jamie to one day live and work independently. Jamie has previous work experience at the local K-Mart, but after overdrawing his cash register, he was let go. Despite having a year of employment in an environment that he enjoyed, the experience of being let go left Jamie feeling defeated, and now, 6 months later, he is unemployed and searching for work. He has been working closely with his job coach through the Department of Rehabilitative Services (DRS) and community case manager through the local community services board to find both employment and living arrangements. However, both Jamie and his job coach admit that the recent downfall in the economy adds another challenge to obtaining employment.

Jamie had one interview since starting his job search, but he was not hired. He is left wondering about his future and whether he can accomplish many of his dreams and goals. He wonders about his math skills and whether they have improved enough to where an employer would hire him and accept his abilities. He also wonders if he should enroll in a community college and whether his Special Diploma is sufficient for enrollment in a community college. Should he abandon his goal of working in retail and business? These are questions that Jamie and many individuals with intellectual disabilities consider when dreams appear to be not in sight.

Jamie's DRS counselor proposes that he enroll in a specialty center for employment, like the Woodrow Wilson Rehabilitation Center, that will help provide career development services, but Jamie wavers about his life and what is the direction that will provide him with the life he seeks. Outwardly, he believes that he is ready for a career, but internally, he has to decide whether he should go with what his DRS counselor suggests, or his father's recommendations to find work so he can live on his own, or whether he believes enough in his abilities to rebound from his challenges and follow his own path.

Michelle   Michelle is a 19-year-old graduate with a mild intellectual disability. She has a very strong desire to find full-time work in the child care field. Her passion of working with children landed her a part-time job (10 hours per week) through her church on-site child care program. She is hoping that this part-time work at her church will help to boost her résumé in hopes of finding full-time work at a child care center.

Over the past 6 months since graduating from high school, Michelle has remained positive on her course to find full-time employment. She had one interview at a neighborhood child care center, but later learned that there were more than 20 applicants for the position. In spite of not finding full-time employment yet, she remains encouraged. She is even thinking about enrolling in the local community college program that has specialized programs to assist individuals with disabilities to advance their careers. Her plan is to enroll in 1 year if she is not successful with finding full-time work.

Michelle has several questions regarding her future. She wonders if she has enough experience and training to find full-time employment. If she enrolls in school, how will this impact her schedule for the next 2–3 years? If she enrolls in school, will this guarantee her the future she desires? Are her academic skills strong enough to overcome the challenges she will face in the work and community college environments?

Michelle keeps in contact with both her teacher/case manager from high school and her rehabilitation counselor. They both have encouraged Michelle and her mother to have Michelle enter the community college training program. The resources as the community college will provide Michelle with formal academics and experience that will assist her with finding full-time employment. Michelle admits that her math and reading levels are low, but she has learned to express what working accommodations she needs to complete certain tasks. Although she is often apprehensive when she has to read to the children or help them with purchases at the church, she knows that working with children is what she wants to do with her life and the right job for her is out there waiting for her to find it.

Despite their challenges, both Jamie and Michelle and other youth with intellectual disabilities demonstrate the potential to become contributing members of society (President's
Committee on Intellectual Disabilities, 2010). Positive outcomes for individuals with intellectual disabilities have not easily occurred in the 21st century. Many people can make
the case that the challenges that individuals with intellectual disabilities face have simply
transformed into new challenges when one considers how much research has been conducted. Many people with intellectual disabilities were seen as incompetent and unable
to make civilized contributions to society. The history of mistreatment and institutionali-
zation of people with intellectual disabilities is deeply rooted. However, since that time,
this population has made steps forward nationally in all facets of life as society embraces
the idea that people with intellectual disabilities can make positive contributions to their
communities, to the economy, and to their families and that they exhibit self-worth. The
support that they receive from a key circle of people in their lives is an important factor
and influence in making these adjustments.

Individuals with intellectual disabilities may not learn as quickly as the average
student, but, with well-placed help and support, many limitations in vocational performance, residential living, and social adjustment can be successfully overcome. With this
assistance, many people with intellectual disabilities are becoming competitively employed and living independently.

This chapter describes ways to help people with intellectual disabilities manage the
challenges inherent in any community and make a successful transition from school to the
world of adulthood.

Who Are Individuals with Intellectual Disabilities?

In 2007, the American Association on Intellectual and Developmental Disabilities (AAIDD),
formerly the American Association on Mental Retardation, ushered in a new, more socially acceptable name for its organization. The significance of this change is reflective of
the progress people with intellectual disabilities are making and the pitch in terminology
also signals a new standard for characterizing and addressing this population. In addition to the terminology, the definition of *intellectual disability* (previously *mental retardation*)
has been discussed considerably and has progressed to incorporate the concepts of supports and how they are provided to individuals with intellectual disabilities (Shogren &
Turnbull, 2010). Table 16.1 shows the historical definitions of mental retardation through
AAIDD.

Shalock, Luckasson, and Shogren (2007) explained that, though the definition of intellectual disability has remained the same and may remain the same for the foreseeable
future, the definition does not stand alone; the following five assumptions are considered
essential when applying the definition (Luckasson, Borthwick-Duffy, Buntinx, Coulter,
Craig, Reeve, et al., 2002, p. 1):

1. The present functional limitations of the individual must be considered in the context of community environments that are typical of the individual's age peers and
   culture.

2. Valid assessments must consider the cultural and linguistic diversity of the individual, including any differences in communication, sensory, motor, and behavioral
   factors.

3. Within an individual, there are both limitations and strengths that may often coexist.

4. A vital reason for describing the individual's limitations is to develop a profile of
   supports that are needed.

5. With appropriate supports over a sustained period, the life functioning of a person
   with intellectual disability will generally improve.

Table 16.1. Historical definitions of *mental retardation*

Year	Author	Definition
1959	Herber	Mental retardation refers to subaverage general intellectual functioning, which originates during the developmental period and is associated with impairment in one or more of the following: 1) maturation, 2) learning, 3) social adjustment. (p. 3)
1961	Herber	Mental retardation refers to subaverage general intellectual functioning, which originates during the development period and is associated with impairment in adaptive behavior. (p. 3)
1973	Grossman	Mental retardation refers to significantly subaverage general intellectual functioning existing concurrently with deficits in adaptive behavior, and manifested during the developmental period. (p. 1)
1983	Grossman	Same as 1973 (p. 1)
1992	Luckasson et al.	Mental retardation refers to substantial limitations in present functioning. It is characterized by significantly subaverage intellectual functioning, existing concurrently with related limitations in two or more of the following applicable adaptive skill areas: communication, self-care, home living, social skills, community use, self-direction, health and safety, functional academics, leisure, and work. Mental retardation manifests before age 18. (p. 1)
2002	Luckasson et al.	Mental retardation is a disability characterized by significant limitations both in intellectual functioning and in adaptive behavior as expressed in conceptual, social, and practical adaptive skills. This disability originates before age 18. (p. 1)
2011	Luckasson et al.	Same as 2002

From Schalock, R.L., Luckasson, R.A. & Shogren, K.A. (2007). The renaming of mental retardation: Understanding the change to the term intellectual disability. *Intellectual and Developmental Disabilities, 45*(2), 123. (Intellectual and developmental disabilities: publication of the American Association on Intellectual and Developmental Disabilities by American Association on Mental Retardation; American Association on Intellectual and Developmental Disabilities Copyright 2007 Reproduced with permission of AMERICAN ASSOCIATION ON INTELLECTUAL DEVELOPMENTAL DISABILITIES in format Textbook and Other book via Copyright Clearance Center.).

The five assumptions are a critical part of the definition of intellectual disability because they both clarify and explain the origin and application of the definition. These assumptions also provide a basis for diagnosis and entitlement to services.

Supports are a key aspect of helping people with disabilities achieve their goals and succeed (e.g., Polloway, 2004), and they are a guiding principle of this book. Supports also are a significant way that people with intellectual disabilities are defined (Thompson et al., 2009). This most recent definition gets further away from the traditional medical model, which focused on what is wrong with a person, and moves closer toward an individualized, strengths-based model. Philosophies espoused in recent years reflect that the success of people with intellectual disabilities is directly based on the availability and quality of supports in their homes, communities, and workplaces (e.g., Wallace & Rogan, 2007; Grigal & Hart, 2010a); it is a serious departure from the way services have been traditionally provided and provides a new vista of hope.

Employment and School Participation for Youth with Intellectual Disabilities

The varying levels of supports for people with disabilities may be as simple as government policies such as the Americans with Disabilities Act (ADA) of 1990 (PL 101-336), which prohibits job discrimination, or much more sophisticated supports that provide technological accommodations for specific workplace or school needs. The U.S. Equal Employment Opportunity Commission (EEOC) enforces the mandates stipulated through ADA and provides an important support for people with intellectual disabilities to enter the workplace using different accommodations (McMahon, Edwards, Rumrill, & Hursh, 2005; McMahon, West, Shaw, Waid-Ebbs, & Belongia, 2005; Unger, Campbell, & McMahon, 2005).

The EEOC provides an important framework to avoid unlawful termination and discrimination of individuals with disabilities. Recent charges by the EEOC demonstrate their efforts to enforce job discrimination against individuals with disabilities. For example, the EEOC recently charged a Texas-based company after reports that, for more than 20 years, they severely abused and discriminated against workers with intellectual disabilities. According to the lawsuit, the workers' legal rights were being denied and they were unknowingly exploited because of their intellectual disabilities, which made them vulnerable. More specifically, the workers were allegedly subjected to verbal abuse, being called "retarded," "dumb ass," and "stupid" by employees of the company; the owner denied the workers lawful wages, physically harassed them, restricted their freedom of movement, and failed to provide clean living conditions and medical care (EEOC, 2011). EEOC Chair Jacqueline Berrien believes that this case was a reminder of the job of EEOC in enforcing the rights of individuals with disabilities and the legal polices of ADA.

School Involvement

The federal mandate of the Individuals with Disabilities Education Act (IDEA) 2004 requiring that children with disabilities be educated with their typical peers to the maximum extent appropriate has implications in the modern shift toward a federally mandated and socially acceptable practice of serving students with disabilities in general education environments. The IDEA legislation has contributed to the more-inclusive movement of educational institutions as states and school districts search out a process for meeting this requirement. Before federal mandates for providing a higher quality of service to students with disabilities, individuals with intellectual disabilities were almost exclusively serviced in restrictive classroom environments, and, quite often, the characteristics of these students were similar in gender, race, culture, socioeconomic status, behavior, and academic achievement. Litigation that challenges the disproportionate placement of students belonging to cultural minority populations in special education (Wehman, 2005) and school officials' recognition of the overrepresentation of minorities diagnosed and placed in more restrictive environments have also contributed to more students in regular education environments.

Although there has been increased awareness and caution with the identification and placement of students with intellectual disabilities, the fact remains that African American students continue to be disproportionately diagnosed and serviced in special education (Skiba, Ploni-Staudinger, Gallini, Simmons, & Feggins-Azziz, 2006). According to Parrish (2002), African American students are the most overrepresented group placed in special education in almost every state in the country, and they are disproportionately overrepresented in each state in the category for intellectual disability. The overrepresentation is despite African American students representing only 15% of the K–12 public school population; they account for more than 20% of the students who are enrolled in special education and are between 2.5 and 3 times more likely to be diagnosed with an intellectual disability (Vallas, 2009). The overrepresentation of African American students with intellectual disabilities both diagnosed and who are serviced in more restrictive classroom environments does not come without significant consequences. Most important is that services do not meet the needs of each student, which can have a devastating impact on a student's future.

There is no question that the inappropriate identification and overrepresentation of African American students in special education and any inappropriate practices to have these students identified and placed in restrictive environments must come to an end (Green, McIntosh, Cook-Morales, & Robinson-Zañartu, 2005). The system policies and legislation must continue to improve and protect students from being wrongfully diagnosed because of their race, culture, or other demographic status. In 1954, the *Brown v. Board of Education* decision ensured equity in public schools. Almost 60 years after this promising decision to ensure equity in public schools, African American students continue to experience inequality through the disproportionate placement in special education that also has implications on African American students having higher dropout rates and lower academic achievement (U.S. Department of Education, 2007b). It is critical that effective reform and litigation continue to both challenge and encourage appropriate interventions to meet the needs of African American students.

Challenges of Working with Youth with Intellectual Disabilities

There are numerous obstacles and challenges to community integration and employment for youth with intellectual disabilities. Not surprising, these issues are often identical to the interests and desires that youth without disabilities ponder. Thoughts of employment, living arrangements, academic challenges, and social and community concerns often dominate as youth-based issues. However, youth with intellectual disabilities also face a range of challenges that they will need to overcome that youth without disabilities may not have to face. Because each of these circumstances is very different, it is important that each person is looked at individually. For example, it is impossible to predict or create universal plans for employment or academic desires and interests because they differ from person to person.

One of the main objectives of the individualized education program (IEP) and transition-planning process is to consider the unique needs and to plan education, employment, and living services for individuals with disabilities (see Chapter 2). The process of meeting individual needs becomes far less effective when generic plans are created based solely on a disability label or when the same goals and plans are designed for groups of students based on their disability. This generic IEP planning practice can be common in some school districts. However, for effective planning, each student must be considered for his or her unique circumstance. In addition, it is important that plans are designed not by one individual but by the student, parents, and professionals who know and have the best interest of the student in mind should be included in the planning and design during the process. The support of this team can help foresee and minimize challenges for the student.

The team may have differences in the academic and transition plan needed to meet the needs of the student. Academically, concerns regarding the curriculum may be discussed based on the scholastic needs, functional skill needs, and even diploma track that the student is on. The passage of No Child Left Behind (NCLB; 2001; PL 107-110), which introduced a higher standard for education requirements for all students, saw a shift with more rigorous curriculum, striking a balance between the academic and transition/functional training, which may require more careful conversation and decision by the team. There have been many suitable frameworks for curriculum attempting to meet the needs of individual transition/functional needs of students under IDEA while continuing to meet the academic standards under NCLB. Thoma, Bartholomew, and Scott (2009) proposed a new strategy to help educational planners meet the goal of linking transition and functional goals with academic standards through the implementation of what they call Universal design for transition (UDT; Table 16.2).

There is little doubt that students with intellectual disabilities require specialized services and consideration with transition-based planning. Although IDEA lists specific requirements for transition planning and services, such as postsecondary education services, vocational education, and independent living, it is often left to the school and team to consider the students' needs and how the academic and special services will be determined.

Table 16.2.   Universal Design for Transition characteristics

Multiple life domains	• Focus is on the transition to a complete, integrated plan for life rather than on multiple, divided life segments.
	• Includes a focus on the typical transition/life domains of employment, community living, postsecondary education, transportation, recreation and leisure, and community integration, but supports are examined for the range of applicability—for example, instruction in writing for employment (creating a résumé and cover letter), writing for the transition to postsecondary education (writing a college admissions essay, writing for an advanced placement class), writing for community living (writing a letter of complaint to a landlord), and/or writing for recreation/leisure (writing in a journal).
Multiple means of assessments	• Focus on collecting an array of information about the student that provides holistic data upon which decisions are made.
	• Assessments include a range of methods and are chosen based on the students' needs and the disparity between student long-range goals and the current information on student strengths/needs and abilities. For example, for a student who is interested in becoming a nurse, assessment should focus on understanding a wide range of skills (aptitude, computer skills, ability to work with others, interest in and awareness of this career). Information should also be gathered in multiple ways (computers, informal and formal, authentic work tasks, on-site employment assessments).
Individual self-determination	• Student is the focus of the process, with his or her preferences and interests serving as the basis for the transition services. Student is the causal agent.
	• Students do not need to do it all themselves, but self-determination needs to be a focus for the entire transition-planning team, ensuring that the student chooses needed supports that achieve his or her long-range adult life goals. Using a person-centered planning method is one way to engage students and plan with them, not for them.
Multiple means of representation	• Transition planning and services are developed so that they include materials, services, and instruction that involve a range of methods.
	• Methods employ a variety of instructional strategies, including the use of authentic learning objectives (i.e., tasks that adults perform in their lives and on the job). For example, rather than have students complete a paper-and-pencil text to demonstrate their understanding of geometry, they could build a walkway by designing its size and shape, determining the amount of materials necessary, and completing the project.
Multiple means of engagement	• Transition planning and services are developed to ensure that there are multiple ways that students can be involved in the process.
	• Instructional design provides opportunities for individuals to be engaged in many different ways to meet multiple objectives. For instance, by involving students in developing a movie, they can demonstrate their knowledge of academic content (in the details of the story line) as well as functional skills such as communication, working with others, and using technology.
Multiple means of expression	• Transition planning and services are developed to ensure that students can communicate their preferences and interests and demonstrate progress in multiple ways.
	• Assessment of student progress can occur in multiple ways, ensuring that students with disabilities are able to demonstrate what they know. These options, when incorporated into transition planning and services, support individual self-determination. For example, students should have the opportunity to express their knowledge and interests in multiple ways, including the use of technology, group work, class and individualized education program, participation, paper-and-pencil work, and authentic task completion.
Multiple resources/perspectives	• Transition planning and services are developed collaboratively, pooling resources (financial, human, and/or material), using natural supports and/or generic community services as well as disability-specific ones.
	• Transition planning and services reflect the range of supports available to individuals with and without disabilities and the best of collaborative planning where stakeholders work together to break down barriers and silos to provide appropriate supports. Employers, peers, community agency representatives, family members, teachers, and guidance counselors are all examples of people who can be included in the transition process and can offer different perspectives in a collaborative process.

From Thoma, C.A. Bartholomew, C.C. & Scott L.A. (2009). *Universal design for learning: A roadmap for planning and instruction.* Baltimore: Paul H. Brookes Publishing; reprinted by permission.

Employment continues to be a major concern for students with disabilities after they have graduated from high school. According to Newman, Wagner, Cameto, and Knokey (2009), only 30% of youth with intellectual disabilities were employed after graduating from high school. Many of the challenges they face in finding and maintaining employment can be addressed with a coordinated schedule of transition services that are mandated as part of IDEA. Effective transition planning and services may offer opportunities for community-based vocational instruction before the student graduates from high school, allowing the student both short- and long-term, paid and unpaid, work experiences that should conclude in employment before the student graduates (Kim & Dymond, 2010). It is critical that the team implement a balanced academic and vocational program for students so that students are given every opportunity to be successful.

Restructuring Schools

For longer than 2 decades, an increased emphasis on improving the academic outcomes of all students has shaped school reform efforts. High-stakes testing has been an overwhelming factor in assessing student outcomes, and how students with intellectual disabilities participate in these assessments has been a source of controversy (Katsiyannis, Zhang, Ryan, & Jones, 2007). Under NCLB, states are required to establish performance standards in the core subjects and develop or adopt tests that will assess student performance to demonstrate 100% proficiency with adequate yearly progress (AYP) by 2013–2014. Schools are held accountable for the performance of individuals with disabilities in meeting their AYP standards, whereas the consequences it has on students with intellectual disabilities who need intense vocational, community integration, and functional skill support is still of concern for schools and other stakeholders (Katsiyannis et al., 2007).

Choice and Empowerment

By now, most individuals are aware of the link between self-determination and the increased quality it can have on the life of people with intellectual disabilities (Lachapelle et al, 2005). More emphasis is now being placed on practices for educating students with intellectual disabilities on learning and implementing strategies that will help them become more self-determined individuals. Emphasis on student-directed learning strategies, such as the student-directed IEP approach, has been documented as an effective way to involve students not only in leading their IEP meetings but also to have a strong voice in employment, independent living, and education decisions. For students with intellectual disabilities, taking a leadership role in their IEPs is critical to empowering them to become self-determined individuals who have control over their own lives.

The most important thing to remember while working with students with intellectual disabilities is that they can and should make their wants and desires known (Grigal & Hart, 2010). The student-directed IEP process encourages student leadership, participation, and development of the IEP and can be utilized to work with youth with intellectual disabilities to promote transition planning and self-determination skills (Hawbecker, 2007; Thoma & Wehman, 2010.

Agran and Hughes (2008) reviewed the importance of self-determination and its link to strategies such as the student-directed IEP and explained that the IEP meeting itself provided a natural and practical experience for students to apply self-determination skills. This type of experience and empowerment for students with intellectual disabilities offers an opportunity to transfer power and control over their values, decisions, choices, and directions of human services from external entities (e.g., government agencies, service providers, social forces) to the consumers of services (i.e., the individuals with disabilities themselves).

Full Participation

The extent to which students with intellectual disabilities are included in regular education classrooms will have a strong bearing on their chance to practice and live as self-determined individuals. Although full inclusion of students with intellectual disabilities has been slow (Smith, 2007), research indicates how important an opportunity it is for individuals with intellectual disabilities to be educated alongside students without disabilities (Idol, 2006; Smith, 2007; Baer, Daviso, Flexer, Queen, & Meindl, 2011). Smith's (2007) analysis of the progress of including students with intellectual disabilities in the regular education classroom environment showed that, nationally, 11% of students with intellectual disabilities were receiving education in the regular education classroom for more than 79% of the time according to data from 2002–2003 school years. This is an increase from previous reporting but an indication that more in terms of policy and practice has to be done to focus on including students with intellectual disabilities in the regular classroom.

Assessment of Youth with Intellectual Disabilities

Youth with intellectual disabilities are often evaluated on their general intelligence and adaptive behavior or functional skills (Siegel & Allinder, 2005). The assessment will often help to determine the placement and programming for students with intellectual disabilities. These assessments will also be used in program development for the students' IEP decisions in conjunction with achievement tests that measure the students' academic skills. Additional standardized norm-referenced and nonformal tests are administered for the evaluation of vocational and transition evaluation of students (see Chapters 8 and 10).

Vocational and transition assessments are major contributors for life during and beyond the classroom in transition domains including employment, community living, and functional and postsecondary achievement of students with intellectual disabilities. These assessments can help identify specific strengths, weaknesses, and training needs and programs that are suitable for students during school and with postschool goals. In addition, these assessments are increasingly helping teachers develop and design academic instruction that will have functional meaning for students with intellectual disabilities.

Curriculum Strategies for Youth with Intellectual Disabilities

Many students with intellectual disabilities will have some difficulties with the curriculum requirements in the core content subjects (Browder, Spooner, Ahlgrim-Delzell, Harris, & Wakeman, 2008). The challenges students with intellectual disabilities face with the curriculum go beyond the classroom as it has implications in employment, independent living, and their ability to access the community. Therefore, research on instructional strategies and interventions are often targeted at methods for teaching reading, math, and other curriculum categories that address learning difficulties for individuals with intellectual disabilities that have an impact on their academic and broader life needs (Bucholz & Brady, 2008).

Research into teaching literacy to students with intellectual disabilities has exploded since the early 2000s in part because of NCLB legislation emphasis on all students showing progress in reading, beginning as early as the third grade. Before NCLB, for a student with intellectual disabilities, literacy instruction was minimal, and, when taught, the focus was often on sight words that were required for daily living requirements. Browder and her associates (2009) noted three possible reasons why reading instruction has historically been disregarded for students with intellectual disabilities. One reason they noted prefaced the historical belief that individuals with intellectual disabilities were incompetent and simply could not learn to read. A second reason they gave as to why reading instruction has been disregarded is again based on the supposition that this population can only learn some functional sight words needed for daily activities versus learning how to decode. The third explanation is regarding the issues with language and communication that have major implications on their ability to receive effective reading instruction. Browder and associates provide excellent counterarguments to each of the three possible reasons to why reading instruction has been disregarded, noting the recent requirement of legislation that holds states accountable to teach reading skills, advances in assistive technology and resources that create alternative ways for the population to participate in literacy instruction, and advances and emphasis on early literacy skills that offer early literacy opportunities. Browder's work lends credence to college participation for youth with intellectual disabilities evidenced by Grigal and Hart (2010).

The efforts made in teaching diverse curriculum, including literacy skills, are showcased through brilliant research and resources that propose new interventions, frameworks, and strategies for overcoming the reading challenges for youth with intellectual disabilities. Bucholz and Brady (2008) and Browder et al. (2009) present great interventions and strategies to teach literacy to students and provide a foundation, model, and procedures for establishing literacy interventions for this population. Browder et al. (2009)'s model of literacy for students with severe disabilities provides one of many excellent examples of the types of literacy models proposed that show how students with significant disabilities can access literature through a planned sequence and program. The literacy models are a representation of literacy instruction that advances the optimism to teach meaningful reading to students with disabilities that will increase their independence and promote a better quality of life in all areas.

The National Center on Secondary Education and Transition (NCSET) and the National Secondary Transition Technical Center (NSTTC) provide excellent strategies, resources, and related research to help with transition planning and with approaches to address curriculum strategies for youth with disabilities. The topic of Universal design for learning (UDL) is an example of an excellent curriculum concept discussed by the organizations to support students with disabilities' access to the general curriculum and as a support in achieving required academic standards. Wehmeyer (2006b) has conducted research regarding youth with intellectual disabilities' access to the general curriculum and notes UDL as a way for this population to make progress with the general curriculum. Furthermore, he conceptualized a model to help IEP team members consider access to the general curriculum for students with intellectual disabilities in his research. Figure 16.1 shows how the IEP team decision-making process can encourage access to the general curriculum for youth with intellectual disabilities.

Table 16.3 lists curriculum recommendations for youth with disabilities. Most curriculum guides present activities in general terms, but good teachers can design creative ways to involve members of the community in the learning process, especially for instruction in vocational, community, and recreational domains. Table 16.4 contains examples of questions one might ask to generate a student profile that could help in setting transition goals.

Self-Determination

Self-determination has also received significant attention since the early 1980s and is recognized as a recommended practice in special education and transition services (Cobb,

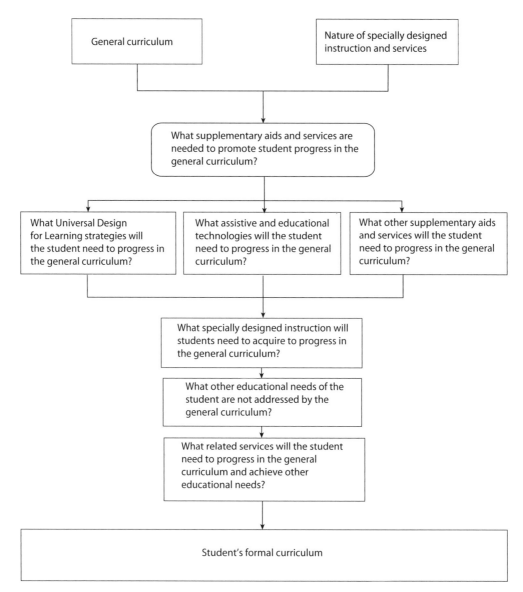

Figure 16.1. Individualized education program team decision-making process to promote student progress in the general education curriculum. (From Wehmeyer, M. [2006]. Universal design for learning, access to the general education curriculum and students with mild mental retardation. *Exceptionality, 14*(4), 225–235; reprinted by permission of the publisher [Taylor & Francis Ltd; http://www.tandf.co.uk/journals].)

Lehmann, Newman-Gonchar, & Alwell, 2009; Eisenman, 2007; Fowler, Konrad, Walker, Test, & Wood, 2007; Wehmeyer et al., 2007) as well as in design and delivery of adult supports and services (Wehman, 2011a). Most of the research in this area focuses on identifying recommended practices to promote self-determination in educational settings (Cobb et al., 2009; Fowler et al., 2007), identifying environmental characteristics that impact the expression of self-determination by youth and adults with disabilities (Van Gelder, Sitlington, & Pugh, 2008), and perceptions of self-determination held by special educators, family, and support staff (Carter, Lane, Pierson, & Stang, 2008; Zhang, 2005).

Until a recent study by Shogren and Broussard (2011), within the perception-related research, most has focused on experiences of youth with learning disabilities and the role of self-determination in transitioning from school to adult life (Trainor, 2005) and college success (Anctil, Ishikawa, & Scott, 2008; Getzel & Thoma, 2008).

Table 16.3.   Curriculum recommendations for children with disabilities

Dos

1. Ask each student the types of activities and skills that he or she would like to work to develop during part of every day.
2. Actively involve students in career education and job-seeking activities.
3. Invite outside speakers from different careers to come into the classroom and share information about their jobs. Encourage students to visit different jobs to gain an understanding of what is involved in holding a job.
4. Teach students how to complete job applications.
5. Teach skilled students how to develop résumés.
6. Make sure every student has a Social Security card.
7. Teach students how to look for jobs in the classified advertisements.
8. Teach students how to find different recreational activities and events in the newspaper. Take them to some of these activities and events and teach them to involve themselves in community activities.
9. Teach students how to get around town by using public transportation or learning how to identify a network of people who will give car rides.

Don'ts

1. Rely heavily on workbooks, which are essentially simulations of what the real work activity is.
2. Rely on large volumes of ditto sheets and desk work.
3. Try to simulate regular education academic-based curricula.
4. Spend extensive time doing blackboard work.
5. Let students repeatedly fail tasks or activities. Instead, try to modify the tasks or make them easier or more interesting.
6. Segregate the more capable from the least capable students in class. Slower students can learn from more capable students. Also, it is not necessarily true that, because students are slow in one area, they will be slow in another area or they will stay slow in a given area.
7. Plan curricula on the basis of a curriculum guide or book that comes from a state agency or book publisher. Plan curricula around the students' needs and interests.
8. Arrange teaching environments so the teacher does all the teaching and the students do all of the listening. Design environments where students are heavily involved in the learning process.
9. Mass-duplicate individualized education programs.

Table 16.4.   Questions to generate student profile data

Interests and preferences	What are (student's name)'s favorite things to do at home?
	What does (student's name) dislike doing at home?
	Describe your dream job for (student's name).
Skills and abilities	What type of chores does (student's name) perform?
	When (state home activity), how long does (student's name) stay on task before needing a break?
	How long is the break?
	How quickly does (student's name) do it; would you say at a slow pace, average pace?
	What equipment or tools does (student's name) use at home?
	Related to learning something new, what are (student's name)'s greatest accomplishments?
	How long did it take (student's name) to learn it?
	How was he or she taught?
On-the-job supports	What accommodation(s) does (student's name) use at home?
Ideas for future work (these questions are most suitable for students in their last year of school)	Name businesses where you would like to see (student's name) employed. Do you have a connection at any of these businesses?
	What days of week and times of day are (student's name) available to work?
Student evaluation and curriculum development	Does the student have insight into what type of work he or she would like to perform?
	What skills can be taught or practiced to promote a successful vocational future?

Shogren and Broussard (2011) explored perceptions of individuals with intellectual disabilities. Overall, they found their perceptions confirmed the importance of promoting personal development of skill set attitudes associated with self-determination and systems change to create environmental opportunities for self-determination and causal agency. Of note, the participants emphasized that "they cannot be self determining in an environment that is not supportive of self determination. And furthermore, even if the environment is supportive, they cannot be self determined unless they have the skills, attitudes and support to be a causal agent" (p. 99). Although the sample size was small, the study confirms and extends the understanding of self-determination and its impact on individuals with intellectual disabilities. There is a critical need to continue research, practice initiatives to promote self-determination, and reform the disability service system.

Functional Community Skills

IDEA mandates that IEP goals address both the academic and the functional proficiency of the student (Collins, Hager, & Galloway, 2011). Functional skill content is often those abilities that are immediate for daily living and functional content is frequently an objective when one is delivering community-based instruction. Some of the key qualities that define a functional skill include the following:

- It is performed within the context of a "real" activity.
- The activity is meaningful to the individual.
- People without disabilities believe the activity serves a purpose.
- If the person is unable to perform the skill for himself or herself, then it will need to be completed by another individual.
- The skill will be utilized throughout the individual's life.

Functional skills can include a number of daily life activities. Ayres, Lowrey, Douglas, and Sievers (2011) provide great examples of the most effective and successful functional skills and curriculum activities that are generally taught to individual students who are learning functional skills. Through their extensive investigation of functional life skills, the researchers identified consumer, office and vocational, safety, and domestic skills as focused activities that could be performed in the functional content. For example, some functional skills that may be performed in the community may include consumer skills such as shopping and ordering food at a restaurant. Other community skills may include learning office and vocational skills. Some domestic and self-help skills activities may include learning how to prepare meals and learning how to dress and do laundry. All of these functional skills are generally considered essential life skill activities that are addressed in functional curriculum. In common, students with disabilities who receive functional curriculum instruction have improved independent life skill outcomes in both their present and their future settings (Snell & Brown, 2006).

Community-Based Instruction

In discussing curriculum strategies and functional curriculum for youth with intellectual disabilities, one must also consider the impact of community-based instruction (CBI), especially for those students with greater support needs (Dymond, 2011). One main purpose of CBI is to provide the mechanism to teach the critical functional skills to students in the community, which serves as the classroom. CBI is defined as the involvement of instructors, therapists, paraprofessionals, and other personnel teaching instructional objectives in natural environments such as nonprofit agencies, restaurants, shopping malls, recreation centers, worksites, and other age-appropriate settings in the neighborhood and community. For example, students may learn to locate grocery items at the local Walmart, learn how to make a bank transaction at Bank of America, or even learn the rules for safety while at the community mall. CBI provides a meaningful way for students to experience the real world.

The main rationale and benefits of CBI are that it

1. Teaches skills that allow the individuals to more fully participate in activities outside the school and adult center setting with peers and family members

2. Exposes individuals to a variety of experiences, thus broadening the choices available to them and increasing their ability to affect their environment

3. Provides opportunities to learn social skills with members of the greater community (not just family, school, or training center staff, and other customers)

4. Enhances quality of life by increasing community inclusion, independence, and participation

5. Prepares individuals for adulthood by teaching skills that will have longitudinal use

6. Raises the family's expectations for their family member with a disability

7. Increases the community's expectations for individuals with disabilities

8. Helps the school and other team members to determine preferences and plan for community-based opportunities that reflect those preferences

CBI can provide learning opportunities to teach vocational instruction to students with disabilities. Community-based transition (CBT) and **community-based vocational instruction** (CBVI) education and programs emphasize vocational preparation encouraged through legislation such as IDEA that mandated more coordinated transition for students with disabilities. Through programs like CBT and CBVI, students are able to experience multiple jobs aimed at increasing their career knowledge while developing the job skills necessary to find work before or after graduation (Renzaglia, Hutchins, Dymond, & Sheldon, 2008). Kim and Dymond noted that

> CBVI is an effective instructional approach for individuals with disabilities. Training in real world environments is critical for students with disabilities, because they may not generalize skills learned in school to community work sites. By allowing exposure to diverse job tasks, CBVI can help students build vocational competence and appropriate work behaviors (Luecking & Fabian, 2000) and promote self-determination (Benz et al., 2004). In addition CBVI provides opportunities to both learn and apply academic knowledge, social skills, and general and specific work skills in the actual settings in which they will be used. (2010, p. 314)

Students with disabilities who participate in programs such as CBT and CBVI are more likely to be employed after they exit high school (Benz, Lindstrom, & Yovanoff, 2000). Despite the connection, challenges with implementing CBI programs are existing and can often involve issues with transporting students to work sites, legal and liability issues once the student is off school grounds, funding, and students missing academic instruction in class (Kim & Dymond, 2010). Careful planning by the IEP team and community setting can help to negate these issues.

Cimera (2010a) investigated the potential impact that community-based, high school transition programs have on the cost-efficiency of individuals with disabilities when they become adults. Outcomes achieved by 246 supported employees were compared. Results indicated that supported employees who participated in CBT programs in high school were more cost efficient from the taxpayers' perspective than were individuals who received only in-school transition services or no transition services at all.

Supported employees who received CBT services also kept their jobs in the community significantly longer than did individuals from the comparison groups.

Developing and Selecting Diploma Types

Diploma types are set by the state education agency and that agency sets the requirements for each diploma category (Swanson, 2008). According to Swanson (2008), about 24 states offer advanced standing diplomas for students who achieve beyond the requirements of the regular high school diploma. In most states, students who do not earn a regular diploma may earn alternative high school credentials or diplomas. They may be in the form of a special type of diploma for students with disabilities who have met the criteria of their IEP and a modified version of the standard diploma for students who may be looking to enter the work force. It is important that the IEP team discuss and consider the student diploma status when considering CBI to ensure that the academic content required to complete his or her diploma is correctly balanced and not jeopardized. With appropriate planning by the IEP team, students can pursue their academic requirements while being challenged with an academic schedule appropriate for their needs. Table 16.5 lists diploma types and options for youth with disabilities.

According to IDEA 2004, students with disabilities are required to participate in state- and district-wide assessments with appropriate accommodations and modifications when necessary. The data on the performance of students with disabilities on these assessments indicate that they are not performing well compared with their general education peers. As a result, some states are issuing alternate exit documents from high school in the form of occupational diplomas, general educational development diplomas, and certificates of attendance, achievement, or completion. Hartwig and Sitlington (2008) interviewed a random sample of employers, asking them if they were willing to hire prospective employees with these types of alternate diplomas. Employers were least willing to hire individuals with certificates of attendance, achievement, or completion and most willing to hire those with occupational diplomas and GEDs.

Table 16.5.   Diploma types

Diploma option	Description
Honors diploma/diploma of high distinction (advance diploma)	For students who achieve at a high academic level. Often, this diploma requires a certain grade-point average (GPA).
Standard diploma (regular diploma)	For students who complete a certain number of credits and obtain a minimum GPA to receive a diploma.
Certificate of completion/attendance	For students who have not received the grades necessary to obtain a standard or advance diploma; demonstrates that a student completed a set number of classes or that a student qualifies for a diploma because of sufficient attendance in a set period of time
Certificate of achievement	For students who demonstrate that they achieved a certain level of performance. This type of diploma certifies that the student was present and performed to the best of his or her ability but did not attain the necessary grades and/or credits to obtain a regular or advance diploma.
IEP/special education diploma	For students receiving special education services and those who have an individualized education program (IEP). Requirements are usually set by the student's IEP team and are therefore unique to each student. Students must meet their IEP requirements.
Occupational diploma	For students who are enrolled in vocational programs, this type of diploma certifies that a student has demonstrated a specific level of competence in an occupational area.

From Johnson, D., Thurlow, M., Cosio, A., & Bremer, C. (2005). Diploma options for students with disabilities. Minneapolis: The National Center on Secondary Education and Transition. NSCET Information Brief, 4(1); reprinted by permission.

Implementing Transition Individualized Education Programs for Youth with Intellectual Disabilities

During the 1980s and early 1990s, much attention was focused on the postschool adjustment of special education students—a movement that stems from the discouraging patterns of postsecondary employment of youth with disabilities. The IDEA Amendments of 1997 (PL 105-17) and 2004 (PL 108-446) include transition planning as one of the services that should be accessible to all special education students. *Transition services* are defined as coordinated sets of activities for students designed with an outcomes-oriented process that promotes smooth movement from school to postschool activities.

In transition planning, it is particularly important that these students be included in all of the planning stages. In many cases, these students have distinct opinions about what they want to do vocationally, socially, academically, and residentially. However, students sometimes have unrealistic views about the types of jobs they can perform. The teacher's role is to help these students to understand the requirements and expectations of various jobs and to identify realistic goals by including career exploration and assessment opportunities into the curriculum. While helping the student to develop realistic job expectations, teachers should also take into consideration the types of jobs about which the student exhibits interest or distaste. For example, many students find work in fast-food restaurants to be stigmatizing and demeaning but are very comfortable working in hotels because they are less likely to run into their peers while working. Implementing career exploration and assessment goals into IEPs can help target appropriate vocational and community training objectives and alleviate unrealistic expectations about job choices.

Social skills training should also be a part of the transition-planning process for students with intellectual disabilities, many of whom have problems with managing their behavior appropriately (Crites & Dunn, 2004). Transition-planning goals should reflect the teacher's effort to work with students to develop coping strategies and to identify community services that may further alleviate problems.

Finally, postsecondary education is a realistic outcome of transition training for some students with intellectual disabilities (Grigal & Hart, 2010). For cases in which the student and his or her family have chosen higher education as a transition-planning outcome, vocational and community-referenced skills should continue to be taught; however, academic preparation is very important. Teachers must be sure that students are prepared to take minimum competency and other tests that are offered in general classrooms.

Once a student's wishes and desires have been obtained, an interagency transition team should be formed to design a transition plan. These representatives should be from the local school division (e.g., administration, special and vocational education), vocational rehabilitation (VR), mental health and mental retardation agencies, private rehabilitation facilities, and postsecondary education institutions, and parents, students, and employers. Individuals with intellectual disabilities usually require these resources, or at least some of them, during the transition-planning process.

Each education team member has a role in planning transition. The roles interact, resulting in a collaboration of ideas and resources with each role being equally important. The special education teacher is responsible for the provision of functional school- and community-based training, and retrieval and analysis of data, and serves as the educational consultant to the team. The rehabilitation counselor's role is to provide funding for adaptive equipment and transportation needs related to employment and to participate in the assessment process. The school administrator's role includes facilitating CBI and transportation and promoting parent, personnel, and public awareness training programs. The role of the service coordinator involves providing follow-along services after graduation; advising all parties about policies associated with Social Security benefits, medical benefits, and employment incentives; and working closely with families throughout the transition process. The role of the vocational education teacher includes providing specific training skills, locating job training sites, and assisting in the collection and analy-sis of data from vocational evaluations. The employer provides input regarding business community needs and access to job training sites. All of these representatives of various agencies work together to plan and project the most efficient and productive outcomes for students and their families (Thoma & Wehman, 2010).

The student and his or her family are the most important partners in the transition-planning process. With foresight and planning of transition services, students with dis-abilities can look forward to brighter futures. Students should provide information about the jobs they want, how they want to spend free time, and how they wish to spend their money (Wehman & Kregel, 2004). Parents' and students' responsibilities to the planning team include conducting home training, advocating for full community integration, and participating in the selection of IEP transition planning processes.

As the evaluation is completed, professionals, parents, and students should feel that something special has been accomplished in the entire planning process (see Chapter 3). These visions need to take into account the different ways to include youth with intellec-tual disabilities into the mainstream of school activities as well as classrooms. Inclusion must be planned—it will not happen by chance.

Peter   Peter is a 19-year-old senior labeled with mild intellectual disabilities. He has a full-scale Wechsler Adult Intelligence Score of 66. Peter's family transferred from Kansas to Virginia last summer. His adoptive parents are professionals and have given him many advantages. Peter was adopted at the age of 8. His mother was a behavioral technician at a group facility for people with disabilities when she met Peter. His father is a lawyer. Peter's biological mother had intellectual disabilities and was only 15 when he was born.

Peter has a driver's license and works part time stocking shelves at Toys "R" Us. He will be 20 when he graduates from high school. His parents would like to see him go to vocational–technical school or to a VR-sponsored program for training. His mother has done a wonderful job of training Peter for independ-ent living: he cooks, cares for his own clothes, irons, cleans, and shops. Peter uses a calculator for math and is ready for more sophisticated computations. This past year, he was an assistant trainer for football, ran track, and also belonged to the Nautilus Club. Peter's parents think he will eventually live independ-ently with support and are in no hurry to see him move out. A trust was established when Peter was adopted to provide for him when his parents have passed on. There are no siblings, and other relatives are distant.

Evaluating Transition Outcomes for Youth with Intellectual Disabilities

Finding employment, advancing education, and furthering other postsecondary op-portunities are critically important to youth with intellectual disabilities as they exit high school. It has been reported that securing postsecondary opportunities, such as employment, can increase the overall psychological well-being and quality of life for individuals with intellectual disabilities (Rose, Perks, Fidan, & Hust, 2010). However, for youth with disabilities, the outcomes of employment and postsecondary education outcome below those of their nondisabled peers (Williamson, Robertson, & Casey, 2010). In fact, in a report by Hensel, Kroese, and Rose (2007) on factors associated with finding employment for individuals with intellectual disabilities, the researchers indicated that less than 10% of individuals with intellectual disabilities are employed. Transition out-comes in other postsecondary opportunities for youth with intellectual disabilities are additionally low. Individuals are leaving educational programs and exiting to waiting lists and an adult services system unprepared for the quality or quantity of needed services (Sitlington & Clark, 2006).

The majority of postschool outcome assessments analyze the employment, post-secondary school enrollment, and residential status of individuals with disabilities (Wittenburg & Maag, 2002). Most employment surveys ask questions regarding employment status, current wages, hours worked, benefits received, and employment history. Independent living outcomes are measured by where and with whom the individual lives. Postsecondary education questions center on enrollment in courses and completion of degree and certificate requirements. For individuals with significant intellectual disabilities, these measures should be expanded to include an analysis of the quality of life and the community integration of the individual. Only then can the success of transition be truly assessed.

In one study, Grigal, Hart, and Migliore (2011) described a secondary analysis of variables from the National Longitudinal Transition Survey-2 (NLTS-2) database. Specifically, students with intellectual disability were compared with students with other disabilities regarding postschool transition goals listed on their IEPs/transition plans, contacts/referrals made to outside agencies during transition planning, participation of other agencies/organizations in transition planning (e.g., VR and higher education representatives), and postsecondary education employment outcomes. Students with intellectual disability were less likely to have postsecondary education or competitive employment goals and outcomes and more likely to have sheltered and supported employment goals and outcomes compared with students with other disabilities. Contacts with and participation of external professionals in IEP/transition-plan meetings also differed between the two groups of students.

In the area of employment, workplace inclusion is critical to success (Chadsey, 2008), and the following questions must be answered during outcome evaluation: Are individuals with significant intellectual disabilities merely working alongside co-workers without disabilities or are they truly socially integrated into the culture of the workplace? Do individuals with significant intellectual disabilities have the opportunity to develop friendships and establish social networks? Is the employment environment conducive to the development of such relationships? What effect does inclusion have on individuals, their co-workers, and the business? Do individuals with disabilities have friendships and supports outside the workplace? Answers to these questions need further research and would be useful in developing future programs and priorities.

Evaluation of successful community inclusion should be done with validated measurements (Verdonschot, de Witte, Reichrath, Buntinx, & Curfs, 2009). These questions may include the following: Who decides how income is spent? Who does the grocery shopping? To which environments outside the home do individuals with significant intellectual disabilities have access? How frequently do individuals participate in outside activities? With whom do they spend the majority of time? Do they have friends? Do they spend time with friends without disabilities? Are recreational activities planned by others? Are the recreational activities ones in which the general community participates or are they planned specifically for individuals with disabilities?

As responses to these questions are being addressed, many national programs are being developed to address the needs of community inclusion for youth with intellectual disabilities. For example, take a rapidly spreading national program called Best Buddies, which pairs people with intellectual disabilities in one-to-one friendships with college students. In the past, many individuals with intellectual disabilities have not had the opportunity to have friends outside their own environment. By becoming a College Buddy, volunteers offer a student with an intellectual disability the chance to explore a new way of life (West, Wehman, & Wehman, 2005).

Best Buddies Colleges is the premise on which the international organization of Best Buddies began (http://www.bestbuddies.org). Social experiences and relationships are a part of life; unfortunately, individuals with intellectual disabilities have historically been excluded from many of the social opportunities that most people enjoy. College chapters are active in more than 360 campuses worldwide. Each chapter is a registered student organization on its college campus and is led by a college buddy director.

Helping Individuals with Intellectual Disabilities Enter Inclusive Employment

Supported employment is intended for individuals with disabilities such as intellectual disabilities who are traditionally unemployed or underemployed or who have difficulty maintaining employment because of significant disabilities (Inge & Moon, 2011). In this approach, the person goes to work in a competitive job in an integrated work setting earning at least minimum wage. To understand the uniqueness of this approach to VR, it is important to take a brief look at how supported employment evolved. For many years, individuals with significant disabilities were served within a continuum model of VR, which included day centers, sheltered workshops, and transitional programs. The premise behind this approach was to teach individuals with disabilities the skills needed to become "ready to work." However, movement out of these segregated settings into employment in the community rarely took place and, eventually, the system came under criticism (Wehman et al., 2007). At this time, the belief that all individuals including those with significant intellectual disabilities should have the opportunity to achieve as much independence as possible including working in their communities was also beginning to flourish. In addition, a number of researchers were demonstrating that people with moderate to severe intellectual disabilities could learn complex real work tasks and, furthermore, that these tasks could and should be taught on the job (Bellamy, Horner, & Inman, 1979; Rusch & Schutz, 1979; Gold, 1972a 1972b, 1978; Wehman, Hill, & Koehler, 1979; Wehman, 1981) instead of in segregated settings. The approach used **applied behavior analysis** and **systematic instruction** and required breaking tasks down into stimulus response chains and using prompting hierarchies and reinforcement to teach them (Wehman, 2006b).

Because of this advancement, individuals with intellectual disabilities and other significant disabilities were no longer required to learn prerequisite skills in segregated settings before going to work. Instead of training an individual with a disability outside a workplace to get ready to work (i.e., work readiness) and then try to locate employment, now research backed the effectiveness of a model that emphasized the effectiveness of obtaining employment first and then training the newly hired employee the skills needed on the job. In the years that followed, a number of projects were funded that demonstrated the effectiveness of training individuals with significant disabilities on the job. The results of these efforts revealed promising practices for a supported employment approach to assist individuals with intellectual disabilities with employment. Then came the passage of legislation, such as the Developmental Disabilities Assistance and Bill of Rights Act of 1984 (PL 94-103), and Title VI, Part C of the Rehabilitation Act Amendments of 1986 (PL 99-506), in combination with systems change grants funded through Title III of the Rehabilitation Act that provided the basis for the initiation of a series of federal- and state-funded demonstration projects designed to provide opportunities and supports for individuals with severe or significant disabilities to work alongside their fellow citizens in their communities.

Through the years, the supported employment approach has been used to assist individuals with intellectual disabilities with gaining and maintaining "real work for real pay" (Wehman, Inge, Revell, & Brooke, 2007). Key to the successful implementation of the supported employment are workplace support services provided and/or facilitated both on and off the job by a VR professional known as a job coach or employment specialist. In the individual approach, the job coach works one to one with the individual with the disability to assist him or her with identifying vocational strengths. Next, the job coach represents the individual to employers in hopes of creating a viable work opportunity for the job seeker. When the job seeker is hired, the coach provides or facilitates an array of workplace supports that typically includes on-the-job skills training and a guarantee to the employer to complete the work while the new hire in getting up to speed. Eventually, when the employee is able to meet the employer's job performance expectations, the coach fades from the job site; however, he or she continues to monitor how things are going and provides or facilitates additional support either on or off the job if needed throughout the life of person's job (Wehman et al., 2007; Targett & Wehman, 2009).

Supported employment is heavily based on research that started in the 1970s. Some of the highlights of the more recent findings include those of Jahoda, Kemp, Riddel, and Banks (2007) who found that individuals with intellectual disabilities in competitive employment enjoyed a higher level of job satisfaction and higher self-esteem than those who went to sheltered work settings. In addition, there have been numerous studies on the cost-effectiveness of the supported employment approach over the years. In 2000, Cimera reviewed 21 cost studies and found that, at the individual level, the cost–benefit ratio is almost always positive, regardless of level of disability. Later, Cimera (2007a) investigated the cumulative costs for supported versus sheltered employment for individuals with intellectual disabilities. Again, supported employment was shown to be more cost-effective. In a more recent study, Cimera (2010b) took a comprehensive look at 231,204 supported employees funded by VR throughout the entire United States from 2002 to 2007. One remarkable finding extrapolates to more than $1.5 billion in cost benefits from supported employment if applied to the total number of U.S. individuals with disabilities served in segregated day placements. However, the author notes that supported employment services "will need to assist individuals with obtaining work that allows them to earn a 'livable wage'" (Cimera, 2010b, p. 25).

Finally, Cimera (2010c) also explored the outcomes achieved by 104,213 individuals with intellectual disabilities who were served by state VR agencies and wished to be enrolled in supported employment. Results found that 62.08% of participants became employed within their community via supported employment and that these individuals, on average, received greater monetary benefits from working (i.e., wages earned) than monetary costs (i.e., taxes paid, foregone wages, reduction in governmental subsidies). Further, this result was found regardless of the number of disabling conditions present and the state in which they received services. However, employment outcomes (i.e., rates of employment, wages earned, hours worked, and cost efficiency) varied significantly among states.

There is little doubt that benefits gained by people with intellectual disabilities by working in integrated employment settings are immense. These include higher wages, greater independence and economic self-sufficiency, greater integration with people without developmental disabilities in the workplace and the community, more opportunities for choice and self-determination, and expanded career options and increased job satisfaction (Wehman et al., 2007). And, although it is clear that, since its inception, supported employment has assisted individuals with significant disabilities with achieving positive employment outcomes, challenges still persist. Some of the challenges faced by those who want to work include conversion of day programs to integrated work options, expansion of program capacity, the need to ensure consumer choice and self-determination, and the achievement of meaningful employment outcomes. In addition, greater attention needs to be paid to employers and what it will take to convince and motivate them to hire a young person with intellectual disabilities. A closer examination of ways to create work opportunities to meet the needs of business and highlight the potential employee's abilities is long overdue, too. By becoming aware of supported employment as a VR option, teachers and other professionals involved in transition of youth with intellectual disabilities can help steer families and students away from sheltered settings and toward real work for real pay. When these primary stakeholders finally say no to segregated settings, it is likely that we will move much closer to a world where everyone (regardless of severity of disability) will have the opportunity for real work for real pay.

Conclusion

Transition planning benefits all parties involved. It benefits the individual with intellectual disabilities because it ensures that appropriate adult options and support mechanisms are in place before the individual graduates so that an integrated lifestyle can be maintained. The school district benefits because graduates attain productive and satisfying lives—one of the goals of public education. Transition planning benefits the service delivery system by examining the effectiveness of current programs and by becoming the driving force for the development of new opportunities for individuals with intellectual disabilities. Without transition planning, there is a higher probability that the individual will exit into waiting lists, sheltered workshops, and segregated living options without the appropriate services or supports.

Implementing transition for individuals with intellectual disabilities is both challenging and complex. Conducting future-planning activities before the development of transition IEPs is one of the ways in which local school districts can begin to address the process. However, the development of a transition IEP alone does not ensure that students with intellectual disabilities will exit into integrated community lives as adults. School districts still must provide appropriate curriculum, vocational training in community settings, integrated age-appropriate school environments, and interagency linkages for transition planning to be successful. Most important, parents and individuals must be empowered with the skills and knowledge to make the best decisions. Only then will the vision of full participation in the community for the individual with intellectual disabilities become a reality.

Study Questions

1. Describe the historical progression and key supports that define and are essential for youth with disabilities.

2. What are some important take-aways from the overrepresentation of African American students with disabilities? What can legislative and school systems do to improve the outcomes for African American students with disabilities?

3. What are some challenges to community integration and employment for youth with disabilities? How can these challenges be minimized to improve community and employment outcomes for youth with disabilities?

4. What considerations should be made when one is developing curriculum and providing effective instruction for students with disabilities? How can current practices such as universal design for transition and self-determination impact the development and implementation of instruction?

5. What considerations should be made when one is developing and implementing transition plans for students with disabilities?

Online Resources

National Center on Secondary Education and Transition: http://www.ncset.org

National Secondary Transition Technical Assistance Center: http://www.nsttac.org

Center on Disability and Development: http://cdd.tamu.edu

Paula's Special Education Resources: http://www.paulabliss.com

Applications for Youth with Learning Disabilities

ELIZABETH EVANS GETZEL
AND JOHN J. GUGERTY

17

After completing this chapter, the reader will be able to

- Understand controversies and complexities surrounding different approaches to defining and documenting an individual's learning disabilities
- Describe the perceptions and feelings of young people with learning disabilities
- Understand techniques for assessment of transition planning for youth with learning disabilities
- Describe universal design for learning strategies that can be useful for youth with learning disabilities
- Understand how to work with students with multiple cultural backgrounds

This chapter provides information and resources to help readers understand the challenges students with learning disabilities (LD) face as they move from secondary education to the community. It includes an overview of the experiences of students with LD and ideas on how to better meet their transition needs and stresses recognition of the importance of student involvement throughout the transition process. We encourage educators and other professionals working with students with LD to use a strength-based approach. Helping students to understand their strengths is critical. Too often, these students cannot articulate their strengths or the accommodations, learning strategies, and technologies they need to meet their specific challenges (Getzel, 2008; Getzel & Thoma, 2006). Using strategies and techniques described in this chapter will hopefully expand one's understanding of the transition for students with LD and spark new ideas and approaches to ensure that these students are fully involved in this process and maximize their chances of success as they undertake adult roles.

Defining Learning Disabilities

LD can be viewed from both the clinical and the personal perspectives. Although a working knowledge of definitions and fluency in the administration and interpretation of assessment protocols is critical, professionals who wish to develop a more accurate understanding of LD and the manifestations of LD in personal, social, and work situations must develop and internalize an understanding of how LD affects the lives of real people. Persons facing issues presented by LD, even in "mild" manifestations, face severe problems in developing and maintaining employment, independence, and interpersonal relationships.

Differences in the identification of LD flow from different disciplinary or professional perspectives, the techniques and measures used in diagnosis, and institutional or organizational constraints (Gregg & Scott, 2000). Defining LD remains an issue in the field as a result of the lack of changes to the definition in the past 40 years (Kavale, Spaulding, & Beam, 2009). As a result, problems exist in the field, particularly in the identification of LD (Kavale et al., 2009; McLoughlin & Lewis, 2005). Although in the Individuals with Disabilities Education Act (IDEA) 2004, the definition of specific learning disabilities (SLD) remained intact, regulations published in 2006 changed both the evaluation criteria and the identification criteria to align them with regulations implementing the No Child Left Behind Act (2001; PL 107-110). As noted by the Learning Disabilities Association of America, this change put "the emphasis on identifying students who are not achieving adequately for the child's age or the attainment of State-approved grade-level standards, not abilities. In effect, the new criteria virtually eliminated a great many students with SLD, including some who have high academic achievement in some areas but markedly low achievement in other areas" (2010, p. 1). In response to this change, the Learning Disabilities Association of America sought input from 56 experts in SLD identification and intervention. Their conclusions, based on both professional expertise and empirical evidence were as follows:

1. Maintain the SLD definition [contained in the Individuals with Disabilities Education Improvement Act of 2004; PL 105-17] and strengthen statutory requirements in SLD identification procedures.
2. Neither ability or achievement discrepancy analyses nor failure to respond to intervention (RTI) alone is sufficient for SLD identification.
3. To meet SLD statutory and regulatory requirements, a "third method" approach that identifies a pattern of psychological processing strengths and deficits, and achievement deficits consistent with this pattern of processing deficits, makes the most empirical and clinical sense.
4. An empirically validated RTI model could be used to prevent learning problems in children, but comprehensive evaluations should occur whenever necessary for SLD

identification purposes, and children with SLD need individualized interventions based on specific learning needs, not merely more intense interventions designed for children in general education.

5. Assessment of cognitive and neuropsychological processes should be used not only for identification but for intervention purposes as well, and these assessment intervention relationships need further empirical investigation. (Learning Disabilities Association of America White Paper, 2010, p. 2)

Unique Challenges Presented by Youth with Learning Disabilities

Many people with LD have portrayed their own unique experiences in secondary and postsecondary school settings.

Secondary School Experiences

Some high school students with LD describe their experiences in vivid and colorful language:

"My head is just like a television set except it has no channel selector. So I get all the programs on my screen at the same time."

"When I sit in class, I keep having these 'mind drifts.' I never know when my mind is gonna drift away so I lose what's happening."

"I like to move around a lot. When I sit still, I get tired. I get bored. I need action."

College Experiences

Carolee Reiling (1990), while a freshman at Stanford University, felt she needed more information about the learning challenges she was experiencing in college. The following are her descriptions of the problems she was facing.

Writing

- *Tendency to work out specific parts of the paper laboriously instead of focusing on the paper as a whole.* (p. 4)
- *Sentences seem to vanish before being written down*—This is a problem that contributes greatly to my problems with writing because often when I finally think of a good way to express something, it is a race for me to get it written down before it disappears, never to come back. It is really frustrating because I will get the first part and then just put a bunch of question marks for the second part. (p. 5)

Spelling

- *Reversals [are] common* (—e.g., *b* instead of *d, freind* instead of *friend, probably* instead of *probably,* 0137 instead of 0317). (p. 7)
- *Frequently dropping, adding, or reversing letters and word parts* ([e.g., *now* instead of *know, dab god* instead of *bad dog*])—This is a very broad category and embodies a lot of the mistakes that I make. I averaged about 31.2 times doing this a day, with a low of 20 and a high of 62. (p. 7)

Testing

- *Difficulty with multiple-choice questions; difficulty filling in the bubbles on forms*—This is something that I could never seem to do, but I thought that it was that way for everybody.

By the time I even located the correct bubbles, I had forgotten which one I was supposed to fill in. (p. 8)

- *Misinterprets directions or questions on examinations*—This is something that I seem to do on every test without fail. It ends up costing me a lot of time and usually a lot of points. On my Physics 61 midterm last quarter, I wasted about 45 minutes of a 2-hour exam by mis-reading just a couple of words, which completely changes a problem. ... But by [the] time [I realized my mistake,] I was so flustered and frustrated that the test just went downhill for me from there. (p. 8)

Concentration

- *Focusing requires extraordinary effort*—It has always been extremely hard for me to concentrate completely, especially when reading, studying, or listening. I have the attention span to read about 3–4 pages. I constantly have to set goals with myself, like saying after I read 5 more pages I can take a short break. ... I intersperse reading with math, which helps break up the monotony and dread of reading. I can never stay focused in my classes, but if I get the notes I can understand the rest later. (p. 9)
- *Easily distracted by noise and movement*—This is a problem that I always associated with my inability to focus for periods of time. ... Noises that really bother me a lot are ticking of clocks or people making noises like flicking their pens because of nervous habits. ... Movement also does not allow me to concentrate. (p. 9)

Speech

- *Difficulty in communicating ideas clearly*—I often say something exactly the opposite of how I should have said it (e.g., 'Does the dog have the ball?' = 'Does the ball have the dog?'). I have gotten into the habit of going over in my head what I have just said hoping to catch stuff like that, and sometimes I do. ... I also have problems conveying my ideas to others even if I say them how I meant to. This is why I am terrified of public speaking or even talking to a group of peers. (p. 10)

Orientation

- *Feeling lost in a familiar setting; becoming disoriented easily*—I always seem to get lost. ... I cannot count the number of times that I have gotten lost running. One afternoon first quarter I was out for 1 hour and 45 minutes because I got lost and could not figure out how to get back. I finally had to ask someone and they showed me the road I was looking for was about 300 feet in front of me. (p. 11)

Everyday Manifestations

- *Feeling constantly behind*—Even if I am caught up on all my work, I never find myself at a loss for something to do. Just because I read the chapter once doesn't mean that I remember any of it. (p. 14)
- *Isolation resulting from fear of being misunderstood*—I have a very difficult time communicating my thoughts, especially when I am speaking to more than just one person and all of the attention is on me. Needless to say, I feel very isolated when ideas that are all so clear in my mind cannot be made understandable to others. I often get a similar feeling when things that others say go so far above my head that they are beyond my reach. (p. 15)

These quotes from Reiling (1990) illustrate what it is like going through life when one cannot rely on the accuracy of what one reads or expresses either in speech or in writing. This too reflects the author's personal experiences when talking to students with similar challenges and reports from others who support these students. It documents the anxiety and stress that an individual with LD experiences and the energy that he or she must expend to cope with tasks that most people perform automatically, accurately, and with minimal effort. In the absence of assistance from knowledgeable professionals, many individuals with LD—even those who were identified in primary or secondary school—have a very incomplete understanding of their disabilities, few use self-monitoring or compensatory strategies, and most have little awareness of how their disabilities influence their abilities to obtain employment and perform successfully on the job (Getzel, 2008; Getzel & Thoma, 2006).

Learning disabilities have often been called the "hidden" disabilities. Students with LD make up about half of all students with disabilities (Shaw, Madaus, & Dukes, 2010) and have the second highest dropout rate compared with other secondary education students with disabilities (U.S. Department of Education, 2006). Because these disabilities are not readily visible, students with specific LD often report that it is difficult to make others understand and accept the problems they experience. As a result, educators form inaccurate perceptions of students with LD, which leads to inadequate preparation and planning for transition from school to the community (Brinckerhoff, McGuire, & Shaw, 2002; Getzel & Thoma, 2006; Shaw et al., 2010). To illustrate this lack of understanding and the misconceptions about students with LD, one student commented, "No one understood my disability, and I was told I could not attend college" (Getzel & Thoma, 2008, p. 80).

The impact of LD affects all areas of an individual's life in school and in the community. Students with LD typically experience difficulties in learning and social interactions, which can impact their success living independently in the community (Smith, Polloway, Patten, & Dowdy, 2004; Kochhar-Bryant, Bassett, & Webb, 2009). It is essential that educators understand the pervasive impact of this disability on the lives of individuals and the need for appropriate accommodations and supports to enable them to successfully make the transition into the community with the skills to pursue employment or higher education.

Understanding One's Disability

The correlation between postsecondary success and self-determination skills is an important one, especially given the fact that other researchers have linked postsecondary education with improved employment outcomes for individuals with disabilities (Stodden & Dowrick, 2000). Therefore, teaching self-determination skills to students with LD is a critical component that will allow them to gain a greater understanding of themselves and learn how to communicate their strengths and accommodation needs both in school and in the community (Getzel & Thoma, 2006; Webb, Patterson, Syverud, & Seabrooks-Blackmore, 2008). Students with LD who are able to understand their skills, effective learning strategies, and how to acquire information or services are able to obtain a sense of control over their lives (Getzel & Thoma, 2006; Kochhar-Bryant et al., 2008; Shaw et al., 2010; Webb et al., 2008). Incorporating self-determination skills as part of a student's learning experience is critical. In secondary schools, accommodations may be part of the students' experience, but in most postsecondary or employment settings, the student or worker with disabilities is part of the mainstream and must self-advocate to obtain accommodations (Brinckerhoff et al., 2002; Getzel & Briel, 2008b; Getzel & Wehman, 2005; Kochhar-Bryant et al., 2008; Shaw et al., 2010).

Wehmeyer (1992) defined *self-determination* as "acting as the primary causal agent in one's life free to make choices and decisions about one's quality of life, free from undue influence or interference" (p. 302). Hoffman and Field (1995) conceptualized self-determination as "one's ability to define and achieve goals based on a foundation of knowing and valuing oneself" (p. 136). College students with disabilities participating in a self-determination project defined it as being able to advocate for what you need, understanding your disability and how it impacts your learning, having self-confidence, being independent, and adjusting your schedule to make sure things get done (Finn, Getzel, & McManus, 2008).

It is clear that the goal of transition planning is to prepare students with disabilities for their lives after high school by teaching skills they will need in the new settings. Parents, educators, friends, and other significant individuals should foster the personal growth and independence of individuals with LD throughout the individual's life (Getzel, 2008; Getzel & Thoma, 2006; Finn et al., 2008; Thoma & Wehmeyer, 2005). Strategies that have been found effective with students in their overall development include (LD Online, 2000)

1. Focus on student strengths, not weakness.
2. Provide structure and let the student know what is expected.
3. Foster self-esteem by providing opportunities for the student to experience success.
4. Ensure that a plan is in place to reinforce the student's positive behavior across environments (e.g., school, home, community).

An important method for assisting students with disabilities to take ownership to achieve their goals is through the development of their individualized education programs (IEPs). All too often, students are not active members in their IEP meetings, even though they attend them (Thoma & Wehman, 2010; Wehman & Wittig, 2009). Students with LD need to become active participants in the IEP process by thinking about what they want for the future, communicating their ideas and feelings with parents and teachers to determine realistic goals, and showing responsibility by following up on objectives that they are responsible for completing (Getzel & Thoma, 2006; Lerner, 2003; Thoma & Wehman, 2010). To assist in the development of self-determination skills for students with LD and their participation in the IEP process, the Virginia Department of Education funded the development and implementation of the I'm Determined project. Resources and information to assist educators, students with LD, and their families can be found on the project's web site, http://www.imdetermined.org. A number of resources on this web site are available to enable educators to incorporate self-determination activities into their curriculum. Two examples of resources that can assist students with LD to become a more active partner in the IEP process are the *One Pager* and the *My Good Day Plan*. *The One Pager* provides an opportunity for students to describe their strengths, interests, preferences, and needs. Students can prepare and distribute this document before an IEP meeting. A second tool is the *My Good Day Plan*, which allows students to describe what happens on a good day, identify positive behaviors, assess if it is happening, problem solve what actions are needed to reach goals, and identify who can assist in this process.

Problem-Solving and Decision-Making Skills

Students with LD need skills that enable them to identify problems or tasks that must be completed, to list the choices or options involved with problems or tasks, to determine possible outcomes or consequences, and to select the best course of action. As one student with LD commented, "It is important to find out what works for you, how to get around problems." Another student with LD stated, "You need to work through problems one step at a time" (Getzel & Thoma, 2006, p. 36). The amount of practice and hands-on experience that these students receive in accepting environments increases the likelihood that they will use these skills in all areas of their lives (Getzel, 2008; Getzel & Thoma, 2006; Thoma & Wehmeyer, 2005).

Students with LD may experience difficulties managing their time. They may miss appointments or other scheduled events. Time management is one of the skills among the self-management skills needed by students with LD. Other skills include organizational skills, study skills, and goal setting. Lack of these skills can result in such challenges as setting priorities or establishing goals. Although these students may appear organized if they keep lists or other techniques to organize their activities (Finn et al., 2008; Getzel, Briel, & Kregel, 2000), they are often unable to determine what to do first. They spend a great deal of time on relatively insignificant tasks and do not focus on the essentials. Many students with LD have difficulty with final decisions and obtaining closure for issues (Smith et al., 2004). Teaching self-management skills while in secondary school in the areas of problem identification, goal setting, self-monitoring, self-evaluation, and self-reinforcement can be strategies to encourage student participation in learning and to help develop skills that can be generalized to other settings (Finn et al., 2008; Getzel, 2008; Getzel, McManus, & Briel, 2004; Getzel & Thoma, 2006; Hadley, 2006).

Another issue confronting many students with LD is the inability to remember something that has been taught previously, even on a daily basis (Smith et al., 2004; Womack, Marchant, & Borders, 2011). Often, these students have been labeled as passive learners, meaning they are not actively involved in the learning process (Lane, Carter, Pierson, & Glaeser, 2006; Scheeler, Macluckie, & Albright, 2010; Shaw et al., 2010; Womack et al., 2011), which is necessary for acquiring problem-solving skills. Short-term memory problems can also contribute to difficulties in remembering information over a period of time (Lerner & Johns, 2009; McLoughlin & Lewis, 2005; Smith et al., 2004).

Social and Communication Skills

Social skills can present particular challenges to people with LD (Kochhar-Bryant et al., 2008; Lerner & Johns, 2009; Shaw et al., 2010). As a result of perceptual difficulties, these individuals may have problems understanding others. They may not be able to differentiate between a stare and a thoughtful glance or other social cues (Womack et al., 2011). They may appear to be rude by breaking into conversations or making inappropriate remarks (Lerner & Johns, 2009). Individuals with auditory problems may have problems telling the difference between angry and excited voices or find that they must concentrate so intently on what is said that they miss the nonverbal messages that accompany spoken words (Lerner & Johns, 2009; Price, 2002). Because of this, they may respond incorrectly. In addition, individuals with LD may appear inattentive because they are easily distracted or maintain poor eye contact with the person who is speaking (Lerner & Johns, 2009; Scheeler et al., 2010).

Because of the inability to socialize with their peers, these students tend to isolate themselves, which delays social development and can result in immature social skills development (Miller, Lane, & Wehby, 2005; Scheeler et al., 2010; Zambo, 2010). Students need feedback about behaviors that create problems for them if they are to learn creative ways to overcome communication obstacles (Lane et al., 2006; Scheeler et al., 2010). One method for providing this kind of support is through the use of mentors. Students or adults who are mentors can offer advice or feedback on how to interact with others in employment or school settings (Brown, Takahashi, & Roberts, 2010; Getzel & Briel, 2008; Scheeler et al., 2010). If students understand the impact they have on others and know how to improve their skills, then they will be able to increase their self-esteem—an essential asset for pursuing goals (Whelley, Radtke, Burgstahler, & Christ, 2003).

Assessment for Transition

Assessments of all kinds are part of the transition experience for youth with identified LD. School personnel who are responsible for arranging or conducting assessments can enhance their value by keeping the following points in mind:

1. Do not assume that an individual has a thorough, accurate understanding of his or her disability or its ramifications. Support staff members at many postsecondary schools

have discovered that students with previously identified LD cannot articulate what having an LD means or describe its implications to others (Getzel, 2008; Getzel et al., 2000, 2004).

2. Explain using specific terms so that the individual can understand why more tests are necessary, what will happen, and what can be learned from these tests. Remember that individuals with communication difficulties may need several explanations, presented in different ways. (Assurances of understanding must be verified.)

3. After all testing has been completed, review the results with the individual. Again, remember to accommodate any perceptual and communication difficulties. Do not accept assurances of understanding without verifying that the individual does, in fact, comprehend.

4. If you purchase assessments from other agencies or independent professionals, discreetly check that the person performing the assessments understands testing accommodations that must be made for the individual. Advanced degrees alone do not guarantee that understanding. In addition, some private testing organizations and professionals actually have psychometricians or paraprofessional staff members administer the assessments while the highly credentialed professional reviews the results and writes the reports. Sometimes, the importance of appropriate testing accommodations and environments is not fully appreciated by those actually carrying out the assessment. It is also important to check the testing environment, in person if necessary, to see that it is free of distractions. A surprising number of testing environments are noisy or contain visual distractions (e.g., ceiling fans, intricate wallpaper, large windows overlooking busy streets). Validity and, thus, relevance of assessments requires that all involved pay close attention to the details of test administration, the details of an individual's known strengths and weaknesses, and the details of the environment in which the assessments occur.

5. Many individuals with LD perform well in the quiet, orderly, systematic environments of classrooms but fail in the noisy, hectic environments of jobs. These latter environments may be replete with interruptions, incomplete or overwhelmingly extensive information, and fluid (i.e., fluctuating, changing) responsibilities. Understanding the conditions under which tasks must be performed is a critical component for success of many individuals with disabilities in the work world.

6. Because it is very possible that other members of the individual's family may also experience LD, take great care to ensure that the purpose, procedures, results, and implications of assessment are conveyed completely and accurately to the individual's parents. Do not rely on the individual to do this unless no other option is possible. When an individual with perceptual or communication problems communicates with others (e.g., parents) who may also have perceptual or communication problems, serious misunderstandings may occur. Preventive actions may result in good working relationships with families and few hostile confrontations.

7. Be sure to address social and interpersonal skills in assessments for transition-planning purposes.

8. Review the eligibility criteria for adult services agencies and comply whenever possible to minimize repetitive and unnecessary testing. If these requirements are met as part of a multidisciplinary team process, then the individual is saved from another, frequently onerous, testing situation; the service delivery process is more efficient; and cooperating agencies' resources are used more efficiently.

The following questions, developed by Dr. Pamela Leconte, George Washington University, and presented to participants in the Consolidated High School District 230 Transition Enhancement Project (Leconte, 2011) can provide a framework of value and relevance upon which educators can build using print, situational, electronic, and observational assessment approaches. These questions can also help those involved in developing and implementing age-appropriate assessments for transition to add value to each student's learning and growth:

1. Whose needs are being met?
2. What is the student learning from assessment? Is it helpful, meaningful, and positive—does it lead to growth?
3. What are we learning from the assessment process?
4. Where are we recording the information?
5. Where are gaps in transition planning?
6. Does the youth understand the "whys" (individualized purposes) of assessment?
7. Are his or her goals realistic, and, if not, how can they become so?
8. Which stakeholders (family, adult service providers, career-technical education instructors, general education teachers, related service personnel) can assist in assessing, identifying gaps, and implementing steps to positive outcomes?
9. How are assessment activities/goals integrated into IEPs?
10. How are assessment outcomes integrated into IEPs and Summaries of Performance?
11. Have we created and/or selected the most appropriate assessment activities?
12. Are "next steps" (planning) based on assessment information?
13. Are "next steps" clearly apparent to all stakeholders and the youth regarding assessment and transition implementation?
14. Did "next steps" work?
15. Do we need to reassess and readjust planning?
16. What additional assessment is needed, if any?
17. Is assessment accessible to all—starting with a Universal Design for Learning framework?
18. Is the youth helping plan and direct his or her own assessment?

Assessment Reports

Assessments are only as good as the information they generate, and reports are useful only to the extent that they contain information that guides the design of transition programs and implementation of services. Assessment reports should include a description of the individual's functional strengths and limitations in executive processing skills, a description of how the individual learns or acquires information, coping and compensation strategies used by the individual, demonstrated basic and vocational skills (including the conditions under which performance was measured), social and interpersonal skills, self-advocacy skills, and the vocational implications of all of these items. At the end of the chapter are resources to help the reader navigate the complex and evolving issues surrounding age-appropriate transition assessment.

Setting Transition Goals

Many youth with LD leave secondary education with insufficient vocational, functional, or academic skills to be successful in either career entry jobs or postsecondary education (Briel & Getzel, 2001; Getzel et al., 2004; Shaw et al., 2010). Improved transition planning while in high school is critical to ensure that these students exit school with the necessary skills and knowledge to acquire the needed supports and services (Brinckerhoff et al., 2002; Kochhar-Bryant et al., 2008; Wehman & Wittig, 2009). Establishing postschool goals helps to provide a framework for the curriculum that students with LD will pursue while in high school and to identify independent living skills that students will need in the community. It is critical that students with LD are actively involved in this process by discussing their interests and postschool goals and planning activities with the IEP team that will assist students in identifying outcomes that will help them reach these goals (Steere & Cavaiuolo, 2002; Thoma & Wehman, 2010; Wehman & Wittig, 2009). Greene and Kochhar-Bryant (2003) identified five important questions to assist students with disabilities to participate in the development of transition goals:

1. What are my school, work, and community-living interests and skills?
2. Where do I want to go to school, live, or work after high school?
3. What courses do I take to prepare for the future?
4. What are my strengths, and what do I need to improve?
5. What do I need to learn to make my goals after high school happen?

Universal Design for Learning

Several factors should be considered when one is determining appropriate teaching strategies for students with LD. These factors can be divided into three categories. The first area focuses on the student. The development of specific teaching strategies is based on the unique learning characteristics of the student as identified through formal or informal assessments (Deshler et al., 2001; Hammill & Bartel, 2004; McLaughlin & Lewis, 2005). The cultural backgrounds of the students and their effects on learning should also be considered (Black, Mrasek, & Ballinger, 2003; Lerner, 2003).

The second category concerns the transition and postschool goals of the students. For some students with LD, further education in a postsecondary setting is a goal. Others may seek employment after leaving school. Teaching strategies and the emphasis on what these students must know differs depending on their transition goals. No matter what their goals are, however, many students need assistance with daily living skills so they can live independently in the community (Getzel et al., 2004; Patton & Trainor, 2004; Thoma & Wehman, 2010; Wehman & Wittig, 2009).

The classroom environment is the final category to consider when selecting teaching strategies. Helping students to feel motivated to learn is especially important for students with LD (Klassen, 2006; Lerner & Johns, 2009; Lane et al., 2006). Many of these students have not had positive experiences in school and, by the time they reach high school or postsecondary settings, are likely to have negative self-images and poor self-concepts and lack motivation (Lerner & Johns, 2009; Smith et al., 2004; Seo, Abbott, & Hawkins, 2008). Creating an atmosphere that reinforces the strengths of the students and helps them to feel comfortable with learning enables these students to feel they can achieve in certain academic or vocational areas (Getzel & Thoma, 2006; Lerner & Johns, 2009; Lane et al., 2006). Educators can assist students with LD to gain invaluable tools to cope with the many decisions they will make as they move from school to the community.

Instructing Students

Secondary education classrooms comprise a diversity of learners whether or not these learners have disabilities. To meet the educational needs of all students, the use of universal design for learning techniques and strategies enables educators to incorporate a variety of learning modalities throughout their instructional activities (Casper & Leuchovius, 2005; Burgstahler, 2008; Lerner & Johns, 2009). Universal design for learning helps to create curriculum, materials, resources, and environments accessible for all individuals without requiring adaptations or specialized design (Schelly, Davies, & Spooner, 2011). What do educators need to consider when determining the use of universal design for learning techniques? Burgstahler and Cory (2008) suggest some instructional strategies developed by Bowe (2000) using universal design for learning techniques. Some of the suggestions include

1. Providing students with options for demonstrating knowledge and skills
2. Informing students about the availability of digitized texts
3. Translating important information into other languages
4. Ensuring that the classroom space is accessible for all students.

Universal design for learning does not "water down" curriculum or remove academic challenges; the use of these strategies enhances the access to learning and retaining information in classroom settings. As a result, by offering students a variety of ways to learn material, all students may learn more effectively (Getzel & Finn, 2005; Thoma, Bartholomew, & Scott, 2009).

Universal design for learning incorporates the variety of learning modalities that all learners possess and can assist students with LD to access materials and demonstrate their knowledge in their areas of strength. Universal design for learning strategies can provide students with LD greater opportunities to access the general curriculum. For example, students with LD who are more visual learners need assistance with "visualizing" information provided through lecture. These students need to turn spoken words into pictures. Whenever possible, lectures should include visual cues to help students understand the information that is being presented. Providing students lecture outlines or PowerPoint presentations before class helps them to prepare for class and review the material after it is presented (Burgstahler & Cory, 2008). When presenting class material, a variety of visual aids should be used to reinforce information. Examples of techniques include (Burgstahler & Cory, 2008; Getzel et al., 2004; Thoma et al., 2009)

1. Software programs that diagram information
2. Using PowerPoint presentations that are highly visual, incorporating maps or graphs
3. Incorporating video clips into lessons
4. Providing demonstrations of skills, concepts, and ideas

Students should also be encouraged to complete assignments with graphs or drawings to illustrate their comprehension of the material.

When students are reading class materials, they should be encouraged to underline or highlight key points. They should also be taught how to take notes that clearly separate different concepts using a color-coding system. Students who are visual learners should get into the habit of using a planner or hand-held technology to record assignment due dates, testing dates, important meetings, and other important class-related information.

Universal design for learning strategies that assist students who have strong auditory learning skills include emphasizing sound when presenting material and speaking slowly and clearly. Students should be taught to listen for cues when information is given. For example, phrases such as, "The most important point is ..." or "To summarize, we have discussed ..." are cues that extra attention should be given. Students should be permitted to tape-record information presented in class to review what was presented. Visual cues, such as maps or charts, can also be used as long as the information is accompanied by a clear explanation (Burgstahler, 2008).

Auditory learners may benefit from oral tests or role play (Getzel et al., 2004; Patton & Trainor, 2004). In role play, students present information to other class members and answer questions they may have. This technique is helpful because the student verbalizes or practices the information obtained (Swanson & Deshler, 2003; Getzel et al., 2004). Students should be encouraged to join or form study groups to reinforce material learned in class. This will also help to identify areas of confusion about the material, which can be later addressed in class. For students who have difficulty with memory, students can use various recording technologies or hand-held technologies to input ideas or important dates to have immediate access to this information. In addition, the use of text-to-speech software provides students with the ability to convert digital text into computerized speech (Burgstahler & Cory, 2008; Getzel, 2008; Webb et al., 2008). Because this software provides material in multimodality method (speech, written text, and the ability to manipulate the text), this software is also very helpful for students who are visual or tactile learners.

Students who learn best through hands-on experiences are tactile learners. For them, educators should structure learning situations to include a variety of activities (Burgstahler, 2008). These students need to be highly involved with class materials by using such techniques as highlighting information, developing flashcards, or demonstrating acquisition of information through the development of projects.

Creating Positive Learning Environments

By the time students with LD reach the secondary school setting, they are often discouraged about school, have negative self-concepts, and lack motivation for learning (Getzel & Thoma, 2006; Thoma & Wehmeyer, 2005). These feelings typically result from a series of negative experiences associated with school. It is important for educators to create classroom environments that are nonthreatening and to build on the strengths and capabilities of the students. Some examples of how educators can help to create a supportive environment include

1. Serving as good role models
2. Being prepared and organized
3. Developing equitable grading policies
4. Using varying teaching styles
5. Encouraging teamwork among students to develop skills

Creating an environment that enables students with LD to feel motivated about learning and that builds their self-esteem is important (Lerner & Johns, 2009). To increase their chances of success in the community, students with LD need many opportunities to learn and practice appropriate behaviors before and during the transition process. If students are given these opportunities in settings that allow them to feel comfortable with making mistakes, asking questions, and acquiring new skills, then they become more involved in their preparation for transitioning into the community. The attitudes and beliefs of teachers regarding their students are fundamental for developing positive learning settings (Lerner & Johns, 2009).

Instructing Students in a Multicultural Classroom

When discussing teaching strategies, it is important to consider working with culturally diverse students with LD (Lerner & Jones, 2009). Careful and comprehensive evaluations should be performed to ensure that these students are not incorrectly identified as having LD as a result of language differences or other cultural influences (Smith et al., 2004). When one is assessing the needs of students who are members of cultural or ethnic groups, information should be gathered concerning all of the developmental domains, cultural and linguistic influences, and family and community data (Black et al., 2003; Xu, Purvis, & Terpstra, 2010). Some suggestions for educators to consider when teaching students with LD from other culturally diverse backgrounds (Bos & Vaughn, 2006) include

a. Demonstrate ideas or concepts
b. Build on the students' previous learning

c.   Repeat important information and stress key words

d.   Provide cooperative learning experience using small groups

Assistive Technology

In recent years, the speed and breadth of technology developments have resembled the proverbial weather in the Pacific Northwest: "Wait 10 minutes and it will change." A strong emphasis on universal design for learning in technology development has opened doors for individuals who in previous years would have needed specialized assistive technology developed to meet the individual's learning and other accommodation needs. For these reasons, it is suggested that educators and other professionals focus on three areas:

1.   The principles embodied in the nondiscrimination requirements of Section 504 of the Rehabilitation Act as amended, and the Americans with Disabilities Act (ADA) of 1990 as amended by the ADA Amendments Act of 2008 (PL 110-325)

2.   Key questions to ask when adding or replacing existing technology

3.   Resources for additional information and training about technology's accessibility

The core principles of Section 504 and Title II of the ADA are equal opportunity, equal treatment, and the obligation to make modifications to avoid disability-related discrimination. As presented by the U.S. Department of Education, Office of Civil Rights (2011), educators should address accessibility issues during the technology acquisition planning process and acquisition procedures. Questions educators should ask include the following (U.S. Department of Education, 2011):

1.   What educational opportunities and benefits does the school provide through the use of this technology?

2.   What can the school do to provide students with disabilities equal access to the educational benefits or opportunities provided through the use of the technology?

3.   How will the educational opportunities and benefits provided to students with disabilities compare with the opportunities and benefits that the technology provides to students without disabilities?

4.   Are all the educational opportunities and benefits that are available through the use of the technology equally available to students with disabilities through the provision of accommodations or modifications (i.e., do students with disabilities have the opportunity to acquire the same information, engage in the same interactions, and enjoy the same services as other students)?

5.   Are the educational opportunities and benefits provided to students with disabilities in as timely a manner as those provided to students without disabilities (i.e., do the time frames under which opportunities and benefits are received by students meet the requirement that students with disabilities be provided benefits and opportunities in an equally effective and equally integrated manner)?

6.   Will it be more difficult for students with disabilities to obtain the educational opportunities and benefits than it is for students without disabilities (i.e., does ease of use for students with disabilities meet the requirement that students with disabilities be provided benefits and opportunities in an equally effective and equally integrated manner)?

Finally, to keep abreast of the rapidly changing world of technology, it is important to become familiar with several sources of up-to-date information. Examples include

•   U.S. Department of Education Office of Educational Technology, National Education Technology Plan: http://www.ed.gov/technology/netp-2010

•   Advisory Commission on Accessible Instructional Materials in Postsecondary Education for Students with Disabilities: http://www2.ed.gov/about/bdscomm/list/aim/index.html

- National Instructional Materials Access Center: http://www.nimac.us
- Bookshare for Education: http://www.bookshare.org
- Described and Captioned Media Program: http://www.dcmp.org
- Learning Ally (formerly Recording for the Blind & Dyslexic): http://www.learningally.org
- National Instructional Materials Accessibility Standard Center: http://aim.cast.org/collaborate/NIMASCtr
- The World Wide Web Consortium: http://www.w3.org/standards/
- The Center for Implementing Technology in Education: http://www.cited.org
- The Family Center on Technology and Disability: http://www.fctd.info
- National Center on Accessible Instructional Materials: http://aim.cast.org

Preparing for Transition
Postsecondary Settings

To ensure that students with LD are prepared to enter postsecondary education programs, educators should focus on transition planning by actively working with students with LD to help promote their success in higher education. This is especially important because students with LD are less likely to earn an advanced degree than their peers without disabilities (Gonzalez, Rosenthal, & Kim, 2011). Students must be prepared to academically meet the required coursework by taking challenging courses in high school that prepare them not only to enter college but also to progress through their program of study (Getzel & Wehman, 2005; Kochhar-Bryant et al., 2008; Shaw et al., 2010). In addition, planning efforts must also include direct skills instruction in self-advocacy, independent living, decision making, and working with students to identify career goals to help them establish a career and make future choices for education and training (Getzel, 2008; Hadley, 2006; Kochhar-Bryant et al., 2008; Shaw et al., 2010; Thoma & Wehman, 2010). Because of the importance of postsecondary education as a transition goal for students with disabilities, Chapter 15 provides a thorough discussion on working with students with disabilities to help them successfully make the transition from secondary to postsecondary education.

Employment

It is essential that students with LD are prepared for employment in light of recent statistics reported by the U.S. Department of Labor (2011) where 29% of youth with disabilities between the ages of 21 and 24 are employed compared with 61% of their peers without disabilities. For individuals with LD, their employment record is typically sporadic and they are frequently employed as unskilled workers (Gonzalez, Rosenthal, & Kim, 2011). It is important for students with LD and educators to understand the critical factors that contribute to individuals with LD maintaining employment. These factors include self-monitoring strategies, accommodations, and self-efficacy rather than such objective characteristics as aptitude or abilities (Seo et al., 2008). Therefore, it is vital that students with LD not only participate in activities that assist them in career-related decisions but also are provided opportunities to strengthen work-related skills that enhance their ability to self-monitor their work performance, understand their accommodations needs in employment settings, and other skills that enable them to work effectively with their co-workers (Briel & Getzel, 2005; Briel & Wehman, 2005; Getzel & Briel, 2008). Some suggested activities for students with LD to engage in while in high school to strengthen their skills include (Briel & Getzel, 2001; Briel & Getzel, 2005)

- Develop an awareness of the range of career opportunities and the requirements for those careers
- Create opportunities for career exploration and work experience during high school, even for students who are planning to attend a postsecondary school
- Obtain part-time employment or volunteer experiences to help develop work habits, enhance social skills, and explore specific career-related interests

In addition, as documented by Madaus, Gerber, and Price (2008), it is crucial that educators and other service providers instill in job seekers with LD a working knowledge of the ADA as amended; decision-making strategies on factors surrounding disclosure of one's disability in the workplace (disclose or not, and, if yes, when, to whom, and how); accommodation options (to request or not, and, if yes, how, when, and to whom); and the self-determination/ self-advocacy skills that will provide the crucial framework and foundation to survive and thrive in workplace settings. In his survey of 500 university graduates with LD, Madaus (2008) reinforced the importance of attention to these issues. He found that, although 73% of the respondents reported that LD affected their job in some way, only 55% reported self-disclosing and only 12% reported that they requested accommodations.

Strategies can be incorporated in the curriculum that include academic and career–technical educators working together to incorporate academic competencies into career–technical courses or to make academic curricula more relevant by using career-specific examples when teaching academic subjects. Cooperation among school personnel is essential to ensure that students' academic and specific career-related skills are integrated. This can be challenging with the increased focus on high-stakes testing and meeting performance standards in which greater emphasis is now placed on academic content, making it difficult to incorporate more specific career-focused classes into students' course schedules.

Conclusion

This chapter has presented a number of experiences from the perspective of the individual with LD. Readers should understand the complexity of the problems and issues that these individuals face and how their disabilities can affect all aspects of their lives. A number of ideas, strategies, and resources have been discussed for use when working with these students and their families as they move from school to the community. Individuals with LD are too often viewed in terms of what they are unable to do and not provided the opportunities to develop their skills and talents. Through appropriate services and supports and a shared commitment, these students can pursue their dreams and aspirations as they enter their adult lives.

Study Questions

1. How can LD affect a student's life in the academic, interpersonal, and employment arenas?
2. Interview a teacher and family member about why having self-determination skills is critical in achieving successful transition into adulthood.
3. Describe the most useful types of assessment strategies and reports that can be helpful to parents and educators of students with LD.
4. Describe the concept of universal design for learning and some of the strategies that can benefit students with LD in the general curriculum.
5. Meet with a local college or university's disability services office to learn about the major issues involved in preparing for transition into postsecondary setting such as college. Be sure to include issues related to employment and career advancement.

Online Resources

Casey Life Skills Assessments: http://www.caseylifeskills.org

Center for Implementing Technology in Education: http://www.cited.org

Center for Research on Learning at the University of Kansas: http://www.kucrl.org

Going to College: http://www.going-to-college.org

I'm Determined: http://www.imdetermined.org

The Learning Disabilities Association of America: http://www.ldanatl.org

Leconte, P. Transition assessment in practice: From mandate to meaning (February 15–16, 2007). Presented at the Fourth Annual Transition Conference, Stevens Point, WI: http://www.wsti.org/documents/Conference%20Handouts/Transition%20Assessment%20Manda-teto%20meaning.ppt

Misunderstood Minds: http://www.pbs.org/wgbh/misunderstoodminds

Smart Kids with LD: http://www.smartkidswithld.org

TeachingLD: http://www.dldcec.org

ThinkCollege!: http://www.thinkcollege.org

Timmons, J., Podmostko, M., Bremer, C., Lavin, D., & Wills, J. (2005, October). *Career planning begins with assessment: A guide for professionals serving youth with educational and career development challenges.* **Washington, DC: National Collaborative on Workforce and Disability for Youth, Institute for Educational Leadership:** http://www.ncwd-youth.info/career-planning-begins-with-assessment

Walker, A.R., Kortering, L.J., Fowler, C.H., & Rowe, D. (2010). *Age-appropriate transition assessment guide.* **(2nd ed.). Charlotte, NC: National Secondary Transition Technical Assistance Center, University of North Carolina at Charlotte:** http://www.nsttac.org

Applications for Youth with Emotional and Behavior Disorders

18

PAUL WEHMAN, KEVIN SUTHERLAND,
AND EDWIN O. ACHOLA

After completing this chapter, the reader will be able to

- Understand the mental health needs of students with emotional and behavior disorders
- Describe six characteristics of students with emotional and behavior disorders
- Understand how work experience and employment can benefit youth with disabilities
- Discuss the role of student choice in transition planning and vocational placement
- Be aware of several types of self-control and techniques for teaching self-control
- Discuss supported employment outcomes for individuals with emotional and behavior disorders

There are many young people in this country like James (see case study) who present challenging emotional and behavioral support needs. In fact, children and youth who are classified as having emotional and behavior disorders (EBD) represent the fourth largest category of students with disabilities in the United States, following only those with speech impairments, intellectual disabilities, and learning disabilities (U.S. Department of Education, National Center for Educational Statistics, 2007). The problems for young people with behavior disorders are complex and at times can appear insurmountable (Karpur, Clark, Caproni, & Sterner, 2005). One of the greatest obstacles to providing transition services is that 51% of these students drop out of school (Sitlington & Neubert, 2004; Newman, Wagner, Cameto, Knokey, & Shaver, 2010). These percentages are close to twice as great as those for all students with disabilities. Many of these problems begin for children at a young age when help is essential (Simpson et al., 2011). Early identification of problems leads to greater odds of successful intervention efforts. Early identification refers to both identifying problems in children as well as identifying early signs of problem behavior later on. There is evidence that early signs of difficulties are detectable (Dunlap, Strain, Fox, Carta, Conroy, Smith, et al., 2006; Fiedler, Simpson, & Clark, 2007). Unfortunately, the trend has been a reluctance to screen for problems in young children, and the tendency is to accept minor misbehavior even as it escalates until the problem is severe and no longer manageable. Because addressing meaningful educational and adult transition goals in a student's individualized education program (IEP) is impossible when the student is no longer attending school, early transition planning becomes imperative.

Transition from school to work can be a very therapeutic way for student with EBD to improve his or her outcomes. For many youth, acquiring and maintaining a job is a step to independence and gaining control over one's life that affords them a sense of self-worth and self-esteem. Unfortunately, Newman, Wagner, Cameto, Knokey, and Shaver (2010) report data that reveals that youth with EBD are still lagging behind their peers in employment. For example, the employment rates at the time of the interview for those in the EBD category ranged from 59.4% in 1990 to 40.5% in 2005, which marked an 18.9% decrease.

This report also compared perceptions of how well youth with EBD were paid, how well they were treated by others on the job, and whether they had many chances to advance in their work across disability category. The percentage of youth with EBD who reported they were "pretty well" paid for their work was 79.2% in 1990 and dropped to 70.7% in 2005. The percentage of youth who reported they were treated "pretty well" by others was 99.6% in 1990 and 92.8% in 2005. The percentage of youth who reported they had "lots of chances to work their way up" was 73.5% in 1990 and 75.4% in 2005. It is not exactly clear why these data demonstrate these declines and plateaus. It is possible that the economic slowdown in the early 2000s helped magnify this problem.

It is also interesting to take a look at these students' college experiences. A comparison across time of postsecondary school enrollment by disability was also reported. It indicated that individuals in four of the nine disability categories experienced significantly higher postsecondary enrollment rates in 2005 than in 1990, including those with emotional disturbances (35% versus 18%; $p < .001$ for all comparisons). Despite the significantly higher enrollment rates experienced by youth with EBD in 2005 compared with 1990, youth with EBD remained among those disability categories least likely to attend postsecondary school. In 2005, only 35% of those with EBD ever had enrolled in a postsecondary program.

There is increasing research literature available on how students with EBD learn in school, despite the inevitable measurement problems that exist in the evaluation of level of inclusion into general education classrooms (Simpson, Peterson, & Smith, 2011). Exposing learners with EBD to instructional practices that are deemed most promising in general education remains a challenge for many general education teachers. Landrum, Tankersley, and Kauffman (2003) suggested that many of these antecedent-based promising practices require consistency in delivery, monitoring, and adaptations beyond what most teachers find feasible. In addition, Levy and Vaughn (2002) found that, even in a special education setting, reading instruction often failed to reflect validated instructional procedures.

Efforts to identify the directionality of students' learning and behavioral problems have proven elusive. Most authorities agree that the two cannot be separated. Sutherland, Lewis-Palmer, Stichter, and Morgan (2008) noted that poor academic achievement and high rates of maladaptive behavior patterns are highly correlated, although the exact nature of that relationship is unknown. Whatever the etiology, it is becoming increasingly clear that effective intervention for students with EBD requires that behavioral and academic deficits be addressed simultaneously (Simpson, Peterson, & Smith, 2010).

Obviously, one way to improve outcomes is to ensure that teachers of students identified as EBD possess the knowledge and skills required to address the myriad challenges associated with this population of students. Simpson et al. (2011) asserted that well-trained and competent teachers are the most important part of successful programs for students with EBD. In addition, evidence-based practices that are applicable to students with EBD (e.g., Dunlap et al., 2006; Simpson et al., 2011; Yell, Meadows, Drasgow, & Shiner, 2009) have been recommended.

Even so, a gap remains between research and practice (Yell et al., 2009). So, although some progress has been made in areas including academic intervention, least-restrictive environment, and identification for services, there is much more to be done.

This chapter describes how to improve transition for students with EBD.

James   James is a 20-year-old man who was diagnosed with anxiety and depression while in high school. Even though he followed his medication schedule, James experienced debilitating mood swings. At times, he had difficulty getting up in the morning or getting out of the car at various destinations. When James would begin to feel under stress, he would often manage his stress by leaving a situation, saying that he did not feel well. His one previous job at a grocery store ended after a public outburst.

James elected to pursue a college education and majored in health and community wellness. He did not disclose his disability to the Services for Students with Disabilities Office but self-accommodated by completing two classes per semester and finishing his academic requirements in 8 years. The final requirement for graduation was to complete a 400-hour internship at a community health club. James's mother initiated an appointment with the university career education program, which was designed to assist college students with disabilities with individualized career planning and placement. James preferred part-time hours and felt that he would work best in the morning. He had visited several clubs without success. It was determined that he needed direct job development assistance to secure an internship.

Several local athletic clubs were contacted before one agreed to work with the Career Connections Program. The fitness director, James, and program staff initially met to develop a work schedule that gradually increased in days and hours. The groundwork was laid to assess and identify effective learning strategies and stress management techniques with the assistance from program staff. On the second day of work, James told the fitness director he was not feeling well and went home early. Program staff came onsite on the third day to further assess the work environment and assist with identifying stress management strategies. Preliminary assignments included observing fitness evaluations, orienting to weight machines, and reading the policy manual. More specific duties were identified that could be completed by James throughout the day, such as helping at the front desk or cleaning equipment. These tasks were identified to help James fill any unstructured time.

Program staff talked with James about what helps him to relieve stress. He identified doing exercises, taking a break, and reading. With assistance, James initiated a discussion with the fitness director about his disability and his need for an accommodation when he is feeling stressed. He selected excusing himself for a few minutes and walking outside in the parking lot as one of his primary strategies. This strategy also proved effective for having James get out of the car in the morning when he and his mother arrived at the job site.

As James neared completion of his internship, he decided to apply for services with the Department of Rehabilitative Services to secure a job coach. Informational interviews were arranged and conducted with employers at health clubs, YMCAs, and recreation centers. Successful strategies used at the internship site and potential job leads were shared with the job coach at an informal meeting with the student and the program staff. Through an informational interview, James was able to secure a part-time position as a program assistant at a YMCA near his home. Effective strategies identified during the internship placement were modified to fit the environment at his new job in the aquatics department.

Who Are Youth with Emotional Disturbance?

According to the U.S. Department of Education (2006), more than 416,000 teachers provide instruction to almost 6.5 million students with disabilities between the ages of 3 and 21 years. These students are classified according to 13 different disability categories. Among the most challenging group of students are the 475,000 that make up the category identified by the U.S. Department of Education as emotional disturbance. Among other terms, these students may be referred to as youth with emotional disabilities, behavior disorders, and EBD. In this chapter, we use the term EBD.

The Individuals with Disabilities Education Improvement Act (IDEA; 2004; PL 108-446) identifies emotional disturbance as

[A] condition exhibiting one or more of the following characteristics over a long period of time and to a marked degree that adversely affects a child's educational performance—

(a)   An inability to learn that cannot be explained by intellectual, sensory, or health factors.
(b)   An inability to build or maintain satisfactory interpersonal relationships with peers and teachers.
(c)   Inappropriate types of behavior or feelings under normal circumstances.
(d)   A general pervasive mood of unhappiness or depression.
(e)   A tendency to develop physical symptoms or fears associated with personal or school problems (Code of Federal Regulations, Title 34, §300.7[c][4][i])

As defined by IDEA, emotional disturbance includes schizophrenia but does not apply to children who are socially maladjusted, unless it is determined that they have an emotional disturbance (Code of Federal Regulation, Title 34, § 300.7[c][4][ii]).

Mooney, Denny, and Gunter noted:

Students identified with emotional disturbance have, by definition, educational difficulties resulting in "an inability to learn which cannot be explained by intellectual, sensory, or health factors …" (Individuals with Disabilities Education Act § 300.7 [b][91]). The educational difficulties of these students, whether a product of their undesirable social behaviors or the cause of them result in their generally experiencing a lifetime of less than desirable social and economic outcomes. (2004, p. 22)

Young people with EBD can be overwhelmed by demands in the community and the workplace, making the transition from school to adulthood particularly difficult. These are not typical children who have periodic behavior problems at different points in their lives. Their problems (e.g., disruptive, withdrawn behavior) tend to present themselves over the long term with significantly higher frequencies of occurrences than those seen in children without behavior disorders.

The most important challenge for the majority of these youth is the ability to better control their behavior—specifically, their impulses to do unusual or bizarre things. Reactions to anxious or stressful situations usually lead to behavior that is inappropriate and viewed negatively by peers or adults. These behavioral manifestations exist within a wider network of relationships between behavior disorders and other disabilities, or what is typically referred to as comorbidity (Dietz & Montague, 2006). Lindsay, Dockrell, and Strand (2007) described the effects and prevalence of coexistence of behavior disorders, attention-deficit and hyperactivity disorders, and language-related disabilities and noted that comorbidity elevates the level of risk for unsatisfactory school and postschool outcomes. They also indicated that language difficulties may in part explain the frustration and impaired social interaction observed in learners with behavior difficulties. Acknowledging the coexistence of other disorders is therefore critical to optimal intervention and treatment for learners with behavior disorders. As a matter of fact, comorbidity or two disability levels is not uncommon for this category, and 25%–35% of students with EBD also have characteristics of students with learning disabilities and more than 80% have academic and behavior problems (Webber & Plotts, 2008).

Therefore, it is not unusual for youth with EBD to display a number of difficulties in both academics and behavior. Students with EBD are likely to display high levels of noncompliance, aggression, poor social problem-solving skills, a tendency toward negative interactions with teachers and peers, and a lack of academic motivation (Walker, Ramsey, & Gresham, 2004). Academically, these students frequently demonstrate below-grade achievement, especially in reading (Lane, 2004; Kauffman & Landrum, 2009). Furthermore, students with emotional disabilities fail to progress academically at a rate equal to their nondisabled peers (Simpson et al., 2011).

Learning and Performance Issues

Difficulty Processing Information

Cognitive difficulties are one of the most common employment obstacles for people with some types of mental illness, particularly schizophrenia, which typically causes difficulty in screening input, sorting out what is important and what is not, and taking action on the input. This causes problems with following directions, sequencing tasks, and making decisions.

Trouble Initiating Action

Slowness in initiation or reluctance to initiate action causes people to look as if they are not motivated. This may be attributable to difficulty processing the information available in the environment—missing or misunderstanding cues. Trouble with initiation can also be attributable to a fear of making mistakes, fear of failure or success, or preoccupation with internal ruminations or hallucinations.

Difficulty Concentrating and Distractibility

This may be a symptom of an illness or a side effect of the medications that are taken to treat the illness. It may be caused by hallucinations or delusions experienced by the individual and demanding attention or a result of difficulty in sorting through and prioritizing environmental input. Changes in distractibility levels can be important feedback for the worker and/or employment specialist to give the medical consultant regarding levels of medication or possible decompensation. Additional structure and/or stronger cues may be needed for the individual to be successful on the job.

Interpersonal Issues

Social Isolation and Alienation from Feelings

An appearance of apathy, slovenliness, emotional dullness, and nonmotivation is a common residual symptom of mental illness. People may also feel anxious in the presence of others and resist interpersonal involvement. This anxiety may interfere with task completion in that the worker may appear distracted and perform poorly because he or she is focusing on how uncomfortable it makes him or her to have to interact with others. Students and workers who are socially isolated also miss out on important information regarding the (usually unwritten) behavioral rules of the classroom and workplace.

Variability of Functioning Level

Students with mood disorders generally have periods of at least relative stability between episodes of illness. The frequency of these episodes must be taken into account when one is helping people select employment. For example, a person who generally becomes ill every spring but who otherwise is able to maintain stability with medication and counseling may need to take a week or two off every year to deal with the illness, but may not need a lot of other accommodations. Another person who experiences rapid cycling and many more residual symptoms may need flexibility in the classroom.

Negative Behavior

Many students with emotional disabilities engage in negative behavior (e.g., acting out; disruptive, aggressive behavior) (Kerr & Nelson, 2010; Kauffman & Landrum, 2009; Simpson et al., 2011). In many instances, the magnitude of the problem necessitates a formal **functional behavioral assessment (FBA)** and positive plan of intervention and support (Yell et al., 2009). Furthermore, with nationwide attention on response to intervention (RTI) and positive behavior interventions and supports (PBIS) in place in more than 10,000 schools, more and more importance will be attached to function-based academic and nonacademic intervention. The same can be said about peer-mediated intervention, conflict resolution, and peer-assisted learning, each of which represents an evidence-based practice (Kerr & Nelson, 2010; Yell et al., 2009).

Classroom Strategies

In recent years, a number of researchers have begun to identify instructional practices that are effective with students with EBD (Lane, 2004). Reading (Nelson, Benner, & Mooney, 2008), writing (Mastropieri et al., 2008), and math strategies proven effective with students with emotional disturbance (Templeton, Neel, & Blood, 2008) are becoming more readily available. In addition, some researchers are attempting to identify interventions that address both academic and behavior problems (e.g., Kern & Clemens, 2007; Sutherland & Snyder, 2007).

Today, a growing number of students with EBD receive all or some of their instruction in general education classrooms (Wagner et al., 2006; Webber & Plotts, 2008). This means both special education and general education teachers must be prepared to address the diverse academic and nonacademic needs of students with EBD. In addition, federal legislation, namely No Child Left Behind (2001; PL 107-110) and IDEA (2004), has put tremendous pressure on schools to improve educational outcomes for all students by requiring both general and special education teachers to rely on evidence-based instructional practices (e.g., Kauffman & Landrum, 2009). However, as previously noted, few evidence-based practices have found their way into the classroom, and, when they do, they are not always correctly implemented (Kauffman & Landrum, 2009; Odom et al., 2005). In fact, national survey data suggest that only 24% of elementary teachers, 30% of middle school teachers, and 31% of high school teachers feel qualified to work with students with EBD (Wagner et al., 2006).

In 2010, Gable et al. conducted a review of the literature to develop a survey to assess the current status of the knowledge and skills of educational professionals in Virginia related to recommended practices with students with EBD. A list of the items included is provided in Table 18.1.

Table 18.1.   List of evidence-based practices

1. A climate that supports successful teaching and learning
2. A program of peer-mediated intervention to promote positive behavior skills
3. A conflict-resolution program
4. An anger-management program
5. Social skills instruction taught as part of regular class instruction
6. Mental health services as appropriate
7. A behavior support/management plan as appropriate
8. A system of positive behavior support
9. Academic supports and curricular/instructional modifications
10. Specialized instruction to promote learning and study skills
11. A crisis intervention plan for emergency situations
12. Materials that reflect gender, cultural, and linguistic differences among students
13. The use of peer reinforcement to promote appropriate student behavior
14. Instruction in self-monitoring of student academic performance
15. Instruction in self-monitoring of nonacademic behavior
16. A systematic approach to cooperative learning
17. Choice-making opportunities for students
18. A formal procedure to develop function-based intervention
19. A systematic approach to data collection, graphing, and analysis for intervention plans
20. Behavior contracts
21. Group-oriented contingency management
22. Peer-assisted learning
23. Clear rules/expectations
24. Precorrection instructional strategies
25. A program to transition students from preschool to elementary school, from elementary to middle school, from middle to high school, or from high school to postsecondary education and/or employment

Note: The list also included the use of physical restraint and seclusion.
From Gable, R.A., Tonelson, S.W., & Walker-Bolton, I. (2010, August 23). A survey of classroom skills of special education teachers, general education teachers, and state directors of special education for students with emotional disabilities in Virginia (pp. 12–13). In I. Walker-Bolton, R.A. Gable, S.W. Tonelson, P. Woolard, & M.K. Gable (Eds.), *Summit on better serving students with emotional disabilities sponsored by the Virginia Department of Education, Charlottesville, VA*. Richmond, VA: Virginia Department of Education; reprinted by permission. (The Virginia Department of Education is the sole copyright owner of the material and reserves all rights to the material, including, but not limited to, the rights to reprint, reproduce, transmit, copy, or distribute the material. A third party who wishes to use the material in any manner must contact the Virginia Department of Education for specific written permission unless that party falls within one of the exceptions specified in the department's policy. Any materials requested that contain copyrighted information from other parties may not be used without the expressed written consent of the person or entity that owns the copyright. These materials, product, or curriculum are not a product of or endorsed in any way by the Virginia Department of Education and have not been reviewed by that department.)

And, although implementing evidence-based practices is critical, there is another key component to providing quality education for students with EBD. Because students with EBD pose a significant challenge to their teachers, some may respond by lowering their expectations, providing easier work with fewer opportunities to respond, delivering lower rates and less contingent praise and positive reinforcement, or diverting their attention to other students (Sutherland, Conroy, Abrams, & Vo, 2010). In addition, this may be coupled with negative exchanges between students with EBD and their teachers (Sutherland & Oswald, 2005). This not only deters the student's education but can also lead to a cycle of failure (Kauffman, 2005).

Special education teachers' skills with classroom organization and behavior management affect the emergence and persistence of behavior problems as well as the success of inclusive practice for students with EBD. Simonsen et al. (2008) evaluated 81 studies and identified 20 general recommended practices in classroom management. These fell into five broad categories:

1. Maximize structure and predictability.
2. Post, teach, review, and provide feedback on expectations.
3. Actively engage students in observable ways.

4. Use a continuum of strategies to acknowledge appropriate behavior.

5. Use a continuum of strategies to respond to inappropriate behavior.

In a more recent study, Oliver and Reschly (2010) conducted a study to examine the extent to which special education teacher preparation programs provide teachers with adequate instruction in these areas (classroom organization and behavior management techniques). Course syllabi from 26 special education teacher preparation programs were reviewed. Results indicated a highly variable emphasis on classroom organization and management among programs. Programs tended to emphasize reactive procedures. Only 27% ($n = 7$) of the university programs had an entire course devoted to classroom management. The remaining 73% ($n = 19$) of university programs had content related to behavior management dispersed within various courses.

Unique Challenges and Issues for Youth with Emotional and Behavior Disorders

The challenges and issues for youth with EBD are at times overwhelming (Katsiyannis & Yell, 2004). Millions of children and youth experience significant psychological and behavior problems (Zhang, Katsiyannis, & Herbst, 2004). The most revealing evidence about the difficulties that these youth experience comes from the evaluations of disciplinary exclusions of all students with disabilities. Zhang et al. noted:

> Students with disabilities are more likely to commit offences resulting in exclusion because of poor social skills, judgment, and planning as well as being less adept in avoiding detection (Leone, Mayer, Malmgren, & Meisel, 2000). According to Leone and colleagues, data from various sources, including Gun-Free School reports and individual states (i.e., Kansas, Kentucky, Maryland, Delaware, Minnesota), revealed that students with disabilities were disproportionately represented in disciplinary exclusions: While approximately 11% of all students ages 6 to 21 receive services under IDEA, close to 20% of students who are suspended are students with disabilities. The data sources, however, did not involve nationally representative data and only occasionally reported exclusions by disability. (2004, p. 37)

Over the years, some structured programs have begun to emerge that are targeted at the prevention of dropouts or helping dropouts get back into school (Hoover & Stenhjem, 2003). The percentage of students with emotional disturbance, ages 14–21 years, served under IDEA, Part B, who dropped out of school, by disability category and year, 1995–1996 through 2004–2005, are reported respectively at 69.9% and 48.2%. Although these figures illustrate an improvement in the dropout rate, as an aggregate group, youth with EBD hold the highest dropout rate among the students within the different disability groups reported (U.S. Department of Education, 2006). Sitlington and Neubert (2004) indicated that only 34%–54% of students with behavior disorders out of school 3–5 years were enrolled in postsecondary education compared with 68% of students in general education. And perhaps one of the most telling statistics of all is that only 40% of adults with behavior disorders are employed—a stark contrast to the employment rate for the general population of adults and students (Newman et al., 2010).

Work as a Way to Manage Disability

As noted earlier, a major challenge that educators and counselors must face in working with these students is helping them to obtain both paid and nonpaid work experiences while still in school. We know that productive work is therapeutic, meaning it can help manage depression, anger, and frustration (Bond, McHugo, Becker, Rapp, & Whitley, 2008; Cook, Blyler, et al., 2008; Drake & Bond, 2008). Hence, it is critical that individuals with EBD are not kept from work because of behavior problems but instead are supported at the job site with appropriate behavioral interventions (Wehman, Inge, Revell, & Brooke, 2007). Improved postschool employment outcomes for students with disabilities who have participated in work-based training have been reported by many researchers (Krupa, 2004). Owens-Johnson and Johnson (1999) wrote an excellent summary on the postschool prospects for students with behavior disorders. They noted that the American dream of education, employment, and responsible citizenship is likely to be an elusive proposition for students who have not developed the necessary skills to be successful in school, let alone on the job. Successful employment outcomes for this population are positively correlated with variables such as vocational education coursework. Sitlington and Neubert (2004) favor inclusion of learners with EBD in career–technical education, increased parent involvement, paid work experience, and counseling in high school to boost the prospects of positive adult outcomes.

Positive Behavior Support

The second challenge professionals face is providing humanistic, nonaversive behavioral and psychological interventions in natural environments for young people with behavior disorders. Training in the community, instructing in the workplace, and teaching mobility within the community are essential elements for promoting transition. Also, use of typically developing peers to avoid behavior problems (Brown, Odom, McConnell, & Rathrel, 2008) is another strategy that is therapeutic and constructive. Often, however, designing and implementing behavioral interventions in natural environments is preempted for training in controlled environments, such as classrooms or institutions. Zuna and McDougall observed:

> One of the most frequent concerns expressed by teachers and administrators is how to manage behavioral problems in the classroom. Behavior that disrupts instruction is problematic for teachers and students, in part, because we have known for quite some time that the amount of time students engage actively in academic tasks is positively correlated to how much they learn (Black, 2004). Functional assessment and positive behavioral support (PBS) are two management approaches that are extensions of applied behavior analysis. Unlike some classroom management practices that rely heavily on aversive consequences, these approaches use more proactive techniques to manage challenging behavior and increase students' active engagement in learning. (2004, p. 18)

The entire issue of physical restraint and also use of seclusion as methods of controlling highly inappropriate and at time dangerous social behavior has been addressed by the Council for Exceptional Children's Division on Behavior Disorders (2009, pp. 223–243). The document provides policy recommendations that include

a.   An introduction to the problem

b.   A declaration of principles

c.   A clear statement of recommendations regarding the use of physical restraint and/or seclusion in school settings

As a result of the challenging behavior of students with EBD (Kerr & Nelson, 2010, Simpson et al., 2011), thousands of schools are implementing RTI and/or PBIS for both learning and behavior problems. The fact that some teachers indicated that they lacked adequate preparation in formal procedures to develop function-based interventions is disconcerting. In addition, the same can be said about other evidence-based practices such as peer-mediated intervention, conflict resolution, and peer-assisted learning (Kerr & Nelson, 2010; Yell et al., 2009). Finally, most general education teachers indicated that they seldom give students choice-making opportunities and neither special educators nor general educators attached much importance to or made much use of group-oriented contingency management strategies. Both of these strategies are relatively easy to implement and have strong empirical support (e.g., Kerr & Nelson, 2010; Landrum et al., 2003). The analysis of the responses of directors of special education suggests a similar knowledge/skill gap with regard to the research literature on a number of evidence-based practices in programs of students with EBD.

Horner and colleagues (1990) were among the first to provide a description of positive behavior interventions and support (PBIS). Since then, leaders such as Reid and Parsons (2003) have extended PBIS with extensive curricula. There have been many additional compilations of applied literature and practical applications of PBIS. Several researchers have evaluated program-wide PBIS models (Hemmeter, Fox, Jack, Broyles, & Doubet, 2007) and classroom-based PBIS models (Sutherland, Conroy, Abrams, & Vo, 2010). These works, along with the emergence of a journal specifically devoted to positive behavior support (i.e., *Journal of Positive Behavior Interventions*), can be argued to constitute evidence of a field that has emerged from that of applied behavior analysis. This latter point was discussed further by Carr and colleagues, who described PBIS as the "evolution of an applied science" (2002, p. 4), one that has emerged primarily from applied behavior analysis, the normalization/inclusion movement, and person-centered values. In summary, PBIS has been an evidence-based approach for dealing with young children's problem behaviors. However, because PBIS has been primarily a conceptual approach for service delivery, several critical factors make examining its efficacy challenging. For instance, the lack of a standardized definition of PBIS, clear measures of implementation fidelity by teachers within classrooms, validation of technical assistance and professional development programs, and taking the procedures to scale have remained pressing issues for the field (Marshall, Brown, Conroy, & Knopf, 2011).

Individualizing Curricula

A third challenge is individualizing curricula to meet the unique and specific psychological and educational needs of students with behavior disorders (Kline & Silver, 2004). Teachers must be able to address the psychological needs of each student in conjunction with his or her educational and vocational needs, ideally with concrete instruction in real-life environments. Instead of trying to solve and eradicate the student's underlying problems, time is better spent developing an array of competent vocational and community skills, especially for those with autism, as the limited data on this population show. Regardless of disability, it is critical that teachers understand and follow this approach in transition planning (Wehman, 2002a).

Owens and Dieker (2003) examined how students with EBD look at their teachers and evaluated what is important in their teaching abilities. Table 18.2 lists rich curriculum, positive behaviors, and student-centered connections.

Table 18.2. Student recommendations on effective teaching

Rich curriculum	• Allow for more group activities and projects.
	• Show enthusiasm when teaching.
	• Allow for more discussion and expression of students in class.
	• Relate the information to your students' lives (current and future).
Embracing positive behaviors	• Hold high expectations.
	• Explain the "rules" clearly and provide consistent consequences regardless of labels or race.
	• Encourage students to do their best regardless of their label or race.
Weaving student-centered connections	• Understand issues students face today.
	• Get to know students and their families.
	• Get to know students in and out of school.
	• Communicate with students at their level.
	• Identify and connect students with services within and outside the school setting.

From Owens, L., and Dieker, L.A. (2003). How to spell success for secondary students labeled EBD: How students define effective teachers. *Beyond Behavior, 12*(2), 19–23. Copyright 2003 by the Council for Children with Behavioral Disorders. http://www.ccbd.net. Reprinted with Permission.

Dropout Issues

Youth with EBD have the highest dropout rate among students with disabilities (U.S. Department of Education, 2006). In 2005, the National Longitudinal Transition Study-2 also reported a high dropout rate stating that 52.6% of youth with EBD did not complete high school. In fact, it has been estimated that between 43% and 56% of adolescents with EBD either drop out or are expelled from school (Webber & Plotts, 2008).

The poor outcomes students with EBD demonstrate in school appear to accrue as they transition to postsecondary educational programs or to the workplace in the community as adults. Few students with EBD pursue a postsecondary education (Kauffman & Landrum, 2009; Webber & Plotts, 2008). Only students with multiple disabilities have lower rates of postsecondary education. Furthermore, youth and young adults with EBD exhibit the highest rate of unemployment of any disability category. In fact, 3–5 years after leaving high school, approximately half are unemployed (Rosenberg, Westling, & McLeskey, 2008). Those who do have jobs are employed in relatively low-status and high–turnover jobs (Rosenberg et al., 2008) and do not live independently (Webber & Plotts, 2008).

Despite these outcomes, secondary schools continue to implement academic curricula and allocate resources as if to prepare students exclusively for college rather than employment. This is much further complicated by the demands for high-stakes testing success (see Chapter 7; also Sitlington & Neubert, 2004). For many students, particularly those with disabilities, to make a successful transition from school to work, educators must provide them with vocational training and meaningful work experiences. Vocational success depends on three types of skills: job-related academic skills, job-related vocational skills, and job-related social skills (Schoen & Nolen, 2004).

With the growing number of evidence-based practices, we now have the knowledge and skills to better serve students with EBD and decrease dropout rates. Van Acker (2010) provided a number of recommendations related to professional development and support. For example,

a. In-service professional development programs must focus attention on evidence-based practices.

b. Both general education and special education teachers must not only be adequately prepared but also have strong administrative and collegial support in their efforts to provide a quality education to all students.

In addition, Van Acker (2010) reported that effective systems of peer feedback need to be introduced into our schools to facilitate teacher–pupil interactions that promote both academic and social–emotional success. We also must also increase our efforts to employ strength-based interventions that build upon the positive attributes of the student.

Van Acker (2010) listed additional recommendations:

a. Find more effective assessment tools and assessment practices to increase our ability to identify students with emotional disabilities.

b. Researchers must continue to identify empirically based interventions to address both the academic and the behavioral problems of students with EBD.

c. Work to identify classroom variables that might serve to either add to or detract from the effectiveness of various interventions.

d. Find ways to create a classroom environment that is conducive to successful teaching and learning.

Simpson, Peterson, and Smith (2011) also described critical education program components for students with EBD:

a. Qualified and committed professionals

b. Utilitarian environmental supports

c. Effective behavior management plans

d. Valid social skill and social interpretation training and social interaction programs

e. Proven academic support systems

f. Strong parent and family involvement programs

g. Coordinated community support mechanisms

h. Ongoing evaluation of essential program components and student outcomes and progress

Juvenile Justice

More and more students with EBD are finding their way into the juvenile justice system. They have to go into the courts for consequences associated with inappropriate or illegal community behavior. Juvenile detention homes function like jails, providing secure confinement for youths awaiting trial who are at risk to themselves or to the community. According to the Coalition for Juvenile Justice (*Richmond Times Dispatch*, 2004), between 300,000 and 600,000 young people cycle through juvenile detention each year. The length of time they spend incarcerated ranges from 1 day to several months. Zhang, Hsien-Yuan, Katsiyannis, Barrett, and Song (2011) reported on a sample of 5,500 juveniles with disabilities with a common pattern of recidivism. Zhang et al. (2010) also observed that truancy remains a persistent concern, with serious consequences for the individual, family, and society, as truancy is often linked to academic failure, disengagement with school, school dropout, and delinquency. This study analyzed large-scale data covering multiple years of cohorts of delinquent youths born between 1981 and 1988. Truancy offenders tend to be referred to the juvenile justice system at an earlier age, be juveniles with a family criminal history, and have received special education services. Caucasians, girls, juveniles from lower-income families, and juveniles who did not use drugs were more likely to be referred for truancy offenses than for other offenses. Implications of these findings for practice and future research were addressed.

Some youth are incarcerated because they have failed to appear for their court hearing or did not comply with the rules imposed by the judge or probation officer. Consider the case of Lawrence, who is 15. He was convicted of petty larceny, stealing from a clothing store with his friends. He attended only one group session to which he was ordered and has been irregular in his school attendance. His absences, not the theft, led to his first incarceration.

Some youth are confined while they await a permanent placement outside their homes; occasionally, some are detained simply because they have no other place to go. Lucinda, for instance, has been in and out of foster care; she is currently waiting for a space in a group home. At 15, she is a chronic runaway; the last time she left, she stole her stepfather's wallet. Both Lawrence and Lucinda are troubled but hardly dangerous. They require consequences that will change their behavior positively; incarceration most likely will have the opposite effect.

Once youngsters are confined, their parents frequently let them linger there, as they are often overburdened and relieved to have them off the streets. While in detention, these youths are exposed to—and often intimidated by—those charged with crimes that range from car-jacking to assault to murder. Like any adolescent, they seek to fit in, and they begin to develop a new sense of identity influenced by the maladaptive norms and social pecking order of a correctional institution (Lane, Wehby, Little, & Cooley, 2005a, 2005b).

Griller-Clark and Unruh (2010) noted that reentry outcomes for formerly incarcerated youth are dismal. The challenges these youth face are even further intensified when they have learning or emotional and behavioral disabilities. Successful transition services need to be initiated in the correctional facility and continue in the community.

In a recent work, Nelson, Jolivette, and Leone (2010) reported on the current status of at-risk and adjudicated youth with behavioral challenges, noting that this provides a context for addressing needed future directions for research and practice in fields that impact this population. This context includes the myriad characteristics and complex needs of these youth, the programs and services currently available in communities and secure settings, and youth outcomes following incarceration.

The authors state at the forefront that there must be a fundamental change in the attitudes and behavior of adults, from those in direct contact with children and youth in schools, courts, and day and residential settings to those who make public policy and those who vote for policy makers. They offer some recommendations anchored within the mission of Council for Children with Behavioral Disorders (CCBD)—the premier organization advocating the appropriate education and delivery of opportunities for youth with and at risk for EBD.

The first recommendation is to initiate a social marketing campaign. The authors believe that a vigorous public awareness and education campaign could be based on the cost savings of keeping youth in school and preventing their incarceration and of providing services during incarceration that offer valid evidence of effectiveness in reducing recidivism.

The next recommendation is to initiate a juvenile justice focus within CCBD. As part of the current efforts to reenergize the organization, it would seem prudent to reach out to members who are working with youth with EBD who are incarcerated or at risk of incarceration, as well as to recruit new members who are doing so. Linking with other organizations and disciplines that advocate for and serve incarcerated juveniles also would increase visibility and political clout.

They also recommend promoting implementation of evidence-based practices in secure settings. Today, there are few empirical studies of the effects of academic and social evidence-based practices in secure settings. They state the framework for this continuum should be based on the three-tiered PBIS model and involve RTI decisions made from youth academic and social data as well as their transition goals. Much work is needed across academic subjects, topographies of behavior, and academic, social, and transition goals. Additionally, PBIS should be viewed as a facility-wide intervention in secure settings as a means to unify consistent expectations and services across all systems (e.g., education, housing, security, recreation, vocation, mental health).

Another recommendation is to launch a new federal juvenile justice EBD initiative. The national Emotional Disability Juvenile Justice Center had a productive, if brief, history. It also marked the extraordinary collaboration between two federal bureaucracies—the Department of Education and the Department of Justice—as well as multiple universities, research, and policy centers. Given the issues and trends noted previously, it may be time to propose another national center focused on moving forward an agenda that promotes more effective strategies for

a. Preventing delinquency and incarceration

b. Addressing programming needs in secure facilities

c. Reintegrating youth back into their local schools and communities

d. Supporting policy changes with high-quality research

The final recommendation focuses on professional development. Specifically, they recommend that the U.S. Department of Education, U.S. Department of Justice, and CCBD or other partnerships promote, fund, and support research and development of multimedia instructional technology that also embeds follow-up components to assess for effects as well as fidelity of implementation.

Bullying, Victimization, and Aggressive Behavior

Bullying, peer victimization, and aggressive behavior in the school context are associated with a host of negative consequences that impact not only adjustment but also academic outcomes of youth with EBD. To illustrate, studies indicate that peer victimization is significantly related to increased internalizing (e.g., Hawker & Boulton, 2000; Paul & Cillessen, 2003) and externalizing (e.g., Hodges, Boivin, Vitaro, & Bukowski, 1999; Sullivan, Farrell, & Kliewer, 2006) behaviors. Both victims and aggressors are also at risk for becoming disengaged from school as reflected by lower levels of support from students and teachers, increased absenteeism, and academic failure (e.g., Orpinas & Horne, 2006). One study found that victimized students reported increased school avoidance and decreased class participation and that these behaviors mediated relations between victimization and lower academic achievement (Buhs, Ladd, & Herald, 2006).

Bullying refers to the systematic use of physical or psychological power by a stronger child against a weaker child (Olweus, 2001). Aggression is commonly defined in broader strokes, usually including primarily behavioral topographies. "According to Brain (1994), an aggressive act must a) have the potential to harm, b) be accompanied by arousal, c) be intentional, and d) be aversive for the victim" (Gumpel & Sutherland, 2010). Accordingly, bullying and aggression are not synonymous: All bullies are aggressors, but not all aggressors are bullies. Despite the fact that the empirical differentiation between bullying and aggressive behavior is at times unclear, a large body of research has conceptualized bullying as a subset of general youth aggression (Boulton, Bucci, & Hawker, 1999). In general, it appears that intentionality may be a relevant and defining feature (Arora, 1996; Gumpel & Meadan, 2000), where bullying is intentional; however, aggression as a more general category may or may not be intentional and can be either instrumental or reactive. In the present context, physical bullying is a subset of physical aggression.

Because of the negative consequences of bullying, victimization, and aggression for children and adolescents, it is concerning that studies suggest that youth with disabilities are at higher risk than their typically developing peers for experiencing peer victimization and/or engaging in aggressive behavior (e.g., Kaukiainen et al., 2002; McNamara, Willoughby, & Chalmers, 2005). For example, in a national study of more than 20,000 adolescents in grades 7–12, adolescents with learning disabilities (LD) were at significantly higher risk for involvement in aggression, as both victims and perpetrators, than youth without LD (Svetaz, Ireland, & Blum, 2000). Also, in a study of 230 adolescents with LD, 92 with comorbid LD and attention-deficit/hyperactivity disorder (ADHD), and 322 adolescents without disabilities, both the groups with LD and LD/ADHD were at elevated risk for peer victimization compared with the group without disabilities (McNamara et al., 2005). Similarly, Kaukiainen et al. (2002) examined experiences of bullying and victimization among 141 early adolescents including youth with and without LD. A distinct group of children with LD emerged who scored high on bullying behavior and also tended to be victimized.

Research on exposure to school violence (as both perpetrators and victims) and students with EBD is scarce but has shown that characteristics of students identified and diagnosed with EBD might predispose them to experience school violence at rates greater than those of their peers, both with and without disabilities (Gumpel & Sutherland, 2010). Students with EBD present challenging behaviors to peers and adults, including relationship problems, aggression, and oppositionality (Webber & Plotts, 2008; Sutherland et al.,

2010). Antisocial behavior patterns that characterize students with EBD include both externalizing (e.g., aggression, delinquency) and internalizing (e.g., anxiety, depression, withdrawal) behavior. Externalizing behaviors, which are typical of many students identified
as EBD, tend to be more stable, be more resistant to intervention, and, consequently, have a
worse prognosis for remediation relative to internalizing behaviors (Hinshaw, 1992). Both
externalizing and internalizing behaviors have been linked to increases in peer-reported
victimization (Hodges et al., 1999) and victimization predicted increases in externalizing
and internalizing behaviors for children without a mutual best friendship.

Characteristics typically associated with students with EBD (e.g., disruptive, aggressive, anxious, withdrawn) are strikingly similar to characteristics used to describe bully–
victims (e.g., impulsive, provocative behavior, low social status; Gumpel & Sutherland,
2010). The social deficits of students with EBD may predispose them to being school aggressors and/or bullies, being targeted by bullies, and, in combination with tendencies for
aggressive and impulsive behavior, students with EBD may also be more likely to become
reactive aggressors. Furthermore, estimates for the prevalence of EBD in the total school
population range from 3% to 6% (Kauffman, 2005), which closely approximates current
estimates of aggressor–victims (3% and 7% for girls and boys, respectively; Gumpel, 2008).

Recently, Rose, Monda-Amaya, and Espelage (2011) conducted an excellent review of
the literature on bullying and victimization. These authors provide an up-to-date review
of this growing problem in the schools.

Implications for Intervention

Although it is hypothesized that students with EBD would be overrepresented in the
bully–victim category, research is sorely needed to test this hypothesis (Gumpel &
Sutherland, 2010). Certainly not all students with EBD are "reactive aggressors," but research and treatment implications for those that do fall in this category are significant.
For example, social skills and social competence training programs that target specific
deficits of reactive aggressors might be combined with interventions targeting classroom
and school social structures, as well as professional development for teachers and administrators, to help modify contexts that support bullying behavior and serve as antecedents for reactive aggression. This is particularly relevant for teacher training, as classroom
environments may either encourage or inhibit bullying behaviors (Espelage & Swearer,
2003; Rodkin & Hodges, 2003). For example, Rodkin and Hodges pointed out that children
may accept, but not internalize, adult-generated rules regarding bullying and aggression.
Thus, teachers must be aware of peer ecologies and social strata in the classroom to maximize the impact of preventative interventions. Given the role of the classroom context, and
specifically the role that the classroom teacher may play in the development of bullying
behavior, students with EBD may be at even greater risk because of the severe shortage of
teachers for this population (U.S. Department of Education, 2001). To illustrate further, by
failing to attract and retain qualified teachers, school districts are often forced to hire un-
qualified teachers (George, George, Gersten, & Grosenick, 1995), resulting in many teachers of students with EBD being young and inexperienced (Stempien & Loeb, 2002). Hence,
the question arises: To what extent are school aggressors a function of individual psychopathology and to what extent are they a function of school variables? Or, to what extent are
schools more prone to violence than are children (Gumpel & Sutherland, 2010)?

An additional implication for research and training involves the social roles that students inhabit in their classroom and school ecologies. Rodkin and Hodges (2003) pointed
out, for example, that social skills training programs, which have emphasized the acquisition of social skills, have evolved from the hypothesized link between peer rejection and
aggression. Recent research has indicated, however, that aggressive students, including
students with disabilities, can be well-integrated into the classroom social structure, affili-
ating with groups of students who are made up of more than 50% nonaggressive children

(Estell, Farmer, Cairns, & Cairns, 2002; Farmer, 2000; Farmer et al., 2002). Herein lies both a potential explanation for the small effect sizes associated with social skills training and students with EBD (Mathur, Kavale, Quinn, Forness, & Rutherford, 1998) and LD (Forness & Kavale, 1996), as well as implications for future research involving social skills training. For example, some have recommended that preventative interventions target not only aggressive students but also the peer context, including nonaggressive peers that might support aggressive behavior (Farmer et al., 2002). Rodkin and Hodges noted that "children who are neither bullies or victims can be a part of the solution or part of the problem" (2003, p. 395).

Research has also shown that the presence of friends helps to buffer children from bullies (American Medical Association, 2002; Baugh, 2003). Experts must encourage students to demonstrate leadership in recognizing bullying, refusing to participate, and coming to the aid of victims skillfully and nonviolently. However, to do so, we must promote a safe, caring environment in which youth feel comfortable in speaking out against bullying, and adults must, therefore, respect youth's voices and perspectives on their personal experiences with bullying.

Today, schools typically respond to bullying, or other school violence, with reactive, punitive measures. However, metal detectors, cameras, or hiring police has no tangible positive results. "Zero tolerance" policies rely on exclusionary measures (suspension, expulsion) that have long-term negative effects. Instead, researchers advocate school-wide prevention programs that promote a positive school and community climate. Such programs require the participation and commitment of students, parents, educators, and members of the community. Effective school programs include early intervention, parent training, teacher training, and a positive school climate.

Discipline and Functional Assessment

Discipline and functional assessment is a key aspect of required skills and services for youth with EBD. IDEA 2004 addressed FBA for students with special behavior needs after much discussion.

The debate surrounding the 2004 reauthorization of IDEA testifies to educators' growing concerns about the rights of students with disabilities as they relate to school discipline (Gable, 1999; Skiba & Peterson, 2000). It appears that, as schools increase the number of students with disabilities in general education settings (U.S. Department of Education, 2002), they also exclude them rather quickly for misbehavior. In response to the reported rise in youth violence (Gumpel & Sutherland, 2010), local school boards and state legislatures frequently mandate school discipline programs that focus on the reduction of violent or aggressive behavior through punishment (e.g., expulsion, suspension, and time out). As a result, schools must increasingly balance the provisions of school disciplinary codes with students' rights to a free appropriate public education as detailed in IDEA 2004.

As a way to assess behavior of students with EBD, functional assessment was included originally in IDEA 1997 (PL 105-17) as well as IDEA 2004. Despite some concerns about the validity of this approach for public policy decisions (Conroy, Alter, & Scott, 2009), the law requires schools to recognize the relationship between student behavior and classroom learning. This legislation compels education authorities to deal positively with the discipline, invoking the behavior of students with disabilities. Functional behavioral assessment is enhanced through functional analysis of behaviors. The term *functional analysis* is used to describe the systematic manipulation of antecedent and/or consequent events that are hypothesized as being related functionally to the occurrence of the problem behavior. Functional analyses are done most often under controlled experimental conditions rather than in applied (i.e., clinical, educational) contexts. FBA is the process of identifying established operations, antecedent variables, and consequent events that control target behaviors. In other words, an FBA identifies when, where, and why problem behaviors occur and when, where, and why they do not occur.

Literature regarding FBA in general education environments has been critical of the paucity of research in such settings, given the complex and often time-consuming nature of FBA (Scott, Alter, & McQuillan, 2010). Less complex team-based FBA processes have been suggested as a realistic alternative for general education environments and Scott et al. (2010) suggested that simplifying practices and language associated with FBA will allow teachers and other practitioners to use this technology more effectively. These authors propose and illustrate a model that maintains the integrity of the primary components of the FBA process while providing clear procedures for implementation in school-based settings.

The Need for Highly Qualified Teachers

Cook, Landrum, Tankersley, and Kauffman stated that "there is little or no systematic, institutionalized support for teachers attempting to implement effective practices" (2003, p. 353). Available research appears to question the current capacity of teachers in the field to implement and sustain effective instruction procedures within the general education setting (e.g., Vaughn, Klingner, & Hughes, 2004). In addition, Wehby, Lane, and Falk (2003) noted that there is a growing body of evidence to support the significant academic and social benefits gained when teachers display more competence in the instructional procedures utilized. For example, Sutherland, Alder, and Gunter (2003) indicated that teacher instructional behavior could be improved by providing regular feedback regarding critical teaching behaviors to the teacher and then having the teacher observe data representing the rate of performance of those behaviors. These data were subsequently graphed at the rate at which those behaviors were observed.

Smith and Daunic discussed the merits of prevention research in the behavior disorder field. They are under way with a major study to examine how peers without disabilities can influence positive behavior in students with behavioral challenges. They observed

> Teaching students with EBD alongside typically functioning peers can minimize stigmatization, facilitate monitoring and social skill reinforcement, and maximize generalization throughout the school day. Using a theoretically based, randomized, controlled prevention trial approach, we are studying the effects of a universal cognitive-behavioral intervention designed to help students develop positive solutions to social problems in anger-provoking situations. Our research, however, requires a blend of requisite social science with practical considerations. (2004, p. 72)

Most teachers and education personnel who work with students with EBD possess experience and training only in special education. Furthermore, most educators are not trained well enough to know how to help these students.

How special education teachers are trained is also important. For example, Nougaret (2002) examined the teaching behavior of teachers with limited preparation. In this investigation, it was seen that first-year teachers who had participated in a traditional education program greatly outperformed first-year teachers with emergency provisional licensure on observational ratings of planning and preparation, classroom environment, and instruction. Results from this study supported earlier studies that reported higher levels of competence in traditional teacher preparation programs, extending these findings to the field of special education. The study illustrates the importance of systematic training in developing special education teachers who are highly qualified in pedagogy as well as content.

Transition Assessment

The philosophy of assessing the vocational and transition needs of youth with EBD is similar to that of all students with disabilities. The focus must be on a community-referenced approach to assessment that specifically asks students about their career and vocational goals. Because of difficulties with the reliability of their responses, it is important to ask about career goals several times and, more important, to observe what their preferences seem to be. Figure 18.1 lists questions that teachers and vocational counselors can ask students; their answers should be shared with parents or guardians. Positive vocational experiences can lead to positive adjustments in the transition process as job motivation and interest are key factors in job satisfaction, which can improve many negative behaviors.

After determining each student's career and vocational interests, teachers must ascertain each student's community living, mobility, recreation, and personal goals. Assessing curriculum targets within these areas is the key to designing good secondary special education programs and effecting positive transitions. Without such an assessment, disgruntlement, boredom, and exacerbation of the student's problems are likely to occur, which often leads to suspension, expulsion, or dropping out.

After making a reliable determination of students' choices and needs, efforts should be channeled into vocational situational assessments (Inge & Moon, 2011). Situational assessments (i.e., the objective quantitative evaluation of student performance in different work settings) are valuable for determining work responses under varied conditions. By varying the stress conditions of the work assessments and modifying the nature of commands and tasks, work performance data can be compiled and potential can be determined. Real-life vocational situational assessments that yield more practical information are recommended over the use of standardized vocational evaluations.

Vocational assessments should help to obtain information about a student's aptitudes, interests, work habits, socialization skills, work attitudes, and work tolerance and can also be used to help structure students' planning and preparation for further postsecondary training (Inge & Moon, 2011). Vocational assessments provide information in response to the following questions:

- Where is the student in the vocational awareness, exploration, or preparation process?
- In what type of occupations does the student show the greatest interest?
- In what occupational area(s) does the student show aptitude and ability?
- Are there specific learning requirements that will need to be incorporated into a student's educational program to help him or her prepare to enter a specific line of work?

Table 18.3 lists eight recommendations for transition assessment that the educator needs to consider when planning for transition.

Teaching for Transition

Many teachers who work with youth with EBD focus their curricula and instructional efforts exclusively on academic skills, neglecting career and vocational education

---

Values are the qualities, characteristics, or ideas that we feel strongly about. What are your values and what would it take for you to be happy at work?

What are your strengths? How do these relate to work?

What are your bad habits or weaknesses? What impact will these have on employment? What changes can you make to help correct these challenges?

What type of work interests you, and why?

What type of work does not interest you, and why?

Describe your ideal job. What does it look like? How does it feel?

Describe your ideal work day.

What technical skills do you have?

What skills do you have that are transferable from your life experiences (e.g., being on time, communication, getting along with others, organization)?

What personality characteristics do you possess that will make you a valued employee?

Figure 18.1. A sample career planning questionnaire. (From HAMILL, D., TEACHING STUDENTS WITH LEARNING AND BEHAVIOR PROBLEMS, 5th Edition, © 1990. Reprinted by permission of Pearson Education, Inc., Upper Saddle River, NJ.)

Table 18.3.   Recommendations for transition assessments

1. Select assessment instruments and procedures first on the basis of how they address these key questions in a student's individual transition planning: Who am I? What do I want in life, now and in the future?
2. Make transition assessment ongoing.
3. Use multiple types and levels of assessments.
4. Make 3-year psychoeducational reevaluations count for all students.
5. Think of assessment procedures in terms of efficiency as well as effectiveness.
6. Develop a transition assessment approach that is not only fair but also enhanced in terms of gender, culture, and language.
7. Organize assessment data for easy access in individualized education program planning and instructional programming.
8. Someone in the school needs to take primary responsibility for arranging and coordinating various kinds of assessments and evaluations for transition planning.

From Clark, G.M. (1998). *Assessment for transition planning: Transition series* (pp. 72–74). Austin, TX: PRO-ED; reprinted by permission.

curriculum. The following list of units of instruction provides teachers with ideas for developing opportunities to participate in community activities:

- Financial and legal aspects of employment
- Attitudes and skills that may lead to promotion
- Job applications and interviews
- Requirements of different occupations
- Occupational interests
- Private and other employment agencies
- Managing time and activities
- Getting along with co-workers
- Coping with frustration and failure at a job
- Identifying different sources of employment
- Understanding employer and supervisor expectations

Creative teachers turn these units into real-life experiences for students, using guest speakers, such as students with disabilities who are working effectively in the community, and panels of professionals. The optimal way to teach these skills, however, is through placement in paying jobs. Concrete actions and practices are particularly important for students with behavior disorders. These students usually have the necessary skills to determine whether an activity is real or simulated. For example, a 3-day internship at a dry cleaning shop, in which a teacher can help the student to manage his or her frustrations and develop work motivation, is far more useful to students than viewing videos or PowerPoint presentations in the classroom. Students learn best when they experience repeated practice and reinforcement, especially when learning how to manage their own behavior. It is essential that teachers, job coaches, counselors, aides, volunteers, or university students provide frequent on-site communication with employers and students.

Unfortunately, students with EBD tend to lack real-life opportunities to develop work-related skills. To illustrate, Carter, Trainor, Cakiroglu, Swedeen, and Owens (2010) surveyed administrators at 34 high schools across 26 school districts and found an average of 14 career development activities available to students with EBD and other disabilities during the previous school year. However, these authors noted that the three career development activities that have the most potential for youth with EBD (school-based enterprises, job placement services, and workplace mentorship opportunities) were the least commonly offered activities in the surveyed high schools. Economic self-sufficiency and greater independence in controlling personal finances should be tackled after the student is performing reasonably well in his or her job. Examples for lessons in this area include

1. Managing money through budgeting
2. Learning how to shop by using catalogs
3. Understanding costs of goods and services
4. Considering price versus quality factors when shopping
5. Comparing prices of different brands or sizes
6. Grocery shopping
7. Understanding sales
8. Reading advertisements
9. Making simple home furnishing purchases
10. Caring for personal possessions
11. Understanding banking services
12. Understanding credit and bank loans
13. Understanding and selecting insurance
14. Saving money

These skills are necessary for competent and well-adjusted transitions. Because many students with EBD are not intellectually slow or delayed, they can acquire many of these skills. They must, however, be taught in a stimulating and creative fashion with an emphasis on competence, not process. Carter, Trainor, Owens, et al. (2010) noted that the poor postschool outcomes experienced by youth with EBD are associated with, among other things, the career development and vocational experiences they are or are not provided during high school.

Teaching Self-Control and Self-Management Strategies

Self-control training can take place in the community, where the process of independent living presents many decision-making situations. Self-control may be required in the following activities:

1. Maintaining a balanced diet
2. Staying on a regular work schedule
3. Washing and caring for clothes
4. Managing money
5. Using discretion in choosing friends and deciding whom to trust

Situations that arise in public places where frustration tolerance may be low are perfect opportunities to practice self-control, such as riding crowded buses, waiting in lines, following directions, dealing with cab drivers, and interacting with hostile service clerks.

Self-management strategies can also be utilized in the workplace. For vocational adjustment, self-control should be used in task performance and social skills. Social behavior, such as the proper use of break time, being prompt, and giving appropriate social greetings, can be incorporated into curriculum objectives. It may also be appropriate to allow students to determine their own work criteria in conjunction with their employer and then self-administer some form of reinforcement. Frequent self-reinforcement for gradually doing more work shapes improved performance.

Martin et al. (2003) conducted an important study to determine if secondary school–age students could use self-determination contracts to regulate the correspondence between their plans, work, self-evaluations, and adjustments on academic tasks. The authors examined the impact of these contracts on the plan, work, evaluation, and adjustment behaviors of eight secondary school–age students with EBD. The students completed daily self-determination contracts to schedule their work on academic tasks, plan for work outcomes, evaluate progress, and adjust for the next day's activity. One-way repeated measures of ANalysis Of VAriance (ANOVAs) yielded 15 significant effects for the correspondence between plan and work, between work and evaluation, between evaluation and adjustment, and between adjustment and the next day plan. Significant academic improvement occurred from pre- to postassessment.

Self-management is driven by self-determination (see Chapter 2) and usually entails instructing the student to independently self-monitor by facilitating natural cues or adding external cues and prompts, compensatory strategies, assistive technology devices, and so forth. Instruction can be provided by co-workers, friends, family members, or the employment specialist, depending on the student's needs. For instance, a family member may assist the student in learning how to check off days on a calendar to determine when he or she goes to work. A co-worker may assist the individual by telling him or her when it is lunchtime, and the employment specialist may train the worker to use a timer and external cues to monitor production.

In vocational settings, employment specialists, rehabilitation counselors, employers, and family members may all help the individual with a disability to develop a plan appropriate to a particular situation. To be effective, however, the designers should be competent in the development of behavior management programs and involve the individual who will be implementing the program.

Self-Determination

Findings from numerous empirical studies have strengthened calls to focus targeted efforts toward promoting self-determination among students with disabilities (Algozzine, Browder, Karvonen, Test, & Wood, 2001; Cobb, Lehman, Newman-Gonchar, & Alwell, 2009; Test, Mazzotti, et al., 2009). For example, a number of potential outcomes are associated with being more self-determined, including enhanced academic performance (Mooney, Ryan, Uhing, Reid, & Epstein, 2005), increased school engagement (Hadre & Reeve, 2003), greater postsecondary involvement (Field, Sarver, & Shaw, 2003), improved postschool employment outcomes (Halpern, Yovanoff, Doren, & Benz, 1995; Wehmeyer & Palmer, 2003), and enhanced quality of life (Wehmeyer & Schwartz, 1997). Although still emerging, extant research suggests a potential link between enhanced self-determination and improved student outcomes

For students with EBD, self-determined behavior may represent an especially germane instructional domain. Assessment studies indicate that educators rate youth with EBD as having limited knowledge about self-determination and diminished capacity to engage in behaviors that enhance self-determination relative to students with learning disabilities (Carter, Lane, Pierson, & Glaesar, 2006; Carter, Trainor, Owens, Sweeden, & Sun, 2010). Furthermore, youth with EBD are more likely than other disability groups to have difficulties in persistence and self-advocacy (Wagner, Marder, et al., 2003). For those with or at risk for EBD who receive services in alternative educational settings, self-determination prospects may be even more limited (Van Gelder, Sitlington, & Pugh 2008). These findings suggest that the instructional needs for students with EBD may even be more imperative than those of other students with high-incidence disabilities.

With recognition of the association between self-determination and improved educational and postschool outcomes for children and youth with or at risk for EBD, increased attention has focused on efforts to promote the skills and attitudes that enhance self-determination. Carter, Lane, et al. (2011) conducted a comprehensive, systematic review of school-based intervention studies, addressing nine component elements of self-determination for students with and at risk for EBD. These 81 studies primarily addressed a narrow range of self-determination elements as intervention components (e.g., self-management and self-regulation, problem solving, goal setting and attainment) or outcome measures (e.g., self-efficacy, problem solving), with relatively few studies addressing students from culturally diverse backgrounds. The authors concluded that additional research is needed to address key gaps related to the school contexts within which these interventions have been delivered.

Teaching Social Skills

Most students with behavior disorders lack social skills. Teachers working with these youth must teach these skills in addition to academic and vocational skills. Social skills should be taught in a variety of community settings as well as in inclusive high schools in interactions with peers without disabilities. Table 18.4 gives tips for inclusion that can be infused into the curriculum resources listed next. In Chapter 11, Carter and Hughes provide more detail on social skills development.

Teachers must keep in mind, however, that effect sizes of social skills training on relevant outcomes of students with EBD are consistently small (Kavale, Mathur, Forness, Rutherford, & Quinn, 1997; Quinn, Kavale, Mathur, Rutherford, & Forness, 1999). Farmer, Quinn, Hussey, and Holohan (2001) noted that these small effect sizes should not be interpreted as an indictment of social skills training; however, these authors argue that the multiple risk factors faced by youth with EBD (which they termed "correlated

Table 18.4. Tips for inclusion of youth with behavior disorders

Instructional strategy	Description	Advantages	Disadvantages
1. Modeling	Exposing target student to prosocial behavior	Easy to implement	Not sufficient if used alone
2. Strategic placement	Placing target student in situations with other students who display prosocial behaviors	Employs peers as change agents, facilitates generalization, is cost-effective	Research data inconclusive when used alone
3. Instruction	Telling students how and why they should behave a certain way and/or giving rules for behavior	Overemphasizes norms/expectations	Not sufficient if used alone
4. Correspondence training	Positively reinforcing students for accurate reports regarding their behavior	Facilitates maintenance and generalization of training, is cost-effective	Very little documentation of effectiveness
5. Rehearsal and practice	Structured practice of specific prosocial behavior	Enhances skill acquisition	Not sufficient to change behavior if used alone
6. Positive reinforcement or shaping	Prosocial behaviors or approximations followed by a reward or favorable event	Strong research support for effectiveness	Maintenance after treatment termination is not predictable
7. Prompting and coaching	Providing students with additional stimuli/prompts that elicit the prosocial behavior	Particularly effective after acquisition to enhance transfer to natural settings	Maintenance after treatment termination is not predictable
8. Positive practice	A consequence strategy in which student repeatedly practices correct behavior	May produce immediate increases in prosocial behavior	Long-term effectiveness not documented; less-restrictive approaches should be used first
9. Multimethod training packages	Multicomponent instructional package that incorporates several behavioral techniques	Greater treatment strength and durability; applicable to a range of children and settings	

From Carter, J., & Sugai, G. (1989). Social skills curriculum analysis. *Teaching Exceptional Children, 22,* 38; reprinted by permission.

constraints") highlight the need for focus of intervention across various systems of influence. For example, a critical component of teaching social skills must be attention to the context in which the student is encouraged to use learned skills, be it the classroom, the lunchroom, or on a job placement. During social interactions in these contexts, there is an ongoing calibration between the propensities of the self and the demands of others (Cairns, 2000). This means that a youth's internal capacities (e.g., social–cognitive skills, activity rates, and emotional and behavioral regulation) and the characteristics of his or her social context (e.g., peer groups, available social roles, social norms) influence each other as they collectively contribute to the development of distinct patterns of social behaviors and skills (Farmer et al., 2001). Thus, the limited effects of social skills training for youth with EBD may be less related to acquisition of taught skills and more related to key environmental factors that may limit their use and effectiveness. Teachers and other professionals should keep these factors in mind as they program for the career development of youth with EBD, with a particular focus on social skills performance.

Supported Employment Outcomes for Individuals with Emotional and Behavior Disorders

As noted in earlier chapters, supported employment (SE) is one very successful way to help youth and adults enter the labor force (Inge & Moon, 2011). This is true for youth with EBD as well. There have been many excellent studies to support outcomes (Drake & Bond, 2008) for individuals with mental illness.

What Is Effective in Supported Employment?

Over the years, SE has been implemented in a variety of ways for people with severe mental illness. From this research, a number of principles that are consistently related to better employment outcomes (Bond et al., 2001; Cook & Razzano, 2000) were identified. Later, this led to the development of evidence-based SE that mirrors the earlier **Individual Placement and Support (IPS)** models (Becker, Swanson, Bond, & Merrens, 2008). The following seven principles emerged as indicators of successful programs:

1. All individuals served are encouraged to consider employment and are offered SE, but the person with mental illness is who ultimately determines if and when to participate. Eligibility is not based on factors (e.g., readiness, abstinence) that have excluded people from employment services.

2. SE is integrated with mental health treatment. The team usually includes the psychiatrist, the caseworker, the employment specialist, and other people who relate to the person.

3. SE is regular employment—real work for real pay. Employment specialists assist individuals with obtaining competitive employment.

4. Emphasis is on a rapid job search, not on activities designed to prepare a person for work (i.e., job readiness training). Together, the employment specialist and the job seeker immediately develop an employment plan that is consistent with job seeker's work goals and the plan is revised over time if needed.

5. Job search efforts are geared to locate or create work that matches the job seeker's preferences, strengths, experiences, and unique challenges. Job finding, disclosure of mental illness, and job supports follow clients' preferences and choices.

6. Follow-along supports are ongoing (Bond & Kukla, 2008). The types and amounts of support vary and must be individualized to the unique situation on hand (Bond et al., 2001).

7. Benefits counseling is used to educate individuals on the effect of earnings on benefits (Bond, 2004).

The critical ingredients of evidence-based SE have been well described and a fidelity scale was developed. The scale differentiates SE programs from other types of vocational services (Becker et al., 2008). Research shows that the scale, which is grounded in evidence-based principles, is practical and widely used and can improve program implementation.

More recently, some of the best evidence on effective ways of supporting people with severe mental illness to gain and maintain employment is found in reviews by Marshall, Bond, and Huxley (2009); Becker, Xie, McHugo, Halliday, and Martinez (2006); and Becker, Whitley, Bailey, and Drake (2007b). The primary outcome measure was the number of individuals who worked. Secondary outcome measures included other employment-related outcomes such as length of employment, clinical outcomes, and costs. Comparisons were made between different methods of vocational rehabilitation including SE, psychosocial rehabilitation, prevocational training such as Clubhouses, and standard clinical care. The studies concluded that SE and in particular the IPS approach was more effective than other forms of vocational rehabilitation in securing paid employment.

The authors concluded that the IPS model of SE appears to be the most effective method of supporting individuals with mental illness who want to work in their communities. Vocational support is best provided by employment specialists based within a treatment center working alongside a clinical lead for vocational rehabilitation. Services must be flexible and individualized to support individuals at various stages of the employment process (Drake & Bond, 2008).

In a recent study, Roberts et al. (2010) examined the relationship between specific techniques for developing social support (i.e., person-centered planning) and job-related outcomes among 110 individuals with psychiatric disabilities receiving SE services in a Northeastern state. The authors found a positive relationship between total days employed and the number of nonpaid supporters an individual reported having; a negative relationship existed between total days employed and number of paid supporters; and there was a positive correlation between total days employed and person-centered planning techniques used at 9 and 12 months.

As educators, guidance counselors, vocational rehabilitation counselors, and other professionals work together to determine how to evaluate outcomes appropriately, several variables should be considered:

1. Does the student have a job? Having a job in which one works a minimum of 15 hours per week, receives at least minimum wage, and learns how to get along with co-workers should be a priority of any transition evaluation checklist.

2. What are the student's self-esteem, confidence, and happiness levels? Does he or she seem excited and motivated by the prospect of coming to school, participating in community-based training, and having a job? If not, then activities such as teaching self-management and exposing students to the positive consequences of work can be very beneficial.

3. What level of behavior is the student exhibiting daily? Are there periodic outbursts of frustration or frequent unpredictable and explosive outbursts? Clearly, the likelihood of a satisfactory level of confidence and self-esteem should be influential in reducing these types of negative behaviors.

4. How many important community living skills does the student gain competence in during a 1-year span?

As we close out this chapter, it is reasonable to examine how two young people with significant emotional disabilities developed their own business (see case studies). They took the best of what we learned in Chapter 11 with what we know about how SE can work and overcome barriers to success.[1]

Edward and Jack, and thousands of others like James at the beginning of this chapter, can work, and work can help to manage behavioral problems and issues. The training technology is there—we need only to learn it and use it.

Edward   Edward is a young man in his early 30s living in a small town in the Northwest. For more than a decade, between hospitalizations and stretches of unemployment, he worked for the three glass installation businesses in his hometown of 15,000. His erratic behavior cost him all those jobs, but not before he learned the ins and outs of the trade. Most important, Edward recognized his former employers' lapses in customer service and set out to start a business that accommodated the symptoms of his bipolar disorder and addressed the needs of construction companies and homebuilders seeking high-quality windows and glazing.

Edward's state employment counselor rejected his business idea, but by working with a U.S. Department of Labor–funded disability demonstration project and the local Small Business Development Center funded by the Small Business Administration, he secured grant money to launch his enterprise. After an initial investment of less than $20,000, Edward's business grossed more than $100,000 each quarter after the first hard year and is projected to generate $800,000 during its second year of operation.

Jack   Jack is 22 years old and lives in a community of 50,000. He has several diagnostic labels. His strong psychotropic medicine slows him down a bit. His local vocational rehabilitation counselor recognized Jack's love of music and woodworking and sent him away to a community college that certified him as a violin repair professional. For the past 6 months, Jack has been marketing his services locally and refining his production methods. His long-term strategy is to carve a niche that includes intense attention to customer service. Typically, customers are high school and college music teachers who temporarily patch their student's broken instruments to get them through the school term. Violin repair shops are inundated with rush orders over Christmas break and during the summer because sending a broken instrument in during the academic year often means a student has no violin to use for weeks.

Jack's simple, yet elegant, solution is to buy and repair an inventory of used violins and keep them as ready replacements for broken ones. He will advertise to music teachers and provide a loaned instrument, shipped overnight, to be used while he repairs the student's violin. This presents an immediate solution to the music teacher and the student and allows Jack to spread his work out over the year instead of creating high-anxiety periods of production over the holidays and the summer. His unique customer service niche accommodates his disability perfectly.

Conclusion

Work experience, paid work, self-employment, and high levels of activity at community-based instruction sites are very important vehicles for improving the quality of behavior in students with EBD. This is how high levels of inappropriate behaviors are reduced. Establishing meaningful work behaviors provides an alternative way to manage these antisocial behaviors. New skills and activities are generated that provide important ways to reduce aberrant behavior therapeutically in this population, regardless of the level of behavior disorder, emotional disturbance, or autism. Self-management, self-control, self-reinforcement, and self-observation strategies are underutilized by educators. Students with behavior disorders must feel that they have control over their environments and help to choose what they want to do. They need choices as well as explicit structure. In addition, there are a number of important behaviors associated with job seeking and employment—travel, training, use of money, banking, and social and personal skills at the

---

[1]Reprinted with permission from Griffin, C., & Hammis, D. (2003). *Making self employment work for people with disabilities.* Baltimore, MD: Paul H. Brookes Publishing Co.

job site—that are important curriculum material for teachers who are responsive to individual transition needs.

Study Questions

1. What are the possible characteristics that indicate that a student may have an EBD?
2. Describe some of the challenges with which youth with EBD are faced.
3. With what challenges are educators and counselors faced in working with students with EBD?
4. What do educators need to consider when planning for transition for students with EBD?
5. Describe five strategies for teaching self-control and self-management to students with EBD.
6. Describe programs that teach social skills to students with EBD.
7. What are some categories of jobs for which youths with EBD might be considered?
8. Describe how effective SE can be for people with EBD.

Online Resources

Council of Exceptional Education: Behavior Disorders and Emotional Disturbance: http://www.cec.sped.org/AM/Template.cfm?Section=Behavior_Disorders_Emotional_Disturbance

National Alliance on Mental Illness: http://www.nami.org

American Academy of Child and Adolescent Psychiatry: http://www.aacap.org/cs/root/facts_for_families/facts_for_families_keyword_alphabetical

PACER Center: Emotional or behavioral disorders: http://www.pacer.org/ebd/

National Dissemination Center for Children with Disabilities: Emotional disturbance: http://nichcy.org/disability/specific/emotionaldisturbance

Applications for Youth with Autism Spectrum Disorders

19

CAROL SCHALL, PAMELA TARGETT,
AND PAUL WEHMAN

After completing this chapter, the reader will be able to

- Identify the characteristics of individuals with autism spectrum disorders (ASDs) in adolescence and young adulthood including the primary and secondary challenges

- Describe the process of completing a functional behavior assessment and developing a positive behavior support plan for a person with an ASD

- Describe evidence-based practices for high school students with ASDs

- Describe required components of excellent transition programs that prepare students with ASDs for higher education and employment

Rashaun   Rashaun is 16 years old and is preparing for graduation from high school in a few years. He has a diagnosis of autism. Despite his challenges, he has accomplished a great deal in his academic career. He passed the state standardized tests in the ninth grade. In addition, he had committed to memory more than 200 historical events from a history time line including the dates and years of passage of every amendment to the U.S. Constitution. He also remembers the birthday of every person who has ever worked with him. He does not remember, however, to ask for help when he is frustrated or confused. Instead, he shakes his head and whines. When he was younger, he sometimes hit others and threw his materials.

Minor changes in his schedule and routine, being told "no" to requests, and correction frustrate him. He also takes verbal cues and directions very literally. After learning the word "flexible," he imitated the picture on the worksheet where the word was defined and did a back bend in his high school cafeteria while proclaiming, "Rashaun is FLEXIBLE!"

Rashaun has created routines for every aspect of his day, from about 4:00 in the morning when he wakes up to wave at the paper deliverer to 8:30 at night when his father tells him, "About time, young man!" which is his cue to go to bed. His parents worry that he will not find a job or live independently because of his insistence on following minor routines. Rashaun also has many odd behaviors that make him stand out from others in school. When he walks, he shakes his head from side to side, and he rocks back and forth when sitting. He does not like loud noises and will become upset at high school pep rallies and assemblies.

Rashaun's family worries about his future. They do not know what he is able to do. It takes him a long time and repeated practice to master everyday skills such as making a sandwich. Even though he has some academic skills, he has very few life skills. They cannot imagine him working or living independently. They do not know what his future holds.

Now that Rashaun's school career is nearing the end, what will he do? Will he be able to find a job and work, or will his routines and subsequent behavior challenges interfere with his independence? Will he be able to live on his own and manage his own financial affairs? These are the critical questions that Rashaun and his parents are facing as they prepare for life after high school graduation. They, like so many other families who have an adolescent with an ASD, are facing one of the most difficult times in their lives.

On one hand, Rashaun seems to be able to do cognitive tasks that are quite impressive. On the other hand, he has significant social communication challenges. This scattered profile, where a person appears very skilled and competent in some areas and challenged in other areas, is very common for individuals across the autism spectrum. During such a transition, though, it is the challenges related to behavioral difficulties that can be most difficult for families and support providers. Despite these challenges, people with ASDs are able to work successfully with the proper supports (Barnhill, 2007; Cimera & Cowan, 2009; Hillier et al., 2007; Lawer, Brusilovskiy, Salzer, & Mandell, 2009; Schall, 2010; Schall & McDonough, 2010; Shaller & Yang, 2005; Taylor & Seltzer, 2011).

This chapter explores the primary and secondary characteristics of ASDs, particularly as they relate to transition from high school to postsecondary education, employment, and adult living. In addition, this chapter explores some of the specialized supports and technology that help individuals like Rashaun cope with the social and personal demands of learning, work, and adult living. Finally, we discuss the specific life and job supports that help individuals with ASDs adjust to life beyond the classroom.

Characteristics of Youth with Autism Spectrum Disorders

There are three reasons for the increased interest in autism in the recent past. They include an increase in the prevalence of ASDs, an understanding that the challenges presented by the disorder are unique among other disabilities, and an understanding of the specialized supports that individuals with autism require (Schall & McDonough, 2010; Wehman, Smith, & Schall, 2009). Currently, ASD is the fastest-growing developmental disability. The Centers for Disease Control and Prevention (2012), report that 1 in 88 children in the

United States has an autism spectrum disorder. This figure is based on 2008 data and represents a 78% percent increase from what was reported ten years ago. According to officials, the rise may be related to better diagnosis, and broader definitions of the disability.

The Assistant Secretary for Special Education and Rehabilitative Services of the U.S. Department of Education, Alexa Posny, said

> The majority of individuals with ASD are currently elementary or middle school age. Yet, those young children and youth will grow to adolescence and adulthood. Thus, providers of secondary education, postsecondary education, and adult services must increase their knowledge and improve the delivery of evidence-based strategies to support this group of students. (U.S. Department of Education, 2011)

Finally, as noted by Assistant Secretary Posney, people with ASD desire to lead "rich, active, connected lives." To accomplish this important task, transition and rehabilitation specialists must implement excellent programs to meet the needs of youth and young adults with ASD.

Notably, recent research has shown that transition planning for students with autism is inadequate. These conclusions are based on a review of survey responses of around 2,000 parents of special education students, which included data on 500 students with autism that was conducted by Shattuck, Narendorf, Cooper et al (2012). The researchers found that more than 50% of young adults with autism were not working or attending postsecondary education 2 years after leaving high school. Notably, the rate of participation was the lowest among the other disability groups studied (i.e., speech-language impairment, learning disabilities, or intellectual disability). Six years after high school, 35% were either unemployed or not furthering their education. One factor that enhanced the likelihood of employment or attending school was the individual coming from a family with a higher income. However, this was less common among Blacks and Hispanics even when the severity of the person's disability was controlled. Among young adults from households with an annual earnings of $75,000 a year, 18% were not working or attending post secondary education. That is compared to 55% of those individuals from families making under $25,000 a year. Shattuck et al (2012) indicated one reason for this may relate to the social connectedness of parents with higher incomes, which may enable them to "help" their child locate work. The researchers concluded that more research is needed to improve outcomes for young adults with autism.

Diagnostic and Behavioral Characteristics of Individuals with Autism Spectrum Disorder

Autism is a lifelong developmental disability that profoundly affects how an individual interacts with the world. Problems in communication and social skills make it difficult for the person to interact with those around them. Some individuals with autism do not speak and do not compensate for a lack of speech by using gestures, pantomime, or eye gaze to communicate. Those who speak may have great difficulty initiating, maintaining, repairing, and ending conversations. They may respond to the initiations of others in unusual ways (e.g., repeat what the person has just said), repeat familiar phrases or songs (functional echolalia), or not speak at all. Even those persons with autism who do speak may not easily share accomplishments or enjoyment with others. These problems make having and keeping friends difficult, thus, further isolating the individual. Compounding the situation, many persons with autism have difficulty in processing sensory information, making it difficult for them to make sense of and react to the world around them. They may be hyper- or hyposensitive to touch, taste, smell, sight, and/or hearing. For example, some may find certain frequencies of sound painful, and others may have difficulty eating certain food or wearing certain clothes. To cope with sensory problems, many engage in repetitive self-stimulatory behavior such as rocking or hand flapping (Carter, Sisco, Chung, & Stanton-Chapman, 2010; Wehman et al., 2009). Still others, like Rashaun, may be extremely bound to routines, making it difficult for them to cope with changes. In addition, they may be extremely anxious, especially in situations that are unpredictable. Many of the classic characteristics of autism are present in Rashaun's difficulty communicating, his social skill challenges, and his demand that routines remain unchanged.

Although persons with autism have some global characteristics in common such as problems communicating and socializing, each person with autism is *unique*. They may have particular strengths and weaknesses that are very different from someone else with the same disability. In fact, autism is a spectrum disorder, which includes individuals who require some support to those who require very substantial support. Regardless of the intensity of support required, all individuals with an ASD present an array of behavioral symptoms that include deficits in social communication and restricted or repetitive patterns of behavior, interests, or activities (APA, 2000). The social communication deficits are wide ranging and include every possible communication difficulty from those who do not talk at all to those who talk but fail to follow standard social communication conventions. In addition, individuals with ASD may have difficulty understanding nonverbal communication such as gestures and may have difficulty developing peer relationships. Finally, the restricted or repetitive patterns of behaviors, interests, or activities describe a wide category of unusual characteristics. This category includes odd, repetitive, and persistent motor movements such as rocking, spinning objects, or hand flapping; a preoccupation with particular subjects; a preoccupation with parts of objects (spinning wheels of a toy car instead of pretending to drive a toy car); or unusual responses to sensory stimuli (APA, 2000; Schall & McDonough, 2010).

For a diagnosis of autism to be verified, these behavioral characteristics must be present before the age of 3 years. Nevertheless, diagnosis may occur after the age of 3 because of a failure to recognize the complex pattern of behaviors that make up the disorder. ASDs are more prevalent among males, affecting four males to every female (Schall & McDonough, 2010). It is possible to have autism co-occur with other disorders such as (but not limited to) Down syndrome, seizure disorders, cerebral palsy, depression, attention-deficit/hyperactivity disorder, and anxiety disorders (Ward & Russell, 2007).

In addition to the primary or core characteristics, individuals with ASD very often exhibit secondary symptoms that are particularly challenging (White, Ollendick, & Bray, 2011). In Rashaun's example, he exhibited some problem behaviors when his routine was changed. Specifically, he would whine and complain. In addition, Rashaun can communicate much about history or birthdays but does not ask for help or express his frustration. In other words, his communication deficits and social skills difficulties combined to create problem behaviors. Table 19.1 lists a number of behaviors associated with ASD.

Autism as a Multidimensional Disorder

Very often, when thinking of disabilities, we think in terms of one dimension and characterize the person by that dimension. When we describe someone as "high-functioning," we generally mean that such a person has higher-than-average cognitive skills compared with his or her peers with disabilities. Such a single discrimination does not seem to apply for persons with ASD. In fact, ASD is multidimensional rather than reflecting a single dimension. Thus, to serve a youth with ASD well, the teacher and support staff must understand the entire person from a multidimensional perspective. The important dimensions to consider when serving a person with autism follow.

Communication Skills and Abilities

Professionals must understand both the forms of communication (e.g., words, pictures, sign language, gestures) and the function of communication (e.g., getting one's needs met, engaging in conversation with others, adjusting conversations based on the social situation). Instead of observing the social cues that tell him that his communication partner is

Table 19.1.   Behavioral characteristics associated with autism spectrum disorder

Speech and communication deficits
- Nonverbal individuals may use sounds or gestures, may use pictorial cues
- Limited ability to express self
- Limited ability to understand thoughts, beliefs, or feelings of others
- Difficulty following instructions
- Unable to follow lengthy conversations or participate in back-and-forth exchanges
- Difficulty understanding abstract concepts
- Interprets figurative phrases literally
- Difficulty understanding nonverbal communication such as eye contact or gestures
- Difficulty entering, maintaining, following, and closing conversations
- Difficulty answering open-ended questions
- Abnormal speech rhythm
- Monotone speech
- Repeatedly and persistently speaks about the same topic or asks same question
- Repeats back verbatim phrases and sentences from conversations or television either immediately or well after hearing the phrase or sentence
- Uses the pronoun "you" instead of using the word "I"
- May use behaviors (self-injurious behavior, tantrum, aggression) to communicate (e.g., get attention, escape task, protest change, or regulate social interaction in predictable manner)

Personal relationships and social skill deficits
- Appears to have lack of interest in other people in the environment
- Difficulty making friends
- Difficulty engaging in social interactions
- Appears withdrawn or appears to prefer to be alone
- May not acknowledge others or engage in traditional greetings
- May not use social amenities (i.e., please, thank you, you're welcome)
- Might invade other people's personal space (e.g., stands too close to others when communicating)
- Appears immature
- Talks loudly to self
- Talks about preferred topics
- May ask embarrassing personal questions (e.g., How old are you?; Are you married?; Why not?)
- May talk too much or ask too many questions
- May display abnormal verbalizations (e.g., scream, hoot, yell, or hum)
- May avoid eye contact and/or fails to orient body toward person speaking

Unusual responses to sensory stimulation and repetitive motor movements
- Appears unaware of important sensory stimuli, may even appear to be deaf or hard of hearing
- Seeks out objects or activities that offer desired stimulation to the exclusion of other activities
- Attends to unusual sensory stimuli (e.g., things that spin, shiny objects, or certain textures)
- Focuses on minute details and appears unaware to rest of the environment
- Has difficulty attending to auditory and tactile input and prefers visual or vestibular channels
- Engages in repetitive behaviors that provide sensory stimulation (e.g., repetitive noise making, hand flapping, rocking, pacing, finger flicking, tapping, spinning, or jumping up and down)
- Has averse or fearful reaction to certain stimuli (e.g., certain noises, food textures, fluctuations in lighting) that are not necessarily threatening
- Reacts to certain sounds that others cannot hear
- Fails to react to painful or uncomfortable stimuli
- Engages in self-injurious behaviors (e.g., skin scratching, head banging, hits or bites self)

Note: Not all persons with autism spectrum disorder exhibit all listed symptoms.

tired of talking, Rashaun talks too much about his topic of interest. As a result, he is not able to get his needs met with communication and is easily frustrated.

Social Skills and Abilities

Professionals must understand the degree to which the person with autism is able to assess the social situation and select appropriate responses. In fact, challenging behaviors are often the result of deficit social skills. Rashaun did not know how to negotiate with his staff and resorted to arguing, complaining, and noncompliance. When he tried to discuss the concept of "flexibility," he performed a back bend in the high school cafeteria.

Cognitive Abilities

Professionals must carefully assess the cognitive skills and abilities of persons with ASD; otherwise, they may make errors about the person. Individuals with autism frequently have a "scattered" profile where they have very high abilities in some areas and deficits in others. Rashaun has some very strong cognitive abilities. Yet, he has significant skill needs. A good transition program would address both strengths and needs.

Ability to Focus and Attend in Learning and Work Situations

Individuals with ASD across the spectrum frequently have difficulty attending and focusing on tasks in the presence of distractions. Professionals must understand each individual's response to various environmental conditions and make reasonable adjustments to increase the person's ability to attend. In Rashaun's case, he has variable abilities to focus and attend. He would not be successful in an unstructured environment with frequent changes in his routine. In fact, he would be very challenging in such a situation.

Ability to Regulate Emotions in Stressful Situations

Finally, it is very important that professionals serving individuals with ASD understand the person's ability to regulate his or her emotional state. Many individuals with ASD will resort to challenging behavior (e.g., tantrums, aggression) when they are pushed under stress. This does not mean that they cannot work or be in the community; rather, it means that support staff must understand the conditions that cause stress and methods for teaching the person to regulate his or her own emotional state. Very often, there are sensory and organizational supports that can be in place for persons with autism. Rashaun would do well with calming time after he has to be in a noisy and chaotic environment.

Describing Rashaun based on the arbitrary distinction of high- or low-functioning is not helpful in understanding his strengths and needs. As a consequence, successful programs would begin with an analysis of a person's strengths and needs in each dimension. In fact, this multidimensional variability creates the greatest challenges and confusion for support staff. When we assume that a person's abilities are singular in dimension based on cognitive abilities, we make errors of intention. Support staff who assumed that Rashaun is bright, therefore he is in perfect control of his behavior, might blame him for his difficulties when his routine changes. Likewise, staff who assumed that an individual with ASD is low functioning because of his or her inability to talk using words might miss his or her abilities in other areas such as working on a computer. This could result in support teams ignoring the possibilities of office work or alternative communication systems for such a person (Ostryn, Wolfe, & Rusch, 2008).

Unique Challenges of Transition-Aged Youth with Autism Spectrum Disorder

Adolescence is a time of major change for all of us. Physical, psychological, and social changes make this time both challenging and rewarding for adolescents and those around them. Persons with autism face similar changes; however, difficulties in socialization and communication can make this an extremely demanding time for them. Adolescents with autism change physically in ways similar to their peers, but the discrepancy between the complex social behavior of a typical adolescent and that of someone with autism may become quite large (Carter, Sisco, Chung, & Stanton-Chapman, 2010; Wehman et al., 2009). The adolescent with autism may have a similar desire to have a girlfriend or boyfriend but may have difficulties in developing and maintaining these relationships. In some cases, the adolescent may be increasingly aware of his or her differences, which may result in increasing his or her anxiety or may lead to bouts of depression. As well, adolescents with autism may not be adequately prepared for the physical and social changes that they will face, thus, furthering the challenge for them to cope with adolescence (Schall & McDonough, 2010).

Families frequently experience greater anxiety once their child with autism enters adolescence. The recognition that the child is now nearing adulthood and will likely require lifelong supports, combined with the need to make arrangements for such supports, creates increased stress on the family (Barker et al., 2011).

These concerns can and should be part of the overall planning related to transition services. In fact, the transition plan should include goals and activities that address family concerns directly through training and indirectly through linking the individual and family with community-based supports and services.

Although all of the ASDs are lifetime disorders, there is evidence that, as the person ages, some of the specific symptoms may improve or abate. Schall and McDonough (2010) reviewed the literature related to changes in ASD in adolescence and found that adolescents and adults with ASD appeared to improve in their communication and social skills while their restricted and repetitive interests and stereotypic behaviors seemed to abate somewhat, especially when, as children, they have the opportunity to interact with their peers without disabilities. This does not mean, of course, that improvement should nullify the need for ongoing supports. Seltzer et al. noted, "That the disorder changes in its manifestation over the life course does not, therefore, indicate that affected individuals have any less of a need for services and supports as they move through adolescence into adulthood and midlife than they did in childhood. Rather, developmentally appropriate services are needed for adolescents and adults with ASD diagnoses" (2003, p. 579). Thus, it should be the goal of professionals supporting individuals with ASD to develop and measure the effects of programs serving transition-aged youth with ASD to ensure long-term success through adulthood.

Outcomes for Individuals with Autism Spectrum Disorder

The reported prognosis for individuals with ASD has changed over time with increased research and improvements in early identification, intensive early intervention, and behaviorally based special education. As a group, however, individuals with ASD, across the entire spectrum of ability, do not achieve employment, independent living, or connected lives at the same rate as individuals with similar disabilities. A primary source of information about postsecondary outcomes for students with ASD is the National Longitudinal Transition Study-2 (NLTS-2). The NLTS-2 followed a large representative sample of youth enrolled in special education as they transitioned into young adulthood from 2001 to 2009, with an age range of 13–26 years. From the overall sample ($n = 11,000$), 922 youth were from the autism category. Cameto (2005) reported that students with ASD participated in general education only about 33% of the time, with most coursework provided in special education (62%). Even though the majority of time modifications to the curriculum were in place in general education settings, students with ASD were substantially less engaged than their typical peers in general education settings. In a recent study, Shattuck, Wagner, Narendorf, Sterzing, and Hensley (2011) examined patterns of service use among youth with ASD from the NLTS-2 sample. Data analysis on youth who exited high school revealed that 32% attended postsecondary education schools, 6% had competitive jobs, and 21% had no employment or education experiences at all. Furthermore, 80% of these individuals were living with their parents, 40% reported having no friends, and only 36% had a driver's license. In addition, there was a dramatic decline in service use upon exiting high school, and the uninsured rate more than doubled from high school to after high school (from 4% to 9%). Unfortunately, youth from families with lower socioeconomic levels had worse outcomes on all measures.

Nevertheless, emerging literature documents practices and programs that result in much better outcomes for individuals with ASD where they achieve and benefit from employment, independent living, and friendships (Barnhill, 2007; Cimera & Cowan, 2009; Hillier et al., 2007; Lawer et al., 2009; Schall, 2010; Schall & McDonough, 2010; Shaller & Yang, 2005; Taylor & Seltzer, 2011). In other words, it behooves all service providers of individuals with ASD in secondary education, postsecondary education, employment, and adult living to learn to implement better services for these students as they transition to adulthood so that they can achieve enviable lives.

Because of the concerns related to outcomes for persons with ASD, it is critical that professional staff have efficient and effective ways to provide supports and education to prepare them for life beyond school. The next section reviews the literature related to evidence-based practices that result in better educational outcomes for students with ASD.

Characteristics of Excellent Transition Programs for Students with Autism Spectrum Disorder

The transition from school to adulthood is a process for all students, regardless of their abilities or diagnoses, that begins when students and their parents begin planning for their post–high school life. For most students without diagnoses, this begins in preschool as children identify their strengths, preferences, and interests. Most students continue to develop their strengths, preferences, and interests through school and extracurricular experiences, culminating with an identified career path in high school. For students with ASD, this process of career development does not seem to happen as readily as it does for students without disabilities. This is likely attributable to the impact that the disorder has on students' ability to engage in social observation and in using their imagination to project themselves into different careers. As a consequence, students with ASD frequently enter this final transition period with little sense of their strengths, interests, and preferences related to work, recreation, and friendship. In fact, as noted in Chapters 3 and 4, youth with disabilities must have a say in their own transition-planning process. If students with ASD enter transition without a sense of their own self or the ability to speak for and determine their own desired path, they will not be able to participate meaningfully in the course of their own lives. Thus, transition programs for youth with ASD must include rich school *and* community-based experiences that will help the youth develop a sense of his or her own career and life path regardless of the student's academic course load.

Schall and Wehman (2009) identified eight essential characteristics of excellent programs for youth with ASD:

1. Providing systematic, structured instruction that results in student engagement and skill development

2. Designing and using environmental and organizational supports that make expectations, schedules, and environments clear

3. Providing specialized education in social communication skills that will increase the students' success at work, home, and in their community

4. Identifying the function of problem behavior and developing **behavior intervention plans** that teach replacement skills over plans that suppress problem behavior

5. Ensuring that functional life and community skills that are necessary for students' long-term success are taught along with required academic skills

6. Ensuring generalization of skills from school-based environments to community, home, and work environments

7. Involving families in the transition process, including educating them about the transition process and the roles adult agencies can play in the life of their student

8. Coordinating connections with adult services agencies to ensure a smooth transition from school to work

The Emerging Use of Technology in Environmental and Instructional Design for Youth with Autism Spectrum Disorder

Technology represents an emerging area of program quality that is becoming readily available to youth with ASD. Specifically, handheld personal digital assistants and tablet computers have been used to teach skills and provide some of the environmental modifications and accommodations (Gentry, Wallace, Karvfordt, & Bodisch Lynch, 2010; Reed, Hyman, & Hirst, 2011, Mechling, 2011). This area holds great promise for its portability, flexibility, and appeal, particularly in modern youth culture. Such devices have been used to teach academic skills and social skills, provide schedules, provide behavioral programs and prompts, and provide video models in environments in subtle and socially acceptable ways. The application of this portable technology has yet to be fully explored and will certainly continue to be an adaptable tool for continued use in the education of students with ASD.

Transition Team Building for Youth with Autism Spectrum Disorder

To implement a transition program that includes all of these characteristics, the person with ASD requires team members who have knowledge or expertise that can assist the young person with ASD. The team must support the young person in acquiring skills and learning behaviors that will increase their success in adulthood. The team should include a number of different perspectives and skills. Thus, instead of thinking about professional titles, teams should consider the skills required to support the team and seek out persons who can contribute those skills to the team. The required skills that make up a sound educational team include

- Teaching social skills
- Teaching communication skills
- Analyzing behavior and developing positive behavior intervention plans
- Coordinating communication and services between school and community-based service providers
- Addressing environmental, sensory, behavioral, and/or mental health concerns
- Identifying potential careers and employers and connecting the person with work experiences to expand their understanding of careers and work
- Teaching work behaviors, job skills, and community living skills
- Facilitating a person-centered visioning process
- Ensuring fidelity of implementation and data collection to ensure the success of the plan

Although this list is daunting, individual team members may be able to contribute multiple skill sets to the team.

The final ingredient in an excellent transition program is the development of a sound transition individualized education program (IEP) for students with ASD. Once a student reaches middle school, the IEP team must begin to contemplate the student as an independent adult worker and consider his or her strengths and needs from the perspective of adulthood and not from the perspective of missed developmental milestones and deficits related to his or her disability. The Virginia Department of Education's guide, *Autism Spectrum Disorders and the Transition To Adulthood,* lists the following questions should guide IEP development during the student with ASD's transition years in middle school and high school.

- To what degree is the student "self-determined"?
- What is the student's or his or her family's[1] vision for the future?
- What are the academic, vocational, recreational, and community-based components and skills that would create an enviable life for this student?
- What academic, functional, daily living, communication, and social skills does the student currently possess that would match his or her vision for himself or herself?
- What academic, functional, daily living, communication, and social skills and abilities does the student require to be able to accomplish his or her vision for himself or herself?
- What additional training or education after high school will the student need to be able to accomplish his or her vision for himself or herself?
- Is this person able to live independently on his or her own in an apartment or house, get around in the community, and/or budget his or her money wisely?
- What is the depth of this student's experiences in the world of work?
- What resources are available to her or him that increase the likelihood that he or she will achieve this vision?
- What skills and abilities will this student need to learn between now and high school graduation that will assist him or her in achieving his or her vision?
- What work and community experiences does this student need to inform his or her decision making to prepare for life beyond high school?
- What experiences, resources, and new agencies will increase the likelihood of a smooth transition into work or postsecondary education and adult life?

When IEP teams consider these questions and use them to guide IEP goal development for students with ASD, they will ensure that the IEP is based on student's preferences, interests, and future vision for himself or herself.

Identifying the Vision for Students with Significant Communication Deficits

This is important for students at all ability levels who have ASD. In the case of students with ASD who may have difficulty articulating their interests because of an intellectual disability or difficulty communicating with words, teachers and family members may have to rely on observation of the student's preferences to identify meaningful activities for that student. For example, imagine a student who likes to be outside. Some potential meaningful activities would include gardening, horseback riding, or boating. Some potential jobs could be in landscaping or working on a dock or on a farm. Table 19.2 demonstrates how narrow student preferences could be shaped into meaningful activities and work.

---

[1]For students with ASD who are unable to communicate their vision for themselves, family members or caregivers may act as a proxy.

Table 19.2.   Translating student preferences into meaningful activities

Preference	Possible activities	Possible work site	Possible recreation/leisure site
Being outdoors Moving things Loves motion	Gardening Landscaping Boat rides Horseback riding	Nursery Dock Farm	Nursery Home Farm Park
Water Baths Smells	Swimming Laundry Dish washing	Hotel Restaurant Candle store	Pool
Vibrations	Baking/cooking Vacuuming Bike riding Amusement rides	Hotel restaurant Bike store Theme park	Theme park Bike trail
Moving things Pushing things People	Shopping Cleaning Delivering things Pushing a stroller Rowing machine	Mall Grocery store Day care Post office	Gym Mall

Curriculum, Literacy, and the Individualized Education Program

When one is considering moving from preferences and interests to IEP goals and academic curriculum, it is important to consider the type of curriculum through which a student will acquire math and reading literacy skills. Snell and Brown (2006) identified four potential ways to address the curricular needs of students with disabilities. They are presented in Table 19.3.

Any given student could receive instruction in different curricula for different subject areas. The student with ASD who has strength in mathematics might receive instruction from the *general education curriculum with adaptations,* whereas that same student might receive instruction from the *embedded academic skills usable in specific life routines curriculum* for reading or language arts. The teacher should always be prepared to offer guidance on what skills and curricula are necessary to maximize future levels of independency.

Thus, students who have intellectual disabilities in addition to ASD and receive their education in a functional life skills program continue to require instruction in basic math and reading literacy. Teams should embed academic content into functional activities to ensure that students who have ASD and intellectual disabilities have their academic and

Table 19.3.   Four curriculum approaches to teaching functional academics

Curriculum	Learning outcome
General education curriculum with or without adaptations	Student will master grade-level material with outcomes similar to those of classmates.
Functional, generalized skills usable across life routines	Student will master critical skills for use in home, community, school, and work settings. Students in this curriculum may perform between a second- and a fifth-grade level in academic content areas.
Embedded academic skills usable in specific life routines	Student will acquire academic skills in the context of his or her daily routine (e.g., reading the menu choices at lunch, counting the coins to make a vending machine purchase).
Adaptations to bypass academic skills	Students will use community-based functional adaptations to academic skills such as matching coins and bills to a money placket, using picture menus to order food at restaurants, following picture schedules to read.

Source: Snell and Brown (2006).

Table 19.4. Embedding academic skills into functional activities

Sample high school standards	Functional activities in which the standard can be taught
The student will read and comprehend a variety of informational materials. a. Identify questions answered in the materials. b. Make, confirm, or revise predictions. c. Use context to determine meanings of unfamiliar words and technical vocabulary. d. Draw conclusions and make inferences based on explicit and implied information.	While reading newspaper articles about their high school's sports teams, students with autism spectrum disorder learn how to master the skills in this standard. Students who do not have reading skill use picture clues and writing with symbols to read a simplified version of the article.
The student will read and demonstrate comprehension of nonfiction. a. Use text organizers, such as type, headings, and graphics, to predict and categorize information. b. Identify structural patterns found in nonfiction. c. Identify cause-and-effect relationships. d. Identify new information gained from reading.	On their community-based job site, students will read signs and written instructions in the environment to gain information regarding the rules at work. For students who do not have reading skill, the teacher created picture representations to assist them in comprehending nonfiction work.
The student will identify representations of a given percentage and describe orally and in writing the equivalence relationships among fractions, decimals, and percentages.	While delivering the school's newspapers, students calculate the percentage of newspapers delivered and yet to be delivered by using fractions, decimals, percentages, and simple ratios.
The student will investigate and understand different sources of energy. Key concepts include a. The sun's ability to produce light and heat energy b. Sources of energy (sunlight, water, wind) c. Fossil fuels (coal, oil, natural gas) and wood d. Renewable and nonrenewable energy resources	While completing community-based training, students will identify how different environments are heated including buildings, cars, outdoor areas, and homes.
The student will identify examples of making an economic choice and will explain the idea of opportunity cost (what is given up when making a choice).	While completing community-based shopping tasks, students will make purchase choices based on the amount of money they have available to them.

functional skill needs met in their educational programs. Table 19.4 demonstrates how academic standards can be embedded into functional skills.

In summary, individuals with ASD display many different characteristics and behaviors that are unique to the disability and to each individual. As they prepare for adulthood, individuals with ASD can learn to compensate for many of those behaviors that are most problematic at work and in adult life. Secondary programs should address the needs of youth with ASD by providing a quality transition program and developing team skills that will result in success.

Curriculum and Students with Autism Spectrum Disorder Who Work Toward a Standard or Advanced Studies Diploma

Too often, students with ASD who have the academic skill to graduate with a standard or higher designation diploma do not receive specialized instruction in important social communication and functional living skills that would increase their success in higher education and employment. Thus, too many students with higher academic abilities are not able to achieve successful employment or independent living because of the lack of specialized instruction in these important areas. A student with ASD who is able to manage complex academic work should not have to sacrifice his or her academic goals to receive instruction in functional and social skill needs. They should not have to choose between receiving specialized instruction in functional work and daily living skills and academic rigor. Instead, IEP teams should be flexible and take advantage of the extra time provided to students with disabilities to meet their functional *and* academic instructional needs. Table 19.5 demonstrates how one IEP team delayed graduation for Matthew, a student with ASD, who had advanced academic skills and significant social and functional skill needs, to develop a comprehensive educational plan and extend his high school career by 1 year.

On a final note to support providing functional experiences for students with ASD, as learners, students with ASD need extensive practice to be able to generalize skills learned in one environment to a new environment. This is true no matter where along the autism spectrum the student's diagnosis falls. The best way to avoid having to teach and reteach skills in every new environment is to teach skills in the environment where they will ultimately be used. For transition-aged students, this is most important. After all, nearly all of the skills a transition-aged student learns will be used in other environments. As a consequence, whenever possible, instruction should be provided in the community where the student lives and in businesses frequented by the student and his or her family. This will ensure that the student has opportunities to socialize in the community and learn skills that will be applicable in the student's community environment. In community-based instruction, educational objectives are taught in natural community environments, such as worksites, shopping malls, and restaurants. Where other students rely on textbooks, computer web sites, and teacher lectures to learn skills, students with ASD require community-based instruction to learn skills. These are not field trips. Instead, educators should consider these community experiences as though they are the textbooks to teach necessary skills.

Table 19.5. Matthew's high school plan to meet his advanced academic needs and his functional employment and social skill needs

High school Year 1	English 9
	Social studies 9
	Earth science
	Basic computer
	Programming elective
	Education for employment 1
	Social skills for success 1
High school Year 2	English 10
	Algebra II (he completed algebra I in middle school honors class)
	Computer programming
	Biology
	Education for employment 2
	Social skills for success 2
High school Year 3	English 11
	Calculus
	Chemistry
	Elective
	Work study—2 periods
High school Year 4	Trigonometry
	Computer elective—dual enrollment at the community college
	Western civilization
	Elective
	Work study—2 periods
High school Year 5	English 12
	Math elective—dual enrollment at the community college
	Computer elective—dual enrollment at the community college
	Science elective—dual enrollment at the community college
	Work study—3 periods
Summer classes in high school Years 1, 2, and 3	Physical education and health
	Physical education, health, and driver's education
	Computer animation

Scientifically Based Practices for Educating and Supporting Youth and Young Adults with Autism Spectrum Disorder

Up to this point, this chapter has reviewed important aspects of education for transition-aged youth with ASD. Specifically, transition-aged students with ASD have been described (*who*). The identification of educational goals based on student interests and preferences has been discussed (*what*). A balanced approach to educational placement and the importance of community-based instruction has been illustrated (*when* and *where*). The last and perhaps most important aspect of transition programming is to teach the skills in the transition IEP and structure community-based experiences to maximize learning (*how*). This section reviews evidence-based teaching strategies for youth with ASD.

Systematic instruction is the set of teaching strategies and techniques that can empower young people with autism to be more independent and capable. These learning strategies need credible empirical research that confirms these strategies as worthy of the student's educational time. In addition to empirical evidence, strategies used to teach students with ASD should also be measured to ensure efficacy. Efficacy means that the instructor collects data to verify that the strategy produced the desired effect for that individual. All evidence-based strategies involve data collection to verify the success of the instructional method. In fact, Figure 19.1 shows how data inform educational practice and instructional strategies through the instructional process.

Using an evidence-based teaching strategy does not guarantee instructional success. Instead, teachers have to collect data either to verify the success of the instructional strategy or to revise the strategy. Thus, the instructional process is continual until the skill is mastered. Following this instructional process moves beyond relying solely on scientific evidence and ensures that teaching strategies are efficacious as well.

Scientifically Based Strategies for Teaching Youth with Autism Spectrum Disorder

According to the National Autism Center, there is only one package of interventions that achieves the scientifically based standard of "established treatment" for youth with ASD between the ages of 19 and 21. That package is the "behavioral package." In the document *National Standards Report*, the behavioral package is described by noting, "These interven-

Figure 19.1. The instructional process.

tions are designed to reduce problem behavior and teach functional alternative behaviors or skills through the application of basic principles of behavior change" (2009, p. 45). When extending the ages down to 15–18 years, there are an additional three packages that have substantial evidence to merit the designation of "scientifically established." These intervention packages are the antecedent, modeling, and self-management packages. Thus, out of 11 packages that have been established through scientific rigor, only four packages are scientifically established for youth between the ages of 15 and 21, and only one package is scientifically established for young adults between the ages of 19 and 21 (National Standards Report, 2009). Nevertheless, a number of instructional strategies do result in increased independence and skill acquisition for middle and high school students with ASD (National Standards Report, 2009; National Professional Development Center on ASD, 2010). Table 19.6 presents a list of those strategies that have been demonstrated as evidence-based according to the National Professional Development Center on Autism Spectrum Disorders for this age group and details the type of skills best matched to the strategy.

As the Table 19.6 demonstrates, there are some individual strategies that are scientifically based and applicable for transition-aged youth. This is an important point for

Table 19.6.   Evidence-based instructional strategies for transition-aged youth with autism spectrum disorder

Evidence-based strategy	Brief description of strategy	Skills best taught or intervention addressed by strategy
Antecedent-based interventions	Modifying the environment, antecedents, or setting events to prevent the need for challenging behavior	In response to problem behavior and after a functional behavior assessment has been completed
Computer-aided instruction	Use of a computer to teach communication or academic skills; there are some programs currently being used to teach social skills as well	Communication skills Academic skills Limited evidence for social skills
Functional behavior assessment	Using indirect and direct methods of assessment to identify the function of a specific problem behavior	In response to problem behavior
Naturalistic intervention	Providing cues, prompts, and instruction in natural environments to elicit and reinforce communication and social behaviors	Communication skills and behaviors Social skills and behaviors
Pivotal response training	Applying the principles of applied behavior analysis to natural environments to teach pivotal behaviors including motivation, responding to multiple cues, social interaction, social communication, self-management, and self-initiation	Social communication and interaction behaviors
Prompting procedures	Verbal, gestural, physical, model, and visual prompts and prompting systems including least-to-most prompts, simultaneous prompts, and graduate guidance	A wide variety of skills
Reinforcement	Strengthening any behavior by providing a consequence that increases the likelihood that the behavior will occur again; includes reinforcement, tokens, point systems, graduated reinforcement systems	A wide variety of behaviors
Self-management	A wide array of interventions to increase appropriate behaviors and decrease problem behaviors for learners across the spectrum including social conversation, sharing, giving, compliments, anger management, habit reversal, and so forth	Behaviors that are able to be defined and practiced by the person with autism spectrum disorder
Social skills groups	Up to eight individuals with autism spectrum disorder practice social skills and social interactions in a group with an adult facilitator	Social skills
Task analysis	Teaching skills with many steps a few steps at a time with reinforcement following each step	A wide variety of skills
Visual supports	Providing an array of information in visual formats including the daily schedule and steps to complete a task, social behaviors, communication supports, how to transition between activities	A wide variety of skills

Source: National Professional Development Center on Autism Spectrum Disorders (2009).

transition-aged youth with ASD. At the same time, there is a paucity of research on evidence-based practices for youth with ASD. To wit, these 11 practices were culled from a list of 24 practices that had a stronger evidence base for use with elementary school–aged students.

Regardless of the curriculum or instructional strategy used, many students with ASD require specialized instruction in communication, social interaction, and social skills. These skills are critical to lifelong success for persons with ASD. Once the IEP team selects skills, then the transition team must implement evidence-based instruction to ensure that the student acquires the necessary skills for success beyond high school.

Because of the evidence base available for the strategies listed in Table 19.6, teachers can feel confident implementing any of these strategies, provided that they are able to implement the strategy with fidelity and that they have applied it appropriately to the correct skill or skill set. Finally, there are 11 teaching strategies that can be implemented with confidence, but it is, again, important to verify the efficacy of the strategy through data collection. In other words, if a teacher is attempting to teach a student with ASD how to ask for time off from his or her supervisor, and he finds that the task analysis is not resulting in sufficient progress, then the teacher should alter the teaching plan. That alteration could include changing the teaching strategy from task analysis to video modeling or pivotal response training.

Also, all of these strategies apply the principles of applied behavior analysis (ABA). When teachers use these strategies to teach functional skills documented in the IEP and they collect data to verify the efficacy of instruction, they are using ABA. Thus, ABA is not a singular curriculum designed to teach young children with ASD only. Instead, ABA is the manipulation of antecedent events and the application of reinforcement designed to strengthen target behaviors.

Finally, observe that a notable ABA strategy, discrete trial training, is not on this list of scientifically based practices for middle and high school youth with ASD. This is because, although discrete trial training is a scientifically based practice for younger children with ASD, there is not enough research to document its applicability to adolescents and young adults. Therefore, it is not included on this list at this time.

Behavior Challenges, Functional Behavior Assessment, and Behavior Intervention Plans

Rashaun   Rashaun continued to make tremendous progress in many academic areas in school, yet, midway through his first year in high school, he began to display challenging behavior. His teacher, Mr. Yohe, noted that Rashaun threw his work, most often in the afternoon during math. On some days, he would throw his work, whine, and cry for the entire math period. This behavior troubled Mr. Yohe and he worried that Rashaun would not be able to continue in his current program with this disruptive behavior. He turned to the school psychologist, Dr. Jaegar, for help in designing a behavior intervention plan (BIP) to address this behavior challenge. To develop a sound BIP, Dr. Jaeger knew that she first needed to complete a functional behavior assessment (FBA) to understand the communicative function of Rashaun's behavior. Through interviews, observation, and hypothesis development, Dr. Jaeger collaborated with Mr. Yohe, Rashaun, and Rashaun's parents, Mr. and Mrs. Nixon, to develop a BIP based on the function of his behavior.

Most behavior, problem or adaptive, serves a specific function in the life of the person in question. To change that behavior, we must assess the function of problem behavior and replace it with a functional communication or social skill that will accomplish the same outcome for the person (O'Neill et al., 1997). In Rashaun's case, to develop the most comprehensive BIP, Dr. Jaeger completed an FBA to identify the function of his behavior.

With this view, it is important to understand that problem behavior is not something that has to be suppressed. Instead, problem behavior is a form of communication that has a function in the life of the person who displays it. Using the laws of behavior, we can narrow the messages that a behavior is communicating down to four basic messages (Cooper, Heron, & Heward, 2007; Schall, 2012):

1. Seeking attention from others
2. Seeking something tangible such as an item, activity, or food
3. Seeking sensory input from the action itself
4. Avoiding a person, task, item, or environment

These consequences, also known as *reinforcement*, make behavior stronger. According to ABA, behavior that is *reinforced* with one of these four basic consequences is made stronger (Cooper, Heron, & Heward, 2007). Thus, problem behavior has been reinforced, probably unknowingly, by one or more of those four consequences. As a result, problem behavior becomes established as a way of "requesting" a particular consequence. For us to replace that behavior with a different behavior, we have to figure out which of the four basic consequences is relevant to an individual with ASD's particular behavior and teach that person a new way to ask for that consequence. In Rashaun's case, part of this assessment begins by collecting information about when (in the afternoon) and where (in math class) the behavior is most likely to occur.

In addition to understanding the consequences that are present after a problem behavior has occurred, we also have to understand the events preceding the behavior that trigger its occurrence. These events, called *antecedents*, will help us understand which of the four consequences result in the problem behavior. For example, if a problem behavior mostly happens after an individual with ASD is left alone, we might guess that individual is seeking attention. If his or her problem behavior usually happens after the individual is given a task he or she does not like, then we might guess that he or she is avoiding that task. While observing Rashaun, Dr. Jaeger noted that Rashaun threw his materials in math class after being assigned independent seat work.

Functional Behavior Assessment

In this discussion of problem behavior, we have proposed that problem behavior might serve a particular function. To identify the function of a particular behavior, we will have to perform an FBA. FBA includes three different phases. They are indirect assessment, direct assessment, and hypothesis development (Bambara & Kern, 2005, Bambara & Knoster, 2009; Carr et al., 1999, Carr et al., 2002; Hieneman, Childs, & Sergay, 2006; Kincaid et al., 2002; Snell, Vorhees, & Chen, 2005). Table 19.7 defines each phase and describes the way data are collected to assess the function of problem behavior.

The culmination of an FBA is to develop a *competing behavior model* (O'Neill et al., 1997). This model is the first step in developing a BIP. Figure 19.2 provides an example of the competing behavior model for an escape-motivated and an attention-motivated behavior.

In Figure 19.2, there is one antecedent and three possible behaviors that lead to two different outcomes. In plain terms, the escape-motivated example could be described as follows:

1. When Rashaun is asked to complete a task he does not like, he will scream, fall to the floor, and throw his materials to avoid the task.
2. His teacher, Mr. Yohe, will first teach him to ask for a break to replace screaming, falling to the floor, and throwing his materials.
3. Once Rashaun has mastered the replacement behavior, asking for a break, his teacher will teach him to tolerate completion of the undesired task by increasing positive reinforcement for task completion.

Table 19.7. Three phases of functional behavior assessment

Phase	Type of data collected	How data are collected
Indirect assessment	• Understanding of the person's likes, dislikes, long-term goals • Definition of problem behavior • History of problem behavior • Person's and/or family members' perspectives on possible antecedents and function of problem behavior • Team members' perspectives on possible antecedents and function of problem behavior	• Review of person's educational and behavioral records • Interview with person and team • Review of incident reports • Review of behavioral data
Direct assessment	• Antecedent, behavior, consequence • Patterns • Interval counts • Frequency counts • Measures of intensity of problem behavior • Current strategies and their effectiveness	• Observations of the person in environments where he or she works, learns, communicates, interacts with others, and lives
Hypothesis development	• Antecedents associated with problem behavior • Functions of problem behavior • Locations where problem behavior occurs	• Summarize findings from data collected through indirect and direct assessment

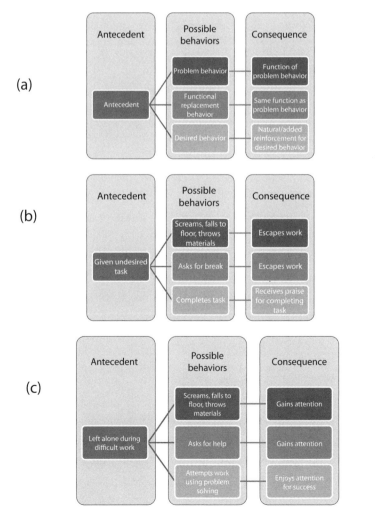

Figure 19.2. a) The competing behavior model; b) example of competing behavior model for escape-motivated behavior; c) example of competing behavior model for attention-seeking behavior.

Likewise, the attention-motivated behavior could be described as follows:

1. When Rashaun is left alone during difficult tasks, he will scream, fall to the floor, and throw materials to gain his teacher's attention.
2. His teacher, Mr. Yohe, will first teach him to ask for help to replace his problem behavior.
3. Once Rashaun has mastered the replacement behavior, asking for help, his teacher will teach him to attempt his work using problem-solving strategies before asking for help.

Notice that, in each case, the behaviors are the same, but the strategies to change behavior vary. This is because the function of each behavior is different. That is an important point to remember when one is developing an intervention to change behavior. That is, there is no "treatment," per se, for specific problem behaviors. Instead, the real key to changing problem behavior is to understand and treat the function of the problem behavior. In Rashaun's case, Dr. Jaeger concluded after completing the three phases of FBA that his behavior was motivated by a desire to escape difficult math tasks. Also, notice that, by completing the competing behavior model, Rashaun's educational team actually begins to assimilate the information collected from the FBA and develop a BIP.

Behavior Intervention Plan

Through the competing behavior model, the educational team identifies new behaviors that can replace the problem behavior. At the same time, there are other strategies that the team should consider. In fact, at minimum, a BIP should include three essential building blocks (Bambara & Kern, 2005; Carr et al., 2002):

1. Prevent the problem behavior from occurring.
2. Teach new behaviors that will replace the problem behavior.
3. Respond differently when the new behaviors and the problem behaviors occur.

These three building blocks are depicted in Figure 19.3.

As a result of this work, Rashaun's team decided to implement the following strategies to prevent the behaviors from occurring:

• Minimize the impact of antecedent, independent math work by pairing it with a desired item, event, or activity. In Rashaun's case, they provided headphones with desired music on an MP3 device while he was completing independent math work.

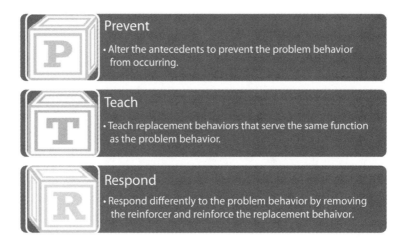

Figure 19.3. Three essential building blocks for a behavior intervention plan. (*Source:* Dunlap, Iovannone, Wilson, Kincaid, & Strain, 2010.)

- Mr. Yohe interspersed mastered work with work that presents more challenge to Rashaun. By interspersing mastered work with challenging work, Rashaun relaxed a bit more when asked to do work.

- Provide frequent breaks to minimize stress around problem situations. This is an important antecedent strategy, particularly for students whose problem behavior functions to avoid work. In Rashaun's case, this was a critical strategy. Mr. Yohe gave him a "take a break" card. Whenever Rashaun showed the card, Mr. Yohe removed the work for a minute or two. Then Mr. Yohe would reintroduce the work while providing additional assistance to Rashaun.

- Offer more choices to the student across the day. This simple strategy makes a huge difference in the lives of students. Offering choices of activities, tasks, materials, location to complete work, and other similar choices frequently results in fewer problem behaviors across the day for the student. Mr. Yohe offered Rashaun the choice of working on independent math for 8 minutes, 9 minutes, or 10 minutes. This choice helped Rashaun relax a bit more while completing math.

- Increase predictability. Many students with communication difficulties and intellectual disabilities have difficulty predicting their own daily schedule. By providing them with visual schedules, teams can increase that student's tolerance of less-desired activities. This is because the student can see what activity is coming next. Picture schedules work best when the student can see that work is followed by a break or desired activity (Bambara & Kern, 2005; Bambara & Knoster, 2009). This was also a very effective strategy for Rashaun and resulted in further reductions in the problem behavior.

These prevention strategies were enhanced by the use of the schedule feature on the mp3 device. In fact, because of Mr. Yohe's own interest in using technology, he was able to implement many technological tools in this part of Rashaun's plan. Specifically, Rashaun used the schedule feature as well as the timer on the MP3 device to implement most of these strategies.

All of these strategies resulted in reduced problem behavior, but Dr. Jaeger also implemented a teaching strategy to replace the problem behavior. Without this aspect of the plan, Rashaun would not become independent in managing his own behavior. For Rashaun, because the team concluded that his throwing behavior was really a request for a break, they decided they had to find a new way for him to request a break. He learned to "ask for 5" when he became frustrated. This is perhaps the most critical aspect of Rashaun's plan. By teaching him to request a break, Mr. Yohe and Dr. Jaeger in fact increase his independence. Because Rashaun's problem behavior was reinforced by avoiding work tasks and the new behavior results in avoiding work tasks, there was no need to purchase expensive trinkets or set up different reinforcement alternatives; Mr. Yohe can give him the same outcome he sought with his problem behavior (Hieneman, Childs, & Sergay, 2006). Thus, the final piece of his behavior intervention was to reinforce the new behavior by giving Rashaun a break when he requests one. This was the "respond" part of the plan described in Table 19.8.

This plan resulted in success. Rashaun increased asking for a break instead of throwing his materials. In addition, because of the other elements of the plan, he also increased the amount of time he spent completing his work. Instead of throwing, he seemed to trust that his teacher would give him breaks, so he was not so stressed throughout the day. This change was not attributable to any one element in the plan. Instead, it seemed to result from all the changes the team made. Table 19.8 lists the essential elements of Rashaun's BIP.

It is important to note that this plan was individualized for Rashaun. This plan would probably not work for another student, especially if that student's behavior serves a different function. If the function of another student's problem behavior were to seek attention, then teaching that person to request a break would not result in the same outcome for that student.

Table 19.8. Rashaun's behavior intervention plan

Preventing setting event and antecedent strategies	Teaching functional replacement behavior strategies	Responding reinforcement strategies
Make sure that Rashaun has his daily schedule with breaks and choices on his MP3 device.	Remind Rashaun to "ask for 5" whenever he begins to whine about his work.	Give Rashaun a break when he asks for one with his picture card.
Offer Rashaun choices regarding how much time he will work on independent work. Set the timer on his MP3 device.	Teach Rashaun to set the timer and input his schedule on his MP3 device.	If he begins to cry or yell, remind him to request a break by handing the "take 5" card to him.
Offer Rashaun breaks when completing difficult work.		
Let Rashaun listen to music on the MP3 device when completing math.		
For every two difficult problems give Rashaun three easy problems.		

Transition Services for Individuals with Autism Spectrum Disorder

As noted previously in this chapter, when provided with intensive support and high-quality educational services, individuals with ASD can achieve. These programs use a combination of autism-specific supports (such as those described in the previous section) and quality job support services that are universal for individuals with disabilities. As a result, more programs have demonstrated that individuals with ASD are successful in community employment settings. In fact, some businesses are leading the way with specialized programs such as Project SEARCH® and revised business models at Walgreens and Specialisterne continue to demonstrate that individuals with ASD enhance the workplace with their unique gifts and talents. (See Chapter 15 for an in-depth discussion of some of these models; see also Beard, 2011; Rutkowski, Daston, Van Kuiken, & Riehle, 2006; Wehman, McDonough, Schall, Molinelli, & Riehle, in press.)

As a consequence, secondary transition programs serving students with ASD must include the full array of transition services including community-based job exploration and training; community-based life skills instruction; instruction in personal management, hygiene, and leisure and recreation skills; and instruction in functional academic skills. Finally, and most importantly, such programs must think widely about potential job supports and services for persons with ASD. The last section of this chapter reviews the types of community job support and services that assist students with ASD in finding and securing employment.

Job Supports for Individuals with Autism Spectrum Disorder

It was previously thought that the employment prospects for people with autism were bleak; however, experience has shown that, with the proper intervention and supports, individuals with ASD can work in a variety of businesses for minimum wage or better. Supported employment is used to assist people with severe disabilities such as ASD with gaining and maintaining employment. Supported employment is founded on the belief that all people regardless of the severity of their disability should have the opportunity to work.

Supported employment was designed to give these individuals with severe disabilities tailored assistance that can make going to work a reality. Using supported employment, the person with the ASD is assisted by a vocational rehabilitation specialist or designated school personnel with identifying vocational strengths and potential support needs, locating a real job for real pay in the community, providing one-to-one on-the-job support and skills training, providing long-term follow-up, and assisting with job retention services. When support staff implement evidence-based practices, the student with ASD will be employed when he or she leaves school. As a consequence, the transition is a simple handoff from one set of support providers to another (school to adult vocational service provider). Garcia-Villamisar, Wehman, and Navarro (2002) found that supported employment resulted in greater quality of life for persons with autism across a 4-year period of time than employment for individuals in sheltered environment. Thus, community-based vocational training programs can and should be developed to assist students with exploring jobs and creating a vision for future employment, learning work values and skills in actual work settings, and becoming employed before leaving school.

Very often, individuals with autism require special job matching that takes into account the effects of the disability on the person in varied environments. Careful matching to desired jobs means that the school and vocational rehabilitation providers must consider the required job skills as well as the social environment. Rashaun would not do well in a chaotic environment with daily changes in his schedule, even if the job skills required in that environment were to his liking. Thus, it is critical to consider the strengths and interests as well as the work environment needs of each person with autism. Division TEACCH, an autism program at the University of North Carolina Chapel Hill, identifies appropriate vocational settings as those that have jobs that are predictable, have potential for clearly defined work tasks, and can be adapted to the individual's need for structure. They seek employers and co-workers who are receptive to training and who are willing to create an environment where an individual is more likely to succeed. Finally, they identify job settings in which there is potential to utilize individual strengths (Chapman, 2004). Careful consideration of all of these components has led to a highly successful supported employment program for individuals with ASD.

A few sources have addressed the needs of individuals with ASD when they are seeking and engaging in community-based paid employment (Hagner & Cooney, 2005; Hawkins, 2004; Lattimore, Parsons, & Reid, 2003; Meyer, 2001). They identify very specific steps that are necessary to ensure successful employment for individuals with autism:

- *Assessing job and task preferences carefully before placement:* As a group, individuals with autism are much more likely to be successful when they engage in preferred tasks regularly in their job. In fact, many sources recommended that jobs be modified to address the persons' work preferences (Hagner & Cooney, 2005; Lattimore et al., 2003).

- *Assessing social, communication, and job skill needs:* This is the one area where persons with autism struggle most. Müller, Schuler, Burton, and Yates (2003) found that persons with ASD were frequently fired from jobs because of social and communication difficulties, not an inability to perform job skills.

- *Making a careful match between the job, the person's preferences, the social and communication demands in the environment, and the tolerance of co-workers for diversity*: This step is critical to developing a successful job placement. Frequently, persons with ASD have difficulty with jobs that require a high degree of interaction with others. Nevertheless, they may be able to tolerate such interaction better with training and matching with a supportive environment. Thus, this is a critical step when seeking employment opportunities for persons with ASD (Meyer, 2001).

- *Teaching the social and communication skills required in the job, in addition to the actual job skills:* The "hard skills" in a job—how to do the job itself—is frequently not difficult for most persons with ASD. The "soft skills" in a job—how to interact with the supervisor and co-workers, how to tolerate change, how to make requests in the environment, how to take a break, and so on—are frequently areas that cause great stress and discord for persons with ASD. Thus, teaching these skills is as important as, if not slightly more important than, teaching the job skills themselves (Müller, Schuler, Burton, & Yates, 2003).

- *Preparing employers and co-workers for the diverse behaviors that a person with autism may display, if necessary:* At times, it may be necessary to prepare co-workers and employers for some of the nonharmful, but odd, behavior or movements in which a person with autism may engage. Not every case requires such intervention; nevertheless, it is possible that, when placing a person with ASD in a work environment, the support provider may have to educate co-workers and employers about the person and his or her different behavior (Howlin, Goode, Hutton, & Rutter, 2004).

- *Teaching co-worker/employee/employer relationship behaviors to the person with ASD:* The communication and social skill deficits in persons with ASD across the entire spectrum are such that they may not understand differences in how to interact with friends, co-workers, or supervisors. In the modern workplace, a simple social error, such as hugging a co-worker, could result in termination of employment. A person with ASD may unknowingly engage in forbidden behavior and not understand the resulting consequence. Thus, it is essential that the person receive support from job-placing professionals in understanding acceptable and unacceptable behavior (Meyer, 2001).

- *Making modifications and adaptations in the job environment to meet the social and communication needs of the worker:* Persons with ASD may require that jobs be modified to meet their individual communication, social, and sensory needs. Such modifications and adaptations may include

  - Providing a consistent schedule

  - Decreasing or developing predictable social interactions

  - Providing visual organizers for job tasks

  - Providing direct supervisory feedback instead of subtle communication about job expectations and performance

  - Explaining and preparing the person for changes at the work site before they occur

  - Encouraging co-workers in initiating interactions with the person

  - Explaining that the failure to say "hi" is not an intentional slight, but a disability-specific oversight

- Providing job coach contact and follow-along during the entire tenure of employment

- Such support makes the challenges of ASD less of an issue in work environments (Hagner & Cooney, 2005; Müller et al., 2003).

- *Supporting the person through job challenges and crises:* All humans who work have bad days at work. For the average person without a disability, such days are measured against the many good days that a person has. For the person with ASD who tends to have great difficulty maintaining perspective and insight, such a regular occurrence as a bad day at the office can become a crisis. As a consequence, persons with ASD frequently need support from co-workers, friends, family, and paid support providers in balancing and coping with everyday work challenges (Müller et al., 2003).

Conclusion

As noted before, persons with ASD present unique challenges and, as such, require specific supports in work environments. Very often, persons with ASD are very successful in completing the skills for jobs but have difficulty managing the social environment for work. Nevertheless, mindful implementation of supports and services frequently results in highly successful employment for persons with ASD.

The critical steps to achieving employment are early exposure to the world of work and training in a variety of community-based job experiences. To achieve steady and successful employment, persons with ASD need a combination of specialized services tailored to meet the challenges of the disorder, universal services designed to assist the person in acquiring the necessary job skills, and involvement from the person's team. Experience has demonstrated that individuals with ASD are successful in adult life when their educational team, family, and community service providers collaborate to plan early, consider the person through person-centered planning, and match the educational curriculum to meet the person's needs.

Study Questions

1. How does the dramatic increase in the prevalence of children and youth with autism impact transition programs for youth with disabilities?

2. What are the three primary characteristics of ASD?

3. What are some of the secondary characteristics and behaviors of ASD?

4. Describe the multidimensional perspective of autism and list and describe the five dimensions that must be considered when one is serving a person with an ASD.

5. What are the three phases a team must execute when completing an FBA and developing a BIP?

6. Describe the competing behavior model and why it is important when one is developing a BIP.

7. What are the three essential building blocks of a BIP?

8. Meet with a teacher or transition coordinator to discuss some ways technology is being used to support students with ASD in transition.

9. What are the characteristics of excellent programs for individuals with ASD?

10. What are two ways that transition teams can identify the necessary communication and social skills a person with ASD may need to learn?

11. Describe the types of experiences that are necessary to prepare a person with ASD for life after school.

12. Meet with someone involved in assisting youth with employment to discuss some steps that ensure successful job placement for a person with ASD. Compare and contrast this information with the eight critical steps presented.

Online Resources

Virginia Commonwealth University Autism Center for Excellence: http://www.vcuautismcenter.org

Association for Positive Behavior Support: http://www.apbs.org

Global Autism Collaboration: http://www.autism.org

Autism Society of America: http://www.autism-society.org/

National Professional Development Center on Autism Spectrum Disorders: http://autismpdc.fpg.unc.edu/

Applications for Youth with Traumatic Brain Injury and Other Health Impairments

20

PAUL WEHMAN, MICHAEL D. WEST,
PAMELA TARGETT, AND CHARLES DILLARD

After completing this chapter, the reader will be able to

- Describe orthopedic and other health impairments and traumatic brain injury (TBI) including definition, etiology, incidence, prevalence, and the unique challenges

- Discuss the unique challenges student may present for transition-planning teams and possible ways to alleviate them

- Describe a functional approach to assessment

- Explain strategies that may assist students with learning work tasks and work-related activities

- Explain the differences in time-limited and advocacy-level services

- Describe ways to evaluate transition services

Since the 1970s, adult services providers and education organizations serving people with disabilities have attempted to design programs around certain values, among them inclusion in a variety of community settings and activities, normalized lifestyles, enhanced quality of life, productive employment with meaningful wages, and, most recently, choice and empowerment. Education personnel are becoming increasingly aware of the need to prepare youth with disabilities for the same goals as youth without disabilities: the advancement of students' own educational and employment goals and goals to live, work, and participate as independently as possible in their home communities after leaving school. School systems often fail to meet this obligation adequately, as shown by the cases of Roberta, Jose, Linda (see case studies), and many others.

Unfortunately, there are many school-age children who are experiencing situations similar to those of Roberto and Jose. Many individuals with mild brain injuries, like Roberto, recover quickly and return to school with no immediate evidence of complications. However, problems may develop, even after mild brain injuries. Problems with academic achievement may not be apparent for a year or more after injury. When problems are detected, they may not initially be associated with the injury or patients and families may deny the presence of mild impairments until more severe problems develop. Often, students with mild brain injuries find that fatigue and attention deficits contribute to failure in the classroom. Although some students with mild injury will need help, most with moderate to severe injuries, like Jose, will require more intensive educational assistance.

Helping Linda and others is challenging yet absolutely essential. A health impairment is an ongoing long-term problem, but it is not and should not be an insurmountable barrier to work, successful school experiences, community living, and adult adjustment. Like all other special needs that most children and youth face, each barrier must be brainstormed for a solution that can work.

This chapter discusses issues and guidelines related to school-to-work transitions and postsecondary education for youth with TBI, orthopedic impairments, and other health impairments, presenting examples of the transition process in action.

Roberto and Jose   On a cold, late, winter afternoon, 15-year-old Roberto, his twin brother, Jose, his mother, Rose, and his father, John, were traveling home from their annual pilgrimage to the boys' grandmother's house when it began to sleet and snow. Because they were only about an hour's drive from home, John decided to keep traveling, but to substantially slow down the pace. About 1 hour later, and only 10 minutes from their final destination, visibility became extremely poor as the weather deteriorated and nighttime approached. Everyone in the car was quiet and tense as they continued on their journey home. Suddenly, there was a severe impact from behind. The light blue sedan careened off the road and crash-landed upside down at the bottom of a steep embankment. In the previous moments, a truck traveling at a high rate of speed had suddenly swerved from the passing lane into the other one in an attempt to miss a fast-braking vehicle. Unfortunately, although this prevented one accident, it caused another.

The truck's driver pulled over and called 911 for help. It took about 20 minutes for the rescue team to arrive. Rose and John were released from the hospital later that evening with minor injuries, but the twins were not so fortunate. Roberto had experienced a broken leg and collar bone as well as a minor TBI. He had lost consciousness for 1 hour. He spent 4 days in the hospital and returned to school a couple of weeks later. Before his injury, Roberto was an average student with plans to attend a technical institute to pursue a career as a computer programmer. When discharged from the hospital, the doctor instructed Roberto to contact him if he had any problems and to follow up in 3 months. Soon after returning to school, Roberto experienced many problems such as frequent headaches, fatigue, and lapses in memory. His grades dropped. He also experienced significant depression as he began to do poorly, lose touch with his friends, and worry about his brother's recovery.

Jose was less fortunate. He experienced a punctured lung, damage to his spleen, and severe TBI. He was in a coma for 6 weeks and afterward began intensive rehabilitation. Spring came and went, but Jose had not returned to school. Before his injury, Jose was an above-average student with plans to attend the local university to pursue a career as an architectural engineer. That summer, he was discharged from the hospital to day rehabilitation where he continued to receive services until the insurance company would no longer authorize payment. On the last day of rehabilitation, the staff gave Jose a small going-away party and reminded him to use the various compensatory memory strategies he had learned. Jose returned to school that fall and experienced a multitude of problems. Specifically, he lacked the ability to initiate activities and had a poor memory that affected his ability to retain information and learn. He also experienced extreme emotional outbursts on a regular basis over seemingly trivial matters. In addition, he did not use the strategies he had been taught in the rehabilitation environment because he was not able to generalize their use to this real-life setting.

Linda   Linda was diagnosed with cerebral palsy (CP) soon after birth. She learned to walk with the assistance of a walker but uses a wheelchair for long distances. Her speech is difficult to understand, and she has only limited use of her hands. She received her early education in a special school operated by a private service organization. When she was 14, she asked her parents if she could go to the general high school in her neighborhood, and they agreed. Her first year there was difficult; the counselors, principal, and teachers had little experience with students who have physical impairments, and the school building itself, built before the Americans with Disabilities Act (ADA) of 1990 (PL 101-336), was not very accessible for students with mobility issues.

Over the next few years, the school made accommodations for Linda: adjusting classes so that she would not have to encounter many stairs or long walks, modifying classroom setups so that she could move about more easily, modifying her classwork and examinations to better suit her abilities, and working with Linda to locate and train peer assistants. Overall, it was a positive experience, and Linda was able to complete the requirements for a diploma and made a few close friends along the way.

However, the school did not adequately plan for Linda's adjustment from high school to adulthood. She graduated and had no place to go. Employment seemed an impossible goal, and she did not feel that she could handle the physical and mental demands of college. It was not until 5 years after graduation that she enrolled in community college, taking classes in computer programming. With adaptations, she was able to use a keyboard and joy-stick mouse. She later transferred to a 4-year college and received services and accommodations related to her disabilities. She earned her degree in information systems over a longer period of time than most students because her physical limitations prevented her from taking a full class load. After graduation, it took her another 3 years to land her first job. In all, the time from high school graduation to her first job amounted to 15 years. At the time that Linda's peers were well along in their careers and building their earning capacity, Linda was just beginning.

Who Are Individuals with Traumatic Brain Injury, Orthopedic Impairments, and Other Health Impairments?

Obviously, understanding a student will vary and require an understanding of his or her unique characteristics and personality; this is critical. However, to serve youth with these disabilities, educators should have some basic knowledge about it. The following section offers an overview of some of the most relevant ones including a definition, the etiology, report on incidence and prevalence, and information on the unique challenges faced.

Traumatic Brain Injury

A TBI, sometimes referred to as an acquired brain injury (ABI), is caused by a bump, blow, or jolt to the head that disrupts the normal function of the brain. Trauma is the major cause of death and disability in children older than 1 year of age (Krach, Gormley, & Ward, 2010). TBI is an important public health issue that has far-reaching consequences that affect the daily lives of those injured as well as the lives of their families. This is often complicated by the fact that children's outward appearance may appear like it did before the accident, yet they may be having significant cognitive, emotional, and functional deficits.

According to the Centers for Disease Control and Prevention (CDC, 2010), the estimated average annual number of TBIs that occur among children ages 0–14 years is 511,257, resulting in 473,947 emergency department visits, 35,136 hospitalizations, and 2,174 deaths. With almost half a million emergency department visits for TBI annually by children ages 0–14 years, it is estimated that one in every 20 emergency department visits at pediatric hospitals is for a TBI, making it more common than burns or poisoning (Anderson & Yeates, 2010). Very young children ages 0–4 years had the highest rate of TBI-related emergency department visits (1,256 per 100,000 population), followed by older adolescents ages 15–19 years (757 per 100,000). Put another way, by the 10th grade, one in 30 students would have had a TBI (Crowley & White-Waters, 2010). The leading causes of TBI are falls, motor vehicle, struck by/against events, and assaults. Falls cause half (50%) of the TBIs among children ages 0–14 years.

In a recent review of the literature, Arango-Lasprilla and Kreutzer (2010) found that African American and Hispanic persons have worse functional outcomes and community integration and are less likely to receive treatment and be employed than white persons after a TBI. Emerging research detects racial and ethnic differences in marital stability, emotional/neurobehavioral complications, and quality of life outcomes; however, more research is needed to corroborate significant findings. African American and Hispanic caregivers express more burden, spend more time in a caregiving role, have fewer needs met, and use different types of coping strategies than white counterparts. Therefore, the racial and ethnic differences noted in this literature review are an indicator that minorities are at disproportionate risk for poorer outcomes. The authors suggested that postacute interventions should specifically target minorities to diminish inequities that exist.

Direct medical costs and indirect costs such as lost productivity of TBI totaled an estimated $60 billion in the United States in 2000, with $1 billion in hospital charges generated for TBI patients younger than 17 years of age (Schneier, Shields, Hostetler, Xiang, & Smith, 2006).

The majority of the injuries to children or adolescents are mild, but TBI can lead to myriad cognitive, motor, and behavioral deficits that may contribute to poor postschool outcomes (McNamee, Walker, Cifu, & Wehman, 2009). Children with TBI may have short- or long-term consequences that affect thinking, perception, language, or emotions, and these consequences may not be readily apparent. Cognitive deficits include problems with attention, memory, problem solving, orientation, thought organization, executive function, and communication impairment. Motor deficits include balance, coordination, response speed, and motor tone abnormality. Behavioral issues include impulsivity and emotional lability. In association with these impairments, functional outcomes are also affected with evidence of low school attainment, reduced vocational opportunities, poor adaptive skills, and lowered quality of life. In addition to deficits that are apparent immediately in the months after injury, TBI during childhood can interrupt normal development and full consequences may not be apparent until years later (Krach et al., 2010).

Long-term follow-up studies of children conducted during the K–12 school years suggest that problems associated with TBI tend to persist or worsen as children progress through school. A critical issue in service delivery for students with TBI is the significant discrepancy between the incidence of TBI and the identification of children with TBI for special education services. Glang, Todis, Thomas, Hood, Bedell, and Cockrell (2008) examined factors that influence identification and service practices for students with TBI. Parents of 56 youth with TBI completed a questionnaire and interview about the hospital–school transition and educational services provided within the first year of school reentry. Results documented that 25% of the sample were identified for formal services (via individualized education program or 504 Plan) whereas more than 41% received informal supports (e.g., schedule change, extra time on tests). Results suggested that injury severity and hospital–school transition services (e.g., written or verbal communication between hospital and school) were related to the provision of formal special education or 504 services. A critical factor contributing to the identification of students with TBI for special education is the link between hospital and school.

Spinal Cord Injury

Injuries to the spinal cord can have profound effects on children, leading to deficits in muscle function, bowel and bladder problems, and skin issues. In addition, there can be profound cognitive, emotional, and psychological issues stemming from the loss of this function. These injuries can be congenital, known as meningomyelocele (MMC) or spina bifida, or acquired spinal cord injury (SCI).

MMC is a developmental birth defect of the neural tube, resulting in an open spinal cord lesion, most often in the lumbar or sacral spine. It is caused by a failure of closure of the embryonic caudal neural tube in the first 4 weeks of gestation (this is significant as the injury occurs often before the mother is aware she is pregnant; McMahon, 2011). The exact causes are unknown, but it is thought to be attributable to a mix of maternal and environmental factors including maternal folic acid deficiency, maternal medication use, and genetic factors. Each year, about 1,500 babies are born with spina bifida. The overall prevalence of spina bifida among children and adolescents 0–19 years of age was 3.1 cases per 10,000, which represents about 24,860 children and adolescents living with spina bifida in the United States in 2002 (Shin et al., 2010). It is the second-most-common congenital motor disorder, behind CP (Pico, Wilson, & Haas, 2010).

Paralysis of the lower legs (paraplegia) or all four extremities (tetraplegia) can be caused by an injury to or an abnormality with the spinal cord. Traumatic causes include motor vehicle accidents, falls, sports, and acts of violence. Nontraumatic causes include infection, tumor, juvenile rheumatoid arthritis, skeletal dysplasia, and transverse myelitis. About 265,000 people are living in the United States with an SCI. Every year, 40 per million or 12,000 new cases occur. It is estimated that children younger than 15 years account for around 5% of new SCIs and 20% of injuries occurred in those aged younger than 20 years (National Spinal Cord Injury Statistical Center, 2011). SCI is classified by the Neurologic Level of Injury (the lowest level with intact sensory and motor function, i.e., C5) and as either complete (with no muscle activity or sensation below the level of injury) or incomplete (some motor or sensory function below the level of injury).

Because of the similar nature of the injury, both SCI and MMC can present some comparable challenges to patients and families. Depending on the severity and level of the injury to the spinal cord, mobility can be significantly affected and children may be dependent on adaptive orthotics, assistive devices, and wheelchairs. Many children can also have neurogenic bowel and bladder and have difficulty with continence. This may require the use of catheters intermittently to empty the bladder and suppositories to stimulate bowel evacuation. Pressure ulcers are also prone to develop because of abnormal pressures on skin attributable to impaired mobility. Children may develop contractures in the ankles and knees, particularly those who do not ambulate and spend significant time in their wheelchair. Scoliosis is also extremely common in both disorders (Pico et al., 2010; Nelson & Hornyak, 2010). Latex allergies have been noted for years to occur in individuals with MMC and have recently been noted to be increasing in children with SCI (Majed et al., 2009).

There are some things that may be different with each patient population. More than 85%–90% of children with MMC will have hydrocephalus and require ventriculoperitoneal shunts (Dirks et al., 2005). Many children will also have cognitive deficits and display what is commonly known as cocktail syndrome, in which children are very verbose and articulate about certain subjects that interest them but lack an overall depth of knowledge.

Children with SCI may experience autonomic dysreflexia, which is a dysfunction of the autonomic nervous systems after SCI. After SCI, a disconnect between the sympathetic and the parasympathetic regulatory system exists. Some noxious stimuli (e.g., urinary tract infection, ingrown toenail, pressure ulcer) will cause an outflow of sympathetic activity leading to dangerous hypertension and bradycardia causing headache, red splotches, and nasal congestion. This can be a medical emergency and must be treated as soon as possible (Nelson & Hornyak, 2010).

Although SCI does not necessarily affect the brain and alter cognition, it should be remembered that trauma that causes SCI may also cause injury to the brain. It is estimated that 10% of children who receive a TBI will also have an SCI (Nelson & Hornyak, 2010). Children should be screened for TBI in the acute period after injury and monitored for late cognitive deficits.

Cerebral Palsy

CP is the most common motor disorder in children. It is defined as a group of disorders of the development of movement and posture, causing limitations that are attributed to non-progressive disturbances that occurred in the developing fetal or infant brain (CDC, 2011). For a child to be diagnosed with CP, they must have three things: a neuromotor control deficit that alters movement or posture, a static brain lesion or injury (usually seen on a magnetic resonance image [MRI] of the brain), and acquisition of this injury in the first few years of life (McMahon, Pruitt, & Vargus-Adams, 2010). This is a very broad disorder that has a very wide spectrum of affected children; from those mildly affected who may only wear a small brace inside one shoe to a child who is more severely affected and is totally dependent for all mobility, activities of daily living, and function. Although it is true that CP is a nonprogressive disorder, children can often grow into their CP—the abnormal muscle forces on their bodies can lead to muscle contracture, joint dislocations, and bony deformities that can lead to pain and loss of function if not treated properly.

Resulting limits in movement and posture cause activity limitation and are often accompanied by disturbances of sensation, depth perception, and other sight-based perceptual problems, communication ability, and sometimes even cognition; sometimes, a form of CP may be accompanied by epilepsy. CP, no matter what the type, is often accompanied by secondary musculoskeletal problems that arise as a result of the underlying etiology (Paneth, 2007).

Establishing an etiology for children with CP is often difficult, particularly those born at full term (Kulak, Okurowska-Zawada, Sienkiewiez, Paszko-Patej, & Krajewska-Kulak, 2010). There are several risk factors for CP; these include prematurity, infection, inflammation, and coagulopathy (Odding, Roebroeck, & Stam, 2006), with the greatest risk factor being prematurity (infants being born before 37 weeks' gestation).

A CDC study shows that the average prevalence of CP is 3.3 per 1,000 8-year-old children or one in 303 children. This report of the prevalence and features of CP, the most common cause of motor disability in childhood, is from select communities that included Alabama, Georgia, Missouri, and Wisconsin. These four sites reported higher prevalence among boys than girls and the most common type of CP across all four sites was spastic CP (81%; http://www.cdc.gov/Features/CerebralPalsy/). Even though there have been tremendous advances in medicine over the same time period, these numbers have remained relatively stable for several decades. This is because, although the survival rate for babies born extraordinarily early (23 and 24 weeks gestation) has improved, those infants are much more susceptible to the neurological injuries that can lead to CP.

Several different classification systems have been developed for children with CP. Children can be classified by the pattern of their body parts that are affected, how their muscles work, or by what they can do functionally. There are three main categories based on pattern of body parts: hemiparesis (one side of body, e.g., left arm and leg), diparesis (usually both legs), and quadriparesis (all four extremities). Muscle movement can be broken down by too much muscle tone (children with spasticity or dystonia), too little muscle tone (hypotonia), abnormal coordination (ataxia), and mixed forms. The Gross Motor Functional Classification System (GMFCS) classifies children with CP into five groups, based on their gross motor skills (Palisano et al., 1997) with skills ranging from a GMFCS I (who can walk indoors and outdoors and climb stairs without limitations) to GMFCS V (children have no means of independent mobility).

Even though CP is primarily a motor disorder, because it is an injury to the brain, there can be many associated disorders. These include sensory impairments, visual impairments, hearing impairments, cognitive impairments, psychological impairments, seizures, oromotor impairments, nutritional disorders, genitourinary disorders, respiratory disorders, and orthopedic deformities of hips, ankles, spine, and upper extremities. Many children with CP *can* have one or several of these issues, but it is important to remember that, just because a child has CP, he or she does not *have* to have any of these (McMahon et al., 2010). A description of associated disorders is provided in Table 20.1.

Neuromuscular Disorders

Neuromuscular disorders are inherited or acquired disorders that affect any or all aspects of the neuromuscular system at the level of the muscle, nerves, neuromuscular junction (where the nerve meets and delivers signal to the muscle), or motor neurons (nerves in the spinal cord controlling muscles). All of these disorders are progressive and result in muscle weakness (Muscular Dystrophy Association [MDA], 2008). Some may affect additional organ systems, including the heart and lungs. Others may have cognitive deficits as well. In addition, some treatments to preserve muscle function may have other significant side effects (e.g., corticosteroids used to treat Duchenne muscular dystrophy [DMD] and Becker muscular dystrophy [BMD] can cause weight gain and behavioral issues).

There are more than a million people in the United States affected by some form of neuromuscular disease, and about 40% of them are younger than 18 years (MDA, 2008). Some of the diseases are present at birth, whereas others will appear in adolescence or adulthood. Because so many of these disorders are inherited, several family members may be affected as well. Life span varies greatly depending on each specific disorder or

Table 20.1. Description of disorders associated with cerebral palsy

Associated disorders	Description (McMahon et al., 2010)
Sensory impairments	Deficits in two-point discrimination, proprioception, stereogenesis
Visual impairments	Strabismus, amblyopia, myopia
Hearing impairments	Rare; sensorineural hearing loss associated with infections, meningitis, and ototoxic drugs
Cognitive impairments	Common but hard to quantify and qualify
Psychological impairments	Variety of behavior and emotional problems possible: attention-deficit/hyperactivity disorder, anger, sadness, impulsivity, emotional lability, anxiety
Epilepsy	More common in more severe cerebral palsy and in children with quadriparesis versus diaparesis
Oromotor impairments	Problems handling secretions, poor swallowing coordination, speech articulation disorders
Genitourinary disorders	Urinary incontinence, urinary hesitancy, urinary retention
Respiratory disorders	Increased risk for infections because of poor cough, impaired control of respiratory muscles
Foot/ankle deformities	Equinus (foot pointed down) and equinovarus (foot pointed down and in)
Knee	Flexion contractures because of tight hamstrings and sitting all the time
Hip	Hip subluxation, dislocation
Spine	Scoliosis
Upper extremity	Elbow and wrist contractures

subtype of each disorder. Pulmonary or cardiac compromise can often be the cause of death. Table 20.2 offers an overview of neuromuscular diseases.

Table 20.2. Overview of neuromuscular diseases

Disorder	Definition	Etiology	Prevalence and incidence	Unique features
Duchenne muscular dystrophy (DMD)	Debilitating myopathic disorder that presents with progressive muscle wasting and diffuse muscle weakness	X-linked recessive disorder, located on Xp21, causing lack of production of dystrophin	Incidence: 1:3,500 to 1:6,000 male births (Matthews, 2011)	Presents as early as 3 years old, males much more affected than females, steady decline in strength after 6–11 years, stop ambulating by age 9–15 but steroids can prolong ambulation, cognitive ability compromise, life span beyond 30 rare (Matthews, 2011)
Becker muscular dystrophy (BMD)	Muscular dystrophy with a similar pattern of weakness seen in DMD but with a later onset and slower rate of progression	X-linked recessive disorder, located on Xp21, causing a reduced amount or production of abnormal dystrophin	Incidence: 5:100,000 Prevalence: 17–27 per 1 million (Joyce 2011a)	Later presentation (between age 5 and 15 years) and slower progression compared with DMD, loss of ambulation > 15 years, scoliosis rare, most survive beyond 30, cardiomyopathy may occur before skeletal muscle weakness (Joyce, 2011a)
Charcot-Marie-Tooth (CMT)	Group of inherited disorders of the peripheral nerve that cause significant progressive neuromuscular impairment	More than 20 genes have been linked to different types of CMT affecting different parts of the nerve; inheritance varies based on type	Prevalence: 1 per 2,500–3,000 (Morozova, 2011); most common genetic neuropathy	Onset usually in first or second decade of life, affects both motor and sensory nerves, weakness starts in hands and feet and can slowly progress to hips, knees, elbows, and shoulders; patients often have a normal life span (Morozova, 2011)
Limb-girdle muscular dystrophy (LGMD)	Group of (at least 19) inherited disorders sharing a progressive pattern of weakness in shoulders and hips (the limb girdles)	Different subtypes each have a different affected production of muscle proteins; inheritance also varies by type	Prevalence: 8–70 per million (Joyce, 2011b)	Can present in childhood, adolescence, young adulthood, or later; both genders affected equally; progressive disorder but rate of progression varies; weakness starts proximally and can extend distally; different subtypes can have cardiac, cognitive, and/or pulmonary involvement (Joyce, 2011b)
Myasthenia gravis (MG)	Disorder of the neuromuscular junction (NMJ) leading to abnormal neuromuscular transmission leading to fluctuating muscle weakness and fatigability (Deshpande, 2011)	Can be neonatal MG (when antibodies from mother attack NMJ), congenital MG (inherited), or acquired MG (autoimmune disorder)	Neonatal: transient in 10%–15% of mothers with MG Congenital: prevalence of 1:500,000 Acquired: incidence of 2:1,000,000 and prevalence of 100 per million (Deshpande, 2011)	Weakness that improves with rest, "droopy" eyes, difficulty swallowing and speaking, respiratory compromise; treatments include medicines and surgery (removal of thymus)
Guillain-Barré syndrome (GBS)	Inflammatory process of the peripheral nervous system resulting in demyelination of nerve axons (Kinnett, 2011)	Commonly occurs after a respiratory or gastrointestinal infection, when immune system attacks nervous system	Incidence: 1:100,000 (Kinnett, 2011)	Diagnosis is made by electromyogram and nerve conduction studies (EMG/NCS) as well as lumbar puncture; treatments can include corticosteroids, plasma exchange, or intravenous immune globulin; recovery is usually excellent (Tekgul, Serdaroglu, & Tutuncuoglu, 2003)

Attention-Deficit Disorder and Attention-Deficit/Hyperactivity Disorder

Attention-deficit disorder and attention-deficit/hyperactivity disorder (ADD/ADHD) are behavioral disorders with which, as of 2006, 4.5 million children in the United States have been diagnosed at some time (Bloom & Cohen, 2006). The defining characteristics are inattention and/or impulsivity and hyperactivity, which can have a significant impact on behavior and performance, both at school and at home (National Institute of Mental Health, 2009, p. 2).

Reviews of epidemiological studies have reported that 3%–7% of school-aged children have ADD/ADHD (Barkley, 2006). In approximately 80% of children with ADD/ADHD, symptoms persist into adolescence and may even continue into adulthood (Faraone, Sergeant, Gillberg, & Biederman, 2003; Harpin, 2005). ADD/ADHD significantly affects the individual throughout childhood and well into adult life, especially if not managed optimally. Adults with ADD/ADHD tend to have a lower occupational status, have poor social relationships, and are more likely to commit criminal offenses and develop substance abuse problems (Faraone, Sergeant, Gillberg, & Biederman, 2003; Harpin, 2005).

A review of outcome studies by Harpin (2005) found that adolescents and young adults with ADD/ADHD face many challenges. They may display oppositional behaviors that result in frequent disciplinary actions at school and may have few or no friends among their peers, both of which likely contribute to high rates of school dropout. As many as 60% of adolescents with ADD/ADHD continue to display symptoms as adults, often clashing with supervisors and co-workers, experiencing frequent terminations and/or resignations, and so forth. For many transitioning students with ADD/ADHD, it may be difficult to find employment situations that are "right" for them. On a more positive note, early identification and treatment predicted positive outcomes related to employment (Halmony, Bentfasmer, Gillberg, & Haavik, 2009).

Among those who go on to college, only half of those identified report receiving adequate accommodation (Chew, Jensen, & Rosen, 2009). In addition, more students with ADD/ADHD report struggling compared with their non-ADD/ADHD peers; for example, a study by Blase et al.(2009) found that students who had a previous or current diagnosis of ADHD self-reported significantly greater concerns in academic, social, and emotional areas and also self-reported significantly higher use of alcohol, cigarettes, and cocaine than did students without a diagnosis of ADHD.

Epilepsy

Epilepsy is one of the most common neurological disorders in children and is manifested by seizure brought about by excessive synchronous neuron activity in the brain. Because it is not uncommon for children to have seizure activity, particularly during periods of illness, the term *epilepsy* is defined as two or more unprovoked seizures more than 24 hours apart in a child older than 1 month of age (Commission on Epidemiology and Prognosis, 1993). A review of epidemiological studies (Shinnar & Pellock, 2002) found that epilepsy affects approximately 0.5%–1% of all children through the age of 16 years. Each year, approximately 300,000 individuals seek medical attention for newly recognized seizures, with approximately 40% (120,000) being children younger than 18 years. Of these, between 20,000 and 45,000 children are confirmed as having epilepsy. The median age of seizure onset is between 5 and 6 years. Epilepsy is often associated with other disabilities and conditions, such as intellectual disability, CP, and autism.

Although the term *epilepsy* is typically associated with tonic-clonic seizures, there are a number of different types of epileptic seizures and syndromes (Table 20.3). Most children are treated with antiepileptic medications, singularly or in combinations; if

Table 20.3.   Common types of seizures resulting from epilepsy

Primary generalized seizures (involve both halves of brain)	Partial seizures (localized to specific areas)
• Absence seizure: Staring, "blanking out," mind wandering, lasts from a few seconds to 20 seconds • Myoclonic seizure: Brief, shocklike jerks of a muscle or a group of muscles • Atonic seizure: Muscles suddenly lose strength; the person may drop things and often falls to the ground • Tonic seizure: Body, arms, or legs make sudden stiffening movements, most often occur during sleep • Clonic seizure: Rhythmic jerking movements of the arms and legs, sometimes on both sides of the body • Tonic-clonic seizure: Both tonic and clonic symptoms	• Simple partial seizure: Abnormal movements; changes in senses of smell, taste, or hearing; psychic feelings of being "outside the body" • Complex partial seizure: Usually starts in a small area of the temporal lobe or frontal lobe of the brain, quickly involves other areas of the brain that affect alertness and awareness; may involve staring and purposeful movement • Secondary generalized seizure: A partial seizure that spreads throughout the brain, becoming generalized

medication fails to control seizure activity, other treatments include surgery and putting the child on a ketogenic diet (Guerrini, 2006; Wheless, Clarke, & Carpenter, 2005).

Although the long-term prognosis for treatment of epilepsy is usually good, there are often educational, social, and employment-related difficulties, even for those whose epilepsy is treatable (Shinnar & Pellock, 2002). The reasons for this are not clear, but there is speculation that seizure-induced brain damage, medications, and public perceptions about epilepsy may contribute to poor outcomes for these children as they approach adulthood.

This section has described some of the more prevalent orthopedic and health impairments of children and youth. Educators will undoubtedly encounter many others in their classrooms, including asthma, heart disorders, leukemia, and other cancers. In many of these types of conditions, the primary educational and transition considerations are related to children being easily fatigued, limited in physical activity, and, in some cases, having a need for frequent treatments and hospitalizations. These needs should be considered carefully in seeking postschool employment and educational options.

Assessment for Transition: Unique Challenges

Students may present many unique challenges for transition-planning teams. Two major challenges for these students are 1) the need for personal assistance services in postschool environments and 2) the need for compensatory strategies (especially for those with cognitive problems such as those faced after a TBI; Wehman, Goodwin, McNamee, & Targett, 2011), assistive technology (AT), and rehabilitation engineering in postschool environments (Webb, Patterson, Syverud, & Seabrooks-Blackmore, 2008). In addition, student self-advocacy is necessary for an effective transition.

Personal Assistance Services and Transition

The World Institute on Disability defines personal assistance services (PAS) as "assistance, under maximum feasible user control, with tasks that maintain well-being, comfort, safety, personal appearance, and interactions within the community and society as a whole" (Holt, Chambless, & Hammond, 2006). In general, PAS is used by persons with disabilities to perform tasks that the person would perform for himself or herself if he or she did not have a disability. It can include tasks that range from reading, communication, and performing manual tasks (e.g., turning pages) to bathing, eating, toileting, personal hygiene, and dressing (Silverstein, 2003).

The primary value of PAS is that they allow people with severe physical or health impairments to participate more fully in community settings and activities, including employment. A personal assistant can fill in the gaps between the requirements or demands of a particular setting and the functional limitations of the individual.

In the past, PAS have been viewed as an essential way of supporting individuals with physical disabilities in their independent living. The use of PAS has been an important extension of empowering individuals with disabilities to live at home and to move about the community with a greater degree of independence. Without PAS, thousands of people with physical and other significant disabilities would be confined to institutionalized nursing home environments or other segregated living situations that were predicated on the need for group care. Fortunately, since the 1980s, there has been both a philosophical and a programmatic move away from institutional living arrangements and an understanding that a personal assistant can play a critically vital role in allowing improved quality of community living for many people with significant disabilities.

During childhood and adolescence, the personal assistance needs of students with orthopedic and health impairments are typically filled by parents and other family members; in school, teachers, aides, or other students provide assistance. During the transition process, personal assistance needs as they relate to the workplace and other community-based environments are of prime interest to the student and his or her family (Turner, 2007a).

The transition individualized education program (IEP) team should identify the anticipated personal assistance needs of the student, as well as the available resources, formal and informal, for meeting those needs. For many daily functions, family, friends, or volunteers can provide work-related assistance without stigmatizing the student. For example, transportation to and from work can be provided by a family member or co-worker. In many, if not most, workplaces, supportive co-workers can be found who will assist the student with getting from one area to another or with eating; however, it is unusual to find co-workers willing to assist with toileting at work, to clean up after toileting accidents, to administer injections, or to take care of other personal and medical needs. A paid assistant is a viable option for those students who would feel stigmatized by having a family member come to the workplace for these purposes (Turner, 2007b). Although the use of a personal assistant in the workplace may initially seem unusual to co-workers, the arrangement should eventually become accepted, particularly if the student hires, trains, and pays the assistant.

Compensatory Strategies, Assistive Technology, Rehabilitation Engineering, and Transition

Students with TBI can learn to use a variety of compensatory strategies and other interventions to help with cognitive and behavior problems. These strategies may be related to enhancing cognitive abilities such as sustaining attention, problem solving, mental flexibility, and new learning. For example, students who have problems recognizing errors may be taught to use a formal self-checking routine to detect errors. Or a student with attention and concentration problems may be taught to create a quiet environment for himself or herself by shutting a door or moving to a quiet zone. Students who have difficulties with problem solving and organization may be taught how to use some type of formal problem-solving framework, which systematically directs the student through a series of cognitive steps. In addition, students may learn to use self-management techniques and a checklist may be taught to increase independence and the ability to adhere to a routine schedule.

Inappropriate social behavior and poor judgment may be related to many things including lack of knowledge or ability to perform the necessary social skills, lack of awareness about one's own behavior, difficulty recognizing social cues and feedback, or reduced behavioral self-control. Some students may benefit from immediate and direct feedback. Role playing can also be useful to help the student develop a repertoire of appropriate social responses.

For students with ADD/ADHD, McIntosh, Filter, Bennett, Ryan, and Sugai (2009) recommended clearly defining and teaching behavioral expectations, adjusting the physical environment to support positive behavior, individualizing instruction to foster engagement and teaching, and reinforcing prosocial skills. Evidence has also supported the use of learning supports, action-oriented and highly structured tasks, explicit and multisensory instruction, enhanced stimulation, modified assignments, note taking, adaptive technology, positive reinforcement, and study skills. The use of positive behavior support has also been recommended (Bradshaw, Koth, Bevans, Lalongo, & Leaf, 2008; Algozzinne & Algozzinne, 2009; McIntosh et al., 2009).

Students with severe orthopedic and health impairments use specialized equipment and procedures to gain more control, independence, and efficiency in day-to-day activities and to participate more fully in community-based vocational and social activities (Wehmeyer, Palmer, et al., 2006). When technology is used by people with disabilities, it is termed *assistive technology*. When AT is used in education, employment, or independent living settings, it is frequently termed *rehabilitation engineering*. In most states, this is a service offered by vocational rehabilitation (VR) agencies.

Examples of technological support for students with health impairments are ventilators to aid respiration, intravenous nutrition, and mobility aids. For students with orthopedic impairments, technology can include an array of assistive devices, from very simple pointing devices to motorized wheelchairs, robotic limbs, and voice- and eye gaze–activated computer programs that help users achieve greater independence in communication and environmental control.

For students with complex communication needs, the use of augmentative and alternative communication strategies such as speech-generating devices, written messages, gestures, sign language, and communication displays help support their interactions with the world and enable them to take on greater responsibility for expressing their needs. This could include a student with CP or TBI. Students with TBI may experience a broad range of motor, sensory, cognitive, and linguistic difficulties making it difficult for them to communicate effectively. After a year postinjury, some have persistent deficits in comprehension of both vocabulary and grammar (Zetterqvist & Jennische, 2010). Implementing augmentative and alternative communication devices can address their needs (Costello, Patak, & Pritchard, 2010). Pediatric rehabilitation specialists are playing key roles in assisting students with complex communication needs with learning skills to have their health concerns addressed. Obtaining quality habilitation/rehabilitation and medical services as adults is of utmost importance and demands special attention. This includes teaching the student how adult services are organized, as well as health literacy, communication, and collaboration skills to ensure successful outcomes (McNaughton, Balandin, Kennedy, & Sandmel, 2010).

Independence and efficiency are important factors in today's workplace. Many of the accommodations made on the job are aimed at increasing autonomy and productivity. AT is a viable complement and/or alternative to a personal assistant for many who are seeking to become more efficient and independent in completing their job requirements. Although AT certainly will not replace the personal assistant, it can sometimes serve to reduce the number of hours that the personal assistant is needed on the jobsite.

Students must have an understanding of AT to apply it effectively in the classroom, home, or workplace. According to the Technology-Related Assistance for Individuals with Disabilities Act of 1988 (PL 100-407), the legal definition of *assistive technology* is any device, piece of equipment, or product system, whether acquired commercially modified, customized, or homemade, that is used to increase, maintain, or improve functional capabilities of individuals with disabilities (2[b][1]). This broad definition is appropriate because of the varied nature of AT applications. AT can be high-tech—which refers to equipment that is expensive and frequently has a computer component. Examples of such equipment include a voice-activated software system, an augmentative communication device, and an electric wheelchair. Now, technology is generally more easily obtained and less expensive. The range of low-tech devices includes everything from Velcro to an electric stapler. Sometimes, the simplest interventions can make a world of difference. For example, Andy, who was responsible for opening mail and entering billing information into a computer, found it extremely difficult to turn on his equipment in the morning. To turn on an electric letter opener, a computer, and a monitor took him about 10 minutes. A simple solution was identified: a power strip was added that all devices were plugged into. The power strip was fastened with Velcro inside a top drawer; he had only to pull open the drawer and flip one switch, reducing the time for completing this task from 10 minutes to 1 minute. Thinking outside the box allowed Andy to become more efficient and effective in this seemingly simple task for the cost of about $10.

In any given situation where a technological intervention may be beneficial, there may be many solutions, so research is essential. If the prospective user has a clear understanding of the options available, then he or she is able to choose the device(s) that best fits the situation. Perceived stigmas associated with using AT may play a lead role in guiding a person's decision. A user must be comfortable with the technology selected or it will be abandoned.

Assessment for Transition Needs

Regardless of a student's academic skills and educational goals, assessment for transition needs should take a very functional approach. School- and community-based work experience programs are ideal for assessing functional abilities and limitations in work environments. This section briefly describes assessment questions that should be addressed by transition IEP teams (Wehman, 2011b).

Bathroom Use

Many students have problems with incontinence, accidents, catheterization, transferring to toilets, and using handheld urinals and require assistance with toileting and other personal needs. Those who use wheelchairs also require accessible bathrooms. Transition planning, therefore, involves educating students about their needs, assessing future bathroom needs, and planning for their provision (Filce & Lavergne, 2011).

Work Endurance

Students often experience fatigue. During school-based work experiences, a student's endurance can be assessed on a multitude of tasks, which drive job placement decisions and adaptation needs.

Eating and Drinking

The amount of assistance required for eating and drinking must be assessed. This includes time requirements, messiness, special diets, and any implications of these factors in transition to work or postsecondary education.

Communication

Meeting communication needs requires an assessment of the means of communication the student uses and the student's proficiency in receptive and expressive communication. Secondary communication modes may need to be developed if those within the student's repertoire are not functional in work settings.

Grooming

Grooming includes the student's personal hygiene and the type and appearance of clothing. Grooming can be problematic for some students because of limited use of hands and arms, visual or perceptual problems, or simply lack of experience with taking care of one's appearance. Because drooling or toileting accidents can occur, assessment should be conducted at the beginning of and throughout the work period.

Hand Use

Hand use assessment includes the ability to grasp and manipulate objects, hand and arm strength, and amount of control over hands and arms.

Medical Needs

Health limitations and the ongoing need for medical monitoring may be issues in future employment for some students. For example, a student with a seizure disorder who experiences tonic-clonic seizures may need to have a place at the job where he or she can go to rest following a seizure or work-time adjustments for unpredictable breaks because of seizures. The transfer from pediatric- to adult-oriented medicine is one of the many transitions that students must accomplish on their way to adulthood. For students with disabilities and special health care needs, access to quality adult-oriented medical care and the ability to manage their own health care needs play a fundamental role in building their capacity to successfully carry out mandated transition activities and other responsibilities that come with adulthood (Betz & Nehring, 2007). School personnel should include plans to bridge the gap between pediatric and adult health services and financing as a part of the transition IEP process (Betz & Nehring, 2007; Repetto, Gibson, Lubbers, Gritz, & Reiss, 2008; Heller & Avant, 2011).

Mobility

Mobility assessment areas include the means that the student uses, distances that can be safely or independently traversed, and needs for accessible entrances, elevators, and so forth. Mobility assessment should also include the need for assistance from others and the need for adaptations to work areas because of limited range of motion or other motor impairments.

Transportation

Getting to and from work is a critical issue for some students—particularly if the student uses a wheelchair or walker or lives in an area with limited or no public transportation. The transition IEP team may need to develop creative solutions to transportation problems, such as ride-sharing.

Social Interaction

Assessment of social interaction includes appropriate and inappropriate social behaviors and responses to stress, criticism, pressure to perform, and so forth. Social assessment should occur in a variety of community-based environments, not just in educational settings.

Academic Skills

An assessment of reading, writing, and mathematics skills leads the transition IEP team in targeting jobs and adaptation strategies. Academic assessments should also help the transition IEP team to identify appropriate postsecondary education or training needs and goals.

Learning

An assessment of how the student learns will lend insight into possible workplace supports for those who have cognitive difficulties such as those experienced after a TBI. It will be important to assess the extent of the difficulties (especially related to attention and concentration, memory, and executive functioning) and the student's insight into current abilities and the best ways to teach the student new information including what types of compensatory strategies may be useful at home, at work, and while out in the community.

Teaching Strategies and Supports for Transition to Work

As with assessment, teaching strategies for students in transition should take a very functional approach. Sharpton and West summarized this approach: "If a work skill or task can be taught, teach it; if it can't be taught, adapt it; if it can't be taught or adapted, support it" (1991, p. 16).

For students with TBI, because of cognitive difficulties and possible problematic social behaviors, jobsite interventions may focus on specific training of tasks and the use of compensatory strategies as well as social skills training. Conversely, for students with orthopedic and health impairments, jobsite interventions focus less on training in specific job tasks and more on adaptations of the work environment or job duties and support for the student/worker, the supervisor, and co-workers.

Cognitive Difficulties

Because of cognitive problems, students with TBI will most likely need intense job skills training on how to perform various job functions and particularly on how to use specific compensatory strategies. Instructional strategies that have been used to teach employees with TBI on the job and help them gain access to various supports are provided in Table 20.4. The most important thing to keep in mind is that instructional strategies must be individualized to the learner and the work setting as well as to the task being taught.

Transition IEP team members should also explore the feasibility of compensatory strategies to enhance a student's learning and promote the ability to perform independ-

Table 20.4.   Examples of instructional strategies for youth with traumatic brain injury

Strategy	Possible uses	Examples
Modeling: Trainer provides the learner with a correct and positive model to follow.	• Training series of steps in task • Training physical skills • Training behaviors difficult to explain or describe with words	• Greeting customers • Folding boxes • Arranging a reservation with a specialized transportation provider for a ride to work
Role playing: Trainer explains how a situation should be handled and gives learner a chance to practice the correct response. (Trainer and learner take turns/switch roles.)	• Developing face-to-face interactions • Developing verbal interactions with others	• Meeting co-workers • Responding to supervisory feedback • Answering the telephone
Least prompts: Trainer provides the least amount to most amount of assistance in the form of a prompt, using a prompting hierarchy.	• Training series of steps in a task	• Filing medical charts • Using a cash register • Learning to use a map to orient to various work areas

ently at a jobsite. For example, a student may be provided with a tool to help him or her remember what to do and how to do it (e.g., a worksheet outlining the steps needed to balance a cash drawer, a map that outlines a route to follow when cleaning apartment grounds, detailed written instructions to follow when cleaning plants). Development and implementation of compensatory memory strategies usually occur when an individual encounters difficulty in learning a new task, shows great variability in task performance, or is unable to meet the required production standard.

To increase their effectiveness, compensatory strategies must be functional and un-obtrusive in work settings and they should be developed in conjunction with the student. Here are some additional examples of strategies that can be used in employment settings to help foster independence:

- Use lists to compensate for memory problems. Information can be written in a pocket notebook or an appointment book or listings posted where a particular task or behav-ior is to occur. Checklists can be used to remind the student that certain activities have been completed.

- Use individual auditory or visual cues. Tape-recorded messages or instructions are ex-cellent auditory cues. Different-colored containers can serve as visual cues for specific items. Structure the environment to enhance functioning.

- Accommodate endurance levels and stress tolerance by sequencing tasks (e.g., sched-ule more difficult tasks first to alleviate fatigue).

- Change the environment, if possible, to decrease stress that may result from excessive noise or temperatures.

The three case studies provide examples of how students were supported at work.

Physical Limitations

The use of adaptations and support strategies in work settings for students with physical limitations has been labeled *jobsite enabling* (Sowers & Powers, 1991; Wood, 1988), a term that captures the importance of adaptation and support for future employment success. For problems or performance impairments in each of the functional areas described in the preceding section, the transition IEP team members should explore the feasibility of the following adaptation and support strategies (Inge & Moon, 2011):

- Redesign the sequence of the task or activity to eliminate difficult steps.

- Determine alternative means of performing the task or activity that are within the student's physical capacity.

- Rearrange the environment to permit easier access to work areas and materials.

- Position the equipment or materials to make the job easier for the individual to reach or manipulate.

- Enhance existing cues (e.g., signs, buttons, instructions) or develop alternative types of cues that the student can discriminate.

- Make or purchase assistive devices that alleviate difficulties with mobility, movement, discrimination, work speed, visual acuity, and so forth.

- Have a co-worker or other support person complete tasks that the student cannot.

Strategy Development

No matter what type of strategy is put in to place, it is important that the student perceive the usefulness of strategies and participate in the planning process. The team may find

Table 20.5. Guidelines for developing work-related compensatory strategies

1. Determine student's strengths and preferred learning style.
2. Commend performance to date in areas in which the individual does well.
3. Ask student to describe performance in certain areas to gauge insight into knowledge of areas that are not presenting difficulties. If student recognizes a problem area, then solicit ideas on possible ways to improve and go to Step 7.
4. If student does not recognize a problem, then set up an opportunity for problem to present itself. When it occurs, bring it to the student's attention and go to next step.
5. Have student state concerns and identify ways to enhance performance.
6. Review data, indicate the individual's current performance, and explain the importance of accomplishing task/improving performance.
7. Brainstorm ideas on potential strategies to use to enhance performance.
8. Reinforce student's ideas. If ideas are unrealistic, then guide the individual through a decision-making process that will lead to the agreed-upon objective.
9. Whenever possible, give the student control (e.g., what size the checklist should be, what color notebook it should be, what words are used).
10. Commend the student for selecting a strategy and explain that strategies may be removed at some point in time.
11. Discuss the positive aspects of using the strategy (e.g., continued employment and independence) with the student and reinforce.
12. Train the student to use the strategy (if tangible, item training should include where to store it and a back-up strategy if it is lost).

the guidelines listed in Table 20.5 to be useful when discussing the development and use of work-related compensatory strategy, adaptation, modification, or job restructuring with a student.

Designing and Implementing Individualized Transition Plans

Although the transition-planning process is generally perceived as focusing on the move from school to work, it is important to recognize that transition planning involves not only the student's future job and work environment but also his or her living situation, recreational and social activities, community mobility, and use of community services. This is illustrated in the case of Judith.

Judith   Judith has congenital spastic diplegia CP but is mobile with Canadian crutches or a scooter. She has a learning disability and a visual impairment that cause her to walk looking down at all times, resulting in problems with balance and frequent falls. Judith attended school at a special education center until she reached high school age, at which point, she was mainstreamed into general education classes with resource help provided as needed.

Judith had some difficulty adjusting to life in high school. The size of the school (1200+ students) overwhelmed her. She had difficulty maneuvering around the building and was frequently late for classes, which tended to upset her more than her teachers. Judith was initially reluctant to ask for help from the resource staff but did when she found it was necessary to do so to keep up with other students in her classes. She was able to maintain average grades.

Judith's high school has two types of transition-program options. One option is a self-contained classroom in which students work on required subjects for graduation as well as job readiness and life skills. The second option is Job Opportunity and Basic Skills (JOBS), a program that includes general high school classes in addition to a job readiness class. Students begin JOBS in their junior year and frequently work a portion of each day by their senior year. Transition options are supported by the VR system, and students are assigned by a VR counselor.

During her junior year, at age 17, Judith was referred to the transition program and the VR agency. She worked with the VR counselor to establish a program that would result in employment after graduation. She was enrolled in the JOBS program that met at 7:30 a.m. (Judith eventually came to hate the early morning and initially wanted a job that began at noon.) During Judith's junior year, the JOBS class included exploring types of jobs and careers and preparing mentally and physically for work. A transition team, which met quarterly during the year, was established that included Judith, her parents, the VR counselor, her JOBS teacher, and her high school guidance counselor.

After attending a job fair sponsored by the VR agency, Judith and her parents were enthusiastic about a clerical skills training program at the local community college and job placement assistance through VR. They discussed this option with the transition team, and another meeting was arranged with a representative from the training program. The program includes 6 months of individualized training, meeting every day for 6 hours. The next session began in July, but Judith still had 1 year of school left before graduation. The program staff arranged for Judith to begin full-time training with the class in July until school began in September. Then, she would attend the training for a half day during the entire school year. She would attend training during the morning and be back at the high school for afternoon classes. She would continue to attend the 7:30 a.m. JOBS class at the school. A school bus would be provided to get her to the training by 9:00 a.m.

In July, Judith began the clerical training program with 12 other people. She was very enthusiastic and enjoyed the contact with others in the class. Her courses included office etiquette, basic bookkeeping, word processing, and receptionist techniques.

In September, Judith started her senior year in high school. She attended JOBS class from 7:30 a.m. to 8:30 a.m. at the school, then took a school bus to the clerical training program at 9:00 a.m., which picked her up again at noon to return to school. She had lunch and, at 12:45 p.m., began her afternoon classes. Because of the structure of the training, it was decided that the process should be reversed during the second semester.

Monthly meetings were held with the transition IEP team, which now included the training instructor from the clerical program. As graduation and completion of the clerical program approached, the focus shifted to finding jobs. The job developer from the training program worked with the VR counselor, the JOBS teacher, and Judith in selecting types of employment situations appropriate for her skills. Judith did very well at filing and receptionist tasks. Her typing was slow as a result of the spasticity in her hands, but it was very accurate. They made a list of employers who could possibly use Judith's skills and made appointments with several of the employers on the list. The job developer from the training program made the initial contacts with the employers. After 2 months of searching, a job was found for Judith as a receptionist with a large agency. She would be the first person encountered by visitors, signing them in and out and monitoring people entering and leaving the building. In addition, she would answer incoming calls to the general information number, switch callers to extension numbers, and take messages on a computer.

The starting date was set for September 1. This provided some time to work on another of the family's requests—helping Judith to move out of her parents' home. Judith had been associated with an agency that provided residential services, and she qualified for a community independent living program. She and a roommate moved into their own apartment in August. Together, they were able to take care of most of their needs, requiring an aide only 3–4 hours per day.

When Judith began work, several adaptations were needed: very simple additions to the computer, a telephone headset, and an enlarged office directory. The job developer from the training program made weekly visits to help Judith to make a smooth transition to work. After several months, visits were reduced to one per month. This visiting schedule continues.

Transition from School to Work

Some students will be able to go to work with instruction and guidance. Others will not. These individuals will require more intensive or advocacy level work support services such as those offered in a supported employment approach (Wehman, 2011a). An overview of these approaches follows.

Instructional Services and Time-Limited Support

In many cases, individuals with severe physical disabilities are able to locate, obtain, and maintain employment without specialized services or through time-limited vocational education or VR services that teach job-seeking and interviewing skills and provide career exploration, work experience, or work adjustment training. Individuals with orthopedic and health impairments may also need occasional assistance from co-workers, friends, and general employee assistance programs to complete tasks and solve work-related problems.

Time-limited services are for those students who appear to need some type of intervention, but not an extensive intervention. Usually, these individuals do not assimilate information quickly and require assistance with carrying out a job search but, once employed, may need no or limited assistance on the job. Often, these individuals participate in classes designed to get ready or prepared for conducting either an independent job search or a job search with some limited assistance from a job placement specialist. Of note, this approach is usually not very effective for persons with significant cognitive disability such as those who have TBI because most of the training takes place in a classroom-type setting. Usually classes are conducted to teach job seeking and maintenance skills. For instance, students learn about various occupations and how to analyze themselves and the job market to choose an appropriate career path or receive information on how to complete employment applications or learn how to interview for a job.

For a person with a TBI, an inordinate amount of time could be expended trying to get the person ready to conduct a job search, when in reality it is highly unlikely that the learning that takes place in the classroom will ever generalize into the real world. Instead, some of these students will require individualized assistance to gain and maintain employment.

Outcomes-Based Planning

Although models range from the practical to the esoteric, transition planning typically focuses on finding and obtaining employment, not necessarily achieving quality-of-life outcomes (e.g., reduced financial dependence, friendships, increased self-esteem and self-direction). Steere, Wood, Pancsofar, and Butterworth (1990) presented an outcomes-based planning model of transition for students with disabilities—based on a career planning model—that is still relevant today and can be useful in identifying and achieving quality-of-life outcomes for all students with disabilities.

The outcomes-based model has three appealing features for students with disabilities. First, this model does not assume that employment is an end in itself but that it is instead a means of achieving a happy and productive adulthood for the student. Second, with the outcomes-based planning model, IEP goals and processes related to transition are consumer-driven, based on the desired outcomes of the student and his or her family. Third, this planning process encourages the transition IEP team to explore transition creatively to achieve an array of potential postsecondary outcomes. The six-step approach to outcome-based planning is as follows:

1. During an orientation session, the team members are introduced, along with the student and family members, and a team leader is named to coordinate the efforts of the group. The steps of outcomes-based planning and a rationale for integrated employment are given during this orientation.

2. A brief biographical sketch of the student is presented that details his or her noteworthy characteristics and achievements. This may also include likes and dislikes, special interests, and support needs. The intent is not necessarily to identify skill limitations, but to focus on ways of building competencies.

3. A brainstorming session is initiated for generating possible quality-of-life outcomes with input from the student. This may involve some interpretations of the student's communication abilities and behaviors and possibly some preconference discussions

with the student. From this brainstorming, a priority list of outcomes and definition statements, or descriptors, is generated through team consensus.

4. A measurement system is then identified for determining whether desired outcomes are being or have been attained.

5. The list of outcomes, descriptors, and standards is then used for initial compatibility screening with potential employment situations as they become available. As each is considered, team members also consider possible barriers and challenges that impede movement to the position. Possible solutions and action plans may be developed to serve as a framework for achieving optimum employment experiences.

6. The members of the team continue to meet to follow up on progress in the completion of action plans and meeting desired outcomes. The process can be repeated as deemed necessary to accommodate the student's growth and changing needs.

This method of planning can be used in when planning for transition. It can also serve as a guide for helping determine future goals.

Advocacy-Level Services

Individuals with physical disabilities have motor impairments related to a variety of diagnoses including CP, muscular dystrophy, multiple sclerosis, rheumatoid arthritis, TBI, and SCI. In addition, many individuals have secondary or, in the case of TBI, primary perceptual or cognitive deficits and concomitant disabilities, such as sensory or medical conditions. This may translate into multiple needs, and some students will require assistance in mobility, communication, learning, self-care, or decision making. Many of these individuals will benefit from a supported employment approach. For a more detailed explanation, the reader should refer to Chapter 13.

In the individual approach, a support person often called a job coach or employment specialist works one to one with the person who has a severe disability to assist him or her with gaining and maintaining a job in the community (Wehman, 2011a; Targett & Wehman, 2011). And, although there will be variation in the approach, typically it goes something like what follows. First, the employment specialist and the job seeker begin to spend time getting to know one another. This is when the employment specialist learns about the person's or the job seeker's vocational interests, strengths, and potential work support needs. Next, the employment specialist goes out to meet with employers to learn about operations and their needs. Then, as possible, the job seeker is represented to a potential employer. This activity continues until a job opportunity is developed. Afterward, the job seeker is consulted and, if agreeable, interviews for the job. Then, once hired, the employment specialist accompanies the new employee to work to provide and facilitate an array of workplace supports that typically includes on-the-job skills training. At this time, depending on the nature of the work and the new hire's abilities to get the job done, the employment specialist may also help ensure the work is completed. Eventually, as the employee begins to meet the employer's job performance standards and expectations, the employment specialist fades his or her presence away from the jobsite; however, he or she continues to monitor how things are going and provides or facilitates additional support either on or off the job as needed (Wehman, 2011a; Targett & Wehman, 2011).

Other Considerations

Employment issues for individuals with only physical disabilities can be quite different from individuals with TBI or those who experience both physical and cognitive disabilities. The term *jobsite enabling* (Inge & Moon, 2011) is frequently used, which focuses less on jobsite training and more on modifications, adaptations, and compensatory strategies to assist an individual with functioning more independently. Other services from an occupational therapist, physical therapist, or speech-language therapist may be needed to assist with positioning, mobility, adaptive equipment, and communication needs. Because of the lack of a single agency being assigned responsibility for the coordination of services for individuals with physical disabilities, employment specialists may find themselves identifying and gaining access to services from other agencies or service providers, normally the role of a service coordinator. In a similar way, not having an agency responsible for the delivery of services has created additional limitations with funding, administering, and staffing ongoing, follow-along services essential for supported employment.

Transportation problems can further restrict employment options because specialized services or lift-equipped buses are often necessary.

Decisions regarding employment choices are also affected by the same issues confronted during service delivery. Communication, motor, and sensory impairments can make it difficult for an individual to express his or her preferences and be accurately understood by another person. The use of augmented communication systems and adaptive equipment can enhance one's ability to express choices and participate in the ongoing decision-making process. Emphasizing the physical environment (e.g., calm, comfortable, free of stress) and providing ample time (e.g., not rushing, waiting during pauses) are critical for valid choice making. Slow or uncontrolled motor movement and unclear speech should not be interpreted as an inability to choose but, rather, as a signal to the employment specialist to utilize adaptations, modifications, or other techniques to make communication easier for the individual. Often, just spending time together, listening to how an individual speaks, and observing his or her mannerisms of expression can eliminate the need to utilize additional supplemental aids.

The planning process for transition to work is similar to planning for the transition to unsupported competitive employment. Planning for these needs is critical because the level of support needed for the student to obtain and keep employment is high. Sowers (1991) recommended a three-step process for developing an employment support plan that is still relevant today:

1. A student's work skills, experiences, and anticipated support needs in the areas of toileting assistance or bathroom accessibility, work endurance, eating and drinking, communication, grooming, hand use, vision and hearing, medical needs, mobility, transportation to and from work, social interactions and behaviors, and academic skills are summarized.

2. During a transition-planning meeting attended by the student, his or her family, educational staff, and adult services agency representatives, the student's available resources are identified, including both formal and informal support mechanisms.

3. The transition-planning team develops a plan for identifying appropriate employment options, the types and minimum amounts of supports to be provided, and the providing and funding entities.

It often happens that an individual who has severe functional limitations cannot perform some of the tasks that an employer expects of his or her employees. For example, an employee with mobility impairments may be able to complete work at a computer or copier but not deliver finished products or visit customers. One technique that is often used in this type of situation is called *job carving* (see Chapter 14), which entails selecting a supported employee's work duties based on his or her strengths and abilities and reassigning those tasks that are too difficult or impossible. Job carving does not create a new position for the employee with a disability but allows an employer to reshuffle job duties to accommodate the worker with disabilities and, in the process, make operations more efficient (Targett & Wehman, 2011).

This approach is also useful for individuals with cognitive disabilities. Finding ways to create a work opportunity in a way that highlights the use of an individual's skills and meets a business needs is often required. Supportive and emerging technologies, such as AT, job carving, workplace accommodations, and supported employment can help mitigate the effects of cognitive, physical, and psychosocial impairments resulting from physical and cognitive disabilities.

Sandy   Sandy has CP that causes unsteady movement in both hands and arms. She was offered a position at a university student identification center as a customer service representative and camera operator. The camera is operated through a computer, which Sandy had never used. She spent the first week learning to operate the computer, while the job coach performed the other functions of the job. After that week, she was comfortable enough to begin adding other tasks to her repertoire.

Several accommodations had to be made to ensure that Sandy could perform her job independently. The first accommodation was to extend the focus knobs on the camera. This reduced her need to reach and made them easier for Sandy to manipulate. Next, an office chair that swiveled was purchased to make getting up and down easier. The chair also had arms to increase her stability. Finally, fine motor skills such as writing take Sandy a great deal of time to complete. To increase her speed in keeping track of who she photographed, a typewriter was obtained. Finally, a trackball was purchased to replace the standard mouse.

Sandy used cheat sheets to remind herself how to operate the office machinery, such as the encoder and the cash register. She also received a great deal of support from her co-workers. Sandy had problems manipulating money. She used a small tray to assist in carrying money back and forth to the register. This worked especially well when large amounts of change were involved. She also had to balance her drawer both before and after her work shifts. She was able to complete this without AT, but it was very hard on her muscles. To make the job less cumbersome, the job coach arranged for the donation of a surplus currency counter from a local bank. This technology made all the difference in Sandy's confidence on her job.

Joe   Joe is an 18-year-old who sustained a TBI caused by a head-on collision with another car. He was in a coma for 21 days and was hospitalized for 6 weeks. Because of the injury, Joe has severe memory problems and difficulties with attention, concentration, and executive functioning. He has a leg brace and walks with a cane. He is not able to control the tremors in his right hand and has difficulty seeing out of his left eye. He also has a history of seizures but is currently taking medication for prevention.

Before his injury, Joe worked part-time as a grocery clerk during the summer. After returning to school, during his IEP meeting, Joe indicated a desire to work in some type of job that would take advantage of his numerical acumen. The transition specialist referred Joe to the State's Department of Vocational Rehabilitation Services. Because of the severity of his disability, a decision was made to refer him to a service provider for supported employment. This service provides individualized vocational assistance to help individuals with severe disabilities with gaining and maintaining employment. Services are provided by a VR specialist known as a job coach.

The job coach helped Joe locate a 20-hour-per-week job as an auditor's assistant at a large accounting firm. The job involved processing expense and merchandise checks and digitally storing documents. Joe, with intensive skills training from the job coach, learned how to do the job in 20 days. Of note, because Joe was not able to meet the employer's expectations from day one, the coach also helped make sure the work was done. This provided some assurance to the employer and allowed Joe the extra time needed to learn how to do the job.

Despite Joe's rapid skill acquisition, problems with work quality and skill maintenance occurred. These problems included forgetting the steps involved to perform certain duties, slow production rate, difficulty in operating the equipment, and sequencing and addition errors. The following job modifications and adaptations were introduced and helped Joe improve his job performance:

1.   Written notes related to the most missed steps were posted as visual cues.

2.   Written procedures on how to perform daily tasks were typed up and placed in a reference manual.

3.   Large paper clips were substituted for small ones.

4.   An electric stapler replaced the manual one.

Joe also had some relationship problems at work. He often hugged his female co-workers and kept asking one girl out. One day, she became so upset with his advances and the guilt she felt due to the lack of interest because of his disability that she went to her manager crying and threatening to quit her job. The manager had to report the incident to personnel. The human resources director informed Joe and the job coach that his behavior could be perceived as sexual harassment and indicated that future infractions would lead to disciplinary action and, further, that three infractions would lead to termination from work. The job coach worked with Joe to come up with a compensatory strategy to help remind Joe to keep his distance. This strategy was teaching him to think and say the phrase "an arm's length away will let me stay"; while stretching out his left arm. In addition, the coach helped him apply for membership at a gym and join a young professionals association.

As Joe demonstrated proficiency at work, the job coach faded her level of assistance from the site. When he left school, he was offered a full-time job with benefits at the accounting firm. Today, Joe lives independently in a small home behind his grandmother's house. His work quality remains stable, according to the job coach who remains in touch with Joe and the employer.

Transition from School to Postsecondary Education and Training

Students with disabilities are enrolling in postsecondary schools in increasing numbers, although the exact proportion is not known because disability disclosure is voluntary. Students with disabilities continue to lag far behind those without disabilities in terms of participation in postsecondary education and training, however (Getzel & Wehman, 2005).

The transition-planning process includes decisions about to which educational institutions the student will apply for admission—decisions made on the basis of physical accessibility, available accommodations, and the student's educational goals and abilities. The student and his or her family should be encouraged to arrange visits to schools to meet with service coordinators, tour the campus and buildings in which the student will have classes, and talk with instructors and other students with disabilities. If student housing will be needed, then the accessibility of rooms and the availability of domestic assistance can be assessed. These site visits provide more valid information than any college catalog.

After acceptance at a postsecondary school, the coordinator of services for students with disabilities at that school should be invited to become a member of the transition-planning team so that proactive planning can occur, even if services will not be sought immediately upon admission. If the student's health or physical condition worsens and problems with attendance or classwork arise, then previous knowledge of the student and his or her disability will help the service coordinator to make arrangements with the instructors before the student's grades are affected.

Cary Cary is a 19-year-old man with sickle-cell anemia, resulting in jaundice, fatigue, infections, and occasional vaso-occlusive episodes requiring medical care and even hospitalization. Despite periodic absences during relapses and treatments, he maintained good grades in high school and wanted to attend college to pursue a business degree. Cary's parents were supportive of his goals and willing to finance his education to the extent they were able.

During Cary's junior year, his high school guidance counselor convened a transition IEP team to help him and his family select a university. During the first meeting, the team members established three criteria:

1. The university they select should offer a business program up to the graduate level in case Cary decides to pursue a master's of business administration.

2. The campus should be designed so that Cary could get around without excessive fatigue.

3. The faculty should be willing to make allowances for Cary's periodic absences from class.

Cary also stated during the meeting that he wanted to attend an out-of-town university. When questioned, he stated that he felt overprotected by his parents and wanted to gain more independence. Although surprised by his request, his parents agreed to consider not only the two universities in their city but also any other state-supported schools as well.

Over the course of his junior year, Cary and his parents visited four universities, meeting with business faculty and service coordinators. The fourth university they visited, located approximately 2 hours from his hometown, seemed ideal, and they decided to concentrate their efforts on getting Cary enrolled there. Several factors led them to choose this university. Although the campus was large, it had an extensive bus system that connected the residence halls, library, and most of the buildings in which Cary would have classes. The university had comprehensive student health services with on-campus clinics. Faculty members of the school of business met with Cary and his parents and assured them that they would accommodate Cary's absences and would help him to keep up with his courses. The disability services coordinator impressed them with her knowledge of sickle-cell anemia and its implications for Cary's educational career. She also assured them that she could arrange for notetakers or other assistance on short notice when Cary would have to miss class or could not get out to do library research or other class requirements. She had also made arrangements before their visit for them to talk with a student with a coronary disorder who had received similar services.

During Cary's senior year, the other members of the transition IEP team helped him and his family with the application process by planning for unforeseen contingencies. The disability services coordinator joined the transition IEP team and was instrumental in identifying problems they might encounter. For instance, Cary had applied for on-campus housing, but the service coordinator informed them that there are never enough dormitory rooms to meet the demand. In case on-campus housing was unavailable, their contingency plan was that Cary and his family would find an apartment on a bus route and advertise for a roommate to share expenses. Fortunately, Cary was accepted for a residence hall, and the contingency plan was not needed.

Another problem area was finances. Cary's parents could afford his tuition, housing, and meal plan, but not much else. The service coordinator brought financial aid applications to the transition IEP meeting for Cary to complete and Cary applied for scholarships and work-study. Between transition IEP meetings, the service coordinator met with the university's work-study coordinator and identified available jobs that would not fatigue Cary and were flexible enough to allow for periodic absences. Cary's transition went very smoothly, thanks to the thorough troubleshooting and contingency planning of the transition IEP team. Cary is now in his sophomore year and is still in the business program. He works 15–20 hours per week in a computer lab, helping other students learn to use word processing, graphics, and spreadsheet programs. His health has been relatively stable, and he has not missed many classes for health reasons; his 7:30 a.m. classes, however, are another story.

The Power of Technology

Technology is advancing exponentially, with each day bringing new advances, products, and uses. Many products have been developed specifically for youth and adults with disabilities, but even those designed for the public at large can be used by those with disabilities to meet educational and transitional needs (Alper & Raharinirina, 2006; Mechling, 2007).

As an example, DePompei et al. (2008) and Gentry, Wallace, Kvarfordt, and Lynch (2008) describe practical applications of use of personal digital assistants (PDAs), smartphones, and other digital devices for students and adults with TBI that compensate for deficits in memory, concentration, and attention. Among those uses are

- Personal calendars with alarms for reminders of important events, meetings
- Contact lists with automatic dialing for reaching peers, family members, employers
- Handy tools such as a calculator, clock, compass
- Cameras for assigning a face to contacts to aid in recognition

- Games that can improve the student's memory, concentration, fine motor coordination, spatial relationships, and visual–perceptual skills
- Global positioning system (GPS) that can assist with wayfinding in the community

Of course, one of the benefits of these devices is that they are ubiquitous—just about everyone has one—and they are relatively inexpensive in relation to many products developed exclusively for individuals with disabilities. Thus, they are far less likely to stigmatize the student than are disability-specific technologies and are much more financially practical for students and their families.

Evaluation of Transition Outcomes

Evaluating transition programs includes process and outcome evaluation. Process evaluation involves determining whether individual students are participating in transition planning and are meeting transition objectives. Outcome evaluation involves conducting follow-up or follow-along studies of students who have been through the program. There are four purposes of conducting outcome evaluations:

1. To assess the postsecondary employment or educational status of students who have received transition services
2. To assess adaptive behavior competence of students who have made transitions
3. To evaluate the degree of coordination of different agencies in the community and their effects on the adjustment of special education graduates
4. To evaluate the satisfaction of students and their families with the transition services they have received and to solicit their suggestions for improving transition

These evaluations help to determine how students are performing and whether the school and family network is helping them on their journey to work and community adjustment.

In sum, students with disabilities are making transitions into an economic and social climate that is equally favorable or inhospitable to students with and without disabilities. Surveying representative samples of students without disabilities is suggested as another desirable feature for outcome studies. For students with the disabilities discussed here, primary questions for follow-along surveys include student mobility within the workplace and the community; use of and need for compensatory memory strategies; AT and rehabilitation engineering services; use of and need for job coaches, personal assistants, or volunteer assistants on the job; involvement in postsecondary education and training; and satisfaction with transition services and the quality of adult life. Answers to these questions allow transition programs to individualize services for their communities and students.

Conclusion

This chapter has reviewed issues and strategies for successful transitions for students with TBI and orthopedic and other health impairments to work and postsecondary educational environments. Key issues include the need for compensatory memory strategies, AT, and personal assistants; self-advocacy; and the identification of appropriate postschool environments. In addition, students and their families should learn the rights and assurances provided to them under the Individuals with Disabilities Education Improvement Act (2004; PL 108-446) and other disability-related legislation, such as the Rehabilitation Act (1973; PL 93-112) and the American with Disabilities Act (1990; PL 101-336). They should also learn about employment services such as supported employment and effective means of advocating for those rights and services.

Study Questions

1. What are the common manifestations of TBI and orthopedic and other health impairments?

2. Why is it challenging for many youth to access personal assistance services? What can be done during the transition process to make sure personal assistant needs are met after graduating from high school?

3. Use the Internet to conduct a search of some compensatory memory strategies and AT that may be helpful to youth in workplace.

4. Meet with an educator or transition specialist and investigate why empowerment and choice making should be promoted in transition planning.

5. What is a functional assessment?

6. Meet with a vocational rehabilitation counselor who serves transition-aged students to discuss the similarities and differences in supported employment and time-limited services.

7. Meet with a disability service office representative to discuss some special considerations for students who choose to pursue postsecondary education.

8. What are the steps involved in conducting an outcome evaluation?

Online Resources

For TBI: http://www.biausa.org and http://www.cdc.gov/TraumaticBrainInjury/

For CP: http://www.ucp.org

For spina bifida: http://www.spinabifidaassociation.org

For SCI: http://www.spinalcord.org

For ADD/ADHD: http://www.webmd.com/add-adhd/default.htm

References

Achieve, Inc. (2006). Creating a longitudinal data system: Using data to improve student achievement. Retrieved from http://www.achieve.org/node/547

Advocates for Special Kids v. Oregon State Board of Education, (cite unavailable, D. Ore. 1999). Cited in Margolis, Leslie Seid (December, 2003). High-Stakes testing, diploma options, and students with disabilities: Negotiating the quagmire of politics, policy, rhetoric, law, and emotion. Maryland Disability Law Center. Retrieved from http://www.gogle.com/url?sa=t&rct=j&q=&esrc-s&source=web&cd=1&ved=0CCgQFjAA&url=http%3A%2F%2Fwww.msde.state.md.us%2FCompHSA%2Fdocs%2FHigh%2520Stakes%2520Testing%2520napas.doc&ei=mrk-T42eGqKy0AH91OioBw&usg=AFQjCNEeCpGc_ujXH2ZRG168Ik5VCvyKQ&sig2=s0EWWm4AaWFsSMFDANmwA, February, 2012.

Agran, M., Blanchard, C., & Wehmeyer, M.L. (2000). Promoting transition goals and self-determination through student self-directed learning: The Self-Determination Model of Instruction. *Education and Training in Mental Retardation and Developmental Disabilities, 35*(4), 351–364.

Agran, M., Cavin, M., Wehmeyer, M., & Palmer, S. (2006). Participation of students with moderate to severe disabilities in the general curriculum: The effects of the self-determined learning model of instruction. *Research and Practice for Persons with Severe Disabilities, 31*, 230–241.

Agran, M., & Hughes, C. (2008). Asking student input: Students' opinions regarding their individualized education program involvement. *Career Development for Exceptional Individuals, 31*(2), 69–76.

Agran, M., Kings-Sears, M.E., Wehmeyer, M.L., & Copeland, S.R. (2003). *Student-directed learning.* Baltimore: Paul H. Brookes Publishing Co.

Agran, M., & Krupp, M. (2011). Providing choice making in employment programs: the beginning or end of self determination. *Education and Training in Autism and Developmental Disabilities, 46*(4), 565–575.

Agran, M., Wehmeyer, M.L., Cavin, M., & Palmer, S. (2008). Promoting student active classroom participation skills through instruction to promote self-regulated learning and self-determination. *Career Development for Exceptional Individuals, 31*, 106–114.

Agran, M., Wehmeyer, M., Cavin, M., & Palmer, S. (2010). Promoting active engagement in the general education classroom and access to the general education curriculum for students with cognitive disabilities. *Education and Training in Autism and Developmental Disabilities, 45*(2), 163–174.

Albus, D., Lazarus, S.S., Thurlow, M.L., & Cormier, D. (2009). *Characteristics of states' alternate assessments based on modified academic achievement standards in 2008* (Synthesis Report 72). Minneapolis: University of Minnesota, National Center on Education Outcomes.

Algozzine, B., & Algozzine, K.M. (2009). Facilitating academic achievement through school-wide positive behavior support. In W. Sailor, G. Dunlap, G. Sugai, & R.H. Horner (Eds.), *Handbook of positive behavior support* (pp. 521–550). New York: Springer.

Algozzine, B., Browder, D., Karvonen, M., Test, D.W., & Wood, W.M. (2001). Effects of interventions to promote self-determination for individuals with disabilities. *Review of Educational Research, 71*, 219–277.

Allen, S.K., Smith, A.C., Test, D.W., Flowers, C., & Wood, W.M. (2001). The effects of "self-directed IEP" on student participation in IEP meetings. *Career Development for Exceptional Individuals, 4,* 107–120.

Allor, J.H., Champlin, T.M., Gifford, D.B., & Mathes, P.G. (2010). Methods for increasing the intensity of reading instruction for students with intellectual disabilities. *Education and Training in Autism and Developmental Disabilities, 45,* 500–511.

Almond, P.J., Lehr, C., Thurlow, M.L., & Quenemoen, R. (2002). Participation in large-scale state assessment and accountability systems. In G. Tindal & T.M. Haladyna (Eds.), *Large-scale assessment programs for all students: Validity, technical adequacy, and implementation* (pp. 341–370). Mahwah, NJ: Lawrence Erlbaum and Associates.

Alper, S., & Raharinirina, S. (2006). Assistive technology for individuals with disabilities: A review and synthesis of the literature. *Journal of Special Education Technology, 21*(2), 47–64.

Alverson, C.Y., Naranjo, J.M., Yamamoto, S., & Unruh, D.K. (2010). Methods for collecting postschool outcomes data on young adults with disabilities: A literature synthesis. *Career Development for Exceptional Individuals, 34,* 95–106.

Alwell, M., & Cobb, B. (2009a). Functional life skills curricula intervention for youth with disabilities: A systematic review. *Career Development for Exceptional Individuals, 32,* 82–93. doi: 10.1177/0885728809336656.

Alwell, M., & Cobb, B. (2009b). Social and communicative interventions and transition outcomes for youth with disabilities. *Career Development for Exceptional Individuals, 32,* 94–107.

American Association on Intellectual and Developmental Disabilities. (2007). *Intellectual disability and the AAIDD definition.* Washington, DC: Author.

American Guidance Service. (2001). *Everyday life skills.* Circle Pines, MN: Author.

American Heritage Dictionary of the English Language. (2000). New York: Houghton Mifflin Company.

American Medical Association. (2002, May). *Educational forum on adolescent health: Youth bullying.* Chicago: Author.

American Psychiatric Association. (2000). *Diagnostic and statistical manual of mental disorders* (4th ed., text revision). Washington, DC: Author.

Americans with Disabilities Act (ADA) of 1990, Pub. L. No. 101-336 (July 26, 1990), Title 42, U.S.C. 12101 et seq.: *U.S. Statutes at Large,* 104-327–378.

Americans with Disabilities Act Amendments Act (ADAAA) of 2008, Pub. L. No. 110-325, 42 U.S.C. §§ 12101 et seq.

Anctil, T.M., Ishikawa, M.E., & Scott, A.T. (2008). Academic identity development through self-determination: Successful college students with learning disabilities. *Career Development for Exceptional Individuals, 31,* 164–174.

Anderson, D., Dumont, S., Jacobs, P., & Azzaria, L. (2007). The personal costs of caring for a child with a disability: A review of the literature. *Public Health Reports, 122,* 3–16.

Anderson, J.L., Bruinlinks, R.H., Morreau, L.E., & Gilman, C.J. (1991). *Adaptive living skills curriculum.* Itasca, IL: Riverside Publishing.

Anderson V., & Yeates, K.O. (2010). *Pediatric traumatic brain injury: New frontiers in clinical and translational research.* Cambridge, UK: Cambridge University Press, 1–5.

Ankeny, E.M., Wilkins, J., & Spain, J. (2009). Mothers' experiences of transition planning for their children with disabilities. *Teaching Exceptional Children, 41,* 28–36.

Ansell, S.E. (2004, January). *Put to the test.* Retrieved February 12, 2003, from Education Week web site: http://www.edweek.org/sreports/qc04/reports/17teaching-t1b.cfm

Apple, A.L., Billingsley, F., & Schwartz, I.S. (2005). Effects of video modeling alone and with self-management on compliment giving behaviors of children with high functioning ASD. *Journal of Positive Behavior Interventions, 7*(1), 33–46.

Arango-Lasprilla, J., & Kreutzier, J. (2010). Racial and ethnic disparities in functional, psychosocial, and neurobehavioral outcomes after brain injury. *Journal of Head Trauma Rehabilitation, 25*(2), 128–136.

Arora, C.M.J. (1996). Defining bullying: Towards a clearer general understanding and more effective intervention strategies. *School Psychology International, 17*(4), 317–329.

Assistive Technology Act of 1998, as amended, Pub L. No. 108-364, Section 3, 188 stat 1707 (2004).

Ayres, K.M., & Langone, J. (2005). Intervention and instruction with video for students with autism: A review of the literature. *Education and Training in Developmental Disabilities, 40,* 183–196.

Ayres, K.M., & Langone, J. (2007). A comparison of video modeling perspectives for students with autism. *Journal of Special Education Technology, 22*(2), 15–30.

Ayres, K.M., & Langone, J. (2008). Video supports for teaching students with developmental disabilities and autism: Twenty-five years of research and development. *Journal of Special Education Technology, 23*(3), 1–8.

Ayres, K.M., Lowrey, K.A., Douglas, K.H., & Sievers, C. (2011). I can identify Saturn but I can't brush my teeth: What happens when the curricular focus for students with severe disabilities shifts. *Education and Training in Autism and Developmental Disabilities, 46,* 11–21.

Ayres, K.M., Maguire, A., & McClimon, D. (2009). Acquisition and generalization of chained tasks taught with computer based video instruction to children with autism. *Education and Training in Developmental Disabilities, 44*(4), 493–508.

Baer, R., Daviso, A., Flexer, R., Queen, R., & Meindl, R. (2011). Students with intellectual disabilities: Predictors of transition outcomes. *Career Development of Exceptional Individuals, 34*(3), 132–141.

Baer, R.M., Flexer, R.W., Beck, S., Amstutz, N., Hoffman, L., Brothers, J., et al. (2003). A collaborative follow-up study on transition services utilization and post-school outcomes. *Career Development for Exceptional Individuals, 26,* 7–25.

Bailey, D.B., Jr., Skinner, D., Rodriguez, P., Gut, D., & Correa, V. (1999). Awareness, use, and satisfaction with services for Latino parents of young children with disabilities. *Exceptional Children, 65,* 367–381.

Baker, D.L., Miller, E., Dang, M.T., Yaangh, C., & Hansen, R.L. (2010). Developing culturally responsive approaches with Southeast Asian American families experiencing developmental disabilities. *Pediatrics, 26,* S146–S150.

Barker, E.T., Hartley, S.L., Seltzer, M.M., Floyd, F.J., Greenberg, J.S., & Orsmond, G.I. (2011). Trajectories of emotional well-being in mothers of adolescents and adults with autism. *Developmental Psychology, 47;* 551–561.

Bambara, L.M., & Kern, L. (2005). *Individualized supports for students with problem behaviors: Designing positive behavior plans.* New York: Guilford Press.

Bambara, L.M., & Knoster, T.P. (2009). *Designing positive behavior support plans* (2nd ed.). Washington, DC: American Association on Mental Retardation.

Bandura, A., & Cervone, D. (2000). Self-evaluative and self-efficacy mechanisms of governing the motivational effects of goal systems. In E.T. Higgins & A.W. Kruglanski (Eds.), *Motivational science: Social and personality perspectives. Key reading in social psychology* (pp. 202–214). Philadelphia: Psychology Press.

Banerjee, M., & Brinckerhoff, L.C. (2010). Helping students with disabilities navigate the college admissions process. In S.F. Shaw, J.W. Madaus, & L.C. Dukes (Eds.), *Preparing students with disabilities for college success: A practical guide to transition planning* (pp. 229–256). Baltimore: Paul H. Brookes Publishing Co.

Barkley, R.A. (2006). Primary symptoms, diagnostic criteria, prevalence and gender differences. In R.A. Barkley (Ed.), *Attention deficit hyperactivity disorder: A handbook for diagnosis and treatment* (3rd ed., pp 122–183). New York: Guilford.

Barnhill, G.P. (2007). Outcomes in adults with Asperger syndrome. *Focus on Autism and Other Developmental Disabilities, 22*(2), 116–126.

Bassett, D., & Kochhar-Bryant, C. (2006). Strategies for aligning standards-based education and transition. *Focus on Exceptional Children, 39*(2), 1–19.

Bates-Harris, C., & Decker C. (2011). Segregated and exploited. *Journal of Vocational Rehabilitation.*

Baugh, T. (2003). *Bystander focus groups: Bullying: Roles, rules, and coping tools to break the cycle.* Washington, DC: The George Washington University.

Bauminger, N. (2002). The facilitation of social-emotional understanding and social interaction in high-functioning children with autism: Intervention outcomes. *Journal of Autism and Developmental Disorders, 32*(4), 283–298.

Bauminger, N. (2007a). Brief report. Group social-multi-modal intervention for HFASD. *Journal of Autism and Developmental Disorders, 37,* 1605–1615.

Bauminger, N. (2007b). Brief report: Individual social-multi-modal intervention for HFASD. *Journal of Autism and Developmental Disorders, 37,* 1593–1604.

Beard, R. (2011, June 30). For some with autism, jobs to match their talents - NYTimes.com. *Opinion - Opinionator - NYTimes.com.* Retrieved July 7, 2011, from http://opinionator.blogs.nytimes.com/2011/06/

Becker, D., Swanson, S., Bond, G., & Merrens, M. (2008). *Evidence-based supported employment fidelity review scale and manual.* Concord, NH: Dartmouth College, Dartmouth Psychiatric Research Center.

Becker, D., Whitley, R., Bailey, E., & Drake, R. (2007). Long-term employment outcomes of supported employment for people with severe mental illness. *Psychiatric Services, 58,* 922–928.

Becker, D., Xie, H., McHugo, G., Halliday, J., & Martinez, R. (2006). What predicts supported employment outcomes? *Community Mental Health Journal, 42,* 303–313.

Bellamy, G.T., Horner, R.H., & Inman, D.P. (1979). *Vocational rehabilitation of severely retarded adults: A direct service technology.* Baltimore: University Park Press.

Bellini, S. (2006). *Building social relationships: A systematic approach to teaching social interaction skills to children and adolescents with autism spectrum disorders and other social difficulties.* Overland Park, KS: AAPC Publishing.

Bellini, S., & Akullian, J. (2007). A meta-analysis of video modeling and video self-modeling inter-ventions for children and adolescents with autism spectrum disorder. *Exceptional Children, 73,* 264–287.

Bender, M., Valletutti, P.J., Baglin, C.A., & Hoffnung, A.S. (1996). *A functional curriculum for teaching students with disabilities.* Austin, TX: PRO-ED.

Bender, W.N., & McLaughlin, P.J. (1997). Violence in the classroom: Where we stand. *Intervention in School and Clinic, 32,* 196–198.

Benz, M., & Kochhlar, C. (1996). School-to-work for all students: A position statement of the

Division on Career Development and Transition. *Career Development for Exceptional Individuals, 19*, 31–48.

Benz, M., Lindstrom, L., & Yovanoff, P. (2000). Improving graduation and employment outcomes of students with disabilities: Predictive factors and student perspectives. *TEACHING Exceptional Children, 66*, 509–529.

Benz, M.R. (2002). Phases of career development: case studies of young women with learning disabilities. *Exceptional Children. 69*(1), 67–83.

Benz, M.R., Lindstrom, L., & Latta, T. (1999). Improving collaboration between schools and vocational rehabilitation: The youth transition program model. *Journal of Vocational Rehabilitation, 13*, 55–63.

Benz, M.R., Lindstrom, L., Unruh, D., & Waintrup, M. (2004). Sustaining secondary transition programs in local schools. *Remedial and Special Education, 25*(1), 39–50.

Benz, M.R., Lindstrom, L., & Yovanoff, P. (2000). Improving graduation and employment outcomes of students with disabilities: Predictive factors and student perspectives. *Exceptional Children, 66*, 509–529.

Bernad-Ripoli, S. (2007). Using a self-as-model video combined with social stories to help a child with Asperger syndrome understand emotions. *Focus on Autism and Other Developmental Disabilities, 22*(2), 100–106.

Bernard-Opitz, V., Sriram, N., & Nakhoda-Sapuan, S. (2001). Enhancing social problem solving in children with autism and normal children through computer-assisted instruction. *Journal of Autism and Developmental Disorders, 31*(4), 377–398.

Betz, C.L. & Nehring W. (2007). *Promoting health care transition for adolescents with special health care needs and disabilities.* Baltimore: Paul H. Brookes Publishing Co.

Beyth-Marom, R., Fischhoff, B., Quadrel, M.J., & Furby, L. (1991). Teaching decision making to adolescents: A critical review. In J. Baron & R.V. Brown (Eds.), *Teaching decision making to adolescents* (pp. 19–59). Mahwah, NJ: Lawrence Erlbaum Associates.

Bigge, J. (1988). *Curriculum based instruction for special education students.* Mountain View, CA: Mayfield.

Black, R.S., Mrasek, K.D., & Ballinger, R. (2003). Individualist and collectivist values in transition planning for culturally diverse students with special needs. *The Journal for Vocational Special Needs Education, 25*(2, 3), 20–29.

Black, R.S., & Ornelles, C. (2001). Assessment of social competence and social networks for transition. *Assessment for Effective Intervention, 26*, 23–39. doi: 10.1177/073724770102600403

Black, S. (2004). Teachers can engage disengaged students. *The Education Digest, 69*, 39–44.

Blackorby, J., & Wagner, M. (1996). Longitudinal outcomes for youth with disabilities: Findings from the National Longitudinal Transition Study. *Exceptional Children, 62*, 399–419.

Blase, S.L., Gilber, A.N., Anatopoulus, A.D., Costello, J., Hoyle, R.H., Swartzwelder, H.S., et al. (2009). Self reported ADHD and adjustment in college: Cross-sectional and longitudinal findings. *Journal of Attention Disorders, 13*, 297–309.

Blessing, C. (2011). Person centered planning education site. Retrieved from http://www.ilr.cornell.edu/edi/pcp/index.html

Block, N., & Dworkin, G. (Eds.). (1976). *The I.Q. controversy.* New York: Random House.

Bloom, B., & Cohen, R.A. (2006). Summary of health statistics for US Children: National Health Interview Survey. National Center for Health Statistics. *Vital Health Statistics, 10*, 234.

Blue-Banning, M., Turnbull, A., & Pereira, L. (2000). Group action planning as a support strategy for Hispanic families: Parent and professional perspectives. *Mental Retardation, 38*, 262–275.

Board of Education v Ambach, 436 N.Y.S. 2d 564 (N.Y. Sup.) (1981).

Bolles, R.N. (2009). *What color is your parachute?* Berkeley, CA: Ten Speed Press.

Bond, G., Drake, R., & Becker, D. (2008). An update of randomized controlled trials of evidence-based supported employment. *Psychiatric Rehabilitation Journal, 31*(4), 280–290.

Bond, G., & Kukla, M. (2008). Service intensity and job tenure in supported employment. In P. Wehman, J. Kregel, & K. Inge. (Eds.), *Workplace supports and job retention: Promoting an employer driven approach to employment of people with disabilities.* Richmond, VA: VCU Rehabilitation Research and Training Center on Workplace Supports and Job Retention.

Bond, G., McHugo, G., Becker, D., Rapp, C., & Whitley, R. (2008). Fidelity of supported employment: Lessons learned from the National Evidence-Based Practice project. *Psychiatric Rehabilitation Journal, 31*, 300–305.

Bond, G., Wehman, P., & Wittenburg, D. (2005). Evidence-based practices that promote employment of people with disabilities. Report submitted to National Council on Disability, Social Security Study Consensus Validation Conference, Washington DC. Available at http://www.worksupport.com/resources/viewContent.cfm/505

Bond, G.R. (2004). Supported employment: Evidence for an evidence-based practice. *Psychiatric Rehabilitation Journal, 27*, 345–359.

Bond, G.R., Becker, D.R., Drake, R.E., Rapp, C.A., Meisler, N., Lehman, A.F., et al. (2001). Implementing supported employment as an evidence-based practice. *Psychiatric Services, 52*(3), 313–322.

Bond, R., & Castagnera, E. (2006). Peer supports and inclusive education: An underutilized resource. *Theory Into Practice, 45*, 224–229.

Bos, C.S., & Vaughn, S. (2006). *Strategies for teaching students with learning and behavior problems* (6th ed.). Boston: Pearson Education, Inc.

Bottsford-Miller, N., Thurlow, M.L., Stout, K.E., & Quenemoen, R.F. (2006). *A comparison of IEP/504 accommodations under classroom and standardized testing conditions: A preliminary report on SEELS data* (Synthesis Report 63). Minneapolis, MN: University of Minnesota, National Center on Educational Outcomes.

Bouck, E.C. (2004). The state of curriculum for secondary students with mild mental retardation. *Education and Training in Developmental Disabilities, 39,* 169–176.

Bouck, E.C. (2006). *When Denver is not a country, but a state: Studying the enactment of functional curriculum in two rural categorical secondary programs.* (Unpublished doctoral dissertation). Michigan State University, East Lansing, MI.

Bouck, E.C. (2008). Factors impacting the enactment of a functional curriculum in self-contained cross-categorical programs. *Education and Training in Developmental Disabilities, 43,* 294–310.

Bouck, E.C. (2009a). Functional curriculum models for secondary students with mild mental impairment. *Education and Training in Developmental Disabilities, 44,* 435–443.

Bouck, E.C. (2009b). No Child Left Behind, the Individuals with Disabilities Education Act and functional curricula: A conflict of interest? *Education and Training in Developmental Disabilities, 44,* 3–13.

Bouck, E.C. (in press). The impact of secondary curriculum on postschool outcomes for students with moderate/severe intellectual disabilities. *Journal of Intellectual Disabilities Research.*

Bouck, E.C., Bassette, L., Taber-Doughty, T., Flanagan, S.M., & Szwed, K. (2009). Pentop computers as tools for teaching multiplication to students with mild intellectual disabilities. *Education and Training in Developmental Disabilities, 44,* 367–380.

Bouck, E.C., & Flanagan, S. (2010). Functional curriculum—evidence-based education? Considering secondary students with mild intellectual disabilities. *Education and Training in Autism and Developmental Disabilities, 45,* 487–499.

Bouck, E.C., & Joshi, G.S. (in press). Functional curriculum and students with mild intellectual disabilities: Exploring postschool outcomes through the NLTS2. *Education and Training in Autism and Developmental Disabilities.*

Bouck, E.C., & Wasburn-Moses, L. (2010). The implementation of an alternate route to a diploma in one state. *Remedial and Special Education, 31,* 175–183.

Boudah, D.J., Knight, S.L., Kostohryz, C., Welch, N., Laughter, D., & Branch, R. (2000). Collaborative research in inclusive classrooms; an investigation with reflections by teachers and researchers. *Teacher Education and Special Education, 23*(3), 241–252.

Boulineau, T., Fore III, C.J., Hagan-Burke, S., & Burke, M. (2004). Use of story map instruction to increase story grammar text comprehension for elementary school students with learning disabilities in a resource setting. *Learning Disability Quarterly, 27,* 105–121.

Boulton, M.J., Bucci, E., & Hawker, D.D. (1999). Swedish and English secondary school pupils' attitudes towards, and conceptions of bullying: Concurrent links with bully/victim involvement. *Scandinavian Journal of Psychology, 40*(4), 277–284.

Bowe, F.G. (2000). *Universal design in education: Teaching nontraditional students.* Westport, CT: Bergin & Garvey.

Braddock, D., Hemp, P., & Rizzolo, M. (2008). *The state of the states in developmental disabilities: Seventh Edition* (pp. 8–66). Washington, DC: American Association on Intellectual and Developmental Disabilities.

Braddock, D., Hemp, R., Rizzolo, M., Coulter, D., Haffer, L., & Thompson, M. (2010). *The state of the states in developmental disabilities 2005.* Boulder, CO: University of Colorado at Boulder, Coleman Institute for Cognitive Disabilities.

Braddock, D., Rizzolo, M., & Hemp, R. (2010). Most employment services growth in developmental disabilities during 1988-2002 was in segregated settings. *Mental Retardation, 42*(4), 317–320.

Bradshaw, C.P., Koth, K., Bevans, K.B., Lalongo, N., & Leaf, P.J. (2008). The impact of school wide positive behavioral supports on the organizational health of elementary schools. *School Psychology Quarterly, 23,* 462–473.

Brain, P. (1994). Hormonal aspects of aggression and violence. In A. Reiss, Jr., K. Miczek, & J. Roth (Eds.), *Understanding and preventing violence* (Vol. 2, pp. 173–244). Washington, DC: National Academy Press.

Branstad, T., Acosta, A., Bartlett, S., Berdine, W., Butterfield, P., Chambers, J., et al. (2002). *A new era: Revitalizing special education for children and their families.* Washington, DC: Department of Education.

Bremer, C., Kachgal, M., & Schoeller, K. (2003). *Self-determination: Supporting successful transition.* Retrieved April 2, 2005, from http://www.ncset.org/publications/viewdesc.asp

Briel, L.W., & Getzel, E.E. (2001). Internships in higher education: Promoting success for students with disabilities. *Disability Studies Quarterly, 21*(1), 38–48.

Briel, L.W., & Getzel, E.E. (2005). Internships and field placements. In L. Getzel & P. Wehman (Eds.), *Going to college: Expanding opportunities for students with disabilities* (pp. 271–290). Baltimore: Paul H. Brookes Publishing Co.

Briel, L.W., & Getzel, E.E. (2009). Postsecondary options for students with autism. In P. Wehman, M.D. Smith, & C. Schall (Eds.), *Autism & the transition to adulthood: Success beyond the classroom* (pp. 189–207). Baltimore: Paul H. Brookes Publishing Co.

Briel, L.W., & Wehman, P. (2005). Career planning and placement. In L. Getzel & P. Wehman (Eds.), *Going to college: Expanding opportunities for students with disabilities* (pp. 291–306). Baltimore: Paul H. Brookes Publishing Co.

Brighouse, H., & Swift, A. (2008). Putting educational equity in its place. *Education Finance and Policy, 3*(4), 444–466.

Brinckerhoff, L.C., McGuire, J.M., & Shaw, S.F. (2002). *Postcondary education and transition for students with learning disabilities* (2nd ed.). Austin, TX: PRO-ED.

Brolin, D.E. (2004). *Life centered career education.* Arlington, VA: Council for Exceptional Children.

Bronfenbrenner, U. (1979). *The ecology of human development.* Cambridge, MA: Harvard University Press.

Bronfenbrenner U. (Ed.). (2005). *Making human beings human: Biological perspectives on human development.* Thousand Oaks, CA: Sage.

Brooke, V., Revell, G., & Wehman, P. (2010). Quality indicators for competitive employment: What special education teachers need to know in transition planning. *Teaching Exceptional Children, 41*(4), 58–66.

Brookhart v Illinois State Board of Education, 697 F. 2d 179 (7th Circuit) (1983).

Brooks-Lane, N., Hutcheson, S., & Revell, G. (2005). Supporting consumer directed employment outcomes. *Journal of Vocational Rehabilitation, 23*(2), 123–124.

Browder, D., Spooner, F., Ahlgrim-Delzell, L., Flowers, C., Algozzine, B., & Karvonen, M. (2003). A content analysis of the curricular philosophies reflect in states' alternate assessment performance indicators. *Research & Practice for Persons with Severe Disabilities, 28,* 165–181.

Browder, D.M., & Cooper-Duffy, K. (2003). Evidence-based practices for students with severe disabilities and the requirement for accountability in "No Child Left Behind." *Journal of Special Education, 37,* 157–163.

Browder, D.M., Gibbs, S.L., Ahlgrim-Delzell, L., Courtade, G., Mraz, M., & Flowers, C. (2009). Literacy for students with severe developmental disabilities: What should we teach and what should we hope to achieve? *Remedial and Special Education. 30*(5) 269–282.

Browder, D.M., & Spooner, F. (2003). Potential benefits of the adequate yearly progress provision of NCLB for students with significant disabilities. *TASH Connections,* 12–17.

Browder, D.M., Spooner, F.H., Ahlgrim-Delzell, L., Harris, A., & Wakeman, S.L. (2008). A meta-analysis on teaching mathematics to students with significant cognitive disabilities. *Exceptional Children, 74*(4), 407–432.

Browder, D.M., Spooner, F., Wakeman, S., Trela, K., & Baker, J.N. (2006). Aligning instruction with academic content standards: Finding the link. *Research and Practice for Persons with Severe Disabilities, 31,* 309–321.

Browder, D.M., Wakeman, S.Y., Flowers, C., Rickelman, R.J., Pugalee, D., & Karvonen, M. (2007). Creating access to the general curriculum with link to grade-level content for students with significant cognitive disabilities: An explication of the concept. *The Journal of Special Education, 41,* 2–16.

Browder, D., Wakeman, S., & Jimenez, B. (2006). Creating access to the general education curriculum with links to grade level content for students with significant cognitive disabilities. Presentation at the 2006 Office of Special Education Programs Project Directors Meeting, Washington, DC. Retrieved from http://education.uncc.edu/access/ppt/CreatingAccess.pdf

Browder, D.M., Wakeman, S.Y., Spooner, F., Ahlgrim-Delzell, L., & Algozzine, R. (2006). Research on reading instruction for individuals with significant cognitive disabilities. *Exceptional Children, 72,* 392–408.

Brown v Board of Education, 347 U.S. 483 (1954). Retrieved from FindLaw.com on July 18, 2011.

Brown, S.E., Takahashi, K., & Roberts, K.D. (2010). Mentoring individuals with disabilities in postsecondary education: A review of the literature. *Journal of Postsecondary Education and Disability, 23*(2), 98–111.

Brown, W.H., Odom, S.L., McConnell, S.R., & Rathrel, J. (2008). Social competence interventions for preschoolers with developmental difficulties. In W.H. Brown, S.L. Odom, & S.R. McConnell (Eds.), *Social competence of young children: Risk, disability and evidence based practices* (2nd ed., pp. 141–163). Baltimore: Paul H. Brookes Publishing Co.

Brownell, M.T., Ross, D.D., Colon, E.P., & McCallum, C.L. (2005). Critical features of special education teacher preparation: A comparison with general teacher education. *The Journal of Special Education, 38,* 242–252.

Bruyere, S.M. (2000). *Disability employment policies and practices in private and federal sector organizations* (technical report). Ithaca, NY: Cornell University, Program on Employment and Disability, School of Industrial Labor Relations.

Bryant, B., Bryant, D., & Reith, H. (2002). The use of assistive technology in postsecondary education. In L. Brinckerhoff, J. McGuire, & S. Shaw (Eds.), *Postsecondary education and transition for students with learning disabilities* (pp. 389–429). Austin, TX: PRO-ED.

Bucholz, J.L., & Brady, M.P. (2008). Teaching positive work behavior with literacy-based behavioral interventions: An intervention for students and employees with developmental disabilities. *Teaching Exceptional Children, 41*(2), 50–55.

Buhs, E.S., Ladd, G.W., & Herald, S.L. (2006). Peer exclusion and peer abuse: Processes that mediate the relation between peer group rejection and children's classroom engagement and achievement? *Journal of Educational Psychology, 98,* 1–13.

Bui, Y.N., & Turnbull, A. (2003). East meets West: Analysis of person-centered planning in the context of Asian American values. *Education and Training in Mental Retardation and Developmental Disabilities, 38,* 18–31.

Bullis, B., & Davis, C. (1996). Further examination of job-related social skills measures for adolescents and young adults with emotional and behavioral disorders. *Behavioral Disorders, 21,* 160–171.

Bureau of Labor Statistics. (2010a). Economic news release: Table A-6. Employment status of the civilian population by sex, age, and disability, not seasonally adjusted. Washington, DC: Bureau of Labor Statistics, U.S. Department of Labor. Retrieved from http://www.bls.gov/news.release/empsit.t06.htm

Bureau of Labor Statistics. (2010b). Persons with a disability: Labor force characteristics. Modified August 25, 2010. Table 1. Employment status of the civilian noninstitutional population by disability status and selected characteristics, 2009 annual averages. Retrieved from http://www.bls.gov/news.release/disabl.t01.htm

Bureau of Labor Statistics. (2011, June 24). News release: Persons with a disability: Labor force characteristics–2010. Retrieved December 29, 2011, from http://www.bls.gov/news.release/pdf/disabl.pdf

Burge, P., Ouellette-Kuntz, H., & Lysaght, R. (2007). Public views on employment of people with intellectual disabilities. *Journal of Vocational Rehabilitation, 26,* 29–37.

Burgstahler, S. (2005). The role of technology in preparing for college and careers. In E.E. Getzel & P. Wehman (Eds.), *Going to college: Expanding opportunities for people with disabilities* (179–198). Baltimore: Paul H. Brookes Publishing Co.

Burgstahler, S. (2008). Universal design in higher education. In S. Burgstahler & R. Cory (Eds.), *Universal design in higher education: From principles to practice* (pp. 3–20). Boston: Harvard Education Press.

Burgstahler, S., & Comden, D. (2011). Computer and cell phone access for individuals with mobility impairments: An overview and case studies. *Neurorehabilitation, 29,* 35–50.

Burgstahler, S. & Cory R. (2008). *Universal design in higher education: From principles to practice.* Boston: Harvard Education Press.

Burkhauser, R.V., & Daly, M.C. (2011). *The declining work and welfare of people with disabilities.* Washington, DC: American Enterprise Institute for Public Policy Research.

Burling, K. (2007). *Pearson Educational Measurement Bulletin, 4.* Retrieved from http://ebookbrowse.com/bulletin-4-final-pdf-d255889677

Butterworth, J., & Callahan, M. (2010). Reestablishing TASH's leadership in employment for persons with severe disabilities. *Research and Practice for Persons with Severe Disabilities, 35,* 1–4.

Butterworth, J., Smith, F.A., Hall, A.C., Migliore, A., & Winsor, J.E. (2009). *StateData: The national report on employment services and outcomes.* Boston: Institute for Community Inclusion. Retrieved July 12, 2011 from http://www.communityinclusion.org/article.php?article_id=250&staff_id=2#trendsA

Butterworth, J., Smith, F., Hall, A.C., Migliore, A., & Winsor, J. (2010). Just do it: Are we making progress in improving employment outcomes? *TASH Connections, 36*(2), 24–26.

Buxton, V. (2004). Customized employment makes dreams come true, *Making a Difference 4*(5), 18–21. Atlanta, GA: Governor's Council on Developmental Disabilities.

Cairns, R.B. (2000). Developmental science: Three audacious implications. In L.R. Bergman, R.B. Cairns, L-G. Nilsson, & L. Nystedt (Eds.), *Developmental science and the holistic approach* (pp. 49–62). Mahwah, NJ: Lawrence Erlbaum Associates.

Calabrese, R., Patterson, J., Liu, F., Goodvin, S., Hummel, C., & Nance, E. (2008). An appreciative inquiry into the Circle of Friends program: The benefits of social inclusion of students with disabilities. *International Journal of Whole Schooling, 4*(2), 20–29.

Callahan, M. (2010). The productivity fallacy: Why people are worth more than just how fast their hands move. *TASH Connections, 36*(2), 21–23.

Cameto, R. (2005). The transition planning process. *National Longitudinal Transition Study 2, 4*(1). Minneapolis: National Center on Secondary Education and Transition, University of Minnesota.

Capizzi, A. (2008). From assessment to annual goal engaging a decision-making process in writing measurable IEPs. *Teaching Exceptional Children, 41*(1), 18–25.

Capps, R., Fix, M., Murray, J., Ost, J., Passel, J., & Herwantoro, S. (2005). *The new demography of America's schools: Immigration and the No Child Left Behind Act.* Washington, DC: The Urban Institute.

Carey, A.C., DelSordo, V., & Goldman, A. (2004). Assistive technology for all: Access to alternative financing for minority populations. *Journal of Disability Policy Studies, 14*(4), 194–203.

Carey, A.C., Potts, B.B., Bryen, D.N., & Shankar, J. (2004). Networking towards employment: Experiences of people who use augmentive and alternative communication. *Research & Practice for Persons with Severe Disabilities, 29*(1), 40–52.

Carr, E.G., Dunlap, G., Horner, R.H., Koegel, R.L., Turnbull, A.P., Sailor, W., et al. (2002). Positive behavior support: Evolution of an applied science. *Journal of Positive Behavior Interventions, 4,* 4–16.

Carr, E.G., Horner, R.H., Turnbull, A.P., Marquis, J.G., McLaughlin, D.M., McAtee, M.L., et al. (1999). *Positive Behavior Support for People with Developmental Disabilities: A Research Synthesis.* Washington, DC: AAMR.

Carter, E.W. (2011). Supporting peer relationships. In M.E. Snell & F. Brown (Eds.), *Instruction of students with severe disabilities* (7th ed., pp. 431–460). Upper Saddle River, NJ: Merrill.

Carter, E.W., Austin, D., & Trainor, A. (in press). Predictors of postschool employment outcomes for young adults with severe disabilities. *Journal of Disability Policy Studies.*

Carter, E.W., Austin, D., & Trainor, A. (2011). Factors associated with the early work experiences of adolescents with severe disabilities. *Intellectual and Developmental Disabilities, 49*(4), 233–247.

Carter, E.W., Cushing, L.S., Clark, N.M., & Kennedy, C.H. (2005). Effects of peer support interventions on students' access to the general curriculum and social interactions. *Research and Practice for Persons with Severe Disabilities, 30*(1), 15–25.

Carter, E.W., Cushing, L.S., & Kennedy, C.H. (2009). *Peer support strategies for improving all students' social lives and learning.* Baltimore: Paul H. Brookes Publishing Co.

Carter, E.W., Ditchman, N., Sun, Y., Trainor, A.A., Swedeen, B., & Owens, L. (2010). Summer employment and community experiences of transition-age youth with severe disabilities. *Exceptional Children, 76,* 194–212.

Carter, E.W., & Hughes, C. (2006). Including high school students with severe disabilities in general education classes: Perspectives of general and special educators, paraprofessionals, and administrators. *Research & Practice for Persons with Severe Disabilities, 2,* 174–185.

Carter, E.W., & Hughes, C. (2007). Social interaction interventions: Promoting socially supportive environments and teaching new skills. In S.L. Odom, R.H. Horner, M. Snell, & J. Blacher (Eds.), *Handbook on developmental disabilities* (pp. 310–329). New York: Guilford Press.

Carter, E.W., Hughes, C., Guth, C., & Copeland, S.R. (2005). Factors influencing social interaction among high school students with intellectual disabilities and their general education peers. *American Journal on Mental Retardation, 110,* 366–377. doi: 10.1352/0895-8017(2005)110[366:FISIAH]2.0.CO;2

Carter, E.W., & Kennedy, C.H. (2006). Promoting access to the general curriculum using peer support strategies. *Research and Practice for Persons with Severe Disabilities, 31*(4), 284–292.

Carter, E.W., Lane, K.L., Crnobori, M., Bruhn, A.L., & Oakes, W.P. (2011). Self-determination interventions for students with and at risk for emotional and behavioral disorders: Mapping the knowledge base. *Behavioral Disorders, 36,* 100–116.

Carter, E.W., Lane, K.L., Pierson, M.R., & Stang, K.K. (2008). Promoting self determination for transition-age youth: Views of high school general and special educators. *Exceptional Children, 75*(1), 55–70.

Carter, E.W., Lane, K.L., Pierson, M.R., & Glaeser, B. (2006). Self-determination skills and opportunities of transition-age youth with emotional disturbance and learning disabilities. *Exceptional Children, 72*(3), 333–346.

Carter, E.W., Lane, K.L., Pierson, M.R., & Stang, K.K. (2008). Promoting self-determination for transition-age youth: Views of high school general and special educators. *Exceptional Children, 75*(1), 55–70.

Carter, E.W., Moss, C.K., Hoffman, A., Chung, Y., & Sisco, L.G. (2011). Efficacy and social validity of peer support interventions for high school students with severe disabilities. *Exceptional Children, 78,* 107–125.

Carter, E.W., O'Rourke, L., Sisco, L.G., & Pelsue, D. (2009). Knowledge, responsibilities, and training needs of paraprofessionals in elementary and secondary schools. *Remedial and Special Education, 30*(6), 344–359.

Carter, E.W., Owens, L., Swedeen, B., Trainor, A.A., Thompson, C., Ditchman, R., et al. (2009). Conversations that matter: Engaging communities to expand employment opportunities for youth with disabilities. *Teaching Exceptional Children, 41,* 38–46.

Carter, E.W., Owens, L., Trainor, A.A., Sun, Y., & Swedeen, B. (2009). Self-determination skills and opportunities of adolescents with severe intellectual and developmental disabilities. *American Journal on Intellectual and Developmental Disabilities, 114,* 179–192.

Carter, E.W., & Pesko, M.J. (2008). Social validity of peer interaction intervention strategies in high school classrooms: Effectiveness, feasibility, and actual use. *Exceptionality, 16,* 156–173.

Carter, E.W., Sisco, L.G., Brown, L., Brickham, D., & Al-Khabbaz, Z.A. (2008). Peer interactions and academic engagement of youth with developmental disabilities in inclusive middle and high school classrooms. *American Journal on Mental Retardation, 113,* 479–494. doi: 10.1352/2008.113:479–494

Carter, E.W., Sisco, L.G., Chung, Y., & Stanton-Chapman, T.L. (2010). Peer interactions of students with disabilities and/or autism: A map of the intervention literature. *Research and Practice for Persons with Severe Disabilities, 35*(3–4), 63–79.

Carter, E.W., Sisco, L.G., Melekoglu, M.A., & Kurkowski, C. (2007). Peer supports as an alternative to individually assigned paraprofessionals in inclusive high school classrooms. *Research and Practice for Persons with Severe Disabilities, 32*(4), 213–227.

Carter, E.W., Swedeen, B., Moss, C.K., & Pesko, M. (2010). "What are you doing after school?" Promoting extracurricular involvement for transition-age youth with disabilities. *Intervention in School and Clinic, 45,* 275–283. doi: 10.1177/1053451209359077

Carter, E.W., Swedeen, B., & Trainor, A.A. (2009). The other three months: Connecting transition-age youth with disabilities to meaningful summer experiences. *Teaching Exceptional Children, 41,* 18–26.

Carter, E.W., Swedeen, B., Walter, M.J., Moss, C.K., & Hsin, C. (2011) Perspectives of young adults with disabilites on leadership. *Career Development for Exceptional Individuals, 34*(1), 57–67.

Carter, E.W., Trainor, A.A., Cakiroglu, O., Cole, O., Swedeen, B., & Ditchman, N. (2009). Exploring school-employer partnerships to expand career development early work experiences for youth with disabilities. *Career Development for Exceptional Individuals, 32*(3), 145–159.

Carter, E.W., Trainor, A.A., Cakiroglu, O., Swedeen, B., & Owens, L.A. (2010). Availability of and access to career development activities for transition-age youth with disabilities. *Career Development for Exceptional Individuals, 33*(1) 13–24.

Carter, E.W., Trainor, A.A., Ditchman, N., Swedeen, B., & Owens, L. (2011). Community-based work experiences of adolescents with high-incidence disabilities. *Journal of Special Education, 45,* 89–103. doi: 10.1177/0022466909353204

Carter, E.W., Trainor, A.A., Owens, L., Swedeen, B., Sun, Y. (2010). Self-determination prospects of youth with high-incidence disabilities: Divergent perspectives and related factors. *Journal of Emotional and Behavioral Disorders, 18*(2), 67–81.

Carter, E.W., Trainor, A.A., Sun, Y., & Owens, L. (2009). Assessing the transition-related strengths and needs of adolescents with high-incidence disabilities. *Exceptional Children, 76,* 74–94.

Carter, E.W., & Wehby, J.H. (2003). Job performance of transition-age youth with emotional and behavioral disorders. *Exceptional Children, 69,* 449–465.

Carter, J., & Sugai, G. (1989). Social skills curriculum analysis. *TEACHING Exceptional Children, 22,* 38.

Casner-Lotto, J., & Barrington, L. (2006). *Are they really ready to work? Employers' perspectives on the basic knowledge and applied skills of new entrants to the 21st century USA workforce* (report). The Conference Board, Corporate Voices for Working Families, the Partnership for 21st Century Skills, and the Society for Human Resource Management, available at: http://www.vtsbdc.org/assets/files/21st_century_skills_standards.pdf

Casper, B., & Leuchovius, D. (2005). *Universal design for learning and the transition to a more challenging academic curriculum: Making it in middle school and beyond.* Parent Brief: National Center on Secondary Education and Transition, University of Minnesota, Minneapolis, MN.

Caspi, A., Wright, B.R.E., Moffitt, T.E., & Silva, P.A. (1998). Early failure in the labor market: Children and adolescent predictors of unemployment in the transition to adulthood. *American Sociological Review, 63,* 424–451.

Causton-Theoharis, J., & Malmgren, K.W. (2005). Increasing peer interactions for students with severe disabilities via paraprofessional training. *Exceptional Children, 71*(4), 431–444.

Causton-Theoharis, J.N. (2009). The golden rule of providing support in inclusive classrooms: Support others as you would wish to be supported. *Teaching Exceptional Children, 42,* 36–43.

Causton-Theoharis, J.N., Giangreco, M.F., Doyle, M.B., & Vadasy, P.F. (2007). Paraprofessionals: The "sous-chefs" of literacy instruction. *Teaching Exceptional Children, 40*(1), 56–62.

Cavanaugh, R., Heward, W., & Donelson, F. (1996). Effects of response cards during lesson closure on the academic performance of secondary students in an earth science course. *Journal of Applied Behavior Analysis, 29,* 403–406.

Cawley, J.F., Foley, T.E., & Doan, T. (2003). Giving students with disabilities a voice in the selection of arithmetic content. *Teaching Exceptional Children, 36*(1), 8–16.

CDC Online Newsroom. (2012). *1 in 88 Children in the United States has been identified as having an autism spectrum disorder* [press release]. Retrieved June 1, 2012, from http://www.cdc.gov/media/releases/2012/p0329_autism_disorder.html

Center for Applied Special Technology. (2010). *Options that increase individual choice and autonomy.* Retrieved from http://www.cast.org/library/UDLguidelines/version1.html

Center for Mental Health in Schools. (2011, March). *Understanding community schools as collaborative for system building to address barriers and promote well-being.* Los Angeles: UCLA.

Center for Universal Design. (1997). *Environments and products for all people.* Raleigh, NC: North Carolina State University, Center for Universal Design. Retrieved January 30, 2004, from http://www.ncsu.edu/project/design-projects/udi/

Center on Education Policy. (2009a). *High school exit exams: Trends in test programs, alternate pathways, and pass rates.* Washington, DC: Author.

Center on Education Policy. (2009b). *State test score trends through 2007-08, part 4: Has progress been made in raising achievement for students with disabilities?* Washington, DC: Author.

Center on Education Policy. (2010). *State high school tests: Exit exams and other assessments.* Retrieved from http://www.cep-dc.org/cfcontent_file.cfm?Attachment=CEP%5FHSEE10report%5F01%2E05%2E11%2Epdf

Centers for Disease Control and Prevention. (2010, March 17). *Injury prevention and control: Traumatic brain injury.* Available at http://www.cdc.gov/TraumaticBrainInjury/statistics.html

Centers for Disease Control and Prevention. *Cerebral palsy.* Retrieved May 25, 2011, from http://www.cdc.gov/Features/CerebralPalsy/

Certo, N., & Luecking, R.G. (2011). Transition and employment: Reflections from a 40 year perspective. *Journal of Vocational Rehabilitation, 35*(3), 157–161.

Certo, N.J., Luecking, R.G., Murphy, S., Brown, L., Courey, S., & Belanger, D. (2008). Seamless transition and long-term support for individuals with severe intellectual disabilities.

Research and Practice for Persons with Severe Disabilities, 33, 85–95.

Certo, N.J., Mautz, D., Pumpian, I., Sax, C., Smalley, K., Wade, H., et al. (2003). A review and discussion of a model for seamless transition to adulthood. *Education and Training in Developmental Disabilities, 38*(1), 3–17.

Certo, N.J., Sax, C., Pumpian, I., Mautz, D., Smalley, K., Wade, H.A., et al. (2002). Transition service integration model: Ensuring that the last day of school is no different than the day after (pp. 119–131). In C. Sax & C.A. Thoma (Eds.), *Transition assessment: Wise practices for quality lives.* Baltimore: Paul H. Brookes Publishing Co.

Chadsey, J. (2008). *Social inclusion at work. Innovations research to practice.* M. Agran & M. Wehmeyer (Eds.). Washington, DC: American Association on Intellectual and Developmental Disabilities.

Chambers, C.R., Hughes, C., & Carter, E.W. (2004). Parent and sibling perspectives on the transition to adulthood. *Education and Training in Developmental Disabilities, 39*(2), 79–94.

Chapman v California Department of Education, No. C 01-01780 CRB, N.D. California, February 21, 2002.

Chew, B.L., Jensen, S.A., & Rosen, L.A. (2009). College students' attitudes toward their ADHD peers. *Journal of Attention Disorders, 13*, 271–276.

Chiak, D.F., & Schrader, L. (2008). Does the model matter? Comparing video self-modeling and video adult modeling for task acquisition and maintenance by adolescents with autism spectrum disorders. *Journal of Special Education Technology, 23*(3), 9–20.

Childre, A., & Chambers, C.R. (2005). Family perceptions of student centered planning and IEP meetings. *Education and Training in Developmental Disabilities, 40*(3), 217–233.

Chubb Group of Insurance Companies. (2011). Business case for diversity. Retrieved from http://www.chubb.com/diversity/chubb4450.html

Chun, M., & Witt, J. (2008). System to enhance educational performance. Retrieved July 7, 2008, from http://www.isteep.com/index.html

Cihak, D.F., Wright, R., & Ayres, K.M. (2010). Use of self-modeling static-picture prompts via a handheld computer to facilitate self-monitoring in the general education classroom. *Education and Training in Autism and Developmental Disabilities, 45*(1), 136–149.

Cimera, R.E. (2000). The cost-efficiency of supported employment programs: A literature review. *Journal of Vocational Rehabilitation, 14*, 51–61.

Cimera, R.E. (2007a) The cumulative cost-effectiveness of supported and sheltered employees with mental retardation. *Research and Practice for Persons with Severe Disabilities, 32*(4), 247–252.

Cimera, R.E. (2007b). Utilizing natural supports to lower the cost of supported employment. *Research and Practice for Persons with Severe Disabilities, 32*(3), 184–189.

Cimera, R.E. (2008). The cost-trends of supported employment versus sheltered employment. *Journal of Vocational Rehabilitation, 28,* 5–20.

Cimera, R.E. (2010a). Can community-based high school transition programs improve the cost-efficiency of supported employment. *Career Development for Exceptional Individuals, 33*(1), 4–12.

Cimera, R.E. (2010b). National cost efficiency of supported employees with intellectual disabilities: 2002-2007. *American Journal on Intellectual and Developmental Disabilities, 115,* 19–29.

Cimera, R.E. (2010c). Supported employment's cost-efficiency to taxpayers: 2002 to 2007. *Research and Practice for Persons with Severe Disabilities, 34*(2), 13–20.

Cimera, R.E. (2010d). The national cost-efficiency of supported employees with intellectual disabilities: The worker's perspective. *Journal of Vocational Rehabilitation, 33,* 123–131.

Cimera, R.E. (2011). Does being in sheltered workshops improve the employment outcomes of supported employees with intellectual disabilities? *Journal of Vocational Rehabilitation, 35,* 1–7.

Cimera, R.E., & Cowan, R.J. (2009). The costs of services and employment outcomes achieved by adults with autism in the US. *Autism, 13*(3), 285–302.

Citron, T., Brooks-Lane, N., Crandell, D., Brady, K., Cooper, M., & Revell, G. (2008). A revolution in the employment process of individuals with disabilities: Customized employment as the catalyst for system change. *Journal of Vocational Rehabilitation, 28,* 169–179.

Clark, G.M. (1996). Transition planning assessment for secondary-level students with learning disabilities. In J.R. Patton & G. Blalock (Eds.), *Transition and students with learning disabilities: Facilitating the movement from school to adult life* (pp. 131–156). Austin, TX: PRO-ED.

Clark, G.M. (1998). *Assessment for transitions planning: Transition series.* Austin, TX, PRO-ED.

Clark, G.M., & Patton, J.R. (2004). *Transition planning inventory.* Austin, TX: PRO-ED.

Clark, H.B., & Davis, M. (2000). *Transition to adulthood: A resource for assisting young people with emotional or behavioral difficulties.* Baltimore: Paul H. Brookes Publishing Co.

Coalitions for juvenile justice. *Richmond Times Dispatch,* November 7, 2004.

Cobb, B., & Alwell, M. (2009). Transition planning/coordinating interventions for youth with disabilities. *Career Development for Exceptional Individuals, 32,* 70–81.

Cobb, B., Lehmann, J., Newman-Gonchar, R., & Alwell, M. (2009). Self-determination for students with disabilities: A narrative meta-synthesis. *Career Development for Exceptional Individuals, 32*(2), 108–114.

Cobb, M.C., Rabren, K., & Eaves, R. (2011). Post-school satisfaction levels of individuals with disabilities: The effects of geographic location, race, and gender. Manuscript submitted for publication.

Coelho, A.L. (2003, November 4). *Disability matters* [VoiceAmerica internet radio broadcast]. Retrieved from http://paychecksnotpity.com/radiocaption/110403VA.html

Cohen, M.R. (2011). *Social literacy: A social skill seminar for young adults with ASDs, NLDs, and social anxiety.* Baltimore: Paul H. Brookes Publishing Co.

Cole, C.M., Waldron, N., & Majd, M. (2004). Academic progress of students across inclusive and traditional settings. *Mental Retardation, 42*(2), 136–144.

Cole, M. (2010). What's culture got to do with it? Educational research as a necessarily interdisciplinary enterprise. *Educational Researcher, 39,* 461–470.

College Board. (2011). *About PSAT/NMSQT for students.* Retrieved on June 13, 2011, from http://www.collegeboard.com/student/testing/psat/about.html

Collins, B.C., Evans, A., Creech-Galloway, C., Karl, J., & Miller, A. (2007). Comparison of the acquisition and maintenance of teaching functional and core content sight words in special and general education settings. *Focus on Autism and Other Developmental Disabilities, 22,* 220–233.

Collins, B.C., & Griffen, A.K. (1996). Teaching students with moderate disabilities to make safe responses to product warning labels. *Education and Treatment of Children, 19,* 30–45.

Collins, B.C., Hager, K.L., & Galloway, C.C. (2011). Addition of functional content during core content instruction for students with moderate disabilities. *Education and Training in Autism and Developmental Disabilities, 46,* 22–39.

Collins, B.C., Kleinert, H.L., & Land, L.E. (2006). Addressing math standards and functional math. In D.M. Browder & F. Spooner (Eds.), *Teaching language arts, math, & science to students with significant cognitive disabilities* (pp. 197–227). Baltimore: Paul H. Brooks Publishing Co.

Collins, B.C., & Stinson, D.M. (1995). Teaching generalized reading of product warning labels to adolescents with mental disabilities through the use of key words. *Exceptionality, 5,* 163–181.

Combs-Richardson, R., & Mead, J. (2001). Supporting general educators' inclusive practices. *Teacher Education and Special Education, 24*(4), 383–390.

Commission on Epidemiology and Prognosis, International League Against Epilepsy. (1993). Guidelines for epidemiologic studies of epilepsy. *Epilepsia, 34,* 592–596.

Common Core State Standards Initiative. (2010a). *Application to students with disabilities.* Retrieved from http://corestandards.org/assets/application-to-students-with-disabilities.pdf

Common Core State Standards Initiative. (2010b). *Introduction to the Common Core State Standards.* Retrieved from http://corestandards.org/assets/ccssi-introduction.pdf

Conley, R.W. (2003). Supported employment in Maryland: Success and issues. *Mental Retardation, 41*(4), 237–249.

Connolly, K.A. (2005). In search of the American dream: An examination of undocumented students, in-state tuition, and the DREAM act. *Catholic University Law Review, 55,* 193–226.

Conroy, M.A., Alter, P.J., & Scott, T.M. (2009). Functional behavioral assessment and students with emotional/behavioral disorders: When research, policy, and practice collide. In T.E. Scruggs & M.A. Mastropieri (Eds.), *Policy and Practice: Advances in Learning and Behavior Disabilities, 22,* 135–168. Bingley, UK: Emerald.

Conroy, M.A., Sutherland, K., Snyder, A., Al-Hendawi, M., & Vo, A. (2009). Creating a positive classroom atmosphere: Teacher's use of effective praise and feedback. *Beyond Behavior, 18*(2), 18–26.

Cook, B.G., Landrum, T.J., Tankersley, M., & Kauffman, J.M. (2003). Bringing research to bear on practice: Effecting evidence-based instruction for students with emotional or behavioral disorders. *Education and Treatment of Children, 26,* 345–361.

Cook, C.R., Gresham, F.M., Kern, L., Barreras, R.B., Thornton, S., & Crews, S.D. (2008). Social skills training for secondary students with emotional and/or behavioral disorders: A review and analysis of the meta-analytic literature. *Journal of Emotional and Behavioral Disorders, 16,* 131–144. doi: 10.1177/1063426608314541

Cook, J.A., Blyler, C.R., Leff, H.S., McFarlane, W.R., Goldberg, R.W., Gold, P.B., et al. (2008). The Employment Intervention Demonstration Program: Major findings and policy implications. *Psychiatric Rehabilitation Journal, 31,* 291–295.

Cook, J.A., & Razzano, L.A. (2000). Vocational rehabilitation for persons with schizophrenia: Recent research and implications for practice. *Schizophrenia Bulletin, 26*(1), 87–103.

Cooney, B.F. (2002). Exploring perspectives on transition of youth with disabilities: Voices of young adults, parents, and professionals. *Mental Retardation, 40,* 425–435.

Cooper, J.O., Heron, T.E., & Heward W.L. (2007). *Applied behavior analysis* (2nd ed.). Upper Saddle River, NJ: Prentice Hall.

Cooper, K.J., & Browder, D.M. (1998). Enhancing choice and participation for adults with severe disabilities in community-based instruction. *Journal of the Association for Persons with Severe Handicaps, 23,* 252–260.

Copeland, S.R., Hughes, C., Carter, E.W., Guth, C., Presley, J., Williams, C.R., et al. (2004). Increasing access to general education: Perspectives of participants in a high school peer support program. *Remedial and Special Education, 26,* 342–352. doi: 10.1177/07419325040250060201

Cormier, D.C., Altman, J.R., Shyyan, V., & Thurlow, M.L. (2010). *A summary of the research on the effects of test accommodations: 2007-2008* (Technical Report 56). Minneapolis: University of Minnesota, National Center on Educational

Outcomes. Available from http://www.cehd. umn.edu/NCEO/OnlinePubs/Tech56/TechnicalReport56.pdf

Corcoran, T., & Silander, M. (2009). Instruction in high schools: The evidence and the challenge. *The Future of Children, 19*(1), 157–183.

Costello, J.M., Patak, L., & Pritchard, J. (2010). Communication vulnerable patients in pediatric ICU: Enhancing care through augmentative and alternative communication. *Journal of Pediatric Rehabilitation Medicine: An Interdisciplinary Approach, 2,* 289–301.

Cote, D., Pierce, T., Higgins, K., Miller, S., Tandy, R. & Sparks, S. (2010). Increasing skill performance of problem solving to students with intellectual disabilities. *Education and Training in Autism and Developmental Disabilities, 45,* 512–524.

Council for Exceptional Children. (2003). Advocacy in action: CEC members speak out against No Child Left Behind. *CEC Today, 10*(4), 4,7.

Council for Exceptional Children. (2008). *What every special educator must know: Ethics, standards, and guidelines* (6th ed.). Arlington, VA: Author.

Council for Exceptional Children. (n.d.). *New flexibility in testing students with disabilities a positive step.* Retrieved from http://www.cec. sped.org/AM/Template.cfm? Section=Home& CONTENTID=6247&TEMPLATE=/CM/ContentDisplay.cfm

Council for Exceptional Children, Division on Behavior Disorders. (2009). Retrieved from http://www.ccbd.net/publications,

Council of Chief State School Officers and the National Governors Association Center for Best Practices. (2010, June). *Common Core. State standards initiative: Preparing America's students for college and career.* Suwanee, GA: Authors. Retreived from: http://www.nga.org/ cms/render/live/en/sites/NGA/home/newsroom/news-releases/page_2010/col2-content/ main-content-list/title_national-governorsassociation-and-state-education-chiefs-launchcommon-state-academic-standards.html

Countino, M.J., Oswald, D.P., & Best, A.M. (2006). Differences in outcomes for female and male students in special education. *Career Development for Exceptional Individuals, 29*(1) 48–59.

Courtade, G.R., Spooner, F., & Browder, D.M. (2007). Review of studies with student with significant cognitive disabilities which link to science standards. *Research & Practice for Persons with Severe Disabilities, 32,* 43–49.

Cox, M.L., Herner, J.G., Demczyk, M.J., & Nieberding, J.J. (2006). Provision of testing accommodations for students with disabilities on statewide assessments: Statistical links with participation and discipline rates. *Remedial and Special Education, 27*(6), 346–354.

Craddock, G., & Scherer, M. (2002). Assessing individual needs for assistive technology. In C.L. Sax & C.A. Thoma (Eds.), *Transition assessment: Wise practices for quality lives.* (p. 100). Baltimore: Paul H. Brookes Publishing Co.

Crane, K., Gramlich, M., & Peterson, K. (2004). Putting interagency agreements into action. *National Center on Secondary Education and Transition (NCSET), Issue Brief, 3*(2).

Crane, K., & Mooney, M. (2005). *Essential tools: Community resource mapping.* Retrieved from http://www.ncset.org/publications/essentialtools/mapping/default.asp

Crews, D.E., & Zavotka, S. (2006). Aging, disability and frailty: Implications for universal design. *Journal of Physiological Anthropology, 25,* 113–118.

Crites, S.A., & Dunn, C. (2004). Teaching social problem solving to individuals with mental retardation. *Education and Training in Developmental Disabilities, 39*(4), 301–309.

Croke, E.E., & Thompson, A.B. (2011). Person centered planning in a transition program for Bronx youth with disabilities. *Children & Youth Services Review, 33*(6), 810–819.

Crone, E.A., Vendel, I., & van der Molen, M.W. (2003). Decision-making in disinhibited adolescents and adults: Insensitivity to future consequences or driven by immediate reward? *Personality and Individual Differences, 35*(7), 1625–1641.

Cronin, M.E. (1996). Life skills curriculum for students with learning disabilities. *Journal of Learning Disabilities, 29,* 53–68.

Cronin, M.E., & Patton, J.R. (1993). *Life skills instruction for all students with special needs: A practical guide for integrating real-life content into the curriculum.* Austin, TX: PRO-ED.

Cross, T., Cooke, N.L., Wood, W.M., & Test, D.W. (1999). Comparison of the effects of MAPS and ChoiceMaker on students' self-determination skills. *Education and Training in Mental Retardation and Developmental Disabilities, 34,* 499–510.

Crowley, J.A., & White-Waters, K. (2010). Psychological assessment in pediatric rehabilitation. In M.A. Alexander & D. Matthews (Eds.). *Pediatric rehabilitation: Principles and practice* (4th ed., pp. 22–52). New York: Demos Medical Publishing.

Cushing, L.S., & Kennedy, C.H. (1997). Academic effects on students without disabilities who serve as peer supports for students with disabilities in general education classrooms. *Journal of Applied Behavior Analysis, 30,* 139–152.

Cushing, L.S., Kennedy, C.H., Shukla, S., Davis, J., & Meyer, K.A. (1997). Disentangling the effects of curricular revision and social grouping within cooperative learning arrangements. *Focus on Autism and Other Developmental Disabilities, 12,* 231–240. doi: 10.1177/108835769701200405

Daniel, S., Walsh, A., Goldston, D., Arnold, E., Reboussin, B., & Wood, F. (2006). Suicidality, school dropout, and reading problems among adolescents. *Journal of Learning Disabilities, 39*(6), 507–514.

Data Accountability Center. (2008). *Individuals with Disabilities Education Act (IDEA) data.*

Number and percentage of students ages 6 through 21 served under IDEA, Part B, by disability category, educational environment and state: Fall 2008. Retrieved from https://www.ideadata.org/arc_toc10.asp#partbLRE

Data Quality Campaign. (2008). *Tapping into the power of longitudinal data: A guide for school leaders.* Retrieved from http://www.dataquality campaign.org/files/publications-tapping_into_the_power_of_longitudinal_data-a_guide_for_school_leaders-010108.pdf

Data Quality Campaign. (2009). *The next step: Using longitudinal data systems to improve student success.* Retrieved from http://www.dataqualitycampaign.org/files/NextStep.pdf

Datillo, J., & Hoge, G. (1999). Effects of a leisure education program on youth with mental retardation. *Education and Training in Mental Retardation and Developmental Disabilities, 34,* 20–34.

Davidsen, D., & Streagle, K. (2011). Developing the transition curriculum. In P. Wehman (Ed.), *Essentials of transition planning.* Baltimore: Paul H. Brookes Publishing Co.

Davies, D.K., Stock, S., Holloway, S., & Weh-meyer, M. (2010). Evaluating a GPS-based transportation device to support independent bus travel by people with intellectual disability. *Intellectual and Developmental Disabilities, 48*(6), 454–463.

Davies, P.S., Rupp, K., & Wittenburg, D. (2009). A life-cycle perspective on the transition to adulthood among children receiving supplementary securing income payment, *Journal of Vocational Rehabilitation, 30,* 133–151.

Debra P. v Turlington, 654 F 2d 1079 (5th Circuit) (1981).

deFur, S.H. (2003). IEP transition planning— From compliance to quality. *Exceptionality, 11,* 115–128.

Delgado-Gaitan, C. (2004). *Involving Latino families in schools.* Thousand Oaks, CA: Corwin.

Dell, A., Newton, D.A., & Petroff, J.G. (2008). *Assistive technology in the classroom: Enhancing the school experiences of students.* Upper Saddle River, NJ: Pearson.

Denton, C.A. (2010, February). *The impact of instructional variables on outcomes in tier 2 first grade reading intervention.* Paper presented at the annual Pacific Coach Research Conference, Coronado, CA.

Denton, C.A., & Al Otaiba, S. (2011). Teaching word identification to students with reading difficulties and disabilities. *Focus on Exceptional Children, 43*(7), 1–15.

DePompei, R., Gillette, Y., Goetz, E., Xenopoulus-Oddsson, A., Bryan, D., & Dowds, M. (2008). Practical applications for use of PDAs and smartphones with children and adolescents who have brain injury. *NeuroRehabilitation, 23,* 487–495.

Deschamps, A. (2004). Traveling the road from high school to college: Tips for the journey. *Transition Voice, 8*(1), 6–7.

Deshler, D., Schumaker, J., Lenz, B., Bulgren, J., Hock, M., Knight, J., et al. (2001). Ensuring content-area learning by secondary students with learning disabilities. *Learning Disabilities Research and Practice, 16*(2), 96–108.

Deshpande S. (2011). Myasthenia gravis. In Nelson MR (Ed.), *Pediatrics* (1st ed., pp. 151–152). New York: Demos Medical Publishing.

DiCecco, V.M., & Gleason, M.M. (2002). Using graphic organizers to attain relational knowledge from expository text. *Journal of Learning Disabilities, 34*(4), 306–321.

Dietz, S., & Montague, M. (2006). Attention deficit hyperactivity disorder comorbid with emotional and behavior disorders and learning disabilities in adolescents. *Exceptionality, 14*(1), 19–33.

DiLeo, D. (2007). *Raymond's room: Ending the segregation of people with disabilities.* St. Augustine, FL: Training Resource Network, Inc.

Dillion, M. (1997, October). *Preparation: A key to college success.* Paper presented at the meeting of the Division of Career Development and Transition International Conference, Overland Park, KS.

Dirks, P.B., Drake, J.M., Lambert-Pasculli, M., Rutka, J.T., Humphreys, R.P., & McDonald, P. (2005). Falling ventriculo-peritoneal shunt rates in myelomeningocele. *Child's Nervous System, 19,* 607.

Dogue, M., & Banda, D.R. (2009). Review of recent research using constant time delay to teach chained tasks to persons with developmental disabilities. *Education and Training in Developmental Disabilities, 44,* 177–186.

Doll, B., & Sands, D.J. (1998). Student involvement in goals setting and educational decision making: Foundations for effective instruction. In M.L. Wehmeyer & D.J. Sands (Eds.), *Making it happen: Student involvement in education planning, decision making, and instruction.* Baltimore: Paul H. Brookes Publishing Co.

Doll, R.C. (1989). *Curriculum improvement: Decision making and process* (8th ed.). Boston: Allyn & Bacon.

Domzal, C., Houtenville, A., & Sharma, R. (2008). *Survey of employer perspectives on the employment of people with disabilities: Technical report.* (Prepared under contract to the Office of Disability and Employment Policy, U.S. Department of Labor). McLean, VA: CESSI.

Dorn, S., & Fuchs, D. (2004). Trends in placement issues. In A.M. Sorrells, H.J. Rieth, & P.T. Sindelar (Eds.), *Critical issues in special education* (pp. 57–72). Boston: Pearson.

Downing, J.E., & Eichinger, J. (2003). Creating learning opportunities for students with severe disabilities in inclusive classrooms. *Teaching Exceptional Children, 36*(1), 26–31.

Downing, J.E., & Peckham-Hardin, K.D. (2007). Inclusive education: What makes it a good education for students with moderate to severe disabilities? *Research and Practice for Persons with Severe Disabilities, 32*(1), 16–30.

Downing, J.E., Ryndak, D.L., & Clark, D. (2000). Paraeducators in inclusive classrooms: Their own perceptions. *Remedial & Special Education, 21*(3), 171.

Drake, R., & Bond, G. (2008). The future of supported employment for persons with severe mental illness. *Psychiatric Rehabilitation Journal, 31*(4), 367–376.

Dukes, C., & Lamar-Dukes, P. (2009). Inclusion by design engineering inclusive practices in secondary schools. *Teaching Exceptional Children, 41*(3), 16–23.

Dunlap, G., Strain, P.S., Fox, L, Carta, J., Conroy, M., Smith, B.J., et al. (2006). Prevention and intervention with young children's challenging behavior: Perspective regarding current knowledge. *Behavioral Disorders, 32*, 29–45.

Dyda, D.J. (2008). Jobs change lives: Social capital and shared value exchange. *Journal of Vocational Rehabilitation, 29*, 147–156.

Dymond, S. (2011). Community participation. In P. Wehman & J. Kregel (Eds.), *Functional curriculum for elementary, middle, and secondary age students with special needs* (pp. 259–291). Austin, TX: PRO-ED.

Dymond, S., Renzaglia, A., Gilson, C.L., & Slagor, M.T. (2007). Defining access to the general curriculum for high school students with significant disabilities. *Research and Practice for Persons with Severe Disabilities, 32*(1), 1–15.

D'Zurilla, T.J., & Goldfried, M.R. (1971). Problem solving and behavior modification. *Journal of Abnormal Psychology, 8*, 107–126.

Eaves, R., Rabren, K., & Hall, G. (2011). *Construct validity of the post-school outcomes transition survey.* Manuscript submitted for publication.

Eckes, S., & Ochoa, T. (2005). Students with disabilities: Transitioning from high school to higher education. *American Secondary Education, 33*(3), 6–20.

Education for All Handicapped Children Act of 1975, Pub. L. No. 94-142, 20 U.S.C. § § 1400 et seq.

Eisenberg, D. (2002, May 6). The coming job boom, *Time*, 41–42.

Eisenman, L.T. (2000). Characteristics and effects of integration academic and occupational curricula for students with disabilities: A literature review. *Career Development for Exceptional Individuals, 23*, 105–119.

Eisenman, L.T. (2007). Self-determination interventions: Building a foundation for school completion. *Remedial and Special Education, 28*, 2–8.

Eisenman, L.T., Pleet, A.M., Wandry, D., & McGinley, V. (2011). Voices of special education teachers in an inclusive high school: Redefining responsibilities. *Remedial and Special Education, 32*(2), 91–104.

Eisenman, L.T., Tanverdi, A., Perrington, C., & Geiman, A. (2009). Secondary and postsecondary community activities of youth with significant intellectual disabilities. *Education and Training in Developmental Disabilities, 44*, 168–176.

Espelage, D.L., & Swearer, S.M. (2003). Bullying in American schools: A socio-ecological perspective on prevention. *Journal of Primary Prevention, 26*(5), 467–468.

Estell, D.B., Farmer, T.W., Cairns, R.B., & Cairns, B.D. (2002). Social relations and academic achievement in inner-city early elementary classrooms. *International Journal of Behavioral Development, 26*, 518–528.

Fabian, E. (2004). *Psychiatric vocational rehabilitation. Directions in rehabilitation counseling*, Long Island City, NY: Hatherleigh Company.

Fabian, E.S. (2007). Urban youth with disabilities: factors affecting transition employment. *Rehabilitation Counseling Bulletin, 50*, 130–138.

Fabian, E.S., Lent, R.W., & Willis, S.P. (1998). Predicting work transition outcomes for students with disabilities: Implications for counselors. *Journal of Counseling and Development, 76*, 311–316.

Faherty, C. (2000). *What does it mean to me? A workbook explaining self awareness and life lessons to the child or youth with high functioning autism or Aspergers.* Arlington, TX: Future Horizons.

Falvey, M.A. (Ed.). (1989). *Community-based curriculum: Instructional strategies for students with severe handicaps* (2nd ed.). Baltimore: Paul H. Brookes Publishing Co.

Faraone, S., Sergeant, J., Gillberg, C., & Biederman, J. (2003). The worldwide prevalence of ADHD: Is it an American condition? *World Psychiatry, 2*(2), 104–113.

Farmer, T.W. (2000). The social dynamics of aggressive and disruptive behavior in school: Implications for behavior consultation. *Journal of Educational & Psychological Consultation, 11*(3–4), 299–321.

Farmer, T.W., Leung, M.-C., Pearl, R., Rodkin, P.C., Cadwallader, T.W., & Van Acker, R. (2002). Deviant or diverse groups? The peer affiliations of aggressive elementary students. *Journal of Educational Psychology, 94*, 611–620.

Farmer, T.W., Quinn, M.M., Hussey, W., & Holahan, T. (2001). The development of disruptive behavioral disorders and correlated constraints: Implications for intervention. *Behavioral Disorders, 26*, 117–130.

Ferguson, H., Miles, B., & Hagiwara, T. (2005). Using a personal digital assistant to enhance the independence of an adolescent with Asperger syndrome. *Education and Training in Developmental Disabilities, 40*, 60–67.

Ferri, B.A., & Connor, D.J. (2005). Tools of exclusion: Race, disability, and (re)segregated education. *The Voice of Scholarship in Education, 7*(28), 1–13.

Fichten, C.S., Asuncion, J.V., Barile, M., Fossey, M.E., Robillard, C., & Wolforth, J. (2001). Computer technologies for postsecondary students with disabilities II: Resources and recommendations for postsecondary service providers. *Journal of Postsecondary Education and Disability, 15*(1), 59–83.

Fiedler, C., Simpson, R., & Clark, D. (2007). Parents and families of children with disabilities. Upper Saddle River, NJ: Pearson.

Field, S., & Hoffman, A. (1994). Development of a model for self-determination. *Career Development for Exceptional Individuals, 17,* 159–169.

Field, S., Hoffman, A., & Sawilowsky, S. (2004). *Self-Determination Assessment Battery.* Detroit, MI: Wayne State University.

Field, S., Sarver, M.D., & Shaw, S.F. (2003). Self-determination: A key to success in postsecondary education for students with learning disabilities. *Remedial and Special Education, 24*(6), 339–349.

Finn, D., Getzel, E.E., & McManus, S. (2008). Adapting the self-determined learning model of instruction for college students with disabilities. *Career Development for Exceptional Individuals, 31*(2), 85–93.

Fish, W.W. (2006). Perceptions of parents of students with autism towards the IEP meeting: A case study of one family support group chapter. *Education, 127*(1), 56–68.

Fish, W.W. (2008). The IEP meeting: Perceptions of parents of students who receive special education services. *Preventing School Failure, 53*(1), 8–14.

Fisher, D., Sax, C., & Pumpian, I. (1999). *Inclusive high schools: Learning from contemporary classrooms.* Baltimore: Paul H. Brookes Publishing Co.

Fisher, S., & Eskow, K.G. (2004). Getting together in college: An inclusion program for young adults with disabilities. *Teaching Exceptional Children, 36*(3), 26–32.

Flannery, K.B., Yovanoff, P., Benz, M.R., & Kato, M.M. (2011). Improving employment outcomes of individuals with disabilities through short-term postsecondary training. *Career Development for Exceptional Individuals, 31*(1) 26–36.

Flexer, R.W., Daviso III, A.W., Baer, R.M., Queen, R.M., & Meindl, R.S. (2011). An epidemiological model of transition and postschool outcomes. *Career Development for Exceptional Individuals, 34,* 132–141. Development: 10.117710885728810387922. Retrieved from http://cde.sagepubs.com/content/early/2011/01/14/0885728810387922

Flippo, K.F., & Gardner, J.F. (2011). Perspectives: Employment: It is everybody's business. *Intellectual and Developmental Disabilities, 49*(4), 300–304.

Flores, S.M. (2010). State Dream Acts: The effect of in-state resident tuition policies and undocumented Latino students. *Review of Higher Education, 33,* 239–283.

Fogg, N.P., Harrison, P.E., & McMahon, B.T. (2010). The impact of the great recession upon the unemployment of Americans with disabilities. *Journal of Vocational Rehabilitation, 33,* 193–202.

Forbush, D.E., & Morgan, R.L. (2004). Instructional team training: Delivering live, internet courses to teachers and paraprofessionals in Utah, Idaho and Pennsylvania. *Rural Special Education Quarterly, 23*(2), 9–17.

Ford, A., Schnorr, R., Meyer, L., Davern, L., Black, J., & Dempsey, P. (1989). *The Syracuse community-referenced curriculum guide for students with moderate and severe disabilities.* Baltimore: Paul H. Brookes Publishing Co.

Foreman, P., Arthur-Kelly, M., Pascoe, S., & King, B.S. (2004). Evaluating the educational experiences of children with profound and multiple disabilities in inclusive and segregated classroom setting: An Australian perspective. *Research and Practice for Persons with Severe Disabilities, 29,* 183–193.

Forness, S.R., & Kavale, K.A. (1996). Treating social skills deficit in children with learning disabilities: A meta-analysis of the research. *Learning Disability Quarterly, 19*(1), 2–13.

Fowler, C., Konrad, M., Walkker, A.R., Test, D.W., & Wood, W.M. (2007). Self-determination interventions' effects on the academic performance of students with developmental disabilities. *Education and Training in Developmental Disabilities, 42,* 270–285.

Fox, S. (2011). *Americans living with disability and their technology profile. Pew Internet and American Life Project.* Retrieved May 6, 2011, from http://www.pewinternet. org/~/media//Files/Reports/2011/PIP_Disability.pdf

Fraker, T., & Rangarajan, A. (2009). The social security administration's youth transition demonstration projects. *Journal of Vocational Rehabilitation, 30,* 223–240.

Frank, A.R., & Sitlington, P.L. (2000). Young adults with mental disabilities—Does transition planning make a difference? *Education and Training in Mental Retardation and Developmental Disabilities, 35*(2), 119–134.

Frankel, B. (2009, May 4). *The DiversityInc top 10 companies for people with disabilities list.* Retrieved from http://diversityinc.com/the-diversityinc-top-50-companies-for-diversity/diversityinc-top-50-lists-2001-2010/

Fremstad, S. (2009). Half in ten: Why taking disability into account is essential in reducing income poverty and expanding economic inclusion. *CEPR Reports and Issue Briefs,* no. 30, Washington, DC.

French, N.K. (2001). Supervising paraprofessionals: A survey of teacher practices. *Journal of Special Education, 35*(1), 41.

Friend, M., & Cook, L. (2003). *Interactions: Collaboration skills for school professionals* (4th Ed.). Boston: Allyn and Bacon.

Fuchs, L.S., Fuchs, D., & Kazdan, S. (1999). Effects of peer-assisted learning strategies on high school students with serious reading problems. *Remedial and Special Education, 20*(5), 309–318.

Fuller, W.E., & Wehman, P. (2003). College entrance exams for students with disabilities: Accommodations and testing guidelines. *Journal of Vocational Rehabilitation, 18*(3), 191–197.

Gable, R. (1999). Functional assessment in school settings. *Behavior Disorders, 24*(3), 246–248.

Gable, R.A., Tonelson, S.W., & Walker-Bolton, I. (2010, August 23). A survey of classroom skills of special education teachers, general education teachers, and state directors of special education for students with emotional disabilities in Virginia (pp. 11–19). In I. Walker-Bolton, R.A. Gable, S.W. Tonelson, P. Woolard, & M.K. Gable (Eds.), *Summit on better serving students with emotional disabilities sponsored by the Virginia Department of Education, Charlottesville, VA*. Richmond, VA: Virginia Department of Education.

Gamoran, A., Porter, A.C., Smithson, J., & White, P.A. (1997). Upgrading high school mathematics instruction: Improving learning opportunities for low achieving, low income youth. *Educational Evaluation and Policy Analysis, 19*, 325–338.

Garcia, S.B., & Dominguez, L. (1997). Cultural contexts that influence learning and academic performance. *Child and Adolescent Psychiatric Clinics of North America, 6*, 621–655.

Garcia, S.B., Perez, A.M., & Ortiz, A.A. (2000). Interpreting Mexican-American mothers' beliefs about language disabilities from a sociocultural perspective. *Remedial & Special Education, 21*, 90–120.

Garcia-Villamisar, D., Ross, D., and Wehman, P. (2000). Clinical differential analysis of persons with autism: A follow up study. *Journal of Vocational Rehabilitation, 14*, p.183-185.

Garcia-Villamisar, D., Wehman, P., & Navarro, M.D. (2002). Changes in the quality of autistic people's life that work in supported and sheltered employment. A 5-year follow-up study. *Journal of Vocational Rehabilitation, 17*, 309–312.

Gay, G. (2000). *Culturally responsive teaching*. New York: Teachers College Press.

Geenen, S., Powers, L., & Lopez-Vasquez, A. (2001). Multicultural aspects of parent involvement in transition planning. *Exceptional Children, 67*, 265–282.

Geenen, S., Powers, L., Lopez-Vasquez, A., & Bersani, H. (2003). Understanding and promoting the transition of minority adolescents. *Career Development for Exceptional Individuals, 26*, 27–46.

Geenen, S.J., & Powers, L.E. (2006). Transition planning for foster youth. *The Journal for Vocational Special Needs Education, 28*(2), 4–15.

Geenen, S.J., Powers, L.E., & Hogansen, J.M. (2007). Youth with disabilities in foster care: Developing self-determination within a context of struggle and disempowerment. *Exceptionality, 15*, 17–30.

Gentry, T. (2008). PDAs as cognitive aids for people with multiple sclerosis. *American Journal of Occupational Therapy, 62*, 18–27.

Gentry, T. (2009). Smart homes for people with neurological disability: State of the art. *Neurorehabilitation, 25*, 209–217.

Gentry, T., Wallace, J., Kvarfordt, C., & Bodisch-Lynch, K. (2010). Personal digital assistants as cognitive aids for high school students with autism: Results of a community-based trial. *Journal of Vocational Rehabilitation, 32*, 101–107.

Gentry, T., Wallace, J., Kvarfordt, C., & Lynch, K.B. (2008). Personal digital assistants as cognitive aids for individuals with severe traumatic brain injury: A community-based trial. *Brain Injury, 22*, 19–24.

George, N.L., George, M.P., Gersten, R., & Grosenick, J.K. (1995). To leave or to stay? An exploratory study of teachers of students with emotional and behavioral disorders. *Remedial and Special Education, 16*, 227–236.

Gerber, P.J., & Price, L. (2003). Persons with learning disabilities in the workplace: What we know so far in the Americans with Disabilities Act era. *Learning Disabilities Research and Practice, 18*(2), 132–136.

Getzel, E.E. (2005). Preparing for college. In E.E. Getzel & P. Wehman (Eds.), *Going to college: Expanding opportunities for people with disabilities*. Baltimore: Paul H. Brookes Publishing Co.

Getzel, E.E. (2008). Addressing the persistence and retention of students with disabilities in higher education: Incorporating key strategies and supports on campus. *Exceptionality, 16*(4), 207–219.

Getzel, E., & Briel, L. (2008a). Experiences of college students with disabilities and the importance of a business mentoring program [Abstract], 157–166. Richmond, VA: Virginia Commonwealth University, Rehabilitation and Training Center.

Getzel, E.E., & Briel, L.W. (June, 2008b). Experiences of college students with disabilities and the importance of a business mentoring program. In P. Wehman, J. Kregel, & V. Brooke (Eds.), *Promoting an employer driven approach to employment of people with disabilities* (pp. 157–167). Richmond, VA: Virginia Commonwealth University, Rehabilitation, Research & Training Center on Workplace Supports and Job Retention.

Getzel, E.E., Briel, L.W., & Kregel, J. (2000). Comprehensive career planning: The VCU career connections program. *Journal of Work, 14*, 41–49.

Getzel, E.E., Deschamps, A., & Thoma, C.A. (2010). Transition individualized education planning and summary of performance. In C.A. Thoma & P. Wehman (Eds.), *Getting the most out of IEPs: An educator's guide to the student-directed approach*. Baltimore: Paul H. Brookes Publishing Co.

Getzel, E.E., & Finn, D.E. (2005). Training university faculty and staff. In E.E. Getzel & P. Wehman (Eds.), *Going to college: Expanding opportunities for people with disabilities*. (pp. 199–216). Baltimore: Paul H. Brookes Publishing Co.

Getzel, E.E., McManus, S., & Briel, L.W. (2004). *An effective model for college students with learning disabilities and attention deficit hyperactivity disorders*. Retrieved January 20, 2004, from http://www.ncset.org/publications/research-topractice/NCSETResearchBrief_3.1.pdf

Getzel, E.E., & Thoma, C.A. (2006). Voice of experience: What college students with learning disabilities and attention deficit/hyperactivity disorders tell us are important self-determination skills for success. *Learning Disabilities, 14*(1), 33–39.

Getzel, E.E., & Thoma, C.A. (2008). Experiences of college students with disabilities and the importance of self-determination in higher education settings. *Career Development for Exceptional Individuals, 31*(2), 77–84.

Getzel, E., & Wehman, P. (Eds.) (2005). *Going to college: Expanding opportunities for people with disabilities*. Baltimore: Paul H. Brookes Publishing Co.

Ghere, G., & York-Barr, J. (2007). Paraprofessional turnover and retention in inclusive programs: Hidden costs and promising practices. *Remedial & Special Education, 28*(1), 21–32.

Giangreco, M.F., Cloninger, C.J., & Iverson, V.S. (1998). *Choosing outcomes for accommodations for children: A guide to educational planning for students with disabilities*. Baltimore: Paul H. Brookes Publishing Co.

Giangreco, M.F., Edelman, S.W., & Broer, S.M. (2001). Respect, appreciation, and acknowledgment of paraprofessionals who support students with disabilities. *Exceptional Children, 67*(4), 485–498.

Gil-Kashiwabara, E., Hogansen, J.M., Geenen, S., Powers, K., & Powers, L.E. (2007). Improving transition outcomes for marginalized youth. *Career Development for Exceptional Individuals, 30*, 80–91.

Glang, A., Todis. B., Thomas, C.W., Hood, D., Bedell, G., & Cockrell, J. (2008) Return to school following childhood TBI: Who gets services? *NeuroRehabilitation, 23*(6):477–486.

Golann, J.W., & Hughes, K.L. (2008, August). *Insight: Dual enrollment policies and practices: Earning college credit in California high schools*. San Francisco: The James Irvine Foundation.

Gold, M. (1972a). Factors affecting production by the mentally retarded: Base rates. *Mental Retardation, 11*, 9–11.

Gold, M. (1972b). Stimulus factors in skill training of the retarded on a complex assembly task: Acquisition, transfer and retention. *American Journal on Mental Deficiency, 76*, 517–526.

Gold, M. (1978). *Try another way: Training manual*. Austin, TX: Marc Gold & Associates.

Gonzalez, R., Rosenthal, D.A., & Kim, J.H. (2011). Predicting vocational rehabilitation outcomes of young adults with specific learning disabilities: Transitioning from school to work. *Journal of Vocational Rehabilitation, 34*, 163–172.

Goodman, J.K., Hazelkorn, M., Bucholz, J.L., Duffy, M.L., & Kitta, Y. (2011). Inclusion and graduation rates: What are the outcome? *Journal of Disability Policy Studies, 21*(4), 241–252.

Gordon, R., Kane, T.J., Staiger, D.O. (2006). *Identifying effective teachers using performance on the job*. Madison, WI: The Hamilton Project, The Brookings Institution, University of Wisconsin.

Gore, J. (2011). Do sheltered workshops teach the disabled skills for the workplace or exploit them for cheap labor? . . . Bare minimum. *Orlando Weekly*, June 10, 2011.

Graham, S., & Harris, K.R. (1989). Improving learning disabled students' skills at composing essays: Self-instructional strategy training. *Exceptional Children, 56*, 231–214.

Greeff, A.P., & van der Walt, K.J. (2010). Resilience in families with an autistic child. *Education and Training in Autism and Developmental Disabilities, 45*(3), 347–355.

Green, J.H., & Brooke, V. (2001) Recruiting and retaining the best from America's largest untapped talent pool. *Journal of Vocational Rehabilitation, 16*, 83–88.

Green, P.E. (2003). The undocumented: Educating the children of migrant workers in America. *Bilingual Research Journal, 27*(1), 51–71.

Green, T., McIntosh, A., Cook-Morales, V.J., & Robinson-Zañartu, C. (2005). From old schools to tomorrow's schools: Psychoeducational assessment of African American students. *Remedial and Special Education, 26*, 82–92.

Greene, G. (2011). *Transition planning for culturally and linguistically diverse youth*. Baltimore: Paul H. Brookes Publishing Co.

Greenwood, C.R., Delquadri, C.J., & Hall, R.V. (1989). Longitudinal effects of class-wide peer tutoring. *Journal of Educational Psychology, 81*, 371–383.

Gregg, N., & Scott, S.S. (2000). Definition and documentation: Theory, measurement, and the courts. *Journal of Learning Disabilities, 33*(1), 5–13.

Gresham, F.M., & Elliott, S.N. (2008). *Social skills improvement system*. Minneapolis, MN: Pearson Assessments.

Gresham, F.M., Lane, K.L., MacMillian, D.L., & Bocian, K.M. (1999). Social and academic profiles of externalizing and internalizing groups: Risk factors for emotional and behavioral disorders. *Behavioral Disorders, 24*(3), 231–245.

Griffin, C., & Hammis, D. (2003). *Making self employment work for people with disabilities*. Baltimore: Paul H. Brookes Publishing Co.

Griffin, C., Hammis, D., & Geary, T. (2007). *The job developers handbook: Practical tactics for customized employment*. Baltimore: Paul H. Brookes Publishing Co.

Griffin, C., Hammis, D., Geary, T., & Sullivan, M. (2008). Customized employment: Where we are; where we are headed. *Journal of Vocational Rehabilitation, 28*(3), 135–139.

Griffin, C., & Targett, P. (2006). Job carving and customized employment. In P. Wehman (Ed.), *Life beyond the classroom* (4th ed., pp. 289–308). Baltimore: Paul H. Brookes Publishing Co.

Griffin, M. (2011). Promoting IEP participation: Effects of interventions, considerations for CLD students. *Career Development of Exceptional Individuals, 34*(3), 153–164.

Griffin, M.M., McMillan, E.D., & Hodapp, R.M. (2010). Family perspectives on postsecondary education for students with intellectual disabilities. *Education and Training in Autism and Developmental Disabilities, 45,* 339–346.

Grigal, M., & Hart, D. (2010a). Postsecondary education; The next frontier for individuals with intellectual disabilities. In M. Grigal & D. Hart (Eds.), *Think college: Postsecondary education options for students with intellectual disabilities* (pp. 1–28). Baltimore: Paul H. Brookes Publishing Co.

Grigal, M., & Hart, D. (2010b). *Think college!: Postsecondary education options for students with intellectual disabilities.* Baltimore: Paul H. Brookes Publishing Co.

Grigal, M., & Hart, D. (2010c). What the future holds. In M. Grigal & D. Hart (Eds.), *Think college: Postsecondary education options for students with intellectual disabilities.* (pp. 291–312). Baltimore: Paul H. Brookes Publishing Co.

Grigal, M., & Hart, D. (2010d). *What's the point? A reflection about the purpose and outcomes of college for students with intellectual disabilities.* Think College Insight Brief, Issue No. 2. Boston: Institute for Community Inclusion, University of Massachusetts Boston.

Grigal, M., Hart, D., & Migliore, A. (2011). Comparing the transition planning, postsecondary education, and employment outcomes of students with intellectual and other disabilities. *Career Development for Exceptional Individuals, 34,* 4–17.

Grigal, M., & Neubert, D.A. (2004). Parents' in-school values and post-school expectations for transition-aged youth with disabilities. *Career Development for Exceptional Individuals, 27,* 65–85.

Griller-Clark, H., & Unruh, D. (2010). Transition practices for adjudicated youth with EBD and related disabilities. *Journal of Behavioral Disorders, 36,* 43–51.

Grossman, H.J. (Ed.). (1973). *A manual on terminology and classification in mental retardation* (rev. ed.). Washington, DC: American Association on Mental Deficiency.

Grossman, H.J. (Ed.). (1983). *Classification in mental retardation* (rev. ed.). Washington, DC: American Association on Mental Deficiency.

Gudykunst, W.B. (2003). *Cross-cultural and intercultural communication.* Thousand Oaks, CA: Sage.

Guerrini, R. (2006). Epilepsy in children. *Lancet, 367,* 499–524.

Gumpel, T.P. (2008). Behavioral disorders in the school: Participant roles and subtypes in three types of school violence. *Journal of Emotional and Behavioral Disorders, 16,* 145–162.

Gumpel, T.P., & Meadan, H. (2010). Children's perception of school based violence. *The British Journal of Educational Psychology, 70*(3), 391–404.

Gumpel, T.P., & Sutherland, K.S. (2010). The relation between emotional and behavior disorders and school based violence. *Aggression and Violent Behavior, 15*(5), 349–356.

Gumpel, T.P., Tappe, P., & Araki, C. (2000). Comparison of social problem-solving abilities among adults with and without developmental disabilities. *Education and Training in Mental Retardation and Developmental Disabilities, 35,* 259–268.

Gutierrez, K.D., & Rogoff, B. (2003). Cultural ways of learning: Individual traits or repertoires of practice. *Educational Researcher, 32*(5), 19–25.

Guy, B.A., Sitlington, P.L., Larsen, M.D., & Frank, A.R. (2009). What are high schools offering as preparation for employment? *Career Development for Exceptional Individuals, 32,* 30–41.

Hadley, W.M. (2006). L.D. students access to higher education: Self-advocacy and support. *Journal of Developmental Education, 30*(2), 10–16.

Hadre, P.L., & Reeve, J. (2003). A motivational model of rural students' intentions to persist in, versus drop out of, high school, *Journal of Educational Psychology, 95,* 347–356.

Hagner, D., & Cooney, B.F. (2005). "I do that for everybody": Supervising employees with autism. *Focus on Autism and Other Developmental Disabilities, 20,* 91–97.

Hall, A.C., Butterworth, J., Winsor, J., Gilmore, D., & Metzel, D. (2007). Pushing the employment agenda: Case study research of high performing states in integrated employment. *Intellectual and Developmental Disabilities, 45,* 182–198.

Hall, A.C., Freeze, S., Butterworth, J., & Hoff, D. (2011). Employment funding for intellectual/developmental disability systems. *Journal of Vocational Rehabilitation, 34,* 1–15.

Halle, J.W., & Dymond, S.K. (2009). Inclusive education: A necessary prerequisite to accessing the general curriculum. *Research and Practice for Persons with Severe Disabilities, 33*(4), 196–198.

Halmoy, A., Bentfasmer, O., Gillberg, C., & Haavik, J. (2009). Occupational outcome in adult ADHD: Impact of symptom profile, comorbid psychiatric treatment: A cross sectional study of 414 clini-cally diagnosed adult ADHD patients. *Journal of Attention Disorders.* 13. doi: 10.1177/1087054708329777, 175-187.

Halpern, A.S. (1985). Transition: A look at the foundations. *Exceptional Children, 51,* 479–486.

Halpern, A.S., Herr, C.M., Wolf, N.K., Doren, B., Johnson, M.D., & Lawson, J.D. (1997). *Next S.T.E.P.: Student transition and educational planning.* Austin, TX: PRO-ED.

Halpern, A., Yovanoff, P., Doren, B., & Benz, M. (1995). Predicting participation in postsecondary education for school leavers with disabilities. *Exceptional Children, 62,* 151–164.

Hamill, L.B. (2002). Teaching students with moderate to severe disabilities: An applied approach for inclusive environments. Upper Saddle River, NJ: Merrill Prentice Hall.

Hammill, D.D., & Bartell, N.R. (2004). *Teaching children with learning and behavior problems*. Boston: Allyn & Bacon.

Hammond, D.L., Whatley, A.D., Ayres, K.M., & Gast, D.L. (2010). Effectiveness of video modeling to teach iPod use to students with moderate intellectual disabilities. *Education and Training in Autism and Developmental Disabilities, 45*, 525–538.

Hanushek, E. (1997). Assessing the effects of school resources on student performance: An update. *Educational Evaluation and Policy Analysis, 19*(2), 141–164.

Hanushek, E.A., & Raymond, M.E. (2002). The confusing world of educational accountability. *National Tax Journal, 54*(2), 365–384.

Haring, T.G., & Breen, C.G. (1992). A peer-mediated social network intervention to enhance the social integration of persons with moderate and severe disabilities. *Journal of Applied Behavior Analysis, 25*, 319–333.

Harper, G.F., & Maheady, L. (2007). Peer-mediated teaching and students with learning disabilities. *Intervention in School and Clinic, 43*, 101–107. doi: 10.1177/10534512070430020101

Harpin, V.A. (2005). The effect of ADHD on the life of an individual, their family, and community from preschool to adult life. *Archives of Disability in Childhood*, (Suppl I), i2–i7.

Harris, D. (2009). Would accountability based on teacher value-added be smart policy? Evidence on statistical properties and comparisons with policy alternatives. *Education Finance and Policy, 4*(4), 319–350.

Harry, B., Kalyanpur, M., & Day, M. (1999). *Building cultural reciprocity with families*. Baltimore: Paul H. Brookes Publishing Co.

Harry, B., & Klingner, J.K. (2006). *Why are so many minority students in special education?* New York: Teachers College Press.

Hart, D., Grigal, M., Sax, C., Martinez, D., & Will, M. (2006). Postsecondary education options for students with intellectual disabilities. *Research to Practice, 45*, 1–4. Retrieved January 10, 2008, from Institute for Community Inclusion Web site: http://www.communityinclusion.org/article.php?article_id=178&staff_id=19

Hart, D., Grigal, M., & Weir, C. (2010). Expanding the paradigm: Postsecondary education options for individuals with autism spectrum disorder and intellectual disabilities. *Focus on Autism and Other Developmental Disabilities, 25*, 134–150.

Hartmann, K.D., Post, K., & Gardner, C. (2010). Technology intervention, using what is there. *OT Practice, 15*, CE-1–8.

Hartnett, H.P., Stuart, H., Thurman, H., Loy, B., & Batiste, L.C. (2011). Employers' perceptions of the benefits of workplace accommodations: Reasons to hire, retain and promote people with disabilities. *Journal of Vocational Rehabilitation, 34*, 17–23.

Hartwig, R., & Sitlington, P. (2008). Employer perspectives on high school diploma options for adolescents with disabilities. *Journal of Disability Policy Study, 19*(1), 5–14.

Harvey, M.W., Yssel, N., Bauserman, A.D., & Merbler, J.B. (2010). Preservice teacher preparation for inclusion: An exploration of higher education teacher-training institutions. *Remedial & Special Education, 31*, 24–33.

Hasnain, R., Sotnik, P., & Ghiloni, C. (2003). Person-centered planning: A gateway to improving vocational rehabilitation services for culturally diverse individuals with disabilities. *Journal of Rehabilitation, 69*(3), 10–17.

Hawbecker, B. (2007). Student-led IEP meetings: Planning and implementation strategies. *Teaching Exceptional Children Plus, 3*(5), 1–19.

Hawker, D.S.J., & Boulton, M.J. (2000). Twenty years' research on peer victimization and psychological maladjustment: A meta-analytic review of cross-sectional studies. *Journal of Child Psychology, 41*(4), 441–455.

Hawkins, G. (2004). *How to find work that works for people with Asperger syndrome: The ultimate guide for getting people with Asperger syndrome into the workplace (and keeping them there)*. London: Jessica Kingsley Publishing.

Heal, L.W., & Rusch, R.R. (1995). Predicting employment for students who leave special education high school programs. *Exceptional Children, 61*, 472–487.

Heath Resource Center. (2010). *Financial aid information 2009-2010 edition*. Washington, DC: George Washington University, Heath Resource Center. Retrieved on June 6, 2011, from http://www.heath.gwu.edu/assets/30/heath_2009_2010_financial_aid_information.pdf

Heber, R. (1959). *A manual on terminology and classification in mental retardation: A monograph. Supplement to the American Journal on Mental Deficiency, 64*(Monograph Suppl.).

Heber, R. (1961). *A manual on terminology and classification on mental retardation* (rev. ed.). Washington, DC: American Association on Mental Deficiency.

Heckman, E.F., Brown, S.E., & Roberts, K.D. (2007). *Mentoring Partnership Project: Exploring mentoring practices for students with disabilities in postsecondary education*. Washington, DC: The George Washington University Heath Resource Center.

Heller, K.W., & Avant, M.J.T. (2011). Health care procedure considerations and individualized health care plans. *Physical Disabilities: Education and Related Services, 30*(1).

Hemmeter, J., Jauff, J., & Wittenburg, D. (2009). Changing circumstances: Experiences of child SSI recipients before and after their age 18 redetermination for adult benefits. *Journal of Vocational Rehabilitation, 30*, 201–221.

Hemmeter, M.L., Fox, L., Jack, S., Broyles, L., & Doubet, S. (2007). A program wide model of positive behavior support in early childhood settings. *Journal of Early Intervention, 29*, 337–355.

Hennessey, M.L., Richard R., Cook, B., Unger, D., & Rumrill, P. (2006). Employment and career development concerns of postsecondary students with disabilities: Service and policy implications. *Journal of Postsecondary Education, 19*(1), 39–55.

Hensel, E., Kroese, B.S., & Rose, J. (2007). Psychological factors associated with obtaining employment. *Journal of Applied Research in Intellectual Disabilities, 20,* 175–181.

Hernandez, B., Keys, C., & Balcazar, F. (2000). Employer attitudes towards disability and their ADA employment rights: A literature review. *Journal of Vocational Rehabilitation, 16,* 83–88.

Heron, T.E., Villareal, D.M., Yao, M., Christianson, R.J., & Heron, K.M. (2006). Peer tutoring systems: Applications in classroom and specialized environments. *Reading and Writing Quarterly, 22,* 27–45.

Heron, T.E., Welsch, R., & Goddard, Y.L. (2003). Applications of tutoring systems in specialized subject areas: An analysis of skills, methodologies, and results. *Remedial and Special Education, 24*(5), 288–300.

Hetherington, S.A., Durant-Jones, L., Johnson, K., Nolan, K., Smith, E., Taylor-Brown, S., et al. (2010). The lived experiences of adolescents with disabilities and their parents in transition planning. *Focus on Autism and Other Developmental Disabilities, 25*(3), 163–172.

Heward, W.L. (2003). Ten faulty notions about teaching and learning that hinder the effectiveness of special education. *The Journal of Special Education, 36*(4), 186–205.

Hieneman, M., Childs, K., & Sergay, J. (2006). *Parenting with positive behavior support: A practical guide to resolving your child's difficult behavior.* Baltimore: Paul H. Brookes Publishing Co.

Hillier, A., Campbell, H., Mastriani, K., Izzo, M.V., Kool-Tucker, A.K., Cherry, L., et al. (2007). Two-year evaluation of a vocational support program for adults on the autism spectrum. *Career Development for Exceptional Individuals, 30*(1), 35–47.

Hinshaw, S.P. (1992). Externalizing behavior problems and academic underachievement in childhood and adolescence: Causal relationships and underlying mechanisms. *Psychological Bulletin, 111*(1), 127–155.

Hitchings, W.E., Retish, P., & Horvath, M. (2005). Academic preparation of adolescents with disabilities for postsecondary education. *Career Development for Exceptional Individuals, 28*(1), 26–35.

Hocutt, A.M., McKinney, J.D., & Montague, M. (2002). The impact of managed care of efforts to prevent development of serious emotional disturbance in young children. *Journal of Disability Policy Studies, 13*(1), 51–60.

Hodges, E.V., Boivin, M., Vitaro, F., & Bukowski, W.M. (1999). The power of friendship: protecting against the escalating cycle of peer victimization. *Developmental Psychology, 35*(1), 94–101.

Hoffman, A., & Field, S. (1995). Self-determination through effective curriculum development. *Intervention in School and Clinic, 30,* 134–141.

Hogansen, J.M., Powers, K., Geenan, S., Gil-Kashiwabara, E., & Powers, L. (2008). Transition goals and experiences of females with disabilities: Perspectives of youth, parents, and professionals. *Exceptional Children, 74*(2), 215–234.

Holbrook, M.D. (August, 2007). *Standards-based individualized education program examples.* Alexandria, VA: National Association of State Directors of Special Education, Project Forum. Available from http://www.nasdse.org/Portals/0/Standards-BasedIEPExamples.pdf

Holburn, S. (2002). The value of measuring person-centered planning. In J. O'Brien & C.L. O'Brien (Eds.), *Implementing person-centered planning: Voices of experience* (pp.79–98). Toronto: Inclusion Press.

Holburn, S., Jacobson, J., Schwartz, A., Flory, M., & Vietze, P. (2004). The Willowbrook futures project: A longitudinal analysis of person-centered planning. *American Journal on Mental Retardation, 109,* 63–76.

Holburn, S., & Vietze, P. (2002). *Person-centered planning: Research, practice, and future directions.* Baltimore: Paul H. Brookes Publishing Co.

Holt, J., Chambless, C., & Hammond, M. (2006). Employment personal assistance services (EPAS). *Journal of Vocational Rehabilitation, 24,* 165–175.

Hood, L.K., & Rubin, M.B. (2004). *Priorities for allocating corporate resources to improve education.* Champaign, IL: Office of Community College Research and Leadership. University of Illinois at Urbana-Champaign.

Hoover, J., & Stenhjem, P. (2003). Bullying and teasing of youth with disabilities: Creating positive school environments for effective inclusion. *National Center on Secondary Education and Transition, 2*(3). Available at: http://ncset.org/publications/default.asp

Horn, C. (2010). Response cards: An effective intervention for students with disabilities. *Education and Training in Autism and Developmental Disabilities, 45*(1), 116–123.

Horner, R.H., Dunlap, G., Koegel, R.L., Carr, E.G., Sailor, W., Anderson, J., et al. (1990). Toward a technology of "nonaversive" behavioral support. *Journal of the Association for Persons with Severe Handicaps, 15,* 125–132.

Howlin, P., Goode, S., Hutton, J., & Rutter, M. (2004). Adult outcome for children with autism. *Journal of Child Psychology and Psychiatry, 45,* 212–229.

Hughes, C. (2009). Postsecondary outcomes in the 21st century—A change is gonna come? *Research and Practice for Persons with Severe Disabilities, 33*(3), 100–102.

Hughes, C., & Avoke, S.K. (2010).The elephant in the room: Poverty, disability and employment. *Research and Practice for People with Severe Disabilities. 35*(1–2), 2–14.

Hughes, C., & Carter, E.W. (2012). *The new transition handbook: Strategies secondary high school teachers use that work.* Baltimore: Paul H. Brookes Publishing Co.

Hughes, C., & Carter, E.W. (2002). Informal assessment procedures. In C. Sax & C. Thoma (Eds.), *Transition assessment: Wise practices for quality lives* (pp. 51–69). Baltimore: Paul H. Brookes Publishing Co.

Hughes, C., & Carter, E.W. (2008). *Peer buddy programs for successful secondary school inclusion.* Baltimore: Paul H. Brookes Publishing Co.

Hughes, C., Copeland, S.R., Agran, M., Wehmeyer, M.L., Rodi, M.S., & Presley, J.A. (2002). Using self-monitoring to improve performance in general education high school classes. *Education and Training in Mental Retardation and Developmental Disabilities, 37,* 262–271.

Hughes, C., Copeland, S.R., Guth, C., Rung, L.L., Hwang, B., Kleeb, G., et al. (2001). General education students' perspectives on their involvement in a high school peer buddy program. *Education and Training in Mental Retardation and Developmental Disabilities, 36,* 343–356.

Hughes, C., Fowler, S.E., Copeland, S.R., Agran, M., Wehmeyer, M.L., & Church-Pupke, P.P. (2004). Supporting high school students to engage in recreational activities with peers. *Behavior Modification, 28,* 3–27. doi: 10.1177/0145445503259215

Hughes, T., & Fredrick, L. (2006). Teaching vocabulary with students with learning disabilities using classwide peer tutoring and constant time delay. *Journal of Behavioral Education, 15*(1), 1–23.

Hughes, C., Golas, M., Cosgriff, J., Brigham, N., Edwards, C., & Cashen, K. (2011). Effects of a social skills intervention among high school students with intellectual disabilities and autism and their general education peers. *Research and Practice for Persons with Severe Disabilities, 36,* 46–61.

Hughes, C., Lorden, S.W., Scott, S.V., Hwang, B., Derer, K.R., Rodi, M.S., et al. (1998). Identification and validation of critical conversational social skills. *Journal of Applied Behavior Analysis, 31,* 431–446.

Hughes, C., Rodi, M.S., Lorden, S.W., Pitkin, S.E., Derer, K.R., Hwang, B., et al. (1999). Social interactions of high school students with mental retardation and their general education peers. *American Journal on Mental Retardation, 104,* 533–544.

Hughes, C., Rung, L.L., Wehmeyer, M.L., Agran, M., Copeland, S.R., & Hwang, B. (2000). Self-prompted communication book use to increase social interaction among high school students. *Journal of the Association for Persons with Severe Handicaps, 25,* 153–166.

Idol, L. (2006). Toward inclusion of special education students in general education: A program evaluation of eight schools. *Remedial and Special Education, 27*(2), 77–94.

Improving America's Schools Act of 1994, Pub. L. No. 103-382. Retrieved from http://www2.ed.gov/legislation/ESEA/toc.html

Individual with Disabilities Education Act of 1990, Pub. L. No. 101-476, 20 U.S.C. §§ 1400 *et seq.*

Individuals with Disabilities Education Act Amendments 1997. Retrieved January 4, 2004 from http://www.ed.gov/offices/OSERS/Policy/IDEA/the_law.html

Individuals with Disabilities Education Improvement Act of 2004, Pub. L. No. 108-446, 20 U.S.C. §§ 1400 *et seq.*

Inge, K., & Moon, S. (2006). Vocational preparation and transition. In M. Snell & F. Brown (Eds.), *Instruction of students with severe disabilities* (6th ed., pp. 569–609). Upper Saddle River, NJ: Merrill.

Inge, K., & Moon, S. (2011). *Preparing students with low incidence disabilities to work in the community.* In J. Kauffman & D. Hallahan (Eds.), *Handbook of special education* (5th ed., pp. 611–623). New York & London: Routledge International.

Inge, K.J., & Shepherd, J. (1995). Assistive technology applications and strategies for school system personnel. In K.F. Flippo, K.J. Inge, & J.M. Barcus (Eds.), *Assistive technology: A resource for school, work, and community* (pp. 133–166). Baltimore: Paul H. Brookes Publishing Co.

Inge, K.J., Wehman, P., Revell, G., Erickson, D., Butterworth, J., & Gilmore, D. (2009). Survey results from a national survey of community rehabilitation providers holding special wage certificates. *Journal of Vocational Rehabilitation, 30*(2), 67–85.

The Institute of Education Sciences. (2008). *Reducing behavior problems in the elementary classroom.* Washington, DC: author.

Interstate New Teacher Assessment and Support Consortium. (2001, May). *Model standards for licensing general and special education teachers of students with disabilities: A resource for state dialogue.* Washington, DC: Council of Chief State School Officers. Retrieved November 18, 2004, from http://www.ccsso.org/intasc.html

Iovannone, R., Dunlap, G., Huber, H., & Kincaid, D. (2003). Effective educational practices for students with autism spectrum disorders. *Focus on Autism and Other Developmental Disabilities, 8*(3), 150–165.

Ispen, C., Arnold, N., & Colling, K. (2005). Self-employment for people with disabilities: enhancing services through interagency linkages. *Journal of Disability Policy Studies, 15*(4), 231–239.

Izzo, M.V., McArrell, B., Yurick, A., & Murray, A. (2010). *EnvisionIT.* Columbus: Ohio State University Nisonger Center.

Jackson, L.B., Ryndak, D.L., & Wehmeyer, M.L. (2009). The dynamic relationship between context, curriculum, and student learning: A case for inclusive education as a research-based practice. *Research and Practice for Persons with Severe Disabilities, 33*(4), 175–195.

Jahoda, A., Kemp, J., Riddel, S., Banks, P. (2007). Feelings about work: A review of the socio-emotional impact of supported employment on people with intellectual disabilities. *Journal of Applied Research in Intellectual Disabilities, 21*(1), 1–18.

Jamentz, K. (2003). *The instructional demands of standards reform*. Washington, DC: American Federation of Teachers.

Janiga, S.J., & Costenbader, V. (2002). The transition from high school to postsecondary education for students with learning disabilities: A survey of college service coordinators. *Journal of Learning Disabilities, 35*(5), 462–468.

Janney, R., & Snell, M.E. (2006). *Social relationships and peer support* (2nd ed.). Baltimore: Paul H. Brookes Publishing Co.

Jitendra, A.K., & Gajria, M. (2011). Reading comprehension instruction for students with learning disabilities. *Focus on Exceptional Children, 43*(8), 1–16.

Johnson, C.E., & Viramontez Anguiano, R.P. (2004). Latino parents in the rural southeast: A study of family and school partnerships. *Journal of Family and Consumer Sciences, 96*(4), 29–33.

Johnson, D.R., Stodden, R.A., Emanuel, E.J., Luecking, R., & Mack, M. (2002). Current challenges facing secondary education and transition services: What research tells us. *Exceptional Children, 68*, 519–531.

Johnson, D.R., & Thurlow, M.L. (2003). *A national study on graduation requirements and diploma options for youth with disabilities* (Technical Report No. 36). Minneapolis: University of Minnesota: National Center on Educational Outcomes. Retrieved from http://education.umn.edu/NCEO/OnlinePubs/Technical36.htm

Johnson, D.R., Thurlow, M., Cosio, A., & Bremer, C.D. (2005, February). *Diploma options for students with disabilities*. (NCSET Information Brief Vol. 4 No. 1). Minneapolis: University of Minnesota.

Johnson, D.R., Thurlow, M.L., & Stout, K.E. (2007). *Revisiting graduation requirements and diploma options for youth with disabilities: A national study*. (Tech. Rep. No. 49). Minneapolis: University of Minnesota, National Center on Educational Outcomes. Retrieved April 2011, from http://www.cehd.umn.edu/NCEO/Online pubs/Tech49/default.html

Jokinen, N.S., & Brown, R.I. (2005). Family quality of life from the perspective of older parents. *Journal of Intellectual Disability, 49*(10), 789–793.

Joyce, B., & Weil, M. (1980). *Models of teaching* (2nd ed.). Upper Saddle River, NJ: Prentice Hall.

Joyce N.C. (2011a). Muscular dystrophy: Becker. In M.R. Nelson (Ed.), *Pediatrics* (1st ed., pp. 137–138). New York: Demos Medical Publishing.

Joyce N.C. (2011b). Muscular dystrophy: Limb-girdle. In M.R. Nelson (Ed.), *Pediatrics* (1st ed., pp. 149–150). New York: Demos Medical Publishing.

Kalyanpur, M., & Kirmani, M.H. (2005). Diversity and technology: Classroom implications of the digital divide. *Journal of Special Education Technology, 20*(4), 9–18.

Kamens, M. (2007). Learning about co-teaching: A collaborative student teaching experience for preservice teachers. *Teacher Education and Special Education, 30*, 155–166.

Karan, O.C., DonAroma, P., Bruder, M.B., & Roberts, L. (2010). Transitional assessment model for students with severe and/or multiple disabilities: Competency-based community assessment. *Intellectual and Developmental Disabilities, 48*(5), 387–392.

Karger, J., & Pullin, D. (2002). *Exit documents and students with disabilities: Legal issues* (Issue Brief 2). College Park, MD: University of Maryland, Educational Policy Research Reform Institute, Institute for the Study of Exceptional Children and Youth.

Karp, M.M., & Hughes, K.L. (2008). Study: Dual enrollment can benefit a broad range of students. *Techniques: Connecting Education and Careers, 83*(7), 14–17.

Karpur, A., Clark, H.B., Caproni, P., & Sterner, H. (2005). Transition to adult roles for students with emotional/behavioral disturbances: A follow-up study of student exiters from steps-to-success. *Career Development for Exceptional Individuals, 28*(1), 36–46.

Karvonen, M., Test, D., Wood, W.M., Browder, D., & Algozzine, B. (2004). Putting self-determination into practice. *Exceptional Children, 71*, 23–41.

Katsiyannis, A., & Yell, M.L. (2004). Critical issues and trends in the education of students with emotional or behavioral disorders. *Behavioral Disorders, 29*(3), 209–210.

Katsiyannis, A., Zhang, D., Ryan, J.B., & Jones, J. (2007). High-stakes testing and students with disabilities: Challenges and promises. *Journal of Disability Policy Studies, 18*, 160–167.

Katsiyannis, A., Zhang, D., Woodruff, N., & Dixon, A. (2005). Transition supports to students with mental retardation: An examination of data from the National Longitudinal Transition Study 2. *Education and Training in Developmental Disabilities, 40*(2), 109–116.

Kauffman, J.M. (2005a). *Characteristics of children's behavior disorders* (8th ed.). Columbus, OH: C.E. Merrill Publishing Co.

Kauffman, J.M. (2005b). *Characteristics of emotional and behavioral disorders of children and youth*. Upper Saddle River, NJ: Merrill/Prentice Hall.

Kauffman, J.M., & Hallahan, D.P. (Eds.). (2011). *Handbook of special education*. New York: Routledge Taylor and Friends Group.

Kauffman, J.M., & Hung, L.Y. (2009). Special education for intellectual disability: Current trends and perspectives. *Current Opinion in Psychiatry, 22*, 452–456.

Kauffman, J.M., & Landrum, T.J. (2009). *Characteristics of emotional and behavioral disorders of children and youth* (9th ed.). Upper Saddle River, NJ: Pearson.

Kauffman, J.M., Mock, D.R., Tankersley, M., & Landrum, T.J. (2008). Effective service delivery models. In R.J. Morris & N. Mather (Eds.), *Evidence-based interventions for students with learning and behavioral challenges* (pp. 359–378). Mahwah, NJ: Erlbaum.

Kauffman, J.M., Nelson, C.M., Simpson, R.L., & Mock, D.R. (2011). Contemporary issues. In J.M. Kauffman & D.P. Hallahan (Eds.), *Handbook of special education* (pp. 15–26). New York: Routledge Taylor and Friends Group.

Kaukiainen, A., Salmivalli, C., Lagerspetz, K., Tamminen, M., Vauras, M., Mäki, H., et al. (2002). Learning difficulties, social intelligence, and self-concept: connections to bully-victim problems. *Scandinavian Journal of Psychology, 43*(3), 269–278.

Kavale, K.A. (1990). Effectiveness of differential programming in serving handicapped students. In M. Wang, M. Reynolds, & H. Walberg (Eds.), *Special education: Research and practice* (pp. 33–35). New York: Pergamon Press.

Kavale, K.A., Mathur, S.R., Forness, S.R., Rutherford, R.B., Jr., & Quinn, M.M. (1997). Effectiveness of social skills training for students with behavior disorders: A meta-analysis. In T.E. Scruggs & M.A. Mastropieri (Eds.), *Advances in learning and behavioral disabilities* (Vol. 11; pp. 1–26). Greenwich, CN: JAI

Kavale, K.A., Spaulding, L.S., & Beam, A.P. (2009). A time to define: Making the specific learning disabilities definition prescribe specific learning disability. *Learning Disability Quarterly, 32,* 39–48.

Kaye, H.S. (2000). Disability and the digital divide. *Disability Statistics Abstract.* San Francisco: Disability Statistics Center, University of California, San Francisco; and Washington, DC: U.S. Department of Education, National Institute on Disability and Rehabilitation Research.

Kaye, H.S. (2003). *Improved employment opportunities for people with disabilities.* Washington, DC: National Institute on Disability and Rehabilitation Research.

Kaye, H.S., Jans, L.H., & Jones, E.C. (2011). Why don't employers hire and retain workers with disabilities? *Journal of Occupational Rehabilitation,* online March 13, 2011, Springer.

Keefe, E.B., Moore, V., & Duff, F. (2004). The four "knows" of collaborative teaching. *Teaching Exceptional Children, 36*(5), 36–41.

Kef, S., & Dekovic, M. (2004). The role of parental and peer support in adolescents well-being: a comparison of adolescents with and without a visual impairment. *Journal of Adolescence, 27,* 453–466. doi:10.1016/j.adolescence.2003.12.005

Kellems, R.O., & Morningstar, M.E. (2010). Tips for transition. *Teaching Exceptional Children, 43*(2), 66–68.

Keller, C.L., Bucholz, J., & Brady, M.P. (2007). Yes, I can! *Teaching Exceptional Children, 39*(3), 18–23.

Kennedy, C.H. (2004). Social relationships. In C.H. Kennedy & E. Horn (Eds.), *Inclusion of students with severe disabilities* (pp. 100–123). Boston: Allyn & Bacon.

Kennedy, C.H., & Fisher, D. (2001). *Inclusive middle schools.* Baltimore: Paul H. Brookes Publishing Co.

Kern, L., & Clemens, N.H. (2007). Antecedent strategies to promote appropriate classroom behavior. *Psychology in the Schools, 44*(1), 65–75.

Kerr, M.M., & Nelson, C.M. (2010). *Strategies for addressing behavior problems in the classroom.* (6th ed.). Upper Saddle River, NJ: Pearson.

Kessler Foundation/National Organization of Disability. (2010). *Survey of employment of Americans with disabilities.* Retrieved May 6, 2011, from http://www.2010DisabilitySurveys.org/octsurvey/pdfs/surveyresults.pdf

Khemka, I. (2000). Increasing independent decision-making skills of women with mental retardation in simulated interpersonal situations of abuse. *American Journal on Mental Retardation, 105,* 387–401.

Kiernan, W., Mank, D., & Wehman, P. (June 8, 2011). Presentation at the American Association of Intellectual and Developmental Disabilities, Minneapolis, MN.

Kiernan, W.E., Hoff, D., Freeze, S., & Mank, D.M. (2011). Perspectives: Employment First: A beginning not an end. *Intellectual and Developmental Disabilities, 49*(4), 300–304.

Kilbane, J., & Sanderson, H. (2004). "What" and "how": Understanding professional involvement in person centered planning styles and approaches. *Learning Disability Practice, 7*(4), 16–20.

Killion, W.K. (2003). *Functional independence skills handbook: Assessment and curriculum for individuals with developmental disabilities.* Austin, TX: PRO-ED.

Kim, K.H., & Turnbull, A. (2004). Transition to adulthood for students with severe intellectual disabilities: Shifting toward person-family interdependent planning. *Research and Practice for Persons with Severe Disabilities, 29*(1), 53–57.

Kim, R., & Dymond, S. (2010). Special education teachers' perceptions of benefits, barriers, and components of community-based vocational instruction. *Intellectual and Developmental Disabilities, 48,* 313–329. doi: 10.1352/1934-9556-48.5.313

Kim-Rupnow, W.S., & Burgstahler, S. (2004). Perceptions of students with disabilities regarding the value of technology-based support activities on postsecondary education and employment. *Journal of Special Education Technology, 19*(2), 43–56.

Kincaid, D., Chapman, C., Shannon, P., Schall, C., & Harrower, J.K. (2002). Families and the Tri-State Consortium on positive behavior support. In J.M. Lucyshyn, G. Dunlap, & R.W. Albin (Eds.), *Families & positive behavior support:*

Addressing problem behavior in family contexts. Baltimore: Paul H. Brookes Publishing Co.

King, G., Lawm, M., King, S., Rosenbaum, P., Kertoy, M.K., & Young, N.L. (2003). A conceptual model of the factors affecting the recreation and leisure participation of children with disabilities. *Physical & Occupational Therapy in Pediatrics, 23*(1), 63–90. doi:10.1080/J006v23n01_05

King-Sears, M.E. (2001). Three steps for gaining access to the general education curriculum for learners with disabilities. *Intervention in School and Clinic, 37*(2), 67–76.

Kinnett, D.G. (2011). Guillain-Barre syndrome. In M.R. Nelson (Ed.), *Pediatrics* (1st ed., pp. 105–106). New York: Demos Medical Publishing.

Klassen, R.M. (2006). Using predictions to learn about the self-efficacy of early adolescents with and without learning disabilities. *Contemporary Educational Psychology, 32,* 173–187.

Kline, F.M., & Silver, L.B. (2004). *The educator's guide to mental health issues in the classroom.* Baltimore: Paul H. Brookes Publishing Co.

Kober, N., Zabala, D., Chudowsky, N., Chudowsky, V., Gayler, K., & McMurrer, J. (2006). *State high school exit exams: A challenging year.* Retrieved from http://www.centerforcsri.org/research/improvement.cgi?st=s&sr=SR005389

Kochhar-Bryant, C., Bassett, D.S., & Webb, K.W. (2009). *Transition to postsecondary education.* Thousand Oaks, CA: Corwin Press.

Kochhar-Bryant, C.A., & Bassett, D.S. (2002). Challenge and promise in aligning transition and standards-based education. In C.A. Kochhar-Bryant & D.S. Bassett (Eds.), *Aligning transition and standards-based education: Issues and strategies* (pp. 1–23). Arlington, VA: Council for Exceptional Children.

Kochhar-Bryant, C.A., & Greene, G.A. (2009). *Pathways for successful transition for youth with disabilities: A developmental process.* Columbus, OH: Allyn & Bacon/Merrill.

Kochhar, C.A., West, L.L., & Taymans, J.M. (2000). *Successful inclusion: Practical strategies for a shared responsibility.* Columbus, OH: Merrill.

Koedel, C., & Betts, J. (2009). Value added to what? How a ceiling in the testing instrument influences value-added estimation. *Education Finance and Policy, 5,* 54–81.

Kohler, P.D. (1993). Best practices in transition: Substantiated or implied? *Career Development for Exceptional Individuals, 16,* 107–121.

Kohler, P.D., & Field, S. (2003). Transition-focused education: Foundation for the future. *The Journal of Special Education, 37,* 174–183. doi: 10.1177/00224669030370030701

Konrad, M., Fowler, C.H., Walker, A.R., Test, D.W., & Wood, W.M. (2007). Effects of self-determination interventions on the academic skills of students with learning disabilities. *Learning Disabilities Quarterly, 30*(2), 89–113.

Konrad, M., & Test, D. (2004). Teaching middle school students to use IEP template. *Career Development for Exceptional Individuals Spring,* 27(1),101–124.

Kotlikoff, L., & Burns, S. (2005). *The coming generational storm: What you need to know about America's economic future.* Cambridge, MA: MIT.

Krach, L.E., Gormley, M.E., & Ward, M. (2010). Traumatic brain injury. In M.A. Alexander, D. Matthews (Eds.), *Pediatric rehabilitation: Principles and practice* (4th ed., pp. 231–260). New York: Demos Medical Publishing.

Kraemer, B.R., McIntyre, L.L., & Blacher, J. (2003). Quality of life for young adults with mental retardation during transition. *Mental Retardation, 41,* 250–262.

Kregel, J. (2012). Work incentives planning and assistance program: Current program results document the program's ability to improve employment outcomes, reduce dependence of benefits, and generate cost savings for SSA. *Journal of Vocational Rehabilitation, 36*(1).

Kregel J., Dean D., & Wehman P. (Eds.). (2002). *Achievements and challenges in employment services for people with disabilities: The longitudinal impact of workplace supports.* Richmond, VA: Virginia Commonwealth University.

Kregel, J., & O'Mara, S. (2011) Work incentives counseling as a workplace support. *Journal of Vocational Rehabilitation, 35*(2), 73–83.

Kreider, H., Caspe, M., Kennedy, S., & Weiss, H. (2007). *Family involvement in middle and high school students' education. Involvement makes a difference: Evidence that family involvement promotes school success for every child of every age.* Cambridge, MA: Harvard Family Research Project, Harvard University.

Krentz, J., Thurlow, M.L., Shyyan, V., & Scott, D. (2005). *Alternative routes to the standard diploma (Synthesis Report 54).* Retrieved from http://education.umn.edu/NCEO/OnlinePubs/Synthesis54.html

Krupa, T. (2004). Employment, recovery, and schizophrenia: Integrating health and disorder work. *Psychiatric Rehabilitation Journal, 28*(1), 8–15.

Kulak, W., Okurowska-Zawada, B., Sienkiewicz, D., Paszko-Patej, G., & Krajewska-Kulak, E. (2010). Risk factors for cerebral palsy in term birth infants. *Advances in Medical Sciences, 55*(2), 216–221.

Kurtz, A., Elliott, S.N., Wehby, J.H., & Smithson, J.L. (2010). Alignment of the intended, planned, and enacted curriculum in general and special education and its relations to student achievement. *Journal of Special Education, 44,* 131–145.

Kurtz, J. (2011). Tools for computer access. *AOTA Technology Special Interest Section Quarterly, 21,* 1–3.

Lachapelle, Y., Wehmeyer, M., Haelewyck, M-C., Courbois, Y., Keith, K., Schalock, R., et al. (2005). The relationship between quality of life and self-determination: an international study. *Journal of Intellectual Disability Research, 49*(10), 740–744.

Laluvein, J. (2010). School inclusion and the "community of practice." *International Journal of Inclusive Education, 14*(1), 35–48.

Lamar-Dukes, P. (2009). Reaching the hard to reach: A review of an initiative aimed at increasing participation and supports for people of color with disabilities and their families in disability organizations. *Research and Practice for Persons with Severe Disabilities, 34,* 76–80.

Landmark, L., Zhang, D., & Montoya, L. (2007). Culturally diverse parents' experiences in their children's transition: Knowledge and involvement. *Career Development for Exceptional Individuals, 30,* 68–79.

Landmark, L.J., Ju, S., & Zhang, D. (2010). Substantiated best practices in transition: Fifteen plus years later. *Career Development for Exceptional Individuals, 33*(3), 165–176.

Landrum, T.J., Tankersley, M., & Kauffman, J.M. (2003). What is special about special education or students with emotional or behavioral disorders? *Journal of Special Education, 37,* 148–156.

Lane, K. (2004). Academic instruction and tutoring interventions for students with emotional and behavioral disorders. In R. Rutherford, M. Quinn, & S. Mathur (Eds.), *Handbook of research in emotional and behavioral disorders* (pp. 462–486). New York: Guilford.

Lane, K.L., & Carter, E.W. (2006). Supporting transition-age youth with and at risk for emotional and behavioral disorders at the secondary level: A need for further inquiry. *Journal of Emotional and Behavioral Disorders, 14*(2), 66–70.

Lane, K.L., Carter, E.W., Pierson, M.R., & Glaeser, B.C. (2006). Academic, social, and behavioral characteristics of high school students with emotional disturbances or learning disabilities. *Journal of Emotional and Behavioral Disorders, 14*(2), 108–117.

Lane, K.L., Pierson, M.R., & Givner, C.C. (2004). Secondary teachers' views on social competence: Skills essential for success. *The Journal of Special Education, 38,* 174–186. doi: 10.1177/00224669040380030401

Lane, K.L., Wehby, J.H., & Cooley, C. (2006). Teacher expectations of students' classroom behavior across the grade span: Which social skills are necessary for success? *Exceptional Children, 72,* 153–167.

Lane, K.L., Wehby, J.H., Little, M.A., & Cooley, C. (2005a). Academic, social, and behavioral profiles of students with emotional and behavioral disorders educated in self-contained classrooms and self-contained schools: Part I. Are they more alike then different? *Behavioral Disorders, 30*(4), 349–361.

Lane, K.L., Wehby, J.H., Little, M.A., & Cooley, C. (2005b). Students educated in self-contained classrooms and self-contained schools: Part II. How do they progress over time? *Behavioral Disorders, 30*(4), 363–374.

Latham, G.P., & Locke, E.A. (1991). Self-regulation through goal setting. *Organizational Behavior and Human Decision Processes, 50*(2), 212–247.

Lattimore, L.P., Parsons, M.B., & Reid, D.H. (2003). Assessing preferred work among adults with autism beginning supported jobs: Identification of constant and alternating task preferences. *Behavioral Interventions, 18,* 161–177.

Lauer, A., Longenecker-Rust, R., Smith, R.O. (2006). *ATOMS Project technical report—Factors in assistive technology abandonment: Replacing "abandonment" with "discontinuance."* Madison, WI: University of Wisconsin-Madison. Retrieved September 22, 2011, from http://www.r2d2.uwm.edu/atoms/archive/technicalreports/tr-discontinuance.html

Lawer, L., Brusilovskiy, E., Salzer, M.S., & Mandell, D.S. (2009). Use of vocational rehabilitative services among adults with autism. *Journal of Autism and Developmental Disorders, 39,* 487–494.

Lawrence-Brown, D. (2004). Differentiated instruction: Inclusive strategies for standards-based learning that benefit the whole class. *American Secondary Education, 32,* 34–62.

Lazarus, S.S., Thurlow, M.L., Christensen, L.L., & Cormier, D. (2007). *States' alternate assessments based on modified achievement standards (AA-MAS) in 2007* (Synthesis Report 67). Minneapolis: University of Minnesota, National Center on Educational Outcomes.

Lazarus, S.S., Thurlow, M.L., Lail, K.E., Eisenbraun, K.D., & Kato, K. (2006). *2005 state policies on assessment participation and accommodations for students with disabilities* (Synthesis Report 64). Minneapolis: University of Minnesota, National Center on Educational Outcomes.

Learning Disabilities Association of America. (2010). *The Learning Disabilities Association of America's white paper on evaluation, identification, and eligibility criteria for students with specific learning disabilities.* Pittsburgh, PA: Author. Retrieved from http://www.ldaamerica.org/pdf/LDA%20White%20Paper%20on%20IDEA%20Evaluation%20Criteria%20for%20SLD.pdf

Leblanc, M., Ricciardi, J.N., & Luiselli, J.K. (2005). Improving discrete trial instruction by paraprofessional staff through an abbreviated performance feedback intervention. *Education & Treatment of Children, 28*(1), 76.

Leconte, P. (May 9, 2011). *Assessment for transition planning.* Presented at the Consolidated High School District 230 Transition Enhancement Project Training Workshop, Tinley Park, IL.

Lee, E., & Lee, S. (2009). Effects of instructional rubrics on class engagement behaviors and the achievement of lesson objectives by students with mild mental retardation and their typical peers. *Education and Training in Developmental Disabilities, 44,* 396–408.

Lee, S., Daniels, M., Puig, A., Newgent, R., & Nam, S. (2008). A data-based model to predict postsecondary attainment of low-socioeconomic-status students. *Professional School Counseling, 11*(5), 306–316.

Lee, S., & Will, M. (2010). The role of legislation, advocacy, and systems change in promoting postsecondary opportunities for students with intellectual disabilities. In M. Grigal & D. Hart (Eds.), *Think college!: Postsecondary education options for students with intellectual disabilities* (pp. 29–48). Baltimore: Paul H. Brookes Publishing Co.

Lee, S.H., Palmer, S.B., & Wehmeyer, M.L. (2009). Goal setting and self-monitoring for students with disabilities: Practical tips and ideas for teachers. *Intervention in School and Clinic, 44,* 139–145.

Lee, S.H., Wehmeyer, M.L., Soukup, J.H., & Palmer, S.B. (2010). Impact of curriculum modifications on access to the general education curriculum for students with disabilities. *Exceptional Children, 76*(2), 213–233.

Lee, V.E., & Ready, D.D. (2009). U.S. high school curriculum: Three phases of contemporary research and reform. *The Future of Children, 19*(1), 135–156.

Lee, Y., Wehmeyer, M., Palmer, S., Williams-Diehm, K., Davies, D., & Stock, S. (2011). The effect of student-directed transition planning using a computer-based reading support program on the self-determination of students with disabilities. *Journal of Special Education, 45,* 104–117.

Lehr, C., & Thurlow, M. (2003). *Putting it all together: Including students with disabilities in assessment and accountability systems* (Policy Directions 16). Minneapolis: University of Minnesota, National Center on Educational Outcomes.

Leone, P.E., Mayer, M.J., Malmgren, K., & Meisel, S.M. (2000). School violence and disruption; Rhetoric, reality, and reasonable balance. *Focus on Exceptional Children, 33*(1), 1–20.

Lerner, B. (1991). Good news about American education. *Commentary, 91*(3), 19–25.

Lerner, J. (2003). *Learning disabilities: Theories, diagnosis, and teaching practices.* Boston: Houghton Mifflin Company.

Lerner, J., & Johns, B. (2009). *Learning disabilities and related mild disabilities: Characteristics, teaching strategies, and new directions* (11th ed.). Boston: Houghton Mifflin Harcourt Publishing Company.

Levine, P., & Edgar, E. (1994). Respondent agreement in follow-up studies of graduates of special and regular education programs. *Exceptional Children, 60,* 334–343.

Levinson, J.C., & Perry, D.E. (2009). *Guerrilla marketing for job hunters 2.0: 1001 unconventional tips, tricks and tactics to land your dream job.* Hoboken, NJ: John Wiley and Sons Inc.

Levy, S., & Vaughn, S. (2002). An observational study of teacher's reading instruction for students with emotional or behavioral disorders. *Behavioral Disorders, 27,* 215–235.

Lian, M.-G.J., & Fontanez-Phelan, S.M. (2001). Perceptions of Latino parents regarding cultural and linguistic issues and advocacy for children with disabilities. *Journal of the Association for Persons with Severe Handicaps 26,* 189–194.

Lieberman, L.M. (1985). Special education and regular education: A merger made in heaven? *Exceptional Children, 51*(6), 513–516.

Lindsay, G., Dockrell, J.E., & Strand, S. (2007). Longitudinal patterns of behavior problems in children with specific speech and language difficulties: Child and contextual factors. *British Journal of Educational Psychology, 77,* 811–828.

Lindstrom, L.E., Benz, M.R., & Johnson, M.D. (1996). Developing job clubs for students in transition. *Teaching Exceptional Children, 29*(2), 18–21.

Lindstrom, L., Doren, B., Metheny, J., Johnson, P., & Zane, C. (2007). Transition to employment: Role of the family in career development. *Exceptional Children, 73,* 348–366.

Lindstrom, L., Doren, B., & Miesch, J. (2011). Waging a living: Career development long-term employment outcomes for young adults with disabilities. *Exceptional Children, 77*(4) 423–434.

Lindstrom, L.E., Flannery, B.K., Benz, M.R., Olszewski, B., & Slovic, R. (2009). Building employment partnerships between vocational rehabilitation and community colleges. *Rehabilitation Counseling Bulletin, 52,* 189–201.

Linn, R.L. (2001). *The design and evaluation of educational assessment and accountability systems.* Los Angeles: National Center for Research on Evaluation, Standards, and Student Testing (CRESST).

LoPresti, E., Mihailidis, A., & Kirsch, N. (2004). Assistive technology for cognitive rehabilitation: State of the art. *Neuropsychological Rehabilitation, 14,* 5–39.

Longwill, A., & Kleinert, H. (1998). The unexpected benefits of high school peer tutoring. *Teaching Exceptional Children, 30*(4), 60–65.

Lopez, J.K. (2007). *The DREAM act.* Retrieved from http://www.unc.edu/world/2007_Latin_Amer/Materials/The%20DREAM%20Act.pdf

Loprest, P., & Maag, E. (2001). *Barriers and supports for work among adults with disabilities: Results from the NHIS-D.* Washington, DC: The Urban Institute.

Lubbers, J.H., Repetto, J.B., & McGorray, S.P. (2008). Perceptions of transition barriers, practices and solutions in Florida. *Remedial and Special Education, 29*(5), 280–292.

Luckasson, R., Borthwick-Duffy, S., Buntinx, W.H.E., Coulter, D.L., Craig, E.M., Reeve, A., et al. (2002). *Mental retardation: Definition, classification, and systems of supports* (10th ed.). Washington, DC: American Association on Mental Retardation.

Luckasson, R., Coulter, D.L., Polloway, E.A., Reese, S., Schalock, R.L., Snell, M.E., et al. (1992). *Mental retardation: Definition, classification, and systems of supports* (9th ed.). Washington, DC: American Association on Mental Retardation.

Luckasson, R., & Reeve, A. (2001). Naming, defining, and classifying in mental retardation. *Mental Retardation, 39,* 47–52.

Luecking, R. (2008). Emerging employer views of people with disabilities and the future of job development. *Journal of Vocational Rehabilitation, 29,* 3–13.

Luecking, R. & Fabian, E.S. (2000). Paid internships and employment success for youth in transition. *Career Development for Exceptional Children, 23*(2), 205–221.

Luecking, R., Reihle, E., & Donovan, M. (2004). *Working relationships: creating career opportunities for job seekers with disabilities through employer partnerships.* Baltimore: Paul H. Brookes Publishing Co.

Luecking, R., & Tilson, G. (2009). Job development in a tough economy: Mission impossible?. *The Advance (APSE), 1*(2), 3–4.

Luecking, R. (2009a). *The way to work: How to facilitate work experiences for youth in transition.* Baltimore: Paul H. Brookes Publishing Co.

Luecking, R.G. (2009b). Work-based learning and work experiences as indispensable educational tools. In R.G. Luecking, *The way to work: How to facilitate work experiences for youth in transition* (pp. 9–25). Baltimore: Paul H. Brookes Publishing Co.

Luecking, R.G. (2011). Connecting employers with people who have intellectual disabilities. *Intellectual and Developmental Disabilities, 49*(4), 261–273.

Luecking, R.G., Fabian, E.S., & Tilson, G.P. (2004). *Working relationships: Creating career opportunities for job seekers with disabilities through employer partnerships.* Baltimore: Paul H. Brookes Publishing Co.

Luft, P., Brown, C., & Sutherin, L. (2007). Are you and your students bored with the benchmarks? Sinking under the standards? Then transform your teaching through transition! *Teaching Exceptional Children, 39*(6), 39–46.

Luke, S., & Schwartz, A. (2007). Assessment and accommodations. *Evidence for Education, 2*(1), 1–11.

Mack, J. (2010, September). Higher expectations for Class of 2011: Most rise to meet new standards, but Algebra II a concern, Michigan educators say. *Kalamazoo Gazette.* Retrieved from http://www.mlive.com/news/kalamazoo/index.ssf/2010/09/ higher_expectations_for_class.html

Madaus, J.W. (2003). What high school students with learning disabilities need to know about college foreign language requirements. *Teaching Exceptional Children, 36*(2), 62–66.

Madaus, J.W. (2005, January/February). Navigating the college transition maze: A guide for students with learning disabilities. *Teaching Exceptional Children, 36*(2), 32–37.

Madaus, J.W. (2008). Employment self-disclosure rates and rationales of university graduates with learning disabilities. *Journal of Learning Disabilities, 41*(4), 291–299.

Madaus, J.W., Banerjee, M., & Hamblet, E.C. (2010). Learning disability documentation decision making at the postsecondary level. *Career Development for Exceptional Individuals, 33,* 68–79.

Madaus, J.W., Gerber, P.J., & Price, L.A. (2008). Adults with learning disabilities in the workforce: Lessons for secondary transition programs. *Learning Disabilities Research and Practice, 23*(3), 148–153.

Majed, M., Nejat, F., Khashab, M.E., Tajik, P., Gharagozloo, M., Baghban, M., et al. (2009). Risk factors for latex sensitization in young children with myelomeningocele. Clinical article. *Journal of Neurosurgery Pediatrics, 4*(3), 285–288.

A manifesto on the employment of Minnesotans with disabilities in the integrated, competitive workforce: A consensus report, June 12, 2007, from the Minnesota Work First Summit. Retrieved from http://www.mnapse.org/Employment-First-Report.pdf, on July 12, 2011.

Mank, D. (2008). Alderbrook 2007. *Journal of Vocational Rehabilitation, 29*(2), 1–10.

Mann, W.C., & Lane, J.P. (1991). *Assistive technology for persons with disabilities. The role of occupational therapy.* Rockville, MD: American Occupational Therapy Association.

Mannix, D. (1995). *Life skills activities for secondary students with special needs.* San Francisco: Jossey-Bass.

Marshall, K., Brown, W.H., Conroy, M.A., & Knopf, H. (2011). Early intervention and prevention of disability. In J.M. Kauffman & D.P. Hallahan (Eds.). *Handbook of special education.* New York: Routledge.

Marshall, M., Bond, G.R., & Huxley, P. (Issue 2, 2009). *Vocational rehabilitation for people with severe mental illness (Review).* The Cochrane Collaboration. New York: Wiley.

Martin, J.E., & Marshall, L.H. (1995). Choice-Maker: A comprehensive self-determination transition program. *Intervention in School and Clinic, 30,* 147–156.

Martin, J.E., Marshall, L.H., & Sale, P. (2004). A 3-year study of middle, junior high, and high school IEP meetings. *Exceptional Children, 70,* 285–297.

Martin, J.E., Mithaug, D.E., Cox, P., Peterson, L.Y., Van Dycke, J.L., & Cash, M.E. (2003). Increasing self-determination: Teaching students to plan, work, evaluate, and adjust. *Exceptional Children, 69*(4), 431–447.

Martin, J.E., Van Dycke, J.L., Christensen, W.R., Greene, B.A., Gardner, J.E., & Lovett, D.L. (2006a). Increasing student participation in their transition IEP meetings: Establishing the self-directed IEP as evidenced-based practice. *Exceptional Children, 72,* 299–316.

Martin, J.E., Van Dycke, J.L., Greene, B.A., Gardner, J.E., Christensen, W.R., Woods, L.L., et al. (2006b). Direct observation of teacher-directed IEP meetings: Establishing the need for student IEP meeting instruction. *Exceptional Children, 72*(2), 187–200. Retrieved from http://ezproxy.lib.ucf.edu/login?URL=http://search.ebscohost.com/login.aspx?direct=true&db=aph&AN=19467719&site=ehost-live

Martin, J.E., Van Dycke, J.V., D'Ottavio, M., & Nickerson, K. (2007). The student directed summary of performance: Increasing student and family involvement in the transition planning process. *Career Development for Exceptional Individuals, 30,* 13–26.

Martorell, A., Gutierrez-Recacha, P., Perda, A., & Ayuso-Mateos, J.L. (2008). Identification of personal factors that determine work outcome for adults with intellectual disability. *Journal of Intellectual Disability Research, 52*(12), 1091–1101.

Maryland State Department of Education. (2010). *Maryland Race to the Top: Application draft.* Retrieved from http://www.maryland-publicschools.org/NR/exeres/D82C142D-779A-4059-9F25-4208E3161459,frameless.htm?Year=2010&Month=4%%3E

Mason, C., Field, S., & Sawilowsky, S. (2004). Implementation of self-determination activities and student participation in IEPs. *Exceptional Children, 70,* 441–451.

Mason, C., McGahee-Kovac, M., Johnson, L., & Stillerman, S. (2002). Implementing student-led IEPs: Student participation and student and teacher reactions. *Career Development for Exceptional Individuals, 25,* 171–192.

Mastropieri, M.A., & Scruggs, T.E. (2000). *The inclusive classroom: Strategies for effective instruction.* Upper Saddle River, NJ: Prentice-Hall.

Mastropieri, M.A., Scruggs, T.E., Cuenca-Sanchez, Y., Irby, N., Mills, S., Mason, L., et al. (2008). Persuading students with emotional disabilities to write: A design study. In M. Mastropieri & T.E. Scruggs (Eds.), *Literacy and learning: Advances in learning and behavior disabilities* (vol. 23, pp. 237–268). Binsley, UK: Emerald Publishing Group.

Mastropieri, M.A., Scruggs, T.E., Mills, S., Irby, N., Cuenca-Sanchez, Y., Allen-Bronaugh, D., et al., & Regan, K. (2009). Persuading students with emotional disabilities to write fluently. *Behavioral Disorders, 35,* 19–40.

Mastropieri, M.A., Scruggs, T., Mohler, L., Beranek, M., Spencer, V., Boon, R.T., et al. (2001). Can middle school students with serious reading difficulties help each other and learn anything? *Learning Disabilities Research and Practice, 16*(1), 18–27.

Mastropieri, M.A., Scruggs, T., Norland, J.J., Berkeley, S., McDuffie, K., Tornquist, E.H., et al. (2006). Differentiated curriculum enhancement in inclusive middle school science: Effects on classroom and high-stakes tests. *Journal of Special Education, 40,* 130–137.

Mastropieri, M.A., Scruggs, T.E., Spencer, V., & Fontana, J. (2003). Promoting success in high school world history: Peer tutoring versus guided notes. *Learning Disabilities Research and Practice, 18*(1), 52–65.

Mathur, S.R., Kavale, K.A., Quinn, M.M., Forness, S.R., & Rutherford, R.B. (1998). Social skills interventions with students with emotional and behavioral problems: a quantitative synthesis of single-subject research. *Behavioral Disorders, 23*(3), 193–201.

Matthews, D.J. (2011). Muscular dystrophy: Duchenne. In M.R. Nelson (Ed.), *Pediatrics* (1st ed., pp. 143–144). New York: Demos Medical Publishing.

Mazzotti, V.L., Rowe, D.A., Kelley, K.R., Test, D.W., Fowler, C.H., Kohler, P.D., et al. (2009). Linking transition assessment and postsecondary goals key elements in the secondary transition planning process. *Teaching Exceptional Children, 42*(2), 44–51.

Mazzotti, V.L., Wood, C.L., Test, D.W., & Fowler, C.H. (2010). Effects of computer assisted instruction on students' knowledge of the self determined learning model of instruction and disruptive behavior. *Journal of Special Education,* published online March 2010, pp. 1–11.

McDonall, M.C., & Cruden, A. (2009). Factors affecting the successful employment of youth with visual impairments and blindness. *Journal of Visual Impairment & Blindness, 103,* 329–341.

McDonnell, J., Wilcox, B., & Hardman, M.L. (1991). *Secondary programs for students with developmental disabilities.* Boston: Allyn & Bacon.

McDonnell, L.M., McLaughlin, M.J., & Morison, P. (Eds.). (1997). *Educating one and all: Students with disabilities and standards-based reform.* Washington, DC: National Academy Press.

McDougall, J., DeWit, D.J., King, G., Miller, L.T., & Killip, S. (2004). High school-aged youths' attitudes toward their peers with disabilities: The role of school and student interpersonal factors. *International Journal of Disability, Development and Education, 51,* 287–313. doi: 10.1080/1034912042000259242

McGahee, M., Mason, C., Wallace, T., & Jones, B. (2001). *Student-led IEPs: A guide for student involvement.* Alexandria, VA: Council for Exceptional Children.

McGahee-Kovac, M. (2002). *A student's guide to the IEP.* Washington, DC: The National Information Center for Children and Youth with Disabilities. Retrieved from http://www.nichcy.org/InformationResources/Documents/NICHCY%20PUBS/st1.pdf

McGuire, J.M. (2010). Considerations for the transition to college. In S.F. Shaw, J.W. Madaus, & L.L. Dukes (Eds.), *Preparing students with disabilities for college: A practical guide for transition* (pp. 7–35). Baltimore: Paul H. Brookes Publishing Co.

McIntosh, K., Filter, K.J., Bennett, J.L., Ryan, C., & Sugai, G. (2009). Principles of sustainable prevention: Designing scale up of schoolwide behavior support to promote durable systems. *Psychology in the Schools, 47*(1), 5–21. doi:10.1002pits.20448

McLaughlin, M.J. (2010). Evolving interpretations of educational equity and students with disabilities. *Exceptional Children, 76*(3), 265–278.

McLaughlin, M.J., Henderson, K., & Rhim, L.M. (1997). *Snapshots of reform: A report of reform in 5 local school districts.* Alexandria, VA: Center for Policy Research on the Impact of General and

Special Education Reform, National Association of State Boards of Education.

McLaughlin, M.J., Krezmien, M., & Zablocki, M. (2009). Special education in the new millennium: Achieving educational equity for students with learning and behavioral disabilities. *Advances in Learning and Behavioral Disabilities, 22,* 1–31.

McLaughlin, M.J., & Thurlow, J. (2003). Educational accountability and students with disabilities: Issues and challenges. *Journal of Educational Policy, 17*(4), 431–451.

McLoughlin, J.A., & Lewis, R.B. (2005). *Assessing students with special needs* (6th ed.). Upper Saddle River: NJ: Pearson Education, Inc.

McMahon, B.T. (2011, August 28). Hiring people with disabilities would help the economy [Letter to the editor]. *The Washington Post.* Retrieved September 7, 2011, from http://www.washingtonpost.com/opinions/hiring-the-handicapped-would-help-the-economy

McMahon, B.T., Edwards, R., Rumrill, P.D., & Hursh, N. (2005). An overview of the national EEOC ADA research project [guest editorial]. *Journal of Vocational Rehabilitation, 25*(1), 1–7.

McMahon, B., Wehman, P., Brooke, V., Habeck, R., Green, H., & Fraser, R. (2004). *Business, disability and employment: Corporate models of success: A collection of successful approaches reported from 20 employers.* Richmond: Virginia Commonwealth University, Rehabilitation Research & Training Center on Workplace Supports and Job Retention.

McMahon, B.T., West, S.L., Shaw, L.R., Waid-Ebbs, K., & Belongia, L. (2005). Workplace discrimination and traumatic brain injury: The national EEOC ADA research project. *Journal of Vocational Rehabilitation, 25*(1), 67–75.

McMahon M. (2011). Myelodysplasia/spina bifida. In M.R. Nelson (Ed.), *Pediatrics* (1st ed.. pp. 153–155). New York: Demos Medical Publishing.

McMahon, M., Pruitt, D., & Vargus-Adams, J. (2010). Cerebral palsy. In M.A. Alexander & D. Matthews (Eds.), *Pediatric rehabilitation: Principles and practice* (4th ed., pp. 165–198). New York: Demos Medical Publishing.

McManus, S., Smith, F., & Jones, S. (2010). Assistive technology. In C.A. Thoma & P. Wehman (Eds.), *Getting the most out of IEPs: An educator's guide to the student-directed approach* (pp. 139–156). Baltimore: Paul H. Brookes Publishing Co.

McMorris, F.A. (2000, March 10). Discrimination is hard to prove if a book treats everyone badly. *Wall Street Journal,* pp. B2, B4.

McNamara, J.K., Willoughby, T., & Chalmers, H. (2005). Psychosocial status of adolescents with learning disabilities with and without comorbid attention deficit hyperactivity disorder. *Learning Disabilities Research and Practice, 20*(4), 234–244.

McNamee, S., Walker, W., Cifu, D.X., & Wehman, P. (2009). Minimizing the effect of TBI-related physical sequelae on vocational return. *Journal of Rehabilitation Research and Development, 46,* 893–908.

McNaughton, D., Balandin, S., Kennedy, P., & Sandmel, T. (2010). Health transitions for youth with complex communication needs: The importance of health literacy and communication strategies. *Journal of Pediatric Rehabilitative Medicine: An Interdisciplinary Approach, 3,* 311–318.

McPherson, S. (2009). A dance with the butterflies: A metamorphosis of teaching and learning through technology. *Early Childhood Education Journal, 37*(3), 229–236. doi:10.1007/s10643-009-0338-8

Meadan, H., Stoner, J.B., & Angell, M.E. (2010). Review of literature related to the social, emotional, and behavioral adjustment of siblings of individuals with autism spectrum disorder. *Journal of Developmental and Physical Disabilities, 22,* 83–100.

Mechling, L.C. (2007). Assistive technology as a self-management tool for prompting students with intellectual disabilities to initiate and complete daily tasks: A literature review. *Education and Training in Developmental Disabilities, 42(3),* 252–269.

Mechling, L.C. (2011). Review of twenty-first century portable electronic devices for persons with moderate intellectual disabilities and autism spectrum disorders. *Education and Training in Autism and Developmental Disabilities, 46,* 479–498.

Mechling, L.C., Gast, D.L., & Seid, N.H. (2009). Using a personal digital assistant to increase independent task completion by students with autism spectrum disorder. *Journal on Autism and Developmental Disorders, 39,* 1420–1434.

Mechling, L.C., & O'Brien, E. (2010). Computer-based video instruction to teach students with intellectual disabilities to use public bus transportation. *Education and Training in Autism and Developmental Disabilities, 45,* 230–241.

Mechling, L.C., & Ortega-Hurndon, F. (2007). Computer-based video instruction to teach young adults with moderate intellectual disabilities to perform multiple step, job tasks in a generalized setting. *Education and Training in Developmental Disabilities, 42*(1), 24–37.

Mechling, L.C., & Seid, N.H. (2011). Use of a hand-held personal digital assistant (PDA) to self-promote pedestrian travel by young adults with moderate intellectual disabilities. *Education and Training in Autism and Developmental Disabilities, 46,* 220–237.

Mellard, D.F., Stern, A., & Woods, K. (2011). RTI school-based practices and evidence-based models. *Focus on Exceptional Children, 43*(6), 1–15.

Meyer, R.N. (2001). *Asperger syndrome employment workbook: An employment workbook for adults with Asperger syndrome.* London: Jessica Kingsley Publishing.

Michaels, C.A. (2007). Sustaining the dream: A response to excessive positivism in person-centered planning. *Research and Practice for Persons with Severe Disabilities, 32*(3), 177–180.

Michaels, C.A., & Barr, V.M. (2002). Best practices in career development programs for post secondary students with learning disabilities: A ten-year follow-up. *Career Planning and Adult Development, 18*(1), 61–79.

Michaels, C.A., Pollack Prezant, F., Morabito, S.M., & Jackson, K. (2002). Assistive and instructional technology for college students with disabilities: A national snapshot of postsecondary service providers. *Journal of Special Education Technology, 17*(1), 5–14.

Migliore, A., & Butterworth, J. (2008). Trends in outcomes of the vocational rehabilitation program for adults with developmental disabilities: 1995-2005. *Rehabilitation Counseling Bulletin, 52*, 35–44.

Migliore, A., Butterworth, J., & Hart, D. (2009). *Postsecondary education and employment outcomes for youth with intellectual disabilities. Fast facts series, No. 1.* Boston: Institute for Community Inclusion.

Migliore, A., Cohen-Hall, A., Butterworth, J., & Winsor, J. (2010). What do employment specialists really do? A study on job development practices. *Research and Practice for Persons with Severe Disabilities, 35*(1–2), 24–30.

Migliore, A., Grossi, T., Mank, D., & Rogan, P. (2008). Why do adults with intellectual disabilities work in sheltered workshops? *Journal of Vocational Rehabilitation, 26*, 5–19.

Migliore, A., Mank, D., Grossi, T., & Rogan, P. (2007). Integrated employment or sheltered workshops: Preferences of adults with intellectual disabilities, their families, and staff. *Journal of Vocational Rehabilitation, 26*(1), 5–19.

Miller, A.D., Barbetta, P.M., & Heron, T.E. (1994). Start tutoring: Designing, training, implementing, and adapting tutoring programs for school and home settings. In R. Gardner, III, D. Sainato, J.O. Cooper, T.E. Heron, W.L. Heward, J. Eshleman, et al. (Eds.), *Behavioral analysis in education: Focus on measurably superior instruction* (pp. 265–282). Monterey, CA: Brooks-Cole.

Miller, J., & Arango, J. (2011a). Racial ethnic minorities and post-injury employment: African Americans with TBI. Issue 6. *Points of Empowerment Fact Sheet.* Retrieved from http://www.vcu-projectempowerment.org

Miller, J., & Arango, J. (2011b). Racial ethnic minorities and post-injury employment: Hispanics with TBI. Issue 5. *Points of Empowerment Fact Sheet.* Retrieved from http://www.vcu-projectempowerment.org

Miller, L., O'Mara, S., & Getzel, E.E. (2009). Saving for postsecondary education: Strategies for individuals with disabilities. *Journal of Vocational Rehabilitation, 31*, 167–174.

Miller, L., O'Mara, S., & Kregel, J. (2012). Social security, work incentives and benefits planning: Navigating the future. In P. Wehman, & J. Kregel (Eds.), *Functional curriculum* (pp. 239–266). Austin, TX: PRO-ED.

Miller, M.J., Lane, K.L., & Wehby, J.H. (2005). Social skills instruction for students with high incidence disabilities: An effective, efficient approach for addressing acquisition deficits. *Preventing School Failure, 49*, 27–40.

Milner, H.R. (2003). A case study of an African American English teacher's cultural comprehensive knowledge and self-reflective planning. *Journal of Curriculum and Supervision, 18*, 175–196.

Minnesota APSE. (2007, June 12). The Minnesota Employment First Summit: A manifesto on the employment of Minnesotans with disabilities in the integrated, competitive workforce. Retrieved from http://www.mnapse.org/Employment-First-Report.pdf

Mithaug, D.E., Mithaug, D., Agran, M., Martin, J., & Wehmeyer, M.L. (Eds.). (2003). *Self-determined learning theory: Construction, verification, and evaluation.* Mahwah, NJ: Lawrence Erlbaum Associates.

Mithaug, D.E., Wehmeyer, M.L., Agran, M., Martin, J.E., & Palmer, S. (1998). The self-determined learning model of instruction: Engaging students to solve their learning problems. In M.L. Wehmeyer & D.J. Sands (Eds.), *Making it happen: Student involvement in education planning, decision making and instruction* (pp. 299–328). Baltimore: Paul H. Brookes Publishing Co.

Monson, M.P., & Monson, R.J. (1993). Who creates curriculum: New roles for teachers. *Educational Leadership, 51*, 19–21.

Montgomery, W. (2001). Creating culturally responsive, inclusive classrooms. *Teaching Exceptional Children, 33*(4), 4–9.

Moon, M.S., Luedtke, E.M. & Halloran-Tornquist, E. (2010). *Getting around town: Teaching community mobility skills to students with disabilities.* Reston, VA: Council for Exceptional Children.

Moon, M.S., Simonsen, M.L., & Neubert, D.A. (2011). Perceptions of supported employment providers: What students with developmental disabilities, families, and educators need to know for transition planning. *Education and Training in Autism and Developmental Disabilities, 46*(1) 94–105.

Mooney, P., Denny, R.K., & Gunter, P.L. (2004). The impact of NCLB and the reauthorization of IDEA on academic instruction of students with emotional or behavioral disorders. *Behavioral Disorders, 29*(3), 237–246.

Mooney, P., Ryan, J.B., Uhing, B.M., Reid, R., & Epstein, M.H. (2005). A review of self-management interventions targeting academic outcomes for students with emotional and behavioral disorders. *Journal of Behavioral Education, 14*, 203–221.

Morgan, R. (2003). Test-retest reliability and criterion validity of a motion video, CD-ROM program designed to allow youth with disabilities to select preferred jobs. *Career Development for Exceptional Individuals, 26*(1), 67–84.

Morgan, R. (2011). Job matching assessment: Inter-rater reliability of an instrument assessing employment characteristics of young adults with intellectual disabilities. *Journal of Vocational Rehabilitation, 34,* 25–33.

Morgan, R., & Alexander, M. (2005). The employer's perception: Employment of individuals with developmental disabilities. *Journal of Vocational Rehabilitation, 23,* 39–49.

Morgan, R., & Ellerd, D.A. (2005). Development and evaluation of a video CD-ROM program for individuals with developmental disabilities to determine job preferences. *Journal of Vocational Rehabilitation, 23*(1), 1–10.

Morgan, R.L., Gerity, B.P., & Ellerd, D.A. (2000). Using video and CD-ROM technology in a job preference inventory for youth with severe disabilities. *Journal of Special Education, 15(3),* 25–33.

Morgan, R., & Horrocks, E. (2011). Correspondence between video based preference assessment and subsequent community job performance. *Education and Training in Autism and Developmental Disabilities, 46*(1), 52–61.

Morningstar, M.E., Frey, B.B., Noonan, P.M., Ng, J., Clavenna-Deane, B., Graves, P., et al. (2010). A preliminary investigation of the relationship of transition preparation and self-determination for students with disabilities in postsecondary educational settings. *Career Development for Exceptional Individuals, 33*(2), 80–94.

Morningstar, M.E., & Liss, J.M. (2008). A preliminary investigation of how states are responding to the transition of assessment requirements under IDEIA 2004. *Career Development for Exceptional Individuals, 31,* 48–55.

Morozova O. (2011). Hereditary motor sensory neuropathy Charcot Marie Tooth disease. In M.R. Nelson (Ed.), *Pediatrics* (1st ed., pp.112–113). New York: Demos Medical Publishing.

Morris, K., & Reinson, C. (2010). A systematic review of the use of electronic memory aids by adults with brain injury. *AOTA Technology Special Interest Quarterly, 20,* 1–4.

Morrison, G.S. (1993). *Contemporary curriculum K-8.* Boston: Allyn & Bacon.

Mull, C.A., & Sitlington, P.L. (2003). The role of technology in the transition to postsecondary education of students with learning disabilities: A review of the literature. *Journal of Special Education, 37*(1), 26–32.

Müller, E., Schuler, A., Burton, B.A., & Yates, G.B. (2003). Meeting the vocational needs of individuals with Asperger syndrome and other autism spectrum disabilities. *Journal of Vocational Rehabilitation, 18,* 163–175.

Murawski, W.W., & Dieker, L.A. (2004). Tips and strategies for co-teaching at the secondary level. *Teaching Exceptional Children, 36*(5), 52–58.

Murnane, R.J., Willett, J.B., & Levy, F. (1995). The growing importance of cognitive skills in wage determination. *Review of Economics and Statistics, 78*(2), 251–266.

Muscular Dystrophy Association. (2008). *What is a neuromuscular disease? A teacher's guide to neuromuscular disease.* MDA Publications Department; p. 11.

Nagle, K.M. (2004). *Emerging state-level themes: Strengths and stressors in educational accountability reform* (Topical Review No. 4). University of Maryland: College Park Educational Policy Reform Research Institute. Available from http://www.eprri.org

National Alliance for Secondary Education and Transition. (2005). *National standards and quality indicators: Transition toolkit for systems improvement.* Minneapolis: University of Minnesota, National Center on Secondary Education and Transition.

National Association of Counselors and Employers. (2004, January 14). Employers identify the skills, qualities of the "ideal candidate" [Web press release]. Retrieved February 7, 2004, from http://www.via.tcu.edu/PDF/AppendixI/AppendixILink6.pdf

National Center for Education Statistics. (2001). *Digest of education statistics 2000.* Washington, DC: U.S. Department of Education.

National Center for Education Statistics. (2007). *Description and employment criteria of instructional paraprofessionals* (Issues Brief). Washington, DC: Author.

National Center for Education Statistics. (2009). *NAEP – 2009 Reading: Grade 4 National Results.* Retrieved from http://nationsreportcard.gov/reading_2009/nat_g4.asp?subtab_id=Tab_6&tab_id=tab1#tabsContainer

National Center for Education Statistics. (2010a). *The condition of education 2010 (NCES 2010-028).* Washington, DC: U.S. Department of Education. Retrieved from http://nces.ed.gov/fastfacts/display.asp?id=65

National Center for Education Statistics. (2010b). *Digest of Education Statistics: 2009.* Retrieved from http://nces.ed.gov/programs/digest/d08/tables/dt08_051.asp

National Commission on Excellence in Education. (1983). *A nation at risk.* Washington, DC: Author.

National Council of Teachers of Mathematics. (2000). *Principles and NCTM standards for school mathematics.* Reston, VA: Author.

National Council on Disability. (2009, March 31). *National disability policy: A progress report.* Retrieved from http://www.ncd.gov/progress_reports/Mar312009

National Council on Disability. (2010). The state of housing in America in the 21st century: A disability perspective. Available at: http://indfit.org/files/NCD_Housing_Report508.pdf

National Dissemination Center for Children with Disabilities. (n.d.). *Supports, modifications, and accommodations for students.* Retrieved from http://www.nichcy.org/EducateChildren/Supports/Pages/default.aspx

National Employer Leadership Council. (2001, March/April). Employer involvement in school-to-work is widespread and expanding. *Employer Focus, 2*(1), 3.

National Governors Association. (2005). *Graduation counts: A report of the National Governors Association Task Force on state high school graduation data: Redesigning the American high school.* Washington, DC: Author. Available from http://www.nga.org/Files/pdf/0507GRAD.PDF

National Institute of Mental Health. (2009). *Attention deficit hyperactivity disorder* (p. 2). Retrieved May 25, 2011, from http://www.pinetech.edu/assets/files/pdf/ADHD.pdf

National Longitudinal Transition Study-2. (2007). *Transition plan* [Data file]. Retrieved from http://www.nlts2.org/data_tables/chooseTopic.jsp

National Organization on Disability. (2004). *Survey of Americans with disabilities.* Washington, DC: Author. Retrieved from http://www.nod.org/research_publications/

The National Professional Development Center on Autism Spectrum Disorders. (n.d.). *Evidence-based practice briefs.* Retrieved on March 1, 2010, from http://autismpdc.fpg.unc.edu/content/briefs

National Secondary Transition Technical Assistance Center. (2007). *Indicator 13 training materials.* Charlotte, NC: Author.

National Spinal Cord Injury Statistical Center. (2011). *Spinal cord injury facts and figures at a glance.* Available at: https://www.nscisc.uab.edu/

Neal, D., & Johnson, W. (1996). The role of premarket factors in black-white wage difference. *Journal of Political Economy, 104*(5), 869–895.

Neece, C., Kraemer, B., & Blacher, J. (2009). Transition satisfaction and family well being among parents of young adults with severe intellectual disability. *Intellectual and Developmental Disabilities, 47,* 31–43.

Neel, R.S., & Billingsley, F.F. (1989). *Impact: A functional curriculum handbook.* Baltimore: Paul H. Brookes Publishing Co.

Neely-Barnes, S., Graff, C., Marcenko, M., & Weber, L. (2008). Family decision making: Benefits to persons with developmental disabilities and their family members. *Intellectual & Developmental Disabilities, 46,* 93–105.

Nelson, B. (2005). Creating positive outcomes for deafblind youth and young adults: A personal futures planning transition model. *Review: Rehabilitation Education for Blindness and Visual Impairment, 36*(4), 173–180.

Nelson, C.M., Jolivette, K., & Leone, P.E. (2010). Meeting the needs of at-risk and adjudicated youth with behavioral challenges: The promise of juvenile justice. *Behavior Disorders, 36*(1), 70–80.

Nelson, J.R., Benner, G.J., & Mooney, P. (2008). *Instructional practices for students with behavioral disorders: Strategies for reading, writing, and math.* New York: Gilford Press.

Nelson, J.R., Roberts, M., Mathurs, S., & Rutherford, R. (1999). Has public policy exceeded our knowledge base? A review of the functional behavioral assessment literature. *Behavior Disorders, 24*(2), 169–179.

Neubert, D., Moon, S., & Grigal, M. (2002). Postsecondary education and transition services for students ages 18–21 with significant disabilities. *Focus on Exceptional Children, 34*(8), 1–9.

Neubert, D.A., Moon, M., & Grigal, M. (2004). Activities of students with significant disabilities receiving services in postsecondary settings. *Education and Training in Developmental Disabilities, 39,* 16–25.

Newman, L., Wagner, M., Cameto, R., & Knokey, A.M. (2009). *The post-high school outcomes of youth with disabilities up to 4 years after high school. Report of findings from the national longitudinal transition study 2* (NCSER 2009-3017). Menlo Park, CA: SRI International. Retrieved March 30, 2010, from http://www.nlts2.org/reports/2009_04/index.html.

Newman, L., Wagner, M., Cameto, R., Knokey, A.M., & Shaver, D. (2010). *Comparisons across time of the outcomes of youth with disabilities up to 4 years after high school. A report of findings from the National Longitudinal Transition Study (NLTS) and the National Longitudinal Transition Study-2 (NLTS2)* (NCSER 2010-3008). Menlo Park, CA: SRI International.

Niemiec, B., Lavin, D., & Owens, L. (2009). Establishing a National Employment First agenda. *Journal of Vocational Rehabilitation, 31,* 139–144.

Nietupski, H., Hamre-Nietupski, S., Curtin, S., & Shrikanth, K. (1997). A review of curricular research in severe disabilities from 1976 to 1995 in six selected journals. *The Journal of Special Education, 31,* 59–60.

Nietupski, J., Hamre-Nietupski, S., Donder, D., Houselog, M., & Anderson, R. (1988). Proactive administration strategies for implementing community-based programs for students with moderate/severe handicaps. *Education and Training in Mental Retardation, 23*(2), 138–146.

No Child Left Behind Act of 2001, Pub. L. No. 107-110, 115 Stat. 1425, 20 U.S.C. §§6301 *et seq.*

Nolet, V., & McLaughlin, M.J. (2000). *Accessing the general curriculum: Including students with disabilities in standards-based reform.* Thousand Oaks, CA: Corwin Press, Inc.

Nolet, V., & McLaughlin, J.J. (2005). *Accession the general curriculum: Including students with disabilities in standards-based reform* (2nd ed.). Thousand Oaks, CA: Corwin Press.

Noon v Alaska State Board of Education, A04-0057 (U.S. District Court) (2004).

Noonan, P.M., Morningstar, M.E., & Erickson, A.G. (2008). Improving interagency collaboration: Effective strategies used by high performing local districts and communities. *Career Development for Exceptional Individuals, 31*(3), 132–142.

Nota, L., Ferrari, L., Soresi, S., & Wehmeyer, M.L. (2007). Self-determination, social abilities, and the quality of life of people with intellectual disabilities. *Journal of Intellectual Disability Research, 51*, 850–865.

Nougaret, A.A. (2002). *The impact of licensure status on the pedagogical competence of first-year special education teachers.* Unpublished doctoral dissertation, George Mason University, Fairfax, VA.

Noyes, D.A., & Sax, C.L. (2004). Changing systems for transition: Students, families, and professionals working together. *Education and Training in Developmental Disabilities, 39*(1), 35–44.

Nuehring, M.L., & Sitlington, P.L. (2003). Transition as a vehicle: Moving from high school to an adult vocational service provider. *Journal of Disability Policy Studies, 14*(1), 25–35.

O'Boyle, B. (2011, February 22). Disabled jobs program a model to follow. *The Times Leader.* Retrieved from http://www.timesleader.com/news/Disabled-jobs-program-a-model-to-follow-.html

O'Brien, D. (2007). Planning with open eyes and open hearts: An alternative to excessive positivism. *Research and Practice for Persons with Severe Disabilities, 32*(3), 173–176.

O'Brien, D., Revell, G., & West, M. (2003). The impact of the current employment policy environment on self-determination of individuals with disabilities. *Journal of Vocational Rehabilitation, 19*(2), 105–118.

O'Brien, J. (2002). Person-centered planning as a contributing factor in organizational and social change. *Research and Practice for Persons with Severe Disabilities, 27*(4), 261–264.

O'Brien, J., & Callahan, M. (2010). Employment support as knowledge creation. *Research & Practice for Persons with Severe Disabilities, 35*(1–2), 1–8.

O'Brien, J., & Pearpoint, J. (2003). *Person centered planning with MAPs and PATH: A workbook for facilitators.* Toronto: Inclusion Press.

Odding, E., Roebroeck, M.E., & Stam, H.J. (2006). The epidemiology of cerebral palsy: incidence, impairments and risk factors. *Disability and Rehabilitation, 28*(4), 183–191.

Odom, S.L., Brantlinger, E., Gersten, R., Horner, R.H., Thompson, B., & Harris, K.R. (2005). Research in special education: Scientific methods and evidence-based practices. *Exceptional Children, 71*, 137–148.

Ohtake, Y., & Chadsey, J.G. (2003). Facilitation strategies used by job coaches in supported employment settings: A preliminary investigation. *Research & Practice with Severe Disabilities, 28*(4), 214–227.

Okilwa, N.S.A., & Shelby, L. (2010). The effects of peer tutoring on academic performance of students with disabilities in grades 6 through 12: A synthesis of the literature. *Remedial and Special Education, 31*(6), 450–463.

Oliver, R., & Reschly, D. (2010). Special education teacher preparation in classroom management: Implications for students with emotional and behavioral disorders. *Behavioral Disorders, 35*(3), 188–199.

Olson, L. (2003). Quality of coursework rises since 1983. *Education Week, 22*(32), 1, 14–17.

Olweus, D. (2001). Bullying at school: tackling the problem. *Observer, 225,* 24–27.

O'Neill, R., Horner, R., Albin, R., Sprague, J., Storey, K., & Newton, S. (1997). *Functional assessment and program development for problem behavior: A practical handbook* (2nd Ed.). Pacific Grove, CA: Brooks/Cole Publishing Company.

O'Reilly, M.F., Lancioni, G.E., & O'Kane, N. (2000). Using a problem solving approach to teach social skills to workers with brain injuries in supported employment settings. *Journal of Vocational Rehabilitation, 14,* 187–194.

Orpinas, P., & Horne, A.M. (2006). Bullying prevention: Creating a positive school climate and developing social competence. *Adolescence, 41*(163), 591–592.

Ostryn, C., Wolfe, P.S., & Rusch, F.R. (2008). A review and analysis of the picture exchange communication system (PECS) for individuals with autism spectrum disorders using a paradigm of communication competence. *Research and Practice for Persons with Severe Disabilities, 33*(1), 13–14.

Owens, L., & Dieker, L.A. (2003). How to spell success for secondary students labeled EBD: How students define effective teachers. *Beyond Behavior, 3,* 20.

Owens-Johnson, L., & Johnson, J. (1999). The local employer survey project: An effective school-to-work curriculum. *Teaching Exceptional Children, 31*(5), 18–23.

PACER Center. (1997). *Natural supports: The emerging role of business in employment of people with moderate and severe disabilities.* Minneapolis, MN: Author.

Galuppi, B., Palisano, R., Rosenbaum, P., Walters, S., Russell, D., & Wood, E. (1997). Development and reliability of a system to classify gross motor function in children with cerebral palsy. *Developmental Medicine and Child Neurology, 39*(4), 214–223.

Palmer, M. (2011). Disability and poverty: A conceptual review. *Journal of Disability Policy Studies, 21*(4), 210–218.

Palmer, S.B. (2010). Self-determination: A lifespan perspective. *Focus on Exceptional Children, 42*(6), 1–16.

Paneth, N., Leviton, A., Goldstein, M., Bax, M., Damiano, D., Dan, B., et al. (2007). Definition and classification of cerebral palsy, Feb 2007. *Developmental Medicine and Child Neurology, 49*(8), 8–14. doi:10.1111/j.1469-8749.2007.tb12610.x.PMID 17370477.

Park, J., Turnbull, A.P., & Park, H.S. (2001). Quality of partnerships in service provision for Korean American parents of children with disabilities: A qualitative inquiry. *Journal of the Association for Persons with Severe Handicaps, 26,* 158–167.

Parrish, P., & Stodden, R. (2009). Aligning assessment and instruction with state standards for children with significant disabilities. *Teaching Exceptional Children, 41*(4), 46–56.

Parrish, S.L., Rose, R.A., & Andrews, M.E. (2010). TANF's impact on low income mothers raising children with disabilities. *Exceptional Children, 75*, 71–92.

Parrish, T. (2002). Racial disparities in the identification, funding, and provision of special education. In D.J. Losen & G. Orfield (Eds.), *Racial inequity in special education* (pp. 15–37). Cambridge. MA: Harvard Civil Rights Project.

Parent, W. & Wehman, P. (2011). Writing the Transition Individualized Education Program. In Wehman, P. *Essentials of Transition Planning.* Maryland: Paul H. Brookes Publishing Co.

Partnership for 21st Century Skills. (2004). *Partnership for 21st century skills.* Retrieved from http://www.p21.org/

Patton, J.R., Cronin, M.E., & Jairrels, V. (1997). Curricular implications of transition: Life skills as an integral part of transition education. *Remedial and Special Education, 18*, 294–306.

Patton, J.R., & Trainor, A. (2002). Using applied academics to enhance the transition process in standards-based education. In C. Kochhar-Bryant & D.S. Bassett (Eds.), *Aligning transition and standards-based education: Issues and strategies.* Arlington, VA: Council for Exceptional Children.

Patton, J.R., & Trainor, A. (2004). Transition from school to independent living. In D.D. Hammill & N.R. Bartel (Eds.), *Teaching students with learning and behavior problems* (pp. 325–368). Austin, TX: PRO-ED, Inc.

Paul, J.J., & Cillessen, A.H.N. (2003). Dynamics of peer victimization in early adolescence: Results from a four-year longitudinal study. *Journal of Applied School Psychology, 19*(2), 25–43.

PCI Education. (n.d.). *Academic curriculum framework.* Retrieved from http://www.pcieducation.com/acf/

Pearman, E., Elliott, T., & Aborn, L. (2004). Transition services model: Partnership for student success. *Education and Training in Developmental Disabilities, 39*(1), 26–34.

Perner, D. (2007). No Child Left Behind: Issues of assessing students with the most significant cognitive disabilities. *Education and Training in Developmental Disabilities, 42*, 243–251.

Perske, R. (2004). Nirje's eight planks. *Mental Retardation, 42*(2), 147–150.

Phillips, W., Callahan, M., Shumpert, N., Puckett, K., Petrey, R., & Summers, K. (2009). Customized transitions: Discovering the best in us. *Journal of Vocational Rehabilitation, 30*, 49–55.

Pico, E.L., Wilson, P.E., & Haas, R. (2010). Spina bifida. In M.A. Alexander, D. Matthews (Eds.), *Pediatric rehabilitation: Principles and practice* (4th ed., 199–230). New York: Demos Medical Publishing.

Pierson, M.R., Carter, E.W., Lane, K.L., & Glaeser, B.C. (2008). Factors influencing the self-determination of transition-age youth with high-incidence disabilities. *Career Development for Exceptional Individuals, 31*(2), 115–125.

Polloway, E.A. (2004). Eulogy for "mild" retardation? *Division on Developmental Disability Express, 14*(3), 1, 8.

Pogue, D. (2011). Pogue's Post: Apple's Assistive Touch Helps the Disabled Use a Smartphone. *The New York Times.* Retrieved November 14, 2011 from http://pogue.blogs.nytimes.com/2011/11/10/apples-assistivetouch-helps-the-disabled-use-a-smartphone/

Post, M., Campbell, C., Heinz, T., Kotsonas, L., Montgomery, J., & Storey, K. (2010). Collaboration between supported employment and human resource services: Strategies for success. *Research and Practice for Persons with Severe Disabilities, 35*(1–2), 24–30.

Post, M., & Storey, K. (2002). Review of using auditory prompting systems with persons who have moderate to severe disabilities. *Education and Training in Mental Retardation and Developmental Disabilities, 37*(3), 317–327.

Potts, B. (2005). Disability and employment: considering the importance of social capital. *Journal of Rehabilitation, 71*(3), 20–25.

Powers, K., Geenen, S., & Powers, L.E. (2009). Similarities and differences in transition expectations of youth and parents. *Career Development for Exceptional Individuals, 3*(3), 132–144.

Powers, K., Gil-Kashiwabara, E., Geenen, S., Powers, L., Balandran, J., & Palmer, C. (2005). Mandates and effective transition planning practices reflected in IEP's. *Career Development for Exceptional Individuals, 28*, 47–59.

Powers, L.E., Sowers, J., Turner, A., Nesbitt, M., Knowles, E., & Ellison, R. (1996). TAKE CHARGE! A model for promoting self-determination among adolescents with challenges. In L.E. Powers, G.H.S. Singer, & J. Sowers (Eds.), *On the road to autonomy: Promoting self-competence in children and youth with disabilities* (pp. 291–332). Baltimore: Paul H. Brookes Publishing Co.

Powers, L.E., Turner, A., Matuszewski, J., Wilson, R., & Phillips, A. (2001). TAKE CHARGE for the future: A controlled field-test of a model to promote student involvement in transition planning. *Career Development for Exceptional Individuals, 24*, 89–103.

Powers, L.E., Turner, A., Westwood, D., Loesch, C., Brown, A., & Rowland, C. (1998). TAKE CHARGE for the future: A student-directed approach to transition planning. In M.L. Wehmeyer & D.J. Sands (Eds.), *Making it happen: Student involvement in education planning, decision making and instruction* (pp. 187–210). Baltimore: Paul H. Brookes Publishing Co.

President's Committee on Intellectual Disabilities. (2010). *A change we have to keep. A road map to personal and economic freedom for people with intellectual disabilities in the 21st Century.* Rehabilitation Act Amendments of 1986, Pub. L. 99-506, 29 U.S.C. §§ 701 *et seq.*

Prinstein, M.J., & Dodge, K.A. (2008). *Understanding peer influence in children and adolescents.* New York: Guilford Press.

Project SEARCH®. (2011). *Project SEARCH®.* Retrieved from http://projectsearch.us/

Pugach, M.C., & Johnson, L.J. (1995). *Collaborative practitioners: Collaborative schools.* Denver: Love Publishing.

Pugach, M.C., & Warger, C.L. (1993). Cultural considerations. In J.I. Goodlad & T.C. Lovitt (Eds.), *Integrating general and special education* (pp. 125–148). New York: Merrill.

Pugach, M.C., & Warger, C.L. (2001). Curriculum matters: Raising expectations for students with disabilities. *Remedial and Special Education, 22,* 194–196.

Quilty, K.M. (2007). Teaching paraprofessionals how to write and implement social stories for students with autism spectrum disorders. *Remedial & Special Education, 28*(3), 182–189.

Quinn, M.M., Kavale, K.A., Mathur, S.R., Rutherford, R.B., & Forness, S.R. (1999). A meta-analysis of social skills interventions for students with emotional and behavioral disorders. *Journal of Emotional and Behavioral Disorders, 7*(1), 54–64.

Rabren, K., & Johnson, C. (2010) Postschool outcome data collection programs: Examples from two states. *Career Development for Exceptional Individuals, 33*(1) 52–63.

Rabren, K., Dunn, C., & Chambers, D. (2002). Predictors of post high school employment for young adults with disabilities. *Career Development for Exceptional Individuals, 25,* 25–40.

Race to the Top Fund, Final Rule, 34 C.F.R. Subtitle B, Chapter II (November 2009). Retrieved June 2, 2010, from http://edocket.access.gpo.gov/2009/pdf/E9-27426.pdf

Radabaugh, M.P. (n.d.). Technology for access and function. *In NIDRR's Long Range Plan-Technology for access and function research.* Retrieved May 14, 2011, from http://www.ncddr.org/new/announcements/lrp/fy1999-2003/lrp_techaf.html

Ramirez, A.Y.F. (2003). Dismay and disappointment: Parental involvement of Latino immigrant parents. *The Urban Review, 35,* 93–110.

Rao, S., & Kane, M.T. (2009). Teaching students with cognitive impairment chained mathematical task of decimal subtraction using simultaneous prompting. *Education and Training in Developmental Disabilities, 44,* 244–256.

Rappaport, J. (1981). In praise of a paradox: A social policy of empowerment over prevention. *American Journal of Community Psychology, 9,* 1–25.

Rea, P.J., McLaughlin, B., & Walther-Thomas, C. (2002). Outcomes for students with learning disabilities in inclusive and pullout programs. *Exceptional Children, 68*(2), 203–222.

Reardon, S.F., Arshan, N., Atteberry, A., & Kurlaender, M. (2010). Effects of failing a high school exit exam on course taking, achievement, persistence, and graduation. *Educational Evaluation and Policy Analysis, 32,* 498–520. doi: 10.3102/0162373710382655

Reed, F.D., Hyman, S.R., & Hirst, J.M. (2011). Applications of technology to teach social skills to children with autism. *Research in Autism Spectrum Disorders, 5,* 1003–1010.

Rehabilitation Act Amendments of 1978. Pub. L. 95-602.

Rehabilitation Act Amendments of 1986. Pub. L. 99-506.

Rehabilitation Act Amendments of 1992. Pub. L. 102-569.

Rehabilitation Act Amendments of 1998. Pub. L. 105-220, 29 U.S.C. §§ 701 *et seq.*

Rehabilitation Act of 1973, Pub. L. 93-112, Section 504, 29 U.S.C. §§ 794 *et seq.*

Rehabilitation Act of 1973, Pub. L. 93-112, 29 U.S.C. 701 *et seq.*

Reichman, N.E., Corman, H., & Noonan, K. (2008). Impact of child disability on the family. *Maternal and Child Health Journal, 12,* 679–683.

Reid, D.H., & Parsons, M.B. (2003). *Positive behavior support training curriculum. Supervisory Edition.* Washington, DC: American Association on Mental Retardation.

Reid, D.K., & Knight, M.G. (2006). Disability justifies exclusion of minority students: A critical history grounded in disability studies. *Educational Researcher, 35,* 18–23.

Reiling, C. (1990). *How significant is "significant"? A personal glimpse of life with a learning disability.* Columbus, OH: Association of Handicapped Student Service Programs in Postsecondary Education.

Renk, K., & Phares, V. (2004). Cross-informant ratings of social competence in children and adolescents. *Clinical Psychology Review, 24,* 239–254. doi: 10.1016/j.cpr.2004.01.004

Renzaglia, A., Hutchins, M., Dymond, S.K., & Sheldon, D. (2008). Career development: An experiential model for developing basic work skills and employment preferences. In P. Bates, K. Storey, & D. Hunter (Eds.), *The road ahead: Transition to adult life for persons with disabilities* (2nd ed.). St. Augustine, FL: Training Resource Network, Inc.

Repetto, J., McGorray, S.P., Wang, H., Podmostko, M., Andrews, W., Lubbers, J., et al. (2011). The high school experience: What students with and without disabilities report as they leave school. *Career Development of Exceptional Individuals, 34*(3), 142–152.

Repetto, J.B., Gibson, R.W., Lubbers, J., Gritz, S. & Reiss, J. (2008). A statewide study of knowledge and attitudes regarding health care transition. *Career Development for Exceptional Individuals, 31*(1), 5–13.

Retish, P., Hitchings, W., Horvath, M., & Schmalle, B. (1991). *Students with mild disabilities in the secondary school.* New York: Longman.

Reyna, V., & Brainerd, C.J. (2007, March). The importance of mathematics in health and human judgment: Numeracy, risk communication, and medical decision making. *Learning & Individual Differences, 17*(2), 147–159.

Rice, C. (2009). Prevalence of autism spectrum disorders—Autism and Developmental Disabilities Monitoring Network, United States,

2005. Atlanta: Department of Health and Human Services, Centers for Disease Control and Prevention.

Richter, S., & Mazzotti, V. (2011). A comprehensive review of the literature on summary of performance. *Career Development of Exceptional Individuals, 34*(3), 176–186.

Riggs, C.G., & Mueller, P.H. (2001). Employment and utilization of paraeducators in inclusive settings. *Journal of Special Education, 35*(1), 54–62.

Riley, C. (2006). *Disability and business: best practices and strategies for inclusion.* Lebanon, NH: University Press of New England.

Rioux-Bailey, C. (2004, March). *Students with disabilities and access to community college: Continuing issues and new directions.* Heath Resource Center. Retrieved from http://www.docstoc.com/docs/28294943/Students-with-Disabilities-and-Access-to-Community-Colleges

Roberts, K.D., & Stodden, R.A. (2005). The use of voice recognition software as a compensatory strategy for post secondary education students receiving services under the category of learning disabled. *Journal of Vocational Education, 22,* 49–64.

Roberts, M.M., Murphy, A., Dolce, J., Spagnolo, A., Gill, K., Lu, W., et al. (2010). A study of the impact of social support development on job acquisition and retention among people with psychiatric disabilities. *Journal of Vocational Rehabilitation, 33,* 203–207. doi: 10.3233/JVR-2010-0528

Robertson, J., Emerson, E., Hatton, C., Elliott, J., McIntosh, B., Swift, P., et al. (2006). Longitudinal analysis of the impact and cost of person-centered planning for people with intellectual disabilities in England. *American Journal on Mental Retardation, 111*(6), 400–416.

Robertson, J., Emerson, E., Hatton, C., Elliott, J., McIntosh, B., Swift, P., et al. (2007). Person-centered planning: factors associated with successful outcomes for people with intellectual disabilities. *Journal of Intellectual Disability Research, 51*(3), 232–243.

Rodkin, P.C., & Hodges, E.V.E. (2003). Bullies and victims in the peer ecology: Four questions for psychologists and school professionals. *School Psychology Review, 32*(3), 384–400.

Roessler, R.T., Hennessey, M.L., & Rumril, P.D. (2007). Strategies for improving career services for postsecondary students with disabilities: Results of focus group study of key stakeholders. *Career Development for Exceptional Individuals, 30,* 158–170.

Rogan, P., & Rinne, S. (2011). National call for organizational change from sheltered to integrated employment. *Intellectual and Developmental Disabilities, 49*(4), 248–260.

Rogers, C., Lavin, D., Tran, T., Gantenbein, T., & Sharpe, M. (2008). Customized employment: Changing what it means to be qualified in the workforce for transition-aged youth and your adults. *Journal of Vocational Rehabilitation, 28,* 191–207.

Rose, C.A., Monda-Amaya, L.E., & Espelage, D.L. (2011). Bullying perpetration and victimization in special education: A review of the literature. *Remedial and Special Education, 32*(2), 114–130.

Rose, D.H., & Meyer, A. (2002). *Teaching every student in the digital age: Universal design for learning.* Alexandria, VA: Association for Supervision and Curriculum Development.

Rose, H., & Betts, J.R. (2001). *Math matters: The links between high school curriculum, college graduation, and earnings.* San Francisco: Public Policy Institution of California. Available from http://www.ppic.org/content/pubs/report/R_701JBR.pdf

Rose, J., Perks, J., Fidan, M., & Hurst, M. (2010). Assessing motivation in work for people with developmental disabilities. *Journal of Intellectual Disabilities, 14*(2), 147–155.

Rosenberg, M.S., Westling, D.L., & McLeskey, J. (2008). *Special education for today's teachers: An introduction.* Columbus, OH: Merrill/Prentice-Hall Publishers.

Rotter, J.B. (1966). Generalized expectancies for internal versus external control of reinforcement. *Psychological Monographs, 80*(1), 244–248.

Rouse, C.E., & Kemple, J.J. (2009). Introducing the issue. *The Future of Children, 19*(1), 3–15.

Rowe, D., & Test, D. (2010). The effects of computer-based instruction on the transition planning process knowledge of parents of students with disabilities. *Research Practice for Persons with Severe Disabilities, 35*(3–4), 102–115.

Rozalski, M., Katsiyannis, A., Ryan, J., Collins, T., & Stewart, A. (2010). Americans with Disabilities Act Amendments of 2008. *Journal of Disability Policy Studies, 21*(1), 22–28.

K.H. Rubin, W.M. Bukowski, & B. Laursen (Eds.). (2009). *Handbook of peer interactions, relationships, and groups.* New York: Guilford Press.

Rueda, R., Monzo, L., Shapiro, J., Gomez, J., & Blacher, J. (2005). Cultural models of transition: Latina mothers of young adults with developmental disabilities. *Exceptional Children, 71,* 401–414.

Ruef, M.B., & Turnbull, A.P. (2002). The perspectives of individuals with cognitive disabilities and/or autism on their lives and their problem behavior. *Research and Practice for Persons with Severe Disabilities, 27*(2), 125–140.

Rusch, F.R., & Braddock, D. (2004). Adult day programs versus supported employment (1988-2002): Spending and service practices of mental retardation and developmental disabilities state agencies. *Research and Practice for Persons with Severe Disabilities, 29*(4), 237–242.

Rusch, F.R., Hughes, C., Agran, M., Martin, J.E., & Johnson, J.R. (2009). Toward self directed learning, post high school placement and coordinated support: Constructing new transition bridges to adult life. *Career Development for Exceptional Individuals, 32,* 53–59.

Rusch, F.R., & Schutz, R.P. (1979). Non-sheltered employment of the mentally retarded adults:

Research to reality? *Journal on Contemporary Business, 8*(4), 85–89.

Rusch, F.R., & Wolfe, M. (2008). When will our values finally result in the creation of new pathways for change—Change that we can believe in? *Research and Practice for Persons with Severe Disabilities, 33*(3), 96–97.

Rust, K.L., & Smith, R.O. (2005). Assistive technology in the measurement of rehabilitation and health outcomes. *American Journal of Physical Medicine & Rehabilitation, 84*(10), 780–793.

Rutkowski, S., Daston, M., Van Kuiken, D., & Riehle, E. (2006). Project SEARCH®: A demand-side model of high school transition. *Journal of Vocational Rehabilitation, 25*, 85–96.

Ryan, J.B., Hughes, E.M., Katsiyannis, A., McDaniel, M., & Sprinkle, C. (2011). Research-based educational practices for students with autism spectrum disorders. *Teaching Exceptional Children, 43*(3), 56–64.

Ryndak, D., Ward, L., Alper, T., Montgomery, S., Wilson, J., & Storch, J.F. (2010). Long-term outcomes of services for two persons with significant disabilities with differing educational experiences: A qualitative consideration of the impact of educational experiences. *Education and Training in Autism and Developmental Disabilities, 45*(3), 323–338.

Ryndak, D., Ward, T., Alper, S., Storch, J.F., & Montgomery, J.W. (2010). Long-term outcomes of services in inclusive and self-contained settings for siblings with comparable significant disabilities. *Education and Training in Autism and Developmental Disabilities, 45*(1), 38–53.

Ryndak, D.L., Jackson, L., & Billingsley, F. (2000). Defining school inclusion for students with moderate to severe disabilities: What do experts say? *Exceptionality, 8*(2), 101–116.

Ryndak, D.L., Moore, M.A., & Orlando, A.M., Delano, M. (2009). Access to the general curriculum: The mandate and role of context in research-based practice for students with extensive support needs. *Research and Practice for Persons with Severe Disabilities, 33*(4), 199–213.

Sablier, J., Stip, E., & Franck, N. (2009). Cognitive remediation and cognitive assistive technologies in schizophrenia. *L'encephale, 35*, 160–167.

Sands, D.J., Adams, L., & Stout, D.M. (1995). A statewide exploration of the nature and use of curriculum in special education. *Exceptional Children, 62*, 68–83.

Sax, C.L., & Thoma, C.A. (2002). *Transition assessment: Wise practices for quality lives.* Baltimore: Paul H. Brookes Publishing Co.

Schall, C., & Wehman, P. (2009). Understanding the transition from school to adulthood for students with autism. In P. Wehman, M.D. Smith, & C. Schall (Eds.), *Autism and the transition to adulthood; Success beyond the classroom* (pp. 1–14). Baltimore: Paul H. Brookes Publishing Co.

Schall, C.M. (2010). Positive behavior support: Supporting adults with autism spectrum disorders in the workplace. *Journal of Vocational Rehabilitation, 32*, 109–115.

Schall, C. (2011). Positive behavior support. In P. Wehman & J. Kregel (Eds.), Functional *curriculum for elementary, middle and secondary aged students* (3rd ed.). Austin, TX: PRO-ED.

Schall, C.M., & McDonough, J.T. (2010). Autism spectrum disorders in adolescence and early adulthood: Characteristics and issues. *Journal of Vocational Rehabilitation, 32*, 81–88.

Schaller, J., & Yang, N.K. (2005). Competitive employment for people with autism: Correlates of successful closure in competitive and supported employment. *Rehabilitation Counseling Bulletin, 49*(1), 4–16.

Schalock, R.L., Luckasson, R.A., & Shogren, K.A. (2007). The renaming of mental retardation: Understanding the change to the term intellectual disability. *Intellectual and Developmental Disabilities, 45*, 116–124.

Schalock, R.L., Luckasson, R.A., Shogren, K.A., Borthwick-Duffy, W.S., Bradley, V., Buntix, W.H.E., et al. (2007). The renaming of mental retardation: Understanding the change to the term intellectual disability. *Intellectual and Developmental Disabilities, 45*(2), 116–124.

Scheeler, M.C., Macluckie, M., & Albright, K. (2010). Effects of immediate feedback delivered by peer tutors on the oral presentation skills of adolescents with learning disabilities. *Remedial and Special Education, 31*(2), 77–86.

Schelly, C., Davies, P., & Spooner, C. (2011). Student perceptions of faculty implementation of universal design for learning. *Journal of Postsecondary Education and Disability, 24*(1), 17–30.

Schmidt, P. (2005, February 22). Students with mental retardation are knocking on college doors, and colleges are responding. *The Chronicle of Higher Education: Today's News.*

Schneier, A.J., Shields, B.J., Hostetler, S.G., Xiang, H., & Smith, G.A. (2006). Incidence of pediatric traumatic brain injury and the associated hospital resource utilization in the United States. *Pediatrics, 11*(2), 483–492.

Schoen, S.F., & Nolen, J. (Sept/Oct 2004). Action research: Decreasing acting-out behavior and increasing learning. *Teaching Exceptional Children, 37*, 26–29.

Schwartz, A.A., Holburn, S.C., & Jacobson, J.W. (2000). Defining person-centeredness: Results of two consensus methods. *Education and Training in Mental Retardation and Developmental Disabilities, 35*, 238.

Scott, L., Saddler, S., Thoma, C.A., Bartholomew, C., Alder, N., & Tamura, R. (2011). Universal design for transition: A single subject research study on the impact of UDT on student achievement, engagement, and interest. *i-manager's Journal on Educational Psychology, 4*(4), 21–32.

Scott, P. (2007). Rallying relationships: The role of positive visions and possible actions in person-centered planning. *Research and Practice for Persons with Severe Disabilities, 32*(3), 181–183.

Scott, T.M., Alter, P.J., & McQuillan, K. (2010). Functional behavior assessment in classroom settings: scaling down to scale up. *Intervention in School and Clinic, 46*, 87–94.

Scruggs, T.E., Mastropieri, M.A., Berkeley, S., & Graetz, J.E. (2009). Do special education interventions improve learning of secondary content? *Remedial and Special Education, 31*, 437–449. doi: 10.1177/0741932508327465.

Scruggs, T.E., Mastropieri, M.A., Berkeley, S., & Marshak, L. (2010). Mnemonic strategies: Evidence-based practice and practice-based evidence. *Intervention in School and Clinic, 46*(2), 79–86.

Seltzer, M.M., Krauss, M.W., Shattuck, P.T., Orsmond, G., Swe, A., & Lord, C. (2003). The symptoms of autism spectrum disorders in adolescence and adulthood. *Journal of Autism and Developmental Disorders, 33*, 565–581.

Seo, Y., Abbott, R.D., & Hawkins, J.D. (2008). Outcome status of students with learning disabilities at ages 21 and 24. *Journal of Learning Disabilities, 41*(4), 300–314.

Sharpe, M.N., Johnson, D.R., Izzo, M., & Murray, A. (2005). An analysis of instructional accommodations and assistive technologies used by postsecondary graduates with disabilities. *Journal of Vocational Rehabilitation, 22*, 3–11.

Sharpton, W.R., & West, M. (1991). Severe and profound mental retardation. In P. McLaughlin & P. Wehman (Eds.), *Handbook of developmental disabilities: A guide to best practices* (pp. 16–29). Austin, TX: PRO-ED.

Shattuck, P.T., Narendorf, S.C., Cooper, B., Sterzing, P.R., Wagner, M., Taylor, J.L. (2012). Postsecondary education and employment among youth with an autism spectrum disorder. *Pediatrics,* published online May 14, 2012. doi: 10.1542/peds.2011-2864

Shattuck, P.T., Wagner, M., Narendorf, S., Sterzing, P., & Hensley, M. (2011). Post-high school service use among adults with an autism service disorder. *Archives of Pediatric and Adolescent Medicine, 165*, 141–146.

Shaw, S.F., Madaus, J.W., & Dukes, L.L. (2010). *Preparing students with disabilities for college success: A practical guide to transition planning.* Baltimore: Paul H. Brookes Publishing Co.

Shin, M., Besser, L.M., Siffel, C., Kucik, J.E., Shaw, G.M., et al. (2010). Congenital Anomaly Multistate Prevalence and Survival Collaborative. Prevalence of spina bifida among children and adolescents in 10 regions in the United States. *Pediatrics.* [e-published July 12, 2010].

Shinnar, S., & Pellock, J.M. (2002). Update on the epidemiology and prognosis of pediatric epilepsy. *Journal of Child Neurology, 17*, S4–S17.

Shipley-Benamou, R., Lutzker, J.R., & Taubman, M. (2002). Teaching daily living skills to children with autism through instructional video modeling. *Journal of Positive Behavior Interventions, 4*(3), 165–175.

Shippen, M.E., Crites, S.A., Houchins, D.E., Ramsey, M.L., & Simon, M. (2005). Preservice teachers' perceptions of including students with disabilities. *Teacher Education and Special Education, 28*, 92–99.

Shogren, K.A., & Broussard, R. (2011). Exploring the perceptions of self-determination of individuals with intellectual disability. *Intellectual and Development Disabilities, 49*(2), 86–102.

Shogren, K.A., Faggella-Luby, M., Bae, S.J., & Wehmeyer, M.L. (2004). The effect of choice-making as an intervention for problem behavior: A meta-analysis. *Journal of Positive Behavior Interventions, 6*, 228–237.

Shogren, K.A., Lopez, S.J., Wehmeyer, M.L., Little, T.D., & Pressgrove, C.L. (2006). The role of positive psychology constructs in predicting life satisfaction in adolescents with and without cognitive disabilities: An exploratory study. *The Journal of Positive Psychology, 1*, 37–52.

Shogren, K.A., Palmer, S., Wehmeyer, M.L., Williams-Diehm, K., & Little, T. (2010). Effect of intervention with the Self-Determined Learning Model of Instruction on access and goal attainment. Manuscript submitted for publication.

Shogren, K.A., & Turnbull, H.R. (2010). Public policy and outcomes for persons with intellectual disability: Extending and expanding the public policy framework of AAIDD's 11th edition of *Intellectual Disability: Definition, classification, and systems of support. Intellectual and Developmental Disabilities, 48*(5), 375–386.

Shogren, K.A., Wehmeyer, M., Palmer, S., Soukup, J., Garner, N., & Lawrence, M. (2007). Examining individual and ecological predictors of the self-determination of students with disabilities. *Exceptional Children, 73*, 488–510.

Shogren, K.A., Wehmeyer, M.L., Palmer, S.B., Soukup, J.H., Little, T., Garner, N., et al. (2008). Understanding the construct of self-determination: Examining the relationship between The Arc's Self-Determination Scale and the American Institute for Research Self-Determination Scale. *Assessment for Effective Instruction, 33*, 94–107.

Shukla-Mehta, S., Miller, T., & Callahan, K.J. (2010). Evaluating the effectiveness of video instruction on social and communication skills training for children with autism spectrum disorders: A review of the literature. *Focus on Autism and Other Developmental Disabilities, 25*(1), 23–36.

Siegel, E., & Allinder, R. (2005). Review of assessment procedures for students with moderate and severe disabilities. *Education and Training in Developmental Disabilities, 40*(4), 343–351.

Silverstein, R. (2003). *The applicability of the ADA to personal assistance services in the workplace.* Policy Brief, Issue 10. Retrieved June 15, 2011, from http://www.communityinclusion.org/article.php?article_id=21&staff_id=36&style=print

Sim, K.E., Emerson, J., O'Brien, K., Pecora, P.J., & Silva, L. (2008). Post-secondary education and training support utilization by students from foster care: Findings from scholarship recipient interviews. *Journal of Public Child Welfare, 2,* 109–129.

Simonsen, B., Fairbanks, S., Briesch, A., Myers, D., & Sugai, G. (2008). Evidence based practices in classroom management: Considerations for research to practice. *Education and Treatment of Children, 31,* 351–380.

Simonsen, M. (2010). *Predictors of supported employment for transitioning youth with developmental disabilities* (unpublished doctoral dissertation). University of Maryland, College Park.

Simpson, A., Langone, J., & Ayres, K.M. (2004). Embedded video and computer based instruction to improve social skills for students with autism. *Education and Training in Developmental Disabilities, 39*(3), 240–252.

Simpson, R. (2008). Children and youth with autism spectrum disorders: The search for effective methods. *Focus on Exceptional Children, 40*(7), 1–14.

Simpson, R., Peterson, R., & Smith, C. (2011). Critical education components for students with emotional and behavioral disorders: Science, policy and practice. *Remedial and Special Education, 32*(3), 230–242.

Siperstein, G.N., Norins, J., & Mohler, A. (2007). Social acceptance and attitude change: Fifty years of research. In J.W. Jacobson, J.A. Mulick, & J. Rojahn (Eds.), *Handbook of intellectual and developmental disabilities* (pp. 133–154). New York: Springer.

Siperstein, G.N., Romano, N., Mohler, A., & Parker, R. (2006). A national survey of consumer attitudes towards companies that hire people with disabilities. *Journal of Vocational Rehabilitation, 24*(1), 3–9.

Sitlington, P.L., & Clark, G.M. (2006). *Transition education and services for students with disabilities* (4th ed.). Needham Heights, MA: Allyn & Bacon.

Sitlington, P.L., & Neubert, D.A. (2004). Preparing youth with emotional and behavior disorders for transition to adult life: Can it be done within the standards-based reform movement? *Behavior Disorders, 29*(3), 279–288.

Skiba, R.J., & Peterson, R.L. (2000). School discipline at a crossroads: From zero tolerance to early response. *Exceptional Children, 66*(3), 335–347.

Skiba, R.J., Ploni-Staudinger, L., Gallini, S., Simmons, A.B., & Feggins-Azziz, R. (2006). Disparate access: The disproportionality of African American students with disabilities across educational environments. *Exceptional Children, 72*(4), 411–424.

Skiba, R.J., Simmons, A.B., Ritter, S., Gibb, A.C., Rausch, M.K., Cuadrado, J., et al. (2008). Achieving equity in special education: History, status, and current challenges. *Exceptional Children, 74,* 264–288.

Smith, A. (2006). Access, participation, and progress in the general education curriculum in the least restrictive environment for students with significant cognitive disabilities. *Research & Practice for Persons with Severe Disabilities, 31*(4), 331–337.

Smith, C.R. (2000). Behavioral and discipline provisions of IDEA '97: Implicit competencies yet to be confirmed. *Exceptional Children, 66*(3), 403–412.

Smith, P. (2007). Have we made any progress? Including students with intellectual disabilities in regular education classrooms. *Intellectual and Developmental Disabilities, 45*(5), 297–309.

Smith, S.D., & Caruso, J.B. (2010). *The ECAR Study of Undergraduate Students and Information Technology, 2010* (Research Study, Vol. 6). Boulder, CO: EDUCAUSE Center for Applied Research. Retrieved on June 16, 2011, from http://net.educause.edu/ir/library/pdf/EKF/EKF1006.pdf

Smith, S.W., & Daunic, A.P. (2004). Research on preventing behavior problems using a cognitive-behavioral intervention: Preliminary findings, challenges, and future directions. *Behavioral Disorders, 30*(1), 72–76.

Smith, T., & DiLeo, D. (2011). Community action teams: an infrastructure for quality service delivery. *Journal of Vocational Rehabilitation, 35,* 1–7.

Smith, T., Polloway, E., Patton, J., & Dowdy, C. (2004). *Teaching students with special needs in inclusive settings* (4th ed.). Boston: Pearson Education, Inc.

Snell, M.E., Brady, N., McLean, L., Ogletree, B.T., Siegel, E., Sylvester, L., et al. (2010). Twenty years of communication intervention research with individuals who have severe intellectual and developmental disabilities. *American Journal on Intellectual and Developmental Disabilities, 115,* 364–380. doi: 10.1352/1944-7558-115-5.364

Snell, M.E., & Brown, F. (2006). Designing and implementing instructional programs. In M. Snell & F. Brown (Eds.), *Instruction of students with severe disabilities* (6th ed.). Upper Saddle River, NJ: Merrill/Prentice Hall.

Snell, M.E., & Janney, R. (2005). *Collaborative teaming* (2nd ed.). Baltimore: Paul H. Brookes Publishing Co.

Snell, M.E., Vorhees, M.D., & Chen, L.Y. (2005). Team involvement in assessment based interventions with prolem behavior, 1997 to 2002. *Journal of Positive Behavior Intervention, 7,* 140–152.

Snyder, E.P. (2002). Teaching students with combined behavioral disorders and mental retardation to lead their own IEP meetings. *Behavioral Disorders, 27,* 340–357.

Snyder, E.P., & Shapiro, E.S. (1997). Teaching students with emotional/behavioral disorders the skills to participate in the development of their own IEPs. *Behavioral Disorders, 22,* 246–259.

Soukup, J.H., Wehmeyer, M.L., Bashinski, S.M., & Bovaird, J. (2007). Classroom variables and access to the general education curriculum of students with intellectual and developmental disabilities. *Exceptional Children, 74*, 101–120.

Sowers, J., & Powers, L. (1995). Enhancing the participation and independence of students with severe physical and multiple disabilities in performing community activities. *Mental Retardation, 33*, 209–220.

Sowers, J.A. (1991). Transitioning students with physical and multiple disabilities to supported employment. *Journal of Vocational Rehabilitation, 1*(4), 25–37.

Sowers, J.A., & Powers, L. (1991). *Vocational preparation and employment of students with physical and multiple disabilities* (pp. 30–31). Baltimore: Paul H. Brookes Publishing Co.

Spence-Cochran, K., & Pearl, C. (2009). A comparison of hand-held computer and staff model supports for high school students with autism and intellectual disabilities. In K. Spence-Cochran & Howard P. Parette (Eds.), *Assistive technology and autism spectrum disorders:Research-based practice and innovation in the field.* Norman, IL: Special Education Assistive Technology Center at Illinois State University and Assistive Technology Industry Association.

Spooner, F., & Browder, D.M. (2006). Why teach the general education curriculum? In D.M. Browder & F. Spooner (Eds.), *Teaching language arts, math, & science to students with significant cognitive disabilities* (pp. 1–14). Baltimore: Paul H. Brookes Publishing Co.

Spooner, F., Di Biase, W., & Courtade-Little, G. (2006). Science standard and functional skills: Finding the links. In D.M. Browder & F. Spooner (Eds.), *Teaching language arts, math, & science to students with significant cognitive disabilities* (pp. 229–244). Baltimore: Paul H. Brookes Publishing Co.

Spooner, F., Dymond, S.K., Smith, A., & Kennedy, C.H. (2006). What we know and need to know about accessing the general curriculum for students with significant cognitive disabilities. *Research and Practice for Persons with Severe Disabilities, 31*(4), 277–283.

Spriggs, A.D., Gast, D.L., & Ayres, K.M. (2007). Using picture activity schedule books to increase on-schedule and on-task behaviors. *Education and Training in Developmental Disabilities, 42*(2), 209–223.

Stancliffe, R.J. & Lakin, K.C. (Eds.). (2005). *Costs and outcomes of community services for people with intellectual disabilities.* Baltimore: Paul H. Brookes Publishing Co.

Staples, K.E., & Diliberto, J.A. (2010). Guidelines for successful family involvement: Working with parents of students with disabilities. *Teaching Exceptional Children, 42*(6), 58–63.

State Vocational Rehabilitation Services Program: Final Rules. (January 17, 2001). *Federal Register, 66*(11), 4389. Washington, DC: U.S. Government Printing Office.

Stecker, P.M., Fuchs, L.S., & Fuchs, D. (2005). Using curriculum-based measurement to improve student achievement: Review of research. *Psychology in Schools, 42*, 795–820.

Steere, D.E., & Cavaiuolo, D. (2002). Connecting outcomes, goals, and objectives in transition planning. *Teaching Exceptional Children, 34*(6), 54–59.

Steere, D.E., Wood, R., Pancsofar, E.L., & Butterworth, J. (1990). Outcome-based school-to-work transition planning for students with severe disabilities. *Career Development for Exceptional Individuals, 13*, 57–69.

Stempien, L.R., & Loeb, R.C. (2002). Differences in job satisfaction between general education teachers and special education teachers: Implications for retention. *Remedial and Special Education, 23*(5), 258–267

Stenhoff, D.M., & Lignugaris/Kraft, B. (2007). A review of the effects of peer tutoring on students with mild disabilities in secondary settings. *Exceptional Children, 74*(1), 8–30.

Sternberg, L. (Ed.). (1994). *Individuals with profound disabilities instructional and assistive strategies* (3rd ed.). Austin, TX: PRO-ED.

Stodden, R.A., Brown, S.E., Galloway, L.M., Myrazek, S., & Noy, L. (2004). *Essential tools: Interagency transition team development and facilitation.* Minneapolis: University of Minnesota, Institute on Community Integration, National Center on Secondary Education and Transition.

Stodden, R.A., Conway, M.A., & Chang, K.B.T. (2003). Findings from the study of transition, technology and postsecondary supports for youth with disabilities: Implications for secondary school educators. *Journal of Special Education Technology, 18*(4), 29–44.

Stodden, R.A., & Dowrick, P.W. (2000). *The present and future of postsecondary education for adults with disabilities.* Honolulu: University of Hawaii, Rehabilitation Research and Training Center.

Stoner, J.B., Bock, S.J., Thompson, J.R., Angell, M.E., Heyl, B.S., & Crowley, E.P. (2005). Welcome to our world: Parent perceptions of interactions between parents of young children with ASD and educational professionals. *Focus on Autism and Other Developmental Disabilities, 20*, 39–51.

Storey, K. (2002). Strategies for increasing interactions in supported employment settings: An updated review. *Journal of Vocational Rehabilitation, 17*, 231–237.

Storms, J., O'Leary, E., & Williams, J. (2000). *The Individuals with Disabilities Education Act of 1997 transition requirements: A guide for states, districts, schools, universities and families.* Eugene, OR: Western Regional Resource Center.

Stuart, A. (2010). *Goal setting and LD: Enhancing skills for success in life.* Retrieved December 31, 2010, from National Center for Learning Disabilities, http://www.ncld.org/ld-basics/ld-aamp-social-skills/social-aamp-emotional-challenges/goal-setting-and-ld-enhancing-skills-for-success-in-life

Sullivan, T.N., Farrell, A.D., & Kliewer, W. (2006). Peer victimization in early adolescence:

Association between physical and relational victimization and drug use, aggression, and delinquent behaviors among urban middle school students. *Development and Psychopathology, 18,* 119–137.

Sutherland, K.S., Alder, N., & Gunter, P.L. (2003). The effect of varying rates of opportunities to respond to academic requests on the classroom behavior of students with E/BD. *Journal of Emotional and Behavioral Disorders, 11,* 239–248.

Sutherland, K.S., Conroy, M., Abrams, L., & Vo, A. (2010). Improving interactions between teachers and young children with problem behavior: A strengths-based approach. *Exceptionality, 18,* 70–81.

Sutherland, K., Lewis-Palmer, T., Stichter, J., & Morgan, P. (2008). Examining the influence of teacher behavior and classroom context on the behavioral and academic outcomes for students with emotional or behavioral disorders. *Journal of Special Education, 41,* 223–233.

Sutherland, K.S., & Oswald, D. (2005). The relationship between teacher and student behavior in classrooms for students with emotional and behavioral disorders: Transactional processes. *Journal of Child and Family Studies, 14,* 1–14.

Sutherland, K.S., & Snyder, A. (2007). The effects of peer tutoring and self-graphing on the reading fluency and classroom behavior of middle school students with emotional or behavioral disorders. *Journal of Emotional and Behavioral Disorders, 15,* 103–118.

Svetaz, M.V., Ireland, M., & Blum, R. (2000). Adolescents with learning disabilities: Risk and protective factors associated with emotional well-being: Findings from the national longitudinal study of adolescent health. *The Journal of Adolescent Health, 27*(5), 340–348.

Swanson, C.B. (2008). *Cities in crisis: A special analytic report on high school graduation.* Bethesda, MD: Editorial Projects in Education Research Center, April, 1.

Swanson, H.L., & Deshler, D. (2003). Instructing adolescents with learning disabilities: Converting a meta-analysis to practice. *Journal of Learning Disabilities, 36*(2), 124–135.

Swedeen, B.L., Carter, E.W., & Molfenter, N. (2010). Getting everyone involved: identifying transition opportunities for youth with severe disabilities. *Teaching Exceptional Children, 43*(2), 38–49.

Symonds, W.C., Schwartz, R.B., & Ferguson, R. (2011). *Pathways to prosperity: Meeting the challenge of preparing young Americans for the 21st century.* Report issued by the Pathways to Prosperity Project, Harvard Graduate School of Education, Wisconsin.

Taber, T.A., Alberto, P.A., Hughes, M., & Seltzer, A. (2002). A strategy for students with moderate disabilities when lost in the community. *Research & Practice for Persons with Severe Disabilities, 27,* 141–152.

Taber, T.A., Alberto, P.A., Seltzer, A., & Hughes, M. (2003). Obtaining assistance when lost in the community using cell phones. *Research and Practice for Persons with Severe Disabilities, 28,* 105–116.

Tanchak, T.L., & Sawyer, C. (1995). Augmentative communication. In K. Flippo, K. Inge, & J.M. Barcus (Eds.), *Assistive technology: A resource for school, work, and community* (pp. 57–79). Baltimore: Paul H. Brookes Publishing Co.

Tardif-Williams, C.Y, Owen, F., Feldman, M., Tarulli, D., Griffiths, D., Sales, C., et al. (2007). Comparison of interactive computer-based and classroom training on human rights awareness in persons with intellectual disabilities. *Education and Training in Developmental Disabilities, 42*(1), 48–58.

Targett, P., & Wehman, P. (2003). Successful work supports for persons with spinal cord injury. *Psychosocial Process,* 6–11.

Targett, P., & Wehman, P. (2009). Integrated employment. In P. Wehman, M.D. Smith, & C. Schall (Eds.), *Autism and the transition to adulthood: Success beyond the classroom.* (pp. 163–188). Baltimore: Paul H. Brookes Publishing Co.

Targett, P., & Wehman, P. (2011). Return to work after TBI: A supported employment approach. In I.Z. Schutz & E.S. Rogers (Eds.), *Work accommodation and retention in mental health* (pp. 277–294). New York: Springer.

Targett, P., Young, C., Revell, G., Williams, S., & Wehman, P. (2007). Customized employment in one stop career centers. *Teaching Exceptional Children, 40*(2), 6–11.

Tarleton, B., & Ward, L. (2005). Changes and choices: Finding out what information young people with learning disabilities, their parents and supporters need at transition. *British Journal of Learning Disabilities, 33,* 70–76.

Taylor, J.L., & Seltzer, M.M. (2011). Employment and post-secondary educational activities for young adults with autism spectrum disorders during the transition to adulthood. *Journal of Autism and Developmental Disorders, 41,* 566–574.

Technology-Related Assistance for Individuals with Disabilities Act of 1988, Pub. L. 100-407, 29 U.S.C. §§ 2201 *et seq.*

Tekgul, H., Serdaroglu, G., & Tutuncuoglu, S. (2003). Outcome of axonal and demyelinating forms of Guillain-Barré syndrome in children. *Pediatric Neurology, 28*(4), 295–299.

Tekin-Iftar, E. (2008). Parent-delivered community-based instruction with simultaneous prompting for teaching community skills to children with developmental disabilities. *Education and Training in Developmental Disabilities, 43*(2), 249–265.

Templeton, T., Neel, R.S., & Blood, E. (2008). Meta-analysis of math interventions for students with emotional and behavioral disorders, *Journal of Emotional and Behavioral Disorders, 16,* 226–239.

Test, D.W. (2008). Seamless transition for all. *Research and Practice for Persons with Severe Disabilities, 33*(3), 98–99.

Test, D.W. (2011). *Evidence-based instructional strategies for transition*. Baltimore: Paul H. Brookes Publishing Co.

Test, D.W., Browder, D.M., Karvonen, M., Wood, W., & Algozzine, B. (2002). Writing lesson plans for promoting self-determination. *Teaching Exceptional Children, 35*(1), 8–14.

Test, D.W., Fowler, C.H., Richter, S.M., White, J., Mazzotti, V., Walker, A.R., et al. (2009). Evidence-based practices in secondary transition. *Career Development for Exceptional Individuals, 32*, 115–128.

Test, D.W., Fowler, C.H., White, J., Richter, S., & Walker, A. (2009). Evidence-based secondary transition practices for enhancing school completion. *Exceptionality, 17*, 16–29.

Test, D.W., Karvonen, M., Wood, W.M., Browder, D., & Algozzine, B. (2000). Choosing a self-determination curriculum: Plan for the future. *Teaching Exceptional Children, 33*, 48–54.

Test, D.W., Mason, C., Hughes, C., Konrad, M., Neale, M., & Wood, W. (2004). Student involvement in individualized education program meetings. *Exceptional Children, 70*, 391–412.

Test, D.W., Mazzotti, V.L., Mustian, A.L., Fowler, C.H., Kortering, L., & Kohler, P. (2009). Evidence-based secondary transition predictors for improving postschool outcomes for students with disabilities. *Career Development for Exceptional Children, 32*, 160–181.

Test, D.W., & Spooner, F. (2005). Community based instructional support. In M.L. Wehmeyer & M. Agran (Eds.), *Mental retardation and intellectual disabilities: Teaching students using innovative and research-based strategies* (pp. 79–100). Boston: Pearson Custom Publishing.

Thoma, C., Bartholomew, C.C., & Scott, L.A. (2009). *Universal design for transition: A road map for planning and instruction*. Baltimore: Paul H. Brookes Publishing Co.

Thoma, C.A., & Getzel, E.E. (2005). "Self-determination is what it is all about": What post-secondary students with disabilities tell us are important considerations for success. *Education and Training in Developmental Disabilities, 40*, 234–242.

Thoma, C.A., Lakin, K.C., Carlson, D., Domzal, C., Austin, K., & Boyd, K. (2011). Participation in postsecondary education for students with intellectual disabilities: A review of the literature 2001–2010. *Journal of Postsecondary Education and Disability, 24*, 175–191.

Thoma, C.A., Pannozzo, G.M., Fritton, S.C., & Bartholomew, C.C. (2008). A qualitative study of preservice techers' understanding of self-determination for students with significant disabiltiies. *Career Development for Exceptional Individuals, 31*(2), 94–105.

Thoma, C.A., Saddler, S., Purvis, B., & Scott, L.A. (2010). Essentials of the student-directed IEP process. In C.A. Thoma & P. Wehman (Eds.), *Getting the most out of IEPs: An educator's guide to the student-directed approach* (pp. 1–23). Baltimore: Paul H. Brookes Publishing Co.

Thoma, C.A., & Wehman, P. (2010). *Getting the most out of IEPs: An educator's guide to the student-directed approach*. Baltimore: Paul H. Brookes Publishing Co.

Thoma, C.A., & Wehmeyer, M.L. (2005). Self-determination and the transition to postsecondary education. In E.E. Getzel & P. Wehman (Eds.), *Going to college: Expanding opportunities for people with disabilities* (pp. 49–68). Baltimore: Paul H. Brookes Publishing Co.

Thomas, S.B. (2000). College students and disability law. *Journal of Special Education, 33*(4), 248–257.

Thompson, J.R., Bradley, V., Buntinx, W.H.E., Schalock, R.L., Shogren, K.A., Snell, M.E. (2009). Conceptualizing supports and the support needs of people with intellectual disability. *Intellectual and Developmental Disabilities, 47*, 135–146.

Thurlow, M., & Johnson, D. (2000). High-stakes testing of students with disabilities. *Journal of Teacher Education, 51*, 305–314.

Thurlow, M.L. (2004). Biting the bullet: Including special-needs students in accountability systems. In S. Fuhrman & R. Elmore (Eds.), *Redesigning accountability systems for education*. New York: Columbia Teacher's College Press.

Ticket to Work and Work Incentives Improvement Act of 1999, Pub. L. 106-170, 42 U.S.C. 1305 *et seq.*

Tillery, C.Y., Werts, M.G., Roark, R., & Harris, S. (2003). Perceptions of paraeducators on job retention. *Teacher Education & Special Education, 26*(2), 118.

Tilly, D.M., & Haney, J.L. (2010, April). *Progressing monitoring for students with moderate to severe disabilities. Academic curriculum framework: Developmentally sequenced K-12+ core skills program.* Presentation at the Council for Exceptional Children Annual Conference and Expo, Nashville, TN. Retrieved from http://www.pcieducation.com/acf/

Tobias, J. (2003). Information technology and universal design: An agenda for accessible technology. *Journal of Visual Impairment and Blindness, 97*, 592–602.

Tomlinson, C. (1999). *The differentiated classroom: Responding to the needs of all learners.* Alexandria, VA: Association for Supervision and Curriculum Development.

Tomlinson, C. (2003). *Fulfilling the promise of the differentiated classroom: Tools and strategies for responsive teaching.* Alexandria, VA: Association for Supervision and Curriculum Development.

Tomlinson, C.A. (2001). *How to differentiate instruction in mixed-ability classrooms* (2nd ed.). Arlington, VA: Association for Supervision and Curriculum Development.

Trainor, A. (2005). Self-determination perceptions and behaviors of diverse students with LD during the transition planning process. *Journal of Learning Disabilities, 38*, 233–249.

Trainor, A.A. (2007a). Perceptions of adolescent girls with LD regarding self-determination and postsecondary transition planning. *Learning Disability Quarterly, 30,* 31–45.

Trainor, A.A. (2007b). Person-centered planning in two culturally distinct communities: Responding to divergent needs and preferences. *Career Development for Exceptional Individuals, 30*(2), 92–103.

Trainor, A.A. (2008). Using cultural and social capital theory to improve postsecondary outcomes and expand transition models for youth with disabilities. *The Journal of Special Education, 42,* 142–162.

Trainor, A.A., Carter, E.W., Swedeen, B., Cole, O., & Smith, S.A. (2011). Perspectives of adolescents with disabilities on employment and community experiences. *The Journal of Special Education, 45*(3), 157–170.

Trainor, A.A., Lindstrom, L., Simon-Burroughs, M., Martin, J.E., & Sorrells, A. (2008). From marginalized to maximized opportunities for diverse youth with disabilities: A position paper of the Division on Career Development and Transition. *Career Development for Exceptional Individuals, 31,* 56–64.

Troiano, P.F., Leifeld, J.A., & Trachtenberg, J.V. (2010). Academic support and college success for postsecondary students with learning disabilities. *Journal of College Reading and Learning, 40,* 35–44.

Tse, J., Strulovitch, J., Tagalakis, V., Meng, L., & Fombonne, E. (2007). Social skills training for adolescents with Asperger syndrome and high-functioning autism. *Journal of Autism and Developmental Disorders, 37,* 1960–1968. doi: 10.1007/s10803-006-0343-3

Turnbull, R., Turnbull, A., Shank, M., Smith, S., & Leal, D. (2001). Severe and multiple disabilities. In R. Turnbull, A. Turnball, M. Shank, S. Smith, & D. Leal (Eds.), *Exceptional lives: Special education in today's schools* (4th ed., pp. 300–334). Upper Saddle River, NJ: Prentice Hall.

Turner, E. (2007a, August). Finding a workplace personal assistant. *PAS Facts, 2.* Retrieved June 15, 2011, from http://www.worksupport.com/documents/PASFACTSVol2.pdf

Turner, E. (2007b, August). Personal assistance services. *PAS Facts, 1.* Retrieved June 15, 2011, from http://www.worksupport.com/documents/PASFACTSVol1.pdf

U.S. Bureau of Labor Statistics. (2009). *Employment projections: 2008-2018 Summary.* Retrieved May 6, 2011, from http://www.bls.gov/news.release/ecopro.nr0.htm

U.S. Census Bureau. (2005). *Disability and American families: 2000.* Available: http://www.census.gov/prod/2005pubs/censr-23.pdf

U.S. Department of Education. (2001). *Twenty-third annual report to Congress on the implementation of the Individuals With Disabilities Education Act.* Washington, DC: Author.

U.S. Department of Education. (2002). *Evidence-based education.* Presented at the Student Achievement and School Accountability Conference. Retrieved from http://www.ed.gov/nclb/methods/whatworks/eb/edlite-slide003.html

U.S. Department of Education. (2003). Title I-Improving the Academic Achievement of the Disadvantaged; Final Rule, 68 *Federal Registry* 268 (December 9, 2003) (codified at 34 C.R.F. pt. 200).

U.S. Department of Education. (2007a). *Final regulations on modified academic achievement standards.* Retrieved from http://www.ed.gov/policy/speced/guid/modachieve-summary.html

U.S. Department of Education. (2007b). *High school coursetaking: Findings from The Condition of Education 2007.* Retrieved from http://nces.ed.gov/pubsearch/pubsinfo.asp?pubid=2007065

U.S. Department of Education. (2008, October). *A uniform, comparable, graduation rate: How the final regulations for Title I hold schools, districts, and states accountable for improving graduation rates.* Retrieved from http://www2.ed.gov/policy/elsec/reg/proposal/uniform-grad-rate.html

U.S. Department of Education. (2009). *Race to the Top Fund.* Available from http://www2.ed.gov/programs/racetothetop/index.html

U.S. Department of Education. (2010a). *National Education Technology Plan.* Retrieved from http://www.ed.gov/technology/netp-2010/executive-summary

U.S. Department of Education. (2010b). *U.S. Secretary of Education announces winners of competition to improve student assessments.* Available from http://www.ed.gov/news/press-releases/us-secretary-education-duncan-announces-winners-competition-improve-student-asse

U.S. Department of Education. (2011, April 1). *Statement by Assistant Secretary Alexa Posny on the Fourth Annual World Autism Awareness Day on Saturday, April 2.* Retrieved June 15, 2011, from http://www.ed.gov/news/press-releases/statement-assistant-secretary-alexa-posny-fourth-annual-world-autism-awareness-d

U.S. Department of Education, National Center for Education Statistics. (2002). *Characteristics of the 100 largest public elementary and secondary school districts in the United States: 2000-01.* NCES 2002-351. Washington, DC: Author.

U.S. Department of Education, National Center for Education Statistics. (2007). *Digest of education statistics.* NCES 2007-017. Washington, DC: author.

U.S. Department of Education, National Center for Education Statistics. (2009). *Percentage distribution of undergraduate students by citizenship and disability: Preliminary condition or impairment. 2007–2008 National Postsecondary Student Aid Survey.* Washington, DC: Author.

U.S. Department of Education, Office for Civil Rights. (2007). *Students with disabilities preparing for postsecondary education: Know your rights and responsibilities.* Washington DC: Author. Retrieved on June 6, 2011, from http://www.ed.gov/ocr

U.S. Department of Education, Office for Civil Rights. (2011). *Frequently asked questions about the June 29, 2010, Dear Colleague letter.* Washington, DC: Author. Retrieved on June 8, 2011, from http://www2.ed.gov/about/offices/list/ocr/docs/dcl-ebook-faq-201105.pdf

U.S. Department of Education, Office of Educational Technology. (2010). *Transforming American education: Learning powered by technology, National Education Technology Plan 2010.* Retrieved on June 29, 2011, from http://www.ed.gov/technology/netp-2010

U.S. Department of Education, Office of Special Education Programs, Data Analysis System, OMB #1820-0517: *Part B, Individuals with Disabilities Education Act, implementation of FAPE requirements, 2010.* Data updated as of July 15, 2011. Retrieved from https://www.ideadata.org/arc_toc12.asp#partbLRE

U.S. Department of Education, Office of Special Education Programs, Data Analysis System. OMB # 1820-0521: *Children with disabilities exiting special education, 1995–96 through 2004–05.* Data updated as of July 17, 2006.

U.S. Department of Education, Office of Special Education and Rehabilitative Services. (2010). *Thirty-five years of progress in educating children with disabilities through IDEA.* Retrieved December 30, 2011, from http://www2.ed.gov/about/offices/list/osers/idea35/history/idea-35-history.pdf

U.S. Department of Education, Office of Special Education and Rehabilitative Services, Office of Special Education Programs. (2005). *25th annual (2003) report to Congress on the implementation of the Individuals with Disabilities Education Act, 2003,* Vol. 1, Washington, DC: Author.

U.S. Department of Education, Office of Special Education and Rehabilitative Services, Office of Special Education Programs. (2010). *29th annual report to Congress on the implementation of the Individuals with Disabilities Education Act, 2007,* Vol. 1, Washington, DC: Author.

U.S. Department of Education, Office of Special Education and Rehabilitative Services, Office of Special Education Programs. (2007). *27th annual (2005) report to Congress on the implementation of the Individuals with Disabilities Education Act,* Vol. 2, Washington, DC: author.

U.S. Department of Labor. (2010). *Labor force statistics from the Current Population Survey: How the government measures unemployment.* Available from http://www.bls.gov/cps/cps_htgm.htm

U.S. Department of Labor. (2011). *Youth employment rate.* Retrieved May 12, 2011, from http://www.dol.gov/odep/categories/youth/youthemployment.htm

U.S. Department of Labor, Bureau of Labor Statistics. National Longitudinal Survey of Youth 1997. 2001 youth survey, responses for 17- to 21-year-olds.

U.S. Department of Labor, Bureau of Labor Statistics [press release]. (2011). [Table displaying national unemployment rates 2008–2011]. *National Employment Monthly Update.* Go13307. Retrieved from http://www.ncsl.org/?tabid=13307

U.S. Department of Labor, Office of Disability Employment Policy. (n.d.). *Customized employment Q and A.* Retrieved from http://www.worksupport.com/research/viewContent.cfm/502

U.S. Equal Employment Opportunity Commission. *Workers with intellectual disabilities abused by Texas-based company for years, EEOC charges* [EEOC press release]. Retrieved from http://www.eeoc.gov/eeoc/newsroom/release/4-6-11b.cfm or http://www.eeoc.gov

U.S. Government Accountability Office. (2009). *Higher education and disability: Education needs a coordinated approach to improve its assistance to schools in supporting students. Report to the chairman, Committee on Education and Labor, House of Representatives. GAO-10-33.* Washington, DC: Author. Retrieved from http://ezproxy.lib.ucf.edu/login?URL=http://search.ebscohost.com/login.aspx?direct=true&db=eric&AN=ED506945&site=ehost-live

U.S. Senate. (2005). *Report on federal programs for employment of persons with disabilities. Report of the Chairman, Committee on Health, Education, Labor and Pensions.* Washington, DC: Author. Retrieved from http://www.randolph-sheppard.org/legis/chairman-report.pdf

Unger, D. (2001). *National study of employers' experiences with workers with disabilities and their knowledge and utilization of accommodations* (doctoral dissertation). Retrieved from Dissertations and Theses database, Virginia Commonwealth University.

Unger, D. (2002). Employers' attitudes towards people with disabilities in the workforce: Myths or realities? *Focus on Autism and Other Developmental Disabilities, 17,* 2–10.

Unger, D.D., Campbell, L.R., & McMahon, B.T. (2005). Workplace discrimination and mental retardation: The national EEOC ADA Research Project. *Journal of Vocational Rehabilitation, 23*(3), 145–154.

University of Wisconsin. (2011). *Vocational rehabilitation outcomes: A multi-level analysis of economic indicators, VR agency characteristics, and RSA-211 data.* (Phase I Report). Madison, WI: Rehabilitation Research and Training Center, Effective VR Service Delivery Practices.

Unruh, D.K., Waintrup, M., Canter, T., & Smith, S. (2009). Improving the transition outcomes of adolescent young offenders. In H.B. Clark & D. Unruh (Eds.), *Transition of youth and young adults with emotional or behavioral difficulties.* Baltimore: Paul H. Brookes Publishing Co.

Usiak, D.J., Stone, V.I., House, R.B., & Montgomery, M.E. (2004). Stakeholder perceptions of an effective CIL. *Journal of Vocational Rehabilitation, 20*(1), 35–43.

Utley, C.A., Mortweet, S.L., & Greenwood, C.R. (1997). *Peer-mediated instruction and interventions: Focus on exceptional children.* Denver, CO: Love.

Valdes, K., Godard, P., Williamson, C., Van Campen, J., McCracken, M., Jones, R., et al. (2006). *National Longitudinal Transition Study-2 (NLTS2): Waves 1 and 2 data documentation and dictionary* (Vol. 2). Menlo Park, CA: SPR International.

Valenzuela, R.L., & Martin, J.E. (2005). Self-directed IEP: Bridging values of diverse cultures and secondary education. *Career Development for Exceptional Individuals, 28*(1), 4–14.

Vallas, R. (2009). The disproportionality problem: The overrepresentation of black students in special education and recommendations for reform. *Virginia Journal of Social Policy & The Law, 17,* 181–208.

Van Acker, R. (2010). Perspectives on services for students with emotional disabilities: a cause for concern. Summit on Better Serving Students with Emotional Disabilities, Sponsored by the Virginia Department of Education, August 23, 2010, Charlottesville, Virginia.

Van Dycke, J.V., Martin, J.E., & Lovett, D.L. (2006). Why is this cake on fire? Inviting students into the IEP process. *Teaching for Exceptional Children, 38*(3) 42–47.

Van Gelder, N., Sitlington, P.L., & Pugh, K.M. (2008). Perceived self-determination of youth with emotional and behavior disorders: A pilot study of the effect of different educational environments. *Journal of Disability Policy Studies, 19,* 182–190.

Van Reusen, A.K., Bos, C.S., Schumaker, J.B., & Deshler, D.D. (2002). *The self-advocacy strategy for education and transition planning.* Lawrence, KS: Edge Enterprises.

Van Reusen, A.K., Deshler, D.D., & Schumaker, J.B. (1989). Effects of a student participation strategy in facilitating the involvement of adolescents with learning disabilities in individualized education program planning process. *Learning Disabilities, 1,* 23–34.

Vaughn, S., Klingner, J.K., & Hughes, M.T. (2004). Sustainability of research based practices: Implications for students with disabilities. In A.M. Sorrells, H.J. Reith, & P.J. Sindelar (Eds.), *Critical issues in special education* (pp. 135–153). Boston: Allyn & Bacon.

Verdonschot, M.L., de Witte, L., Reichrath, E., Buntinx, W.E., & Curfs, L.G. (2009). Community participation of people with an intellectual disability: a review of empirical findings. *Journal of Intellectual Disability Research, 53*(4), 303–318.

Virginia Assistive Technology System. (2001). A resource guide to assistive technology funding. Richmond, VA: Department of Rehabilitation Counseling. Retrieved May 15, 2011, from http://www.vats.org/atfunding.htm

Virginia Commonwealth University, Benefits Assistance Resource Center. (2012). *Plans for achieving self support briefing paper.* Richmond, VA: Virginia Commonwealth University.

Virginia Department of Education. (October 2010). *Autism Spectrum Disorders and the Transition to Adulthood.* Richmond, VA: Author.

Virginia Department of Education. (2011a). *I'm determined. My good day plan.* Retrieved March 30, 2011, from http://www.imdetermined. org

Virginia Department of Education. (2011b). *I'm determined. Student involvement in the IEP.* Retrieved June 14, 2011, from http://www. imdetermined.org

Vocational Rehabilitation Act of 1918. Pub. L. 65-178. Retrieved from http://www.va.gov/ op3/docs/ProgramEvaluations/DisComp Program/Disability_Comp_Legislative_ Histor_Lit_Review.pdf.

Wagner, M. (2003). An overview of the school programs of secondary students with disabilities. In M. Wagner, L. Newman, R. Cameto, P. Levine, & C. Marder (2003). *Going to school: Instructional contexts, programs, and participation of secondary school students with disabilities. A report from the National Longitudinal Transition Study-2 (NLTS2).* Menlo Park, CA: SRI International. Retrieved from http://www.nlts2. org/reports/2003_12/nlts2_report_2003_12_ch4. pdf

Wagner, M., Cadwallader, T., & Marder, C. (2003). *Life outside the classroom for youth with disabilities.* Menlo Park, CA: SRI International.

Wagner, M., Cameto, R., & Newman, L. (2003). *Youth with disabilities: A changing population: A report of findings from the National Longitudinal Transition Study (NLTS) and the National Longitudinal Transition Study-2 (NLTS2).* Menlo Park, CA: SRI International.

Wagner, M. & Davis, M. (2006). How are we preparing students with emotional disturbances for the transition to young adulthood?: Findings from the National Longitudinal Transition Study—2. *Journal of Emotional and Behavioral Disorder, 14,* 86–98.

Wagner, M., Friend, M., Bursuck, W., Kutash, K., Duchnowski, A., Sumi, W., et al. (2006). Educating students with emotional disturbances: A national perspective on school programs and services. *Journal of Emotional and Behavioral Disorders, 14,* 12–30.

Wagner, M., Marder, C., Blackorby, J., Cameto, R., Newman, L., Levine, P., et al. (2003). *The achievements of youth with disabilities during secondary school.* Menlo Park, CA: SRI International.

Wagner, M., Newman, L., & Cameto, R. (2004). *Changes over time in the secondary school experiences of students with disabilities. A report of findings from the National Longitudinal Transition Study (NLTS) and the National Longitudinal Transition Study-2 (NLTS2).* Menlo Park, CA: SRI International. Available at http://www. nlts2.org/pdfs/ changestime_compreport.pdf

Wagner, M., Newman, L., Cameto, R., Garza, N., & Levine, P. (2005). *After high school: A first look at the postschool experiences of youth with disabilities: A report from the National Longitudinal Transition Study-2 (NLTS-2).* Menlo Park, CA: SRI International.

Wagner, M., Newman, L., Cameto, R., & Levine, P. (2005). *Changes over time in the early postschool outcomes of youth with disabilities. A report of findings from the National Longitudinal Transition Study (NLTS) and the National Longitudinal Transition Study-2 (NLTS2).* Menlo Park, CA: SRI International. Available at: http://www.nlts2.org/reports/2005_06/nlts2_report_2005_06_complete.pdf

Wagner, M., Newman, L., Cameto, R., Levine, P., & Marder, C. (2003). *Going to school: Instructional contexts, programs, and participation of secondary school students with disabilities.* Menlo Park, CA: SRI International. Available from http://www.nlts2.org/reports/2003_12/index.html

Wagner, M., Newman, L., Cameto, R., Levine, P., & Marder, C. (2007). *Perceptions and expectations of youth with disabilities.* Menlo Park, CA: SRI International.

Walker, A.R., Uphold, N.M., Richter, S., & Test, D.W. (2010). Review of the literature on community-based instruction across grade levels. *Education and Training in Autism and Developmental Disabilities, 45*(2), 242–267.

Walker, H.M., & Gresham, E.M. (1997). Making schools safer and violence free. *Intervention in School and Clinic, 32,* 199–204.

Walker, H.M., Ramsey, E., & Gresham, F.M. (2004). *Antisocial behavior in school: Evidence-based practices* (2nd ed.). Belmont, CA: Wadsworth.

Wallace, J., & Neal, S. (1993). *Special topic report: Funding assistive technology.* Richmond, VA: Virginia Assistive Technology System.

Wallace, P., & Rogan, P. (2007). *Make the day matter: Promoting typical lifestyles for adults with significant disabilities.* Baltimore: Paul H. Brookes Publishing Co.

Wallace, T., Shin, J., Bartholomay, T., & Stahl, B.J. (2001). Knowledge and skills for teachers supervising the work of paraprofessionals. *Exceptional Children, 67*(4), 520–533.

Waller, K.S., Houchins, D.E., & Nomvete, P.T. (2010). Establishing a school-based mentoring program for youth who are transition from a secure facility. *Beyond Behavior, 19,* 30–35.

Walsh, J.M., & Jones, B. (2004, May/June). New models of cooperative teaching. *Exceptional Children, 36*(5), 14–20.

Wandry, D.L., & Pleet, A.M. (2009). *Engaging and empowering families in secondary transition: A practitioners guide* (pp. 66–69). Arlington, VA: Council for Exceptional Children.

Wang, P., & Michaels, C.A. (2009). Chinese families of children with severe disabilities: Family needs and available support. *Research and Practice for Persons with Severe Disabilities, 34*(2), 21–32.

Ward, A., & Russell, A. (2007). Mental health services for adults with autism spectrum disorders. *Advances in Mental Health and Intellectual Disabilities, 1*(4), 23–26.

Ward, M.J. (1996). Coming of age in the age of self-determination: A historical and personal perspective. In D.J. Sands & M.L. Wehmeyer (Eds.), *Self-determination across the life span: Independence and choice for people with disabilities* (pp. 3–16). Baltimore: Paul H. Brookes Publishing Co.

Ward, T., Van De Mark, C.A., & Ryndak, D.L. (2006). Balanced literacy classrooms and embedded instruction for students with severe disabilities: Literacy for all in the age of school reform. In D.M. Browder & F. Spooner (Eds.), *Teaching language arts, math, & science to students with significant cognitive disabilities* (pp. 125–169). Baltimore: Paul H. Brookes Publishing Co.

Warnock, M. (2005). *Special educational needs: A new look. Impact No. 11.* London: Philosophy of Education Society of Great Britain.

Warren, S.F., Fey, M.E., & Yoder, P.J. (2007). Differential treatment intensity research: A missing link to creating optimally effective community interventions. *Mental Retardation and Developmental Disabilities Research Reviews, 13*(1), 70–77.

Watanabe, M., & Sturmey, P. (2003). The effect of choice-making opportunities during activity schedules on task engagement of adults with autism. *Journal of Autism and Developmental Disorders, 33,* 535–538.

Weaver, R., Landers, M.F., & Adams, S. (1991). Making curriculum functional: Special education and beyond. *Intervention in School and Clinic, 26,* 284–287.

Webb, K.W., Patterson, K.B., Syverud, S.M., & Seabrooks-Blackmore, J.J. (2008). Evidence based practices that promote transition to postsecondary education: Listening to a decade of expert voices. *Exceptionality, 16,* 192–206.

Webber, J., & Plotts, C. (2008). *Emotional and behavioral disorders: Theory and practice.* Boston: Pearson, Allyn, Bacon, Inc.

Wehby, J.H., Lane, K.L., & Falk, K.B. (2003). Academic instruction for students with emotional and behavioral disorders. *Journal of Emotional and Behavioral Disorders, 11,* 194–197.

Wehman, P. (1981). *Competitive employment: New horizons for severely disabled individuals.* Baltimore: Paul H. Brookes Publishing Co.

Wehman, P. (2002a). A new era: Revitalizing special education for children and their families. *Focus on Autism and Other Developmental Disabilities, 17*(4), 194–197.

Wehman, P. (2002b). *Individual transition plans: The teacher's curriculum guide for helping youth with special needs* (2nd ed.). Austin, TX: PRO-ED.

Wehman, P. (2005). Students with low incidence disabilities. In J. Wood (Ed.), *Adapting instruction in accommodating students in inclusive settings* (5th ed., pp. 56–87). Upper Saddle River, NJ: Prentice Hall.

Wehman, P. (2006a). *Life beyond the classroom: Transition strategies for young people with disabilities,* (4th ed.). Baltimore: Paul H. Brookes Publishing Co.

Wehman, P. (2006b). Individualized transition planning: Putting self-determination into action. In P. Wehman (Ed.), *Life beyond the classroom: Transition strategies for young people with disabilities* (pp. 71–96). Baltimore: Paul H. Brookes Publishing Co.

Wehman, P. (2011a). *Essentials of transition planning.* Baltimore: Paul H. Brookes Publishing Co.

Wehman, P. (2011b). Individual and community transition planning. In *Essentials of transition planning* (pp. 26–28). Baltimore: Paul H. Brookes Publishing Co.

Wehman, P., Brooke, V., & Green, H. (2004). *Public private partnerships: A model for success.* Richmond: Virginia Commonwealth University Rehabilitation Research and Training Center on Workplace Supports and Job Retention.

Wehman, P., Brooke, V., Green, H., Hewett, M., & Tipton, M. (2008). Public/private partnerships and employment of people with developmental disabilities: Preliminary evidence from a pilot project. *Journal of Vocational Rehabilitation, 28*(1), 53–66.

Wehman, P., Brooke, V., & Revell, G. (2007). Real work for real pay: Inclusive employment: Rolling back segregation of people with disabilities. In P. Wehman, K. Inge, G. Revell, & V. Brooke (Eds.), *Real work for real pay* (pp. 3–18). Baltimore: Paul H. Brookes Publishing Co.

Wehman, P., & Getzel, E.E. (2005). *Going to college: Expanding opportunities for people with disabilities.* Baltimore: Paul H. Brookes Publishing Co.

Wehman, P., Goodwin, M., McNamee, S., & Targett, P. (2011). Return to work after a traumatic brain injury. In F. Zollman (Ed.), *Manual of traumatic brain injury management.* New York: Demos Medical.

Wehman, P., Hill, J.W., & Koehler, F. (1979). Placement of developmentally disabled individuals into competitive employment: Three case studies. *Education and Training of the Mentally Retarded, 14,* 269–276.

Wehman, P., Inge, K.J., Revell, W.G., & Brooke, V.A. (2007a). *Real work for real pay: Inclusive employment for people with disabilities.* Baltimore: Paul H. Brookes Publishing Co.

Wehman, P., Inge, K.J., Revell, W.G., & Brooke, V.A. (2007b). *Supported employment and workplace supports: Overview and background.* In P. Wehman, K.J. Inge, W.G. Revell, Jr., & V.A. Brooke (Eds.), *Real work for real pay: Inclusive employment for people with disabilities* (pp. 117–138). Baltimore: Paul H. Brookes Publishing Co.

Wehman, P., & Kregel, J. (2004). *Functional curriculum for elementary, middle, and secondary age students with special needs* (2nd ed.). Austin, TX: PRO-ED.

Wehman, P., & Kregel, J. (2011). *Functional curriculum for elementary, middle, & secondary age students with special needs* (3rd ed.). Austin, TX: PRO-ED.

Wehman, P., McDonough, J., Molinelli, A., Schall, C., Riehle, E., & Ham, W. (in press). Project SEARCH® for youth with autism spectrum disorders: Increasing competitive employment upon transition from high school. *Teaching Exceptional Children.*

Wehman, P., McDonough, J., Schall, C., Molinelli, A., & Riehle, E. (in press). Project SEARCH® implementation at high school level for youth with autism. Submitted to *Teaching Exceptional Children.*

Wehman, P., Revell, W.G., & Brooke, V. (2003). Competitive employment: Has it become the "first choice" yet? *Journal of Disability Policy Studies, 14*(3), 163–173.

Wehman, P., Smith, M., & Schall, C. (2009). *Autism and the transition to adulthood: Success beyond the classroom.* Baltimore: Paul H. Brookes Publishing Co.

Wehman, P., & Thoma, C. (2006). Teaching for transition. In P. Wehman (Ed.), *Life beyond the classroom: Transition strategies for young people with disabilities* (4th Ed., pp. 201–236). Baltimore: Paul H. Brookes Publishing Co.

Wehman, P., & Wittig, K. (2009). *Transition IEPs. A curriculum guide for teachers planning and designing transition programs* (3rd ed.). Austin, TX: PRO-ED.

Wehmeyer, M. (1992). Self-determination and the education of students with mental retardation. *Education and Training in Mental Retardation, 27,* 302–314.

Wehmeyer, M.L. (1996). A self-report measure of self-determination for adolescents with cognitive disabilities. *Education and Training in Mental Retardation and Developmental Disabilities, 31,* 282–293.

Wehmeyer, M.L. (2002). Assessment in self-determination: Guiding instruction and transition planning. *Assessment for Effective Intervention, 26*(4), 41–50.

Wehmeyer, M.L. (2004). Self-determination and the empowerment of people with disabilities. *American Rehabilitation, 28,* 22–29.

Wehmeyer, M.L. (2005). Self-determination and individuals with severe disabilities: Reexamining meanings and misinterpretations. *Research and Practice for Persons with Severe Disabilities, 30,* 113–120.

Wehmeyer, M.L. (2006a). Beyond access: Ensuring progress in the general education curriculum for students with severe disabilities. *Research and Practice for Persons with Severe Disabilities, 31*(4), 322–326.

Wehmeyer, M.L. (2006b). Universal design for learning, access to the general education curriculum and students with mild mental retardation. *Exceptionality, 14*(4), 225–235.

Wehmeyer, M.L., Abery, B., Mithaug, D.E., & Stancliffe, R.J. (2003). *Theory in self-determination: Foundations for educational practice.* Springfield, IL: Charles C Thomas Publisher.

Wehmeyer, M.L., Agran, M., & Hughes, C. (2000). A national survey of teachers' promotion of self-determination and student-directed learning. *Journal of Special Education, 34,* 58–68.

Wehmeyer, M.L., Agran, M., Hughes, C., Martin, J., Mithaug, D.E., & Palmer, S. (2007a). *Promoting self-determination in students with intellectual and developmental disabilities.* New York: Guilford Press.

Wehmeyer, M.L., & Bolding, N. (1999). Self-determination across living and working environments: A matched-samples study of adults with mental retardation. *Mental Retardation, 37,* 353–363.

Wehmeyer, M.L., & Bolding, N. (2001). Enhanced self-determination of adults with intellectual disabilities as an outcome of moving to community-based work or living environments. *Journal of Intellectual Disabilities Research, 45,* 371–383.

Wehmeyer, M.L., & Field, S. (2007b). *Self-determination: Instructional and assessment strategies.* Thousand Oaks, CA: Corwin Press.

Wehmeyer, M.L., Field, S., Doren, B., Jones, B., & Mason, C. (2004). Self-determination and student involvement in standards-based reform. *Exceptional Children, 70*(4), 413–425.

Wehmeyer, M.L., Garner, N., Lawrence, M., Yeager, D., & Davis, A.K. (2006). Infusing self-determination into 18-21 services for students with intellectual or developmental disabilities: A multi-stage, multiple component model. *Education and Training in Developmental Disabilities, 41,* 3–13.

Wehmeyer, M.L., & Gragoudas, S. (2004). Centers for independent living and transition-age youth: Empowerment and self-determination. *Journal of Vocational Rehabilitation, 20*(1), 53–58.

Wehmeyer, M.L., Gragoudas, S., & Shogren, K. (2006). Self determination, student involvement, and leadership development. In P. Wehman (Ed.), *Life beyond the classroom* (4th ed). Baltimore: Paul H. Brookes Publishing Co.

Wehmeyer, M.L., & Kelchner, K. (1995). *The Arc's Self-Determination Scale.* Arlington, TX: The Arc National Headquarters.

Wehmeyer, M.L., Lance, G.D., & Bashinski, S. (2002). Promoting access to the general curriculum for students with mental retardation: A multi-level model. *Education and Training in Mental Retardation and Developmental Disabilities, 37*(3), 223–234.

Wehmeyer, M.L., Lattin, D., & Agran, M. (2001). Achieving access to the general education curriculum for students with mental retardation: A curriculum decision-making model. *Education and Training in Mental Retardation and Developmental Disabilities, 36,* 327–342.

Wehmeyer, M.L., Lattin, D., Lapp-Rincker, G., & Agran, M. (2003). Access to the general education curriculum of middle school students with mental retardation: An observational study. *Remedial and Special Education, 24,* 262–272.

Wehmeyer, M.L., & Lawrence, M. (1995). Whose future is it anyway? Promoting student involve-ment in transition planning. *Career Development for Exceptional Individuals, 18,* 69–83.

Wehmeyer, M.L., Lawrence, M., Kelchner, K., Palmer, S., Garner, N., & Soukup, J. (2004). *Whose future is it anyway? A student-directed transition planning process* (2nd ed.). Lawrence, KS: Beach Center on Disability.

Wehmeyer, M.L., & Palmer, S.B. (2003). Adult outcomes for students with cognitive disabilities three years after high school: The impact of self-determination. *Education and Training in Developmental Disabilities, 38,* 131–144.

Wehmeyer, M.L., Palmer, S.B., Agran, M., Mithaug, D.E., & Martin, J.E. (2000). Promoting causal agency: The Self-Determined Learning Model of Instruction. *Exceptional Children, 66*(4), 439–453.

Wehmeyer, M.L., Palmer, S.B., Lee, Y., Williams-Diehm, K., &Shogren, K.A. (2011). A randomized-trial evaluation of the effect of *Whose future is it anyway?* on self-determination. *Career Development for Exceptional Individuals, 34*(1), 45–56.

Wehmeyer, M.L., Palmer, S.B., Shogren, K., Williams-Diehm, K., & Soukup, J. (2010). Establishing a causal relationship between interventions to promote self-determination and enhanced student self-determination. *Journal of Special Education.* doi: 10.1177/0022 466910392377.

Wehmeyer, M.L., Palmer, S.B., Smith, S.J., Parent, W., Davies, D.K., et al. (2006). Technology use by people with intellectual and developmental disabilities to support employment activities: A single-subject design meta analysis. *Journal of Vocational Rehabilitation, 24,* 81–86.

Wehmeyer, M.L., & Schwartz, M. (1997). Self-determination and positive adult outcomes. A follow-up study of youth with mental retardation or learning disabilities. *Exceptional Children, 63*(2), 245–255.

Wehmeyer, M.L., & Schwartz, M. (1998). The relationship between self-determination and quality of life for adults with mental retardation. *Education and Training in Mental Retardation and Developmental Disabilities, 33*(1), 3–12.

Wehmeyer, M.L., Shogren, K., Palmer, S., Williams-Diehm, K., Little, T., & Boulton, A. (in press). Impact of the Self-Determined Learning Model of Instruction on student self-determination: A randomized-trial placebo control group study. *Exceptional Children.*

Wehmeyer, M.L., Shogren, K.A., Zager, D., Smith, T.E.C., & Simpson, R. (2010). Research-based principles and practices for educating students with autism spectrum disorders: Self-determination and social interactions. *Education and Training in Autism and Developmental Disabilities, 45*(4), 475–486.

Weiner, H.M. (2003). Effective inclusion: Professional development in the context of the classroom. *Teaching Exceptional Children, 35*(6), 12–18.

West, M., & Anderson, J. (2005). Telework and employees with disabilities: Accommodations and funding options. *Journal of Vocational Rehabilitation, 23,* 115–122.

West, M.D., Wehman, P.B., & Wehman, P. (2005). Competitive employment outcomes for persons with intellectual and developmental disabilities: The national impact of the Best Buddies Job Program. *Journal of Vocational Rehabilitation, 23*(1), 51–63.

Westerlund, D., Granucci, E.A., Gamache, P., & Clark, H.B. (2006). Effects of peer mentors on work-related performance of adolescents with behavioral and/or learning disabilities. *Journal of Positive Behavioral Interventions, 8,* 244–251. doi: 10.1177/10983007060080040601

West-Evans, K. (2006). *Imagine the possibilities: VR's future with consumers and businesses.* Retrieved from http://www.rehabnetwork.org/busrel/presentations/archive/2006/NC_2006.pdf

Wheeler, J. (2006). *Community-based vocational training.* Verona, WI: Attainment Co.

Wheless, J.W., Clarke, D.F., & Carpenter, D. (2005). Treatment of pediatric epilepsy: Expert opinion, 2005. *Journal of Child Neurology, 20* (Suppl 1), S1–S56.

Whelley, T.A., Radtke, R., Burgstahler, S., & Christ, T.W. (2003). Mentors, advisers, role models, and peer supporters: Career development relationships and individuals with disabilities. *American Rehabilitation, 27*(1), 42–49.

Whitbread, K.M., Bruder, M.B., Fleming, G., & Park, H.J. (2007). Collaboration in special education: Parent-professional training. *Teaching Exceptional Children, 39*(4), 6–14.

White, N.A., & Loeber, R. (2008). Bullying and special education as predictors of serious delinquency. *Journal of Research in Crime and Delinquency, 45,* 380–397.

White, S.W., Ollendick, T.H., & Bray, B.C. (2011). College students on the autism spectrum: Prevalence and associated problems. *Autism, 15,* 683–701.

Whitman, T.L. (1990). Self-regulation and mental retardation. *American Journal on Mental Retardation, 94*(4), 347–362.

Wiggins, G., & McTighe, J. (2005). *Understanding by design* (2nd ed.). Alexandria, VA: Association for Supervision and Curriculum Development.

Wigham, S., Robertson, J., Emerson, E., Hatton, C., Elliott, J., McIntosh, B., et al. (2008). Reported goal setting and benefits of person centered planning for people with intellectual disabilities. *Journal of Intellectual Disabilities, 12,*143–153.

Wilder, L.K., Ashbaker, B.Y., Obiakor, F.E., & Rotz, E.J. (2006). Building multicultural transitions for ethnically diverse learners with disabilities. *Multiple Voices, 9*(1), 22–33.

Will, M. (1983). *OSERS programming for the transition of youth with disabilities: Bridges from school to working life.* Washington, DC: Office of Special Education and Rehabilitative Services.

Williams-Diehm, K., & Benz, M.R. (2008). Where are they now? Lessons from a single school district follow-up study. *Journal for Vocational Special Needs Education, 30*(2), 4–15.

Williams-Diehm, K., Palmer, S., Lee, Y., & Schroer, H. (2010). Goal content analysis for middle and high school students with disabilities. *Career Development for Exceptional Individuals, 33*(3), 132–142.

Williams-Diehm, K., Wehmeyer, M.L., Palmer, S., Soukup, J.H., & Garner, N. (2008). Self-determination and student involvement in transition planning: A multivariate analysis. *Journal on Developmental Disabilities, 14,* 25–36.

Williamson, R.L., Robertson, J.S., & Casey, L.B. (2010). Using a dynamic systems approach to investigating post-secondary education and employment outcomes for transitioning students with disabilities. *Journal of Vocational Rehabilitation, 33,* 101–111.

Wilson, K., Getzel, E., & Brown, T. (2000). Enhancing the post-secondary campus climate for students with disabilities. *Journal of Vocational Rehabilitation, 14*(1), 37–50.

Wilson, M. (2008). *Math course taking and achievement among secondary students with disabilities: Exploring the gap in achievement between students with and without disabilities.* Unpublished doctoral dissertation, University of Maryland, College Park.

Winsor, J., & Butterworth, J. (2008). Participation in integrated employment and community based nonwork services for individuals supported by state disability agencies. *Intellectual and Developmental Disabilities, 46,* 166–168.

Wittenburg, D., Golden, T., & Fishman, M. (2002). Transition options for youth with disabilities: An overview of the programs and polices that affect the transition from school. *Journal of Vocational Rehabilitation, 17,* 195–206.

Wittenburg, D.C., & Maag, E. (2002). School to where? A literature review on economic outcomes of youth with disabilities. *Journal of Vocational Rehabilitation, 17,* 265–280.

Wittig, K.M. (2009). *Transition IEPs, A curriculum guide for teachers and transition practitioners* (pp. 9–10). Austin, TX: PRO-ED.

Wolman, J., Campeau, P., Dubois, P., Mithaug, D., & Stolarski, V. (1994). *AIR Self-Determination Scale and user guide.* Palo Alto, CA: American Institute for Research.

Womack, S.A., Marchant, M., & Borders, D. (2011). Literature-based social skills instruction: A strategy for students with learning disabilities. *Intervention in School and Clinic, 46*(3), 157–164.

Wood, W. (1988). Supported employment for persons with physical and intellectual disabilities. In P. Wehman & M.S. Moon (Eds.), *Vocational rehabilitation and supported employment* (p. 341–363). Baltimore: Paul H. Brookes Publishing Co.

Wood, W.M., Karvonen, M., Test, D.W., Browder, D., & Algozzine, B. (2004). Promoting student self-determination skills in IEP planning. *Teaching Exceptional Children, 36*(3), 8–16.

Woods, L.L., & Martin, J.E. (2004). Improving supervisor evaluations through the use of self-determination contracts. *Career Development for Exceptional Individuals, 27,* 207–220.

Woods, L.L., Sylvester, L., & Martin, J.E. (2010). Student-directed transition planning: Increasing student knowledge and self-efficacy in the transition planning process. *Career Development for Exceptional Individuals, 33*(2), 106–114.

Workforce Investment Act of 1998, Pub. L. 105-220, 29 U.S.C. 2801 *et seq.*

Worrell, J.L. (2008). How secondary schools can avoid the seven deadly "sins" of inclusion. *American Secondary Education, 36*(2), 43–56.

Xu, Y., Purvis, B., & Terpstra, J.E. (2010). Involving families in the process and multicultural considerations. In C.A. Thoma & P. Wehman (Eds.), *Getting the most out of IEPs: An educator's guide to the student directed approach* (pp. 25–40). Baltimore: Paul H. Brookes Publishing Co.

Yell, M.L. (2006) *The law and special education* (2nd ed.). Upper Saddle River, NJ: Pearson Education, Inc.

Yell, M.L., & Drasgow, E. (2005). *No Child Left Behind: A guide for professionals.* Upper Saddle River, NJ: Prentice Hall.

Yell, M.L., Drasgow, E., & Lowrey, K.A. (2005). No Child Left Behind and students with autism spectrum disorders. *Focus on Autism and Other Developmental Disabilities, 20,*(3), 130–139.

Yell, M.L., Meadows, N.B., Drasgow, E., & Shiner, J.G. (2009). *Evidence-based practices for educating students with emotional and behavioral disorders.* Upper Saddle River, NJ: Merrill.

Ysseldyke, J., Nelson, J.R., Christenson, S., Johnson, D.R., Dennison, A., Triezenberg, H., et al. (2004). What we know and need to know about the consequences of high-stakes testing for students with disabilities. *Exceptional Children, 71*(1), 75–94.

Zaft, C., Hart, D., & Zimbrich, K. (2004). College career connection: A study of youth with intellectual disabilities and the impact of postsecondary education. *Education and Training in Developmental Disabilities, 39*(1), 45–53.

Zager, D., & Alpern, C.S. (2010). College-based inclusion programming for transition-age students with autism. *Focus on Autism and Other Developmental Disabilities, 25,* 151–157. doi:10.1177/1088357610371331

Zigmond, N., Magiera, K., & Matta, D. (2003, April). Co-teaching in secondary schools: Is the instructional experience enhanced for students with disabilities? Paper presented at the Council for Exceptional Children Annual Convention and Expo, Seattle, WA.

Zambo, D.M. (2010). Strategies to enhance the social identities and social networks of adolescent students with disabilities. *Teaching Exceptional Children, 43*(2), 29–35.

Zetterqvist, B., & Jennische, M. (2010). Linguistic difficulties in adolescents after acquired brain injury: A retrospective study. *Journal of Pediatric Medicine: An interdisciplinary Approach, 3,* 251–258.

Zhang, D. (2001). The effect of "Next S.T.E.P." instruction on the self-determination skills of high school students with learning disabilities. *Career Development for Exceptional Individuals, 24,* 121–132.

Zhang, D. (2005). Parent practices in facilitating self-determination skills: The influences of culture, socioeconomic status, and children's special education status. *Research and Practice for Persons with Severe Disabilities, 30,* 154–162.

Zhang, D., Hsien-Yuan, H., Katsiyannis, A., Barrett, D.E., & Song Ju (2011). Adolescents with disabilities in the juvenile justice system: Patterns of recidivism. *Exceptional Children, 33*(1), 283–298.

Zhang, D., Ivester, J.G., Chen, L., & Katsiyannis, A. (2005). Perspectives on transition practices. *Career Development for Exceptional Individuals, 28*(1), 15–25.

Zhang, D., Katsiyannis, A., & Herbst, M. (2004). Disciplinary exclusions in special education: A 4-year analysis. *Behavioral Disorders, 29*(4), 337–347.

Zhang, D., Willson, V., Katsiyannis, A., Barrett, D., Song Ju, & Jiun-Yu Wu (2010). Truancy offenders in the juvenille justice system: A multicohort study. *Behavioral Disorders, 35*(3), 229–242.

Zuna, N., & McDougall, D. (2004). *Teaching Exceptional Children, 37*(1), 18–24.

Glossary

1619(a)   A provision of the Social Security Act whereby people with disabilities (including those with visual impairments as well as those injured at work) who continue to work can still receive Supplemental Security Income (SSI). To qualify, a person must have been eligible for an SSI payment for at least 1 month before beginning working at the substantial gainful activity level, still exhibit evidence of a disability, and meet all other eligibility rules, including the income and resource tests.

1619(b)   A provision of the Social Security Act whereby people with disabilities (including those with visual impairments as well as those injured at work) can continue to receive Medicaid coverage even if their earnings (alone or in combination with other income) become too high for a Supplemental Security Income (SSI) cash payment. To qualify, a person must have been eligible for an SSI cash payment for at least 1 month; would be eligible for cash payment except for earnings; must still exhibit evidence of a disability; must still meet all other eligibility rules, including the resources test; must need Medicaid in order to work; and must have gross earned income that is insufficient to replace SSI, Medicaid, and any publicly funded attendant care.

academic or standards-based curriculum   The general education curriculum either with or without accommodations or curricular adaptation.

accommodations   Changes in teaching methods and materials for students who are working toward the same goals and standards as the rest of the students in the general education classroom.

alternate assessments   An option for students with disabilities to participate in the state's accountability system, where an assessment is designed for a small group of students who are unable to participate in the regular state assessment, even with appropriate accommodations.

Americans with Disabilities Act of 1990 (ADA; PL 101-336)   ADA prohibits discrimination on the basis of disability in numerous venues, including (but not limited to) employment, public entities/transportation, public accommodations, and telecommunications.

applied behavior analysis   The manipulation of antecedent events and the application of reinforcement designed to strengthen target behaviors of students.

apprenticeship   A system whereby new practitioners of a particular skill are trained by master practitioners of the skill.

assistive and instructional technology   An array of school-purchased devices a child uses in the home and other settings if the individualized educational program team determines the child needs it to receive a free appropriate public education.

assistive technology (AT)   According to the federal Assistive Technology Act (ATA; 2004; PL 108-364), "any item, piece of equipment or product system, whether acquired commercially off the shelf, modified, or customized, that is used to increase, maintain, or improve functional capabilities of individuals with disabilities." AT can be as simple as colored tabs to separate sections in a binder or as complex as a computer console that performs word processing based on a user's speech.

attention-deficit disorder, attention-deficit/hyperactivity disorder (ADD/ADHD)   Behavioral disorders that involve inattention and/or impulsivity and hyperactivity, which can significantly impact a person's behavior and performance.

autism spectrum disorder (ASD)   A developmental disability significantly affecting verbal and nonverbal communication and social interaction, generally evident before age 3, that adversely affects a child's educational performance. Other characteristics often associated with autism are engagement in repetitive activities and stereotyped movements, resistance to environmental changes or changes in daily routines, and unusual responses to sensory experiences.

backward design planning   A process used to develop standards-based instruction that includes functional instruction that requires identifying the standards and the desired learning outcomes, determining acceptable evidence of progress toward the standard, and developing instructional plans and learning experiences that aid a student's progress toward the statewide standard.

behavior intervention plan (BIP)   A plan that includes a minimum of three essential building blocks: 1) preventing the problem behavior from occurring, 2) teaching new behaviors that will replace the problem behavior, and 3) responding differently when the new behaviors and the problem behaviors occur.

Benefits Planning, Assistance, and Outreach Initiative   A federally funded initiative to educate and assist individuals with disabilities to understand the benefits and risks of going back to work and/or increasing their work income. There is no cost to consumers for this service.

Blind Work Expense   A Social Security work incentive that is limited to those individuals who receive Supplemental Security Income and who are blind, whereby the Social Security Administration deducts all work expenses, whether or not they are attributable to an individual's disability.

Board of Education v Ambach **(1981) in New York State**   Court ruling that held, in general, that the state had the power to adopt standards requiring the passing of an exit exam for receipt of a diploma and that the denial of diplomas to students with disabilities was not a violation per se of the Education for All Handicapped Children Act (PL 94-142; the forerunner of the Individuals with Disabilities Education Act) or Section 504.

Brookhart v Illinois State Department of Education **(1983)**   Court ruling that found that requiring students with disabilities to pass an exam as a prerequisite for receipt of a diploma was not a violation per se of the Education for All Handicapped Children Act (PL 94-142) or Section 504. They also found that the students' due process rights were violated because they received only a $1\frac{1}{2}$ period of notice before the test requirement was imposed.

Brown v Board of Education **(1954)**   A court case decision that was the catalyst that led to the broadening of education for all people.

Centers for Independent Living   Organizations that provide general information about disability-related resources in the community and offer classes in areas such as financial management, socialization, sexuality, leisure activities, and self-advocacy. Peer counseling and other programs are geared to assist students with building their advocacy skills as well as understanding their rights. Some offer other services including assistance with employment.

cerebral palsy (CP)   A common motor disorder in children that is made up of a group of disorders of the development of movement and posture, causing limitations that are attributed to nonprogressive disturbances that occurred in the developing fetal or infant brain.

Chapman v California Department of Education **(2002)**   Court ruling that found that the California High School Exit Exam violated the rights of students with disabilities under federal law because students were not allowed to use calculators and other accommodations on the assessment.

cognitive and metacognitive strategies   A variety of strategies that teachers can use to support students with and without disabilities to learn from text such as recognizing text structure, cognitive mapping, questioning, identifying main ideas, and summarization, as well as reciprocal teaching and its variants such as collaborative strategic reading (CSR), POSSE (predict, organize, search, summarize, evaluate), and SQ3R (survey, question, read, recite, review).

collaborative teaming   The process by which general educators work cooperatively with special educators in order that education in regular classes may be achieved satisfactorily for students with disabilities; it may also include parental involvement.

community-based instruction   Teaching academics, life skills, and employment skills in a natural environment and the real-life, community-based settings to prepare students with disabilities for adulthood.

community-based transition   Transition that focuses on finding work for people with disabilities in the communities in which they live.

community-based vocational instruction   An approach where students with disabilities (especially those with severe disabilities) receive vocational instruction within community businesses in which they are likely to seek gainful employment.

community-based work experiences   A variety of paid or unpaid work experiences that help students learn about themselves and the world of work as they participate in vocational exploration, vocational assessment, and vocational training within various businesses.

community rehabilitation providers (CRPs)   For-profit or nonprofit businesses that assist people with disabilities to obtain and maintain competitive employment by offering a variety of services such as counseling, assessments, benefits counseling, job placement, and supported employment that are typically funded by a contract or fee-for-service arrangements with an agency such as the states' vocational rehabilitation agency. Some may also have contracts with local developmental disabilities agencies to provide case management services.

community resource mapping   An activity used to acquaint teachers with the target community's culture, resources, transition assets, and needs in order to develop baseline knowledge about the community's current issues and assets that will be used during transition planning.

competitive employment   Full-time or part-time work in a business that pays commensurate wages—at or above minimum wage—and benefits commensurate with those of coworkers.

consultation   An approach where the special educator helps the general education teacher identify instructional and curricular accommodations and modifications to be implemented to support the student with a disability.

co-teaching   A teaching model that is used to increase access to the general education curriculum for students with disabilities, in which the special education teacher provides additional support in the classroom and supplements the content area knowledge of the general education teacher with knowledge and expertise related to teaching students with disabilities.

curriculum adaptation   The modification of the representation or presentation of the curriculum or modification of the student's engagement with the curriculum that is used to enhance access and progress that is used to meet the needs of one or a small number of students with disabilities, which may include modifications to instructional materials, the delivery of instruction, the manner in which a student engages in instruction, or the process of assessing what a student has learned. Or, because many instructional materials are print-based, adaptations to these materials can include books on tape, braille, computer-based work, audiocassette tapes, videotapes, and CD-ROMs.

customized employment   A process for individualizing the employment relationship between a job seeker or an employee and an employer in ways that meet the needs of both.

customized job   The creation of a new or negotiation of an existing job description in a business for an individual with a disability.

day programs and sheltered workshops   Segregated programs that offer skill training, prevocational training, make-work vocational activities, field trips, recreation, and other types of special education–related curricula for individuals with severe disabilities.

Debra P. v Turlington **(1981)**   Court ruling that indicated that the state could not deprive students of a high school diploma on the basis of an exit exam unless the state could prove that the students received adequate notice about the test, that the test was fundamentally fair, and that it covered material actually taught in the classroom.

developmental disability (DD)   A lifelong disability that can be attributed to mental and/or physical impairments and manifests before the age of 18.

differentiated instruction   Instruction that addresses the needs of diverse learners and emphasizes a variety of elements including content, process, and products.

discovery   An assessment process that results in discovering the individual's vocational interests and skills, which form the basis for developing a job for the person in his or her community.

dual enrollment   A collaboration between high schools and colleges that allows high school students to attend and earn credit for college-level classes usually during their junior or senior year; classes may be held on a college campus with postsecondary education students or at a high school with other high school students taught by a college instructor.

Earned Income Exclusion   A process by which the Social Security Administration disregards most of the income that was earned when they calculate the amount of a worker's Supplemental Security Income check.

Education for All Handicapped Children Act of 1975 (EHA; PL 94-142)   EHA was the predecessor of the Individuals with Disabilities Education Act and required public schools that accepted federal education funding to provide education to students with physical and mental disabilities. Schools were also required to assess students with disabilities to evaluate their performance and create an appropriate educational program for them.

emotional disturbance   A condition exhibiting characteristics such as an inability to learn that cannot be explained by intellectual, sensory, or health factors; difficulty building or maintaining satisfactory interpersonal relationships with peers and teachers; inappropriate types of behavior or feelings under normal circumstances; a general pervasive mood of unhappiness or depression or a tendency to develop physical symptoms or fears associated with personal or school problems over a long period of time and to a marked degree that adversely affects a child's educational performance.

Employment First   A concept built upon the notion that competitive employment should be the first choice for all persons with disabilities.

employment specialist   A vocational rehabilitation professional who assists individuals with the most severe disabilities with gaining and maintaining work by using an individualized supported employment approach; also known as a *job coach*.

entitlement   A benefit that, under the law or based on established rights, an individual is allowed or guaranteed to receive. Rights under the Individuals with Disabilities Education Act would be an example of an entitlement.

epilepsy   A common neurological disorder in children that is manifested by seizure brought about by excessive synchronous neuron activity in the brain and further defined as two or more unprovoked seizures more than 24 hours apart in a child older than 1 month of age.

evidence-based practices   Practices that have been substantiated through empirical research that supports a link between results or outcomes and a practice.

free appropriate public education (FAPE)   The right of children with disabilities to be educated at the public expense ("free") in a program that is designed to meet their unique educational needs ("appropriate").

functional analysis   The systematic manipulation of antecedent and/or consequent events that are hypothesized as being related functionally to the occurrence of the problem behavior that is conducted most often under controlled experimental conditions rather than in applied (i.e., clinical, educational) contexts.

functional assessment   The process of identifying established operations, antecedent variables, and consequent events that control target behaviors; it identifies the when, where, and why problem behaviors occur and when, where, and why they do not occur.

functional behavioral assessment (FBA)   A method used to identify the function of a student's particular behavior that includes indirect assessment, direct assessment, and hypothesis development.

functional community-referenced skills   Skills that are critical for students, especially those with severe disabilities, to effectively make the transition to adult living (i.e., working, living, and participating in the community).

functional curriculum   A curriculum that focuses on developing the skills that a student will need to perform independently or with supports in vocational, residential, and community environments.

general large-scale assessments   State accountability assessment where students with disabilities may participate either with or without accommodations.

high tech   A way to describe assistive technology that refers to devices that are complex and typically contain electronic components such as voice output communication aids, electronic wheelchairs, universal remote controls, and computers.

Higher Education Opportunity Act of 2008 (HEOA; PL 110-315)   Act that expanded the opportunities for students with disabilities to access postsecondary education programs such as access for students with intellectual disabilities to federal financial aid including Pell Grants, Supplemental Educational Opportunity Grants, and federal work-study programs.

Home and Community-Based Services Medicaid Waiver (HCBS)   Funding that can be accessed by community service boards and agencies to assist individuals with disabilities with housing, supported living services, and employment supports, that is targeted toward providing services in the community for individuals who, without these services, because of the significant nature of their disability and resulting support needs, would need to live in an institutional setting.

hybrid curriculum model Secondary curriculum that is linked to the content standards but perhaps has a look and feel of incorporating traditionally associated life skills.

Impairment-Related Work Expense (IRWE) A Social Security work incentive that can be used to pay for items that are necessary to work and are incurred because of the individual's disability.

inclusion The placement of a special education student in general education classes full time, with the responsibility for the student's education and progress placed on the general education teacher, supported by whatever continuum of special education services the student needs to succeed.

inclusive individual support model A post–secondary education model that individualizes the services and supports provided and how classes are accessed on campus (e.g., students with intellectual disabilities or other developmental disabilities enroll in classes for credit or audit based on the course offerings in the college catalog).

Indicator 1 One of four indicators from the State Performance Plan, which is related to transition and surrounds high school graduation: "Percent of youth with IEPs graduating from high school with a regular diploma compared to percent of all youth in the State graduating with a regular diploma."

Indicator 2 One of four indictors from the State Performance Plan, which is related to transition and is associated with dropout rates: "Percent of youth with IEPs dropping out of high school compared to the percent of all youth in the State dropping out of high school."

Indicator 13 One of the four indicators from the State Performance Plan: "Percent of youth with IEPs aged 16 and above with an IEP that includes appropriate measurable postsecondary goals that are annually updated and based upon an age appropriate transition assessment, transition services, including courses of study, that will reasonably enable the student to meet those postsecondary goals, and annual IEP goals related to the student's transition services needs. There also must be evidence that the student was invited to the IEP Team meeting where transition services are to be discussed and evidence that, if appropriate, a representative of any participating agency was invited to the IEP Team meeting with the prior consent of the parent or student who has reached the age of majority." (20 U.S.C. 1416[a][3][B])

Indicator 14 One of four indicators from the State Performance Plan: "Percent of youth who are no longer in secondary school, had Individualized Education Programs (IEPs) in effect at the time they left school, and were: A. Enrolled in higher education within one year of leaving high school. B. Enrolled in higher education or competitively employed within one year of leaving high school. C. Enrolled in higher education or in some other postsecondary education or training program; or competitively employed or in some other employment within one year of leaving high school." (20 U.S.C. 1416[a][3][B])

individual placement and support model A model of supported employment that is designed to assist individuals with mental illness with gaining and maintaining work in their communities.

individualized education program (IEP) An education plan for students with disabilities. Each public school student with a disability who receives special education services must have an IEP, which sets the goals and objectives that the student will achieve in the coming school year. The IEP is reviewed and revised on an annual basis by the IEP team.

individualized education program (IEP) team The group of people in a school or other facility that meet to discuss the development and servicing of a student's IEP. By law, the team must include the parents of the student, the student (as appropriate), at least one general education teacher, at least one special education teacher, a representative of the local education agency (e.g., the principal or his or her designee), and anyone else the parents or school have chosen to invite (e.g., related service provider, school psychologist, advocate, other family members).

individualized plan for employment (IPE) A plan designed by a vocational rehabilitation counselor and individual with a disability that documents an individual's vocational goal, and the services to be provided to reach the goal.

Individuals with Disabilities Education Improvement Act of 2004 (IDEA 2004; PL 108-446) An act of Congress signed into law by President George W. Bush on December 3, 2004. It helps to ensure equity, accountability, and excellence in the education of children with disabilities. IDEA 2004 is a reauthorization of the Education of All Handicapped Children Act of 1975 (EHA; PL 94-142) and carries on many of the protections that law established. The law promulgated changes in the individualized education program process, due process, and student discipline. A previous reauthorization of the EHA (1990) and amendments to the law (1997) introduced numerous changes to these areas as well.

infused skills grid A method of providing specialized instruction during general education classes that clearly illustrates where identified skills will be taught during a student's day and which team members have identified particular skills for targeted instruction.

intellectual disability (ID) A generalized disorder, usually appearing in childhood, characterized by impaired cognitive functioning, sometimes measured by below-average performance on tests of mental ability or intelligence. ID is the current preferred term for the disorder, which was, at one time, called *mental retardation*.

job carving The process of analyzing the work performed in a given job and identifying tasks that might be assigned to an employee with severe disabilities. It is more or less synonymous with *job creation* from a supported employment perspective.

job development The process of creating a work opportunity on behalf of a job seeker with a disability that is achieved by earning an opportunity to connect with an employer to learn about business needs and operations and then moving on to propose a job description and get a commitment from the employer to meet and possibly hire the person.

least-restrictive environment (LRE) The movement of students with disabilities away from segregated settings, as stated in the Individuals with Disabilities Education Improvement Act (PL 108-446), "to the maximum extent appropriate, children with disabilities, including those children in public and private institutions or other care facilities, are educated with children who are not disabled, and special classes, separate schooling, or other removal of children with disabilities from the regular educational environment occurs only when the nature or severity of the disability is such that education in regular classes with the use of supplementary aids and services cannot be achieved satisfactorily." (IDEA 2004 [Part B, Sec 612 (a)(5)])

local education agency (LEA) A synonym for a school district or any entity that operates schools in the United States.

low tech A way to describe assistive technology that refers to devices that are passive or simple, with few moving parts, such as picture communication boards, pointers, and switches.

Medicaid A health program for people with limited incomes and resources. Medicaid was established in 1965 by the Social Security Amendments 89-97, 79 Stat. 286. The program is jointly funded by the state and federal governments and is managed by the states.

Eligibility is determined by a means test, which establishes whether an individual is sufficiently indebted or indigent.

Medicare   The United States' social insurance program that was established by the Social Security Act Amendments of 1965 (PL 89-97; signed into law by President Lyndon B. Johnson on July 30, 1965) and is administered by the U.S. Government. It provides health insurance coverage to persons ages 65 years and older, persons younger than 65 with physically disabling conditions or congenital physical disabilities, or others who meet certain legal criteria.

microenterprise   A small business that has fewer than five employees and can start up without great expense (i.e., $30,000 or less).

***Mills v Board of Education of the District of Columbia* (1972)**   A U.S. District Court case that declared that students with disabilities must be given a public education and that the financial limitations of the local education agency could not be a consideration. The case set a precedent that educational services must be made on the basis of children's needs, not on the schools' fiscal capabilities to provide such services.

mixed hybrid model   A postsecondary education model for students with disabilities that is designed to offer social and academic experiences (for credit or audit) on campus with students without disabilities.

modification   A general education practice that involves students with more significant disabilities to work toward different goals (individualized education program goals or alternate learning outcomes) than their peers in the general education classroom.

natural supports   A type of support that is developed and facilitated by an employment specialist after an individual with a disability has been hired that involves empowering workplace personnel such as the supervisor or a co-worker to provide on-the-job training and other individualized assistance to the employee with the disability.

neuromuscular disorders   Neuromuscular disorders are inherited or acquired disorders that affect any or all aspects of the neuromuscular system at the level of the muscle, nerves, neuromuscular junction (where the nerve meets and delivers signal to the muscle), or motor neurons (nerves in the spinal cord controlling muscles).

No Child Left Behind Act of 2001 (NCLB; PL 107-110)   A reauthorization of the Elementary and Secondary Education Act of 1965 (PL 89-10), NCLB is based on the belief that high academic standards should be set for what students learn. States are required to develop assessments to be administered to all students in certain grades as a condition of receiving federal education funding. States set their own achievement standards.

occupational therapist (OT)   A professional who works with individuals with mental, physical, developmental, and/or emotional disabilities using treatments that develop, recover, or maintain clients' activities of daily living. OTs help individuals with disabilities increase and maintain motor function and reasoning ability and also help them compensate for permanent loss of function.

One-Stop Career Center   A U.S. Department of Labor initiative, established under the Workforce Investment Act of 1999 (PL 105-220). One-Stop Career Centers offer assistance to job seekers, including, but not limited to, training referrals, career counseling, and job listings. Job seekers can visit brick-and-mortar centers or connect online to a center's information.

paraprofessional   Paraprofessionals provide individualized student support, under the direction of teachers, by performing various activities such as functional assessments, observing and documenting data, implementing behavior management systems, and instructing students in small groups.

***Pennsylvania Association for Retarded Citizens (PARC) v Commonwealth of Pennsylvania* (1972)**   A U.S. District Court case that secured the right of free appropriate public education for children with intellectual disabilities.

person-centered planning (PCP)   A set of approaches that helps a person with disabilities plan his or her life choices more effectively. The ultimate goal of PCP is the empowerment of the individual for whom the approaches have been designed.

personal assistance services   A service used by persons with disabilities to perform tasks that the person would perform for himself or herself if he or she did not have a disability that range from reading, communication, and performing manual tasks to activities of daily living such as bathing, eating, toileting, personal hygiene, and dressing.

personal supports   A variety of supports that are used to increase the participation of students with disabilities in general education classrooms.

Plan to Achieve Self-Support (PASS)   A provision of the Supplemental Security Income section of the Social Security Act that enables people with disabilities to return to work. PASS allows its users to set aside money and/or items in service of a particular work goal.

Project SEARCH®   A nationwide model for inclusive educational programming designed to prepare students for postsecondary employment that was started in 1996 when the Cincinnati Children's Hospital adopted a major diversity initiative. Students participate in a 1-year on-site internship at the host business. Through these targeted internships, students acquire competitive, marketable, and transferable skills enabling them to apply for related positions upon completion of the program. Students also build communication, teamwork, and problem-solving skills important to their overall development as a young worker.

public–private partnership   A service or business venture that is funded and operated through a partnership of government and one or more private-sector companies.

Rehabilitation Act Amendments of 1978 (PL 95-602)   Amendments that responded to consumer concerns for added involvement by the establishment of independent living centers.

Rehabilitation Act Amendments of 1986 (PL 99-506)   Amendments that enhanced support for rehabilitation engineering, with clear definitions for rehabilitation engineering services. In addition, support for special projects and demonstrations in supported employment were established.

Rehabilitation Act Amendments of 1992 (PL 102-569)   Amendments that clearly outlined the intent of Congress to ensure consumer choice in career opportunities and focused on competitive employment as the desired outcome.

Rehabilitation Act Amendments of 1998 (PL 105-220)   Amendments that govern the vocational rehabilitation programs, and provide federal dollars, matched by state dollars, to all states to give individuals with disabilities assistance with employment. The act required cooperation among educational agencies responsible for the transition from school to employment or postsecondary education. This means that the vocational rehabilitation program works cooperatively with local education authorities to serve transition-age youth and is a primary support resource for adults with disabilities who need employment services. The act mandated ongoing support, including assessment of employment needs, job development and placement service, social skills instruction, and intense services at home or at work to live independently or maintain employment.

Rehabilitation Act of 1973 (PL 93-112)   An act of Congress signed into law by President Richard M. Nixon on September 26, 1973. It prohibits discrimination on the basis of disability in programs conducted by federal agencies, in programs receiving federal financial assistance, in federal employment, and in the employment practices of federal contractors. Section 504 of the act created and extended civil rights protections to people with disabilities. As a direct result of the Rehabilitation Act, many people with disabilities were provided opportunities in education and employment. The act was amended in 1978 (to establish independent living centers), 1986 (to enhance support for rehabilitation engineering), 1992 (to ensure consumer choice in career opportunities), and

1998 (to provide federal funds to assist people with disabilities in finding meaningful employment).

response to intervention (RTI) A three-tiered prevention model that considers a student's response (i.e., progress) to a research-based intervention provided by the school while the child is still in the general education environment. RTI can be instrumental in identifying students who have learning disabilities.

Section 504 A major provision of the Rehabilitation Act that created and extended civil rights to people with disabilities by providing opportunities for children and adults with disabilities in education, employment, and various other settings. It also called for the establishment of the Individual Written Rehabilitation Program today known as Individualized Plans for Employment, which was a major step to ensure the enhanced involvement of a person with a disability in developing his or her vocational rehabilitation program.

Section 504 Plan A written accommodation plan to meet the needs of students with disabilities or health conditions who do not qualify for special education services. A 504 Plan spells out the modifications and accommodations that will be needed for students with disabilities to have an opportunity perform at the same level as their peers. A 504 Plan, which falls under civil rights law, is an attempt to remove barriers and allow students with disabilities to participate freely; like the Americans With Disabilities Act, it seeks to level the playing field so that those students can safely pursue the same opportunities as everyone else. An IEP, which falls under the Individuals with Disabilities Education Act, is much more concerned with actually providing educational services.

self-determination A behavior construct that reflects that a person is capable of acting as his or her own causal agent in making decisions and choices. Self-determination has been a key concept in the normalization, independent living, and self-advocacy movements for people with disabilities.

self-employment Employment option for individuals with disabilities who access support systems to help them operate their own businesses, limited partnerships, or businesses within businesses.

self-prompting technology Any device or system capable of prompting a person through a task analysis, set of directions, or task to complete a designated task, assignment, or job without additional prompting by teachers or instructional staff.

Services for Students with Disabilities Office The postsecondary educational institution's office that is responsible for determining accommodations for students with disabilities; may also be referred to as the Office for Student Disability Services or the Office for Students with Disabilities.

Social Security A social welfare and insurance program more properly known as the Old-Age, Survivors, and Disability Insurance program. Promulgated by the Social Security Act of 1935 (PL 74-271), it has been part of each amendment of the Social Security Act since its inception.

Social Security Administration (SSA) An independent agency of the U.S. Government that administers Social Security benefits.

Social Security Disability Insurance (SSDI) A Social Security Administration program that provides benefits to people with disabilities (including those with visual impairments) who are "insured" by workers' contributions to the Social Security trust fund, based on one's wage earnings (or those of one's spouse or parents) as required by the Federal Insurance Contributions Act (FICA). Title II of the Social Security Act (PL 74-271) authorizes SSDI benefits.

spinal cord injury (SCI) Injuries to the spinal cord that lead to deficits in muscle function, bowel and bladder problems, and skin issues. In addition, there can be profound cognitive, emotional, and psychological issues stemming from the loss of this function. These injuries can be congenital, known as meningomyelocele or spina bifida, or acquired spinal cord injury.

State Developmental Disability Agency   State agencies that offer services to individuals with intellectual and developmental disabilities and may operate under a variety of different names such as the local Community Service Boards. Some states operate these services under direct state supervision of local agencies. These local boards and/or state-directed programs frequently also serve individuals with disabilities based on mental health and/or substance abuse issues. Eligibility for these services is usually based on the presence of a disability that meets specific state guidelines, and these eligibility criteria will vary from state to state and may include case management along with a variety of other services (e.g., housing employment). Case managers can attend transition meetings, both as resources for information and referral and also to help plan for specific transition support services needed by an individual.

state performance plan   A state plan required by Section 616(b) of the Individuals with Disabilities Education Improvement Act of 2004 (PL 108-446) that is submitted to the Office of Special Education that consists, in part, of targets for 20 indicators, as well as activities intended to improve results for students with disabilities. Four indicators related to transition are Indicators 1, 2, 13, and 14. These four indicators provide a method to track what is happening with youth with disabilities, influencing school divisions in all states to improve the way transition planning is developed within individualized education programs.

structured peer tutoring   A teaching strategy that has been used in classrooms to improve the learning of students with and without disabilities that may result in a variety of benefits such as improved academics (e.g., reading, math computation, safety skills), positive work behaviors (e.g., on-task, motivation), and improved social interactions.

student-directed learning   Related to self-determination, student-directed learning is an educational construct that enables students with disabilities to take control of their own learning through antecedent cue regulation (reminders to complete tasks), self-instruction (talking through a problem aloud), self-monitoring (e.g., keeping track of tasks with checklists), self-evaluation (checking the quality of work), and self-reinforcement (administration of rewards to oneself).

student-directed transition individualized education program (IEP)   An approach where person-centered planning is used to enable a student to successfully direct his or her own transition IEP, thereby ensuring a focus and commitment to student's desires, goals, and strengths.

Student Earned Income Exclusion (SEIE)   A Social Security work incentive designed for individuals with disabilities who are younger than age 22 and who are attending school. If qualified, the person can go to work and the Social Security Administration will count even less of total earnings when calculating the Supplemental Security Income benefit.

Substantial Gainful Activity (SGA)   A term used to describe the level of work activity a person has or the earnings one receives. Work is "substantial" if it involves doing significant physical or mental activities or a combination of both. For work activity to be substantial, it does not need to be performed on a full-time basis. "Gainful" work activity is work performed for pay or profit, work of a nature generally performed for pay or profit, or work intended for profit, whether or not a profit is realized.

substantially separate model   A postsecondary education model where students with significant disabilities are on campus but primarily take classes with other students with significant disabilities. Interacting with other college students without disabilities occurs mainly through social activities on campus.

summary of performance   A written summary of the student's academic achievement and functional performance, which includes recommendations on how to assist the student in meeting his or her postsecondary goals, that is required by the Individuals with Disabilities Education Improvement Act (2004; PL 108-446) and provided by the local education agency toward the end of the student's last year in school; this can be used by the student to educate future agencies, employers, and/or supports of his or her academic and functional abilities.

Supplemental Security Income (SSI)   A Social Security Administration program that makes cash assistance payments to people with disabilities (including visual impairments), elderly people, and children who have limited income and resources. The federal government funds SSI from general tax revenues. Title XVI of the Social Security Act authorizes SSI benefits.

support facilitator   An approach where the special educator provides support to a student with a disability in the general classroom by arranging appropriate level and frequency of in-class support or engages others, including paraprofessionals and peers, to provide additional support in the general education classroom.

supported employment (SE)   A federally funded program to facilitate competitive employment in integrated settings for people with moderate to severe disabilities who need ongoing support to succeed in a work environment. Such support could include job coaches, transportation, assistive technology, specialized job training, and individualized supervision.

systematic instruction   A set of teaching strategies and techniques.

text enhancement strategies   A number of strategies that teachers can use to support a student's learning in reading and literacy such as *graphic organizers* that can be used to visually depict relationships between ideas, *advance organizers* that provide an outline of the major components of a lesson, *story maps* that diagram grammar elements in narrative texts, and *mnemonic illustrations* that link unfamiliar information with information in the students' existing knowledge base.

Ticket to Work and Workforce Incentive Improvement Act of 1999 (TWWIIA; PL 106-170)   An act of Congress signed into law by President Bill Clinton on December 17, 1999. TWWIIA creates the Ticket to Work Program administered by the Social Security Administration. This program modernizes employment-related services offered to people with disabilities. Individuals with disabilities can get job-related training and placement assistance from an approved provider of their choice. TWWIIA also expands health care coverage so that people with disabilities will be able work without fear of losing their health insurance.

transition   The life changes, adjustments, and cumulative experiences that occur in the lives of young adults as they move from school environments to independent living and work environments.

transition individualized education program (IEP)   Transition IEP refers to an IEP that focuses on a student's postschool adult life outcomes. Some states have a separate IEP specifically related to transition and call it the transition IEP rather than it being part of the student's IEP.

transition meeting   An individualized education program meeting at which transition goals are discussed, once a student has reached the age of 14.

transition planning   Planning that takes place to develop long-term goals and objectives and the selection of services and instruction that specifically address the student's specific education, training, work, and independent living goals beyond high school.

transition services   A coordinated set of activities for a student with a disability that is focused on improving the academic and functional achievement of the student with a disability to facilitate the student's movement from school to postschool activities, such as employment and community living. They are based on the student's needs; take into account strengths, preferences, and interests; and include instruction, related services, and community experiences, among other things.

traumatic brain injury (TBI) An injury caused by a bump, blow, or jolt to the head that disrupts the normal function of the brain and is sometimes called an *acquired brain injury*.

universal design for learning (UDL) Non–disability-specific teaching methods and best practices that promote achievement among all students in the general education class-room and that are based on multiple and flexible methods of presentation, expression, an d engagement.

universal design for transition (UDT) A strategy that incorporates components of Universal Design for Learning, and the following components: multiple transition/life domains, multiple means of assessment, student self-determination, and multiple resources/perspectives to transition planning.

video modeling (VM) A technique that is used to teach a student a desired behavior, which involves the student observing the desired behavior via an instructional video clip (i.e., of someone modeling the behavior) and then learning to imitate the behavior.

vocational assessment A directed set of assessment activities to assist people with disabilities in finding meaningful occupations. A vocational assessment also takes into account medical, psychological, social, cultural, and economic data in order to provide a realistic appraisal.

vocational rehabilitation (VR) A service provision of the Rehabilitation Act of 1973 (PL 93-112). VR agencies help people with disabilities prepare for employment and look for jobs. States manage their respective VR agencies.

vocational rehabilitation counselor A professional who is a fundamental partner in transition that can assist eligible youth with employment by providing guidance and counseling, vocational assessment, job placement, and/or other services such as support-ed employment for youth with severe disabilities.

workplace and job analysis An analysis of workplace factors and job characteristics that is conducted during job development to examine how an existing position may meet a particular job seeker's abilities and expectations and/or determine possible ways to create or develop a new job description for an individual with a disability that will benefit the business.

Workforce Investment Act of 1998 (WIA; PL 105-220) An act of Congress signed into law by President Bill Clinton on August 7, 1998. The act provides for efforts to develop the U.S. workforce in the following areas: streamlining services through a one-stop service delivery system, empowering job seekers through information and access to training re-sources, providing universal access to core services, ensuring a strong role for local work-force investment boards and the private sector, and improving youth programs.

workplace supports Supports that exist in a workplace that are available to all employees and may be categorized as environmental, procedural, or natural.

Index

Page numbers followed by *f* indicate figures; those followed by *t* indicate tables.